Poverty in Guatemala

THE WORLD BANK
Washington, D.C.

ISBN: 0-8213-5552-X
eISBN: 0-8213-5553-8
ISSN: 0253-2123

Cover Photo by Ximena Traa.

Library of Congress Cataloging-in-Publication Data

Poverty in Guatemala.
    p. cm.—(A World Bank country study)
    Includes bibliographical references.
    ISBN 0-8213-5552-X
    1. Poverty—Guatemala. I. Series.

HC144.Z9P6268 2003
339.4´6´097281—dc21

                                                                    2003053509

CONTENTS

LIST OF TABLES

LIST OF BOXES

LIST OF FIGURES

TECHNICAL BACKGROUND PAPERS

Available on the web at http://www.worldbank.org/guatemalapoverty

1. Livelihoods, Labor Markets, and Rural Poverty, by Renos Vakis

2. Education Sector Review, by Maria Elena Anderson

3. Education and Poverty LSMS Analysis, by John Edwards

4. Perceptions of Education (Qualitative Study), by Martha Rodriguez

5. Health and Poverty, by Michele Gragnolati and Alessandra Marini

6. Malnutrition and Poverty, by Alessandra Marini and Michele Gragnolati

7. Poverty and Modern Utility Services, by Vivien Foster and Caridad Araujo

8. Transport and Poverty: A Profile Using Data from the ENCOVI 2000, by Jyotsna Puri

9. Vulnerability and Vulnerable Groups: A Quantitative and Qualitative Assessment,
   by Emil Tesliuc and Kathy Lindert

10. Social Protection, Private Transfers and Poverty, by Emil Tesliuc and Kathy Lindert

11. Exclusion and Poverty in Guatemala's Rural Villages: The Challenge of Tackling
    Cumulative Barriers, by Carine Clert and Ana-María Ibáñez

12. Social Capital in Guatemala: A Mixed Methods Analysis, by Ana-María Ibáñez,
    Kathy Lindert, and Michael Woolcock

13. Qualitative Poverty and Exclusion Study (QPES), Main Report, by COWI Consulting

ABSTRACT

Poverty in Guatemala is high and deep. In 2000, over half of all Guatemalans lived in poverty. About 16% lived in extreme poverty. Available evidence suggests that poverty in Guatemala is higher than in other Central American countries. Although poverty has fallen over the past decade, its trend recently declined due to a series of economic shocks during 2001 and 2002. The drop of poverty incidence since 1990 is slightly slower than what would have been predicted given Guatemala's growth rates, suggesting that growth has not been particularly "pro-poor." This pattern arises largely because growth in the rural sectors—where the poor are largely concentrated—has been slower than in other areas. Poverty and vulnerability are mainly chronic whereas only a fifth were transient poor. Likewise, while 64% of the population could be considered vulnerable to poverty, the majority of these are vulnerable due to low overall expected consumption rather than high volatility of consumption. The chronic nature of poverty and vulnerability highlights the importance of building the assets of the poor, rather than focusing primarily on the expansion of public safety nets or social insurance. Nonetheless, some public transfers (social assistance) could indeed be desirable to alleviate the poverty and suffering of the *extreme* poor, particularly when linked to participation in health and education activities.

The Peace Accords represented a turning point for Guatemala's development path, paving the way for a transformation to a more prosperous and inclusive nation. Key areas related to economic development and poverty reduction include: a focus on human development, productive and sustainable development, modernization of the democratic state, and strengthening and promoting participation. The rights of the indigenous and women were also highlighted as cross-cutting themes throughout the accords, in an attempt to reverse the historical exclusion of these groups. Given the importance of improving living conditions to lasting peace, poverty reduction has taken center stage on the current social policy agenda. In particular, the Government outlined its poverty reduction strategy in a policy document "Estrategia de Reducción de la Pobreza" (ERP). General principles emphasized in the ERP include: a rural focus, using the poverty map for targeting; efficient and transparent public spending; decentralization; and participation. Key action areas include: (a) promoting growth with equity; (b) investing in human capital (emphasizing health, education and food security); and (c) investing in physical capital (particularly water and sanitation, rural roads, electricity, and rural development). Cross-cutting issues in the ERP include multiculturalism and inter-culturality, gender equity, and vulnerability. The preparation of the ERP helped to introduce some policies, such as improved targeting by using the poverty map, but the dialogue on the poverty reduction agenda and on many of ERP's recommendations should be reactivated and possibly included in the agenda for the new administration.

In the six years since the signing of the Peace Accords, Guatemala has taken important steps on this new development path, with progress in public sector management, public revenues and spending, and improvements in the coverage and equity of education and basic services. Importantly, these steps signal that progress *is* possible, despite the magnitude of the challenge of changing the course of history. Despite progress, households have not perceived significant improvements in living conditions and households are decidedly more pessimistic about changes in their welfare since the Peace Accords. They attribute their perceptions to economic factors, such as a lack of increases in incomes and opportunities (factors that directly affect "their wallets.") Many of the challenges for poverty reduction coincide largely with the remaining actions on the Peace Agenda. In particular, select development-related targets supported by the Peace Accords have not been met, especially those involving outcomes in health, education and economic growth as well as fundamental institutional reforms. The lack of progress in these key development outcomes reflects the need for renewed efforts to achieve poverty reduction and improvements in living conditions, which are crucial for lasting peace. The overlaps between the Peace Agenda and the poverty reduction agenda highlight remaining priority challenges in several key areas: (a) creating opportunities; (b) reducing vulnerability; and (c) improving institutions and empowering communities.

In developing a broad agenda for poverty reduction, three caveats are important to emphasize at the outset: First, while there is no single "blueprint" for poverty reduction, there are some key levers that take central stage for national efforts to reduce poverty. Second, the policy discussion is aimed primarily at the perspective of policy makers and the role of the public sector; hence it emphasizes interventions that both (a) would have a substantial impact on poverty; and (b) merit the use of public resources in a market-oriented economy. Third, poverty reduction is a multi-dimensional and long-term process. There is no single magic bullet to reduce poverty. Rather, efforts should be made to attack the poverty problem from a multitude of angles, including those to foster opportunity, build assets, reduce vulnerability, and improve institutions and empower communities.

The overall purpose of this report is to offer the Government of Guatemala a comprehensive assessment of poverty and of policies that affect the prospects for poverty reduction in the country and to suggest some general guidelines which it is hoped will be helpful for the Government to further develop its strategy to reduce poverty. At the same time, the report is intended to inform civil society in Guatemala and other external donors, and to trigger a dialogue on the path to follow to overcome vulnerability and poverty.

ACKNOWLEDGMENTS

This report is part of a collaborative multi-year program of analytical work and technical assistance that signals the commitment of the World Bank to poverty reduction. The program seeks to (a) conduct a thorough, multi-dimensional analysis of poverty and exclusion in Guatemala using both quantitative and qualitative data; (b) provide relevant policy analysis, advice, and tools on the incidence and impact of public programs, which could serve as inputs into the formulation and implementation of the Government's poverty reduction strategies; (c) contribute to the World Bank's assistance program, including the development of the next Country Assistance Strategy (CAS) and the design of new operations in a variety of sectors; and (d) foster institutional development and capacity building in our counterpart agencies for greater ownership and sustainability of the analysis and results.

The program has been highly collaborative, spanning several years (1998-present) and involving continuous cooperation and numerous missions (over 30 in total). The main phases and activities supported by the program have included: (a) support to the MECOVI[i] Program to develop an integrated system of household surveys and build capacity for survey design, implementation and analysis, including the production and analysis of the Encuesta Nacional de Condiciones de Vida (ENCOVI 2000) (1998-present); (b) qualitative data collection[ii] (field work conducted in 2000); (c) training in poverty analysis (initially in 1999–2000 with data from the ENIGFAM, then in 2001 with data from the ENCOVI); (d) training in, and construction of, poverty maps (occurring in 2000–2001); (e) support to the formulation of the Government's Poverty Reduction Strategy (from mid-2000-early 2002); and finally (f) analysis and preparation of the present report (from mid-2000 to 2002).

This program is collectively called the Guatemala Poverty Assessment Program (GUAPA Program). The main counterpart agencies for the GUAPA Program have been the *Instituto Nacional de Estadística–Guatemala* (INE) and the General Planning Secretariat under the Presidency (SEGEPLAN) in collaboration with the University of Rafael Landívar (URL). The World Bank team extends a heartfelt thanks to the teams from each of these agencies for their fruitful collaboration and partnerships.

An earlier draft of this report was discussed with representatives of the Government (SEGEPLAN, INE, Ministry of Finance, Ministry of Communications, Secretaría Ejecutiva de la Presidencia, the Secretaría de Bienestar Social, the Congreso de la República, FIS, FOGUAVI, INFOM-UNEPAR, and the Ministry of Health), the international community (UNDP, JICA, Costa Rican Embassy, Canadian Embassy, Japanese Embassy, JICA, KfW, and FAO), and the academic community (URL, ASIES, CIEN, FUNDAZUCAR, FLACSO, and IDC) during a series of consultations held in Guatemala in June 2002. We are very grateful for their participation, suggestions, and comments, which we have taken into account in the current draft.

The World Bank's task team included Kathy Lindert (Task Manager), Carlos Sobrado, Renos Vakis, Diane Steele, Caridad Araujo, Carine Clert, John Edwards, Emily Gustafsson-Wright, Vivien Foster, Ana-María Ibáñez, Michele Gragnolati, Alessandra Marini, Jyotsna Puri, Gloria Rubio Soto, Emil Tesliuc, Jean-Philippe Tre, Quentin Wodon, Michael Woolcock. Carlos Becerra and Martha Rodriguez provided valuable inputs in Guatemala. Lerick Kebeck provided task assistance and managed the production and presentation of the report. The Spanish version was translated by LTS translation, with editing and review kindly provided by Lerick Kebeck and Lorena Cohan. Shelton Davis, Peter Lanjouw, Jose Roberto Lopez Calix, and Tomas Rosada Villamar served as Peer Reviewers and Advisors throughout the process. Michael Walton, Alberto Valdés, Indermit Gill, Quentin Wodon, Jeni Klugman, and Jehan Arulpragasam provided additional advice. The team also benefited from the guidance of the management team: Guillermo Perry (Chief Economist), Ana-María Arriagada (Director and Sector Manager), Donna Dowsett-Coirolo and Jane Armitage (Country Directors), Suzana Augusto (Country Officer), Ian Bannon and Felipe Jaramillo

(Lead Economists), Norman Hicks (Sector Manager), Helena Ribe (Sector Leader), Eduardo Somensatto (Resident Representative), and Chris Chamberlin (Sector Manager). Finally, the team benefited from the advice of two "Quality Enhancement Review Panels," one on vulnerability analysis consisting of Lant Pritchett, Lynne Sherburne-Benz, Michael Woolcock, Tamar Manuelyan Atinc, and the other transport and poverty, Christina Malmberg-Calvo, Dominique van de Walle, Robin Carruthers, and Hanan Jacoby along with Guillermo Ruan, our partner on the transport side. In addition, we benefited from the inputs and support of the Multi-Sector Team Learning Initiative, particularly from the assistance of our "coach," Jennifer Sara.

Funding for the study was generously provided by the World Bank (including from the Institutional Development Fund), the Government of Denmark, the Government of Japan, and the Government of the Netherlands. Funding for the MECOVI Program was generously provided by the World Bank, the IDB, CEPAL, USAID, the Soros Foundation, UNDP, UNICEF, and the ILO.

Vice President	David de Ferranti
Country Director	Jane Armitage
LCSPR Director	Ernesto May
LCSHD Director	Ana-Maria Arriagada
Sector Manager-Poverty	Norman Hicks
Sector Manager-Social Protection	Christopher Chamberlin
Sector Leader	Helena Ribe
Resident Representative	Eduardo Somensatto
Task Manager	Kathy Lindert

---

[i]Program for the Improvement of Surveys and Measurement of Living Conditions in Latin America and the Caribbean (MECOVI). Sponsors of the program include the Inter-American Development Bank (IDB), the World Bank (IBRD), and the Economic Committee for Latin America and the Caribbean (CEPAL), as well as USAID, the Soros Foundation, UNDP, UNICEF, and the ILO.

[ii]This initiative, called the "Qualitative Poverty and Exclusion Study" (QPES) was generously sponsored by the Danish Government. The work was carried out by local consultants under a contract with COWI consulting.

ACRONYMS AND ABBREVIATIONS

ANACAFE	National Coffee Association
AP	All poor
ARI	Acute respiratory infections
ASIES	Asociación de Investigación y Estudios Sociales
BNI	Basic Needs Indicators
CA	Central America
CAS	Country Assistance Strategy
CELADE	Centro Latinoamericano y Caribeño de Demografía
CEM	Country Economic Memorandum
CIEN	Centro de Investigaciones Económicas Nacionales
CONRED	Coordinadora Nacional para la Reducción de Desastres
DHS	Demographic and Health Survey
DIGEBI	Dirección General de Educación Bilingüe
DNS	Debt-for-nature swap intercultural
ENCOVI	Living Standards Measurement Survey
ENIGFAM	Encuesta Nacional de Ingresos y Gastos Familiares
ERP	Estrategia para la Reducción de la Pobreza
FAO	Food & Agriculture Organization
FIS	Social Investment Fund
FLACSO	Facultad Latinoamericana de Ciencias Sociales
FOGUAVI	Fondo Guatemalteco para la Vivienda
FPL	Full poverty line
FUNDAZUCAR	Fundación del Azúcar
GUAPA	Guatemala Poverty Assessment Program (World Bank)
HAZ	High by age index (Malnutrition)
HDI	Human Development Index
HH	Household
HIPC	Highly Indebted Poor Countries
ILO	International Labor Organization
IGSS	Instituto Guatemalteco de Seguridad Social
INCAP	Instituto de Nutrición de Centro América y Panamá
INE	National Statistics Institute; Instituto Nacional de Estadística–Guatemala
INFOM-UNEPAR	Instituto de Fomento Municipal–Unidad Ejecutora del Programa de Acueductos Rurales
KA1, KA2	Kaqchiqel communities in QPES study
KI1, KI2	K'iché communities in QPES study
L1, L2	Ladino communities in QPES study
LAC	Latin America and the Caribbean Region
LSMS	Living Standards Measurement Study
M1, M2	Mam communities in QPES study
MAGA	Ministerio de Agricultura, Ganadería y Alimentación
MDG	Millennium Development Goals
MECOVI	Program for the Improvement of Surveys and Measurement of Living Conditions in Latin America and the Caribbean
MINEDUC	Ministry of Education
MINUGUA	United Nations Verification Mission—Misión de Verificación de las Naciones Unidas en Guatemala
MSPAS	Ministry of Public Health and Social Assistance

NGO	Nongovernmental Organization
NP	Non-poor
PRONADE	Programa Nacional de Autogestión para el Desarollo Educativo
PPP	Purchasing Power Parity
PRSP/ERP	Poverty Reduction Strategy Paper
PSU	Primary Sample Unit
PTA	Parent-teachers association (school committees)
QE1, QE2	Q'eqchi communities in QPES study
QPES	Qualitative Poverty and Exclusion Study (ECEP)
SA	Social Assistance
SAS	Secretaria de Asuntos Sociales de la Municipalidad de Guatemala
SBS	Secretaria de Bienestar Social de la Presidencia de la República
SEGEPLAN	Secretaria de Planificación y Programación
SI	Social Insurance
SIAS	Sistema Integral de Atención de Salud
SIAF	Integrated Financial Management System
SOSEP	ecretaria de Obras Sociales de la Esposa del Presidente
SP	Social Protection
UNDP	United Nations Development Program
UNICEF	United Nations International Children's Emergency Fund
URL	Universidad Rafael Landívar
USAID	United States Agency for International Development
VAT	Value Added Tax
WAZ	Weight by age Index (Malnutrition)
WDR	World Development Report
WHO	World Health Organization
XPL	Extreme poverty line
WHZ	Weight by High Index
XP	Extreme poor

CURRENCY EQUIVALENTS
US$1 = Q7.70 (July 1, 2000)
US$1 = Q7.78 (Current)

FISCAL YEAR
December 31–January 1

EXECUTIVE SUMMARY

Objectives of Report. This report is part of a collaborative multi-year program of analytical work and technical assistance (the Guatemala Poverty Assessment Program, or "GUAPA" program). The poverty assessment report itself has three main objectives. The first is to conduct an in-depth, multi-dimensional analysis of poverty building on the framework of the World Bank's World Development Report (WDR) for 2000/2001 using both quantitative and qualitative data. The second is to examine the impact of government policies and spending on the poor. The third is to use the empirical findings to identify options and priorities for poverty reduction in the future. Policy options are outlined not only in general, but for the specific themes and sectors covered. It is hoped that the report will make an empirical contribution to improving the Government's anti-poverty policies and strategies (broadly as well as for specific sectors). The report is also expected to contribute to the definition of the country assistance strategy (CAS) and lending operations of the World Bank and other donors, so as to make these interventions more effective in the future. This type of study is conducted by the World Bank in its client countries on a regular basis with the objective of assessing the poverty situation of the country in question.

Analytical Framework. The GUAPA embraces the conceptual framework developed in the World Development Report (WDR) 2000/2001 that stresses the multi-dimensionality of poverty. Poverty is associated with (a) a low level and productivity of assets, which constrain opportunities; (b) exclusion from institutional, social and political spheres; and (c) vulnerability to risks and shocks. Reducing poverty requires concerted efforts on all of these inter-connected dimensions: expanding the opportunities of the poor, empowering them, and improving the security of their well-being.

Data. An innovative aspect of the GUAPA is its combination of qualitative and quantitative data sources, which are both valuable in their own right but yield important synergies when used together. The primary source of quantitative information is the Living Standards Measurement Survey (*Encuesta Nacional de Condiciones de Vida*, ENCOVI 2000), which was conducted by the *Instituto Nacional de Estadística—Guatemala* (INE) under the auspices of the MECOVI

I

Program.[1] The study also draws on the results of a Qualitative Poverty and Exclusion Study (QPES) covering 10 rural villages of different ethnicities that were also included in the ENCOVI sample. The QPES was designed to complement the ENCOVI with in-depth information of perceptions of poverty, vulnerability, social capital, education, public services, and gender roles.

Collaborative Approach. The approach embraced by the GUAPA/MECOVI program is as important as this report itself. It is based on a highly collaborative process between the Government, the World Bank, and other donors[2] designed to build local capacity for, and ownership of, the analysis of poverty. The process involved continuous cooperation, technical assistance and training with three main counterpart agencies: INE, the planning secretariat (SEGEPLAN), and the University of Rafael Landívar (URL). The process has already generated several outputs, including the ENCOVI and its database; a new and improved Poverty Map designed to serve as a policy tool for targeting public spending and interventions (constructed by the SEGEPLAN-INE-URL technical team with World Bank technical support); the training and capacity building of numerous staff in these agencies; and technical support to the Government's poverty reduction strategy (PRSP).

Guatemala's Poverty Problem is Serious

Poverty in Guatemala is high and deep. In 2000, over half of all Guatemalans—56% or about 6.4 million people—lived in poverty. About 16% lived in extreme poverty. Available evidence suggests that poverty in Guatemala is higher than in other Central American countries, despite its mid-range ranking using per capita GDP (US$3,630 in PPP terms). The costs of reducing poverty are also high. Given average consumption levels of the poor, it is estimated that the minimum *annual* cost to eradicate poverty is equal to about 8% of GDP. To put this in context, total Government spending in 2000 was about 13%. Moreover, these costs are hypothetical; they represent the cost of bringing all the poor up to the poverty line, excluding the inevitable administrative costs or leakages to the non-poor associated with virtually all poverty-alleviation schemes.

Although poverty has fallen over the past decade, it has increased in recent years. Poverty is estimated to have fallen from about 62% in 1989 to 56% in 2000.[3] This drop is slightly slower than what would have been predicted given Guatemala's growth rates, suggesting that growth has not been particularly "pro-poor." This pattern arises largely because growth in the rural sectors—where the poor are largely concentrated—has been slower than in other areas. Moreover, projections suggest that poverty has actually increased slightly in 2001 and 2002, due to a series of economic shocks. These projections are based on estimated growth rates which are estimated to have fallen in those years (with slightly negative per capita growth rates once population growth is taken into account).

Poverty and vulnerability are mainly chronic, not transient. While 56% of Guatemala's population lived in poverty in 2000, the majority of these (79%) were chronically poor, whereas only a fifth were transient poor. Likewise, while 64% of the population could be considered vulnerable to poverty, the majority of these are vulnerable due to low overall expected consumption rather than high volatility of consumption. The chronic nature of poverty and vulnerability highlights the importance of building the assets of the poor, rather than focusing primarily on the expansion of public safety nets or social insurance. Nonetheless, some public transfers (social assis-

---

1. The "Program for the Improvement of Surveys and Measurement of Living Conditions in Latin America and the Caribbean" (MECOVI), is sponsored by the Inter-American Development Bank (IDB), the World Bank (IBRD) under the GUAPA program, and the Economic Committee for Latin America and the Caribbean (CEPAL) with additional funding from a number of other donors, including USAID, the Soros Foundation, UNDP, UNICEF, and the ILO.

2. In particular, the IDB, UNDP, USAID, UNICEF, the Soros Foundation and the ILO.

3. Comparing estimates of poverty over time in Guatemala is complex due to large differences in survey and measurement methodologies (see Chapter 2). The estimates for 1989 are adjusted to make them more methodologically comparable to those for 2000.

tance) could indeed be desirable to alleviate the poverty and suffering of the *extreme* poor, particularly when linked to participation in health and education activities.

Poverty is predominantly rural, and higher among the indigenous. Over 81% of the poor and 93% of the extreme poor live in the countryside. Three quarters of all rural residents live in poverty and one quarter live in extreme poverty. Poverty is also significantly higher among the indigenous (76% are poor) as compared with the non-indigenous population (41% are poor).

While pockets of poverty pepper the country, there is also a significant "poverty belt" in the Northern and North-Western Regions. Poverty in Guatemala is a national problem, with pockets of poverty spread throughout the country. Nonetheless, poverty is significantly lower in the Metropolitan region around the capital, and much higher in the North and Northwest Regions, as well as the Department of San Marcos, which were largely affected by the country's three-decades long civil war.

Inequality is also quite high. With Gini indices for consumption and income of 48 and 57 respectively, Guatemala ranks among the more unequal countries of the world. The population is characterized by a large "low-income" majority and a small high-income minority, with the top quintile accounting for 54% of total consumption. There are significant inequities across ethnic groups. Although the indigenous represent 43% of the population, they claim less than a quarter of total income and consumption.

Malnutrition rates among Guatemalan children are abysmally high—among the worst in the world. Some 44% of children under five are stunted.[4] There is a strong correlation between poverty and malnutrition, as four fifths of malnourished children are poor. Moreover, malnutrition is declining more slowly in Guatemala than in other countries.

Guatemala also ranks poorly for health outcomes. Guatemala ranks among the worst in LAC for life expectancy, infant mortality and maternal mortality. The patterns of health indicators also suggest worse conditions for the poor, rural, and indigenous populations. Though health outcomes have improved over the past 20 years, Guatemala's progress has been slower than the low-income countries of Bolivia, Nicaragua and Honduras.

Although Guatemala's performance in education still lags, with important biases against the poor, progress has been made. With an illiteracy rate of 31%, only Nicaragua and Haiti rank worse in LAC. Likewise, educational attainment is extremely low (4.3 years on average). Nonetheless, Guatemala has made progress in improving the educational stock. Current primary enrollment has also expanded, particularly since the signing of the Peace Accords in 1996. Nonetheless, coverage is still low and biased towards the non-poor.

Progress is also evident for basic utility services, though important gaps and disparities remain. Overall, about 70% of Guatemalan households have piped water and electricity. Almost 90% have some kind of basic sanitation, though fewer than half have sewerage. About 20% subscribe to either a fixed line and/or a cellular telephone service. Expansions in coverage have accelerated since the signing of the Peace Accords in 1996, with a targeted expansion for disadvantaged groups. Nonetheless, important disparities remain, with significant coverage gaps for the poor, particularly in rural areas.

While Poverty is Largely Determined by Household Characteristics and Assets . . .

Poverty is clearly associated with lower levels or productivity of key assets, including labor, education, physical assets (including basic utility services, land, and housing), and social capital. Geographic location and household size are also found to be important correlates of poverty. Disparities in assets also constitute the main sources of inequality, with education accounting for over half of all inequality in Guatemala. The cross-sectional *relationship* between these assets and poverty is similar to that found in other countries.

---

4. According to the Height-for-Age (HAZ) measure.

... Historical and Contextual Factors also Shape Guatemala's Poverty Profile

History and context matter. A combination of historical and contextual factors have fundamentally influenced Guatemala's performance regarding the *levels* of the endowments and characteristic determinants of poverty observed today. They also provide hints about key challenges and potential levers to reduce poverty tomorrow. This report does not purport to conduct an exhaustive review of these historical and contextual factors; rather it seeks to simply highlight the importance of these factors in influencing poverty in Guatemala.

In terms of context, two key features play an important role in shaping the profile of poverty: geographic isolation and ethnic exclusion. First, while Guatemala is a physically diverse country, geographic isolation—due to its complex topography and an inadequate road network—limits opportunities, constrains social networks, and fosters vulnerability. Overall, 13% of households lack any form of adequate motorable road access, with an even higher degree of physical isolation among the poorest quintiles and the indigenous.[5] **Second,** while Guatemala's population is rich in cultural and linguistic diversity, this diversity has historically been accompanied by conflict, exclusion and a dualistic social and economic structure. In a population of over 11 million, about half the population is indigenous, including some 23 ethno-linguistic groups. Internationally, countries with significant indigenous populations tend to have higher overall poverty rates. Within these countries, the indigenous tend to be poorer than the non-indigenous population due to historically exclusionary forces. In this regard, Guatemala is no exception.

In fact, past policies greatly contributed to an exclusionary pattern of development in Guatemala, particularly for land, labor, and education. All of these spheres were intertwined with each other, and with the development of coffee, Guatemala's primary export crop. Policies such as massive land expropriations, forced labor, and exclusion from the education system (as part of a broader political strategy), all sought to promote economic growth, but to the exclusion and detriment of the indigenous population. Women were also excluded from these spheres. As a result of these policies—and despite having almost twice the per capita GDP of Honduras, Nicaragua, or Bolivia—Guatemala already ranked behind these countries by 1960 on several key social indicators. It also lagged significantly behind the collective group of comparable "lower-middle income countries."

The 36-year civil war further imposed costs on the Guatemala's development. Somewhat paradoxically, Guatemala managed to maintain reasonable growth rates in the early phases of the war, though growth did fall during the peak of the conflict in the 1980s. In addition to a large loss of life, the war had serious short- and long-run impacts on Guatemala's development, for the overall economy (lost jobs, productivity, output), human capital (and hence long-run growth), and for life at the village level. THE PEACE ACCORDS SIGNALED A SHIFT TOWARDS A MORE INCLUSIVE DEVELOPMENT PATH

The Peace Accords represented a turning point for Guatemala's development path, paving the way for a transformation to a more prosperous and inclusive nation. Key areas of emphasis related to economic development and poverty reduction include: a focus on human development, goals for productive and sustainable development, a program for the modernization of the democratic state, and strengthening and promoting participation. The rights of the indigenous and women were also highlighted as cross-cutting themes throughout the accords, in an attempt to reverse the historical exclusion of these groups.

Moreover, given the importance of improving living conditions to lasting peace, poverty reduction has taken center stage on the current social policy agenda. In particular, the Government recently outlined its poverty reduction strategy in an important policy document "Estrategia de Reducción de la Pobreza" (ERP),[6] presented at the Consultative Group meetings in

---

5. This statistic refers to households in the ENCOVI questionnaire for which community-level data were available, see Chapter 10 for details.

6. SEGEPLAN (November 2001).

February 2002. General principles emphasized in the ERP include: a rural focus, using the poverty map for targeting; efficient and transparent public spending; decentralization; and participation. Key action areas include: (a) promoting growth with equity; (b) investing in human capital (emphasizing health, education and food security); and (c) investing in physical capital (particularly water and sanitation, rural roads, electricity, and rural development). Cross-cutting issues in the ERP include multiculturalism and inter-culturality, gender equity, and vulnerability.

Progress has Occurred . . . But Challenges Remain

In the six years since the signing of the Peace Accords, Guatemala has taken important steps on this new development path, with progress in public sector management, public revenues and spending, and improvements in the coverage and equity of education and basic services. Importantly, these steps signal that progress *is* possible, despite the magnitude of the challenge of changing the course of history.

However, changing the course of history in such a short time span is not easy in any country. The hierarchical relations, attitudes, and institutional forces that have pervaded for centuries do not disappear over night. Furthermore, recent events (including Hurricane Mitch and political instability) have delayed the implementation of the Peace Agenda.

Moreover, despite progress, households do not perceive significant improvements in living conditions. While communities in the ENCOVI do perceive progress—and attribute it to improvements in basic services—households are decidedly more pessimistic about changes in their welfare since the Peace Accords. They attribute these perceptions to economic factors, such as a lack of increases in incomes and opportunities (factors that directly affect "their wallets").

Many of the challenges for poverty reduction coincide largely with the remaining actions on the Peace Agenda. In particular, select development-related targets supported by the Peace Accords have not been met, especially those involving outcomes in health, education and economic growth as well as fundamental institutional reforms. The lack of progress for these key development outcomes reflects the need for poverty reduction and improvements in living conditions, which are crucial for lasting peace. This overlapping between the Peace Agenda and the poverty agenda highlights remaining priority challenges in several key areas: (a) creating opportunities; (b) reducing vulnerability; and (c) improving institutions and empowering communities.

Key Challenge: Building Opportunities and Assets

Despite Guatemala's historically reasonable *economic growth rates*, current growth is neither sufficiently fast nor oriented towards the poor. Guatemala has historically enjoyed relative macroeconomic stability and reasonable growth (averaging 3.9% over the period from 1950–2000). Nonetheless, growth did not favor the poor because the economy did not generate enough low-skilled jobs. Agriculture, which employs the majority of the poor, experienced below-average growth rates over the past 20 years. In addition, other sectors did not grow fast enough to offer enough employment opportunities for the poor. Reflecting these trends, the estimated decline in poverty over the past decade has been slightly slower than what would have been expected with neutral growth. Moreover, growth has fallen in recent years, and may have caused a slight increase in poverty.

As a result, faster growth and interventions to reach the poor are necessary to reach the Millennium Development Goals (MDGs). Given current growth projections, the record for meeting such targets is likely to be mixed. Targets for most social indicators established by the Government's poverty reduction strategy (ERP)[7] should be met by 2005. Nonetheless, extreme poverty is not expected to fall as ambitiously as anticipated under the ERP due to slower overall growth in 2001 and 2002. Moreover, given projected growth rates, it does not seem likely that Guatemala will meet most of the more ambitious targets for health and education established under the international MDGs (Table 5.6). As a result, faster growth and interventions to boost

---

7. Estrategia de Reducción de la Pobreza (November 2001).

the assets of the poor are clearly needed to improve living conditions enough to meet these goals. As discussed below, further work is needed to define key actions for a pro-poor growth strategy.

The poor are constrained in terms of *opportunities and livelihoods*. The poor are highly dependent on agricultural income (which accounts for about half of the total income of the poorest quintile, as compared with just 3% for the top quintile). Poorer households are fairly homogeneous in their occupations, dividing their labor primarily between agriculture, self-employment, and blue collar jobs (mainly in the informal sector), which all yield significantly relatively lower incomes. Some 87% of the rural poor depend on agriculture, either as small-scale subsistence farmers or agricultural day laborers. Indeed, poverty rates among these groups are significantly higher than among those whose main source of income comes from non-agricultural employment.

Similarly, women and the indigenous face both constrained opportunities and discrimination on the labor market. The indigenous appear limited to lower-paying jobs, primarily in agriculture. Non-Spanish speakers also face considerably lower incomes. While a relatively low share of women participate in the labor market, those that do are highly concentrated in the informal sector, which generates lower incomes. Finally, the indigenous face considerable wage discrimination, even after controlling for human capital and job differences. Women also face wage discrimination, but the wage gap between men and women is smaller than the one between the indigenous and non-indigenous.

Agriculture is unlikely to serve as a major vehicle for poverty reduction. While the poor are highly dependent on agriculture (subsistence farming and agricultural jobs), agriculture is not likely to be a dynamic source of new employment opportunities and will probably continue to shrink as a share of GDP. Agriculture has faced declining growth rates over the past several decades. Within agriculture, traditional crops, such as coffee, which tend to employ a significant number of workers, are contracting in the face of a structural terms-of-trade decline. The production of non-traditional crops has expanded significantly, but not enough to replace the earnings and employment opportunities lost by the coffee crisis. Data from the ENCOVI suggest that relatively few households overall are involved in the production of non-traditional exports, and most are non-poor.[8] Poor farming households are primarily involved in the production of subsistence crops. Similarly, while very few households report having received technical assistance (only 3% overall), over 70% of public technical assistance was reported by non-poor households. As such, although the poor will likely to continue to depend on agriculture as an important source of income, it is unlikely that agriculture will provide the solution to the poverty problem or that many people will escape poverty via agriculture.

Although land is an important asset, its ownership is highly inequitable in Guatemala. Moreover, the holdings of the poor tend to be: (a) quite small, often providing below-subsistence incomes; (b) untitled; (c) poorly located (geographically isolated); and (d) of poor quality. Market-based land reform efforts are promising and should continue to be pursued, although high costs and design issues remain to be addressed.

Non-farm employment opportunities could provide a route out of poverty in rural areas. Multivariate regressions signal a strongly negative correlation between non-farm activities and poverty. Indeed, almost half of the rural non-poor are landless, typically working in a variety of jobs (for example, as self-employed entrepreneurs in commerce or manufacturing or in non-farm salaried jobs). Nonetheless, a variety of barriers constrain access by the poor to non-farm opportunities, particularly geographic location, inadequate infrastructure and education. Additional analytical work should be conducted to further define such a strategy.

Indeed, geographic location is highly correlated with poverty and employment opportunities. The spatial proximity to larger cities offers considerable advantages, with higher poverty rates and fewer employment opportunities in smaller municipalities.

---

8. Though it is possible that some were poor before getting involved in the production of non-traditional exports. The single year nature of data collected in the ENCOVI do not allow for such analysis.

Improving *education* is central to both the Peace Agenda and the poverty agenda. Indeed, education is a crucial determinant of poverty, inequality, and earnings. It also greatly influences health outcomes, malnutrition and fertility rates.

There have been significant improvements in education, particularly since the signing of the Peace Accords in 1996. Notably, (a) the sector has undergone important institutional and structural reforms (including some decentralization and deconcentration); (b) public spending on education has increased significantly since 1996, with the bulk going to the primary level; (c) literacy and educational attainment are increasing over time, with important reductions in disparities between genders, ethnicities, and the poor versus the non-poor; (d) coverage has accelerated at all levels since the Peace Accords, particularly the primary level, and the expansion has been well-targeted to the poor (largely through the PRONADE program); and (e) official statistics on internal efficiency suggest improvements.

Nonetheless, important challenges remain. Significant coverage gaps and disparities remain, particularly for the poor, girls, rural, and indigenous children. Very few poor make it to the secondary level, and inequalities in earnings are largely generated at this level. Despite progress, indicators of internal efficiency suggest serious structural deficiencies in the educational system. Moreover, the low returns to primary school suggest shortcomings in the quality of schooling. Demand-side factors, particularly the direct costs of attending school, are the main constraints to increased coverage at the primary level. Secondary enrollment is constrained by both supply- and demand-side constraints, particularly the direct costs of attending school and opportunity costs (work and domestic duties). The targeting of public spending on education is neutral at best, and highly regressive at the secondary and university levels. PRONADE is the exception: it is highly targeted to the poor (with only 8% of beneficiaries being non-poor). Existing demand-side programs, such as scholarships and the school transport subsidy, are *highly* regressive, with most benefits going to the non-poor. Other programs (for example, school feeding and the *bolsa de utiles* program) are slightly better targeted, but mainly benefit the middle quintiles of the population.

While Guatemala has made some progress in the *health* sector, significant challenges remain for improving health outcomes. Progress has mainly centered on sectoral reforms (for example, some decentralization and deconcentration). In spite of these, key health outcomes (malnutrition, infant mortality, maternal mortality, and morbidity) are not improving as fast as they should, and Guatemala remains among the worst performers in LAC. Health outcomes are worse among the poor, the indigenous, and rural residents, suggesting a need for better targeted interventions. A significant share of the population lacks access to affordable health services, particularly the poor and rural and indigenous residents.

A combination of supply- and demand-side factors appears to be blocking improved health access. On the supply side, services are fragmented; insurance coverage is minimal; inefficiencies in public funding are generated by use of highly-subsidized public facilities by the few who are insured (virtually exclusively the non-poor); and even when facilities are available, they often lack medicines, doctors or staff. Public spending on health has not increased sufficiently and public spending is not well targeted to the poor. On the demand side, economic barriers (direct costs of health care) present the main constraint to improved access. Although public health care is highly subsidized, private health care is relatively expensive. As such, in situations in which only private services are available, disadvantaged groups lack access due to economic constraints. Cultural barriers further constrain access of the indigenous population to health care.

There has been significant progress in expanding the equitable provision of *basic utility services* since the signing of the Peace Accords in 1996. Notably: (a) sectoral reforms have improved competition and efficiency; (b) the volume of resources channeled towards the expansion of rural service provision has increased substantially through a variety of new and existing institutional mechanisms; (c) overall coverage of basic services has accelerated considerably since 1996; and (d) this expansion has been well-targeted, with new connections going disproportionately to traditionally disadvantaged groups.

Nonetheless, significant coverage gaps and disparities in access remain. A significant share of those without access to basic services live in communities where the services are present but do not connect due to demand-side barriers, such as the direct costs of connecting to and using services. As such, demand-side interventions, not just the physical provision of infrastructure will be needed. Given existing rates of expansion, it will take more than eight years to reach universal coverage for all services except sanitation, and the total cost of meeting universality is estimated at between US$1–1.5 billion. In addition, energy subsidies (under the "*tarifa social*") are extremely poorly targeted, benefiting primarily the non-poor. Finally, the quality of piped water services is poor (non-potable and irregular).

Guatemala especially needs to extend the road network and public *transport* to the poor, particularly in rural areas. Rural residents and the poor are relatively more isolated in terms of road and transport access. There is a significant inverse correlation between access to the motorable road network. Year-round access is also crucial, with road closures from rains and landslides further cutting off access to opportunities and services. The poor also lack access to public transportation, which appears to be correlated with a lack of adequate roads in rural areas. Road improvements since the Peace Accords appear to have favored the non-poor and urban residents. The ENCOVI shows that inadequate road access significantly constrains the access of the poor and rural residents to health services, opportunities and institutions, further exacerbating their isolation.

Key Challenge: Reducing Vulnerability by Building Assets

The lack of adequate assets makes the poor vulnerable to shocks. Despite the lack of any major macro shocks in 2000, households in Guatemala report a high incidence of shocks that year, and most experienced multiple shocks with varying duration of impact. The effects of shocks are multi-dimensional, affecting not only income, wealth and consumption, but also community assets, the psychological and social well-being of individuals, families and communities, health and education. The poor are more exposed to natural disasters and agriculture-related shocks. They also have lower resilience to shocks than the non-poor. The cost of shocks is significant. Economic shocks have larger and more severe impacts than other types of shocks. Possible sources of vulnerability in the future include: (a) worsening terms-of-trade and job loss (such as those associated with the crisis in the coffee sector); and (b) natural disasters. All are likely to have lasting and severe impacts on the poor.

Certain sub-groups of the population are inherently or structurally vulnerable due to special circumstances. Specifically, key vulnerable groups include young children, who are vulnerable to malnutrition and lack of development; school-aged children, who are vulnerable due to lack of educational opportunities and child labor; the working poor, particularly those in agriculture, due to low earnings and susceptibility to natural shocks; poor households lacking basic services; seasonal migrants and their families; and poor, rural households living in areas prone to natural disasters.

Faced with shocks, Guatemalan households tend to rely primarily on their own assets, with little Government assistance. The main coping strategies include reduced consumption or self-help. Few households report receiving any formal governmental or non-governmental assistance in the face of shocks. The poor are less equipped than the non-poor to fight shocks, and are more likely to reduce consumption (regrettably, of basic staples) or use existing assets (particularly labor). The non-poor are more likely than the poor to use market-based insurance mechanisms.

Indeed, existing public social protection[9] programs are poorly targeted and inefficient. Social insurance is virtually exclusively limited to (a small share of) the non-poor. Public social

---

9. An adequate social protection system is an important element of a comprehensive strategy to reduce poverty and vulnerability. **Social protection** (SP) has been traditionally defined as "a set of public measures aimed at providing income security for individuals." (Holzmann and Jørgensen 2000). The final goal of public social protection policies is to increase the welfare of the population, and to that end, these schemes have generally included social assistance (SA) and social insurance (SI) programs. **Social assistance** programs are generally designed to help individuals or households cope with chronic poverty or transient declines in income that would cause them to live in a situation of poverty or worsening poverty. As such, they help alleviate poverty and reduce vulnerability to poverty. SA programs as a whole make up what is commonly referred to

assistance programs are scattered across many agencies, with many gaps and duplications in coverage. Moreover, they are generally regressive. Private transfers (such as international and domestic remittances, charity and donations) are an important source of income, accounting for almost half of all transfers received by households in Guatemala. Nonetheless, the current distribution of transfers reveals that they do not go to the poorest groups (and in fact are regressive), and hence do not compensate for inadequacies in the public social safety net.

Key Challenge: Building Institutions and Empowering Communities

Despite some progress, a weak public sector has hampered Guatemala's efforts to improve living conditions and promote a more inclusive society. In addition, it has affected the menu of options for reducing poverty and the ways in which these interventions are carried out. Though there has been some progress in public finances and public expenditure management, significant challenges remain, including: (a) the weak tax base (about 10% of GDP in 2001), which significantly constrains public spending (about 13% of GDP in 2001); (b) public expenditure management needs additional strengthening, with better links to policy, planning, and priorities; (c) public spending is poorly targeted; (d) public sector accountability and responsiveness needs to be improved; (e) the civil service is weak, hampered by inefficient hiring practices; and (f) the Government is highly centralized, especially given the heterogeneity of Guatemala's population and communities.[10]

Governance is also weak. Good governance is important for poverty reduction, and has been linked to higher incomes, lower infant mortality and higher literacy. Guatemala scores poorly on most governance indicators, particularly those for corruption, the rule of law and the justice system, and political instability, all of which damage the climate for growth and investment. The Government has recently undertaken a number of important initiatives designed to improve governance, including issuing a Letter of Intent *(Carta de Intenciones del Gobierno de Guatemala)* to develop a national program to promote transparency and reduce corruption.

At the community level, social capital is limited and concentrated among the more privileged groups in society. Communities have an important role to play in promoting their own development, particularly in light of Guatemala's weak public sector. Social capital can offer significant benefits to community welfare, including managing local public goods, coping with shocks, and leveraging external assistance. Nonetheless, the ENCOVI and QPES suggest that social capital in Guatemala is mainly concentrated in strong horizontal, within-village connections, with weaker bridges to other communities or links to formal institutions. This pattern reflects the physical isolation of many communities and decades of civil war and exclusion. Moreover, the ENCOVI and QPES suggest that social capital appears to be concentrated among the more privileged groups, with women, the poor, and the uneducated significantly less likely to participate at the community level. The recent passage of three laws[11] on decentralization and participation is an important step towards creating a legal framework for the empowerment of local communities. The implementation of these laws should seek to reverse the traditional exclusion of women, the poor, and uneducated from community-level participation.

---

as "the social safety net," and include programs such as transfers (in cash or kind), subsidies, and workfare. **Social insurance** schemes include publicly-provided or mandated insurance for unemployment, old age (pensions), disability, survivorship, sickness, and so forth, which are designed to help mitigate income risks. Private transfers can complement public social protection interventions.

10. Though there is a current move towards greater decentralization, with the passage of three recent laws by the Congress (the *Ley de los Consejos de Desarrollo Urbano y Rural,* the *Código Municipal,* and the *Ley General de Descentralización*).

11. The *Ley de los Consejos de Desarrollo Urbano y Rural,* the *Código Municipal,* and the *Ley General de Descentralización*.

Other actors—particularly the private sector, NGOs, and religious groups—are active players in the fight against poverty. Given the limited size and scope of the public sector, partnerships should be sought with these actors to help advance the poverty-reduction agenda.

A Broad Agenda to Reduce Poverty

In developing a broad agenda for poverty reduction, three caveats are important to emphasize at the outset:

■ **First, while there is no single "blueprint" for poverty reduction, there are some key levers that take central stage for national efforts to reduce poverty,** and these are the emphasis of this report. Nonetheless, efforts should be made to tailor this broad agenda to local conditions, particularly in a country as heterogeneous as Guatemala. To this end, efforts are underway in Guatemala to develop not only a national poverty reduction strategy, but also localized strategies at the department and municipal levels.[12]

■ **Second, the policy discussion is aimed primarily at the perspective of policy makers and the role of the public sector;** hence it emphasizes interventions that both (a) would have a substantial impact on poverty; and (b) merit the use of public resources in a market-oriented economy. Nonetheless, other actors, such as the private sector and other facets of civil society (communities, NGOs, religious organizations), also have an important role to play in reducing poverty. The private sector, in particular, will provide the central arena for economic growth and productive activities, which are crucial for poverty reduction. Other facets of civil society are clear partners in this poverty reduction agenda, and will play crucial roles in prioritization and implementation of public sector actions, as well as the provision of other services and interventions that are beyond the scope of the public sector.

■ **Third, poverty reduction is a multi-dimensional and long-term process.** There is no single magic bullet to reduce poverty. Rather, efforts should be made to attack the poverty problem from a multitude of angles, including those to foster opportunity, build assets, reduce vulnerability, and improve institutions and empower communities. Moreover, poverty reduction does not occur over night. Implementation of key actions to reduce poverty takes time, and often the impact of such actions occurs over an even longer time frame (for example, into subsequent political cycles, or even subsequent generations). That said, the sooner actions are undertaken, the more quickly the inter-generational cycle of poverty can be broken.

■ **Broadly speaking, a concerted strategy should be adopted to reduce poverty in Guatemala** by building opportunities and assets, reducing vulnerability, improving institutions and empowering communities. A broad agenda of actions in these areas is outlined in Table A.

■ **Building opportunities.** Economic growth is crucial, particularly given the relatively small size and capabilities of Guatemala's public sector. Moreover, a recurring theme that arises in the analysis is the fact that the poor, particularly the rural poor, women and the indigenous, are not able to fully participate in, or benefit from, the overall economic system. Therefore, improving employment and earnings opportunities is essential, and this depends largely on the actions of the private sector. The pattern of growth needs to be made more "pro-poor," with an emphasis on building opportunities for the rural poor, women and the indigenous. This will depend on complementary policies in two other key areas: building the assets (education, infrastructure, land and physical capital) of the poor (particularly the rural poor), as well as improving institutions and the investment climate.

■ **Building the assets of the poor.** Given the chronic nature of poverty in Guatemala, existing disparities, and linkages to the other key areas, this is arguably the most important area

---

12. These efforts are being led by SEGEPLAN under the ERP initiative.

TABLE A: MENU OF OPTIONS AND KEY ACTIONS FOR POVERTY REDUCTION

Main Constraints	Main Recommendations	
Key Issues	**Priority**	**Key Actions & Time Period for Actions and Impact**

BUILDING OPPORTUNITIES AND LIVELIHOODS: Priority overall, especially in rural areas

● **Growth has slowed and isn't very "pro-poor."** Economic growth is crucial for reducing poverty and building opportunities, particularly given the relatively small size and limited capabilities of Guatemala's public sector.
● **Households do not perceive improvements,** largely due to constrained opportunities and limited earnings
● **Limited opportunities and earnings** for the poor, particularly the rural poor, women, and the indigenous:
  ✓ Discrimination for women, indigenous
  ✓ Low profitability in agriculture
  ✓ Constrained entry for non-farm opportunities
	▪▪▪▪
	
	▪▪▪▪
	
	▪
	
	▪▪▪▪
	
	▪▪▪
	
	▪
	
	▪
	
	▪
		● Maintaining macroeconomic stability, with a careful plan for allocating public expenditures and strengthening tax collection; ACT: on-going, IMP: ST, MT
		● Improving the climate for growth, including governance and public sector management; ACT: ST, MT; IMP: MT, LT
		● Improving regulation and supervision of financial sector; ST
		● Promoting growth with emphasis in sectors that are likely to generate employment, such as non-agricultural sectors, via education and training, transport, basic infrastructure, and support to SMEs.; ACT: ST, MT; IMP: LT
		● Reducing transactions costs in accessing markets (e.g., with road access, basic services); ACT: ST, MT; IMP: MT, LT
		● Creating mechanisms to discourage labor-market discrimination for women and the indigenous; ACT: MT; IMP: LT
		● Expanding land titling and land markets programs; establishing financial institutions in rural areas; ACT: MT; IMP: MT
		● Expanding seasonal employment creation programs (such as existing food-for-work programs) to provide opportunities for the rural poor; ACT: MT; IMP: MT

BUILDING THE ASSETS OF THE POOR—EDUCATION:
Priority for poor overall, especially for girls, indigenous, rural

● **Disparities, gaps in access:**
  ✓ Pre-primary: all poor, esp. rural
  ✓ Primary: poor, esp. girls, indigenous
  ✓ Secondary: all poor
● **Demand-side constraints** (both primary and secondary)
● **Supply-side constraints** (mainly at secondary)
● **Internal efficiency, quality**
● **Weak targeting of pubic spending, education programs**
● **Health outcomes**—malnutrition, infant and maternal mortality, and morbidity—are inadequate and not improving fast enough
	▪▪▪
	
	▪▪▪▪
	
	▪▪▪
	
	▪▪▪▪
	
	▪▪▪
	
	▪▪▪▪
	
	▪▪▪▪
		● Continuing increases in public spending on education, particularly at primary and pre-primary levels; ACT: ST, MT; IMP: MT, LT
		● Expanding coverage, especially for girls and indigenous. Expansion should be implemented via decentralized PRONADE program using poverty map to replace supply-side restrictions as targeting mechanism; ACT: ST, MT; IMP: MT, LT
		● Lowering official age of entry for primary school from 7 to 6; ACT: ST; IMP: MT
		● Reviewing and improving quality, curriculum and performance standards, particularly at grades 1, 7, and 10 (transition years); ACT: ST, MT; IMP: MT, LT
		● Promoting, expanding, consolidating and improving demand-side programs, with emphasis on girls and indigenous children (e.g., scholarships, school feeding, bolsa de utiles); ACT: ST, MT; IMP: MT, LT
		● Increasing investments in early childhood development; ACT: ST, MT; IMP: MT, LT
		● Using poverty map and other mechanisms, to better target public spending and demand-side programs (e.g., scholarships, school feeding, bolsa de utiles); ACT: ST; IMP: MT

(continued)

TABLE A: MENU OF OPTIONS AND KEY ACTIONS FOR POVERTY REDUCTION (*CONTINUED*)		
Main Constraints	**Main Recommendations**	
Key Issues	**Priority**	**Key Actions & Time Period for Actions and Impact**
BUILDING THE ASSETS OF THE POOR—HEALTH: Priority for poor overall, especially for girls, indigenous, rural		
● **Public spending inadequate and not well targeted** ● **Significant share of population lacks access to affordable health care,** particularly the rural poor and indigenous ● **Supply-side constraints,** including fragmented services, minimal insurance coverage, waste in public spending, lack of medicines, doctors, staff ● **Demand-side constraints,** including cost and cultural barriers	■■■	● Increasing public spending and expanding access to health care combined with better targeting (via poverty maps and health posts/community centers); ACT: ST, MT; IMP: MT
	■■■	● Emphasizing preventative care, infectious and parasitic diseases, reproductive health, ey outcomes (mortality, malnutrition); ACT: ST, MT; IMP: MT
	■■	● Conducting a critical review of existing malnutrition interventions; ACT: ST; IMP: ST
	■■■	● Implementing specific interventions for malnutrition as a top priority: community-based information and behavioral change programs; growth monitoring for pregnant women and children under age two; micro-nutrient supplements. ACT: ST, MT; IMP: MT, LT
	■	● Focusing on demand-side interventions (e.g., conditional transfers) that could be channeled through self-targeted health posts/community centers; ACT: ST, MT; IMP: MT
	■■	● Promoting culturally-sensitive health care practices; ACT: ST, MT; IMP: MT
	■	● Conducting full review of supply-side issues; ACT: ST; IMP: MT
	■	● Developing monitoring system for health outcomes, including better and more regular measurement of infant and maternal mortality; ACT: ST; IMP: MT
	■■	● Adopting measures to improve efficiency and quality of services delivered (see Chapter 8); ACT: MT, LT; IMP: LT
	■■	● Facilitating increased awareness of family planning options so as to reduce Guatemala's high population growth rates, which constrain per capita income growth; ACT: ST, MT; IMP: LT
BUILDING THE ASSETS OF THE POOR—BASIC SERVICES: Priority for poor overall, especially for rural, indigenous		
● **Significant coverage gaps and disparities,** especially among rural poor and indigenous ● **Demand-side factors** (connections costs) ● **Supply-side constraints** (not available) ● **Energy subsidies** poorly targeted ● **Quality of water is poor** (not potable, irregular) ● **Geographic isolation** for rural poor, due to limited road network and public transport services	■■	● Maintaining and, if possible, increasing resources for expansion of services; ACT: ST, MT; IMP: MT
	■■	● Targeting service expansion to poor (particularly rural) using poverty map combined with geographic information on coverage gaps; ACT: ST; IMP: MT
	■■	● Developing strategy for demand-side constraints; ACT: ST; IMP: MT
	■	● Eliminating "tarifa social" energy subsidy and using resources to fund new connections instead; ACT: ST, but gradually; IMP: MT
	■	● Allowing water tariffs to rise to a level that allows water utilities to become financially sustainable and improve the quality of service offered; ACT: ST but gradually; IMP: ST-MT
	■■	● Encouraging social funds and other providers to consider measures to improve quality of water; ACT: ST; IMP: ST
	■■	● Complementing water and sanitation programs with measures to improve household hygiene and water treatment practices; ACT: ST; IMP: ST

TABLE A: MENU OF OPTIONS AND KEY ACTIONS FOR POVERTY REDUCTION (CONTINUED)

Main Constraints — Key Issues	Priority	Main Recommendations — Key Actions & Time Period for Actions and Impact
BUILDING THE ASSETS OF THE POOR—TRANSPORT: Priority for rural poor		
● **Road quality and closures** limit year-round access	■■	● Focusing public spending on transport on rural areas; ACT: ST; IMP: ST, MT
● **Road improvements have favored non-poor, urban areas**	■■■	● Expanding and improving *motorable* road network in rural areas, particularly by improving existing roads (including dirt roads); ACT: ST, MT; IMP: ST, MT
● **Inadequate road access significantly constrains access of rural poor to health services, opportunities, institutions**	■	● Targeting expansion and rehabilitation using combination of poverty map with road maps; ACT: ST, MT; IMP: ST, MT
REDUCING VULNERABILITY: Priority for all poor/vulnerable, particularly rural and specific vulnerable groups		
● **Lack of assets makes poor vulnerable to shocks,** particularly natural disasters and agriculture-related shocks	■■■	● Building assets of poor and key vulnerable groups (see Table B); ACT: ST, MT; IMP: MT, LT
	■■	● Expanding and improving disaster management relief; ACT: ST, MT; IMP: MT
● **Key sources of future vulnerability:** (a) coffee crisis; (b) lost remittances from global slowdown; (c) natural disasters	■	● Introducing catastrophic insurance schemes; ACT: MT; IMP: MT
	■■	● Improving targeting of social protection programs; ACT: ST, MT; IMP: MT
● **Certain sub-groups** are particularly vulnerable due to special circumstances	■	● Eliminating energy subsidy and school transport subsidy; ACT: ST; IMP: ST
● **Faced with shocks, households rely on own assets with little formal assistance**	■■	● Consolidating and improving scholarships and school feeding programs; ACT: ST, MT; IMP: ST, MT
● **Existing social protection programs are poorly targeted and inefficient**	■■	● Improving targeting of *bolsa de utiles* program; ACT: ST, MT; IMP: ST, MT
IMPROVING INSTITUTIONS AND EMPOWERING COMMUNITIES: Priority for all poor		
● **Weak public sector hampers poverty reduction efforts**	■■	● Improving tax base and tax collection; ACT: ST, MT; IMP: ST, MT
✓ Weak tax base, limited public spending	■■■	● Increasing and improving targeting of public spending; ACT: ST, MT; IMP: ST, MT
✓ Public exp. management needs strengthening	■■■	● Improving public expenditure management, with stronger links to policy, planning, and priorities; ACT: ST, MT; IMP: ST, MT
✓ Public spending poorly targeted		
✓ Weak civil service	■■	● Strengthening the civil service; ACT: MT; IMP: MT
✓ Overly centralized	■■	● Improving incentives for better service delivery (e.g., implementing recently-passed laws on decentralization, local *"control social,"* and service "report cards" and client satisfaction surveys); ACT: MT, LT; IMP: MT, LT
● **Governance weak, constrains growth and poverty reduction efforts:** corruption, lack of rule of law, inadequate justice system, political instability.	■■■	● Expanding and building on recent initiatives to fight corruption (e.g., an anti-corruption charter) and making it a top priority. ACT: ST, MT; IMP: ST, MT
● **Social capital limited, concentrated among privileged**	■■■	● Improving rule of law, justice system; ACT: ST, MT; IMP: ST, MT
✓ Limited networks outside villages	■■	● Promoting community-based development but with explicit outreach programs to ensure participation of excluded groups (women, poor, uneducated) in community-decision making; ACT: ST, MT; IMP: ST, MT
✓ Community participation limited for women, poor, uneducated	■■	● Partnering with private sector, NGOs to extend services; ACT: ST, MT; IMP: ST, MT

■■■ = top priority; ■■ = medium priority; ■ = priority; ST = one year period; MT = 1–3 years; LT = more than 3 years; ACT = period for implementation of actions; IMP = period needed for impact on poverty

for poverty reduction. Key assets include: education, health, basic utility services (particularly water and sanitation), rural roads, and land and physical capital.

▪ **Reducing vulnerability.** Again, the central path for reducing vulnerability is to build the assets of the poor, because most vulnerability in Guatemala is associated with low expected earnings (due to weak assets) rather than high volatility of consumption. Nonetheless, disaster management is important, given the poor's exposure to natural and agriculture-related shocks. Moreover, much could be done to improve the efficiency and effectiveness of existing social protection programs. Many of these, such as scholarships, school feeding, could also play a role in building the assets of the poor by easing demand-side constraints to improved coverage. Efforts should be made to consolidate and improve existing programs, particularly with respect to their targeting. Strategic priorities should seek to maintain the current focus of social protection programs on children, given their inherent vulnerabilities and prospects for long-term transmission of poverty.

▪ **Improving institutions and empowering communities.** Weaknesses in the public sector and poor governance strongly shape the menu of feasible options and effectiveness of poverty reduction efforts. They also influence the overall climate for investment and economic growth. As such, improvements in this area are deemed to be of high priority, consistent with the strategic emphasis on "modernization of the state" in the Peace Accords. The role of communities in promoting their own development is also important, as acknowledged in the Peace Accords, and poverty reduction efforts should seek to partner with communities in determining priorities. Nonetheless, explicit efforts should be made to reach out to groups typically excluded from community decision-making (namely, the poor, women, and the uneducated). Partnerships should likewise be sought with private-sector and NGOs to extend and improve service delivery.

These priorities are consistent with the overall principles of the Peace Agenda. Indeed, reducing poverty and improving living conditions is central to lasting peace in Guatemala.

Priority Actions for Poverty Reduction

Certain actions stand out as *top priority.* Within this broad agenda, actions should be further prioritized using the following criteria: (a) likely poverty impact; (b) political, institutional, and administrative feasibility; (c) economic feasibility and costs; and (d) their need and justification for public sector resources. Such prioritization will likely require further dialogue and analysis (for example, institutional assessments, costing of actions, public expenditure analysis). As a first cut, certain actions should be considered as top priority, based on a cursory review of such criteria:

(1) **Promoting economic growth.** Guatemala must raise its rate of economic growth if it is to make significant progress in reducing poverty and achieving key development and peace targets. This is true internationally, but particularly relevant for Guatemala, given the limited scope for public sector action and redistribution. In this context, the main engine of growth is likely to come from the private sector, with the public sector playing a supporting role affecting growth mainly insofar as it stimulates private-sector investment and productive activities. Yet the actions of the public sector in this supporting role are crucial. In particular, *priority actions* include:

   ▪ Maintaining macroeconomic stability;

   ▪ Enforcing a tight fiscal position, with a careful plan for strengthening tax collection and redirecting public spending towards the social sectors so as to build assets that are crucial to both growth and poverty reduction;

   ▪ Fostering a climate that is conducive to private investment and growth, including improvements in governance and public sector management; and

▨ Promoting growth with special emphasis on sectors that are likely to generate substantial employment for the poor. Additional analytical work is needed to define a more comprehensive pro-growth strategy. Nonetheless, while a thorough sectoral analysis of growth is beyond the scope of this study, available data do suggest certain levers that would have stronger impacts on poverty reduction than others for urban and rural areas:

  ◉ In urban areas, this requires policies to support labor-intensive sectors, particularly micro-, small and medium enterprises (MSMEs), as well as education and technical training.

  ◉ In rural areas, this means developing non-agricultural activities that are better remunerated and have better long-term prospects than traditional agriculture. Key interventions to support growth in non-farm activities include: (a) increasing and improving the targeting of investments in education and technical training; (b) increasing investments in transport and basic infrastructure, which are crucial for the diversification, growth and inclusion of the poor in the rural economy and with facilitating the adjustment to the coffee crisis; and (c) policies that promote micro, small and medium enterprises (MSMEs), a segment of the private sector that tends to generate a lot of employment. While agriculture is unlikely to generate enough additional employment opportunities to reduce poverty on a large scale in the medium term, it will continue to be an important source of incomes for the poor (at least in the short run). In this context, diversification efforts should focus on non-traditional products with better demand and price prospects than traditional export crops. Policies should also continue to facilitate productivity improvements (such as technical assistance), so as to boost the earnings of those who remain in agriculture. Investments in infrastructure (such as, rural roads to improve marketing opportunities and education to improve farm-management practices) will likewise be important.

(2) **Investing in education, with priority actions to improve quality and access to pre-primary and primary education.** Both theory and empirical analysis of the ENCOVI demonstrate the crucial role of education in promoting economic growth; reducing poverty and malnutrition; reducing vulnerability by making the labor force more agile and able to adjust to shocks; and reducing inequality, social disparities and exclusion. Since Guatemala is still a "primary" country *on average* (with average attainment of 4.3 years) and since the poor in particular fail to complete primary school, investments should still focus on expanding and improving primary education, at least in the medium-term. In the longer-run, as a larger share of the poor complete primary school, efforts should emphasize expanding access to secondary school. As such, *priority actions* should focus on:

▨ Increasing access to primary education, largely through demand-side interventions, since supply-side constraints are no longer binding for most of the population. However, as supply-side gaps are filled, the Government should consider easing eligibility criteria so as to allow poor communities that already have schools to be eligible for the PRONADE-type community-based school-management model. To target this expansion, the poverty map could be used to identify eligible schools and preserve PRONADE's exemplary targeting record;

▨ Improving the quality of education, curriculum and performance standards so as to improve internal efficiency and the returns to education, particularly at the primary level; and

▨ Investing in early childhood development to promote: (a) improved child nutrition at an early age, since nutritional status is a significant factor in determining enrollment and attainment and since nutritional deficiencies emerge at a young age; and (b) early educational opportunities, including links between traditional schooling and pre-primary schooling.

(3) **Investing in health, with an emphasis on expanding access and usage using both supply- and demand-side interventions.** Again, both theory and empirical analysis using the ENCOVI point to important linkages between health and productivity (economic growth), vulnerability (health shocks), and poverty. Guatemala's health outcomes have lagged significantly behind those in other countries as well as the targets set by the Peace Accords and the MDGs. A significant share of the population still lacks access to health facilities—or fails to use them when available—due to a mix of supply- and demand-side constraints. As such, *priority actions* should seek to improve health outcomes by:

- Expanding access to affordable health care using both supply- and demand-side interventions. Such interventions should be targeted to the poor and priority groups (for example, using the poverty map);
- Emphasizing preventative care, infectious and parasitic diseases, reproductive health, key outcomes (mortality, malnutrition); and
- Expanding access to potable (not just piped) water and improved sanitation to complement the basic health care package.

(4) **Integrating actions to reduce malnutrition into the basic health-care package.** The high and stagnant rates of malnutrition in Guatemala require the highest attention. Their lasting effects also result in inter-generational transmission of poverty. Reducing malnutrition should be designated as a top priority. Malnutrition interventions should be integrated into the MSPAS basic health care package and provided at the community level through outreach workers, so as to improve their effectiveness and reach and foster the integration of malnutrition as a key concern into the health system. The target population for these schemes should be pre-school children (particularly those under 24 months of age) and mothers (including pregnant and lactating women). *Priority actions* include:

- Promotion of proper health, hygiene, and feeding practices;
- Growth monitoring of pregnant women and children under aged two;
- Micronutrient supplementation (particularly for iron); and
- Deworming treatments and oral rehydration therapy.

(5) **Reducing isolation and improving communications by investing in rural transport and roads.** Many communities in Guatemala are still relatively isolated due to a lack of road access. Empirical analysis using the ENCOVI has demonstrated the effects of isolation on opportunities, productivity, vulnerability (shocks), and access to services. Expanded rural transport helps build the assets of the poor, promote economic growth and opportunity, reduce vulnerability, and empower communities. *Priority actions* in this area include focusing on improving and expanding the network of motorable roads in rural areas, particularly those with untapped economic potential *and* a high concentration of poor people.

(6) **Improving governance and the effectiveness of the public sector.** Actions are needed to reduce corruption, improve transparency, improve public expenditure management, and better target existing resources to the poor. Such actions will have multiple benefits, including: (a) making the most of existing scarce resources and improving service delivery; (b) fostering a climate that is more conducive to economic growth; (c) assuring that public resources reach the poor (needed for impact); and (d) improving the credibility of government and its ability to increase revenues in the future (without such improvements, the Government will face continued resistance to tax increases). Priority actions include:

- Improving the tax base and increasing public spending, which will depend on improvements in governance and the effectiveness and credibility of the public sector;
- Improving the targeting of public spending particularly for investments in education, health, basic utility services, and transfers;

- Improving public expenditure management, with stronger links to policy, planning and priorities;
- Expanding and building on recent initiatives to fight corruption (such as adopting an anti-corruption charter);
- Improving incentives for better service delivery (for example, implementing the recently-passed laws on decentralization,[13] local *"control social,"* and service "report cards" and client satisfaction surveys); and
- Improving the rule of law and the justice system.

Priority Target Groups for Poverty Reduction in Guatemala

The broad agenda for poverty reduction can become even more effective by focusing efforts on key priority groups. For example, while economic growth is needed in general, growth that provides opportunities for the rural poor will be even more effective in reducing poverty. While building assets of the poor in general is essential, priority is needed to tackle the issues of malnutrition and the relative disparities against poor women and indigenous residents.

As such, the Government should prioritize among poverty groups, according to the prevalence of poverty, specific risks, and demographic circumstances. Specifically, the analysis reveals several priority groups that should be emphasized in poverty reduction efforts: (a) poor and malnourished children; (b) poor women and girls; (c) poor indigenous households; (d) the rural poor; and (e) specific geographic areas (Table B). Clearly, these groups can have considerable overlaps. For example, a poor or malnourished indigenous girl living in rural areas in the North or North-Western parts of the country would probably qualify for just about any anti-poverty intervention.

- **Poor and malnourished children.** The developmental status of children renders them extremely vulnerable to the risks of living in an impoverished environment. Youth (particularly early childhood) is the point in the life cycle when physical, cognitive, and psychosocial development occurs at its most accelerated pace and is most susceptible to abnormal development from poverty conditions. As such, childhood poverty also increases the likelihood of inter-generational transmission of poverty. Children in Guatemala are particularly disadvantaged and vulnerable: they have relatively higher rates of poverty; close to half are malnourished; infant mortality is alarmingly high; a significant share of children fail to enroll in school, thereby missing crucial opportunities for social and cognitive development; and child labor is common, particularly among poor children, further compromising their chances of attending school. In this context, poverty reduction efforts should confer top priority to poor and malnourished children as a key target group.
- **Poor girls and women.** Girls and women face cumulative disadvantages in Guatemala, reflecting historically exclusionary policies (for example, in land and education) and a general culture of *machismo.* They face limited access to education (with fewer girls attending school even when schools are available), constrained employment opportunities, explicit wage discrimination (even after taking into account differences in endowments), and traditional exclusion from land ownership. Women are also at risk for health shocks, with Guatemala recording extremely high levels of maternal mortality. Furthermore, women participate significantly less in community decision-making (limited social capital networks). Yet women's roles are crucial in promoting long-term development, with a strong influence, for example, on the nutritional status of children.

---

13. Specifically, the *Ley de los Consejos de Desarrollo Urbano y Rural,* the *Código Municipal,* and the *Ley General de Descentralización.*

TABLE B: PRIORITY TARGET GROUPS

Priority Target Groups	Key Constraints/Challenges	Possible Targeting Tools
Poor and malnourished children, especially pre-school (age 0–6) and primary-aged children (7–13)	▨ Poverty ▨ Malnutrition (stunting) ▨ Not enrolled in school ▨ Child labor ▨ Vulnerable phase of life cycle ▨ Inter-generational transmission of poverty	▨ Poverty map combined with information on malnutrition and educational enrollment ▨ Self-targeting via health posts and community health centers (e.g., a growth monitoring program channeled through these facilities) ▨ Community-based targeting ▨ Proxy means testing
Poor women and girls	▨ Historical pattern of exclusion ▨ Less access to education ▨ Constrained in employment and earnings opportunities ▨ Face wage discrimination ▨ Face discriminatory attitudes (culture of *machismo*) ▨ Excluded from participating in community decision making (social capital)	▨ Poverty map ▨ Gender-based targeting (e.g., programs that restrict eligibility to girls, such as scholarships) ▨ Community-based targeting ▨ Proxy means testing
Poor indigenous	▨ Historical pattern of exclusion ▨ Higher poverty and malnutrition ▨ Less access to education, health services ▨ Less coverage by basic utility services ▨ Constrained in employment and earnings opportunities ▨ Face wage discrimination ▨ Face discrimination in treatment by public officials and other service providers	▨ Poverty map combined with language map ▨ Proxy means testing
The rural poor, particularly small land-holders, agricultural day laborers, seasonal migrant agricultural workers	▨ Higher poverty and malnutrition ▨ Less access to education, health services ▨ Less coverage by basic utility services ▨ Geographic constraints (isolation, roads, small municipalities) ▨ Constrained employment and earnings opportunities ▨ Low returns, limited coverage of labor and IGSS benefits ▨ Susceptible to shocks	▨ Poverty map ▨ Vulnerability maps (e.g., natural disasters) ▨ Proxy means testing, with certain proxies emphasized (e.g., land holdings, electricity connections, etc.) ▨ Migration maps (that could be developed from census data) showing municipalities with significant concentrations of seasonal migrants
Specific geographic areas, especially in the "poverty belt" (Norte, Nor-Occidente, San Marcos)	▨ Higher poverty rates, malnutrition ▨ Lower access to basic services ▨ Geographic isolation, limited road network	▨ Poverty map, combined with other asset-specific maps/info. (e.g., gaps in coverage of roads, education, health services, utilities, etc.)

▨ **Poor indigenous households.** The indigenous likewise suffer cumulative disadvantages, reflecting the historical pattern of exclusion and decades of conflict. Poverty is higher among the indigenous. Indigenous children also suffer higher rates of malnutrition and less access to education, which affect their earnings ability in the future. The indigenous also have less access to health and basic utility services. They are further constrained in employment opportunities (particularly those who don't speak Spanish), and face considerable wage discrimination (even after taking into account disparities in endowments). Finally, they also report perceptions of discrimination by public officials and service providers.

▨ **Rural poor.** Poverty is higher in rural areas, and even higher among specific rural sub-groups, including small land-holders, agricultural day laborers, and seasonal migrant agricultural workers. The rural poor (particularly these sub-groups) have relatively limited access to services and infrastructure (education, health, utilities, transport, markets). They also have limited employment and earnings opportunities, particularly those living in more geographically isolated areas and smaller municipalities. They also face lower returns to their labor and are rarely covered by formal labor and IGSS benefits. Finally, they are quite susceptible to shocks, particularly natural disasters, agricultural-related shocks, and recent economic shocks (such as the coffee crisis which has worsened the terms-of-trade for producers and caused job loss for day laborers). The emphasis of the ERP on rural areas is thus correct and should be maintained.

▨ **Specific geographic areas.** While poverty is clearly a national problem in Guatemala, poverty is significantly higher in the "poverty belt" in the Northern and North-Western regions as well as the departments of San Marcos. The poverty map helps further pinpoint specific municipalities with higher incidence of poverty. The ERP's inclusion of the poverty map as a key tool is thus appropriate.

Given budget constraints, certain activities should be actively targeted to the poor. As a "rule of thumb," incremental increases in public spending on areas such as education, health, basic utility services, core communication links, social assistance transfers, or employment schemes should be explicitly targeted to the poor in order to better integrate them into the economy and improve social indicators. Decisions regarding the allocation of investments in other services, such as more intensive infrastructure, institutional support, or banking services, should generally follow indicators of economic potential, which could also be combined with targeting criteria (such as the poverty map). Ideally, a strategy to promote pro-poor growth and reduce poverty would focus on areas that have both a large concentration of poor people, but also a strong potential for future economic activity.

The Government can use a variety of tools to better target programs to priority groups. Improved use of limited public resources is crucial for poverty reduction efforts. Ensuring such resources are channeled to key poverty groups (Table B) is a first step in improving the effectiveness of public spending and poverty reduction efforts. The Government has at its disposition several potentially potent tools for targeting its poverty reduction efforts to these priority groups. **First,** the poverty map, recently constructed by SEGEPLAN-INE-URL, can be extremely useful (alone or with other targeting tools) in ensuring that resources get channeled to municipalities with high concentrations of the poor. **Second,** efforts have been made to develop other maps and geographic-based databases, such as an extensive road network inventory/map, vulnerability maps, conflict maps, municipal-level databases on education and health services, etc. The upcoming census will help update many of these maps. A unified geographic information system could combine the poverty map with these other maps and databases to better target specific interventions to the poor. **Third,** certain services (such as health posts and community health centers) are self-targeted to the poor. Other programs could be channeled through these facilities to take advantage of this inherent self-targeting (and perhaps even promote use of these facilities). **Fourth,** community-based targeting could be used (perhaps after broader program allocations are made using the poverty map) to select specific individuals eligible for programs (such as poor or malnourished children, girls or women). Given the traditional exclusion of certain groups from community decision-making, however, care should be taken to ensure that these patterns are not repeated. **Fifth,** a unified proxy-means database (such as those in Costa Rica or Colombia) could be developed for programs targeted to individuals, though this could require significant administrative capabilities.

Monitoring Poverty Reduction Efforts

Monitoring of both poverty and poverty reduction interventions is necessary, and adequate resources should be made available for this task. First, the MECOVI program seeks to develop an integrated system of household surveys to track living conditions and provide data for the evaluation of the impact of interventions. The system will build on the ENCOVI 2000, and should execute similar surveys every 3–5 years. In addition, INE is currently developing an employment and incomes survey that would be executed on a more regular basis, to fill crucial gaps in Guatemala's information base. Finally, the upcoming Population Census will provide additional information for the monitoring of poverty, including an opportunity to update the poverty map (combined with data from the ENCOVI), as well as infrastructure maps.

Second, SEGEPLAN is also developing tools to monitor actions to reduce poverty under the ERP, including: further elaborating the ERP (fleshing out details for specific sectors and developing department- and municipal-level poverty reduction strategies), and developing a system of monitoring indicators for the targets set by the ERP. Ideally, a goal-based poverty reduction strategy would involve a system that relates actions and external conditions to progress in reaching the goals, incorporating evaluation mechanisms and feedback loops. The development of this type of system should clearly be coordinated with: (a) efforts to gather data (for example, with the MECOVI program); (b) efforts to monitor the targets set by the Peace Accords and the MDGs, (c) the SIAF, which is developing performance monitoring indicators for public expenditure management; and (d) the various executing agencies (such as, sectoral ministries). Adequate financial and technical resources should be made available to the concerned agencies for the purposes of strengthening these two facets of the monitoring system.

CHAPTER I

INTRODUCTION

Context for Report: The GUAPA Program

This report is part of a broader, multi-year program of analytical work and technical assistance that signals the commitment of the World Bank to poverty reduction and seeks to: (a) contribute to filling the crucial information gaps on poverty and living conditions; (b) deliver timely outputs on a regular and on-going basis in response to client requests and data availability; and (c) provide longer-term partnering and collaboration on poverty analysis and strategy. The four main interconnected "prongs" of the program include:

(a) **"GUAPA collaborative,"** which seeks to foster institutional development and capacity building in counterpart agencies for greater ownership and sustainability of the analysis and results. As such, the program adopts a collaborative approach, providing technical assistance and hands-on training to counterpart agencies for poverty measurement, data collection, analysis, and policy and strategy formulation;[1]

(b) **"GUAPA analytical,"** which seeks to conduct a thorough, multi-dimensional analysis of poverty building on the framework of the World Bank's World Development Report for 2000/2001 using both quantitative and qualitative data (the main product is this present report);

(c) **"GUAPA policy,"** which seeks to contribute to the design of the Bank's upcoming Country Assistance Strategy (CAS),[2] as well as the upcoming Country Economic Memo-

---

1. Two grants from the World Bank's Institutional Development Fund (IDF) supported this approach, one to INE for the development of capacity for an integrated household survey system (TF027318) and one to SEGEPLAN for institutional strengthening for poverty analysis and policy and strategy formulation (TF027423).

2. The linkages between the GUAPA and the CAS were greatly strengthened by support from a joint GUAPA-CAS Multi-Sector Team Learning Grant. In particular, this grant supported two retreats (to date) to discuss the findings of the GUAPA and their implications for the CAS, including the majority of the World Bank's Guatemala country team.

randum (CEM), the government's poverty reduction policies and strategies, and the poverty-effectiveness of interventions and policies in Guatemala;

(d) **"GUAPA operational,"** which seeks to forge linkages to lending operations currently under preparation to improve their poverty focus, such as those in social protection, education, and transport.

This program is collectively called the Guatemala Poverty Assessment Program (GUAPA Program), which is intricately linked to the World Bank's support for the MECOVI Program in Guatemala (see Box 1.1). The main counterpart agencies for the GUAPA Program have been the *Instituto Nacional de Estadística—Guatemala* (INE) and the General Planning Secretariat under the Presidency (SEGEPLAN) in collaboration with the University of Rafael Landívar (URL). Beyond this report, some of the outputs already generated with the support of the GUAPA/ MECOVI program include the Living Standards Measurement Survey (*Encuesta Nacional de Condiciones de Vida,* ENCOVI 2000) and its database (see below), the poverty map (see Box 14.1 in Chapter 14), a profile of poverty prepared by the multi-agency technical team from INE-SEGEPLAN-URL, as well as the training and capacity building of numerous staff in these agencies. The work has also provided technical support to the Government's poverty reduction strategy (PRSP).[3]

BOX 1.1: THE MECOVI PROGRAM: FILLING A CRITICAL INFORMATION GAP

Guatemala does not have a strong tradition in collecting statistics on the living standards of its population. This largely reflects the three-decade long civil war which, until recently, made topics such as "poverty," "living conditions," and "social equity" taboo in government circles. As a result, Guatemala has an excessively large gap in terms of recent, systematic, and comprehensive data on poverty, social indicators, and living conditions.

To fill these gaps and generate comprehensive, systematic, and integrated household survey data on living conditions, the Government of Guatemala requested to be incorporated in the "Program for the Improvement of Surveys and Measurement of Living Conditions in Latin America and the Caribbean" (MECOVI), sponsored by the Inter-American Development Bank (IDB), the World Bank (IBRD), and the Economic Committee for Latin America and the Caribbean (CEPAL). The MECOVI-Guatemala program also draws on financial inputs from a number of other donors, including USAID, the Soros Foundation, UNDP, UNICEF, and the ILO. The objectives of this program involve (a) developing an integrated system of household surveys, including two Living Standards Measurement Surveys (ENCOVI 2000 and 2003) and labor and income surveys in interim years (2001 and 2002); and (b) building national capacity for designing, implementing, and analyzing household survey data. One of the elements of the GUAPA Program involves providing both financial and technical support to this MECOVI Program.

Objectives of Report

This poverty assessment report has three main objectives. The first is to conduct an in-depth, multi-dimensional analysis of poverty building on the framework of the World Bank's World Development Report (WDR) for 2000/2001 using both quantitative and qualitative data. The second is to examine the impact of government policies and spending on the poor in key sectors. The third is to use the empirical findings to identify options and priorities for poverty reduction in the future. Policy options are outlined not only in general, but for the specific themes and sectors covered. It is hoped that the report will make an empirical contribution to improving the Government's anti-poverty policies and strategies (broadly as well as for specific sectors). The report is also expected to contribute to the definition of the country assistance strategy (CAS) and lending operations of the World Bank and other donors, so as to make these interventions more effective in the future.

Poverty Assessments are studies conducted by the World Bank in its client countries on a regular basis (usually every 35 years). They are not intended to be a critique of a particular government

---

3. SEGEPLAN: 2001d.

administration; rather, they assess the poverty situation of the country in question. They provide a basis for a collaborative approach to poverty reduction by country officials and the World Bank, and help to establish the agenda of issues for policy dialogue.

Analytical Framework

Poverty is a multi-dimensional phenomenon in terms of its definition, measurement, manifestations, causes, and solutions. The analytical framework adopted for this report embraces this multi-faceted view, which was formalized in the recent World Development Report 2000. The poor are poor because they lack the resources to attain basic necessities (food, shelter, clothing, and acceptable levels of health and education). The poor are also particularly vulnerable to the impact of adverse shocks, with limited assets to be able to cope with them. Finally, a sense of voicelessness and powerlessness, particularly with regards to their representation and interaction with institutions, also characterizes the manifestation of poverty. An important aspect of this framework is the interaction between these factors, which tend to reinforce each other. This analytical framework can be simplified into the following three inter-related facets of poverty (see Box 1.2):[4]

- **Opportunity.** Opportunity (or lack of it) to generate incomes and attain basic necessities is central to the manifestation of poverty. **Economic growth** is essential for expanding economic opportunities for poor people. Growth in turn depends on the functioning of markets, the policy environment, institutions, and initial conditions (such as geography, social fragmentation, initial incomes). The ability of growth to influence the opportunities of the poor depends not only on the pace of growth but also on the pattern of growth in the economy (favoring or disfavoring sectors which employ substantial segments of the poor population). The poor also rely on a portfolio of **assets** in order to forge opportunity, including human capital (their own labor, education, and health), physical assets (basic services, housing and land), financial assets (savings and credit), and social capital (horizontal and vertical connections, informal and formal organizations, etc.). Generally, the poor suffer from an unequal distribution of these assets.
- **Empowerment.** The social and political context in which the poor operate affects their daily lives. A lack of political and social voice, discrimination, social barriers, conflict, inappropriate treatment by public officials, alienation from service providers, language barriers, and a lack of information about services and rights all affect the ability of the poor to achieve their potential and create a sense of voicelessness and powerlessness. Strengthening democratic processes, enforcing the rule of law, promoting participation in political processes and decision making, and removing social barriers are all important steps to empower the poor so that they can expand their opportunities and reach their potential. These contextual factors are particularly important in Guatemala, where a history of conflict, exclusion and discrimination have constrained the mobility of the poor for generations.
- **Vulnerability.** Vulnerability comes from the notion that certain groups in society are more vulnerable to shocks that threaten their livelihood and/or survival. Other groups are so vulnerable that they live in a chronic state of impoverishment where their livelihood remains a constant state of risk (such as street children). The sources of risk may be natural (for example, hurricanes) or the result of human activity (such as job loss, conflicts, or violence). Low levels of assets (see above) make poor people especially vulnerable to the impact of negative shocks. Strengthening the assets of the poor enhances their ability to manage risks and weather shocks. Risk management interventions (such as social insurance or social assistance) can also help the poor mitigate and cope with shocks.

---

4. This analytical framework is largely based on the framework set forth in the World Development Report 2000.

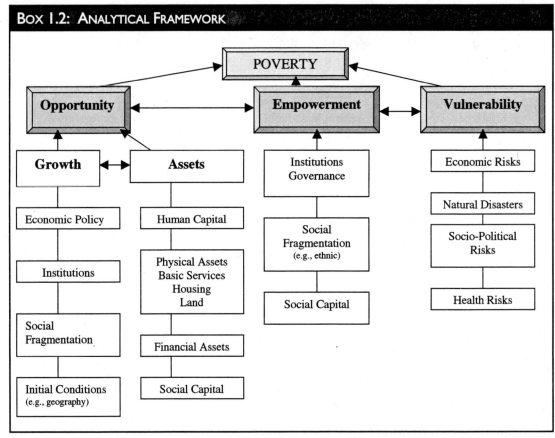

Source: K. Lindert, October 2000 based on WDR 2000.

Information Sources: Integrating Quantitative and Qualitative Data

An innovative aspect of the GUAPA is its *combination* of qualitative and quantitative research methods, which are both valuable in their own right but yield important synergies when used together.

Quantitative Data on Living Conditions. Quantitative household and community surveys are suitable for gathering information that can be quantified, tabulated and analyzed statistically. They have the advantage of providing concrete data on a range of generalizable indicators for a statistically representative sample of the population.

The main source of quantitative information is the Living Standards Measurement Survey (**ENCOVI-2000**), which was conducted under the MECOVI Program (see Box 1.1).[5] The ENCOVI provides a unique opportunity for poverty analysis, providing a comprehensive snapshot of living conditions for a representative sample of the Guatemalan population. The survey was executed by INE, with field work carried out during the period from July–December 2000. It covers a sample of 7,276 households and is statistically representative at the national level and for a number of strata including: (a) urban and rural areas; (b) eight regions[6] (and urban and rural areas in these regions);

---

5. Data from the ENCOVI 2000 are available to the public from by contacting INE at inedifusion@intel-net.net.gt. Documentation and information on the survey is available from the World Bank at http://www.worldbank.org/lsms/lsmshome.html

6. Guatemala, Norte (covering the departments of Baja Verapaz, Alta Verapaz), Nor-Occidental (covering Huehuetenango and Quiche), Sur-Occidental (covering Sololá, Totonicapán, Suchitepequez, Quetzeltenango, Retalhuleu, and San Marcos), Central (covering Chimaltenango, Escuintla, Sacatepequez), Nor-oriental (covering Izabal, Zacapa, Chiqimula, El Progreso), Sur-oriental (covering Santa Rosa, Jalapa, Jutiapa) and Petén.

and (d) ethnic groups according to the language classifications in the 1994 Census including: Ladinos (Spanish speakers), K'iche, Kaqchiqel, Mam, Q'eqchi, other Maya, and "other indigenous."

The ENCOVI is based on the LSMS survey methodology which combines an integrated set of questionnaires to collect data on household living standards with extensive quality control features. The **household questionnaire** gathers information needed to generate monetary measures of poverty (using consumption and/or income). It also collects information on key assets and other living standards indicators, including: labor and migration, housing, land, basic services, transport, health, education, financial assets, household enterprises, agriculture, fertility and nutritional status. The Guatemala ENCOVI also includes a number of non-standard modules designed to collect information on the social dimensions of poverty, including: social capital, participation and citizenship, crime and violence, risks and shocks, and time use. The **community questionnaire** seeks responses from community focus groups about infrastructure and basic services (which allow for control variables), labor market conditions, product markets, formal social capital (e.g., community organizations), and a variety of qualitative issues such as perceptions of services, living standards, crime and violence, and key issues facing the community. A **price questionnaire** also collects necessary information for constructing detailed spatial and temporal price indices.

Qualitative Data. Qualitative instruments, by contrast, are useful for gathering information on the influence of motives, attitudes and preferences on economic behavior, on perceptions, and on the barriers and opportunities that determine poverty and mobility. They are not intended to be statistically representative or reflect measures of central tendency. Rather, they yield information that is primarily descriptive but can broaden the field of inquiry to include questions, issues and factors in the quantitative instruments which are otherwise likely to be missed.

A **Qualitative Study of Poverty and Exclusion (QPES)** provides the main source of qualitative information for GUAPA.[7] The objectives of the QPES are to gather information on perceptions and the nature of constraints to and opportunities for economic mobility so as to better understand the dynamic processes that perpetuate or reduce poverty and exclusion. The QPES collected data in ten rural communities that are also included in the ENCOVI. The configuration of these villages seeks to examine perceptions of poverty and exclusion for a number of ethnicities; as such, the sample includes two villages from each of the following ethnic groups: Mam, K'iche, Q'eqchi, Kaqchiqel, and Ladino (non-indigenous). For the purposes of protecting the anonymity of respondents, each village is given a code name (M1, M2, K1, K2, etc.). The field work covered a number of themes including: perceptions of poverty and welfare; perceptions of risk, shocks and vulnerability; social capital; user perceptions of public programs; community perceptions of education; and gender roles and issues. The main research instruments included: community focus groups, direct interviews, social mapping, and observation. Annex 5 presents a summary of the main findings of each of the ten QPES villages.[8]

Overview of the Report

This report is divided into five sections. Part 1 examines the magnitude and causes of poverty in Guatemala. Chapter 2 finds that poverty rates and inequality are among the highest in the LAC region. Moreover, Guatemala ranks among the worst in the region for various social indicators. Malnutrition rates in particular are abysmally high.[9] Chapter 3 shows that poverty is determined largely by household characteristics and endowments, including key assets such as human capital, physical assets, and social capital. Chapter 4 contends that other factors—both historical and contextual—have also fundamentally shaped Guatemala's performance regarding the levels of these endowments and characteristics. In particular, various forces in Guatemala's historically exclusion-

---

7. Funding was provided by the Government of Denmark (TF039498). Field work was conducted in July and October 2000.

8. The full report is also available on the web at: www.worldbank.org/lacpoverty

9. Particularly for stunting (height-for-age), see Chapters 2 and 8.

ary pattern of development have put Guatemala at a relative disadvantage in terms of its development and key social indicators. Moreover, the long civil war imposed further costs on Guatemala's development. Chapter 4 then contends that the Peace Accords signaled a fundamental shift in Guatemala's pattern of development, paving the way to a more prosperous and inclusive nation. In the six years since the Peace Accords, Guatemala has taken important steps on this new development path, with progress in public sector management, public revenues and spending, and improvements in the coverage and equity of education and basic services. These steps signal that progress *is* possible, despite the magnitude of the challenge of changing the course of history.

Nonetheless, challenges remain. Many of the key challenges for poverty reduction coincide largely with the remaining actions on the Peace Agenda. In particular, progress on the Peace Accords is deficient for key development targets, especially for those involving health and education outcomes, and economic growth. These outcomes reflect the need for poverty reduction and improvements in living conditions, which are crucial for lasting peace. They highlight remaining priority challenges in several key areas—which reveal the significant overlaps between the Peace Agenda and the Poverty agenda: (a) creating opportunities; (b) reducing vulnerability; and (c) improving institutions and empowering communities.

Part 2 examines the first of these key challenges, specifically, the challenge of building opportunities and assets. Specifically, Chapter 5 examines the relationship between poverty and economic growth in Guatemala. Chapter 6 builds on this macro-economic context to further examine the livelihoods and earnings opportunities of the poor from a more "micro," household-level perspective, with a focus on rural livelihoods. The poor also rely on a portfolio of assets in order to forge opportunity, including education (Chapter 7), health (Chapter 8), basic utility services (Chapter 9), land and financial assets (Chapter 6), and access to transport (Chapter 10). Generally, the poor suffer from an unequal distribution of these assets.

Part 3 examines the second challenge area, namely the challenge of reducing vulnerability and improving social protection. In Chapter 11, shocks, particularly natural disasters and economic shocks, are found to have a considerable impact on the poor. Poverty and vulnerability, however, are found to be primarily chronic—rather than transient—in nature, highlighting the importance of building the assets of the poor. Chapter 12 finds that the use of existing resources devoted to social protection could be greatly improved by eliminating certain programs and consolidating, improving the targeting and expanding the coverage of others.

Part 4 examines empowerment as the third key challenge. Chapter 13 contends that these institutional forces are crucial for both the Peace Agenda and the Poverty agenda, influencing the both menu of options available to the Government in future efforts to reduce poverty and the way in which these options are carried out. Indeed, poverty and economic growth are not only driven by economic processes, but also by interacting economic, social and political forces. In particular, they depend on the accountability and responsiveness of state institutions. Social institutions (kinship systems, community organizations, and informal networks) also greatly affect poverty outcomes, helping communities manage public goods, cope with risks and shocks, and leverage external assistance. In light of the importance of these factors for both poverty and the Peace Agenda, this chapter reviews key institutional challenges in the areas of (a) public sector management; (b) governance; and (c) community participation and social capital. The chapter also considers the role of other important actors in development, namely the private sector, NGOs, and religious organizations.

Part 5 (Chapter 14) identifies a menu of priority actions for poverty reduction efforts in Guatemala, building on the in-depth empirical analysis offered by the combination of quantitative and qualitative data from the ENCOVI and the QPES, as presented in preceding chapters. The chapter contends that these priority actions are consistent with the overall principles of Peace Agenda. Indeed, reducing poverty and improving living conditions is central to lasting peace in Guatemala.

PART I

THE MAGNITUDE AND CAUSES OF POVERTY

Part 1 of the report identifies the magnitude of poverty in Guatemala and examines its causes. Reflecting the multi-dimensionality of poverty, Chapter 2 examines the poverty "problem" using an array of monetary and social indicators, as well as perceptions of poverty identified by Guatemalan communities and households themselves. Likewise, echoing its multiple facets, poverty has many causes. In general, poverty is determined by key household endowments and characteristics. These are analyzed in Chapter 3. Yet historical forces and contextual factors also play a crucial role in shaping patterns of poverty. These factors are discussed in Chapter 4.

CHAPTER 2

POVERTY AND SOCIAL INDICATORS OF "THE PROBLEM"

This chapter identifies the magnitude of the poverty problem in Guatemala. A systematic analysis of poverty requires some measure of welfare. Ideally, such a measure would (a) capture the multi-dimensional aspects of poverty; (b) be observable and measurable in a consistent way across households, space and time; and (c) be objective. Since no single measure fully captures all such features, living conditions should be monitored over time using a battery of indicators rather than with a single measure. This report considers both monetary and non-monetary indicators of well-being. The chapter starts with an analysis of poverty and inequality using monetary measures. Non-monetary indicators of poverty and living conditions—including malnutrition, health, education, basic services, composite indices, and perceptions—are then explored. The chapter ends with a summary "report card" of key monetary and non-monetary indicators, for cross-sectoral comparison and easy reference.

The main findings of this chapter are that the magnitude of the poverty problem is quite large. In fact, poverty rates and inequality in Guatemala are among the highest in the LAC region. Moreover, Guatemala ranks the worst in the region—and among the worst in the world—for malnutrition.[1] It also performs poorly for indicators of education, health, and basic utility service coverage, though it has made some progress in expanding the coverage of education and utility services. Finally, the chapter reveals interesting patterns about perceptions of changes in poverty and welfare over time. Specifically, while communities do perceive progress—and attribute this to improvements in basic services—households are decidedly more pessimistic about changes in their welfare since the Peace Accords. These more negative perceptions are attributed to economic factors, such as a lack of improvements in incomes and opportunities.

---

1. Particularly for stunting, see below and in Chapter 8.

Monetary Indicators of Poverty and Inequality in Guatemala[2]

Monetary Measures of Poverty: Consumption and Poverty Lines

Typical monetary measures of welfare include income and consumption. This study primarily uses consumption because (a) it is fairly comprehensive;[3] (b) consumption data tend to be more reliable than income data due to incomplete measurement, underreporting, and seasonality of income; (c) it tends to fluctuate less than income (which can even go to zero in certain months due to seasonality), making it a better indicator of living standards; and (d) consumption is less subjective than basic needs indices (BNI), which rely on some form of subjective weighting across their components.

Using data from the ENCOVI 2000, two poverty lines were calculated: an extreme poverty line and a full poverty line.[4] The **extreme poverty line** is defined as yearly cost of a "food basket" that provides the minimum daily caloric requirement of 2,172.[5] The selected "food basket" is based on the average consumption patterns observed in the ENCOVI 2000 for the entire population.[6] The annual cost of this minimum caloric requirement yields an extreme poverty line of Q.1,912. Below this level of consumption (or income), individuals cannot maintain the minimum level of caloric consumption even if all resources were allocated to food. The **full poverty line** is defined as the extreme poverty line (the cost of food that satisfies the minimum caloric requirement) plus an allowance for non-food items. This allowance is calculated as the average non-food budget share for the population whose food consumption was around the extreme poverty line (Q.1,912).[7] It is assumed that, since these individuals barely meet the minimum caloric requirements, whatever share of total consumption they actually allocate to non-food must be essential. The analysis found the non-food share for this group to be 56%. This method yields a full poverty line of Q.4,319,[8] below which individuals would be considered poor.[9]

Poverty in Guatemala: Levels, Trends and Patterns

Poverty in Guatemala is very high. In 2000, over half of all Guatemalans (56% or about 6.4 million people) lived in poverty (Table 2.1).[10] About 16% lived in extreme poverty. International comparisons of poverty are always difficult due to various methodological differences

---

2. Most of these results come from collaborative work conducted jointly by INE, SEGEPLAN, and URL with technical assistance provided by the World Bank under the GUAPA/MECOVI programs using data from the Encuesta de Condiciones de Vida (ENCOVI 2000), *Instituto Nacional de Estadística—Guatemala*. Detailed tables are included in the Statistical Appendix (Annex 4).

3. In terms of comprehensivity, consumption covers different sources of consumption (purchased and non-purchased including consumption of own-produced products, *autoconsumo*). It also provides wide coverage of the multiple dimensions of welfare, including basic material necessities (such as food, clothing), the current value of physical assets (such as land, housing), and the consumption of basic services (e.g., water, energy), health and education. Other measures, particularly basic needs indices, consider only a fraction of these components (e.g., excluding basic material items such as food and clothing).

4. These poverty lines were calculated using data from the ENCOVI 2000 by an inter-agency technical team from INE, SEGEPLAN, and URL with technical assistance provided by the World Bank under the GUAPA and MECOVI programs.

5. This minimum average daily caloric requirement was estimated by the *Instituto de Nutrición de Centro América y Panamá (INCAP)*, representing a weighted average based on the assumption of moderate activity, taking into account the actual age and gender distribution of the Guatemalan population in accordance with official population projections.

6. The reference group excludes the bottom and top 2% of the population to avoid extreme values.

7. Households with a yearly per capita food consumption within 5% of the extreme poverty line value.

8. Q. 1,912 (44%) for food, and Q. 2,407 (56%) for non-food items.

9. An advantage of this method for calculating the extreme and full poverty lines (in contrast to those methods that use the cost of a pre-determined "normative" basket of food and non-food items) is that it does not impose assumptions about the consumption preferences and patterns of the population. These patterns are empirically observed for the full Guatemalan population (rural and urban alike)—rather than imposed by the analyst.

10. Poverty rates were estimated using data from the ENCOVI 2000, *Instituto Nacional de Estadística—Guatemala* by a multi-agency technical team from INE, SEGEPLAN and URL with technical assistance from the World Bank's GUAPA team. See Annex 4 for additional results on poverty patterns as well as sensitivity analysis.

TABLE 2.1: POVERTY IN GUATEMALA, 2000 Poverty Indicators by Welfare Measure							
	All Poor (below FPL)			**Extreme Poor (below XPL)**			**GNI Per Capita, PPP**
	% Poor[a]	Depth[b]	Severity[c]	% Poor[a]	Depth[b]	Severity[c]	
Using Consumption	56.2%	22.6	11.7	15.7%	3.7	1.3	$3,630
Using Income	65.6%	35.1	25.9	31.9%	15.1	22.2	$3,630

Sources: GNI (gross national income) per capita estimates for 1999 in PPP US$, from World Bank, World Development Indicators 2001. Poverty estimates calculated by INE-SEGEPLAN-URL with technical assistance from World Bank using the ENCOVI 2000, *Instituto Nacional de Estadística—Guatemala.* a. Incidence of poverty or headcount index (% of population whose total consumption or income falls below poverty line, FPL or XPL). All poor includes extreme poor (throughout study). b. The Poverty Depth Index (P1) represents the amount needed to bring all poor individuals up to the poverty line (FPL or XPL), expressed as a percent of the poverty line taking into account the share of the poor population in the national population. c. The Poverty Severity Index (P2) is a derivation of P1 that takes into account the distribution of total consumption among the poor. In other words, it is a measure of the degree of inequality among the population below the poverty line.

(welfare measures, poverty lines, survey samples). Nonetheless, available evidence does suggest that poverty in Guatemala is higher than in other Central American countries, despite its midrange ranking using per capita GDP.[11] It is also generally deeper (P1 measures) and more severe (P2 measures).

The relatively[12] lower incidence of extreme poverty in Guatemala is a reflection of the food consumption patterns of the population. As discussed above, the extreme poverty line is based entirely on the cost of food items. The Guatemalan diet derives a large share (46%) of calories from corn and corn products, which are also the cheapest source of calories (Q.0.00057/calorie). Comparisons with other extreme poverty lines are valid in the sense that they measure the capability of satisfying a minimum caloric requirement, but also taking into account the ability of the population to satisfy this requirement in the most efficient way.[13] As such, by taking into account the observed "cost efficiency" of the minimum caloric intake, the extreme poverty classification is a test that only a small share (15%) of the population fail to meet.

The costs of reducing poverty in Guatemala are high. Given average consumption levels of the poor, it is estimated that the minimum *annual* cost of eradicating poverty represents about Qz.11,121 million, or 8% of GDP (as compared with 5% in Panama and 17% in Nicaragua). Moreover, these costs are hypothetical annual costs. They are calculated as the cost of bringing all poor individuals up to the poverty line, excluding the inevitable administrative costs or leakages to the non-poor associated with virtually all poverty-alleviation schemes. These administrative costs and leakages can be quite high, as discussed in Chapter 12. To put this in context, total Government spending in Guatemala in 2000 was about 13%—and spending on public investments was only 4%. Total public spending on health and education amounted to 3.6% of GDP. Public spending on social protection (assistance and insurance) was 1.8% and with another 1.7% by social funds. Clearly, the task of eliminating—or even reducing—poverty represents quite a challenge.

Poverty appears to have fallen over the past decade. Comparing estimates of poverty over time in Guatemala is complex due to large differences in survey and measurement methodologies

---

11. For example, poverty rates in Nicaragua and Panama were 47.9% and 37.3% respectively (using consumption as a measure of welfare).

12. Relative to the overall incidence of poverty.

13. In other words, sometimes differences in poverty rates reflect not only the economic conditions of the country, but also the endowments and the customs of the population. This characteristic does not diminish the validity of the methodology, but rather enhances it because, since the objective is to measure welfare, it takes into account not only what people have (endowments), but also how they use it (e.g., consuming the relatively cheaper corn).

BOX 2.1: OTHER STUDIES AND SURVEYS OF POVERTY

Three surveys allow for the calculation of poverty rates at the national level over the past decade (a) the 1989 Encuesta Nacional Sociodemografica (ENS); (b) the 1998–99 Encuesta Nacional de Ingresos y Gastos Familiares (ENIGFAM); and (c) the Encuesta Nacional Sobre las Condiciones de Vida (ENCOVI) carried out in 2000. While it is tempting to compare the results of these different surveys, differences in welfare measures (consumption vs. income; different ways to measure both), poverty lines, and samples often render such comparisons meaningless. Using these surveys, various studies of poverty in Guatemala have yielded the following results.

Poverty Estimates for 1989. Using data from the 1989 ENS, CEPAL (1991) and the World Bank (1995) both estimated poverty to be quite high (80% and 75% respectively). The income variable collected in the 1989 ENS, however, was highly under-estimated as it was based on very restricted set of questions on income. Subsequent analyses by UNDP (2000) and the World Bank have attempted to correct for this over-estimation, yielding very consistent estimates (63% and 62% respectively).[14]

Poverty Estimates for 1988–89.[15] Using income as a welfare measure and data from the 1988–90 ENIGFAM, UNDP (2000) estimates poverty at 56.7% and extreme poverty at 26.7%. Comparisons between the results of the ENIGFAM and other surveys are complex, however, due to the fact that the sample for the ENIGFAM was only 20% rural and the survey questionnaire was not designed for the analysis of poverty but for the calculation of weights for consumer price indices (there are substantial differences in measurement of welfare and poverty lines between the ENIGFAM and other surveys). SEGEPLAN (November 2001) reports similar, but slightly lower results in its Estrategia de Reducción de la Pobreza (ERP): 54.3% for full poverty and 22.8% for extreme poverty.[16]

Poverty Estimates for 2000. Using data from the 2000 ENCOVI and consumption as a welfare indicator, a multi-agency team consisting of INE, SEGEPLAN, and URL, estimated poverty at 56.2% and extreme poverty at 15.7%. These are the figures adopted in the present study. The ENCOVI 2000 offers many advantages over previous surveys in terms of poverty measurement and analysis, including a nationally representative sample with extensive rural coverage, detailed questions on consumption and income, and a broad range of topics covering the multi-dimensions of poverty and living conditions. As part of the MECOVI Program, INE expects to repeat comparable ENCOVI surveys every few years to allow for comparable monitoring of poverty and living conditions.

Consistencies in Patterns and Trends Across Studies and Surveys. Despite difficulties in comparison, the various studies and surveys yield fairly consistent patterns. Over time, poverty appears to have fallen from 62–63% in 1989 to between 54–56% by the end of the 1990s. Moreover, all studies suggest similar patterns, such as higher poverty and worse overall living conditions in rural areas and among the indigenous. The consistency of these trends and patterns is more important for policy than the exact number or rate of poverty in any given year.

(Box 2.1). Until recently, the 1989 Socio-Economic Survey provided the only nationally-representative measures of welfare and poverty. Using this survey, poverty in 1989 was estimated at about 75% of the population.[17] These estimates, however, were based on a very simple income question (with only five categories). To get towards better comparability, the ENCOVI 2000 repeated these same exact questions (five categories, as well as other income questions for a more complete measurement). The results suggest that in 2000, the "1989 comparable income aggre-

---

14. The adjustments by the World Bank take advantage of the fact that, for purposes of comparison only, the ENCOVI 2000 repeated the same set of income questions from the 1989 ENS (along with an expanded set for better measurement). An analysis of the "1989 comparable" income aggregate using these comparable questions shows that income was underestimated by about 18%. Hence poverty rates were probably about 18% lower than originally estimated for 1989.

15. The results reported by SEGEPLAN (November 2001) were based on joint work by SEGEPLAN-INE-URL to construct the poverty map by combining data from the 1994 Census and the 1998–99 ENIGFAM. They are based on projected consumption estimates.

16.   The results reported by SEGEPLAN (November 2001) were based on joint work by SEGEPLAN-INE-URL to construct the poverty map by combining data from the 1994 Census and the 1998–99 ENIGFAM. They are based on projected consumption estimates.

17. World Bank (1995).

gate" was about 18% lower on average than the consumption aggregate. As such, poverty rates for 1989 were likely overestimated. Adjusting for these differences, poverty that year was probably around 62%. As such, poverty is estimated to have fallen by about six percentage points from 1989 to 2000 (Figure 2.1). These results are roughly consistent with what would be expected given past growth rates (and growth-poverty elasticities, see Chapter 5).

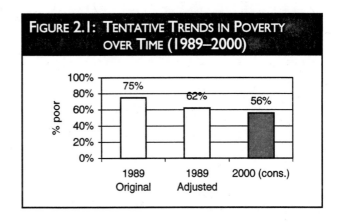

FIGURE 2.1: TENTATIVE TRENDS IN POVERTY OVER TIME (1989–2000)

Nonetheless, with negative growth in GDP per capita, projections suggest that poverty may have increased slightly since 2000. As discussed in Chapter 5, Guatemala's economic growth rates have slowed substantially in recent years, reflecting a series of economic shocks. In fact, taking into account population growth rates, growth has actually declined in per capita terms. As such, poverty has likely increased. Taking into account these trends in the pace of growth, projections using the ENCOVI suggest that poverty likely rose slightly from 56.2% in 2000 to 56.6% in 2001, with extreme poverty rising from 15.7% to 16.0% (see Chapter 5).

About two-thirds of all Guatemalan children live in poverty. Due to higher fertility rates among the poor, a large share of children live in poverty. In fact, 68% of children under six (about 1.7 million) and 63% of all children under 18 (about 3.8 million) live below the poverty line. In contrast, 45% of senior citizens over age 60 live in poverty.[18] This lower share of elderly in poverty (compared with 56% of the overall national population) could reflect lower life expectancy among the poor than the average or non-poor population.

Poverty is not higher among households headed by women. Only a small share of households (14%) in Guatemala report having a woman as household head. Contrary to popular belief, households headed by men have slightly higher poverty rates than those headed by women (Table 2.2). Controlling for other factors, multivariate regressions show no significant difference between male and female household heads in determining poverty status (see Chapter 3).

Poverty is predominantly rural and extreme poverty is almost exclusively rural. A disproportionate share of the poor and extreme poor live in rural areas in comparison with the share of rural residents in the national population (Table 2.2). Over 81% of the poor and 93% of the extreme poor live in the countryside. Three quarters of all rural residents fall below the full poverty line and one quarter live in extreme poverty.

Poverty is significantly higher among the indigenous, but with differences between indigenous groups. As discussed in Chapter 4, Guatemala is a multi-ethnic society, including some 23 different ethno-linguistic indigenous groups (21 of which are Mayan). Although the indigenous represent about 43%[19] of the national population, they account for 58% of the poor and 72% of the extreme poor. Over three-quarters of the indigenous population live in poverty, as compared with 41% of the non-indigenous. Poverty is also deeper and more severe among the indigenous (see Annex 4 for details on these indices). The ENCOVI 2000 also reveals that there are

---

18. All comparisons presented in this report that are based on ENCOVI 2000 data are statistically significant at the 90 percent level or more.

19. This estimate is from the *Instituto Nacional de Estadística—Guatemala* using the expanded sample of the ENCOVI 2000 and updated sample weights based on projections from the 1994 census. Other estimates put the indigenous population as high as 60% (CELADE, 1994).

TABLE 2.2: POVERTY PATTERNS IN GUATEMALA

	% of National Population	Incidence of Poverty Headcount Index (% of pop.)		Contribution to National Poverty (% of category)	
		All Poor	Extreme Poor	All Poor	Extreme Poor
Total Guatemala	100.0	56.2	15.7	100.0	100.0
By Geographic Area					
Urban	38.6	27.1	2.8	18.6	6.9
Rural	61.4	74.5	23.8	81.4	93.1
By Ethnicity					
Non-Indigenous	57.6	41.4	7.7	42.4	28.3
Indigenous	42.6	76.1	26.5	57.6	71.7
Kaqchiqel	8.9	62.6	13.6	9.9	7.7
K'iche	9.4	64.4	19.1	10.8	11.5
Q'eqchi	6.5	83.5	38.0	9.6	15.6
Mam	8.3	89.7	34.2	13.2	18.0
Other Indigenous	9.5	83.6	31.3	14.1	19.0
By Region					
Metropolitana	21.7	18.0	0.6	6.9	0.9
Norte	8.1	84.0	39.1	12.1	20.1
Nororiente	8.2	51.8	8.9	7.6	4.7
Suroriente	8.8	68.6	20.1	10.7	11.3
Central	10.7	51.7	8.7	9.8	6.0
Suroccidente	26.5	64.0	17.0	30.1	28.6
Noroccidente	12.9	82.1	31.5	18.8	25.9
Petén	3.3	68.0	12.9	4.0	2.7
By Gender of Household Head					
Male	85.3	57.6	12.3	87.5	90.8
Female	14.7	47.8	8.4	12.5	9.2

Source: Poverty estimates calculated by INE-SEGEPLAN-URL with technical assistance from World Bank using the ENCOVI 2000, *Instituto Nacional de Estadística—Guatemala*. **Metropolitana** mainly covers Guatemala City (and Department); **Norte** includes the Departments of Baja Verapaz and Alta Verapaz; **Noroccidente** covers the Departments of Huehetenango and Quiché; **Suroccidente** includes the Departments of Sololá, Totonicapán, Suchitepequez, Quetzaltenango, Ratalhuleu, and San Marcos; **the Central Region** covers the Departments of Chimaltenango, Escuintla, and Sacatapequez; **Nororiente** covers the Departments of Izabal, Zacapa, Chiquimula, and El Progreso; **Suroriente** includes the Departments of Santa Rosa, Jalapa, and Jutiapa; and **Peten** covers Petén.

important differences in poverty rates between indigenous groups. The largest indigenous groups are the K'iché, the Kaqchiqel, the Mam, and the Q'eqchi. Among these, the Mam and Q'eqchi have the highest poverty rates.

Pockets of poverty are present throughout the country, but there is also a significant "poverty belt" in the Northern and North-Western Regions. Poverty in Guatemala is a national problem, with pockets of poverty spread across the country (see Figure 2.2).[20] Regionally, the ENCOVI shows that poverty is significantly lower in the Metropolitan region of Guatemala

---

20. This map will be updated using data from the ENCOVI rather than the ENIGFAM for the final version of this report.

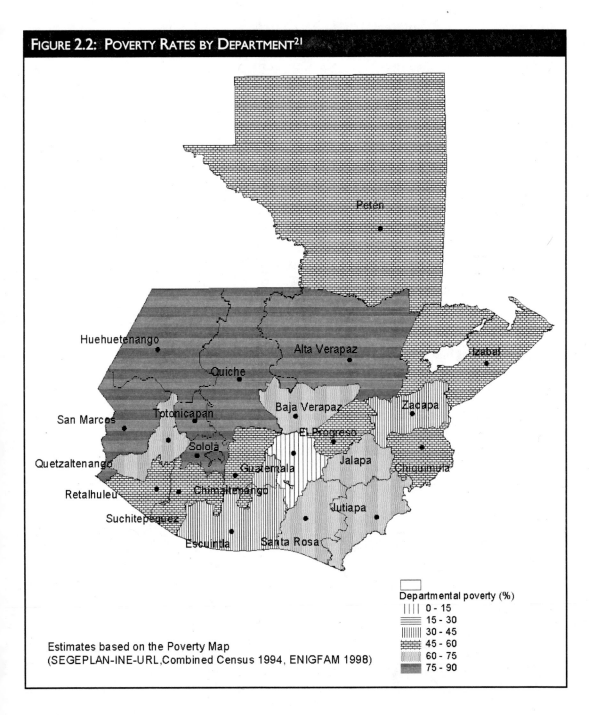

FIGURE 2.2: POVERTY RATES BY DEPARTMENT[21]

Estimates based on the Poverty Map
(SEGEPLAN-INE-URL,Combined Census 1994, ENIGFAM 1998)

Departmental poverty (%)
| | | | 0 - 15
15 - 30
30 - 45
45 - 60
60 - 75
75 - 90

City. It is moderately high in the Nororiente and Central Regions of the country (Table 2.2). It is much higher in the Norte and Nor-Occidente Regions as well as the Department of San Marcos (which collectively comprise a "poverty belt"), which were largely affected by the country's three-decades long civil war (see Chapter 4).

---

21. This map will be updated using data from the ENCOVI rather than the ENIGFAM for the final version of this report.

Inequality in Guatemala:
Levels and Patterns[22]

International evidence suggests that inequality is a handicap to longer-term poverty reduction for two reasons.[23] First, greater income inequality leads to lower investment in physical and human capital and hence slower economic growth— which translates into higher poverty. Second, cross-country evidence suggests that higher inequality results in a lower rate of poverty reduction at any given growth rate.

Guatemala is among the more unequal countries in the world. The Gini indices using consumption and income for Guatemala are 48 and 57 respectively. This is more unequal than most other LAC countries, which as a whole has higher inequality than other regions in the world (Table 2.3).[24]

TABLE 2.3: INEQUALITY
(Gini coefficients)

	Inequality (GINIs)
Using Consumption as Welfare Measure	
Guatemala (2000)	48
Nicaragua (1998)	50
Panama (1997)	49
LAC median	46
Using Income as Welfare Measure	
Guatemala (2000)	57
Nicaragua (1998)	54
Panama (1997)	60
Honduras (1996)	55
El Salvador (1998)	52
Costa Rica (1998)	46
LAC median	55

The population distribution in Guatemala is characterized by a large "low-income" majority and a very small "high-income" minority. As shown in Figures 2.3 and 2.4, income shares climb slowly, with a fairly flat distribution, across the lower quintiles. They then jump up dramatically in the top quintile, which accounts for 54% of total consumption (almost three times higher than the next highest quintile and 11 times higher than average consumption in the bottom quintile).

There are significant inequities across ethnic groups and geographic areas. Although the indigenous represent 43% of the population, they claim less than a quarter of total income and consumption in the country, with the non-indigenous accounting for 75%. Nonetheless, inequality

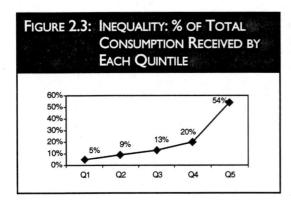

FIGURE 2.3: INEQUALITY: % OF TOTAL CONSUMPTION RECEIVED BY EACH QUINTILE

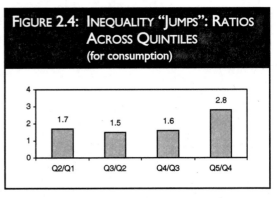

FIGURE 2.4: INEQUALITY "JUMPS": RATIOS ACROSS QUINTILES
(for consumption)

---

22. This section is based primarily on the results of the ENCOVI 2000—*Instituto Nacional de Estadística.* Detailed tables can be found in the Statistical Appendix, Annex 4.

23. See Deininger and Squire (1997), Ravallion and Chen (1997), and Ravallion (mimeo, February 12, 1998) for a survey of cross-country evidence.

24. As for poverty, inferring distributional changes for income over time is a challenging task due to differences in survey designs and methodological issues. Nonetheless, using the "1989 comparable income aggregate," the Gini coefficient for 2000 is 61, compared with 60 for 1989, suggesting that income inequality has slightly increased during the last decade. Source: World Bank calculations using data from the ENCOVI 2000, *Instituto Nacional de Estadística—Guatemala.*

as measured by Gini coefficients is higher among (within) the non-indigenous population than among the indigenous. Likewise, whereas rural residents account for almost two thirds of the nation's population, they claim only about a third of total income and consumption. Inequality within urban areas, however, is higher than among rural residents.

Non-Monetary Indicators of Poverty and Living Conditions in Guatemala

To complement monetary measures of poverty and welfare, this section examines patterns and trends in non-monetary indicators of poverty for a fuller understanding of the multi-dimensionality of poverty. Some non-monetary indicators considered here are topic- or sector-specific, malnutrition (measured by anthropometric data), health, education, and basic services. Others are composite indices, such as the Human Development Index proposed by the UNDP (which is actually a mixed indicator including income, health and education indices).[25]

Malnutrition: A Red Flag! Extremely Poor Performance, Little Progress[26]

Malnutrition among Guatemalan children is extremely high—among the worst in the world. Guatemala has among the worst performances in the world—and *the* worst in LAC—in terms of child growth attainment, with an overall stunting rate of 44% of all children under five.[27] As discussed in Chapter 8, there is a strong correlation between poverty and child malnutrition, as four fifths of malnourished children in Guatemala are poor (height-for-age). Malnutrition is much higher among poor children than non-poor children (64% of extreme poor and 53% of all poor children versus 27% of non-poor children). Malnutrition is also higher among rural and indigenous children than their urban or non-indigenous counterparts, as discussed in more detail in Chapter 8.

   Moreover, malnutrition is declining slower in Guatemala than in other countries. Guatemala has made some progress in reducing malnutrition, with stunting rates falling from 59% in 1987 to 44% in 2000. However, the yearly percentage reduction (1.7%) has been the slowest in the LAC region. This lack of adequate progress paradoxically contrasts with significant progress in other areas (basic services, health, education), as discussed in subsequent chapters.

Health: Poor Performance, with Slow Progress[28]

Guatemala also ranks poorly for health indicators. Life expectancy at birth (65 years) is the lowest in Central America, and far lower than the average for LAC countries (70) or lower-middle income countries (69).[29] Infant mortality (40–45 per thousand)[30] is also the highest in Central America, and far higher than the average for LAC (30) or lower-middle income countries (32).[31] Only Bolivia and Haiti perform worse for life expectancy or infant mortality in LAC; Guatemala does worse than other low-income countries, such as Nicaragua and Honduras. The patterns of health indicators also suggest worse conditions for the poor, rural, and indigenous populations (see Chapter 8). Though Guatemala has improved health outcomes over the past 20 years, its progress has been slower than the low-income countries of Bolivia, Nicaragua and Honduras.

---

25. Other parts of this report do attempt to examine further aspects of living conditions, including crime and violence, justice, isolation and transport, and empowerment, reflecting the multi-dimensionality of poverty and welfare.

26. See GUAPA Technical Paper 6 (Marini and Gragnolati, 2002) for details.

27. These stunting rates (height for age) are consistent for various recent surveys (ENCOVI 2000: 44%; DHS 1998: 46%). See Chapter 8 for additional details on malnutrition in Guatemala.

28. See GUAPA Technical Paper 5 (Gragnolati and Marini, 2002) and Chapter 8 for more details.

29. Source: World Bank (2001b).

30. Estimates of infant mortality for Guatemala vary. The 1998/99 Demographic and Health Survey (DHS) puts the average at 45. The World Bank World Development Indicators (2001), based on official health statistics, puts the estimate for that same year at 40.

31. World Bank (2001b).

Education: Poor Performance With Biases Against the Poor, but With Some Progress[32]
Guatemalan literacy is not only below average in Latin America, it is *far lower*. With an illiteracy rate of 31% in 2000, only Nicaragua and Haiti rank worse. Illiteracy among women, the poor, indigenous, and rural residents is particularly high (see Chapter 7). Despite this poor performance, Guatemala has seen improvements over time, with a slight quickening of the pace since the signing of the Peace Accords in 1996 (see Chapter 7).

Although educational attainment is quite low in Guatemala, with significant gender, ethnic and poverty gaps, there has been some progress over time. Guatemala is still a "primary" country, with an average educational stock of 4.3 years (for those aged 14+). Attainment is even lower among women, the poor, and the indigenous, and these gaps have been narrowing over time (see Chapter 7).

Guatemala has made progress in improving primary enrollment, but coverage is still low and biased towards the non-poor. In the early 1970s, primary schools enrolled just over half[33] of the target population. Net enrollment rates increased dramatically in only one generation, to 79% in 2000.[34] Importantly, progress has been significantly faster in the years since the signing of the Peace Accords in 1996. Notwithstanding its commendable progress, primary coverage is still low by international standards. Guatemala's net enrollment is the lowest in Central America, and lags significantly behind the averages for LAC (91%) and lower-middle income countries (99%). As with other indicators, enrollment is lower among girls, the poor, indigenous, and rural children (Chapter 7). Coverage at the pre-primary, secondary, and superior levels are even lower and more biased against disadvantaged groups than at the primary level (see Chapter 7).

Basic Services: Important Progress in Improving Coverage and Reducing Inequities[35]
Overall coverage for basic services in Guatemala is typical for Central America. Overall, about 70% of Guatemalan households have water[36] and electricity. Almost 90% have some kind of basic sanitation, though fewer than half have sewerage. About 20% subscribe to either a fixed line and/or a cellular telephone service. Around 17% of Guatemalan households do not have access to any kind of modern network utility service. While overall coverage rates are average for Central America, they lag slightly the average for Latin America and other lower-middle income countries.

Coverage has accelerated considerably in recent years, with a targeted expansion for disadvantaged groups. Coverage indices for electricity, water, and sanitation increased far faster following the Peace Accords than in the years leading up to the Accords (see Chapter 9 for details). Moreover, data suggest that this expansion has been well targeted and that the poor, rural, and indigenous households have seen their probability of receiving service more than double following the Peace Accords, increasing more than for other segments of society. Even this substantial improvement, however, has not been enough to offset their historic disadvantage. As such, despite relative progress, in absolute terms, these groups still remain the least likely to receive services and a significant coverage gap remains (as discussed in more detail in Chapter 9).

Composite Measure: The Human Development Index (HDI)
Guatemala has made progress in raising the level of the HDI, but this level remains below what would have been expected given the level of GDP per capita of the country. The UNDP's Human Development Index (HDI) is a composite indicator of well-being that combines a weighted sum of three indices covering life expectancy, educational attainment, and per capita income (the higher the score the better). Because per capita income is included in the HDI, this index is a mixed indicator rather than a purely non-monetary indicator of well-being. On the positive side, Guatemala has improved its HDI since 1975 (Table 2.4). On the negative side, however,

---

32. See Chapter 7 and GUAPA Technical Papers 2, 3, and 4 for details.
33. World Bank WDI 2001.
34. Source: World Bank calculations using ENCOVI 2000—*Instituto Nacional de Estadística Guatemala*.
35. Refer to matrix at end of chapter + Working Paper!!!!
36. Defined as piped water to dwelling or yard. Note that piped water does not guarantee potable water in Guatemala.

TABLE 2.4: TRENDS IN THE HUMAN DEVELOPMENT INDEX, 1975–99									
	PRSP (HIPC) countries in LAC					Non-HIPC Central America countries			
	HO	BO	GUY	NI	All	CR	SV	GUA	PA	All
HDI index **(higher number is better)**									
1975	0.517	0.512	0.678	0.569	0.569	0.745	0.585	**0.505**	0.711	0.637
1980	0.565	0.546	0.681	0.580	0.593	0.769	0.584	**0.541**	0.730	0.656
1985	0.596	0.572	0.670	0.588	0.607	0.770	0.604	**0.554**	0.745	0.668
1990	0.614	0.596	0.676	0.596	0.621	0.789	0.642	**0.577**	0.746	0.689
1995	0.627	0.628	0.699	0.618	0.643	0.807	0.681	**0.608**	0.769	0.716
1999	0.634	0.648	0.704	0.635	0.655	0.821	0.701	**0.626**	0.784	0.733
1999 HDI and GDP ranking **(lower number is better)**									
GDP ranking	112	111	93	113	107	47	86	**92**	67	62
HDI ranking	107	104	93	106	103	41	95	**108**	52	74
GDP-HDI ranking	+5	+7	0	+7	+4	+6	−9	**−16**	15	−12

Notes: HO = Honduras; BO = Bolivia; GUY = Guyana; NI = Nicaragua; CR = Costa Rica; SV = El Salvador; GUA = Guatemala; PA = Panamá.

Source: UNDP (2001).

in absolute terms, the 1999 performance is well below the average for Central American countries. Moreover, despite a higher level of economic development, Guatemala's human development performance is below that of Latin America's Highly Indebted Poor Countries (HIPC). Finally, Guatemala is the only country in Table 2.4 for which the HDI ranking is far worse than its GDP ranking (a difference of 16 positions in the rankings). This suggests that, despite progress over time, the country still lags significantly behind in human development.

Perceptions of Poverty and Welfare in Guatemala

This section considers subjective perceptions of Guatemalan households and communities regarding definitions of poverty and welfare, changes over time, the main causes of these changes, and priorities for the future.

Defining Poverty and Welfare

Multi-Dimensional Perceptions of Welfare. The Qualitative Poverty and Exclusion Study (QPES) gathered perceptions of the concept of welfare from focus groups in 10 rural villages. Despite several interesting cultural and linguistic discussions (Box 2.2), there is considerable consensus across these villages as to the meaning of welfare and, to most, the concept is multi-dimensional.

First, all study villages identify material aspects of welfare (Table 2.5). These include basic material necessities, such as food and clothing. Villagers also identify

---

BOX 2.2: LINGUISTIC APPROXIMATIONS OF "WELFARE"

In some of the indigenous communities in the QPES, focus group participants discussed words that encompass the concept of welfare or well-being. Some examples:

Maaká chik tink'aáuxla—Not having to worry about anything (Q'eqchi village, QE1)
Sa tatwanq—To live well (QE1)
Sahaqinch-ool—To be content (QE1)
Wanq inna'aj—To have somewhere to live (QE1)
Quicotemal—To be content: "Sundays we go to the market and I'm content to go to the market . . . There we buy our salt, sugar, and other things" (K'iché village, KI2)
Q'ino—In general, this term can mean "rich." It is also used for the name of a tropical fruit (*jocote*) which is "sabrosa" (delicious) (Mam village, M2)

TABLE 2.5: PERCEPTIONS OF WELFARE FROM 10 RURAL VILLAGES, QPES										
	Q'eqchi		Mam		K'iché		Kaqchiqel		Ladino	
	QE1	QE2	M1	M2	KI1	KI2	KA1	KA2	L1	L2
Material/Physical Dimensions										
Basic material necessities (e.g., food, clothing)	X	X	X	X	X	X	X	X	X	X
Access and ownership of assets (land, housing)	X	X	X	X	X	X	X	X	X	X
Public and Community Services		X	X	X		X	X	X	X	
Having an Education (knowledge)	X	X		X				X		
Social, Psychological, Spiritual Dimensions										
Having good social relations (family, communal)	X		X	X	X			X	X	X
Spiritual relations, emotional balance		X			X	X				X
Freedom				X				X		

Source: Qualitative Poverty and Exclusion Study (QPES), COWI/World Bank (2001).

incomes (salaries) and health in this rubric, noting the links between health and physical conditions needed for working and generating income. Participants in all study communities also identify access to, and ownership of, land and housing as key material aspects of welfare. Ownership was highlighted in particular by residents of fincas (KA1), who live in homes and work land that is owned by the plantation, but do not own these assets themselves.

Second, all villages identify access to public and communal services as being important aspects of welfare, including health services, water, education, roads, credit and technical assistance. The specific services vary somewhat, sometimes reflecting what the villages currently lack.

Third, several villages equate welfare with having an education. In these cases, the concept of education transcends the merely productive, income-generating aspects, with villagers noting the empowering importance of education for acquiring skills, talents, and especially knowledge to "permit them to think clearly so as to make correct decisions."

Finally, participants in several villages note the social, psychological and spiritual aspects of welfare (Box 2.3). Most villages note the importance of having good social relations within the family and community as contributing to well-being. Examples include having a family life without conflicts, abuse (principally towards women or children), or alcoholism; and harmonious communal relationships (friendships, trust, mutual respect). Some note the importance of spiritual relations, emotional balance and happiness, and freedom (*libertad*).

Perceptions of Poverty. Much like with welfare, the QPES villages all point out the multi-dimensionality of poverty. First, all study villages equate poverty with a lack of basic material necessities, such as food and clothing (Table 2.6). Most also associate it with a lack of access or ownership of assets (land, housing). These results are very similar to those found in an earlier study of perceptions of poverty by von Hoegen and Palma in which 89% of all interviewed (560/627) identified that the absolute priority was food as a productive input ("No tener dinero para comer").[37] A significant share of those interviewed in this earlier study also identified poverty not only with hunger (food), but also with housing ("No tener lote ni vivienda propia"). Second, the majority of villages link poverty to a inadequate public or community services and particularly education. The von Hoegen and Palma study also found a large share of those interviewed attributing poverty to a lack of education and training (368/627 interviews). Third, poverty is associated with a social, cultural, and spiritual dimensions in many of the study communities.

---

37. von Hoegen and Palma (1999).

BOX 2.3: DEFINITIONS OF WELFARE: EXAMPLES FROM QPES VILLAGES

Material/Physical Definitions:
—"What we think about is our work, our *milpa* (corn). We all have this necessity. We are happy because we have enough to eat from our *milpa*. Well-being means having corn and beans." (KI2)
—Welfare is "having money to buy what we need to live well . . . food . . . not suffering from hunger" (M2)
—"Having food . . . having clothing . . . having money . . . living well . . . having a job." (KA2)
—"Having a parcel of land would be adequate . . . Having our own land and house for our family." (KA1, finca village)
—"Having land . . . Having a house with two stories." (QE1)

Public/Community Services:
—"To have water" (KI2); "To have enough water" (M2)
—"To have midwives in the community; to have health centers, hopsitals . . . to have the possibility of credit/borrowing" (M1)
—To have "a good road (un buen camino)." (KA2)

Having an Education:
—"That we have knowledge" (QE1)
—"When children study its to improve their futures." (QE2)
—"To know how to read and write . . . To have an education." (KA2)

Social/Emotional/Spiritual Dimensions:
—"Welfare is that husbands don't hit their women . . . that we don't fight, my husband doesn't fight or hit me" (KA1)
—"Peace . . . that there are no problems . . . that there are no deceptions . . . that there is peace in the family and the community . . . that there is no alcoholism . . . alcoholism creates mistrust." (QE1)
—"Welfare is to look for God . . . although my house might not be good, I look for God . . . Only God can help us." (KA1)
—"To feel good with God . . . Although we don't have anything, yet we are good with God, we participate in church and we have God in our hearts . . . to be at peace . . . to be content." (L2)
—"To have freedom for people small and large. To have freedom to look for work in other communities . . . That the woman has the freedom to participate." (L1)

TABLE 2.6: PERCEPTIONS OF POVERTY FROM 10 RURAL VILLAGES, QPES

	Q'eqchi		Mam		K'iché		Kaqchiqel		Ladino	
	QE1	QE2	M1	M2	KI1	KI2	KA1	KA2	L1	L2
Material/Physical Dimensions										
Lack of basic material necessities (e.g., food,clothing)	X	X	X	X	X	X	X	X	X	X
Lack of access/ownership of assets (land, housing)		X	X	X	X	X	X	X	X	X
Inadequate Public and Community Services	X	X	X	X	X	X		X		
Inadequate Education	X	X	X	X	X			X		
Social, Psychological, Spiritual Dimensions										
Lack of good social relations (family, communal)			X	X	X		X			X
Lack of spiritual relations		X				X	X			X
Lack of freedom, cultural identity			X							

Source: Qualitative Poverty and Exclusion Study (QPES), COWI/World Bank (2001).

BOX 2.4: DEFINITIONS OF POVERTY: EXAMPLES FROM QPES VILLAGES

Lack of Material Necessities/Physical Assets
—"Not having food . . . not having work . . . not inheriting (land) . . . not having a house or having a house in bad condition." (L1)
—Poverty is "when there's not enough to eat . . . when there is no money to buy medicines." (KA2)
—"Not having anything . . . not having work, there is no land." (L2)
—Poverty is "little land; little harvests (*milpa*) . . . due to a lack of inheritance." (M1)

Inadequate Public/Community Services:
—"Not having potable water in all the houses." (M2)
—"Death for not bringing the sick quickly to the health post or hospital." (L1, where there are no health services)

Inadequate Education:
—"Not having an education. The school offers only 6 years . . . the lack of training." (M2)
—Poverty is "the lack of education in the community . . . Many are still illiterate, they can't communicate with everyone else." (K11)

Social/Emotional/Spiritual Dimensions:
—"If we were united, we could look for markets and export our products . . . The rich are always united, we the poor are always disorganized . . . the problem is that we are not united." (K11)
—Poverty is "misunderstanding in marriage . . . when the woman is good and the man is bad or the reverse . . . having a disordered life and not looking for God." (KA1)
—"The ancestors used natural medicines; curing with natural medicine is being lost, now only with doctors and in health centers." The woman is poor because she doesn't worry about this. . . .
—Poverty is "a lack of community organization . . . there are no leaders." (M1)

Perceptions of Changes in Poverty and Welfare Over Time: Possible Paradox?[38]

The ENCOVI 2000 collected data on perceptions of changes in welfare and poverty over the "past five years"(period from 1995–2000). This corresponds with the period following the Peace Accords, and hence offers a unique opportunity to gauge perceptions of progress over this crucial period. Such data were collected in both the household and community questionnaires.

Households and communities report strikingly different perceptions of changes in welfare over time, suggesting a possible disconnect in household and community welfare models. While there is a clear perception of improvements in welfare at the community level, such gains are not perceived at the household level. Perceptions of community-level welfare seem to be based more on the provision of "public goods," such as basic services and education, which indeed have seen improvements since the signing of the Peace Accords (as discussed above). Such progress is not acknowledged at much with respect to household welfare. Perceptions of changes in household welfare seem to be driven primarily by economic factors that more directly affect the "wallets" of consumers (employment, incomes, and prices).

Communities do perceive that *community* **welfare and living conditions have improved over the past five years.** Over half of all communities sampled in the ENCOVI 2000[39] perceive welfare has improved at the community level over the past five years (1995–2000), which spans the period covering the Peace Accords (Figure 2.5). Only 10% perceive that community welfare has worsened, with the remainder perceiving no change in living conditions. These results are almost identical for urban and rural communities alike. Interestingly, with a higher share of indigenous communities surveyed report improvements in welfare than non-indigenous. In particular, a large share of K'iché (72%) and Q'eqchi (63%) communities (which were indeed affected by the war) report perceived improvements in welfare during the period following the Peace Accords.

Communities mainly attribute these gains to improvements in public services and education. Over half of those perceiving improvements in community welfare attribute this progress to

---

38. All statements about perceptions of changes in welfare and poverty over time in this section are based on the results of the ENCOVI 2000. See Annex 4 for details.

39. The ENCOVI community interviews were carried out as focus group discussions with a variety of community members.

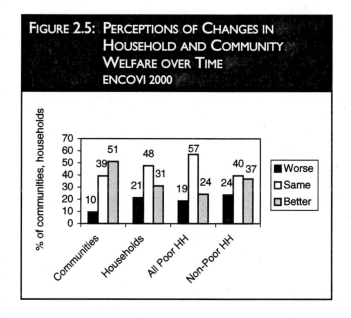

FIGURE 2.5: PERCEPTIONS OF CHANGES IN HOUSEHOLD AND COMMUNITY WELFARE OVER TIME
ENCOVI 2000

improvements in public services, such as water, sanitation, energy, and transport. The next strongest factor is education (13%). These perceptions are indeed consistent with the gains observed for the extension of public services and education (as discussed above and in Chapters 9 and 7 below).

In contrast, perceptions of changes in *household* welfare are decidedly more pessimistic than communities. Interestingly, the same community focus groups that ranked community living standards as having improved were much less positive in their ranking of changes in households welfare over time.[40] The majority of community focus groups in the ENCOVI sample perceive no changes in household welfare, while only a third indicated that household-level welfare had improved over the past five years, with 20% saying household welfare had worsened. Household perceptions of changes in their own welfare are consistently pessimistic (Figure 2.5). The bulk of poor households perceive that living conditions remained stagnant over the past five years, whereas perceptions of non-poor households were spread more across the spectrum (with a larger share perceiving both improvements and a worsening of living conditions).

This more pessimistic view of household welfare is attributed mainly to factors that more directly affect consumption and incomes. Households and communities are quite consistent in their reporting of the factors that cause changes in welfare and poverty at the household level. Both link household welfare to factors that directly affect the purchasing power of consumers. The labor market (unemployment, employment opportunities, and incomes) is by far the top explanatory variable for household welfare and poverty in the view of both households and communities. Prices (cost of living) are the second most cited factor (by both communities and households). Education and corruption/bad government are also mentioned as factors affecting poverty, but by a much smaller share of households. It seems that despite observed progress in basic services and education, Guatemalans are more concerned with factors that more directly affect the "wallets" of consumers in basing their views of household welfare. These findings are consistent with those of the QPES, in which virtually all communities equated welfare with the satisfaction of material necessities, such as food and clothing, as well as the ownership of productive physical assets, such as land and housing (as discussed above). They are also consistent with the findings of the von Hoegen and Palma (1999) qualitative survey of perceptions of poverty in which low incomes, the cost of living, a lack of land, and a lack of employment opportunities were ranked by interviewees as the top four causes of poverty.

Nonetheless, when asked what are the priority problems for communities, households seem to revert to a "public goods" view of state intervention. Despite their emphasis on "livelihoods" as key factors affecting household welfare, very few households (less than 3%) identify labor market factors (employment opportunities, unemployment, incomes and salaries) as priority problems for resolution in their communities. Instead, public services (such as water, energy, telecom, and transport) were the main priorities cited by households (50%), followed by health (11%), social problems (8%, including violence, alcoholism, family problems), and education (5%).

---

40. Both households and communities in the ENCOVI were asked about their perceptions of changes in household welfare. Perceptions of changes in community welfare were only collected in the community survey.

TABLE 2.7: SUMMARY REPORT CARD FOR MONETARY AND NON-MONETARY INDICATORS OF POVERTY AND LIVING CONDITIONS

	Level (most recent year)	International Comparisons	Changes Over Time	Worse for: Poor	Worse for: Rural	Worse for: Indigenous	Worse for: By Region
Poverty (2000)	56%	Worst in Central America (CA), below LAC average	Improving as expected with growth	not applicable	Worse rural: 75% urban: 27%	Worse indig: 76% non-indig.: 41%	National problem Worse for: Norte Noroccidente
Health and Malnutrition							
Malnutrition (2000) children 0–5	44%	Worst in LAC, among worst in world	Little progress (slower than other countries)	Worse poor: 53% non-poor: 27%	Worse rural: 51% urban: 33%	Worse indig.: 58% non-indig: 33%	Same as poverty
Infant mortality 1998/99	40–45 depending on source	Among worst in LAC, worst in CA	Slow progress (slower than other countries)	Mixed results, worse in lower "wealth" quintiles	No	Worse indig. 56% non-indig. 44%	Central, Sur-occidente, Nor-oriente (finca zones)
Diarrhea, children 0–5 (2000)	31.3%	n.a.	Worsening	Worse poor: 33% non-poor: 27%	Worse rural: 35% urban: 25%	Worse indig.: 35% non-indig.: 27%	Norte (much worse)
ARI children 0–5 (2000)	47.9%	n.a.	Worsening	Not strong pattern	Worse rural: 51% urban: 41%	Not significant	Norte, Nor-oriente
Dengue (1999) Cholera (1999)	3.3 per 10,000 18.7 per 100,000	n.a.	Improving	n.a.	n.a.	n.a.	n.a.
Education							
Illiteracy adults aged 14+ (2000)	31% illiterate 22% men 39% women	Worst in LAC except Haiti and Nicaragua	Improving over time, espec. since Peace Accords	Worse poor: 46% non-poor: 17%	Worse rural: 42% urban: 16%	Worse indig. 49% non-ind.: 20% ind. women: 62%	Same as poverty

		International	Over time	Poor vs. non-poor	Rural vs. urban	Indigenous	Regional
Educational Attainment adults aged 14+ (2000)	4.3 years 4.9 men 3.8 women	n.a.	Improving over time	**Worse** poor: 2.4 yrs non-poor: 6.4 yrs	**Worse** rural: 2.7 yrs urban: 6.4 yrs	**Worse** indig: 2.5 years non-ind: 5.5 yrs ind. women: 1.8	Same as poverty
Net enrollment— Primary (2000)	79% 81% boys 76% girls	Lowest in CA Below LAC and lower-middle income averages	Improving, especially since Peace Accords	**Worse** poor: 78% non-poor: 90%	**Worse** rural: 75% urban: 85%	**Worse** indig: 75% non-ind.: 84% ind. girls: 67%	Same as poverty
Basic Services (Coverage all for 2000)							
Piped water in dwelling or yard	69%	Average for CA, below LAC and lower-middle income averages	Improving, especially since Peace Accords	**Worse but improving** poor: 56% non-poor: 79%	**Worse** rural: 53% urban: 87%	**Worse** indig: 62% non-indig.: 73%	Worse in Norte and Petén
Sanitation (latrines, septic tanks, sewerage)	87%	Average for CA, below LAC and lower-middle income averages	Improving, especially since Peace Accords	**Worse but improving** poor: 79% non-poor: 94%	**Worse** rural: 79% urban: 98%	**Worse** indig: 84% non-indig: 88%	Worse in Petén, Suroriente, Nororiente
Electricity	73%	Average for CA	Improving, especially since Peace Accords	**Worse, but improving** poor: 54% non-poor: 89%	**Worse** rural: 56% urban: 95%	**Worse** indig: 61% non-indig: 81%	Worse in Norte, Petén, Nor-occidente, Nor-oriente
Telecommunications	fixed phone: 15% cell phone: 10%	Average for CA	Improving, especially since Peace Accords	**Worse:** poor: 1% non-poor: 27%	**Worse** rural: 3% urban: 31%	**Worse:** indig: 4% non-indig: 22%	Worse in Norte, Petén, Nor-occidente, Sur-oriente

Sources: World Bank calculations using ENCOVI 2000—*Instituto Nacional de Estadística—Guatemala* unless otherwise noted. Other sources: international comparisons mostly come from World Bank World Development Indicators 2001; infant mortality indicators from DHS 1998/99; dengue/cholera from Ministry of Health. All numbers are cited and explained in more detail (along with sources) in the technical papers (Annexes) to this report.

CHAPTER 3

THE DETERMINANTS OF POVERTY AND INEQUALITY: ENDOWMENTS AND HOUSEHOLD CHARACTERISTICS

T his chapter analyzes the relative importance of key household characteristics and disparities in assets as correlates of poverty and inequality in a multi-variate setting. Three key conclusions emerge from the analysis:

- The determinants of poverty and inequality overlap substantially—and most involve crucial policy levers. These same factors also play a role in determining malnutrition, as discussed in Chapter 8.
- Disparities in key assets (human capital, physical assets, and social capital) are indeed strongly correlated with poverty and inequality.
- These factors are similar to the correlates of poverty and inequality in other countries. In other words, the *relationship* between key household characteristics and assets and poverty is similar across countries. Nonetheless, the *level* of endowments held by Guatemalan households is determined by complex historical processes and contextual factors, which shape the poor performance observed in Guatemala today. These historical processes and contextual factors are discussed in Chapter 4.

The Determinants of Poverty

This section analyzes the correlates of consumption in a multi-variate setting. The analysis is useful, first, to verify the relative role of various household characteristics and endowments in determining poverty status, and second, to assess the potential impact that policy-inducing changes in these factors are likely to have on poverty, holding all other factors constant. The correlates of consumption were examined for the nation as a whole, as well as for urban and rural areas.[1] A positive coefficient on a variable in the regressions signals that that variable is associated with higher consumption[2] (and hence lower chances of being poor). The results are presented in Table 3.1 (below).

---

1. The dependent variable is the log of per capita consumption.
2. The direct interpretation of the variable coefficients is the percentage change in consumption due to a change of one in the corresponding variables.

It is important to note the limitations of this analysis at the outset. **First,** the analysis does not capture the dynamic impact of certain causes of poverty over time. For example, historical processes of exclusion cannot be directly captured (though they are revealed to some extent in the *level* of endowments observed). These factors are nonetheless important, and as such are discussed in Chapter 4. In addition, the impact of changes in economic growth—most certainly a key determinant

TABLE 3.1: THE CORRELATES OF POVERTY

Dependent Variable = Natural Log of Yearly per capita consumption			All	Urban	Rural
AREA & REGION		Urban (Rural excluded)	NS	n.a.	n.a.
		North (Metropolitan excluded)	−0.358	−0.352	−0.326
		Northeast Region (Metropolitan excluded)	−0.216	−0.209	−0.159
		Southeast Region (Metropolitan excluded)	−0.415	−0.386	−0.395
		Central Region (Metropolitan excluded)	−0.246	−0.260	−0.195
		Southwest Region (Metropolitan excluded)	−0.287	−0.309	−0.239
		Northwest Region (Metropolitan excluded)	−0.281	−0.344	−0.219
		Peten Region (Metropolitan excluded)	−0.321	−0.281	−0.321
DEMOGRAPHIC	**LANG ETHNICITY**	Spanish speaking household (ability to speak)[c]	0.088	0.091	0.098
		Indigenous Household (self identification)[c]	−0.168	−0.193	−0.147
	SIZE	# of HH Members 0 to 6 years old	−0.228	−0.200	−0.235
		# of HH Members 7 to 24 years old	−0.173	−0.178	−0.169
		# of HH Members 25 to 59 years old	−0.148	−0.195	−0.111
		# of HH Members 60 or more years old	−0.094	−0.147	−0.081
		# of HH Members 0 to 6 years old squared	0.023	0.015	0.023
		# of HH Members 7 to 24 years old squared	0.012	0.011	0.012
		# of HH Members 25 to 59 years old squared	0.009	0.015	NS
		# of HH Members > 60 years old squared	NS	NS	NS
	OTHERS	Female Household Head (versus male)	NS	NS	NS
		Age of Household Head	0.013	0.016	0.008
		Age of Household Head Squared	−0.0001	−0.0002	−0.0001
		% of males in the household	0.001	NS	0.001
EDUCATION	**HIGHEST**	Primary incomplete (Maximum in household)	0.116	NS	0.092
		Primary complete (Maximum in household)	0.233	0.230	0.191
		Secondary incomplete (Maximum in household)	0.280	0.275	0.272
		Secondary complete (Maximum in household)	0.456	0.426	0.452
		University (Maximum in household)	0.472	0.502	0.299
	SECOND HIGHEST	Primary incomplete	0.044	NS	0.084
		Primary complete	NS	NS	0.115
		Secondary incomplete	0.220	NS	0.324
		Secondary complete	0.404	0.297	0.467
		University	0.658	0.530	0.636

(continued)

TABLE 3.1: THE CORRELATES OF POVERTY (CONTINUED)					
Dependent Variable = Natural Log of Yearly per capita consumption			**All**	**Urban**	**Rural**
LABOR	EMPLOYMENT AND SECTOR	1st. No work[d]	0.150	0.262	NS
		1st. Mining/manuf/energy (agr. excluded)[d]	NS	NS	NS
		1st. Construction (agr. excluded)[d]	0.110	0.134	0.121
		1st. Commerce (agr. excluded)[d]	0.128	0.171	0.106
		1st. Transport (agr. excluded)[d]	0.121	0.139	0.183
		1st. Services (agr. excluded)[d]	0.127	0.175	0.104
		2nd. No work[e]	−0.058	NS	−0.074
		2nd. Mining/manuf/energy (agr. excluded)[e]	NS	NS	NS
		2nd. Construction (agr. excluded)[e]	NS	NS	NS
		2nd. Commerce (agr. excluded)[e]	NS	NS	NS
		2nd. Transport (agr. excluded)[e]	NS	NS	NS
		2nd. Services (agr. excluded)[e]	NS	NS	NS
	TYPE OF EMPLOYMENT	1st. White collar (Public excluded)[d]	NS	NS	NS
		1st. Blue collar (Public excluded)[d]	−0.152	−0.143	NS
		1st. Domestic (Public excluded)[d]	−0.120	NS	NS
		1st. Self employed (Public excluded)[d]	NS	NS	NS
		1st. Unpaid (Public excluded)[d]	NS	0.245	NS
		2nd. White collar (Public excluded)[e]	NS	NS	−0.185
		2nd. Blue collar (Public excluded)[e]	NS	NS	−0.232
		2nd. Domestic (Public excluded)[e]	NS	NS	−0.235
		2nd. Self employed (Public excluded)[e]	NS	NS	−0.222
		2nd. Unpaid (Public excluded)	−0.203	NS	−0.361
	UNDER-EMPLOYMENT	1st.: >12 & <=20 hours/week[b]	NS	NS	NS
		1st.: >20 & <=40 hours/week[b]	NS	NS	NS
		1st.: > 40 hours/week[b]	0.055	NS	0.064
		2nd.: >12 & <=20 hours/week[e]	NS	NS	NS
		2nd.: >20 & <=40 hours/week[e]	NS	NS	NS
		2nd.: > 40 hours/week[e]	−0.042	NS	−0.047
HECTARES OF AGRICULTURAL LAND WORKED[a]		0.5–1.5 ha worked (0–0.5 ha excluded)	NS	NS	NS
		1.5–3.5 ha worked (0–0.5 ha excluded)	0.025	NS	0.029
		3.5–10.5 ha worked (0–0.5 ha excluded)	0.016	NS	0.022
		10.5–50 ha worked (0–0.5 ha excluded)	0.005	0.012	0.006
		>50 ha worked (0–0.5 ha excluded)	NS	NS	0.003
HOME OWNERSHIP		House owned and paid (rented excluded)	NS	0.111	NS
		House owned and not paid (rented excluded)	0.114	0.186	NS
		Other House ownership (rented excluded)	NS	−0.085	NS
MUNICIPIO LEVEL BASIC UTILITY SERVICES[b]		Sewage connection	0.120	0.123	NS
		Electricity connection	0.242	0.324	0.232
SOCIAL CAPITAL		Participate Organizations—Bridging	0.049	0.082	NS
		Participate—Bridging activities	0.081	0.081	0.074
		Participate—Linking activities	NS	0.057	NS
		Number of Organizations—Cluster	NS	−0.005	NS

(continued)

TABLE 3.1: THE CORRELATES OF POVERTY (CONTINUED)			
Dependent Variable = Natural Log of Yearly per capita consumption	All	Urban	Rural
Constant	8.621	8.572	8.776
Number of observations	7,275	3,423	3,852
Number of strata	8	8	8
Number of PSUs	737	353	384
Population size	11,383,521	4,395,934	6,987,587
F	86.85	48.19	35.23
Prob > F	0	0	0
R-squared	**0.73**	**0.69**	**0.57**

NS: Not significant at P<=10%; __: Significant at P<=10%; all others: significant at p<=5%
a. The variable used was the reported number of hectares worked for each category (no dummy.) b. Basic service data are taken from the mean values at the municipal level in the census to avoid simultaneity problems. c. For the majority of household members d. 1st = characteristics of the person with the highest labor income in the household. e. 2nd = characteristics of the person with the second highest labor income in the household. Source: World Bank calculations using the ENCOVI 2000, *Instituto Nacional de Estadística–Guatemala*.

Variables excluded due to lack of significance: no partner (wife, husband, et.), participation in any community group, perceived exclusion (from education services, health services, connection to drinking water, training, access to credit, technical assistance, public transport, insurance, sewage connection, road improvement, and justice), and if household perceived exclusion: human capital, social security and physical assets.

of poverty—cannot be assessed using this static, cross-section model. The issue of growth and poverty is discussed in Chapter 5. **Second,** the analysis is limited by the variables available at the household level from the ENCOVI 2000. Other factors, such as social conditions or physical conditions (for example, variations in climate or access to markets), could not be included due to a lack of data at this level. **Finally,** although theory holds that many of the variables included in the analysis do indeed contribute to (cause) poverty (or poverty reduction), the statistical relationships should be interpreted as correlates not as determinants, since in some instances, causality can run both ways.

Poverty is clearly associated with lower levels of key assets, including labor, education, physical assets, social capital and infrastructure characteristics for the municipality. Geographic location and household size are also found to be important correlates of poverty. Key findings are summarized below:

- **Education,[3] particularly higher levels, can serve as an elevator for upward economic mobility.** As discussed in Chapters 2 and 7, educational disparities are quite high in Guatemala. The higher the educational attainment in the household, the higher the household consumption, and hence the lower the chances a household lives in poverty. Overall, having someone in the household who has completed primary schooling raises consumption by 23%[4] (for an average yearly return in total consumption of 3.8% per year of schooling completed). The gains are even stronger with higher levels of education. Having a member of the household who has completed secondary schooling raises consumption by 46% (for an average yearly return in total consumption of 7.5% per year of schooling completed). Having more than one member with an education also significantly increases consumption, and hence reduces the likelihood that a household will be poor. The impact of a

3. The analysis uses the maximum educational attainment of the members with highest and second highest education in the household. Since the education of these members (usually adults) generally precedes their current economic status, it could validly be considered as having a causative influence on poverty status and consumption (whereas the educational levels of young dependents in the household may be low because poverty prevents them from affording an education).
4. Compared to households in which none of the members has any formal education.

second member in the household with formal education is especially strong for completed secondary and university studies (40% and 66%.)

- **Working in agriculture, blue collar jobs or as a domestic servant is strongly correlated with poverty.**[5] Households in which the highest income-earner[6] works in agriculture have significantly lower consumption levels (and hence are more likely to be poor) than those depending on work in other sectors (construction, commerce, transport or services). Likewise, those households in which the highest income-earner has a blue collar or domestic servant job have significantly lower consumption levels than those in other types of jobs. Interestingly, unemployment (no work) and under-employment do not have strong effects on consumption. Rather it is the sector (agriculture) or type of job (blue collar, domestic servant) that drives lower consumption levels and poverty status. These results are not uncommon. Unemployment is rarely associated with poverty in countries with little or no safety net (unemployment benefits). The poor simply cannot afford to be unemployed. They generally work, but in lower paying sectors and jobs—as found in the present analysis.
- **Larger agricultural land holdings[7] are associated with higher consumption in rural areas.**[8] Possessing and working plots of land between 1.5–3.5 hectares raises rural consumption levels from 4.3% to 10.2% total (by 2.9% per hectare[9]) over those with no land. Similarly, working plots between 3.5–10.5 hectares raises rural consumption levels up to 23.1% (by 2.2% per hectare) over those with little or no land. The returns to larger plots are significantly lower on a per hectare basis but the total values are higher: up to 30% for plots between 10.5–50 hectares (0.6% per hectare), and a 0.3% per hectare for larger than 50 hectares plots (see Table 3.1). Small plots (less than 1.5 hectares) are not associated with lower (or higher) consumption levels.
- **Households in municipalities with more access to basic utility services are significantly less likely to be poor.** As discussed in Chapters 2 and 9, disparities in access to basic utility services are quite large. In urban municipalities, the level of access to sewage connections is associated with consumption levels that are up to 12% higher than those without access.[10] Municipal electricity connections is associated with higher consumption levels in both urban (32% higher) and rural (23% higher) areas. The municipality variables can be interpreted as a proxy for local endowments and represent the effect of local characteristics not captured by other variables.[11]
- **Participation in "bridging" social capital is correlated with higher levels of consumption.** As discussed in Chapter 13, bridging social capital refers to the bridges (horizontal connections) that people make with a broader group of people who have comparable economic status, education levels and political power. School groups, professional associations, groups that manage community-level public goods, and social groups are examples of bridging social capital.[12] Households with members who participate in bridging activities

---

5. See Chapter 6 for additional information on labor, incomes and livelihoods.

6. This includes only labor income (since other sources of income can not be directly attributed to specific household members.)

7. The variable used was "holdings of agricultural land worked."

8. See Chapter 6 for additional information on land holdings and poverty.

9. The total percentage is the result of multiplying the 2.9% by the plot size for the group (1.5 and 3.5 hectares.)

10. The 12% refers to households in municipalities with 100% access compared to households in municipalities with 0% access.

11. This variables are included to take into consideration the "locational" or fixed effects into the model.

12. Bridging social capital contrasts with (a) bonding social capital, which refers to more narrow horizontal ties connecting family members, neighbors, close friends and business associates; and (b) linking social capital, which constitutes the vertical ties people have with formal organizations, institutions or people in positions of influence. See Chapter 4 and Technical Paper 12 (Ibáñez, Lindert and Woolcock, 2002) for more information on the different types of social capital.

and organizations tend to have higher levels of consumption. The direction of causality is not clear, however, since households could be better off due to such connections, or they could participate more because they are better off. Nonetheless, the correlation remains between bridging connections and higher economic status.

■ **Even after accounting for disparities in assets and endowments, geographic location is a major factor in explaining poverty in Guatemala.** Households located in any region are more likely to be poor than those residing in the Metropolitan Region. Those residing in the Sur-Oriente, Norte, and Peten regions have significantly lower levels of consumption than those in the capital region (42%, 36%, and 32% respectively). Interestingly, after controlling for other assets and characteristics (such as ethnicity, language ability, agricultural employment, education, region, and municipal infrastructure), residents of rural areas are not significantly more likely to be poor than their urban counterparts.

■ **Spanish speakers and non-indigenous households are less likely to be poor.**[13] Even after accounting for other differences, such as education, ethnically indigenous households and those who do not speak Spanish have lower levels of consumption and are thus more likely to be poor. Spanish-speaking ability raises consumption levels by about 9%, indigenous households tend to have consumption levels that are 17% lower than otherwise similar non-indigenous households. Still, additional analysis suggests that the main source of welfare differences between indigenous and non-indigenous households is due to low asset holdings, as opposed to differences in the marginal returns to these assets.[14]

■ **Larger households tend to be poorer, particularly those with many young children.** Overall, each additional child under six years old lowers total consumption by 23% (higher in rural areas than urban); each additional member from age 7–24 lowers total consumption by 17%. The magnitude of these values suggests that increased awareness and use of family planning methods could have a significant effect on reducing poverty. Interestingly, despite the numerous disadvantages faced by women in Guatemala (such as, access to education, labor returns, as discussed in other chapters), households headed by women are not inherently more likely to be poor than those headed by men once other factors are taken into account.

■ **Shocks—such as natural disasters and economic crises—are also associated with higher poverty.** These are analyzed using additional multivariate regressions in Chapter 11.

The Sources of Inequality

The sources of inequality in Guatemala overlap substantially with the correlates of poverty. As with poverty, disparities in assets and endowments (labor, education, housing, land, and basic services) explain a large share of inequality (Table 3.2 below). Other sources of inequality include geographic location and household size and composition.[15] Three quarters of Guatemala's consumption inequality can be explained by disparities in education, certain services, labor

---

13. A household is classified indigenous when the majority of its members identify themselves (self-identification) as such. A household is classified as Spanish-speaking when the majority of its members can speak Spanish (regardless of where or how often.)

14. By using the Oaxaca-Blinder decomposition, the difference in consumption levels between indigenous and non-indigenous households was decomposed in terms of differences due to asset holdings and in those due to the returns to the assets. The exercise reveled that about 70% of the differential is attributed to asset holding differentials.

15. The analysis reveals that gender is not a relatively important attribute in explaining *between-household* inequality (or poverty) in Guatemala. The unimportance of gender is consistent with international evidence for developing countries (see Ferreira and Litchfield, 1997). It is important to note, however, that inequality *within households* is not captured by ENCOVI data, and intra-household inequality between genders could indeed be significant. In fact, other factors (such as unequal access to education for girls) suggests that it is.

TABLE 3.2: DECOMPOSITION OF INEQUALITY IN GUATEMALA

Variable	Groups	Sub-Groups	% of inequality explained by:
	National	**All Guatemala**	**100.0%**
I	**Geographical**	**2 Areas (Urban/Rural)**	**33.4%**
2		8 Regions	31.5%
3	**HH composition / size**	Number of Members aged 0–24	27.7%
4		**Number of Members aged 0–6**	**25.3%**
5		Household Size (regardless of age)	23.8%
6		Number of Members aged 7–24	12.6%
7		Number of males in household	1.8%
8		Gender of Household Head (male or female)	0.4%
9		Number of Members aged 25–59	0.2%
10		Number of Members aged 60+	0.1%
11	**Education**	**Average education for those aged 13 and older**[a]	**52.5%**
12		Average education for all members[a]	52.5%
13		Average education for those aged 18–59[a]	47.1%
14		Higher education level in the household[a]	46.3%
15		Education of household head[a]	43.9%
16		Literacy (household average)[b]	31.6%
17		Literacy of household head	16.9%
18	**HH services**	**Telephone connection**	**42.6%**
19		Drainage	34.6%
20		Piped water inside house	24.1%
21		Electricity connection	21.3%
22		Home ownership (Owned & paid, Own & not fully paid, renting, other)	8.4%
23	**Labor & Credit**	Stratum (pre-sample classification based on area characteristics)[c]	32.4%
24		Sector (Agric., Mining, Manufacturing, Utilities, Construction, etc.)	28.8%
25		**Work in agriculture**[d]	**24.9%**
26		Job type (Public, White Collar, Blue Collar, Domestic, Self Employment)[d]	16.0%
27		Formal sector work (versus informal sector)[d]	9.8%
28		CREDIT: Household has more than Q.1000 in loans	4.8%
29		Work in the public sector (vs. outside public sector)	3.6%
30	**Ethnicity & Language**	Ethnicity: specific self classification (K'iche,Q'eqchi,Kaqchiquel,Mam, Other Maya, Non-Indig.)	23.4%
31		**Ethnicity: self classification (indigenous versus non-indigenous)**	**21.3%**
32		Language: Spanish speaking ability (Majority of HH members)	17.4%
33		Language: Specific language spoken (Majority of HH members: K'iche, Q'ueqchi, Kaqchiquel, Mam or other indigenous)	10.4%

(continued)

TABLE 3.2: DECOMPOSITION OF INEQUALITY IN GUATEMALA (CONTINUED)			
Variable	**Groups**	**Sub-Groups**	**% of inequality explained by:**
34	Land	**Hectares of agricultural land worked (0,1,2–3,4–6,7–9,>9)**	16.2%
35		Hectares of agricultural land owned (0,1,2–3,4–6,7–9,>9)	9.0%
TOTAL: % of inequality explained by variables 1, 4, 11, 18, 25, 31, 34			**75.9%**

a. Defined by the years of education in groups of: 0, 1–3, 4–6, 7–9,10–12, 13–17 and 18 and more years.
b. In groups of 0%, 1–25%, 26–50%, 51–75%, and 75–100%.
c. The stratum classification is based on the average household characteristics for each Primary Sampling Unit from the latest Census data.
d. Of the highest labor income earner in the household.

Source: World Bank calculations using data from the ENCOVI 2000, *Instituto Nacional de Estadística–Guatemala.* Based on a decomposition of Entropy Measures of Inequality (Theil indices). Figures presented for the E-0 measure of inequality. Those for E-1 and E-2 yield very similar magnitudes and results.

(agricultural work), land, ethnicity, geography, and household size.[16] Education constitutes the single most important determinant of inequality, accounting for over *half* of all inequality in Guatemala. This reflects the large disparities in access to education and the large wage differentials associated with various levels of educational attainment (as discussed in more detail in Chapter 7).

The long-term nature of many of these variables is significant: as international experience has shown, it is very difficult to reduce inequality. Many of these factors are somewhat structural (for example, geography), difficult for Governments to change (land distribution, sectoral employment opportunities), or affect the distribution of consumption mainly in the long run (education and fertility). As such, inequality is a particularly "stubborn" variable, quite resistant to change over time.[17]

16. It is important to note that, with the exception of this "combined" analysis (analyzing the different variables together), the decomposition of inequality using each variable is not additive.

17. Even in Chile, which has aggressively pursued structural policies to promote growth, and reduce poverty and inequality for some time (trade policies, education reform, targeted public investments, etc.), the Gini index of inequality has only fallen by 1.5 percentage points in seven years. See Ferreira and Litchfield (1997) and World Bank (1997).

CHAPTER 4

HISTORICAL AND CONTEXTUAL FACTORS

The last chapter showed that household endowments, assets, and characteristics play an important role in "determining" poverty in Guatemala. From a technical point of view, the "cross-sectional" *relationships* between these variables and consumption (the "betas" in the regressions) are quite similar to those found in other countries.[1] Yet Guatemala's high degree of poverty and exclusion did not emerge over night. This chapter argues that other factors—both contextual and historical—have fundamentally shaped Guatemala's performance regarding the *levels* of the endowments and characteristic determinants of poverty observed today (the levels of the "x's" used in the regressions). This report does not purport to conduct an exhaustive review of these historical and contextual factors; rather it seeks to simply highlight the importance of these factors in influencing poverty in Guatemala.

Specifically, this chapter examines the key contextual and historical factors and their role in shaping Guatemala's poverty profile today, highlighting key challenges for tomorrow. It begins with an overview of two predominant contextual factors in the make-up of Guatemala as a country: rich cultural diversity and geographic isolation. With this context in mind, Section 2 then reviews key exclusionary forces in Guatemala's historical pattern of development: (a) massive land expropriations from the indigenous population which have resulted in one of the most unequal distributions of land in the world; (b) forced labor policies that exploited indigenous labor from the 1800s through the middle of 1900s; and (c) human capital accumulation, which has historically suffered as from exclusionary education policies, as part of a broader political strategy, and as an outcome of land and labor policies. These forces all put Guatemala at a historical disadvantage in terms of its development and key social indicators. Moreover, the long civil war imposed further costs on Guatemala's development, as reviewed in Section 3.

Section 4 then asserts that the Peace Accords, signed in 1996, not only yielded a formal end to the armed conflict, but signaled a fundamental shift in Guatemala's pattern of development, paving

---

1. For a cross-country review in LAC, see Wodon (2000). See also various poverty assessments.

the way for a transformation to a more prosperous and inclusive nation. In the six years since the Peace Accords, Guatemala has taken important steps on this new development path, with progress in public sector management, public revenues and spending, and improvements in the coverage and equity of education and basic services. Importantly, these steps signal that progress *is* possible, despite the magnitude of the challenge of changing the course of history.

Nonetheless, challenges remain. This is to be expected. Changing the course of history in such a short time span is not easy in any country. The hierarchical relations, attitudes, and institutional forces that have pervaded for centuries do not disappear over night. Moreover, events such as Hurricane Mitch and political transitions have delayed the implementation of the Peace Agenda.

Section 4 contends that many of the remaining challenges for the Peace Agenda coincide largely with priorities for poverty reduction. In particular, progress on the Peace Accords is deficient for key development targets, especially for those involving health and education outcomes, and economic growth. These outcomes reflect the need for poverty reduction and improvements in living conditions, which are crucial for lasting peace. They highlight remaining priority challenges in several key areas, which reveal the significant overlaps between the Peace Agenda and the challenge of poverty reduction: (a) creating opportunities; (b) reducing vulnerability; and (c) improving institutions and empowering communities. These challenges are discussed in subsequent chapters.

Diversity, Ethnicity and Isolation

Guatemala is a physically diverse country, with many isolated areas. The country is divided into numerous distinct geographic zones, including forested highlands in the west, fertile lowland coasts, and tropical forests in Peten. Two-thirds of the country is mountainous and volcanic. Most of the population lives on land between 900 and 2,500 meters above sea level. Unfortunately, this natural resource diversity is being increasingly threatened by erosion, deforestation, and population pressures on the land. The country is not physically united and many villages are fairly isolated, with long inter-village distances, due to an inadequate road network (see Chapter 10). About 13% of households in the ENCOVI 2000 sample did not have access to motorable roads;[2] this figure reaches close to 20% in the Nor-Occidente, Nor-Oriente, and Norte regions, which are also among the poorest. Such physical isolation is also higher among the poorest quintiles and the indigenous, than the nonindigenous (see Chapter 10 for details). Village access is further complicated by impassability from road closures (due to landslides, mudslides, flooding, etc.), as discussed in Chapter 10.

Mirroring the physical diversity of the country, Guatemala's population is rich in cultural and linguistic diversity. In a population of over 11 million, about half the population is indigenous, including some 23 ethno-linguistic groups, 21 of which are Mayan.[3] The largest indigenous groups include the K'iche (22% of the indigenous population), the Kaqchiqel (21%), the Mam (19%), and the Q'eqchi (15%).[4] The Mayan population—descendents of the great civilization that created the magnificent pyramids and ceremonial centers of Mexico and Central America—live primarily in hundreds of small, rural communities scattered throughout the western and central highlands.[5] Taking language as a cultural asset, the ENCOVI 2000 reveals that some 84% of the indigenous population (self-identified ethnicity, see Box 4.1), speaks an indigenous language (Table 4.1). This share differs by specific indigenous group, with a higher share of the Mam and Q'eqchi speaking Indigenous languages than the K'iché or Kaqchikel. An inter-generational loss of cultural heritage also seems evident, since a smaller share of indigenous children and youth

---

2. Motorable roads defined as paved, gravel or unpaved roads. Excludes dirt roads, tracks and paths. Estimates are for households in the ENCOVI sample for which community-level information was collected. See GUAPA Technical Paper 8 (Puri, 2002) for additional details.

3. Tovar Gómez (1998).

4. Population estimates by ethnicity based on World Bank calculations using the ENCOVI 2000 (expanded sample), *Instituto Nacional de Estadística—Guatemala*.

5. Davis (1988) and FLACSO (2001).

BOX 4.1: WHO IS "INDIGENOUS"? A HISTORICAL PERSPECTIVE

The history of how many Indigenous people there are in Guatemala is as much an account of efforts by a dominant political group to set itself apart from the general population as it is a description of demographic change. Guatemalan census data have always distinguished between indigenous and non-indigenous people, but the criteria for classification evolved with the maturation of national identity.

The Indian/non-Indian dichotomy was at first unequivocal. When European conquerors first established themselves in the territory, the word "indigenous" was an adjective that meant native-born. However, Spanish law granted full citizenship to anyone born of Spanish parents. This was true even if they were locally born and if only one parent was Spanish. As this new group of locally-born descendents of Europeans grew, its members came to be known as "*Ladinos*." During the colonial period, Indians were subject to a head tax, which provided an economic incentive for classification as Ladinos. Zilberman de Luján (1995) notes that throughout the colonial period the "*Población de Castas*"—later called "Ladinos"—grew in proportion to the Indian population because indigenous people wished to evade the tribute.

The table below shows a fairly steady but very uneven decline in the percentage of "Indians" reported. For instance, between 1893 and 1921 there was almost no change. In both years classification was left up to the interviewer, who was told to "discretely write down the person's race" without asking the subject, for it was believed that asking resulted in "erroneously recording" individuals as Ladinos. Another 30 years later, the recorded percent Indigenous dropped by 11 points when the census instructed the census taker to "use as a basis for classification whatever was the local social perception of that individual." Another 11 point drop resulted in only 14 years, when the local-standards methodology was "cross-checked" with "objective" criteria, including language spoken, dress, whether shoes were worn and whether the person ate bread or corn tortillas. In 1973 and 1981, crosschecking was dropped and the census taker was allowed to decide ethnicity, except in the case of maids, when the *patron's* opinion was to be recorded. The result was that between 1964 and 1973 the proportion recorded as indigenous rose slightly for the first time in Guatemala's history. By 1994 data collection is imbued with the spirit of peace-process democracy and pluralism. The census report notes that "the individual's right to self-identification with an ethnic group was respected. For this reason [ethnicity] was obtained by means of a direct question and not through simple observation." While the ENCOVI 2000 includes numerous possible indicators of ethnicity, including language, self-identification, and language of ancestors, the definition used here is "self-identification" (consistent with the census).

% of Population by Ethnicity, 1893–2000

	Ladinos	Indigenous		Ladinos	Indigenous
1893 Census	35.3%	64.7%	1973 Census	56.2%	43.8%
1921 Census	35.2%	64.8%	1981 Census	58.1%	41.9%
1950 Census	46.4%	53.6%	1994 Census	58.3%	41.7%
1964 Census	57.8%	42.2%	2000 ENCOVI	57.5%	42.6%

Source: Adapted from GUAPA Technical Paper 3, Edwards (2002).

speak the Indigenous languages than the older generations. Moreover, the loss is particularly strong with inter-ethnic marriage: while 90% of those between 7–25 years who boast "full Mayan linguistic lineage" (four Mayan-speaking grandparents and two Mayan-speaking parents) speak indigenous languages, only 41% speak the language if only three grandparents are Mayan speakers (even if both parents are), and only 18% speak indigenous languages if only one parent does (even if all four grandparents do).[6] Taking Spanish-speaking ability as an indicator of economic access, the ENCOVI indicates that, while 89% of the overall population speaks Spanish, only three-quarters of the indigenous population do. This share differs significantly by specific ethnicity and gender, with only a third of the Q'eqchi population and two-thirds of indigenous women reporting that they speak Spanish (Table 4.1). Taking bilingualism (ability to speak both Spanish and indigenous languages) as an indicator of possession of both cultural and economic assets, however, the indigenous are clearly better endowed (Table 4.1).

---

6. Indeed, the language abilities of parents and grandparents were significant determinants of Mayan-speaking abilities in multi-variate regressions. See GUAPA Technical Paper 3 (Edwards, 2002) for details.

TABLE 4.1: LANGUAGE ABILITY BY SOCIO-ECONOMIC GROUP

			Language Spoken		
	Spanish	Indigenous	Monolingual Spanish	Monolingual Indigenous	Bilingual
All Guatemala	89	35	65	11	24
Area					
Urban	97	19	81	2	17
Rural	84	44	56	16	28
Gender					
Male	91	35	65	9	26
Female	87	35	65	13	22
Poverty					
Extreme poor	68	66	34	32	33
All poor	82	60	50	17	33
Non-poor	98	15	85	2	12
Ethnic group					
Non-indigenous	100	1	99	0	1
Indigenous	74	84	16	27	57
Indigenous					
K'iche	79	75	25	21	54
Q'eqchi	37	86	4	63	33
Kaqchiquel	91	75	25	9	65
Mam	87	81	19	13	68
Indigenous male	79	82	18	21	61
Indigenous female	68	85	15	32	53
Age group (for indigenous only)					
7–13	68	77	23	32	45
14–18	77	78	22	23	55
19–25	76	82	18	24	58
26–40	76	84	16	24	60
40+	67	89	11	33	56

Source: World Bank calculations using ENCOVI 2000, *Instituto Nacional de Estadística—Guatemala.*

Unfortunately, Guatemala's diversity has historically been accompanied by conflict, exclusion, and a dualistic social and economic structure. Internationally, countries with significant indigenous populations tend to have higher poverty rates. Within these countries, the indigenous tend to be poorer than the non-indigenous population due to historically exclusionary forces.[7] In this regard, Guatemala is no exception. Indeed, inequality between ethnicities is a pervasive feature in Guatemala. As discussed in Chapter 2, while the indigenous make up about 43% of the population, they account for less than a quarter of total income and consumption. In contrast, economic and political resources remain concentrated among the economic elite of predominantly European descent and the Ladino population. The linkages between these groups have historically been weakened by decades of exclusion and conflict, as discussed below.

Unlike its topography or people, Guatemala's economy is not so diverse. As discussed in Chapters 5 and 6, agriculture still dominates, accounting for a quarter of GDP,[8] and employs 36%

---

7. Psacharopoulos and Patrinos (1994).
8. World Bank macroeconomic database.

of all workers.[9] The economy is still largely based on exports of coffee and sugar, notwithstanding some success in promoting non-traditional exports. Despite a fall in international prices, coffee still accounts for over 25% of export earnings. Sugar, bananas, and cardamom follow as the principal cash crops. The main export crops all require large inputs of seasonal labor for harvest. Subsistence agriculture traditionally revolves around the production of corn and black beans. *Maquila* (free-trade assembly and re-export zones), mining, energy, commerce, and services have all grown fairly rapidly in the past decade. Tourism strengthened in the 1990s and now exceeds coffee or sugar as the main source of foreign exchange, though its success depends largely on political stability and security. Remittances are also an important source of income (see Chapters 5 and 6).

Exclusionary Forces in Guatemala's Historical Pattern of Development

In fact, past policies greatly contributed to an exclusionary pattern of development in Guatemala, particularly for land, labor, and education. All of these spheres were intertwined with each other. They are all also intimately connected with the development of coffee, Guatemala's primary export crop. Such policies sought to promote economic growth, but the indigenous population was excluded from benefiting from this growth. Women were also excluded from these spheres.

Land

The historical practice of expropriating land from the indigenous gained momentum with the development of agricultural exports, particularly coffee. The indigenous have consistently been divested of their land in Guatemala since the conquest and colonial times. Land privatization and expropriation accelerated in the late 1800s, however, with significant changes in the legal environment determining property rights,[10] which coincided with the spread of coffee. Coffee production depended on secure private property rights, and it was only then that coffee developed rapidly. These laws encouraged privatization by simplifying the conversion of communally-held indigenous lands (*ejidos*),[11] into individually titled holdings. A central aim of land privatization and consolidation was the formation of large plantations (*fincas*), with the creation of a class of large landowners at the expense of indigenous cultivators, to take advantage of the expanding world market for coffee.[12] Since the ideal terrain for coffee occurs between 800–1,500 meters of altitude, the indigenous peoples who had been cultivating these lands were compelled to located to higher and less fertile grounds for their subsistence cultivation.[13] Nearly one million acres of land were privatized between 1871, when land privatization decrees were initiated, and 1873 alone.[14] With the shift towards larger plantations, some 3,600 persons received plots averaging 450 hectares each during the period between 1896 and 1921.[15]

---

9. For the population aged 15+. World Bank calculations using the ENCOVI 2000, *Instituto Nacional de Estadística, Guatemala*.

10. A Presidential Decree of 1873 provided for the sale of national lands in individual lots of between 45 and 225 hectares each. Plant (1995).

11. Communal rights to *ejidos* were not entirely abolished, however, for two reasons: (a) it was in the interest of plantation owners unable or unwilling to support a full-time labor force that the Indigenous retain access to some means of subsistence production; and (b) because such lands provided an opportunity for taxation for the Government. Grandin (2000) and UNDP (2000).

12. Although coffee is produced by both large and small farmers in Guatemala (with over 30,000 producers), the bulk of production is from the larger producers. Plant (1995). This model of coffee development based mainly on large plantations is similar to that of El Salvador's, but contrasts with relatively more efficient small-holder production practices in Costa Rica and Colombia. In the late 1800s, close to 80% of coffee in Guatemala was produced on farms greater than 50 hectares, as compared with 58% in El Salvador, 38% in Costa Rica, and only 14% in Colombia. Nugent and Robinson (August 2000).

13. Plant (1995).

14. Nugent and Robinson (2000).

15. Plant (1995).

Such consolidation has continued until recent times, as diversification of exports brought new expropriations from peasants. As discussed above and in Chapter 5, Guatemala's economy has diversified substantially in recent decades, though coffee still dominates. During the country's brief democratic period, from 1944–1954, the Government introduced a series of agrarian reform measures, including laws to protect communal lands. The reforms were aborted in with the military coup in 1954, however, delaying any significant land reforms until the 1990s. Land consolidation continued during this period. While communal lands accounted for 12% of agricultural land in 1950, this share had dropped to 4.8% by 1964 and only 1.1% in 1979 (the year of the last agricultural census).[16] Between 1950 and 1970, the number of farm families—most of them indigenous—possessing parcels of land too small to provide subsistence incomes increased by 37% and the number of landless peasants increased to about one-fourth of the rural workforce.[17] Estimates from 1979 indicate that less than 2% of the population owned at least 65% of the land and less than 1% of all farms were over 2,500 hectares in size and accounted for over 20% of the land, while over 78% of all farms were under 3.5 hectares and accounted for slightly more than 10% of the land.[18] With an estimated Gini coefficient for the distribution of land of 85 in 1979, Guatemala's land inequality is among the most skewed in the developing world.[19] Women have also been consistently denied the right to hold land, both legally and then by tradition. According to INTA, only 8% of land appropriations between 1954 and 1996 went to women.[20] Indeed, tradition still bars women from inheriting land in most of the QPES study villages.

BOX 4.2: LIFE IN A FINCA VILLAGE: THE STORY OF KA1 (QPES)

"Los que nos tratan mal son los encargados de la finca . . . Aquí no hay que hablar de bienestar, sino de pobreza. Aquí todos somos pobres. Son muchos nuestros deseos, pero nada tenemos . . . No nos vamos porque no tenemos a donde ir."

—Villagers of KA1, QPES, July 2000.

The 200-some villagers of KA1 live and work permanently on a coffee plantation (finca).[21] Most were born on the finca, their relatives having migrated there in previous generations. The villagers of KA1 own almost zero physical assets; the finca owns the houses and small plots they are allowed to use for subsistence production (mainly of corn). When their spouses pass away, widows are not allowed to maintain use of these plots or houses, unless they move in with relatives who are actively employed on the finca. The houses are in terrible condition, with incomplete wooden walls and metal roofs. The villagers lack access to most basic services, such as piped water, sanitation, or energy. The only access to the finca comes from an unpaved road, which gets flooded during heavy rains and becomes impassable. Financial capital is virtually non-existent, as the villagers have little opportunity to acquire surplus or borrow. Almost all adults are illiterate, and the single-teacher school only offers through grade three. Child labor prevents many from attending, particularly the boys. There is no health clinic or pharmacy, only a traveling midwife.

Workers on the finca receive benefits according to their labor classification. Permanent workers ("*rancheros*" or "03") do receive benefits. However, many "permanent residents"—particularly union members—have been classified as "volunteers" ("06") and have much more tenuous job security, facing periodic suspensions in an apparent strategy by the finca to avoid paying labor benefits and discourage union affiliation. Their classification

(continued)

---

16. UNDP (2000).

17. Davis (1988).

18. Plant (1995).

19. This compares with land Gini coefficients in other Central American and LAC countries of: 82 for El Salvador, 81 for Panama, 80 for Costa Rica and Nicaragua, 77 for Honduras and Bolivia, and 61 for Mexico. Source: Deininger and Orlinto (2000). The ENCOVI 2000 yields a Gini coefficient of 79 for land, though this survey was designed as a household survey and not an agricultural or land census.

20. UNDP (2000).

21. ANACAFE (2001) estimates that some 300,000 people live and work permanently on coffee fincas in Guatemala.

BOX 4.2: LIFE IN A FINCA VILLAGE: THE STORY OF KAI (QPES) (CONTINUED)

as volunteers (same grouping as temporary migrant workers, or *cuadrillas*) derives from the fact that they seek work on other fincas during periods of suspension. Women on the fincas do not receive labor benefits, despite contributing to the production process, both directly (especially during the harvest) and indirectly by maintaining the workers via household chores and cooking.

Social capital and capacity to engage in collective action is virtually non-existent. The villagers do not feel they belong to the community. Vertical authoritarian relations between the finca administrators and the villagers dictate daily life and discourage the formation of horizontal connections within the village. While some workers do maintain ties to the union, this has been a bit of a mixed blessing due to their reclassification as volunteers (06). In addition to a lack of these basic assets, the villagers of KAI seem to have lost their cultural identity, identifying themselves and their language not as the Mayans (Kaqchiqel and k'iché) that they are, but simply as "natives" of the finca who speak "lengua." Children only speak Spanish, though they do understand the Indigenous languages. Few residents wear traditional Indigenous clothing (*traje*).

On top of their extreme poverty, the villagers of KAI have been subject to several significant shocks, with lasting effects, including the earthquake of 1976 (their homes have still not been repaired), repeated large-scale labor shocks (including vengeful dismissals for union affiliation), and other recurring natural disasters (including flooding and landslides). They have little hope for the future, noting that "everything stays the same on the finca, without water, without lighting, without drainage or latrines" and that "they have no where else to go." Children's aspirations do not go beyond the life they know, with boys indicating that when they grow up they will "work on the coffee harvest and clean the hillside" and girls answering they will "clean the house."

Labor

Guatemala's economy essentially grew on the backs of Indigenous workers who suffered numerous forms of mandatory forced labor, again connected to the expansion of the coffee sector. Indigenous labor in Guatemala has historically been viewed as an exploitable asset. In fact, land policies of the late 1800s had the additional goal of reducing land available to subsistence Indigenous to create a low-wage labor force. In the late 1800s, insufficient cheap labor was a barrier to the expansion of coffee. The expropriation of Indigenous communal lands helped create rural unemployment by forcing families into marginal areas or leaving them without access to sufficient land.[22] Such conditions were precisely the prerequisites for several types of forced labor:

- **Mandamiento.** In 1877, the state instituted its infamous mandamiento forced-labor system in which villages (pueblos) were required to supply coffee plantations with work crews of up to sixty people for periods of fifteen to thirty days.[23]
- **Forced Work on Roads.** In 1873, the *contribución de caminos* decreed that all able male citizens were obliged to provide free labor on public projects to build roads or pay a commutation fee.[24] Supposedly, this free work requirement applied to all, but in practice, only the indigenous population was forced to perform it.[25]
- **Debt Servitude.** Indentured labor was also common. Under this system, advances were provided to workers in anticipation of a certain amount of work; debts were then deducted from the worker's harvest or in cash. Such debts commonly built up to levels high enough that the workers were essentially "owned" by the finca owners (*patrones*).[26] Debts were

---

22. McCreery (1976).

23. This new law was actually a rationalization and expansion of state labor obligations in effect since the 1830s. Gandin (2000). Workers were forcibly recruited unless they could demonstrate from their personal workbooks (*libreto de jornaleros*) that such service had been recently performed. McCreery (1983).

24. The requirement was originally for three days of free labor, but this was extended to two weeks per year in 1910. Grandin (2000).

25. UNDP (2000).

26. Grandin (2000). Nugent and Robinson (2000). UNDP (2000).

monitored by local public authorities who were authorized to arrest any defaulters, as evidenced by debt-recordings in the personal workbooks required for all indigenous peasants.[27]
- **Vagrancy Law.** The 1934 *ley contra vagancia* obliged landless peasants to work at least 150 days per year on plantations. Proof of service was required in the workers' personal workbooks, and the system was monitored and enforced by the State itself.[28] In conjunction with mass land expropriations, an increasing share of indigenous were forced into these conditions.

These forced labor laws remained in effect until the middle of the 20th century. During the country's brief democratic experiment (from 1944–1954), the Government enacted the first Labor Code in 1947, providing for minimum wages and recognizing the freedoms of organization, finca owners were still allowed to pay up to 35% of workers' salaries in food, a practice that even appeared in the Constitution of 1985. An important step occurred with the Agrarian Reform Act of 1952 that prohibited all forms of servitude and slavery. This law was again abandoned, however, in 1954, after the military coup, when a decree permitted landowners to reintroduce the semi-feudal *colono* system under which landowners could avail themselves of a cheap labor force by providing subsistence plots on their plantations in exchange for labor during the harvest season,[29] a practice that continues today (see Box 4.2). Finally, the Constitution of 1985 reestablished most modern labor rights,[30] though as shown in Chapter 6, many are not enforced (for example, labor benefits, minimum wages).

Education and Human Capital
Cross-country evidence[31] **suggests that Guatemala's human capital accumulation—and hence long-term economic growth—suffered as a result of land and labor policies.** In Guatemala, like El Salvador, land and labor policies favored the development of the coffee sector via large plantations. Such an approach reflects the fairly close ties between the landed elite and both the conservative and liberal parties in the 1800s. The subsistence-wage economy that resulted provided little incentive for workers or firms to invest in human capital. In contrast, the economies of Costa Rica and Colombia benefited substantially from policies that protected and promoted the development of coffee based primarily on small-holder production. Small-holders have stronger incentives to accumulate human capital because they are more likely to reap its returns. This structure fostered faster human capital generation, and hence a stronger base for economic growth in the long-run.

Relatively lower human capital accumulation among the indigenous is also an outcome of a historically exclusionary educational system—which reflected a broader strategy of political exclusion. Education in Guatemala was traditionally reserved for "citizens," a status not fully extended to women or the Indigenous until 1945.[32] The liberal government of 1871 instituted a substantial education reform, shifting responsibility for providing education from the Church to the state, and making education free and mandatory. The policy was not implemented, however, as the state lacked the necessary resources (teachers or funds). Nonetheless, some indigenous education centers and secondary schools for women were established during this period. In practice, the education system was ethnically segregated: on the one hand, the state promoted a paternalistic approach to "civilize" and assimilate the indigenous as agricultural producers; on the other hand, the education system continued to exclude the indigenous, being largely reserved for ladino males. As such, virtually the entire indigenous population (and most women) remained illiterate. Illiteracy was then used as a pretext for ineligibility for voting, making the educational policy part of a broader strategy of

---

27. Plant (1995).
28. Plant (1995) and UNDP (2000).
29. Plant (1995).
30. UNDP (2000).
31. Analysis conducted by Nugent and Robinson (August 2000).
32. UNDP (2000).

political exclusion. With the temporary introduction of a more democratic state in 1945 came education reform, including a literacy campaign, the creation of the *Instituto Indigenista Nacional,* and a policy to officialize indigenous languages.[33] Progress was made, and overall literacy rose from 19% in 1930 to 29% in 1950,[34] and to 37% by 1964. Further policy changes were legislated in 1985 under the National Education Law, which emphasized decentralization and participation of indigenous communities in the education system. This was the first time that a law asserted that the education system should be take into account Guatemala's ethnic diversity.[35]

Overall Development

By outbreak of the civil war Guatemala was already far behind in its development, particularly its social indicators. Despite having almost twice the per capita GDP of Honduras, Nicaragua or Bolivia, by 1960, Guatemala ranked worse than these countries on several key social indicators. In particular, Guatemala had the lowest gross primary enrollment rate in LAC, the second shortest life expectancy (second only to Bolivia), and infant mortality rates only slightly lower than Honduras, Nicaragua or Bolivia.[36] Guatemala also lagged significantly behind the collective group of comparable "lower-middle income countries" on these social indicators in the 1960s.

Guatemala's 36-Year Civil War: Significant Costs for Long-Term Development

Guatemala's was one of the longest of Latin America's recent civil wars. Spanning 36 years (from 1960–1996), the war underwent several phases, only later involving the indigenous on a large scale. The first wave broke out in 1960 with a group of army officers revolting against government corruption. Initially, the movement was centered in the eastern region and involved primarily the non-indigenous population. When the revolt failed, the officers fled to the countryside and launched a war against the Government.[37] The second wave broke out in the 1970s, this time in the western highlands, with some Indigenous communities becoming active participants. During the final and longest phase, from the late 1970s into the 1980s, social tensions exploded into a full scale civil war with active indigenous participation (involving close to half a million Mayans during that period).[38] Although Indigenous communities had been undergoing important social changes for more than a century,[39] it was not until this later phase that they became a source of mobilization and support for the country's guerrilla movements, and hence a perceived threat to the country's powerful economic and military elites.[40] The guerrilla military offensive reached its height in 1980–81, gaining 6,000–8,000 armed fighters and 250,000–500,000 active collaborators.

---

33. UNDP (2000).

34. By 1930, literacy had already reached 67% in Costa Rica and 52% in Colombia. It was lower in El Salvador, at 27%, but still higher than in Guatemala. Nugent and Robinson (August 2000).

35. UNDP (2000).

36. World Bank World Development Indicators Database using GDP per capita in constant 1995 US$ (Guatemala = $928, compared with $513, $638, and $827 for Honduras, Nicaragua, and Bolivia respectively); life expectancy at birth (Guatemala = 46 compared with 43 for Bolivia, 47 for both Honduras and Nicaragua; and 56 for LAC overall); gross primary enrollment rates (Guatemala = 45%, compared with 64, 66, and 67 for Bolivia, Nicaragua, and Honduras respectively); and infant mortality (Guatemala = 130 per 1000 live births, compared with 166, 143, and 139 for Bolivia, Honduras, and Nicaragua respectively, 128 for lower-middle income countries, and 105 for LAC).

37. World Bank and the Carter Center (1997).

38. Davis (1988) and Jonas (2000).

39. Davis (1988) describes a widespread "sociological awakening" of Guatemala's indigenous population during this period. The roots of this sociological mobilization can be traced to the political changes (e.g., the formation of political parties, trade unions, and peasant leagues) that took place in Guatemala in the period of popular democracy and social reformism from 1945 to 1954. In the 1970s, opposition political parties, especially the Christian Democratic (CD) party also began to organize and gain influence in the Guatemalan countryside, some even sponsoring successful indigenous candidates for office.

40. Davis (1988).

In response, the military launched a major counterinsurgency effort that reached genocidal proportions in the early 1980s, executing scorched-earth warfare tactics, mandatory paramilitary "civilian self-defense patrols" (PACs), forced resettlement camps, and the militarization of the entire administrative apparatus of the country.[41]

Guatemala's war was also one of the bloodiest in LAC. In total, more than 200,000 people (over 2% of the population) were killed or "disappeared" and another million (10%) were displaced. Over 600 villages were completely destroyed, their residents massacred.[42] The results of the investigation by the Historical Clarification Commission indicate that 93% of the actions of violence were attributable to agents of the state (particularly the military), and that 53% of the victims were Mayan, 11% were Ladino, and 30% were of unregistered ethnicity.

Although Guatemala recorded reasonable economic performance during the early phases of the conflict, the conflict imposed significant costs on the economy and village life. Somewhat paradoxically, despite the war, Guatemala managed to maintain reasonable growth rates during the 1960s and 1970s, though they fell significantly during the 1980s.[43] Nonetheless, in addition to the loss of life, the war had serious short- and long-run impacts on Guatemala's development, for the overall economy and life at the village level (Box 4.3). While it is impossible to quantify the full range of impacts, some are directly quantifiable. The Historical Clarification Commission report estimates that, during the 1980s alone, the costs of the war were equivalent to 15 months of production in Guatemala, or 121% of GDP in 1990. The majority of these costs arise from the loss of productive

---

BOX 4.3: REBUILDING AFTER THE VIOLENCE OF THE 1980S: THE STORY OF KII (QPES)

"Ella ha pasado penas ... el esposo desapareció, ya nunca los vimos ... A mi esposo lo llevaron y como mi hijo tenía 10 meses en el pecho, mamó la tristeza y el niño murió ... Ya no pudimos trabajar ... ya no vimos la cosecha de maíz ... Afectó a los niños, ya no fueron a la escuela ... Ya no se comunicaban entre vecinos y familiares ... Un montón de gente se fue a la capital por miedo."
—Villagers of KII describing the violence of the 1980s, QPES 2000

Although the QPES teams did not explicitly seek out villages that had been subject to substantial violence during the civil war, several happened to fall into the sample. The K'iche village of KII is one of them. The shock was apparently severe, with numerous families losing relatives (killed or missing), girls being raped, and houses being looted. A huge share of the population fled to the capital in fear, returning only in the 1990s. In addition to the obvious psychological trauma suffered by the victims and their families, agricultural production halted, children didn't attend school, and communication between neighbors and families was severed out of fear and lack of trust. "Envious" villagers apparently "wrongfully" accused other residents of being guerrilla members. People were even afraid to talk inside their homes for fear of being listened to and reported by their neighbors. Even today, they still complain of *susto* (post-traumatic stress syndrome) as a lasting effect.

Nonetheless, the community seems to have rebuilt itself substantially since the conflict ended. In terms of village organization and social capital, it boasts numerous committees (for development, water, electricity, stoves, PTA, a cooperative, and a farmers association), though some allege misuse of funds by the water committee. The villagers have fairly strong links to external bodies and are receiving assistance from the municipality, various bilateral agencies, social funds, NGOs, and ministries. On the other hand, there are some religious conflicts and divisions in the community, women are not active in community decision making, the illiterate seem to be excluded ("no one takes them into account") and links between poor and wealthier families are scarce. Land inequality is high, and land conflicts have arisen due to unclear borders between properties. In terms of assets, the community is well-endowed, with extensive road access, water, latrines, electricity, and substantial communal infrastructure (market, mills, 17 churches, sports fields). The village also boasts relatively extensive school coverage, with pre-primary, primary, and secondary schools. Health services are missing, however, and they only have midwives. Major sources of livelihoods are fairly well-diversified, including agriculture (corn and fruits) and non-farm activities (artisan crafts, textiles, commercialization).

---

41. Jonas (2000).
42. Comisión para el Esclarecimiento Histórico (CEH, Truth Commission) (1999).
43. Growth averaged 5.4% p.a. in the 1960s and 5.5 p.a. in the 1970s. It then fell to 0.9% p.a. in the 1980s. Sources: IMF and Banco de Guatemala.

potential and abandoned economic activities due to death, disappearance, or forced displacement. Destruction of physical capital, including private, community and infrastructure assets was also costly (estimated at 6% of GDP in 1990). The engagement of the potential workforce in a military, rather than productive, capacity also further reduced Guatemala's output. UNDP (2000) estimates that the PACs diverted a significant share of the economically active population, with a cost of $3,000 million in 1990 or 39% of GDP for that year. Using time-series models and average growth-poverty elasticities, Lopez (October 2001) estimates that if the armed conflict had not occurred, per capita GDP in 2000 would have been about 40% higher and poverty would have been about 12 percentage points lower. Social indicators lagged even further behind growth, with Guatemala remaining among the worst performers for education and even falling in the rankings behind Honduras and Nicaragua for infant mortality during the period from 1975–1990. Policies and strategies to reduce poverty were essentially non-existent. The mere use of the term "poverty" was considered "taboo" in official circles until the 1990s, since such egalitarian concepts were associated with leftist insurgents.[44] Other impacts include the repression of participation of civil society organizations was discouraged and the (often deliberate) destruction of vast areas of the highlands (e.g., via burning of forests).[45]

The 1996 Peace Accords: Towards a More Inclusive Course of Development

The Peace Accords: A Turning Point for Guatemala's Development Path

The Peace Accords aimed not only to formally end the armed conflict, but to reverse the country's historically exclusionary pattern of development. Recent developments in Guatemala have been shaped in large part by the signing of the Peace Accords in December 1996. The four main areas of the agreements involved (a) resettlement, re-incorporation, and reconciliation issues; (b) an integral human development program; (c) goals for productive and sustainable development; and (d) a program for the modernization of the democratic state, including a strengthening of the capacity of participation and consultations of the distinct segments of civil society. Three cross-cutting themes were also emphasized throughout the accords: the rights of indigenous communities, commitments regarding the rights and position of women, and a strengthening of social participation.[46] Importantly, the main themes on the Peace Agenda were maintained throughout the protracted negotiations process, despite numerous changes in Government, three different peace commissions, and various changes in the military. The endurance of these main themes throughout the peace process bears testimony to their importance as priorities for the country.

The agenda for economic development and the reduction of poverty and exclusion were the focus of two main accords. In particular, the **Accord on the Identity and Rights of Indigenous Peoples,** signed in March 1995, proposed to formally define Guatemala as a multi-ethnic, multi-cultural and multi-lingual nation and recognized that the identities of the indigenous peoples are fundamental to the construction of national unity. The accord contained many provisions to overcome the historic exclusion and exploitation suffered by indigenous peoples, including: proposals for anti-discrimination legislation; the protection of cultural rights; educational reforms (including decentralization and the promotion of multilingual and multicultural education); recognition of the traditional forms of organization and communal land ownership; and the creation of several joint commissions (*comisiones paritarias*) to guide these reforms.[47] Unfortunately, poor voter turnout at a referendum in 1999 resulted in a rejecting of a package of constitutional reforms necessary for full implementation of this accord. The **Socioeconomic and Agrarian Issues (SEA) Accord,** signed in May 1996, established the overall development agenda, with stronger social orientation and a general

---

44. This point was repeatedly emphasized at a workshop on poverty organized by SEGEPLAN in October 2000.

45. Davis (1988) and Jonas (2000).

46. MINUGUA (2001a).

47. Jonas (2000).

goal of closing the huge gap between rich and poor. The accord covered a range of development areas, including: growth, tax revenues, public spending, education, and health, each with specific monitorable targets (see below). It also emphasized broader citizen participation in development and for the decentralization of development projects through "development councils" (*consejos de desarrollo*). With respect to land, rather than endorsing full-fledged land reform, the Accords focused instead on (a) market-assisted land redistribution; (b) the creation of a Land Fund, from which land would be acquired by the Government and made available to landless peasants; and (c) the implementation of a national land survey and land registry. Conspicuously absent from the SEA Accord are specific actions and targets regarding labor markets and job creation (see Chapter 6).[48]

Progress Since the Peace Accords

In the six years since the signing of the Peace Accords, progress has been made in a number of important areas. In addition to bringing formal end to the war, reducing the size of the armed forces and creating a new civilian police force (PNC), progress has been achieved in several areas on the economic development side of the Peace Agenda, including:

- **Improving public financial management.** As discussed in Chapter 13, progress has been made with the introduction and implementation of the Integrated Financial Management System (SIAF) since 1998.
- **Increasing tax revenues.** In August 2001, the Government increased the value added tax rate (VAT) from 10% to 12% in order to increase revenues as a key part of the Peace Agenda. Efforts have also been made to improve the efficiency of the tax collection agency to clamp down on tax evasion. As a result, tax revenues have increased, rising from 8.7% of GDP in 1996 to an estimated 9.8% in 2001, with total revenues rising from 9.2% to 11.1%.
- **Increasing public spending, particularly for certain sectors.** Overall public spending has increased from 10.4% of GDP in 1996 to 13.4% in 2000.[49] Notably, spending on education and basic services (particularly via the social funds) has increased significantly, as discussed in Chapters 7 and 9. Such resources are crucial for Guatemala to be able to invest in improved living conditions.
- **Improving educational coverage.** As discussed in Chapter 7, Guatemala has made progress towards improving educational coverage and narrowing disparities between genders, ethnicities, and poverty groups. Importantly, such progress has accelerated since the signing of the Peace Accords in 1996.
- **Improving the coverage of basic utility services.** As discussed in Chapter 9, Guatemala has likewise made significant advances in extending the coverage of basic utility services (water, sanitation, electricity) and reducing disparities in access to these services.

Progress has also occurred in other areas. For example, for land, numerous entities have been created and initiatives launched, though their reach has been limited to only a few thousand households (see Chapter 6).

These steps signal that progress *is* possible. While Guatemala has not achieved the full set of targets set up by the Peace Accords, it is important to recognize that progress has been made. Given Guatemala's long history of exclusion and conflict, such progress is noteworthy since it essentially constitutes the first steps on a new, more inclusive development path.

Remaining Challenges: Important Overlaps in the Peace Agenda and the Poverty Agenda

Nonetheless, significant challenges remain. Changing the course of history hasn't been easy. The hierarchical relations, attitudes, and institutional forces that have pervaded for centuries will

---

48. Jonas (2000).
49. Source: SIAF/Ministry of Finances (Feb. 12, 2002).

TABLE 4.2: PERFORMANCE OF SELECT PEACE MONITORING INDICATORS
A Snapshot for the Years 2000, 2001

Objective/Target	Base 1995	Target 2000	Actual 2000	Estimated 2001
Economic and Fiscal Targets				
Growth Rate (%)	6.0	6.0	3.3[a]	1.9[a]
Tax Revenues (% GDP)	7.6	12.0	9.6[a]	9.8[a]
Health				
Spending (% GDP)[b]	0.9	1.3	1.1	1.1
Preventive Care (% of health budget)[c]	38	>50	52	n.a.
Education Spending (% of GDP)[b]	1.6	2.5	2.5	2.8
Judicial/Public Min. Spending (% of GDP)[b]	0.2	0.3	0.5	0.6
Military Spending (% of GDP)[b]	1.0	0.7	0.7	0.9
Investment in Rural Development (mn Q.)[c]	n.a.	50	>300	n.a.
Investment in Rural Infrastructure (mn Q.)[c]	n.a.	300	>300	n.a.
Social Targets				
Literacy Rate (%)	64.2 [d]	70.0	68.9[e]	n.a.
Primary Education Coverage				
three years—gross rate[i]	84[c]	100	125[e]	n.a.
three years—net rate[i]	69[c]	100	72[e]	n.a.
Infant Mortality (deaths per 1000 live births)	40[c]	20	40–45[f]	n.a.
Maternal Mortality Rate (per 100,000 giving birth)	97[c]–270[g]	48.5	190[h]–270[g]	n.a.
Vaccination Coverage				
Polio[c]	80	85	88	n.a.
Measles[c]	83	95	83[h]	n.a.

Sources: a. World Bank macroeconomic database. b. SIAF/Ministry of Education (Feb. 12, 2002), based on executed ("devengada") spending figures. c. World Bank (February 2000). d. INE-1994 Census. e. World Bank calculations using the ENCOVI 2000, *Instituto Nacional de Estadística—Guatemala*. f. DHS 1998–99. g. World Health Organization. h. World Development Indicators (2001). i. Note that the Peace Accords targets specified these coverage indicators as being for the first three years, rather than the standard six. Note that the difference between gross and net enrollment rates is primarily the enrollment of over-aged students, aged 10+. **Shading** signifies targets that are under-achieving.

not disappear over night. Moreover, recent events, including reconstruction efforts required after Hurricane Mitch struck in 1998 and instability caused by the political transition in 1999–2000, have delayed the implementation of the Peace Agenda. As such, close to 200 actions on the agenda had to be rescheduled and are now programmed to be implemented over the next three years.[50]

Many of the key challenges for poverty reduction coincide largely with the remaining actions on the Peace Agenda. In particular, key development-related targets supported by the Peace Accords have not been met, especially those involving outcomes in health, education and economic growth as well as fundamental institutional reforms (Table 4.2). The lack of progress for these key development outcomes reflects the need for poverty reduction and improvements in living conditions, which are crucial for lasting peace. This overlapping between the Peace Agenda and the poverty agenda highlights remaining priority challenges in several key areas:

   ▦ **Building Opportunities and Assets.** The most recent peace monitoring report by the
      UN Secretary General and MINUGUA[51] notes uneven progress in the areas of human and

---

50. Comisión de Acompañamiento del Cumplimiento de los Acuerdos de Paz (December 2000).
51. MINUGUA (2001a).

sustainable development. Improving the climate for growth and opportunities and building key assets (such as human capital, access to basic utility services and transport, and land and physical capital) are crucial for meeting targets in this area. These same factors present significant challenges for poverty reduction, as discussed in Chapters 5–10.

- **Reducing Vulnerability.** Improving security (both personal and economic) is crucial for both lasting peace and poverty reduction. Indeed, both poverty and instability can be greatly worsened by the onslaught of shocks (natural, political, economic). The challenges of reducing vulnerability and improving social protection are discussed in Chapters 11 and 12.
- **Improving Institutions and Empowering Communities.** The most recent peace monitoring report also highlights key challenges for modernizing the state and promoting community participation as a means to empower Guatemalan people and bring about a more inclusive society.[52] Such challenges are also crucial for poverty reduction and include: (a) strengthening public sector management; (b) improving governance (particularly corruption and the rule of law); and (c) fostering more inclusive participation at the community level, as discussed in Chapter 13. These institutional factors are important in their own right, but also have a strong influence on the menu of options available to the Government in the other areas in their efforts to reduce poverty.

---

52. MINUGUA (2001a).

PART 2

KEY CHALLENGE: BUILDING OPPORTUNITIES AND ASSETS

C hapters 3 and 4 both emphasize the importance of assets and opportunities as contemporary and historical determinants of poverty. Indeed, opportunity (or lack of it) to generate incomes and attain basic necessities is central to the manifestation of poverty. Promoting growth and development is also crucial for meeting the targets set by the Peace Accords, as discussed in Chapter 4.

The next few chapters seek to examine more deeply the issues relating to poverty and opportunity with a view of informing policy. Specifically, Chapter 5 examines the relationship between poverty and economic growth in Guatemala from a "macro" perspective. Chapter 6 builds on this macro-economic context to further examine the livelihoods and earnings opportunities of the poor at the household level ("micro" perspective), with a focus on rural livelihoods. The poor also rely on a portfolio of assets in order to forge opportunity, including education (Chapter 7), health (Chapter 8), basic utility services (Chapter 9), land and financial assets (Chapter 6), and access to transport (Chapter 10). Generally, the poor suffer from an unequal distribution of these assets.

CHAPTER 5

GROWTH AND POVERTY

Economic growth is essential for expanding economic opportunities for poor people. As countries become richer, the incidence of poverty tends to fall. Other indicators of well-being, such as average levels of education and health, tend to improve as well. For these reasons, economic growth is a powerful force for poverty reduction.[1] The ability of growth to influence the opportunities of the poor depends not only on the pace of growth but also on the pattern of growth in the economy (that is, favoring or disfavoring sectors which employ substantial segments of the poor population). Growth itself is also endogenous, depending on a range of factors, including, *inter alia,* human capital development, success in building more effective, transparent and inclusive institutions (which affect investment levels and allocations), functioning markets, and so forth.

This chapter examines the relationship between poverty and growth in Guatemala. It first reviews the pace and pattern of growth over time, suggesting potential effects on poverty. The chapter then assesses the potential pace of future poverty reduction and improvements in social indicators, taking into account the expected future rate of growth. Such projections are compared to the goals set by the Government's poverty reduction strategy (ERP) and the international millennium development goals (MDGs). While a full analysis of the sources of growth is beyond the scope of this study, the chapter offers some suggestions as to key priorities for promoting pro-poor growth in the future.

Poverty and Growth over Time

Poverty and the Pace of Growth

For much of its recent history, Guatemala has enjoyed relative macroeconomic stability and reasonable growth. Inflation has generally been held back and growth averaged about 3.9% over the period from the 1950s through the 1990s (Table 5.1). The exception occurred during the 1980s, when growth rates slowed to about 1%, in conjunction with the intensification of the civil war and a demise in the international economic environment. Growth attempted a rebound during

---

1. World Bank (2001e).

TABLE 5.1: AVERAGE REAL GROWTH RATES, 1950s–1990s					
	1950s	**1960s**	**1970s**	**1980s**	**1990s**
Average annual change (%)	3.7	5.4	5.5	0.9	4.0

Source: IMF (April 2001) / Banco de Guatemala.

the 1990s, averaging 4%, which is slightly higher than the average for Latin America (3.4% p.a.). Nonetheless, with one of the highest population growth rates in the region (2.6% for the period from 1980–99),[2] per capita growth rates were significantly lower (and even negative during the 1980s), averaging 1.3% p.a. over the past 50 years.

Simulations using the ENCOVI yield an elasticity of poverty to GDP per capita of −0.99%. This estimate is similar to what was estimated using the 1998–99 ENIGFAM and growth-poverty elasticities in other LAC countries.[3] It is important to note, however, that the elasticity was simulated using single year data and assumes that inequality remains constant and that everyone benefits from growth equally (that is, if growth is 1% on average, all individuals see their total consumption increase by 1%, and poverty falls by close to 1%).

In fact, while survey data suggest that poverty has fallen over the past decade, this decline was slightly lower than what would have be expected given observed growth rates during that period. As discussed in Chapter 2, poverty appears to have fallen from 62% in 1989 to about 56% in 2000. However, given average per capita growth rates of 1.4% p.a. over that same period, poverty would have been expected to have fallen to 53% by 2000 (using the simulated elasticities described above). The difference between the observed reduction in poverty from 1989–2000 (6 percentage points) and the predicted reduction in poverty (9 percentage points) could arise due to measurement issues (for example, a lack of comparability between the 1989 and 2000 estimates, as discussed in Chapter 2). More seriously, they could also signal that the pattern of growth was not neutral (as assumed), but rather favored the non-poor. Indeed, the sectoral patterns of employment and growth suggest that growth was not neutral or pro-poor, as discussed below.

Despite longer-term progress in reducing poverty, simulations suggest that poverty may have increased slightly in 2001 due to the recent economic downturn. A number of recent macro-economic shocks have undermined both economic expansion and poverty reduction. In particular, the global economic contraction led by the US recession is expected to negatively influence key sectors of Guatemala's economy (Table 5.2), including exports and tourism as well as private investment and inflows, particularly remittances. Problems in Guatemala's financial sector have also damaged overall confidence and could further put the brakes on investment (though recent legal initiatives could improve the situation). Finally, the coffee sector (Guatemala's main export) is experiencing a structural crisis, facing the lowest prices in several decades (see Chapter 6). In light of these economic shocks, the real growth rate is estimated to have slowed to 1.9% for 2001, implying a contraction in growth per capita of −0.8%. As such, poverty may have increased slightly from 56.2% in 2000 to 56.6% in 2001, with extreme poverty rising from 15.7% to 16.0%.

Poverty and the Pattern of Growth: Pro-Poor?
Growth did not favor the poor because the economy did not generate enough low-skilled jobs. Agriculture, which employs the majority of the poor, experienced below-average growth rates over the past 20 years (Table 5.3). In addition, other sectors did not grow fast enough to offer enough employment opportunities for the poor. As a result, growth was not pro-poor

---

2. World Bank (2001b).
3. Wodon and Narayan (2000).

TABLE 5.2: MAIN MACROECONOMIC INDICATORS, 1997–2001

	Actual			Estimate	
	1997	1998	1999	2000	2001
Annual real growth rates (1958 prices):					
GDP at market prices	4.4%	5.0%	3.8%	3.3%	1.9%
Population Growth	2.67%	2.68%	2.68%	2.68%	2.69%
GDP per capita	1.7%	2.3%	1.2%	0.6%	−0.8%
Consumption	4.5%	4.9%	3.8%	3.5%	2.6%
Exports (GNFS)	7.4%	1.0%	5.5%	4.8%	1.1%
Imports (GNFS)	19.2%	23.2%	1.4%	2.6%	2.7%
Gross domestic investment	18.4%	38.9%	−2.4%	0.9%	−0.3%
GDP Levels					
Nominal GDP (US$ millions)	17,768	19,306	18,225	18,988	20,671
GDP per capita (US$)	1,689	1,788	1,644	1,668	1,768
Trade (US$ millions)					
Exports of GNFS	3,175	3,455	3,466	3,865	3,858
Imports of GNFS	4,188	5,028	5,010	5,358	5,452
Trade balance	−1,013	−1,573	−1,544	−1,494	−1,594
Current account balance (US$ millions)	−686	−1,037	−1,010	−913	−922
Current account as % of GDP	−3.9%	−5.4%	−5.5%	−4.8%	−4.5%
Change in net international reserves (US$ millions)	−232	−243	−121	−674	−344
Investment balances, as % of GDP					
Gross domestic investment	13.7%	17.4%	17.4%	16.8%	16.0%
o/w, Public Sector investment	3.7%	4.5%	5.7%	4.5%	4.1%
Incremental capital-output ratio (ICOR)	2.1	2.1	3.6	3.9	6.6
Central Government savings	3.1%	2.3%	2.4%	1.8%	1.8%
Non government savings	6.7%	9.7%	9.5%	10.1%	9.7%
Gross domestic savings	8.0%	9.3%	8.9%	8.9%	8.3%
Price and exchange rate indicators					
CPI inflation (average)	9.2%	6.6%	5.2%	6.0%	7.0%
Annual average exchange rate (Quetzales/US$)	6.1	6.4	7.4	7.8	7.8
Government finances (% of GDP)					
Total revenues, of which	9.4%	9.7%	10.5%	10.5%	11.1%
Tax revenues	8.8%	8.7%	9.3%	9.6%	9.8%
Total expenditures, of which	10.1%	11.9%	13.3%	12.4%	13.6%
Consumption	3.6%	4.1%	4.4%	4.8%	5.3%
Deficit(−)/Surplus(+), after grants	−0.8%	−2.3%	−2.9%	−1.9%	−2.5%
External debt					
Public Debt / GDP	14.7%	15.0%	18.1%	17.6%	18.6%

Source: Banco de Guatemala, World Bank macroeconomic database. Projections by World Bank.

because the economy did not generate enough low skilled jobs (both agricultural and non-agricultural) to absorb labor surpluses.

Poverty and Growth in the Future: Targets and Projections
Understanding the potential impact of growth on poverty can be useful for projecting poverty outcomes and other welfare indicators. As discussed above, simulations using data from the ENCOVI suggest that a 1% increase in per capita income could result in approximately a 0.99% decline in the headcount index of poverty. This relationship between poverty and growth assumes

TABLE 5.3: PRO-POOR GROWTH? THE SECTORAL PATTERN OF EMPLOYMENT AND ANNUAL GROWTH
(in %)

	Sectoral growth (annual, in %)[a]		Contribution to GDP (in %)[a]	Employment Distribution (% of people in:)[b]		
	1980–1989	1990–2000	For 2000	Poor	Non-poor	Total
GDP at market prices	**1.0**	**4.0**	100	100	100	100
Agriculture	1.1	2.9	24	55	17	36
Industry	0.3	3.9	21	18	24	21
Construction	−1.1	4.3	2	6	6	6
Gas, electricity, water	4.5	9.3	4	0.2	1.0	0.4
Mining and quarrying	4.0	11.2	1	0.2	1.0	0.3
Manufacturing	0.2	2.6	14	12	16	14
Services	1.2	4.4	50	27	59	43
Transportation	2.6	5.8	10	3	4	3
Trade/Commerce/Tourism	−0.2	4.0	26	15	29	22
Banking/Financial	2.4	6.8	6	1	5	3
Public administration	4.5	4.7	8	2	8	5
Other	1.0	3.3	5	n.a.	n.a.	n.a.

Sources: a. World Bank macroeconomic database/Banco de Guatemala; b. World Bank calculations using the ENCOVI 2000, *Instituto Nacional de Estadística—Guatemala.*

FIGURE 5.1: STRUCTURE OF GROWTH, 1965-2000

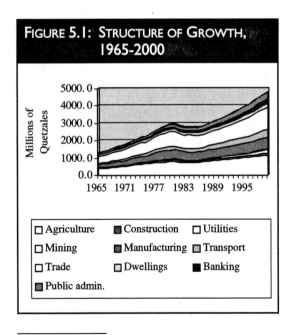

that inequality remains constant and that the pattern of growth is neutral.[4] Using the expected projections for growth, the projected evolution of overall and extreme poverty is presented in Table 5.4 for the period from 2000 to 2020. Overall, poverty is projected to decrease from 56.2% in 2000 to 44.4% by the year 2020. Likewise, elasticities of social indicators to growth and urbanization from a worldwide panel can be used to forecast how growth would affect these other indicators of well-being.[5] Similar to poverty projections, growth yields a significant improvement over time for all indicators (Table 5.5). For example, infant mortality is expected to fall from 40 deaths per 1,000 births in the year 2000 to 26 in the year 2020. Universal coverage of water and sanitation is also expected to be reached during that period.

---

4. As discussed above, this assumption might not hold, since it appears that the pattern of growth has not been neutral, but rather has favored the non-poor.

5. The worldwide panel of elasticities for social indicators and simulation software (SIMSIP) was developed by Wodon and Ryan (2000). The model used here assumes an annual growth rate of 4% (1.3% per capita taking into account the population growth rate of 2.7%), urbanization as projected by the UN. In addition, the expected projections also assume constant inequality and neutral growth.

FIGURE 5.2: STRUCTURE OF ECONOMY, 1965-2000

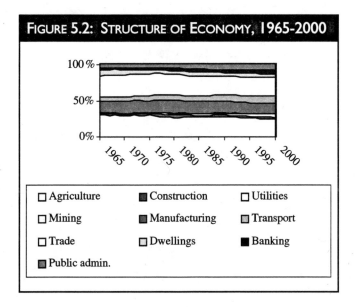

- ☐ Agriculture
- ■ Construction
- ☐ Utilities
- ☐ Mining
- ▨ Manufacturing
- ▨ Transport
- ☐ Trade
- ▨ Dwellings
- ■ Banking
- ▨ Public admin.

Given current growth projections, the record for meeting the targets set by the Government's poverty strategy and the Millennium Development Goals (MDGs) is likely to be mixed (Table 5.6.). Targets for most social indicators established by the Government's poverty reduction strategy (ERP)[6] should be met by 2005. Nonetheless, extreme poverty is not expected to fall as ambitiously as anticipated under the ERP due to slower overall growth in 2001 and 2002. Moreover, given projected growth rates, it does not seem likely that Guatemala will meet most of the more ambitious targets for health and education established under the international MDGs (Table 5.6). Faster growth and interventions to boost the assets of the poor are clearly needed to improve living conditions enough to meet these goals.

Summary of Key Issues and Priorities

The above discussion yields the following main messages:

- **Economic growth is necessary for reducing poverty and improving living conditions.** This is true internationally, but particularly relevant for Guatemala, given the relatively small size and limited capabilities of Guatemala's public sector (see Chapter 13).
- **Despite Guatemala's historically reasonable growth rates, current growth patterns are neither sufficiently fast nor disproportionately oriented towards the poor.** Guatemala's growth rates will not likely be sufficient to reach the international MDGs. Moreover, the poor do not seem to be benefiting from the existing pattern of growth.
- **As such, steps should be taken to improve both the pace of growth and make it more pro-poor.** In this context, the main engine of growth is likely to come from the private sector, with the public sector playing a supporting role affecting growth mainly insofar as it

TABLE 5.4: GDP GROWTH AND POVERTY REDUCTION

	2000	2001	2002	2003	2004	2005	2010	2015	2020
	Assumptions								
Real annual growth rates	n.a.	1.9%	2.3%	3.3%	4.0%	4.0%	4.0%	4.0%	4.0%
Population growth	n.a.	2.7%	2.7%	2.7%	2.7%	2.7%	2.7%	2.7%	2.7%
Real annual per capita growth rates	n.a.	−0.8%	−0.4%	0.6%	1.3%	1.3%	1.3%	1.3%	1.3%
	Poverty Projections								
Extreme poverty rates	15.7%	16.0%	16.2%	15.9%	15.5%	15.1%	12.8%	10.4%	8.6%
Overall poverty rates	56.2%	56.6%	56.8%	56.5%	55.8%	55.0%	51.6%	47.8%	44.4%

Note: Projections based on growth elasticity to poverty of −1.

Source: World Bank simulations using data from the ENCOVI 2000, *Instituto Nacional de Estadística—Guatemala.*

6. SEGEPLAN (2001c).

TABLE 5.5: GDP GROWTH AND NON-MONETARY INDICATORS

	2000 (base)	2001	2002	2003	2004	2005	2010	2015	2020
Health Indicators									
Infant Mortality	40.7	39.9	39.0	38.2	37.4	36.6	33.0	29.5	26.3
Under-five Mortality	53.8	52.7	51.6	50.5	49.4	48.4	43.3	38.7	34.3
Life Expectancy	65.3	65.7	66.1	66.5	66.8	67.2	69.1	71.1	73.2
Malnutrition (stunting)	44.0	43.4	42.9	42.3	41.8	41.3	38.7	36.4	34.1
Education Indicators									
Illiteracy Rate	31.0	30.0	29.1	28.3	27.4	26.6	23.3	20.1	17.4
Net Primary Enrollment	79.0	79.2	79.4	79.6	79.7	79.9	80.6	81.5	82.4
Net Secondary Enrollment	25.0	25.5	26.1	26.6	27.2	27.8	30.5	34.0	37.9
Gross Primary Enrollment	99.0	99.4	99.9	100.4	100.8	101.2	102.7	104.7	106.5
Infrastructure Indicators									
Access to Piped Water	69.0	70.9	72.8	74.6	76.4	78.1	82.7	92.0	100.0
Access to Sanitation	87.0	89.0	90.9	93.0	95.0	97.1	100.0	100.0	100.0
Telephone Mainlines	15.0	16.2	17.6	19.0	20.5	22.1	30.4	44.5	65.4

Sources: Malnutrition, all education and infrastructure indicators: ENCOVI 2000, Infant mortality: DHS 1998/1999, Under five mortality: WDI 2000 for 1999, Life expectancy: WDI 2001 for 1999. Simulations by World Bank using SIMSIP software developed by Wodon et. al. based on a worldwide panel of elasticities, average growth and per capita growth rates of 4.0% and 1.3% p.a., population growth rates of 2.7% p.a. and UN projections for urbanization.

TABLE 5-6: MEETING POVERTY STRATEGY AND MILLENNIUM TARGETS: HIT OR MISS?

	ERP Targets	MDG Targets	Model Projections (Table 5.5)	
	2005	2015	2005	2015
Extreme Poverty	Reduce by 3 percentage points	Reduce by 50% of the 1990 level (by 2% p.a.)	Reduced by half a % point	Reduced from 15.7% in 2000 to 10.4% (by 2% p.a.)
Health Indicators				
Malnutrition (hunger, measured as stunting)	None	Reduce by 50% by year 2015 (from 59% to 30%)	41%	36%
Infant Mortality	Reduce to 35 per 1000	Reduce by 66% of the 1990 level (by 2.6% p.a.)	Reduced from 40 in 2000 to 37 per 1000	Reduced from 40 in 2000 to 30 per 1000 (by 1.7% p.a.)
Under-five Mortality	Reduce to 48 per 1000	Reduce by 66% of the 1990 level (by 2.6% p.a.)	48 per 1000	Reduced from 54 in 2000 to 39 per 1000 (by 1.9% p.a.)
Life Expectancy	Increase to 67 years	n.a.	67 years	71 years
Education Indicators				
Illiteracy Rate	Reduce to 20%	n.a.	26.6%	20.1%
Net Primary Enrollment	Reduce to 88%	Universal	79.9%	81.5%
Infrastructure Indicators				
Access to Piped Water	Increase coverage to 60% in rural areas	Universal	Overall coverage 78.1%	Overall coverage 92.0%
Access to Sanitation	Increase coverage to 60% in rural areas	Universal	Overall coverage 97.1%	Overall coverage 100.0%

Model projections based on SIMSIP software developed by the World Bank.

stimulates private-sector investment and productive activities. Yet the actions of the public sector in this supporting role are crucial. While a full analysis of the sources and engines of growth in Guatemala is beyond the scope of this paper, several areas appear to be important priorities:

- Maintaining macroeconomic stability;
- Enforcing a tight fiscal position, with a careful plan for strengthening tax collection and redirecting public spending towards the social sectors so as to build assets that are crucial to both growth and poverty reduction;
- Fostering a climate that is conducive to private investment and growth, including improvements in governance and public sector management (see Chapter 13), as well as the regulation and supervision of the financial system. Without such improvements or a resolution of underlying social conflicts, private investment will remain depressed or will be channeled into low-productivity areas (e.g., linked to corruption), further hampering Guatemala's prospects for growth; and
- Promoting growth with special emphasis on sectors that are likely to generate substantial employment for the poor in both rural and urban areas. Additional analytical work is needed to define a more comprehensive pro-growth strategy. Nonetheless, while a thorough sectoral analysis of growth is beyond the scope of this study, available data do suggest certain levers that would have stronger impacts on poverty reduction than others for urban and rural areas:
  - In urban areas, this requires policies to support labor-intensive sectors, particularly micro-, small- and medium-enterprises (MSMEs), as well as education and technical training.
  - In rural areas, this means developing non-agricultural activities that are better remunerated and have better long-term prospects than traditional agriculture. As discussed in Chapter 6, key interventions to support growth in non-farm activities include: (a) increasing and improving the targeting of investments in education and technical training; (b) increasing investments in transport and basic infrastructure, which are crucial for the diversification, growth and inclusion of the poor in the rural economy and with facilitating the adjustment to the coffee crisis; and (c) policies that promote micro-, small- and medium-enterprises (MSMEs), a segment of the private sector that tends to generate a lot of employment. While agriculture is unlikely to generate enough additional employment opportunities to reduce poverty on a large scale in the medium term, it will continue to be an important source of incomes for the poor (at least in the short run). In this context, diversification efforts should focus on non-traditional products with better demand and price prospects than traditional export crops (as discussed in Chapter 6). Policies should also continue to facilitate productivity improvements (such as technical assistance), so as to boost the earnings of those who remain in agriculture. Investments in infrastructure (e.g., rural roads to improve marketing opportunities and education to improve farm-management practices) will likewise be important.

LIVELIHOODS, LABOR MARKETS, AND RURAL POVERTY

"Poverty is not having anything . . . not having work, there is no land."

Ladino Villager, L2 (QPES)

While the last chapter discussed the general importance of economic growth in reducing poverty from a "macro" perspective, this chapter attempts to examine more closely the livelihoods of the poor from a more "micro" (household-level) perspective, with a view to informing policy-makers of potential paths for promoting opportunities for the poor. Indeed, incomes, livelihoods and opportunities are among the top concerns ranked by Guatemalan households.[1] In fact, despite progress in other areas, a significant share of households do not perceive improvements in welfare since the Peace Accords, and they attribute this primarily to a lack of opportunities (factors that directly affect "their wallets," as discussed in Chapter 2). As such, improving livelihoods, particularly for the rural poor, presents one of the main challenges for both the poverty and peace agendas in Guatemala.

In this context, this chapter begins with a review of income sources in Guatemala. Since labor is the main productive asset for the poor, the chapter then examines the constraints faced by the poor in generating incomes, and how such constraints may exclude them from participating in the overall economic system. In addition, given that these constraints are directly connected to a lack of access to credit, insurance and opportunities, it is important evaluate how these failures relate to vulnerability and exclusion of people or specific groups. Finally, since poverty in Guatemala is highly concentrated in rural areas, the chapter analyzes issues pertaining to rural livelihoods, including land, agriculture and non-farm opportunities. The chapter is mainly based on an analysis of data from the ENCOVI,[2] though most of the findings are also confirmed in the QPES.

Incomes and Inequality
Incomes in Guatemala are unequal both in their distribution and in their sources. As discussed in Chapter 2, income inequality in Guatemala is quite high, with a Gini coefficient of 57.

---

1. Source: World Bank calculations using the ENCOVI 2000, *Instituto Nacional de Estadística—Guatemala*.
2. Vakis (2002).

While the poorest quintile of the population receives only 3% of total income in Guatemala, the top quintile captures 62%. Disparities are also evident in the sources of income (Table 6.1). Specifically:

- **The poor are largely dependent on agricultural income,** reflecting their predominantly rural location. Agriculture accounts for about half of the total income of the poorest quintile, as compared with just 3% for the top quintile. As discussed below, the poor, particularly the extreme poor, seem to lack opportunities outside the agricultural sector, which generates relatively low incomes. Moreover, agriculture (particularly day-labor jobs) offers few labor benefits, such as job security or pensions.
- **In contrast, the non-poor have access to a much more diversified set of employment opportunities,** with significant employment in non-agricultural sectors, such as services. As discussed in Chapter 5, growth rates have been significantly higher in these sectors than in agriculture over the past 20 years.
- **Transfers, both public and private, are important sources of income for the poor.** Private transfers in the form of remittances constitute more than 20% of per capita income for households that receive them. In addition, international remittances (especially from

TABLE 6.1: INCOME SOURCES, BY CONSUMPTION QUINTILES

| | Consumption quintiles | | | | | |
	1	2	3	4	5	Total
Income per capita (Q)	1,429	2,408	3,487	5,064	15,503	5,578
Labor income (%)	77	78	77	76	70	73
Agricultural	49	38	24	14	3	13
Salaries	30	18	11	6	1	6
Formal sector	13	9	6	4	1	3
Informal sector	17	9	5	2	0	3
Net income from production	19	20	13	8	2	7
Non- Agricultural	28	40	53	62	67	60
Salaries	17	25	39	47	46	42
Formal sector	8	13	26	36	42	35
Informal sector	9	12	13	11	4	7
Own business	11	15	14	15	21	18
Formal sector	1	1	1	1	7	4
Informal sector	10	14	13	14	14	14
Non-labor income (%)	22	22	24	26	30	27
Return to capital[a]	10	8	10	11	16	14
Donations, gifts	11	12	12	10	6	8
Remittances	3	4	5	5	4	4
Private	1	2	1	2	1	1
Public	7	6	6	3	1	3
Pensions, indemnizaciones	1	1	1	3	5	3
Other[b]	0	1	1	2	3	2

Percentages may not add up to 100 due to rounding.
a. As interest received was negligible, the return to capital includes: income from rental of equipment, rental of property and the interest received.
b. For example, inheritance or lottery winnings.
Source: World Bank calculations using ENCOVI 2000, Instituto Nacional de Estadística—Guatemala.

the United States and Mexico) are on average twice as large as domestic (see Box 6.1). Simulations of the effects of current adverse shocks in the coffee industry (which is already affecting domestic remittances via the decreases in seasonal employment) and the global economic slowdown (especially in the United States), suggest a sharp decline in per capita income and a slight increase in both overall and extreme poverty (as discussed in Chapter 5). On the other hand, while public transfers represent a higher share of income for the poor (Table 6.1), they are regressive in their absolute levels. These issues stress the need for policies that help affected populations cope with and adjust to shocks (as discussed in Chapters 11 and 12). They also suggest that improving targeting mechanisms while implementing policies for the poor and other vulnerable groups is essential (as discussed in Chapter 11).

Labor Markets

Labor Market Participation

Participation in the labor market depends significantly on gender and education levels. The Guatemalan labor force consists of about four million people (with an additional half a million children that are employed between the ages 7–14). Participation is high among men (89%) and moderate for women (44%). Poor men are more likely to participate in the labor force compared to non-poor men, while for women the opposite is true. In fact, more educated women (who tend to be non-poor) seem to self-select into the labor market, which is not surprising given the higher returns to education for women, as discussed in Chapter 7. Finally, open unemployment is very low but underemployment (based on hours worked) affects about a third of the working population, which is consistent with a number of hypotheses such as exclusionary practices or lack of employment opportunities.

Informality

Labor markets are characterized by a high degree of informality. Informality seems to be growing in Guatemala. Based on available data, it is estimated that an annual average of some 6,400 formal sector jobs were lost during the 1990s.[3] Indeed, the formal sector seems to have been incapable of absorbing the growing labor supply, with surplus workers being pushed into the informal sector.[4] The ENCOVI 2000 shows that more than two thirds of the employed and three quarters of the working poor are engaged in the informal sector. Women are also more likely to work in the informal sector than men (with 71% of female workers engaged in the informal sector, as compared with 62% of male workers). Importantly, the informal sector is very dynamic and heterogeneous in Guatemala, ranging from small scale farmers to textile workers and merchants (Figures 6.1 and 6.2).[5] The structure of the informal sector also differs significantly between rural and urban areas. This diversity implies a variety of paths out of poverty. For example, the negative correlation between non-agricultural informal work and poverty, both in rural and urban areas, highlights the importance of non-agricultural employment opportunities for poverty reduction (as discussed in more detail below).

Labor Policies

Active labor market interventions are not effective instruments for reducing poverty. In fact, existing labor market policies do not benefit the poor since the do not reach them. The dominance

---

3. von Hoegen (2000).
4. Von Hoegen (2000).
5. Figures 6-1 and 6-2 use only those employed in the informal sector older than age 15. "Other" includes mining, basic services, construction, transport and financial jobs. Source: World Bank calculations using ENCOVI 2000, *Instituto Nacional de Estadística—Guatemala*.

BOX 6.1: MIGRATION AND LIVELIHOODS

Migration has long been a dominant feature of Guatemalan life, though migration patterns have shifted over time.

Seasonal Migration. During colonial times, indigenous people migrated to the south coast to work in the production of indigo and salt.[6] Accelerated land expropriations, forced labor mandates and the emergence of coffee in the late 1800s resulted in massive seasonal, and some permanent, migration of the indigenous from the northwest highlands to satisfy labor shortages in the southern coffee region, as discussed in Chapter 4. Today, between 400,000 and 800,000 people migrate temporarily each year.[7] More than two thirds of seasonal migration occurs within Guatemala. Seasonal migration is more common among poor and rural residents, the indigenous, bilingual individuals and among men, according to data from the ENCOVI 2000. Indeed, poverty rates among temporary migrants are high (75% as compared with 55% of permanent migrants and 56% of the overall population). While a lack of income-earning opportunities is the main motive for migration according to migrant households in the ENCOVI, migration is also used as a coping mechanism in response to crises (such as the civil war or Hurricane Mitch).[8] The crisis in the coffee sector and emerging problems in sugar production will definitely affect an already vulnerable population that relies extensively on these activities for their incomes.

International Migration. International migration has grown from about 50,000 people in the 1980's to more than a million people in late 1990s.[9] Destinations vary, but the main recipients are the United States and Mexico. Overall, 9% of all households receive international remittances, though a higher share of the non-poor (12%) receive them than the poor (6%).[10] The QPES suggests that remuneration (both in-kind and in cash) and working conditions are better in the *fincas* in Mexico than those in Guatemala. Moreover, it is apparent that as community members migrate abroad, their remittances contribute substantially to those families that receive them. Indeed, there are obvious differences in the houses of those with family members living in the US and those without. It seems that international migration introduces a certain degree of within-village inequality at the community level due to remittances and goods sent back "home."

Permanent Migration. The ENCOVI shows that permanent migrants are more likely to be non-poor living in urban areas and having completed primary education. They are also predominantly non-indigenous. On the one hand this may reflect limitations faced by the indigenous in finding permanent opportunities and relocating prior to the signing of the Peace Accords, such that permanent relocation was contained among the better off, namely, the non-indigenous. On the other hand, the negative correlation between permanent migration and poverty may also suggest permanent rural-to-urban migration as a possible path out of poverty. While it is impossible to test this hypothesis with ENCOVI data, it may be the case that by migrating, these people managed to take advantage of better opportunities, assets and services in urban areas such that most of them are not poor today.

---

of informal sector jobs among the poor puts poor workers out of reach of such policies.[11] In fact, data from the ENCOVI show that, while about 40% of salaried workers earn less than legal minimum, this share rises to 60% of poor workers.[12] Moreover, only 16% of the poor receive other labor benefits (such as the thirteen month salary bonus). Indeed, villagers in the QPES community KA1 describe the schemes used by employers to avoid paying labor benefits to the *finca* workers (including dismissing them regularly throughout the year so as to maintain them on non-permanent contracting status and hence avoid paying the benefits). Since active labor policies introduce distortions into the labor market, these policies can in fact be counterproductive. As discussed below,

---

6. Ministerio de Salud (1998).

7. Estimating the magnitude of migration is a complex matter. The ENCOVI 2000 estimates the number of seasonal migrant workers to around 400,000 (excluding children under 7). Other sources such as Ministerio de Salud (1998) put this figure closer to 800,000. Such differences may arise from the sample design but also from the survey definition of migration.

8. The QPES and other qualitative work reveal that migration is an important coping mechanism in times of crisis as well as a regular source of earnings for the poor. Other motivations for migration include the search for better social services such as education and health).

9. ASIES (2000).

10. World Bank calculations using the ENCOVI 2000, *Instituto Nacional de Estadística—Guatemala*.

11. However, 26% of formal-sector workers also receive less than the minimum wage.

12. The ENCOVI survey does not distinguish between those who are registered in the Government's minimum wage system versus those who are not registered.

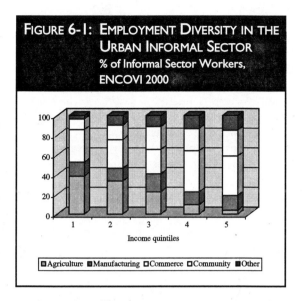

FIGURE 6-1: EMPLOYMENT DIVERSITY IN THE URBAN INFORMAL SECTOR
% of Informal Sector Workers, ENCOVI 2000

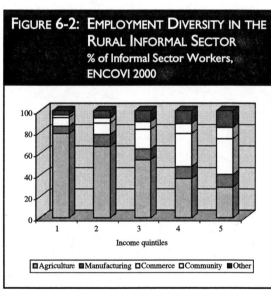

FIGURE 6-2: EMPLOYMENT DIVERSITY IN THE RURAL INFORMAL SECTOR
% of Informal Sector Workers, ENCOVI 2000

policies should instead focus on enabling the poor to participate in the labor market, which requires investments in education, technical training, and infrastructure (such as roads). Such investments will help break down barriers to opportunities *and* improve renumeration.

Opportunities
The poor have fewer opportunities for higher-paid jobs and a limited ability to diversify income sources. The non-poor are twice as likely to work in a higher paying jobs in the public sector or white-collar occupations as the poor. Moreover, the poor are three times as likely to work in agriculture as the non-poor. In fact, poorer households appear to be rather constrained in employment opportunities, dividing their labor between self-employment, blue-collar jobs, and agriculture, which all yield significantly lower incomes than other sectors. In addition, household employment portfolios reveal a pattern whereby poorer households are more homogenous in their occupations (most of the individuals are in agricultural), while for non-poor households there is more diversity among the occupations of working members. While some of this disparity is explained by differences in human capital accumulation, this unequal distribution in opportunities and income-generating possibilities is also attributable to the lack of spatial integration for these groups. Non-Spanish speakers and indigenous populations face similar constraints in employment opportunities.

Geographic location is correlated with poverty and employment opportunities. The spatial proximity to a bigger city may offer a number of advantages to a household such as employment opportunities but also access to services and infrastructure not available in a smaller community. Combining data from the 1994 census (which allows for the construction of municipal population sizes) with those from the ENCOVI reveals that location is central to employment opportunities. First, 75% of the households that reside in small municipalities (less than 10,000 people) are rural, whereas 40% of those living in municipalities with more than 30,000 people are rural. Second, poverty rates are significantly higher among households in smaller municipalities. Third, the share of non-farm income is higher for those households residing in larger municipalities implying that non-farm employment opportunities (that yield higher incomes) are more likely to be available in these areas. In fact in the rural areas, the share of non-farm self-employed income for households living in larger municipalities is almost twice the income of those from smaller municipalities. Therefore, if municipal size is a proxy for opportunities and infrastructure, these correlations imply that integrating households with markets and the rest of the economy is key for allowing the poor to access opportunities.

Wages and Returns to Labor

Real wages have followed a divergent trend between sectors. The evolution of real monthly wages by industry over the last decade reveals two interesting patterns.[13] First, while in the early 1990s, real monthly wage growth was relatively equal among the different industries, dispersion in wages has increased in the late 1990s, as has been observed for many other countries in LAC. The increase in wage inequality could be a response to reforms[14] and trade liberalization, which shifted relative wages in favor of higher skilled jobs (and perhaps has driven the apparent increase in overall inequality, as discussed in Chapter 2). Second, agricultural wages have been increasing much slower than in other sectors since the mid-1990s. Nonetheless, despite lagging levels, wages in agriculture seem to have increased in real terms during the 1990s, probably explaining a good part of the improvements in poverty.

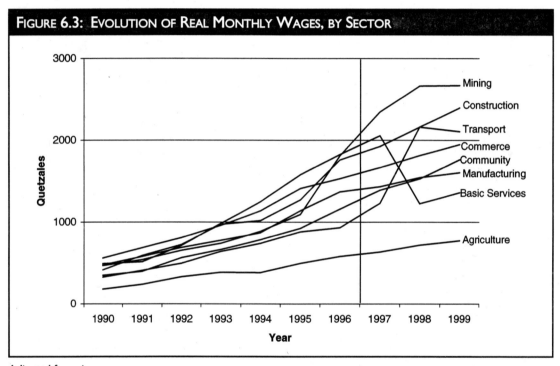

FIGURE 6.3: EVOLUTION OF REAL MONTHLY WAGES, BY SECTOR

Adjusted for prices
Source: ILO (laborsta.ilo.org)

The lowest labor earnings occur in agricultural occupations, rural areas, the informal sector and among marginal groups such as the poor and indigenous. Real hourly wages average Q7.3.[15] Wages are more than twice as high in urban as compared with rural areas and also for the non-indigenous as compared with the indigenous. In addition, the average real wage of Q3.3 in agriculture is almost five times smaller than the Q15.8 wage for financial services. The average hourly wage in the informal sector is less than half of that in formal occupations in the private sec-

---

13. Wages have been adjusted for inflation using the CPI.

14. Indeed, the two sharp changes in monthly wages occurred in 1997 in the basic services and transport sectors, and may be linked to the privatization process of electricity and telecommunications industries that occurred that year (see Chapter 9).

15. Taking into account all labor earnings, whether cash or in-kind, and including gross wages/salaries, the "13th month" salary bonus, the value of tips, etc. Wage data have been adjusted for spatial differences using price indices. See 1, Vakis (2002) for details.

tor. Wages decrease dramatically for poorer individuals and increase with higher levels of education. Similar patterns are also observed for earnings among the self-employed.

Men in lower-skilled occupations receive more than women while there is more wage equality among higher skilled jobs. Discrimination in labor markets is often reflected both in hiring practices but also in the earnings differentials between different groups such as men and women. In Guatemala, wages for men are up to 50% higher than for women in jobs like manufacturing and commerce. This wage differential is smaller and even negligible in the public sector or white-collar occupations, where typically the educational attainments are higher. Yet, as the analysis shows below, wage differentials cannot be fully explained by educational attainments alone, implying that there is a high degree of discrimination.

Ability to speak Spanish is correlated with higher earnings. Men and women who speak Spanish earn more than 30% more than those who do not, even when other factors are taken into account using regression analysis. This is also true for bilingual speakers, indicating the role of language ability. Yet, as shown below, neither educational attainments nor language ability are enough to explain earnings gaps between indigenous and non-indigenous, implying the existence of labor market discrimination.

Wage discrimination is high for indigenous groups. While human capital endowments explain some of the variation in earnings, wage discrimination (based on the unexplained part of the determinants of earnings) is prevalent for the indigenous.[16] The average wage gap between indigenous and non-indigenous workers is 50%. Controlling for differences in human capital endowments, experience, sector of employment and other characteristics, a significant share of this gap can be attributed to wage discrimination (95% for men and 35% for women) against indigenous workers. Similarly, close to half of the wage gap between men and women can be attributed to wage discrimination (controlling for other factors), though the average wage gap between men and women is small (1.3%).

Child Labor

Child labor is common in Guatemala. About half a million children between the ages of 7 and 14 are employed in Guatemala, with a third of them working in plantations (mainly coffee and sugar fincas). Most of these children come from poor households (75%) and reside in rural areas (80%). Boys are more likely to work in agriculture, while girls generally work in both agriculture and commerce. They receive significantly lower wages than adults and work about 30 hours a week, seriously inhibiting the ability to attend school (see Chapter 7).

Rural Poverty and Livelihoods

As discussed in Chapter 2, rural areas have disproportionately higher rates of poverty than urban areas. This section examine the livelihoods of the rural poor, arguing that agriculture and land reform are unlikely to provide significant policy levers to reduce poverty. Subsistence farming and traditional exports such as coffee, in particular, are unlikely to be significant sources of employment growth for the rural poor. Non-traditional exports could serve as a potential source of growth, but their reach has been limited in scope, particularly for the poor. Rather, data from the ENCOVI suggest that non-farm opportunities are likely to drive rural growth and employment opportunities. As such, removing constraints faced by the poor to engage in such occupations is crucial.

Agriculture, Land and Rural Poverty

The vast majority of the rural poor are subsistence farmers or agricultural day laborers. Some 87% of the rural poor depend on agriculture, either as small-scale subsistence farmers or agricultural laborers (Table 6.2). Indeed poverty rates among these groups are significantly higher than those whose main source of income comes from non-agricultural sources. As discussed in Chapter 3, dependence on agriculture is significantly related to lower consumption levels (even after controlling for other differences).

---

16. Based on a Oaxaca-Blinder decomposition.

TABLE 6.2: RURAL POVERTY BY LAND STATUS AND MAIN SOURCE OF INCOME

	% of rural population	% of rural poor	Poverty rate (P0)
All rural	100	100	75
Landowners	54	59	82
0–1 hectares	32	35	81
1–2 hectares	10	12	87
2–5 hectares	7	7	80
5–15 hectares	3	3	74
>15 hectares	2	2	74
Tenants	19	20	80
Landless Households[a]			
Agricultural day laborers	8	8	76
Non-agricultural workers	19	13	49

a. Landless households are divided into those that derive most of their income from agriculture and those that derive most of their income from non-agricultural sources

Source: World Bank calculations using ENCOVI 2000, Instituto Nacional de Estadística—Guatemala.

Access to land is inversely correlated with poverty. Land is not only necessary for agricultural production, but can also serve as collateral, allowing households to obtain credit for input purchases or diversify their income portfolio by engaging in other activities. Nonetheless, land ownership in Guatemala is highly skewed and unequally distributed, as discussed in Chapter 4. The poor tend to have smaller plots and poverty rates are higher among those with smaller plots (Table 6.2). Indeed, larger holdings are significantly correlated with higher consumption in rural areas (even controlling for other factors, as discussed in Chapter 3). Moreover, the relative geographic isolation of the poor suggests that their land is poorly located, further depressing the values of this asset. The plots owned by the poor are also likely to be of lower quality than those owned by the non-poor.

In addition, poor landowners are less likely to have land titles or use land markets. Land titles allow farmers access credit by using their land as collateral for credit (see Box 6.2). They also offer security and even provide incentives for the farmer to be more productive. Overall, only 41% of landowner households possess formal title to their land. Only a third of the poor have land titles compared to almost half of the non-poor. Larger landowners are also more likely to have titles. Moreover, the non-poor use land markets more than the poor. In particular, more than half of the land owned by non-poor households was purchased on the market as compared with only a third of the land owned by extreme poor households (the remainder being acquired by inheritance).

Market-based land reform efforts are promising and should continue to be pursued. However, existing pilot land programs have proved difficult and slow due to their high costs and other design issues (Box 6.3). Further, low agricultural returns in traditional crops require that beneficiaries of these programs look for better prospects in non-traditional alternatives. However, the staggering costs of providing the bulk of the rural poor with good quality parcels and complementary inputs suggest that this is not a feasible option to eradicate mass poverty in the rural sector.

Similarly, agriculture overall is unlikely to provide a significant route out of poverty for the bulk of the rural poor. Agriculture has faced declining growth rates over the past several decades, contracting as a share of GDP (see Chapter 5). Within agriculture, traditional crops such as coffee, which tend to employ a significant number of workers, are contracting in the face of a structural terms-of-trade crisis, as discussed below. Non-traditional crops have increased significantly, but not enough to replace the earnings and employment opportunities lost by the coffee crisis, as discussed below. As such, although the poor will likely to continue to depend on agriculture as an important source of income, it is unlikely that agriculture will provide the solution to the poverty problem or that many people will escape poverty via agriculture.

Traditional Agricultural Exports: Vulnerability and the Coffee Crisis

The worldwide structural change in the coffee industry is seriously affecting Guatemala. Coffee has always played an important role for the Guatemalan economy. It is the most important

BOX 6-2: RURAL CREDIT

Credit can provide an important input to both agricultural and non-farm profitability. Credit allows households to acquire land and other inputs. It also enables households to diversify their income sources by engaging in other activities besides farming. Nonetheless, access to credit in rural Guatemala is minimal. Only 13% of the rural households applied and received any kind of a loan (15% among the non-poor and 13% among the poor). Just 10% of landless households applied and received a loan as opposed to 15% for landowner households, indicating the importance of collateral (as discussed below). Loan sizes were significantly higher for the non-poor than the poor.

Lack of collateral is one of the most frequent reasons households refer to for not applying for a loan. The ENCOVI suggests that about 40% of rural households wanted to receive credit but chose not to apply. Among those who believed they needed credit, the top three reasons for not applying for a loan were: (a) lack of collateral; (b) too expensive; and (c) fear of ineligibility for a loan. In the case of collateral, it is not necessarily the lack of assets *per se* but the lack of formal ownership of the assets that may prevent households to access credit. For example, lack of land titles (discussed above) may disable farmers from obtaining credit even though they do own the land.

Interestingly, it appears that credit institutions do exist in rural areas. However, the fact that that people feel that loans are expensive may be a signal of a non-competitive credit market (for example, a few local informal money lenders). In addition, a lack of information may lead to people with the wrong impressions about their ability to qualify for a loan as well as the costs and risks associated with lending. As such, addressing these issues of information and supply is important. In fact, a recent study on rural financial services in Guatemala recognizes the short supply of formal lending institutions as an important impediment to obtaining credit in rural areas.[17] Indeed, only half of the households that reported receiving loans in the ENCOVI survey obtained them from formal lenders. Furthermore, the poor and landless are more likely to receive credit from informal lenders, corroborating the findings that formal lenders require land titles as collateral and the fact that the poor face constraints in accessing credit from formal institutions. Nonetheless, interventions in credit markets should be complemented by investments in rural infrastructure, education and information access in order to raise living standards in rural areas.

BOX 6.3: LAND REDISTRIBUTION PROGRAMS IN GUATEMALA

Land redistribution is a sensitive topic, both politically and culturally. Since the 1980s, a number of land programs have been at work helping farmers access land in Guatemala. Programs like the "Fundación Guatemalteca para el Desarrollo-Fundación del Centavo" (FUNDACEN), the "Fondo para la Reinserción Laboral y Productiva de la Población Repatriada" (FORELAP), and the "Fondo Nacional de Tierras" (FONATIERRA) have benefited more than 7,000 households. As part of the Peace Accords in 1996, the Guatemalan Government established the Comisión Institucional para el Desarrollo y Fortalecimiento de la Propiedad sobre la Tierra (PROTIERRA) whose responsibilities include: (i) a cadastral-based land registry; (ii) a land fund to promote market-driven land reform; (iii) land conflict resolution mechanisms and free legal services with special attention to land access and land traditional management by rural communities; (iv) a national geographic information system; (v) a comprehensive land tax system; (vi) agricultural development; and (vii) rural investment programs.

The idea of the land fund is to allow poor households to access land via a credit subsidy. The program gives a loan to qualified households that allows them to buy land and inputs. In addition, the participants receive technical assistance. The loan lasts for 4 years and it costs 5% in annual interest. Up to today, about 5,000 households have participated in the program. However, this and previous programs have been criticized for being slow and the overall target of 335,000 (in the case of the land fund) to be unfeasible. In addition, critics mention the lack of incentives to repay the loans as repossessing the land is hard to implement, preferential treatment in the way that land is allocated, the low interest rates charged and the program's possible overcrowding of other land projects as important problems.

Currently, both the government and local agencies are considering alternative market-based mechanisms to facilitate land access. For example, rental markets are likely to be cheaper to implement. In addition, title programs (such as the "Registro General de la Propiedad" (RGP) or pilot programs such as the "Catastro" project may not only allow households to access credit but also enable them to participate in rental programs. Finally, land leasing programs with the option to buy the land are also considered.

Sources: The land fund program, (1998); Carrera (1999)

---

17. The World Bank (1999).

export of the country with receipts of more then $570 million in 2000 (20% of total export earnings), making Guatemala the fifth largest coffee exporter in the world.[18] However, the recent entry of a number of new producers (particularly Vietnam), as well as overproduction in Latin American countries (e.g. Brazil) have severely depressed international coffee prices, resulting in significantly lower revenues for coffee producers in Guatemala. Indeed, the National Coffee Association (ANACAFE) estimates that export volumes in 2001 fell by 1 million bags, to 5.3 million, and receipts by 50% to less than $300 million. As the downward trend in international prices was caused by structural changes on the worldwide coffee market, these changes are likely to be permanent (rather than a temporary price shock).

Coffee production provides a significant source of income for many rural households. The ENCOVI reveals that 11% of rural households produce coffee. About 140,000 rural households receive incomes from coffee production, of which more than 75% are poor.[19] On average, coffee producing households received Q4,526 in coffee sales. Non-poor coffee-producing households received almost five times more in coffee sales than poor households. Coffee income comprises about 25% the total income per capita, irrespective of poverty status (for coffee producing households only). As expected, most coffee producers are landowners.

Many more people depend on coffee production from the demand of agricultural labor. According ANACAFE, there are an estimated 200,000 people permanently employed in the coffee industry. This figure increases to more than 500,000 during coffee harvest season. Most laborers (*jornaleros*) in the coffee sector are seasonal migrants from poor households that depend on the coffee sector to augment their incomes, as discussed in Box 6.1. Indeed, poverty rates among temporary migrants are high (75% as compared with 55% of permanent migrants and 56% of the overall population).

The crisis in the coffee industry will thus affect a significant share of the rural population. Lower revenues are likely to push some coffee producers to dramatically decrease their demand for labor or force them completely out of business. According to the Ministry of Agriculture more than 40,000 coffee production related jobs are expected to be lost in 2002 (ANACAFE puts this figure at 60,000). As most of these jobs are expected to be low-end jobs, the effect on the poor is likely to be significant.

Faced with this crisis, a number policies should be considered. First, for those producers who will be able to survive the crisis as coffee farmers, assistance should be provided to expand Guatemala's presence in well-paid "niche" markets (specialty, organic, "fair trade" coffees) by improving quality, helping extend long-term contracts and establishing contacts with purchasing firms in developed countries. Second, for those who are forced to exit the sector, assistance should be provided to help with diversification in agriculture and non-agriculture, including: developing a large portfolio of substitute crops, livestock activities, service sector activities (for example, commerce, restaurants, tourism, cultural activities), and light manufacturing opportunities (for example, handicrafts, textiles); providing technical assistance to boost the competitiveness of promising activities; and improving the skills of the people displaced from coffee. Programs to address the employment losses also seem necessary in the short run, given the large number of workers that will likely be affected. For example, workfare programs (particularly seasonally-targeted schemes) could be strengthened and expanded to provide alternative employment for those dependent on salaries from (seasonal) labor in the coffee sector.

Crop Diversification and Non-Traditional Agricultural Products
Guatemala's non-traditional agricultural exports sector has grown impressively over the last few years. Over the past decade, exports of various non-traditional crops have increased dramati-

---

18. The World Bank (2001b).

19. It is important to note that, because the ENCOVI is a *household* survey, plantations owned by entities other than households (e.g., corporations, banks) are not captured in the data collected in the survey. The estimates presented here are household-based; conclusions should not be drawn about the poverty status of all coffee producers (e.g., corporations, banks, etc.).

TABLE 6.3: Types of Crops Produced, by Type of Household				
	Types of crops produced:[a]			
	Subsistence only	Both subsistence and traditional exports	Both subsistence and Non-Traditional exports	Traditional exports only
Household population (in 000's)	651	147	23	28
Indigenous (% within crop category)	58	35	75	44
Poverty (within crop category)				
Extreme Poor (%)	20	26	5	14
All Poor (%)	73	79	63	66
Household distribution by land ownership (%)				
Tenants	33	14	17	10
Landowners 0–1 hectares	45	38	54	72
Landowners 1–2 hectares	10	21	17	13
Landowners 2–5 hectares	6	16	9	5
Landowners 5–15 hectares	3	8	2	0
Landowners >15 hectares	3	3	1	2
Total	100	100	100	100

a. Traditional exports crops are coffee, sugar, bananas and cardamom. Non-traditional exports are snow peas, sprouts, broccoli, cauliflower, flowers, mangos, melons, pineapple, papaya, okra and berries. Subsistence crops are the remaining crops (e.g. corn). Classification based on those of the Asociación Gremial de Exportadores de Productos No Tradicionales (AGEXPRONT).

Source: World Bank calculations using ENCOVI 2000, Instituto Nacional de Estadística—Guatemala.

cally. For example, exports of fruits such as mangoes, papaya, berries and melons, increased from US$14 million in 1990 to more than US$300 million in 1999.[20] Traditional exports, such as coffee and sugar, still dominate, however, increasing from US$629 million to US$1,044 million over that same period. Nonetheless, the weakened outlook for revenues from traditional exports combined with the expansion of the production and export of non-traditional crops highlights the potential role of this sector for future opportunities in rural areas.

However, the ENCOVI 2000 reveals that very few farm-households produce non-traditional agricultural products, and most are non-poor. The survey allows for the division of households among those that produce export-related agricultural products (further divided in traditional and non-traditional) and all other products.[21] Only 23,000 households produce non-traditional agricultural crops as opposed to 650,000 that produce subsistence crops (Table 6.3).[22] Households that produce non-traditional agricultural products have better socioeconomic indicators, suggesting that production of these crops may be limited to those households that have better access to resources. Further research could explore the types of constraints that may impede farmers from engaging in the production of these crops.

---

20. AGEXPRONT (2000).
21. Still, due to the survey design, these findings are only suggestive and are not representative.
22. Traditional exports crops are coffee, sugar, bananas and cardamom. Non-traditional exports are snow peas, sprouts, broccoli, cauliflower, flowers, mangos, melons, pineapple, papaya, okra and berries. Non-tradable crops are the remaining crops (e.g. corn). Classification based on those of the Asociación Gremial de Exportadores de Productos No Tradicionales (AGEXPRONT).

Agricultural Technical Assistance
Agricultural extension and technical assistance could serve as potentially levers to promote rural growth and reduce poverty, particularly given the importance of crop diversification and the need to improve farm productivity in Guatemala. Nonetheless, data from the ENCOVI show that only 3% of the farmers in rural Guatemala received such assistance in 2000. While most technical assistance provided by non-public institutions seems to be well targeted to poor households, more than 70% of public technical assistance is received by non-poor households, suggesting inadequate targeting of public interventions.

Non-Agricultural Opportunities: a Potential Route Out of Poverty?
Non-agricultural opportunities may provide a possible channel for escaping poverty. Much of the recent empirical literature on the relationship between non-agricultural incomes and rural poverty clearly indicates a strong relationship between the two.[23] First, by diversifying their income portfolios, rural households can augment their incomes and minimize adverse income shocks from farm activities. Second, as non-agricultural incomes increase the households' cash liquidity, households can access farm inputs easier thus raising farm productivity. Finally, the non-farm sector offers poor landless households (otherwise unable to engage in farm activities) an option for income generation.

Indeed, **rural households that do not depend on agriculture are less likely to be poor.** The ENCOVI reveals a negative correlation between non-agricultural incomes and poverty in Guatemala. Landless households have significantly better socio-economic indicators than those that depend on agriculture: lower poverty rates (see Table 6.2), higher incomes and consumption levels, lower household sizes and higher levels of education for the household head. In fact, almost half of the rural non-poor households are landless, typically working as self-employed entrepreneurs in commerce or manufacturing, or in non-agricultural salaried jobs (e.g., construction, teaching). Only 26% of the landless households are indigenous, which may be an indication that access to specific non-agricultural occupations may be constrained for indigenous households. The earlier findings on indigenous labor-market discrimination via wages also supports the possibility of exclusion.

Given the potential of non-agricultural employment in reducing rural poverty, it is **important to understand the constraints that specific groups face in accessing these jobs.** Numerous constraints are plausible. For example, as the poor generally live in smaller and isolated communities (based on regional population densities), opportunities for non-agricultural jobs may be scarce. In addition, this spatial isolation implies that these communities will be more likely to lack complementary infrastructure (for example, roads, electricity, telephones). In fact, a study on the role of basic services and non-farm enterprise profitability using the ENCOVI finds that: (a) the probability of having a micro-enterprise in rural areas is significantly higher among households with coverage of modern utilities; and (b) micro-enterprises without access to services such as electricity and telephone connections in the rural areas have significantly lower profits that those who have access.[24]

Regression analysis confirms that human capital as well as lack of infrastructure are both important constraints for participation in the non-agricultural sector. In particular, employment-type choice models indicate that low human capital (for example, education) is an important impediment for participation in higher return occupations. In addition, areas where non-agricultural opportunities are more wide-spread increase the probability of being employed in such jobs, suggesting that the role of local infrastructure and access to services is a necessary condition for employment growth in non-agricultural jobs. These findings imply that while the non-agricultural sector could offer an exit path from poverty, overcoming the constraints that are associated with

---

23. For a recent survey see Lanjouw and Lanjouw, 2001.
24. Foster and Araujo (2002).

accessing these jobs is an essential part of a rural poverty reduction policy kit. Still more work could focus on explicitly exploring these constraints to fully understand the dynamics of the non-agricultural sector with the rest of the economy.

Summary of Key Issues and Priorities

This chapter highlights a number of key issues regarding livelihoods and opportunities for the poor:

- The poor, women and the indigenous are constrained in both employment opportunities and earnings, with a high dependence on agriculture and the informal sector and few labor benefits.
- The indigenous face significant wage discrimination; women also face wage discrimination, though the wage gap between men and women is smaller than the one between the indigenous and non-indigenous.
- Geographic location is an important factor in determining both poverty and earnings opportunities, with smaller municipalities offering fewer options.
- While the poor are highly dependent on agriculture (subsistence farming and agricultural jobs), agriculture is not likely to be a dynamic source of new employment opportunities and will continue to shrink as a share of GDP. As such, agriculture is unlikely to serve as a major vehicle for poverty reduction.
- Similarly, although land is an important asset, its ownership is highly inequitable in Guatemala. Moreover, the holdings of the poor tend to be: (a) quite small, often providing below-subsistence incomes; (b) untitled; (c) poorly located (geographically isolated); and of poor quality. In addition, full-fledged land reform is unlikely to serve as a major vehicle for poverty reduction due to the high costs and slow pace of land programs, and low agricultural returns.
- Coffee, Guatemala's traditional export crop, has suffered a long-term structural price shock, further emphasizing the need for diversification. This shock is likely to have substantial impacts on the poor, both as producers and as workers (permanent and seasonal).
- While non-traditional export crops could offer potential opportunities for growth and employment, their scope has been limited to date, with little involvement of the poor.
- Rather, non-agricultural employment could provide an important route out of poverty, though a variety of barriers constrain access to these opportunities, particularly education and geographic location.

These findings suggest a number of priorities for reducing poverty and promoting opportunities:

- **Enhancing opportunities should be at the center of the poverty agenda.** A recurring pattern that arises in the analysis is the fact that the poor and other marginal populations such as the indigenous are not able to fully participate in, or benefit from, the overall economic system. Therefore, addressing the improvement of employment opportunities is necessary. Some specific areas for policy intervention that emerge from the analysis are:
  - **Reducing the human capital gaps between the poor and non-poor.** Education is essential to expand the opportunities of the poor and allow them to access higher-paying jobs. Education and technical training are particularly important to help them access expected growth opportunities in non-agricultural sectors. Investments need to concentrate on expanding the poor's access to education, as well as improving quality so as to boost the returns to education (see Chapter 7).
  - **Lowering transactions costs in accessing markets.** By decreasing the strong spatial disadvantage that many of poor face (especially in the rural areas), marginal populations could see dramatic increase in opportunities via the easier access to product and factor

markets, both in agricultural and non-agricultural sectors. Thus emphasis on investments in road infrastructure and basic services coverage is essential (see Chapters 9 and 10).

- **Creating mechanisms to discourage labor-market discrimination for the indigenous and women.**

■ **A rural development strategy is also key for Guatemala's overall poverty reduction strategy.** As poverty is highly concentrated in rural areas special attention in rural employment and income generation is important. In particular, the two main areas for consideration include:

- **Promoting growth of non-agricultural sectors,** which are likely to be the main engines of rural growth and employment. Despite the potential of the non-farm sector as a vehicle for reducing poverty, numerous barriers prevent the poor from accessing such opportunities, including disparities in education levels, transport and basic infrastructure, lack of access to rural credit, and geographic disadvantages. Interventions should thus focus on removing such barriers, with targeted investments in education and technical training, policies to promote micro-, small- and medium-scale enterprises (MSMEs) which tend to generate employment, and investments in basic services and transport.

- **Increasing agricultural productivity and diversification.** While agriculture is unlikely to generate enough additional employment opportunities to reduce poverty on a large scale in the medium term, it will continue to be an important source of incomes for the poor (at least in the short run). As such, efforts should be made to increase land and labor productivity and to diversify to non-traditional crops. Coffee production should also take greater advantage of markets for specialty coffees. This requires investments in human and physical capital, as well as access to new technologies, financial institutions, and technical assistance.

■ **Finally, safety nets and risk management are important components of a poverty strategy.** Even if a successful poverty reduction program is established, certain groups could remain vulnerable (as discussed in Chapter 11), including:

- **Seasonal migrants** who are already affected by the adverse structural terms-of-trade shock in the coffee industry. While they face the possibility for job loss, the welfare of their families is also affected, as they depend on the remittances that they send. A strengthening and expansion of workfare programs may be needed to help supplement their incomes;

- **Child-laborers,** who face considerable trade-offs in terms of under-investments in education. Exploring mechanisms and incentives to motivate tem to stay in school is crucial since these children represent an important future labor force base;

- The **indigenous,** who seem to have limited access to non-agricultural opportunities and face wage discrimination; and

- **Geographically isolated households,** that may not be able to take advantage of economic growth or employment creation programs due to the high transaction costs and barriers of participating in such programs.

CHAPTER 7

EDUCATION AND POVERTY

"Poverty is the lack of education in the community . . . Many are still illiterate, they can't communicate with everyone else."

K'itché Villager, KI1 (QPES)

Improving education and educational outcomes is central to both the Peace Agenda and the poverty agenda. While previous chapters review the importance of education in determining poverty and inequality, and the historical and institutional situation pertaining to human capital development, this chapter seeks to analyze more deeply the issues pertaining to the current education system, with a view of informing policy and highlighting priorities for poverty reduction. After a brief sectoral overview, the chapter considers the issues of: (a) educational stock (literacy and attainment), coverage and equity issues; (b) internal efficiency; (c) disparities in the quality of education; (d) barriers to increased enrollment and attainment; (e) the returns to education; and (f) public spending and equity. It concludes with a review of progress, key issues and priorities in education for poverty reduction.

The chapter draws on several types of research, including (a) the results of the ENCOVI 2000, which allow for an examination of education issues from a poverty perspective; (b) the results of the QPES, which included an extensive module on the perceptions of education in the ten rural study villages; and (c) an updated sector review, which provides institutional and public spending information.[1]

Sectoral Overview
The education sector has undergone important reforms since the signing of the Peace Accords in 1996. These accords establish education as a means to transmit and develop values and knowledge within a multi-lingual and multi-cultural society, thus the curricula must integrate equally the diverse cultures and languages of the country. They also assert that education and training are key factors to achieve equity, national unity, economic modernization and international

---

1. Much of the analysis of the ENCOVI is presented in GUAPA Technical Paper 3, Edwards (2002). Additional analysis of the ENCOVI (returns to education and supply- and demand-side constraints) was conducted by Renos Vakis (2001) and is contained in Annex 6. The education module of the QPES was designed and analyzed by Rodriguez (2001). The updated sector review was conducted for the World Bank by Anderson (2001).

competitiveness. As discussed in Chapter 4 and below, various targets were set for increasing public spending, and improving literacy and coverage. The Ministry of Education (MINEDUC), which is responsible for regulating, directing, planning, supervising, and evaluating the sector, has been restructured in order to deconcentrate, decentralize, and simplify education administration to promote efficiency and effectiveness. Financial management was deconcentrated under the SIAF program, and since 1998, all central administrative units and Departmental Directorates receive budgetary allocations and are accountable for their use. Important components of decentralization efforts include support to the expansion of the PRONADE program (see Box 7.1), where legally organized communities receive direct transfers of funds to manage the schools; the creation of School Boards (*Juntas Escolares*) in most schools, that also receive a direct transfer of funds annually for school maintenance; and the creation of Teacher Selection Committees (*Jurados de Oposición*) at the municipal and departmental levels, though these latter were abolished in 2000.

The split between public and private provision varies significantly by level of education. Pre-primary and initial education are not required in Guatemala, though a number of programs have developed over the past decade to expand their coverage.[2] Data from the ENCOVI suggest that over three quarters of pre-primary students attend public schools. **Primary education** is compulsory for 7–12 year olds, although many do not enroll and there is a high percentage of over-age students in the primary system (as discussed below). According to the ENCOVI, 88% of all primary students attend public schools, with 79% provided by MINEDUC and 9% under the PRONADE program (see Box 7.1). **Secondary education** is split into two cycles: basic secondary and diversified secondary.[3] Basic secondary provides three years of education (grades 7–9) to those who have completed the sixth grade of primary school. It is expected to provide the academic and technical skills necessary to join the labor force to those who do not further pursue their studies. Diversified secondary provides between 2–4 years (normally, grades 10–12) of schooling for those who have completed grade 9 of basic secondary and consists of four learning tracks: general education, teacher education, commercial education, and technical education. According to the ENCOVI, only 40% of

---

BOX 7.1: THE PRONADE PROGRAM

Organization, Decentralization, and Participation. PRONADE (the Programa Nacional de Autogestión para el Desarollo Educativo) is a decentralized, community-led program that seeks to increase access and improve the quality of primary education, especially in rural, indigenous and remote areas. Under PRONADE, rural communities with no access to education services receive direct financing from MINEDUC. To qualify, communities must meet at least four criteria: (a) the community must find a site and demonstrate ability and interest in managing the new school; (b) the community must be located at least 3 km. from the nearest public school; (c) the community must have at least 20 pre-primary and primary aged children; and (d) the community must not already have any teachers on the official government's payroll. Communities receive financing directly from the Government to cover teacher salaries, learning materials, and school snacks. Specialized NGOs are contracted by PRONADE to cover administrative training. Financing is fully contingent on extensive community participation in all aspects, ranging from hiring teachers to setting the local school calendar. Each community is represented by a school committee (COEDUCA), which is elected locally and comprised of parents and community members.

Outcomes and Impact. Various program evaluations[4] suggest impressive results for PRONADE (compared to other public primary schools), including: longer time spent in the classroom, higher attendance, higher and more informed community participation, and higher grade promotion rates and student retention. Moreover, as discussed below, the ENCOVI 2000 shows that the program is extremely well targeted to the poor.

---

2. These include (a) the Proyecto de Atención Integral al Niño (PAIN), supported by MINEDUC, which has expanded rapidly since the Peace Accords and provides initial education for 0–5 year olds; (b) monolingual and bilingual pre-primary schooling, which is directed to 4–8 year old children and has likewise expanded rapidly since 1996; and (c) CENACEP, an accelerated pre-school program that provides 35 days of basic skills to children over 6.5 years old before they enter first grade. See Anderson (October 2001) for more details on these programs and their coverage.

3. See Anderson (October 2001) for more details.

4. See Anderson (October 2001) for an overview of these various program evaluations.

all secondary students are enrolled in public schools, with the private sector playing a more major role in provision at this level. Public sector schools include Ministry Schools (30% of total secondary enrollment) and Cooperative Schools (10% of total secondary enrollment), which operate primarily in urban areas and involve a tri-partite financing arrangement between MINEDUC, municipal authorities, and legally organized parents' associations. **University education** is provided by one public sector university, San Carlos (USAC) and nine private sector universities. Data from the ENCOVI suggest that just under 40% of all university students are enrolled at the USAC.

Educational Stock, Coverage and Equity

Guatemalan literacy is not only below average in Latin America, it is *far lower.* With an illiteracy rate of 31% in 2000, only Nicaragua and Haiti rank worse. Female illiteracy is particularly high (39%), especially among indigenous women (62%). Progress in teaching women to read and write lags about 20 years behind male literacy. Illiteracy is higher among the poor (46%) than the non-poor (17%) and in rural areas (42%). Regional and ethnic patterns largely mimic those for poverty (Figures 7.1, 7.2). Despite this poor performance, Guatemala has seen improvements over time, with a slight quickening of the pace since the signing of the Peace Accords in 1996 (Figure 7.3).

Although educational attainment is quite low in Guatemala, with significant gender, ethnic and poverty gaps, there has been some progress over time. Guatemala is still a "primary" country, with an average educational stock of 4.3 years (for those aged 14+). Educational attainment is higher among the non-indigenous than the indigenous, with an average "ethnic" gap of three

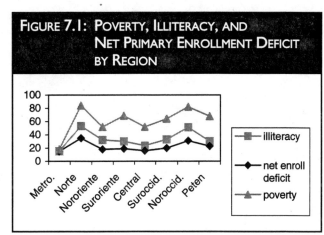

FIGURE 7.1: POVERTY, ILLITERACY, AND NET PRIMARY ENROLLMENT DEFICIT BY REGION

Source: ENCOVI 2000

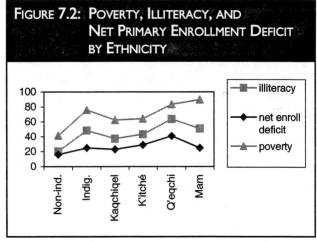

FIGURE 7.2: POVERTY, ILLITERACY, AND NET PRIMARY ENROLLMENT DEFICIT BY ETHNICITY

Source: ENCOVI 2000

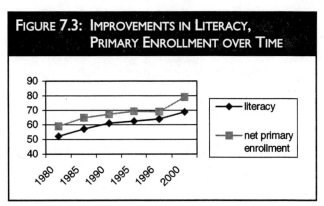

FIGURE 7.3: IMPROVEMENTS IN LITERACY, PRIMARY ENROLLMENT OVER TIME

Sources: Ganuza et. al. (1999); ENCOVI 2000

years. It is lower for women than men, with an average "gender" gap of one year. Indigenous women in particular have completed very few years of schooling (1.8). Yet the largest gap is observed between the poor and the non-poor, with an average "education-poverty" gap of four years. Overall, Guatemala has made significant progress over time, with today's 19–25 year olds having completed an average of 5.6 years as compared with those over 40 years old having completed only 2.9 years (Figure 7.4). Moreover, the "gender," "ethnic" and "poverty" gaps do appear to be narrowing across generations (Figure 7.4).

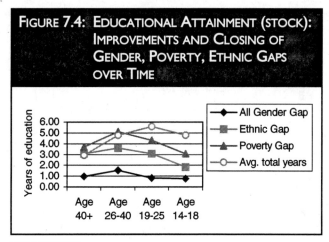

FIGURE 7.4: EDUCATIONAL ATTAINMENT (STOCK): IMPROVEMENTS AND CLOSING OF GENDER, POVERTY, ETHNIC GAPS OVER TIME

ENCOVI 2000

Guatemala has made a sincere effort to improve educational coverage, particularly since the Peace Accords. Using primary enrollment as a yardstick, Guatemala has taken large strides towards universal access. In the early 1970s, primary schools enrolled just over half[5] (World Bank, 2001b) of the target population. Net enrollment rates increased dramatically in only one generation, to 79% in 2000.[6] Importantly, progress has been significantly faster in the years since the signing of the Peace Accords in 1996 (Figure 7.3), reflecting a large increase in public spending on education and ambitious programs to expand coverage.[7] About half of the increase in coverage was achieved through the PRONADE program, with a targeted expansion in rural areas (Box 7.1). Secondary enrollment also rose sharply in that period (by 39%), with rural enrollment increasing as a share of total enrollment (from 12%–19% of the total from 1996–2000). There has also been a significant push to increase girls' enrollment, particularly that of indigenous girls. With USAID and private-sector support, for example, the Ministry of Education initiated a pilot program "Eduque a la Niña" in 1993 to promote the enrollment of indigenous girls via scholarships, educational materials and community promoters. An evaluation of the pilot shows that, compared with a control group of students that were not part of the program, the scholarship program was effective in promoting attendance, retention, and completion of female students in school and that female teachers constitute an incentive for active participation of female students in the classroom.[8]

Nonetheless, important gaps in coverage remain, particularly among girls, the indigenous, rural children, and the poor. Pre-primary coverage is low overall, particularly among rural, indigenous, and poor children (Table 7.1). At the primary level, key gaps include: (a) girls overall, particularly indigenous girls, one third of whom are not enrolled; (b) the indigenous, particularly the Q'eqchi; (c) rural children, a quarter of whom are not enrolled; and (d) poor and extreme poor children (Table 7.1). Ethnic and regional enrollment gaps largely mimic patterns observed for poverty (Figures 7.1 and 7.2). Secondary coverage is quite low overall, with only a quarter of the target population enrolled. Secondary enrollment is even lower among the indigenous, rural youths, and the poor and extreme poor (Table 7.1).

Internal Efficiency

Even when children do enroll in school, they face a number of hurdles as they attempt to advance through the educational system. Symptoms of these obstacles include: (a) delayed initial

---

5. World Bank (2001b).
6. Source: World Bank calculations using ENCOVI 2000—*Instituto Nacional de Estadística Guatemala.*
7. Source: Ministry of Education, Education Statistics Yearbook 1996–2000, as cited in Anderson (2001).
8. Anderson (2001).

TABLE 7.1: NET ENROLLMENT RATES, BY LEVEL AND GROUP
% of target aged children that are enrolled in school

	Pre-Primary			Primary			Secondary		
	All	Male	Female	All	Male	Female	All	Male	Female
Total	23%	22%	25%	79%	81%	76%	25%	26%	24%
Non-Indigenous	27%	27%	28%	84%	71%	86%	32%	32%	33%
Indigenous	18%	16%	20%	75%	82%	67%	14%	18%	11%
K'iche	21%	18%	25%	71%	78%	64%	17%	23%	12%
Q'eqchi	15%	15%	14%	59%	65%	52%	6%	9%	3%
Kaqchiqel	23%	17%	30%	77%	78%	77%	23%	28%	17%
Mam	15%	15%	15%	75%	78%	71%	9%	9%	10%
Other	16%	16%	16%	71%	75%	67%	13%	17%	10%
Urban	35%	32%	38%	85%	88%	82%	46%	48%	44%
Rural	17%	17%	18%	75%	78%	72%	12%	14%	10%
Non-Poor	39%	35%	43%	90%	90%	89%	44%	44%	45%
All Poor	17%	18%	17%	78%	81%	75%	13%	16%	10%
Extreme Poor	13%	13%	12%	58%	65%	53%	3%	3%	2%

Source: World Bank calculations using the ENCOVI 2000, *Instituto Nacional de Estadística—2000.*

enrollment; (b) grade repetition; (c) delayed advancement (late grade-for-age, which reflects both delayed initial entry and repetition); and (d) drop out. Each suggests institutional problems inherent in the education system.

First, a significant share of Guatemalan children delay initial enrollment in primary school, particularly poor, rural, and indigenous children. Enrollment is delayed in Guatemala both by policy and in practice. In terms of policy, the official age of entry for primary school is age seven—a full year later than in most countries. This means that officially, 12-year olds are still in primary school and 13–19 year olds would still be in secondary school. In practice, a substantial share of Guatemalan children initially enroll even later than the official entry age. In fact, the ENCOVI shows that about a fifth of all primary-aged students enrolled in first grade at least one year later than the official entry age.[9] Late initial enrollment is particularly common among rural, indigenous, and poor students (Figure 7.5).

Late enrollment is costly. First, it can lead to truncated schooling as older children face greater opportunity costs on their time and pressures to work. The ENCOVI shows this to be the case for non-indigenous children, for whom late enrollment translates into less total years of schooling upon withdrawal. In contrast, indigenous children who are enrolled late

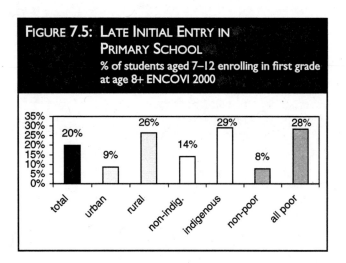

FIGURE 7.5: LATE INITIAL ENTRY IN PRIMARY SCHOOL
% of students aged 7–12 enrolling in first grade at age 8+ ENCOVI 2000

---

9. Share of children ages 7–12 at the time of the ENCOVI 2000 who ever enrolled in school.
Source: World Bank calculations using the ENCOVI 2000, *Instituto Nacional de Estadística—Guatemala.*

are also more likely to be withdrawn at a later age. As such, for indigenous children, late enrollment means delayed overall schooling, but not necessarily less schooling. Second, late initial enrollment is also associated with overall lifetime earnings. For example, calculations using the ENCOVI suggest that a high-school graduate with a two-year enrollment delay earns 15% less over his lifetime than one that started at the official entry age.

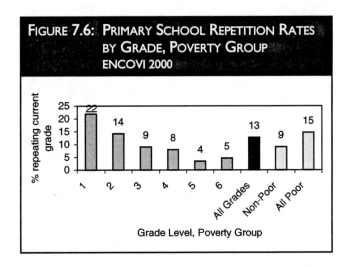

FIGURE 7.6: PRIMARY SCHOOL REPETITION RATES BY GRADE, POVERTY GROUP
ENCOVI 2000

Second, despite progress, a significant share of primary-school children are held back from grade advancement, suggesting deficiencies in the educational system. Data from the ENCOVI suggest that the overall repetition rate for primary school is 12.8%.[10] Official statistics on repetition are slightly higher, but do show some progress since the signing of the Peace Accords in 1996.[11] Nonetheless, repetition rates in the first two grades are so high (Figure 7.6), that they signal serious deficiencies in the educational system. There are several possible factors that commonly explain this sort of repetition pattern: (a) inherent characteristics—such as Spanish language barriers, malnutrition, and a lack of academic support in the home—make it difficult or impossible for many students to perform adequately; (b) the curriculum may be unrealistically demanding; (c) school quality and teacher "seriousness" may be judged by "high standards" that they demonstrate by holding children back; and (d) schools are thought to be "too full," so lower grades are used as filters. The fact that repetition rates fall in the later grades should not be understood to mean that the situation eventually improves in the sense that students finally learn and repeat less. Rather, this is best seen as indirect evidence that many more repeaters drop out of school before reaching those grades (discussed below). Repetition rates are significantly higher for poor children (Figure 7.6) than non-poor children. Almost a quarter of poor students a made to repeat the first grade. The poverty-repetition linkage could reflect inherent characteristics (lack of academic support in the home, malnutrition), school quality issues, or overcrowding in schools. Interestingly, repetition rates do not differ significantly by gender or ethnicity at the primary level.

Likewise, repetition patterns at the secondary level signal problems with transitions between levels and

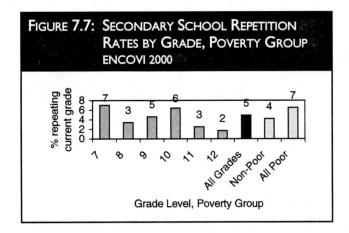

FIGURE 7.7: SECONDARY SCHOOL REPETITION RATES BY GRADE, POVERTY GROUP
ENCOVI 2000

---

10. These ENCOVI 2000 calculations are based on the share of children who are currently in school who report repeating the grade they are currently in. They do not include those who were told they had to repeat, but subsequently dropped out.

11. The Ministry of Education reports a repetition rate of 14.5% in 2000, down from 15.3% in 1996. See Anderson (2001).

cycles. The institutional split between cycles of secondary education (see above) is clearly betrayed in repetition rates across grades, which peak at the beginning of each cycle (in grade 7 and again in grade 10, see Figure 7.7). Likewise, while repetition rates are higher overall for the poor than the non-poor (Figure 7.7), they are even higher for the poor at grade 10 (22% of poor tenth graders compared with only 1% of non-poor tenth graders), signaling that poor children face difficulties in transitioning from the basic cycle to diversified secondary. These discontinuities in repetition rates across grades suggest that students face changing standards, which create bottlenecks at the beginning of each educational cycle. The standards between levels are not harmonized: what for many students constituted a passing level of effort in grade 6 is judged insufficient in grade 7; what was acceptable in grade 9 is suddenly below par in grade 10. Again, several explanations can account for this pattern. There may be successively fewer schools serving higher grade levels, and those schools that do offer higher grade levels tend to be of better quality.[12] In this scenario, students that pass at smaller ("worse") schools find they are unprepared for the standards of the bigger ("better") schools that offer higher grade levels. Another possibility is that the bottom grade at each level acts as a filter in an overcrowded system. Under this view, for instance, the top three secondary school grades serve as a filter for students that are university-bound, where lower quality students are intentionally "flushed out" during the basic education cycle. In any case, the observed discontinuity between cycles is a "red flag" for quality differentials and should be explored more fully.

Third, as a result of late initial enrollment and repetition, a significant share of students are "over-aged" for their grades. Both official statistics and ENCOVI data suggest that late "grade-for-age"—which reflect cumulative schooling delays from all sources (late initial entry, grade repetition, and temporary withdrawals)—is a significant problem in Guatemala. The ENCOVI shows that 19% of all 15-year-olds are still in primary school. Official statistics also point to such a problem: some 11–17% of basic secondary education students were apparently over-aged in 2000, though this figure drops to 2.6% for diversified secondary (purportedly due to the "filtering" forces described above). Multi-variate regressions[13] analyzing the determinants of grade-for-age suggest important links to poverty. Higher household per capita consumption (an indicator of current well-being) and the child's height-for-age (a proxy for past well-being and malnutrition) are both associated with more rapid progress through the school system. Given all other characteristics, girls tend to advance faster than boys. There is also considerable inter-ethnic variation. The non-indigenous, K'iché, Mam and "other indigenous" children all advance through the grades at similar paces. In contrast, Q'eqchi children are about a third of a year behind similar non-indigenous (taking into account other factors), while the average Kaqchiqel student is about one-tenth of a year ahead. Interestingly, grade repetition has about a one-to-one impact on late grade-for-age (repeating one grade translates into almost exactly a one-year delay), whereas the trade-off with late enrollment is less than one-to-one (children whose initial enrollment was delayed by two years are on average less than two years behind those who enrolled at age 7).

Finally, while drop out rates have improved over time, they are still high and a significant share of poor and extreme poor children drop out of the school system before they reach grade 6. Official statistics suggest that drop-out rates have improved somewhat over time, declining from 8.2% in 1996 to 7.0% in 2000 for primary school, and from 4.7% to 3.6% for secondary over the same time period. While it is difficult to calculate drop-out rates directly using the ENCOVI, the data do suggest that they are particularly high for the poor. In the QPES, the main reasons that children drop out were seasonal migration and child labor, domestic responsibilities, and poverty and the costs of attending school, according to parents and teachers in the study villages.

---

12. Anderson (2001) provides descriptions of the sector that are consistent with this explanation.
13. See Edwards (2002) for more details and regression results.

Disparities in the Quality of Education

The quality of education received by poor children lags that received by the non-poor. There are two ways to assess educational quality: the quality of learning (via standard achievement tests) and the quality of inputs (materials, books, teachers, etc.). Results of student testing under the National Program of Evaluation of School Achievement (PRONERE) reveal significant inequities in the quality of the primary education system.[14] While student achievement in reading and math is generally low, it is even lower among rural students, boys, and indigenous students. The evaluations also show that urban schools have more qualified and better trained teachers, better infrastructure and more books. The ENCOVI 2000 and QPES offer several additional signs that the poor lack access to key quality-related inputs:

- Lower **household spending** on books and school supplies among the poor and indigenous suggests lower use of educational materials in their learning process (Table 7.2 below). There is substantial variation in absolute costs by poverty group, ethnicity and geographic area, with much higher spending overall by the non-poor, non-indigenous and urban residents—even in public schools. These differences arise primarily from spending on materials and books. Even in public schools, the non-poor spend close to three times more than the poor on these items. Spending on informal fees (fund-raisers, donations), which contribute to educational and extra-curricular activities, is also higher among the more privileged groups (even in public schools).
- A larger share of the poor and indigenous report not having **textbooks,** which tend to be highly correlated with other indicators of school quality. While only 5% of all primary students and 10% of all secondary students report not having any books, a higher share of the indigenous report not having them. Moreover, even when they report having books, the poor and indigenous spend significantly less on books and materials than the non-poor and non-indigenous, suggesting that these latter groups have access to more (and possibly better or more up-to-date) books and materials than the disadvantaged groups.
- The poor and indigenous children are more likely to belong to communities reporting an insufficient number of **teachers.**[15] The QPES villages also report high student-teacher ratios in multi-grade classrooms, ranging from 31–52 students per teacher in the indigenous villages (average of 38) and 25 in both Ladino communities. Indeed, vacancies and teacher

---

BOX 7.2: SCHOOLING IN GUATEMALA: CHILDREN'S PERSPECTIVES

The QPES interviewed children on their perceptions of their schools. In terms of their **teachers,** children in all but one village (L1) perceive their teacher as an important person in their lives who teaches them, gives them snacks (la refacción), and serves as a second parent. In L1, the children voiced opposing opinions, with some saying the teacher was good because he teaches them, and others saying he was "bad" because he hits them. The children in all ten villages universally identified (a) learning to read and write; (b) learn Spanish (in the indigenous villages); (c) drawing; and (d) singing as their **favorite aspects** of school. Their **least favorite aspects** included (a) fighting between classmates; (b) that they aren't given time to play; and (c) that the schools are dirty. **Physical punishment** was identified as common practice in 9 of the 10 schools (the exception being in KA2 where the teacher takes away "points" as the main form of discipline). In terms of **language of instruction,** the children in the 8 Mayan villages expressed a range of views, with some preferring instruction in Spanish, others preferring bilingual teaching, and others favoring teaching in their maternal indigenous languages. Children in 7/10 of the villages see education as offering them a **better future.** Those who didn't make this linkage belong to the communities of QE2 and KA1 (both *finca* villages), and M2 (also quite poor and highly dependent on seasonal migration to the *fincas* for income).

---

14. The Universidad del Valle was contracted to carry out the testing. Tests were administered to third and sixth graders in 1997, 1999 and 2000. See Anderson (2001) for a summary of key findings.

15. Calculations using the ENCOVI 2000 community questionnaire, which is not representative for all communities in Guatemala, but covers 60% of households in the household survey.

turnover in rural areas are high; this could be associated with the lack of incentives for rural teachers, who face difficult working conditions but do not receive differentiated salaries than their urban counterparts.[16]

▨ Poor and indigenous children are more likely to belong to communities reporting inadequate **school facilities** (infrastructure, classrooms, desks, etc.).[17] Informants in all ten QPES villages also report problems with the physical infrastructure of their schools, including: poor quality and maintenance of the school itself; lack of classrooms; lack of furniture, materials; and a lack of basic services (e.g., water and latrines). Other problems identified in

---

BOX 7.3: LANGUAGE, CULTURE AND EDUCATION

One of Guatemala's great assets is its rich cultural and linguistic diversity. Indeed, a cross-cutting theme in the Peace Accords is the preservation and promotion of Guatemala as a multi-cultural, multi-lingual society. Unfortunately, there are signs of erosion of this cultural asset, with formal education playing somewhat of a detrimental role.

First, fluency in indigenous languages is being lost over time. As discussed in Chapter 4, the ENCOVI 2000 reveals that a smaller share of subsequent generations of ethnically-indigenous people speak indigenous languages (77% for those aged 7–13 compared with 89% for those aged 40+). Moreover, the loss is particularly strong with inter-ethnic marriage: while 90% of those between aged 7–25 who boast "full Mayan linguistic lineage" (4 Mayan-speaking grandparents and 2 Mayan-speaking parents) speak indigenous languages, only 41% speak the language if only 3 grandparents are Mayan speakers (even if both parents are), and only 18% speak indigenous languages if only one parent does (even if all 4 grandparents do). Indeed, the language abilities of parents and grandparents were significant and positive determinants of mayan-speaking abilities in multi-variate regressions.[18]

Second, it appears that education is playing an adverse role in the loss of indigenous languages. Controlling for other factors (including the language abilities of parents and grandparents), there is a 1.8% decline in the probability of native fluency in an indigenous language for each year of schooling completed by the mother and a further 2.4% decline for each year of schooling completed by the child.[19]

Third, some Mayan communities perceive a conflict between traditional oral teachings and modern education. All Mayan communities in the QPES note substantial differences between traditional oral teachings (at home) and modern education (at school). According to elders and parents in the study communities, the main roles of traditional teachings are to teach values, respect (*respeto, saludar*), culture and customs. Most also note that children learn gender roles and skills at home (with boys getting apprenticeships in productive skills and roles and girls learning reproductive, domestic roles). Elders in all ten study communities perceive that these norms are being lost over time. Regarding formal education, most QPES informants perceive that education plays an important economic role (creating opportunities, overcoming poverty), and many point to the importance of acquiring "knowledge" (conocimiento) and to the role formal education plays in helping them overcome ethnic barriers and exclusion so that they may reach the "ladino world" of opportunities (e.g., by learning Spanish at school). Nonetheless, these very benefits of formal education apparently come with a cost. Five of the eight Mayan communities in the QPES perceive a conflict between formal education and traditional oral teachings. This conflict is usually described as the school children losing respect for traditions and elders, becoming "lazy" at home, or having to do homework instead of traditional (gender-based) duties.

The Government has recently undertaken a number of initiatives to preserve and promote Guatemala's cultural heritage in the education system. These include promoting bilingual teaching methodologies under the DIGEBI program, and a new program to prepare a National Cultural Development Plan, deconcentrate the cultural education services of the Ministry of Culture and Sports (MCS), and develop a National Cultural Resources Information System (NCRIS), with the support of the World Bank under the Universalization of Basic Education Project.

---

16. Anderson (2001).

17. Calculations using the ENCOVI 2000 community questionnaire, which is not representative for all communities in Guatemala, but covers 60% of households in the household survey.

18. Edwards (2002).

19. Based on multi-variate regressions of the determinants of indigenous language ability for those ages 7–25 that have at least one indigenous-speaking grandparent. Data from the ENCOVI 2000, analysis by Edwards (2002).

the QPES include: problems with school meals and meal preparation (e.g., lack of a proper kitchen to prepare school meals), lack of parental support for education (identified by the teachers), and irregular pay of teachers.

■ The **returns to education** are fairly low in Guatemala (see below), particularly at the primary level, which could signal deficiencies in quality.

■ While **language barriers** may prevent higher enrollment and advancement—particularly in the early years of primary—potential **language and cultural losses** also need to be taken into account in the national curriculum in order to preserve Guatemala's rich cultural heritage (Box 7.3).

Nonetheless, there has been an important push to improve education quality in Guatemala, particularly since the Peace Accords. The Ministry of Education, with bilateral and multi-lateral financing, has implemented various education models to address quality issues in primary education, including: (a) providing teacher training in multi-grade teaching methodologies (*Nueva Escuela Unitaria*, NEU schools) piloted in several departments; (b) promoting bilingual schools and methodologies in departments with large indigenous populations (Directorate General of Bilingual, Intercultural Education, DIGEBI schools); (c) providing training in bilingual multi-grade methodologies (DIGEBI-NEU combinations) piloted in the Department of Alta Verapaz; and (d) developing the "schools for excellence" piloted in various schools throughout the country. Results of various program evaluations for these pilots are generally positive.[20]

Barriers to Enrollment and Attainment

Many factors contribute to enrollment decisions, including supply-side factors (availability and proximity of schools, quality of schooling), and a range of inter-related demand-side factors, such as the ability to cover direct costs (fees, transport, uniforms, materials, etc.), opportunity costs (earnings from child labor, domestic responsibilities), migration (seasonal or permanent location changes), expected returns, parental education history, household composition, and attitudes and beliefs. This section explores potential barriers to enrollment and attainment, with a view to informing policy as to possible priorities.

Primary School: Supply- vs. Demand-Side Constraints

Demand-side factors—rather than a lack of schools—appear to be the main obstacles to increased primary enrollment. Numerous indicators reveal that a lack of schools is not the main constraint to increased enrollment in Guatemala. **First,** household perceptions point to demand-side factors, rather than a lack of school facilities, as the main barriers to enrollment. Only 7% of non-enrollees at the primary level cited supply-side factors—such as distance to schools, inadequate class space, and lack of facilities—as key obstacles (see Figure 7.9).[21] **Second,** late enrollment and drop-out, for example, both suggest that the children have a school to go to, but they—or their parents—are declining to enroll. **Third,** gender disparities in enrollment rates strongly reveal such choices, given that about half the population is male and half is female, and that boys and girls are randomly distributed among families. Overall, 24% of all primary-aged girls are not enrolled, compared with only 19% of same-aged boys (Table 7.1 above). As such, at least a fifth of all girls who are not enrolled *do* have a school to go to and *could* be enrolled. We know this because their brothers *are* enrolled. Such biases are even more evident among the indigenous: net *non*-enrollment rates are 33% for indigenous girls as compared with 18% for indigenous boys. As such, about 45% of all primary-aged indigenous girls who are not enrolled *do* have access to a school and *could* be enrolled. Likewise, for the poor, about a quarter of all un-enrolled primary-aged girls *could* be

---

20. See Anderson (2001) for details.

21. Other reasons cited—such as age, sickness, migration, and "other" (non-coded)—all individually accounted for small shares of the reasons for not enrolling.

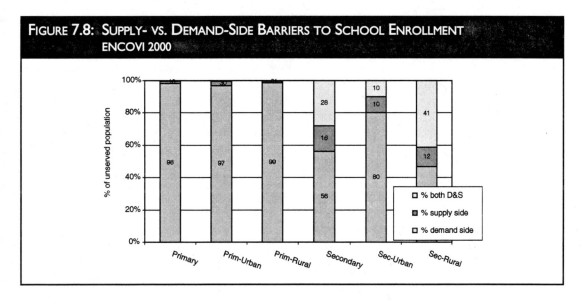

FIGURE 7.8: SUPPLY- VS. DEMAND-SIDE BARRIERS TO SCHOOL ENROLLMENT
ENCOVI 2000

enrolled in the sense of having access to a school.[22] **Finally,** cluster analysis of the ENCOVI strongly suggests that very few children fail to attend due to a lack of facilities. Since households in the ENCOVI were sampled in clusters (within primary sampling units, PSUs), enrollment in school by any child within a cluster signals the existence of a primary school facility. Using such information, non-enrollees can be classified into: (a) those who do not attend because there are no facilities available (pure supply-side gap); (b) those who fail to enroll even when a school is available (pure demand-side constraints); and (c) those who do not enroll because there is no school available, but still would not enroll if school facilities were provided (mixed supply- and demand-side factors).[23] This analysis reveals that only 2% of all non-enrollees lack primary school facilities (and this share is similar in both urban and rural areas, see Figure 7.8). This means that the problem of non-enrollment cannot be solved by building more schools. Rather, policies should seek to ease key demand-side constraints, as discussed below. As discussed above, the quality of schooling should also be addressed as low quality leads to low returns, which in turn lead to low demand for the educational investment.

Primary School: Main Demand-Side Constraints

Indeed, gender, ethnicity, parents' education, and poverty are all important demand-side determinants of enrollment and attainment. Controlling for other factors,[24] girls are less likely to enroll at any age than boys. Likewise, being indigenous reduces the likelihood of enrollment at any given age. Furthermore, if a person has both characteristics, it is even less likely that she will enroll.[25] Paternal and maternal education and total consumption per capita all have positive effects on the likelihood children will enroll. As such, education not only plays a key role in determining current poverty (as discussed in Chapter 3), but also plays a crucial role in the inter-generational transmission of poverty. Education not only begets higher household incomes, but also contributes

---

22. Calculating this as the difference between net "non-enrollment" rates (poor girls: 25% vs. poor boys: 19%) as a share of total net non-enrollment for girls (6/25 = 24%). World Bank calculations using the ENCOVI 2000, *Instituto Nacional de Estadística—Guatemala*.

23. See Annex 6 for additional details on the methodology for decomposing supply- and demand-side constraints to increased coverage of education, health and basic utility services using data from the ENCOVI.

24. This section presents the results of multi-variate "hazard function" regressions which explain the probability that a child will ever enroll as dependent on a variety of individual and household characteristics. For details and results of various specifications, see GUAPA Technical Paper 3 Edwards (2002).

25. In other words, the interaction effect is also significant and negative.

directly to the education—and hence future earnings—of today's children. Even after controlling for per capita consumption, household size and birth order also affect the chances that a child will enroll, with older children (lower birth order) and children in larger households being less likely to enroll. Child malnutrition (height-for-age) is also positively correlated with enrollment and attainment, even after other factors are taken into account. Similar results are observed in multi-variate regressions that examine the determinants of dropping out of school, once enrolled.[26] In this case, girls and indigenous children are significantly more likely to drop out than their boys or non-indigenous counterparts. Interestingly, late-enrolled indigenous children (interaction variable) are less likely to drop-out, signifying that late enrollment delays schooling but does not necessarily translate into less schooling. Again, parental education and household size are also important determinants of drop out.

Guatemalan households point to economic factors as the main constraints to increased primary enrollment. "Lack of money" was the single most common reason given for not enrolling in primary school, accounting for 38% of non-enrollees (Figure 7.9).[27] This pattern did not differ significantly by gender, ethnicity, or area, though it was slightly higher for the poor (39%) than the non-poor (32%). This suggests that direct costs of attending school are prohibitively high, particularly for the poor. Indeed, the costs to households of public schooling are quite high (see below). "Lack of interest" is the second main impediment to primary enrollment, according to Guatemalan households, accounting for 16% of absentees.[28] This might reflect the relatively low returns to education at the primary level (see below), or poor quality of education (not interesting to the children). Economic factors clearly do not explain the significant gender biases observed in Guatemala (particularly given higher female rates of return, as discussed below). As

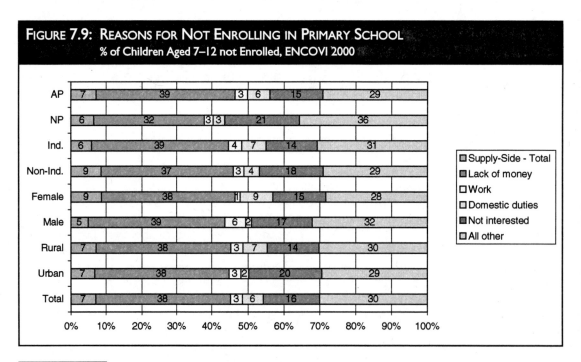

FIGURE 7.9: REASONS FOR NOT ENROLLING IN PRIMARY SCHOOL
% of Children Aged 7–12 not Enrolled, ENCOVI 2000

---

26. Results of multi-variate hazard regressions for dropping out of school, once enrolled (ages 6–25). For details and results of various specifications, see Edwards (2002).

27. Informants in the ENCOVI were asked for the primary reason children did not enroll in school. Percentages are for the target age cohort of non-enrollees (aged 7–12). World Bank calculations using the ENCOVI 2000, *Instituto Nacional de Estadística—Guatemala*.

28. The share was fairly constant across genders, ethnicities, and areas, though was slightly higher for the non-poor (21%) than the poor (15%).

such, a combination of economic, cultural and information/outreach solutions might be needed in order to improve girls' opportunities to attend school.

Secondary School: Supply- vs. Demand-Side Constraints
A combination of supply- and demand-side factors prevent increased enrollment at the secondary level. Cluster analysis[29] of ENCOVI data suggests that less than half of all non-enrollees fail to enroll in secondary school due to a lack of school facilities (Figure 7.8). Demand-side factors are even more dominant in deterring enrollment in urban areas. In contrast, demand- and supply-side factors both prevent rural youths from attending secondary school.[30] Interestingly, in indicating the main reasons for non-enrollment, Guatemalan households tend to downplay the lack of facilities as a deterrent to increased enrollment. In fact, despite the apparent lack of secondary schools in Guatemala, only 3% cited supply-side factors—such as distance to schools, inadequate class space, and lack of facilities—as the main reasons for not enrolling (Figure 7.10). Instead, most attribute non-enrollment to demand side factors, such as the direct costs of schooling or competing demands for their time (work, domestic responsibilities). Indeed, economic factors were by far the main reasons reported in the ENCOVI for not enrolling in secondary school (accounting for 69% of all non-enrollees, Figure 7.10).[31] Specifically, "had to work" was cited by about 29% as the main reason, followed by the direct costs of schooling (25%). Domestic responsibilities accounted for about 15% of non-enrollees. While the share citing direct costs did not vary significantly by gender, ethnicity, poverty group, or area, there were significant variations in the split between work and domestic responsibilities by gender. Close to half of all truant boys cited "work" as the main reason for not enrolling, compared with 14% of girls. Close to 28% of truant girls cited domestic

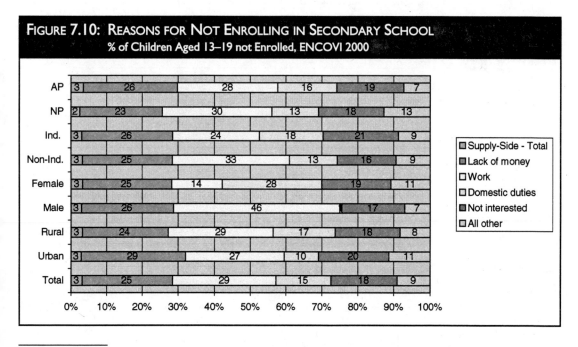

FIGURE 7.10: REASONS FOR NOT ENROLLING IN SECONDARY SCHOOL
% of Children Aged 13–19 not Enrolled, ENCOVI 2000

---

29. See Annex 6 for details on the methodology for decomposing supply- and demand-side constraints to increased coverage of education, health and basic utility services using data from the ENCOVI.

30. The rural and urban decompositions do not necessarily average into the decomposition for the overall country since they rely on different take-up rates for each area as well as different rates for the gap due to supply reasons.

31. Informants in the ENCOVI were asked for the primary reason children did not enroll in school. Percentages are for the target age cohort of non-enrollees (aged 13–19). World Bank calculations using the ENCOVI 2000, *Instituto Nacional de Estadística—Guatemala*.

responsibilities, as compared with only 1% of boys. "Lack of interest" accounted for just under a fifth of all non-enrollees, and this share did not vary significantly across the demographic groups.

Secondary School: Main Demand-Side Constraints

The direct costs of schooling are indeed high. Guatemalan households allocate an average of 5% of total consumption to education, though this share varies significantly between the poor (3%) and the non-poor (6%). Overall, it costs households an average of Q.650 per student to attend primary school, including fees, uniforms, transport, and books and materials. This cost is lower for Ministry schools and *significantly* lower for students at PRONADE schools,[32] as compared with private schools (Table 7.2). Secondary school is considerably more expensive, averaging Q.2,951 per student, or 68% of the annual per capita poverty line.[33] Even public secondary school provided by the MINEDUC is *five* times more expensive than public primary (Table 7.2). Cooperative

TABLE 7.2: THE DIRECT COST OF SCHOOLING
Annual Costs to Households Per Student, Primary and Secondary Schools, Quetzales/Student

	All Schools	Ministry Schools	PRONADE-prim. Cooperative-sec.	Private Schools	Other
Primary—All	650	341	92	3,434	374
Non-Indigenous	905	405	100	4,012	444
Indigenous	262	245	88	1,111	236
Urban	1,352	577	316	3,884	767
Rural	257	222	76	1,747	225
Non-Poor	1,305	554	306	3,913	658
All Poor	206	210	74	731	223
Primary—By Type of Cost (%)					
Fees	35%	5%	3%	58%	44%
Uniforms	9%	13%	13%	6%	7%
Books and Materials	33%	53%	44%	17%	28%
Transport	8%	3%	2%	11%	5%
Other (fundraisers, donations)	15%	26%	39%	7%	17%
Secondary—All	2,951	1,705	1,525	4,017	1,758
Non-Indigenous	3,216	1,618	1,658	4,365	2,296
Indigenous	2,095	2,057	1,343	2,610	1,230
Urban	3,377	1,929	1,546	4,336	2,439
Rural	2,034	1,297	1,504	3,014	1,187
Non-Poor	3,493	2,067	1,762	4,404	2,578
All Poor	1,298	956	1,138	1,845	1,110
Secondary—By Type of Cost (%)					
Fees	41%	9%	26%	51%	30%
Uniforms	6%	8%	8%	5%	2%
Books and Materials	28%	45%	39%	22%	34%
Transport	10%	16%	5%	9%	17%
Other (fundraisers, donations)	15%	23%	22%	13%	18%

Source: World Bank calculations using ENCOVI 2000, *Instituto Nacional de Estadística—Guatemala.*

---

32. Given PRONADE's reliance on community and parental participation, these out-of-pocket costs underestimate the true costs to families to the extent that they do not cover parental contributions in kind and in labor.

33. Poverty line established by INE at Q.4319 per person per year, see Chapter 2.

schools are not much cheaper. This presents a significant barrier to the poor for attending school, as highlighted by Guatemalan households in the ENCOVI (see above).

Opportunity costs to schooling are also high, as evidence by the large prevalence of child labor in Guatemala As discussed in Chapter 6, one in every five children aged 7–14 is employed. Older children are more likely to work, with 29% of children aged 10–14 working as compared with 8% of those aged 7–9. Three quarters of child laborers come from poor households, and about 80% reside in rural areas. About two thirds of child laborers are boys. Importantly, child laborers complete about half the number of years of schooling than their non-working counterparts.[34] The QPES also reveals that working conflicts with schooling: child labor was cited as the main cause of absenteeism and drop out in most of the study communities. Work-school conflicts are often seasonal, increasing during harvest periods which vary by crop (for example, coffee harvests run from November to December, sugar in October to April but especially from November to February, and cardamom twice a year). Such seasonal variations throughout the country suggest that a possible decentralization and tailoring of the school calendar to local conditions might be warranted to reduce the likelihood of work-school conflicts.

The Returns to Education

While the rates of return to primary are education are low, they are higher for secondary school and university, particularly for women. Earnings regressions[35] by level of education completed show that the rates of return to education increase in a non-linear function (Table 7.3). For example, a male who has completed primary education is expected to receive 11% more than a male with no education (which translates into an hourly earnings increase of about 2% per year of primary education). In contrast, the returns to secondary education are much higher. A male with secondary education receives 27% more than a male with no education (or 6% more per year of secondary schooling).[36] This pattern is similar for females,[37] but actual rates of return are higher for women, highlighting the importance of girls' education. The overall low returns to primary education suggest inadequate quality of schooling or lack of opportunities for low-skilled workers. They also corroborate the high share of non-enrollees who indicate that a "lack of interest" is their main reason for not enrolling: the returns perhaps do not justify the costs of the education investment decision.

A lack of ability to speak Spanish is correlated with lower rates of return. Controlling for other factors, men and women who speak Spanish

TABLE 7.3: RETURNS TO EDUCATION, BY GENDER			
	Male	**Female**	**Overall**
Primary completed (%)[1]	11	17	15
Secondary completed (%)[1]	27	54	51
University completed (%)[1]	74	76	74
Overall (%)[2]	3	6	6

Returns to education is the % increase in hourly wages due to educational level increases
1. compared with no education
2. per year of education

---

34. Among 10–14 year olds, those who work complete 1.78 years of schooling as compared with 3.38 for those that don't or 3.35 for those that go to school and work. World Bank calculations using the ENCOVI 2000, *Instituto Nacional de Estadística—Guatemala*.

35. See Edwards (2002) for details on the methodology used for these estimations (based on a Heckman selectivity model).

36. Regressions using the years of education were also estimated. The overall rates of return are 3% per year of schooling for males and 6% for females.

37. Specifically, a female who has completed primary school is expected to receive 17% more than one with no education (or almost 3% per year of primary completed). A woman who has completed secondary school receives an average of 54% more than one with no education (or 9% more per year of secondary completed). See Vakis (2002) for details.

earn more than 30% more than those who do not.[38] This is also true for bilingual speakers, highlighting the importance of language ability.

**Income inequalities emerge from both differences in educational attainment and the
returns to education.** As discussed in Chapter 3, differences in education account for over half of
total inequality in Guatemala. Further analysis suggests that inter-generational inequality is attributable to a combination of (a) inequality in educational attainment (years of schooling), which has
been equalizing over time due to the expansion of educational coverage; *and* (b) inequalities in the
returns to schooling, which could signal disparities in the quality of education.[39] Inequalities seem
to emerge in particular at the secondary level: a very small share of the poor attend secondary
school and the returns to this level far exceed those at the primary level.

**Additional years of schooling are needed to compensate for the low returns to primary
education as a means to escape poverty.** An "education-poverty line" can be calculated taking
into account household size and differences in the *level* of returns by gender and ethnicity.[40] Such
calculations reveal that for a five-person household, a male ladino household head needs 12.5 years
education to earn enough to pull his family out of poverty (more than a secondary education),
assuming he were the only income-earner in the household. For a similar household, if the male
were indigenous, he would need to have completed 17.6 years of schooling (almost a university
education) to earn enough to escape poverty. Ladina women would need 15.1 years, as compared
with Indigenous women who would have had to complete 23.4 years to pull their households out
of poverty. The ethnic and gender differences reflect disparities in the actual levels of returns to
schooling (not the rates).[41]

Public Spending and Equity

Level and Composition of Public Spending on Education
**Guatemala has made substantial progress in increasing public spending on education since
the Peace Accords.** Although still quite low relative to other LAC or lower-middle income countries,[42] public spending on education has expanded by an average of about 20% per year in real
terms since 1996, rising faster than GDP and total government expenditures (Table 7.4).

**Primary schooling absorbs the bulk of public expenditures on education, which is con-
sistent with equity and poverty concerns.** Primary schooling receives close to half of public
spending on education in Guatemala (Table 7.4). Given existing gaps in coverage and the fact that
the majority of the poor still do not complete primary school (discussed above), this allocation
seems appropriate. Moreover, public spending on primary schooling is slightly progressive, largely
due to the impressive targeting of the PRONADE program (see below). Spending on secondary
education is quite low (7% of total public education spending in 2000), much lower than spending
on tertiary education (USAC), which is highly regressive (see below). The spending category that
has grown the most since the Peace Accords is "other," which includes a range of adult education
and special programs.

The Distributional Incidence of Public Spending on Education
**Public spending on pre-primary school is well targeted overall, with an even stronger pro-
poor bias for the PRONADE program.** Over three quarters of public spending on pre-primary
schooling is received by the poor (Table 7.5). This reflects the fact that a substantial share of non-
poor pre-primary students attend private institutions. This share received by the poor is even
higher for spending on the PRONADE Program.

---

38. Edwards (2002).
39. Edwards (2002).
40. Although the *rates* of return per additional year of school are higher for girls, the overall *level* of earnings are lower.
41. See Edwards (2002) for details on these "education-poverty line" calculations.
42. Public spending on education averaged 4% and 5% of GDP for LAC countries and lower-middle
income countries respectively. Source: World Bank World Development Indicators Database.

TABLE 7.4: PUBLIC EXPENDITURES ON EDUCATION						
	1996	1997	1998	1999	2000	Average
Education Expenditures (mn Q.)[a]	1,505	1,900	2,617	3,285	3,629	n.a.
As % of GDP	1.6%	1.8%	2.1%	2.4%	2.5%	2.1%
As % of Total Gov't Exp.	15.2%	15.1%	15.7%	17.1%	18.3%	16.1%
Education Expenditures (mn Q, base year=2000)[b]	1,978	2,307	3,062	3,642	4,054	n.a.
Annual % change	n.a.	16.6%	32.7%	18.9%	11.3%	19.9%
By Level (% of total)[b]						
Pre-Primary	8.0%	9.8%	8.7%	6.0%	7.4%	8.0%
Primary (non-PRONADE)	49.2%	42.0%	40.0%	44.7%	44.2%	44.0%
PRONADE	n.a.	n.a.	3.3%	3.8%	4.9%	4.0%
Basic Secondary	7.8%	4.9%	5.0%	5.3%	5.0%	5.6%
Diversified Secondary	4.0%	6.8%	5.3%	3.0%	1.9%	4.2%
Tertiary (USAC)	14.0%	11.1%	12.1%	10.0%	9.3%	11.3%
Construction[c]	10.2%	9.3%	9.4%	9.2%	9.6%	9.5%
Other[d]	6.8%	16.2%	16.2%	17.9%	17.7%	14.9%
By Economic Classification (% of total)[b]						
Capital Expenditures	21.0%	22.0%	20.1%	26.6%	19.1%	21.8%
Personnel Expenditures	63.0%	61.8%	57.8%	57.7%	64.6%	61.0%
Non-Personnel Recurrent	16.0%	16.2%	22.1%	15.7%	16.3%	17.3%

Sources: a. SIAF/Ministry of Finance; b. Banguat, Ministry of Finance, and MINEDUC (Planning Unit), as reported in Anderson (October 2001). c. Information not available by level of education, but heavily weighted towards primary schools. d. Includes adult education, literacy training, other training programs, special education programs, and miscellaneous expenditures not classified by level of education.

While public spending on primary education is distributionally neutral, spending on the PRONADE program—which accounts for a large share of the recent expansion—is extremely well targeted. Spending on primary education essentially mirrors the distribution of the population: the poor account for about 56% of the population and receive about 54% of public spending on primary education (Table 7.5). Indeed, public spending on primary school is not as well targeted in Guatemala as in other LAC countries (Figure 7.11), reflecting the significant coverage gaps observed among the poor in Guatemala. In contrast, public spending on PRONADE is *extremely* well targeted, with only 8% of all benefits going to the non-poor—one of the best targeting records in LAC. The success of PRONADE targeting is important particularly in light of the fact that PRONADE accounted for a substantial share of new net enrollment since the Peace Accords.

In contrast, public subsidies for secondary and university schooling are highly regressive. The non-poor receive 67% and 94% of public spending on secondary and university edu-

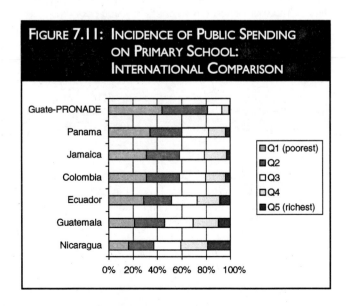

FIGURE 7.11: INCIDENCE OF PUBLIC SPENDING ON PRIMARY SCHOOL: INTERNATIONAL COMPARISON

TABLE 7.5: DISTRIBUTIONAL INCIDENCE OF PUBLIC SPENDING ON EDUCATION AND EDUCATIONAL SUPPORT (DEMAND-SIDE) PROGRAMS
% of total benefits received by each group

	Total	By Quintile					By Poverty Group			By Ethnicity		By Area	
		Q1	Q2	Q3	Q4	Q5	XP	AP	NP	Ind	Non-Ind	Rural	Urban
Education—Total	100	17	21	21	21	21	13	55	45	37	63	59	41
Pre-Primary	100	39	18	24	14	4	30	78	22	64	36	76	24
o/w Ministry Schools	100	35	19	27	14	5	26	76	24	65	35	74	26
o/w PRONADE	100	59	16	10	15	0	49	85	15	60	40	88	12
Primary	100	21	25	23	21	10	16	65	35	42	58	69	31
o/w Ministry Schools	100	18	24	24	22	11	14	62	38	40	60	67	33
o/w PRONADE	100	44	37	12	6	1	37	92	8	65	35	93	7
Secondary	100	3	12	23	31	32	2	33	67	22	78	36	64
o/w Ministry Schools	100	3	12	22	31	33	2	33	67	21	79	35	65
o/w Cooperatives	100	3	16	27	30	25	2	38	62	42	58	51	49
University	100	0	0	6	11	82	0	6	94	37	88	8	92
Demand-Side Programs													
School Feeding	100	16	25	27	20	11	12	63	37	43	57	79	21
Scholarships	100	9	4	23	16	48	3	30	70	47	53	28	72
Bolsa de Utiles (materials)	100	18	24	24	20	13	14	60	40	35	65	69	31
School Transport	100	0	2	15	56	27	0	16	84	8	92	3	97
Memo for Comparison													
Share of total population	100	20	20	20	20	20	16	56	44	43	58	61	39
Share of poor population	100	36	36	29	0	0	n.a.	n.a.	n.a.	58	42	81	19
Share of total consumption	100	5	9	13	20	54	4	24	76	24	76	37	63

Note: XP=Extreme poor; AP=All poor; NP=Non-poor; Ind=Indigenous; Non-Ind=Non-Indigenous.

Source: World Bank calculations using the ENCOVI 2000, *Instituto Nacional de Estadística—Guatemala*. Figures reflect differential unit subsidies by level and program as well as the number of students enrolled in public institutions regardless of their age. Quintiles are individual consumption quintiles.

cation respectively (Table 7.5). Public spending on Cooperative schools at the secondary level is likewise regressive, with 62% going to the non-poor. In fact, the distsribution of public spending at the secondary and university levels is more regressive than in other countries, reflecting extremely low enrollment by the poor in Guatemala (Figures 7.12 and 7.13).

Demand-side interventions (such as school feeding, scholarships and other subsidies) are poorly targeted to the poor. Scholarships in particular disproportionately benefit the non-poor, with close to *half* of all scholarship benefits accruing to the *top* quintile of the population (Table 7.5). The top two quintiles are likewise the main beneficiaries of the school transport subsidy, receiving 83% of total subsidy benefits. School feeding and the *Bolsa de Utiles* (school materials) programs are somewhat better targeted, benefiting primarily the middle quintiles of the population. The targeting of demand-side interventions to the poor is particularly important since such programs represent transfers designed to ease cost-related barriers to enrollment.

Overall, public spending on education is neutrally distributed. Reflecting the sum of the above patterns by level, public spending on education in Guatemala essentially follows population patterns, with a slight bias against the poorest quintile (Table 7.5). It is, however, more progressive than the existing distribution of total consumption in the economy (Table 7.5).

Summary of Key Issues and Priorities

There have been significant improvements in the education sector over time, particularly since the signing of the Peace Accords in 1996. Notably,

- The sector has undergone important institutional and structural reforms, including the deconcentration of financial management and the development of the PRONADE program and school boards, which help decentralize key decisions to the local level;
- Public spending on education has increased significantly since 1996 and the bulk of such spending goes to the primary level;

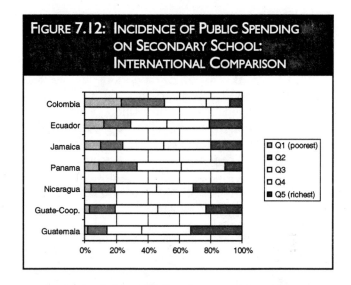

FIGURE 7.12: INCIDENCE OF PUBLIC SPENDING ON SECONDARY SCHOOL: INTERNATIONAL COMPARISON

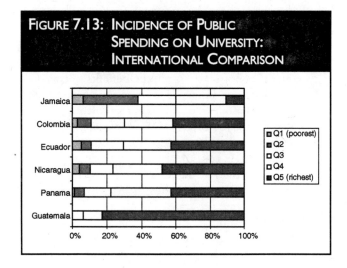

FIGURE 7.13: INCIDENCE OF PUBLIC SPENDING ON UNIVERSITY: INTERNATIONAL COMPARISON

- Literacy and educational attainment are increasing over time—with important reductions in the disparities between genders, ethnicities, and the poor versus the non-poor;
- Coverage has accelerated at all levels since the Peace Accords, particularly the primary level, and about half of the expansion was achieved through the PRONADE program;
- The expansion in coverage appears to have been well-targeted, since much was achieved through the PRONADE program which is extremely well targeted to the poor; and
- Official statistics on indicators of internal efficiency (repetition rates, drop out) suggest improvements.

Nonetheless, important challenges remain. In particular:

- Significant coverage gaps and disparities remain, particularly for the poor, girls, and rural and indigenous children;
- Very few poor even make it to the secondary level (few complete primary school)—and inequalities in earnings are largely generated at this level;

- Despite progress, indicators of internal efficiency (late enrollment, repetition, drop out) suggest serious structural problems in the educational system;
- The low returns to primary education suggest deficiencies in the quality of schooling;
- Beyond a physical lack of schools, key barriers include "demand-side" factors such as the direct costs of attending (at both the primary and secondary levels) and opportunity costs (for example, work and domestic duties which conflict with secondary enrollment)
- Public spending on primary school, which absorbs the bulk of public funds, is distributionally neutral, though spending on the PRONADE program is extremely well targeted. Public spending on secondary and university education is highly regressive.
- Demand-side programs—such as scholarships and the school transport subsidy—are highly regressive, with most benefits going to the non-poor; other programs (such as school feeding and the *bolsa de utiles* program) are slightly better targeted, but benefit mainly the middle quintiles of the population.

In light of these challenges, a number of policy recommendations seem appropriate. Specifically:

- Continued increases in public spending on education are needed to allow for a further expansion of enrollment to cover remaining gaps, particularly at the pre-primary and primary levels;
- Expansion of coverage should be promoted particularly for girls (especially indigenous girls) and indigenous children (for example, by expanding the "Eduque a la niña" programs);
- Expansion should be implemented via the PRONADE program (with quality improvements as necessary) given the benefits of this program in terms of community and parental participation. However, as supply-side gaps are filled, the Government should consider easing eligibility criteria so as to allow poor communities that already have schools to be eligible for the PRONADE-type community-based school-management model. To target this expansion, the poverty map could be used to identify eligible schools and preserve PRONADE's exemplary targeting record;
- Efforts should be made to better target public spending and demand-side programs so as to make more equitable and efficient use of existing resources; the poverty map could be used to help target programs and future interventions;
- The Government should seriously consider lowering the age structure for primary school, such that the official starting age is 6 rather than 7; this would lower the ending age from 12 to 11, which is important since older children face more competition for their time (opportunity costs via work and domestic duties);
- The Government should examine and improve quality, curriculum and performance standards, particularly at grades 1, 7 and 10, so as to improve student retention, transition and grade advancement at those grades; bilingual education (particularly in the early grades) is also important to improve learning, retention, and repetition rates in those transition years;
- As part of its efforts to decentralize key decisions to the local and community levels, the Government should consider decentralizing the school calendar so that communities could adjust to local harvest schedules so as to reduce competition between school and work;
- Demand-side support programs (such as scholarships) should be promoted and expanded at both the primary and secondary levels, as demand-side factors appear to be key constraints at both levels; however, such programs need to be restructured (consolidated, see Chapter 12) and explicitly targeted to the poor; and
- Investments should be made in early childhood development to promote: (a) improved child nutrition at an early age, since nutritional status is a significant factor in determining enrollment and attainment and since nutritional deficiencies emerge at a young age (see Chapter 8); and (b) early educational opportunities, including links between traditional schooling and pre-primary schooling.

HEALTH, MALNUTRITION, AND POVERTY

Poverty results in "death for not bringing the sick quickly to a health post." Ladino Villager, L1 (QPES) "My wife is sick but I can't bring her to a doctor or health center because I don't have money to pay for the visit or the trip (pasaje)"

Mam Villager, M2 (QPES)

This chapter seeks to analyze more deeply the issues pertaining to health and health care, with a view of informing policy and highlighting priorities for poverty reduction. The chapter begins with a review of the main health challenges facing Guatemala. Reflecting the gravity of the problem, it then assesses the problem of malnutrition, a key health challenge in Guatemala. It then explores the issues of coverage and access, concluding that both supply- and demand-side factors explain remaining access gaps. The chapter then reviews some of the key supply-side issues, including reforms and progress since the Peace Accords, public spending in the sector, institutional fragmentation and inefficiencies, and insurance coverage. Demand-side factors are then considered, including utilization patterns of various health services, and demand-side obstacles to greater coverage (particularly economic and cultural factors). Finally, the chapter concludes with a review of progress, key issues, and priorities in health for poverty reduction. The chapter mainly draws on analysis of the ENCOVI 2000,[1] supplemented by institutional information and qualitative data from the QPES.

Main Health Challenges

Unlike many other countries in Latin America, Guatemala is only at the beginning of the demographic and epidemiological transition. The population is very young, with a median age of 18, which is more on par with Africa (median age 18) than LAC (24), and far younger than Europe and North America (37 and 36).[2] The poor population is particularly young, signaling a higher dependency ratio (Figure 8.1). It is also growing rapidly. Fertility (five children per woman) is the highest in Latin America.[3] Guatemala also exhibits the second lowest average age of mothers

---

1. Gragnolati and Marini (2002).

2. Sources: Guatemala: World Bank calculations using ENCOVI 2000, *Instituto Nacional de Estadística— Guatemala;* rest of world: United Nations (2001).

3. Source: Guatemala: DHS 1998. The average is 2.6 for LAC and 2.1 for lower-middle income countries. Source: World Bank (2001b).

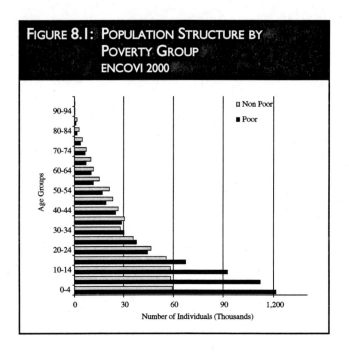

FIGURE 8.1: POPULATION STRUCTURE BY POVERTY GROUP ENCOVI 2000

at first birth in LAC, which internationally has been shown to have deleterious consequences for child health and survival of childbearing. The population growth rate is far higher than the average for LAC or other lower-middle income countries (Table 8.1). In terms of diseases, major causes of death in Guatemala still include treatable and communicable diseases, such as diarrhea, pneumonia, cholera, malnutrition, and tuberculosis. While the incidence of cholera and dengue has decreased rapidly over the past five years, the prevalence of malaria, diarrhea, and acute respiratory infections (ARI) have increased significantly.[4] At the end of 2000, 4,000 cases of AIDS were officially recognized with a potential sub-estimation of 50%. The share of women infected by the virus has increased significantly over time, and the rise in infected women in reproductive age implies that there is also a higher probability of vertical transmission.[5]

Guatemala is among the worst performers in terms of health outcomes in all of Latin America (Table 8.1). Life expectancy at birth is the lowest in Central America, and far lower than the average for LAC countries or lower-middle income countries. Infant mortality (40–45 per thousand)[6] is also the highest in Central America, and far higher than LAC average or the average for lower-middle income countries. Only Bolivia and Haiti perform worse for life expectancy or infant mortality in LAC; Guatemala does worse than other low-income HIPC/IDA countries, such as Nicaragua and Honduras. As discussed below, malnutrition rates are also among the highest in the world. Finally, maternal mortality is extremely high at 270 per 100,000; the only other countries in LAC with higher rates of maternal mortality are Haiti and Bolivia.[7] Guatemala has made some progress in improving health outcomes (such as infant mortality and life expectancy) over the past 20 years, but it's progress has been slower than the low-income HIPC/IDA countries of Bolivia, Nicaragua and Honduras. Progress in reducing malnutrition has been *significantly* slower in Guatemala than in other countries; in fact, it was the slowest in the LAC region.[8]

The patterns of health indicators do suggest worse conditions for the poor, rural, and indigenous populations, but the correlations depend on the indicator. In terms of *demographic behavior*, fertility rates are definitely higher among the poorer regions (Norte, Nor-Occidente, Peten), rural residents, indigenous women, and those with less education (which seems to have the strongest distinguishing effect, with those with no education having fertility rates 2.3 times higher than those with secondary education).[9] In terms of *morbidity*, the prevalence of diarrhea among

---

4. Gragnolati and Marini (2002).
5. Nuñez (2001).
6. Estimates of infant mortality for Guatemala vary. The 1998/99 Demographic and Health Survey (DHS) puts the average at 45. The World Bank World Development Indicators (2001), based on official health statistics, puts the estimate for that same year at 40.
7. World Health Organization.
8. Marini and Gragnolati (2002).
9. Source: DHS 1998/99 (survey does not allow for analysis by poverty group).

TABLE 8.1: INTERNATIONAL COMPARISON OF VARIOUS HEALTH INDICATORS, 1999				
	Infant Mortality	Life Expectancy	Population Growth	Dependency Ratio	GNI/Capita, PPP
Haiti	70	53	2.0	0.8	630
Bolivia	59	62	2.2	0.8	2,300
Guatemala	40–45	65	2.6	0.9	3,630
Dominican Republic	39	71	2.0	0.6	5,210
Peru	39	69	2.0	0.6	4,480
Honduras	34	70	3.0	0.8	2,270
Nicaragua	34	69	2.7	0.8	2,060
Brazil	32	67	1.7	0.5	6,840
El Salvador	30	70	1.5	0.7	4,260
Mexico	29	72	1.9	0.6	8,070
Ecuador	28	69	2.3	0.6	2,820
Paraguay	24	70	2.9	0.8	4,380
Colombia	23	70	2.0	0.6	5,580
Panama	20	74	1.9	0.6	5,450
Uruguay	15	74	0.7	0.6	8,750
Costa Rica	12	77	2.4	0.6	7,880
Chile	10	76	1.6	0.6	8,410
LAC Average	30	70	1.8	0.6	6,620
Lower Middle-Income Countries	32	69	1.4	0.5	4,250
World	54	66	1.6	0.6	6,870

Source: WDI 2001. Infant mortality per 1000 live births. Population growth for 1980–99. Dependency ratio = dependents as % of working age population.

children is higher among those in the poorer quintiles (Figure 8.2), rural residents, indigenous populations, and the poorer regions (e.g., Norte). In contrast, no significant difference is observed in the prevalence of ARI among children by quintile (Figure 8.2) or ethnicity.[10] In terms of *outcomes*, the prevalence of malnutrition is significantly higher among indigenous and rural children, and among those in the poorer quintiles (Figure 8.2), as discussed below. While infant mortality is higher among the indigenous and those with lower education, there is no distinguishable difference between urban and rural areas. Moreover, regional patterns for infant mortality do not closely follow those for poverty, with higher infant mortality in the Central (57), Sur-Occidente (58), and Nor-Oriente (54) regions (which do not have the highest poverty rates in the country). Interestingly, parts of these regions cover the "finca zone" with a significant share of plantations (coffee, sugar, banana)

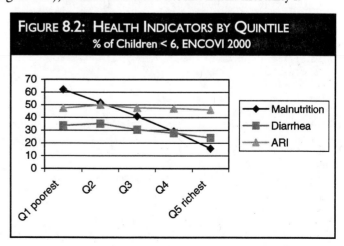

FIGURE 8.2: HEALTH INDICATORS BY QUINTILE
% of Children < 6, ENCOVI 2000

— Malnutrition
— Diarrhea
— ARI

10. Diarrhea and ARI information from World Bank calculations using ENCOVI 2000, *Instituto Nacional de Estadística—Guatemala.*

that serve as catchments for migrant laborers and their families.[11] The 1995 DHS survey, does, however, suggest a correlation between "wealth" and infant mortality, with infant mortality rates for children in the poorest "wealth quintile" that were twice those for their counterparts in the top quintile.[12]

A Focus on Malnutrition: A Red Flag!

Indicators of Malnutrition

Malnutrition among Guatemalan children is extremely high—among the worst in the world. Guatemala has among the worst performances in the world in terms of child growth attainment, with an overall stunting rate of 44% of all children under five (height-for-age, HAZ).[13] With these rates, malnutrition affects a total of 756,000 children under 5 nationwide. Not only is the prevalence of chronic malnutrition (stunting, HAZ) higher in Guatemala than any other country in LAC, it is also twice as high as the second highest rate in the region, observed in Bolivia in 1998 (27%). Guatemala's malnutrition rate is also among the highest in the world. Among those countries for which there is reliable information, only Bangladesh and Yemen have higher stunting rates (55% in 1996/7 and 52% in 1997, respectively). These estimates are consistent across time and across types of surveys (for example data from DHS surveys yield stunting rates (HAZ) for Guatemala of 50% in 1995 and 46% in 1998). Furthermore, they are not the result of some genetic aberration: stunting rates among the population of Southern Mexico—which arguably could have similar genetic heritage as much of the Guatemalan population (particularly the Mayan population)— are *far* lower than those in Guatemala (29% in 1998).[14]

Moreover, **malnutrition is declining slower in Guatemala than in other countries.** Guatemala has made some progress in reducing malnutrition, from 59% in 1987 to 44% in 2000. However, the yearly percentage reduction (1.7% p.a.) has been the slowest in the LAC region. The annual reduction was nearly twice as fast in Bolivia, which was the second slowest at reducing malnutrition in the region; the reduction in Brazil was far faster. This lack of adequate progress paradoxically contrasts with significant progress in other areas (basic services, health, education), as discussed in subsequent chapters. Simulations suggest that, even if malnutrition in Guatemala were to fall at the pace projected by a worldwide panel of elasticities (i.e., faster than its historical pace), it would not improve enough to meet the Millennium Development Goals (MDGs) by the year 2015, as discussed in Chapter 5.

---

11. Infant mortality indicators from DHS 1998/99.

12. Wealth measures include consumer items (e.g., television, cars), dwelling characteristics (e.g., flooring materials, water, toilet facilities), and other assets. Source: Gwatkin, Rutstein, Johnson, Pande, and Wagstaff (2000).

13. These stunting rates (height-for-age, HAZ) are consistent for various recent surveys, as are other measures of malnutrition (weight-for-age, WAZ, and weight-for-height (WHZ)). Specifically, in 1995, the DHS recorded 49.7% for HAZ, 26.6% for WAZ, and 3.3% for WHZ; the 1998 DHS recorded 46.4% for HAZ, 24.2% for WAZ, and 2.5% for WHZ; and the ENCOVI 2000 recorded 44.2% for HAZ, 22.3% for WAZ, and 2.5% for WHZ.

14. Malnutrition indicators for Southern Mexico were as follows: 28.9% stunting (height for age), 1.6% wasting (weight for height), and 11.8% underweight (weight for age) in 1998/99 based on DHS data as reported by the World Health Organization (WHO). In contrast, comparable indicators for Guatemala that same year (DHS data for 1998/99) were: 46.4% stunting, 2.5% wasting, and 24.2% underweight. Estimates for Guatemala from the 2000 ENCOVI were: 44.2% stunting, 2.8% wasting, and 22.3% underweight. Results from the International Biological Programme (Eveleth and Tanner 1976) and from more recent studies (Eveleth and Tanner 1990) reveal that, on a worldwide scale, height differences among children under five years from different countries are relatively small in comparison with large differences between and within countries due to environmental factors. Similarly, Martorell (1985), shows that, while differences due to social class were large, the differences that could be attributed to genetic factors were small (using a sample of height measurements from seven-year old boys from Brazil, Costa Rica, Guatemala, Haiti, Jamaica, Nigeria, India, and Hong Kong). Looking at growth data from well-to-do preschool children of different ethnic groups, Habicht et. al. (1974) reached the same conclusion.

Malnutrition is most serious among children under age two. Since malnutrition is a cumulative phenomenon, malnutrition rates increase with child age. The fastest increases in stunting occur in the first 24 months of life, particularly during the weaning period (from 6–24 months).[15] As such, the most effective nutrition programs should target children under the age of two, rather than at school age, which is the focus of most existing interventions (for example, school feeding).

There is a strong correlation between poverty and child malnutrition. Four fifths of malnourished children in Guatemala are poor. Malnutrition is much higher among poor children than non-poor children (64% of extreme poor and 53% of all poor children versus 27% of non-poor children). Children in the poorest quintile are almost four times more likely to be malnourished than their counterparts in the top quintile (62% and 16% respectively).

The incidence of malnutrition closely mirrors the geographic and ethnic patterns of poverty. As such, anthropometric measures appear to be good objective indicators of living standards. Like for poverty, malnutrition is much higher among rural children than urban (51% vs 32%). It is also much higher among the indigenous than the non-indigenous (58% vs. 33%), and this gap holds true even controlling for other factors, as discussed below. Figures 8.3 and 8.4 show that the patterns of both poverty and malnutrition are quite similar across specific ethnic groups and geographic regions. The only exception is among the Q'eqchi, who have quite high poverty, but relatively lower chronic malnutrition (stunting). Q'eqchi children do, however, have higher acute malnutrition (wasting) and diarrhea rates (which tend be correlated).

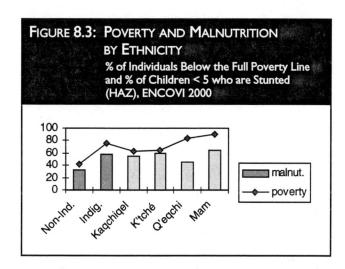

FIGURE 8.3: POVERTY AND MALNUTRITION BY ETHNICITY

% of Individuals Below the Full Poverty Line and % of Children < 5 who are Stunted (HAZ), ENCOVI 2000

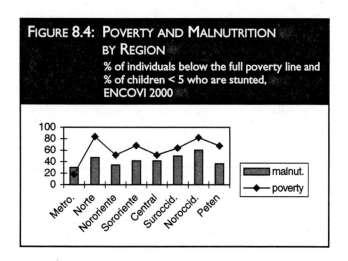

FIGURE 8.4: POVERTY AND MALNUTRITION BY REGION

% of individuals below the full poverty line and % of children < 5 who are stunted, ENCOVI 2000

The Determinants of Malnutrition

Malnutrition is the product of the interaction of many factors, including individual and household decisions and behaviors (such as feeding practices), community infrastructure, the cultural and natural environment, national policies, and international economic conditions. Multi-variate regressions and proximate correlate analyses were used to identify the relative importance of many

---

15. The median duration of breastfeeding in the ENCOVI sample is 16 months, with longer periods among lower quintiles.

of these factors. Based on this analysis, the main determinants of malnutrition for children under age 5 include:

- **Education.** Parental education is among the most important determinants of children's growth attainment, even after controlling for other factors. Education improves parents' ability to manage nutrition, disease and sanitation. It also influences other socioeconomic characteristics, such as parental age at marriage, number of children and their status in the community. In turn, malnutrition among school-aged children (which largely reflects early child malnutrition) has a significant impact on grade advancement in school, as discussed in Chapter 7.
- **Illness.** Morbidities, especially diarrhea and respiratory infections, are both causes and consequences of malnutrition. Stunting rates are much higher among children with frequent and early-age exposure to diarrhea or respiratory infections. In turn, malnourished children are more likely to be susceptible to such diseases. Disease prevention and treatment, together with improving the availability and quality of water and sanitation are critical for fighting chronic malnutrition.
- **Family Planning.** Pregnancies at a young age, numerous children, and short intra-birth spacing—all very common in Guatemala (as discussed above)—are associated with deficient child growth patterns.
- **Mother's Nutritional Status.** Reflecting inherent genetic traits, there is a strong relationship between the mother's height and her child's nutritional status. As expected, the influence of a father's height is significant, but smaller than the mother's height because of the mother's additional effect on children's nutritional status through the womb environment. Including variables for parents' height also controls for genetic factors.
- **Breastfeeding.** Breastfeeding and appropriate weaning practices are one of the most important household behaviors that can influence nutritional outcomes and that can be influenced by policies and programs (e.g., information campaigns). Exclusive breastfeeding for at least the first six months of life provides an adequate source of nutrients and antibodies and eliminates the risks of illness from contaminated utensils or water. It also helps repress fertility by extending the duration of post-partum amenorrhoea. Indeed, breastfeeding proved to be a significant determinant of malnutrition in regression analysis in Guatemala.
- **Basic Utility Services.** The availability of piped water, sanitation, electricity, and garbage collection systems is significantly correlated with better nutritional outcomes.
- **Geography, Ethnicity and Language Ability.** Malnutrition is also worse in rural areas, among the indigenous, and among children whose mothers do not speak Spanish, even after controlling for other factors. As discussed above, malnutrition is almost twice as high among the indigenous as the non-indigenous. Even after controlling for other characteristics,[16] a significant share of this gap is unexplained and likely arises due to health and behavioral factors (for example, weaning practices, hygiene, cooking behaviors).
- **Poverty.** Per capita consumption has a very significant and positive effect on children's nutritional status, though the direction of causality is not clear. Poverty boosts malnutrition by restricting individuals' access to basic services and other assets, increasing exposure to disease, and reducing access to food. On the other hand, high rates of malnutrition jeopardize future economic growth by reducing the intellectual and physical potential of the population.

Malnutrition Interventions

Little funding is devoted to the problem of malnutrition in Guatemala. Nutrition programs received about US$27 million in 2000, most of which was used in school feeding programs for primary-school-aged children. The School Lunch program of MINEDUC received 9.3 million,

---

16. Using the Oaxaca-Blinder decomposition.

while almost US$12 million paid for the school breakfast program sponsored by the Office of the Vice President. Food for preschoolers was administered through PAIN and *Hogares Comunitarios,* both of which covered a total of 42,000 children under five, or 14% of the total number of children under five living in extreme poverty, or 2.8% of the total number of poor children under five.

Moreover, existing resources are misdirected and do not attack the main sources of the problem. Virtually all public funds earmarked for "nutrition" are directed to school feeding programs or short-term emergency assistance (for example, food handouts or food-for-work programs in areas struck by natural disasters). A variety of other grass-roots level schemes exist, but these are small and quite dispersed. While school feeding programs can serve as useful incentive mechanisms to promote increased enrollment and attendance at school, they have little effect on malnutrition because (a) they reach the malnourished or potentially malnourished population too late since they are directed to school-aged children when most stunting or wasting occurs in early phases of life (particularly between 6–24 months of age); and (b) a lack of available food is rarely the main cause of long-term malnutrition. Moreover, while emergency food programs are useful for alleviating short-term acute food security problems, such food handouts are not necessarily the most effective or sustainable solutions to the larger, long-term malnutrition problems.

Past efforts in micronutrient fortification have lagged, and anemia among women is quite high. At one time, Guatemala stood out as a pioneer in micronutrient fortification, as one of the first countries to adopt fortification practices. However, interruptions in fortification, weak regulation and poor targeting have made Guatemala one of the worst performers in terms of implementation of these schemes.[17] Without proper fortification or adequate dietary sources of iron, the percentage of women affected by anemia is the second highest in Central America (35% in 1995), which results in adverse consequences for infant mortality and low-birth weight babies.

An aggressive, integrated approach to malnutrition needs to be adopted in Guatemala. Targeted and concerted actions are needed in the areas of health (particularly child and maternal health), access to basic utility services (e.g., potable water and sanitation), and education (nutrition information). Moreover, specific nutritional interventions are needed. These include: (a) promotion of exclusive breastfeeding, proper health, hygiene, and complementary feeding practices; (b) growth monitoring and promotion of pregnant women and children under age two; (c) micronutrient supplementation (particularly for iron) and reinstating fortification programs; and (d) deworming treatments and oral rehydration therapy. The main target population for these schemes should be pre-school children (particularly those under 24 months of age) and mothers (including pregnant and lactating women). To improve the effectiveness and reach of these programs (and avoid having them get "set aside"), these interventions should be integrated into the MSPAS basic health care package and provided at the community level through outreach workers selected by the community but contracted either by NGOs or the MSPAS. This would also allow for the institutionalization of nutrition activities within MSPAS, which would eventually contribute to the much needed rationalization of the myriads of independent, often incompatible, nutrition efforts in Guatemala. Nonetheless, although institutionalization can be done within MSPAS, strong collaboration should be established with other key ministries and stakeholders at the highest levels, given the multi-faceted nature of malnutrition.

Access to Health Care

Access to health care services is a key determinant of health outcomes. International evidence suggests that access to, and use of, health care services is highly correlated with health outcomes. Other factors (access to potable water, education, and household behaviors) also play important roles.

While estimates vary, a significant share of Guatemalans apparently lack access to health care services. The World Health Organization (WHO) defines access as living within one hour of

---

17. See GUAPA Technical Paper 6, Marini and Gragnolati (2002) for additional details on these schemes.

traveling time to a health care facility. Data from the ENCOVI suggest that average traveling times are about 45 minutes overall, but that they are much higher in rural areas (just under an hour). According to the ENCOVI, about 59% of households lacked access to a health facility (had to travel more than 60 minutes of traveling time).[18] This lack of access was worse among the poor (63%) than the non-poor (52%). It is also worse in rural areas (64%) than urban (48%), and in the Norte, Central, Suroccidente, Sur-oriente, and Peten regions, most of which have very high rates of infant mortality. As discussed in Chapter 9, adequate road access is crucial for rural populations to access health services. Travel times for those without motorable roads are considerably higher (69 minutes)—well beyond the WHO definition of access. Qualitative data also suggest that health services are more lacking than other basic social services. In the QPES, for example, only three of ten rural villages had access to a health clinic or health post, though all ten villages reported access to midwives. In contrast, data from the Ministry of Health (MSPAS) suggest that only 9% of the population lacked access in 1999, coming down from 46% without access at the time of the Peace Accords in 1996, largely due to improved coverage of the SIAS program (including traveling health promoters).

Even when health facilities are present, they are often understaffed and lack medicines and equipment.[19] According to data from the ENCOVI, the poor and indigenous are more likely to live in communities reporting insufficient medicines, medical equipment, beds, ambulances, and medical staff (particularly maternal-child specialists such as gynecologists, obstetricians, and pediatricians). Various qualitative studies also point to these problems.[20] The World Bank World Development Indicators (2001) suggest that there are significantly fewer physicians per capita in Guatemala (0.9) than other lower-middle income countries (1.9) or the LAC region as a whole (1.6). The ENCOVI suggests that waiting times (a sign of understaffing) are considerably long, averaging 46 minutes for all types of facilities. They are substantially longer for public and IGSS hospitals (66 and 87 minutes respectively) and shorter at community centers (33 minutes).

Access is constrained by both supply and demand-side barriers. Two types of indicators support these findings. **First,** the ENCOVI 2000 gathered data on reasons people did not seek treatment when they were ill but judged that treatment was necessary.[21] Demand-side factors (particularly economic constraints) account for the bulk of the coverage gap (Figure 8.5). Nonetheless, supply-side factors (including distance and lack of transport to health facilities, a lack of doctors and nurses, and lengthy waiting times) also appear to present significant constraints to improved access. Overall, these factors accounted for 17% of the coverage gap. These supply-side constraints were higher among those in the poorer quintiles (25% in the poorest quintile compared with 8% in the richest, Figure 8.5). Supply-side constraints were also seven times more frequent in rural than urban areas, reflecting the greater presence of health facilities in Guatemala's cities. **Second,** data on health treatment patterns within "communities" (primary sampling units, PSUs) in the ENCOVI sample allow for a decomposition of coverage gaps between (a) those who did not seek treatment because there were no health care facilities available (pure supply-side gap); (b) those who did not seek treatment even when facilities were available (pure demand-side constraints); and (c) those who did not seek treatment because no health care facilities were available, but still would still not seek treatment if such facilities were provided (mixed supply- and demand-side factors).[22]

---

18. This is based on data gathered for travel time to take children affected by common maladies (diarrhea or ARI). This could underestimate access since it doesn't account for (a) those who didn't seek treatment (perhaps because they lack access); or (b) those who didn't report the illness.

19. Calculations using the ENCOVI 2000 community questionnaire, which is not representative for all communities in Guatemala, but covers 60% of households in the household survey.

20. Annis (1981); Pebley et. al. (1997); QPES (2001).

21. These numbers exclude those who were ill but deemed treatment unimportant (sickness not bad enough to require health care). World Bank calculations using the ENCOVI 2000, *Instituto Nacional de Estadística—Guatemala.*

22. See Annex 6 for additional details on the methodology for decomposing supply- and demand-side constraints to increased coverage of education, health and basic utility services using data from the ENCOVI.

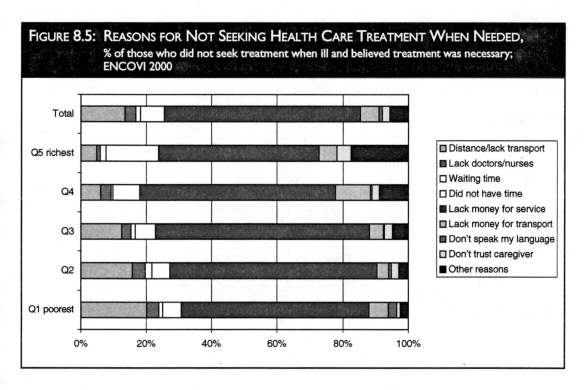

FIGURE 8.5: REASONS FOR NOT SEEKING HEALTH CARE TREATMENT WHEN NEEDED,
% of those who did not seek treatment when ill and believed treatment was necessary;
ENCOVI 2000

Legend:
- Distance/lack transport
- Lack doctors/nurses
- Waiting time
- Did not have time
- Lack money for service
- Lack money for transport
- Don't speak my language
- Don't trust caregiver
- Other reasons

This analysis reveals that overall, about 13% of households do not have access to any health care facility (supply-side constraints), but about half of these would not seek treatment even if facilities were to be made available (mixed supply- and demand-side constraints, see Table 8.2). Demand-side constraints prevented about 87% of the population from seeking health treatment, even when facilities were present. In terms of public facilities, which are significantly cheaper than private (as discussed below), a much larger share of the population lacked physical access to such facilities,

TABLE 8.2: DECOMPOSITION OF COVERAGE DEFICIT—ACCESS TO HEALTH FACILITIES
(for households that do not use facilities)

	Demand side constraints only	Both supply- and demand-side constraints	Supply-side constraints only	Total
Public facility—All	45	44	11	100
Public facility—Urban	55	35	10	100
Public facility—Rural	38	51	11	100
Private—All	69	21	9	100
Private facility—Urban	72	17	11	100
Private facility—Rural	68	25	8	100
Other facility—All	55	35	10	100
Other facility—Urban	41	47	12	100
Other facility—Rural	66	26	8	100
Any facility—All	87	6	7	100
Any facility—Urban	84	8	8	100
Any facility—Rural	89	4	6	100

Source: World Bank calculations using the ENCOVI 2000, Instituto Nacional de Estadística—Guatemala. See Annex 6 for details on methodology.

particularly in rural areas where 62% lack public health facilities (though demand-side constraints would also prevent many of these from seeking treatment). **In conclusion,** a combination of both supply- and demand-side constraints limit the ability of households to seek health care services in Guatemala, with supply-side constraints playing a more dominant role in rural areas than urban. Both demand- and supply-side constraints to improved access are discussed in greater detail below.

Supply-Side Factors

Some Improvements Since the Peace Accords . . . But Little Impact on Health Outcomes
The Peace Accords included significant commitments to improving health and health care services in Guatemala. The main health-related objectives included: (a) increasing public spending on health by 50% from 1995–2000 with at least 50% of the budget devoted to preventative health; (b) reducing infant and maternal mortality by 50%; (c) eradicating measles by 2000 and maintaining polio eradication certification; and (d) decentralizing and deconcentrating health service provision.

Some progress has been made in reforming the system. Important steps have been taken on the institutional side, with health being one of the pilot ministries (along with education) to deconcentrate financial management under the SIAF program, as discussed in Chapter 4. The Government also launched the *Sistema Integrado de Atención de Salud* (SIAS) in response to the Peace Accords in order to expand coverage to the rural and indigenous population and improve health services. The SIAS system is highly decentralized, often working through NGOs, cooperatives, and municipalities. It provides both preventive and curative care with the aim of bringing services closer to communities and promoting community participation. It often sponsors traveling "promotores de salud" in rural areas. The Government also adopted a National Health Plan for the period from 2000–2004 that focuses on (a) decentralization with social and community participation; (b) providing primary health care with an emphasis on promoting information, self-awareness and responsibility; and (c) improving equity, efficiency, quality and sustainability with a focus on the most disadvantaged groups. Finally, available data do suggest a shift in public spending towards preventive care, which is appropriate given Guatemala's epidemiological status and equity concerns.

Despite these efforts, spending and health outcomes have not improved significantly. Although public spending on health has increased slightly, it still falls short of targets set by the Peace Accords (see below). Infant mortality still hovers around 40–45, far from the target for 2000 of 20 per 1,000 live births. Maternal mortality also far exceeds the target of 48.5 per 100,000. Measles vaccinations likewise fell short of their target for 2000 (see Chapter 4). Moreover, malnutrition remains stagnant at an extremely high level, as discussed above. Closely related, Guatemala has seen an increase in the prevalence of diarrhea, malaria, and acute respiratory infections.

Public Spending: Increases Insufficient, Not Well Targeted
Public spending increases have been insufficient. As a share of GDP, total public spending on health has increased over the period from 1995–2000, but still falls short of the Peace Accords targets (Table 8.3). Over the period from 1990–98, total per capita spending on health care (public and private) averaged US$155 in PPP terms, which was far lower than its Central American neighbors,[23] or the averages for LAC (US$452) or lower-middle income countries (US$190).

Nonetheless, the composition and execution of public spending have improved somewhat. Available data suggest that the Government has increased its allocations to preventive health care (over tertiary or other levels of health care), which is vitally important to poverty reduction as it focuses on the main health problems faced by the poor (Table 8.3). Moreover, changes in public expenditure management—including the incorporation of health spending into the SIAF system

---

23. For that same period, the per capita PPP averages were: Honduras US$210, Nicaragua US$266, El Salvador US$298, Panama US$410, and Costa Rica US$509. Source: World Bank (2001b).

TABLE 8.3: PUBLIC SPENDING ON HEALTH, 1995–2000						
	1996	1997	1998	1999	2000	2000-target
Public Spending on Health, mn Q.[a]	627.2	872.1	1177.8	1594.1	1557.7	n.a.
% of GDP	0.7%	0.8%	0.9%	1.2%	1.1%	1.3%
% of Total Public Spending	6.3%	6.9%	7.1%	8.3%	7.9%	n.a.
Capital exp/total public health exp.[b]	30.5	35.3	18.0	23.6	17.6	n.a.
Preventive/total public health exp.[b]	n.a.	43.0	46.0	49.0	52.0	>50
Executed/Planned Spending (ratio)[a]	62.1	91.5	91.6	89.6	94.3	100

Sources: a. SIAF/Ministry of Finance (executed spending). b. World Bank (2000b).

and the deconcentration of financial management—have improved the execution of public health spending somewhat since their introduction in 1997 (Table 8.3). Nonetheless, recurrent spending seems to have edged out capital expenditures over time, thus reducing spending on longer-term investment activities.

Public spending on health is not very well targeted. Overall public health spending benefits the middle quintiles disproportionately more than their share in the population (Table 8.4). This is not dissimilar to other countries in LAC, though Guatemala's poorest quintiles still receive slightly less benefits from public health spending than their counterparts in other countries (Figure 8.6). By poverty group, the poor receive about 53% of total public spending on health, close to their share in the overall population (56%). Nonetheless, public spending on health *is* more progressive than the current distribution of total consumption in the economy (Table 8.4).

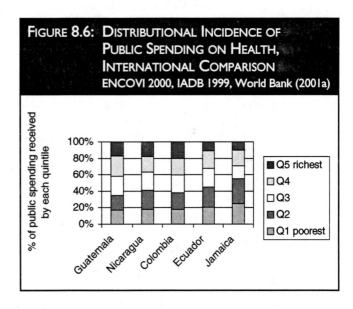

FIGURE 8.6: DISTRIBUTIONAL INCIDENCE OF PUBLIC SPENDING ON HEALTH, INTERNATIONAL COMPARISON
ENCOVI 2000, IADB 1999, World Bank (2001a)

By type of facility, public spending on hospitals is by far the most regressive, with the top two quintiles receiving 51% of total net public subsidies on hospitals, as compared with only 29% for the lowest two quintiles (Table 8.4). In contrast, public spending on health posts and community centers is very well targeted (Table 8.4), reflecting higher usage of these types of facilities by the poor.

Duplications and Fragmentation in the Health Sector
Institutionally, public services are somewhat fragmented between two large providers. The Ministry of Public Health and Social Action (MSPAS) is responsible for providing curative and preventive care for the entire population at practically no charge to users. The largest actor in the sector, MSPAS also has the constitutional mandate for defining sectoral policies and coordinating other actors in the sector. The other large public actor is the Guatemalan Social Security Institute (IGSS), which provides retirement benefits and health services to eligible formal sector workers in their families. The IGSS runs separate facilities from MSPAS. While members of the IGSS can use MSPAS facilities, only affiliated members can use IGSS facilities. As discussed in Chapter 12, coverage of the IGSS is very low, even as a share of formal sector workers. Other providers in the sector

TABLE 8.4: DISTRIBUTIONAL INCIDENCE OF PUBLIC HEALTH SPENDING, BY FACILITY
% of net public subsidies received by each group

| | Total | By Quintile | | | | | By Poverty Group | | | By Ethnicity | | By Area | |
		Q1	Q2	Q3	Q4	Q5	XP	AP	NP	Ind	Non-Ind	Rural	Urban
Health—Total	100	17	18	23	25	17	12	53	47	40	60	64	36
Hospital	100	13	16	21	29	22	9	45	55	33	67	58	42
Health Center	100	20	23	28	20	9	16	65	35	51	49	67	33
Health Post	100	40	22	27	6	5	29	84	16	53	47	98	2
Community Center	100	39	20	23	8	10	34	75	25	71	29	87	13
Memo for Comparison													
Share of total population	100	20	20	20	20	20	16	56	44	43	58	61	39
Share of poor population	100	36	36	29	0	0	n.a.	n.a.	n.a.	58	42	81	19
Share of total consumption	100	5	9	13	24	54	4	24	76	24	76	37	63

Source: World Bank calculations using the ENCOVI 2000, *Instituto Nacional de Estadística—Guatemala.* Figures reflect differential unit subsidies by provider as well as utilization patterns by provider. Quintiles are individual consumption quintiles.

include private providers, including traditional health practitioners (see Box 8.1) and modern providers, which have emerged primarily in urban areas in response to rising incomes and dissatisfaction with the quality of public sector care. The private sector also dominates the provision of pharmaceuticals, with very limited state regulation. NGOs (both international- and national-based) are also active in the health sector. In reality, there is little coordination between providers, with significant duplications and gaps in coverage.

Use of various facilities by the insured also reveals duplications and inefficiencies in coverage. Interestingly, a substantial share of those with private health insurance—who tend to be in the richest quintiles of the population—still use highly subsidized public facilities (public or IGSS hospitals, health posts and centers, Table 8.5). In contrast, an equal share of those covered by IGSS use IGSS hospitals and private hospitals, perhaps reflecting their dissatisfaction with services at IGSS hospitals (which had the longest waiting times of all facilities). Finally, a substantial share of those with no insurance (who tend to be poorer, as discussed below) still used relatively more expensive private hospitals, reflecting gaps in coverage of the public health system and disparities in the quality of care received in public and private facilities.

Inadequate Insurance Coverage
Health insurance coverage of any kind is very low in Guatemala. Only 11% have any kind of health insurance (Table 8.6). Most of those who have insurance are affiliated with IGSS, while the

TABLE 8.5: USE OF DIFFERENT HEALTH FACILITIES BY PEOPLE WITH TYPE OF INSURANCE COVERAGE

Type of Insurance	Public Hospital	IGSS Hospital	Private Hospital	Health Post or Center	Community Center	Pharmacy	Home	Other
Private	5.3	17.0	53.0	7.7	0.3	6.1	8.3	2.3
IGSS	6.0	38.6	37.1	4.6	1.2	6.9	3.0	2.7
No Insurance	10.1	1.3	39.5	26.9	2.2	8.3	5.8	6.1

Source: World Bank calculations using the ENCOVI 2000, *Institutio Nacional de Estadística—Guatemala.*

TABLE 8.6: SHARE OF INDIVIDUALS COVERED BY HEALTH INSURANCE

	Total	Q1	Q2	Q3	Q4	Q5	Urban	Rural
Private insurance	2.2	0.0	0.0	1.0	2.0	9.0	5.5	1.0
IGSS	8.3	3.0	3.0	6.0	12.0	18.0	14.5	5.0
No Insurance	89.0	97.0	97.0	93.0	86.0	73.0	81.0	94.0

Source: World Bank calculations using the ENCOVI 2000, *Institutio Nacional de Estadística—Guatemala.*

rest have private insurance. The great majority of those who have either type of insurance belong to the richest quintiles and live in urban areas (Table 8.6).

Demand-Side Factors

Underutilization of Health Services

The ENCOVI suggests a serious under-utilization of health services among disadvantaged groups. These patterns can be seen for children, individuals and prenatal and delivery care. Specifically:

▨ **Children with diarrhea or ARI lack treatment, particularly the poor, indigenous, and rural children.** Over half of all Guatemalan children with diarrhea or ARI are treated by relatives or non-medically qualified personnel (Table 8.7). Mirroring this pattern, over half are treated at home. A much higher share of children in the poorest quintiles lack treatment by medical professionals. Only in the highest quintile do children have a higher probability of being seen by a doctor than by any other person. Non-indigenous and urban children are twice as likely to be treated by a doctor than indigenous or rural children.

TABLE 8.7: UTILIZATION OF HEALTH SERVICES BY CHILDREN WITH DIARRHEA OR ARI

	Total	By Quintile					By Ethnicity		By Area	
		Q1	Q2	Q3	Q4	Q5	Non-Indigenous	Indigenous	Urban	Rural
Prevalence of Diarrhea[a]	31.3	33.8	35.2	30.5	27.8	24.1	35.6	27.5	24.7	34.5
Prevalence of ARI[a]	47.9	47.4	50.1	47.6	47.2	46.0	48.8	47.0	41.2	51.1
By Personnel[b]										
Non-medically trained	6.4	6.1	5.7	7.5	6.2	5.9	7.9	4.9	6.3	6.4
Nurse/Promotor	17.8	24.1	23.4	17.5	9.4	4.2	20.7	15.2	7.8	22.0
Doctor	25.8	14.1	18.5	22.0	39.4	56.2	18.3	32.7	44.6	18.1
Parent/relative	50.0	55.4	52.4	53.1	45.0	33.8	53.1	47.2	41.3	53.6
By Type of Facility[b]										
Public Hospital	2.3	1.4	1.1	2.4	4.7	3.1	1.7	2.9	3.3	1.9
IGSS Hospital	4.1	1.0	3.2	3.1	8.6	8.6	2.9	5.2	11.0	1.3
Private hospital/clinic	10.8	3.5	4.6	8.0	17.2	38.6	6.6	14.8	19.6	7.3
Health post/center	19.3	21.9	23.9	20.7	14.2	8.2	20.5	18.3	15.1	21.1
Community center	3.2	7.1	2.2	1.7	2.2	0.0	4.0	2.4	1.0	4.2
Pharmacy	4.6	3.7	4.4	5.0	6.1	4.0	5.6	3.7	5.1	4.4
At home	52.7	59.3	55.1	56.0	45.4	36.2	55.7	49.8	42.6	56.8
Other	3.0	2.3	5.5	3.1	1.5	1.1	3.1	2.9	2.8	3.1

Source: World Bank calculations using the ENCOVI 2000, *Institutio Nacional de Estadística—Guatemala.* a. % of children < 6 with diarrhea or ARI in the month preceding the interview. b. % of children with diarrhea or ARI visiting different types of health facilities or personnel.

■ **Overall**, a far smaller share of the poor, indigenous and rural residents are treated by medical professionals. Two thirds of those in the poorest quintile do not seek treatment by medical professionals (doctors, nurses or promotores), versus just over one third of those in the top quintile (Table 8.8). Likewise, whereas over half of urban and indigenous residents each seek treatment from medical professionals, only a third of rural and indigenous residents do.

■ **Professional pre-natal care** is likewise far less likely among disadvantaged groups. The type and quality of pre-natal care during pregnancy and delivery are very important factors for the health of mothers and their children. While a fifth of all women did not seek any form of pre-natal care, the share is much higher among the poorest quintiles (about one third) than those at the top of the spectrum (less than one tenth). Likewise, a higher share of indigenous and rural women do not undergo pre-natal visits. Of those who do seek care, poor, indigenous and rural women are far more likely to be seen by midwives, whereas the non-poor, non-indigenous and urban women are more likely to be treated by doctors (Table 8.9).

■ **An extremely high share of women from disadvantaged groups give birth at home.** Over four fifths of women in the poorest quintile give birth at home, compared with 12% of those in the top quintile (Table 8.9). Similarly, over two thirds of rural women and three quarters of indigenous women deliver at home. Delivery in the home is of particular concern for poor women, since they lack the sanitary conditions needed for safe delivery: as discussed in Chapter 9, half of all households in the poorest quintile lack piped water (and the water is not potable even for those with connections), and over a quarter lack any type of sanitation. The lack of such basic utility services is similar for rural and indigenous households. Only 14% of women in the poorest quintile deliver in the presence of a doctor, nurse or promotor; most (71%) are accompanied by a midwife, and the remainder (15%) are not

TABLE 8-8: UTILIZATION OF HEALTH SERVICES BY INDIVIDUALS

| | | By Quintile | | | | | By Ethnicity | | By Area | |
	Total	Q1	Q2	Q3	Q4	Q5	Indigenous	Non-Indigenous	Urban	Rural
By Personnel[b]										
Non-medically trained	4.8	4.5	4.9	6.6	5.4	3.3	5.9	4.1	3.6	5.7
Nurse/Promotor	9.5	16.5	13.9	11.8	7.8	2.3	13.7	6.6	3.6	13.7
Doctor	36.1	13.6	22.6	32.6	39.0	58.1	24.0	44.4	51.8	25.0
Parent/relative	19.2	29.8	23.0	21.0	17.2	11.0	22.8	16.8	14.7	22.5
Self Medication	19.5	17.2	25.0	18.3	21.5	16.8	20.7	18.8	17.8	20.8
Did nothing	10.9	18.4	10.7	9.7	9.1	8.6	12.9	9.4	8.6	12.5
By Type of Facility[b]										
Public Hospital	9.3	8.5	10.8	10.2	11.8	6.8	8.1	9.9	8.8	9.7
IGSS Hospital	6.8	2.2	3.2	5.7	8.2	9.3	3.7	8.4	10.5	3.2
Private hospital/clinic	40.0	12.6	24.8	26.9	39.6	62.5	30.2	45.4	51.5	29.3
Health post/center	22.8	39.9	35.5	34.3	23.2	5.7	29.6	19.1	13.8	31.4
Community center	2.0	5.4	2.1	2.2	1.7	0.9	3.2	1.3	0.8	3.1
Pharmacy	8.0	8.1	9.2	10.3	9.0	5.5	11.5	6.0	5.6	10.2
At home	5.5	8.2	7.1	4.0	2.0	6.9	6.5	4.9	5.2	5.7
Other	5.7	15.1	7.3	6.4	4.4	2.5	7.3	4.8	3.9	7.5

Source: World Bank calculations using the ENCOVI 2000, *Institutio Nacional de Estadística—Guatemala.* a. % of individuals with illness or accidents in the month preceding the interview.

TABLE 8.9: PRENATAL CARE AND TREATMENT DURING DELIVERY, PREGNANT WOMEN

	Total	Q1	Q2	Q3	Q4	Q5	Indigenous	Non-Indigenous	Urban	Rural
			By Quintile				By Ethnicity		By Area	
Prevalence of Diarrhea[a]	31.3	33.8	35.2	30.5	27.8	24.1	35.6	27.5	24.7	34.5
Prenatal Care										
No Prenatal Checks[a]	21.3	34.2	28.0	22.7	10.2	8.8	26.2	17.3	13.3	26.8
By Personnel[b]										
Non-medically trained	2.4	4.4	2.6	1.8	1.3	2.0	4.2	1.1	1.4	3.0
Midwife	33.7	59.7	45.4	36.3	20.3	6.1	49.2	22.7	14.4	46.7
Nurse/Promotor	11.0	15.7	15.6	12.0	8.6	2.5	12.7	9.8	5.4	14.8
Doctor	52.4	19.5	36.2	49.3	69.8	89.1	32.9	66.2	78.4	34.8
Relative	0.6	0.7	0.2	0.6	0.9	0.2	1.0	0.2	0.4	0.7
By Type of Facility[b]										
Public Hospital	12.5	3.9	9.7	15.6	19.2	12.9	6.6	16.6	16.0	10.1
IGSS Hospital	9.3	1.2	4.1	7.4	13.5	20.9	4.3	12.8	18.0	3.5
Private hospital/clinic	17.0	2.0	4.4	8.1	24.0	48.7	9.4	22.3	30.9	7.6
Health post/center	24.3	25.5	31.8	31.6	21.5	9.6	24.2	24.3	19.1	27.8
Pharmacy	0.2	0.0	0.2	0.6	0.0	0.0	0.4	0	0.0	0.3
Midwife's house	13.5	18.7	16.9	17.3	11.0	2.6	17.2	10.8	7.0	17.8
At home	21.8	45.6	31.3	18.4	9.2	4.8	35.8	11.9	7.8	31.2
Other	1.6	3.1	1.5	1.1	1.6	0.6	2.1	1.3	1.4	1.8
Delivery: Treatment and Place										
By Personnel[b]										
Non-medically trained	2.7	4.1	2.5	3.4	2.2	0.9	3.4	2.2	2.4	2.9
Midwife	47.1	70.5	63.1	49.4	29.8	12.3	63.1	34.8	25.0	60.2
Nurse/Promotor	4.5	3.1	4.8	4.5	6.1	3.9	3.4	5.3	4.3	4.6
Doctor	40.1	11.0	21.5	36.6	61.2	83.0	19.9	55.6	67.6	23.8
Relative	5.6	11.3	8.2	6.1	0.7	0.0	10.2	2.1	0.7	8.5
By Type of Facility[b]										
Public Hospital	25.7	9.8	18.3	30.0	41.2	32.1	13.6	35.1	35.4	20.0
IGSS Hospital	7.6	1.3	3.4	4.7	12.7	19.5	3.5	10.8	15.8	2.8
Private hospital/clinic	8.0	0.1	0.7	2.5	11.7	31.4	3.2	11.6	16.9	2.7
Health post/center	3.3	1.5	3.3	4.9	3.4	3.8	1.8	4.5	4.0	3.0
Midwife's house	3.1	3.4	2.9	4.7	2.9	1.2	3.2	3.1	2.3	3.6
At home	51.8	83.5	70.5	52.3	28.2	11.9	74.5	34.2	25.2	67.4
Other	0.5	0.4	0.8	0.9	0.0	0.3	0.2	0.7	0.4	0.6

Source: World Bank calculations using the ENCOVI 2000, *Institutio Nacional de Estadística—Guatemala*. a. % of non-pregnant women who have been pregnant. Pregnant women are excluded to avoid censoring in the data. b. % of women who had prenatal checks.

seen by any medical professional (Table 8.9). Interestingly, women in the poorest quintile are twice as likely to have complications with birth as those in the top quintile, but women in the top quintile are 13 times as likely to have a cesarean sectioned birth as those in the bottom quintile.[24]

24. Some 17% of women in the poorest quintile report complications, as compared with 7% of those in the top quintile; 23% of women in the top quintile had cesarean sections as compared with 1.8% of women in the poorest quintile. Source: World Bank calculations using the ENCOVI 2000, *Instituto Nacional de Estadística—Guatemala*. See GUAPA Technical Paper 5 (Gragnolati and Marini, 2002) for details.

Barriers to Access

Demand-side factors—particularly economic barriers—limit access to health services. As shown in Figure 8.5 above, 83% of households cite demand-side factors as the primary reasons for not seeking treatment when needed.[25] This share is slightly lower among the poorer quintiles (75%), for whom supply-side constraints figure more prominently. Nonetheless, the primary barrier for *all* quintiles is economic: some 60% do not seek treatment because they lack money to pay for health services. Another 6% do not seek treatment because of the costs of transport to health services.

There are **significant variations in the costs of health care in Guatemala.** Guatemalan households allocate an average of 3.7% of total consumption to health, though this share varies significantly between the poor (1.4%) and the non-poor (4.2%). Service costs vary considerably by provider and level of service. For example, out-of-pocket expenditures per visit to public facilities average Q19, with 66% of all households paying nothing for public services. Within the public domain, these expenditures range from Q7 per visit to public health posts (with 74% paying nothing) to Q43 per visit to public hospitals (with 60% paying nothing, including 54% of those in the top quintile). In comparison, out-of-pocket expenditures per visit to private facilities average Q130 (seven times higher than the average cost of public facilities). The average costs of prenatal care and deliveries likewise vary significantly by provider and level of service (Table 8.10), with private providers being much more costly. Although public facilities are quite cheap (and indeed, many pay nothing per visit), costs may still present a significant barrier to access—as identified by households in the ENCOVI survey—if they lack access to public facilities. Hence access is constrained not only by an availability of health services, but also by an availability of *affordable* (public) services for the poor.

Besides costs, cultural factors, such as language, trust, and perceptions of discrimination, may constitute barriers to access to health services, particularly among the indigenous. Indeed, about 3% of indigenous households cite such barriers as the primary reasons for not seeking services when ill, according to the results of the ENCOVI survey. Qualitative research reveals the need for a culturally sensitive approach to health care. For example, a study by Solares (1997) highlights perceptions of discrimination, the "cold world" of the hospital, and miscommunication and confusion of patients (Box 8.1). Indeed, perceptions of discrimination in hospitals were also identified by villagers in the QPES community of M2. Another reason why Guatemalans do not seek "formal" health care is the widespread practice of traditional medicine (Box 8.1). Indeed, the extensive use of midwives for treatment might reflect not only a lack of alternative medical professionals, but also preferences reflecting a better cultural match between midwives and their clients (Box 8.1).

TABLE 8.10: AVERAGE COSTS OF PRENATAL AND DELIVERY CARE, BY TYPE OF FACILITY

Quetzales	Public Hospital	IGSS Hospital	Private Hospital or Clinic	Health Post or Center	Midwife's House	Own House	Other
Prenatal Care	304	168	635	262	130	89	130
Urban	407	183	747	394	252	334	446
Rural	231	87	354	163	102	62	50
Giving Birth	274	500	3,014	1,262	224	105	120
Urban	349	500	3,471	1,927	161	126	n/a
Rural	218	n/a	956	120	250	100	120

World Bank calculations using the ENCOVI 2000, *Instituto Nacional de Estadística—Guatemala*

---

25. These numbers exclude those who were ill but deemed treatment unimportant (sickness not bad enough to require health care). World Bank calculations using the ENCOVI 2000, *Instituto Nacional de Estadística—Guatemala*.

BOX 8.1: HEALTH AND ETHNICITY: THE NEED FOR A CULTURALLY SENSITIVE APPROACH

Cultural Barriers to Health Care

A qualitative study of ethnicity and health conducted by Solares (1997)[a] reveals perceptions of discrimination, fears of hospitals, and patient miscommunication among the indigenous population. In some cases, these fears lead to practices such as reducing pregnancy weight gain to avoid having to go to the hospital to give birth (as highlighted by Solares below):

*Perceptions of discrimination. *"Los indígenas sienten . . . que en el Puesto de Salud y en el Hospital los tratan mal, los reprenden por causas ajenas a ellos como el no poder llegar a una hora prefijada o no entender bien el castellano. . . . Su incomprensión dentro del Puesto de Salud no sólo depende de no poder hablar ni comprender bien una lengua extranjera como es el castellano, sino que se agrava por razón de su analfabetismo tan acentuado en la población indígena. . . ."*

*The cold world of the hospital. *"Cuando sus parientes quedan encerrados y ocultos en la instalación hospitalaria, se les impide saber de ellos y sólo reciben las vagas indicaciones de acudir otro día. . . . Por eso es que las embarazadas hacen lo posible por reducir su peso a fin de que el niño nazca delgado y le evite así a su madre el tener que acudir al hospital por causa de una 'complicación.' El hospital para la parturienta indígena significa el desarraigo absoluto de su vida familiar, de su núcleo doméstico y de su casa que es donde ocurre el alumbramiento, con la compañia de familiares que las apoyan."*

*Miscommunication and confusion of the patient. *"La práctica médica corriente de callar información al paciente, choca profundamente con la manera tradicional del mundo indígena. . . . Por ejemplo, recetan a la gente pero no les indican el funcionamiento ni qué efectos puede causarles. Todo esto produce una gran confusión (. . . agravada en la mayoría de los casos por la incomunicación lingüística), la cual explica hechos como el de las concepciones erróneas de interpretar las vacunas como medios para "curar" enfermedades indistintamente; el padecer posteriormente alguna afección o el sufrir reacciones normales en las vacunas, pero desconocidas para la familia del pequeño paciente."*

Traditional Medicine

Another reason why Guatemalans do not seek "formal" health care is the widespread practice of traditional medicine. Although modern medicine is becoming increasingly dominant, traditional beliefs about sickness and health continue to inform rural Guatemalans' health ideas and choices. For example, as in other rural areas of LAC, the indigenous ethno-medical framework revolves partly around one primary set of oppositions: between hot and cold. Illness is believed to be caused by an imbalance of hot and cold, and treatment is believed to be effective only if the prescribed medicines or foods are the opposite temperatures of the disorder so as to restore the hot-cold balance.[b] Many people use both traditional and modern medicine, which are usually perceived as complementary rather than in conflict with one another.[c] Recent findings suggest that modern medicine is being used more frequently for the treatment of child illness than traditional remedies.[d]

Traditional Health Practitioners

In the absence of—or as an alternative to—formal health facilities, the *comadrona* (midwife), *curandero* (herbalist) and the *ajq'ij* (Mayan priest) offer traditional and culturally acceptable services, often together with SIAS *promotores de salud* (health practitioners).[e,f] The *comadrona* usually treats pregnant women, serves as a gynecologist, and sometimes as a pediatrician. She is typically a woman in her forties, who shares the same language, values and cultural beliefs as her patients. The *curandero* deals with the physical and psychic well-being of society, and is believed to have special abilities that allow him direct contact with superior forces. He normally treats diseases such as eye problems, anger and indigestion, usually with medicinal plants, candles and animal parts. The *ajq'ij* is not only responsible for the health of the village, but also for upholding customs (e.g., the Mayan calendar and celebrations). He is normally an expert in herbs, including those used in rituals and for medical treatment.[f]

Sources: a. Jorge Solares (1997). b. Logan (1973). c. Cosminsky and Scrimshaw (1980). d. Heuveline and Goldman (1998). e. QPES (2002); f. MSPAS, OPS/OMS (2001).

Summary of Key Issues and Priorities

Guatemala has made some progress on health since the Peace Accords, mainly on sectoral reforms. Notably:

- The Peace accords made significant commitments to improving health and health care services;
- Financial management of public health care was deconcentrated under the SIAF program;
- The Government launched the decentralized *Sistema Integrado de Atención de Salud* (SIAS) program and a National Health Plan; and

- Public spending has shifted towards preventive care, which is crucial for treating the health problems faced by the poor.

Nonetheless, significant challenges remain, particularly for improving health outcomes. Notably:

- Key health outcomes—malnutrition, infant mortality, maternal mortality, and morbidity (e.g., diarrhea, ARI)—are not improving as fast as they should, and Guatemala remains among the worst health performers in LAC. Health outcomes are significantly worse among the poor, indigenous and rural residents, suggesting a need for better targeted interventions;
- The extremely high prevalence of malnutrition—and its resistance—is particularly worrisome and should be deemed a top priority for public action;
- A significant share of the population lacks access to affordable health services, particularly the poor and rural and indigenous residents (especially those who lack access to motorable roads); a combination of supply- and demand-side factors appears to be blocking improved access;
- On the supply side, services are fragmented; insurance coverage is minimal; inefficiencies in public funding are generated by use of highly-subsidized public facilities by the few who are insured (virtually exclusively the non-poor); moreover, even when facilities are available, they often lack medicines, doctors or staff;
- Public spending on health has not increased sufficiently and public spending is not well targeted to the poor;
- On the demand side, economic barriers (direct costs of health care) present the main constraint to improved access. Although public health care is highly subsidized, private health care is relatively expensive. As such, in situations in which only private services are available, disadvantaged groups lack access due to economic constraints;
- Cultural barriers further constrain access of the indigenous population to health care; and
- Complements to health care—access to potable (not just piped) water and improved sanitation—are also lacking in their coverage, further exacerbating adverse health outcomes (see Chapter 9).

In light of these challenges, a number of policy recommendations seem appropriate. Specifically:

- Accelerated increases in public spending on health are needed to allow for improved coverage of public health services, with an emphasis on expanding preventive care, reducing and treating infectious and parasitic diseases associated with poverty, and improving the key outcomes of infant and maternal mortality and malnutrition (including information and behavioral change programs);
- Improving knowledge and access to effective family planning methods, especially in rural areas, would result in both a reduction of population growth and an improvement of reproductive and child health indicators;
- Efforts should be made to better target public spending (and possibly behavior-conditioned demand-side programs) so as to make more equitable and efficient use of existing resources; the poverty map could be used as a tool to help target programs and future interventions; focusing on expanding coverage of, and adequate inputs for, rural health posts, community health centers, and traveling SIAS promoters in remote areas would also result in an improved degree of self-targeting due to the disproportionate use of these services by the poor;
- Efforts should be made to promote culturally-sensitive health care practices, including working with traditional community-based health practitioners, recruiting indigenous

health *promotores,* sensitizing hospital staff towards respectful treatment of indigenous patients, and information outreach programs;

- A critical review of existing malnutrition interventions (across agencies, both public and private) should be conducted with a view towards (a) identifying programs that have worked (both in Guatemala and internationally); (b) streamlining and restructuring existing programs to better focus on young children, growth monitoring, information and behavioral change via community-based interventions.

- Specific interventions should be undertaken to reduce malnutrition as a priority area. These include: (a) promotion of proper health, hygiene, and feeding practices; (b) growth monitoring of pregnant women and children under aged two; (c) micronutrient supplementation (particularly for iron); and (d) deworming treatments and oral rehydration therapy. The target population for these schemes should be pre-school children (particularly those under 24 months of age) and mothers (including pregnant and lactating women). To improve the effectiveness and reach of these programs (and avoid having them get "set aside"), these interventions should be integrated into the MSPAS basic health care package and provided at the community level through outreach workers selected by the community but contracted either by NGOs or the MSPAS. This would also allow for the institutionalization of nutrition activities within MSPAS, which would eventually contribute to the much needed rationalization of the myriads of independent, often incompatible, nutrition efforts in Guatemala.

- Demand-side interventions (transfers conditional on behavioral change, growth monitoring, etc.) should be considered. They could be channeled through self-targeted health posts/community centers.

- A full sectoral review should be conducted to examine more closely supply-side issues, including, *inter alia:* (a) an analysis of the institutional capacity of MSPAS; (b) an evaluation of the SIAS system, with an emphasis on identifying ways in which to improve its impact on health outcomes; (c) an assessment of the provision, gaps and duplication of services by the various health care institutions; (d) a full assessment of access—not only of access in terms of the physical availability of services but also in terms of the availability of *affordable* (public) services in rural areas; and (e) an analysis of the adequacy of complementary inputs such as staffing, medicines and equipment;

- The Government should develop a monitoring system for health outcomes, including better and more regular measurement of maternal and child mortality; an analysis should also be undertaken to further examine the determinants of maternal and child mortality so as to better tailor policy recommendations towards improving these outcomes;

- In the medium term, the Government should seek additional steps to improve the efficiency and quality of services offered, such as: (a) introducing a system of referral and counter-referral; (b) implementing a hospital reform program that leads to a more efficient use of existing human and capital resources in public health care facilities (e.g., by introducing incentive schemes such as performance agreements); (c) charging the population covered by IGSS and private insurance for services received in the MSPAS facilities; (d) allowing the non-IGSS population to use IGSS facilities and charging the client rather than MSPAS for their use; and (d) considering contracting out certain services within IGSS and MSPAS to private services (in addition to those contracted to NGOs to expand the coverage of basic health care)

CHAPTER 9

BASIC UTILITY SERVICES AND POVERTY

"Poverty is not having potable water in all the houses."

Mam Villager, M1 (QPES)

This chapter seeks to analyze more deeply the issues pertaining to the coverage of basic services (electricity, water, sanitation, sewerage, telephone), with a view of informing policy and highlighting priorities for poverty reduction. Specifically, the chapter considers the issues of: (a) the benefits of basic services; (b) recent reforms and increases in financing for basic service expansion since the Peace Accords; (c) access and equity in the coverage of basic services; (d) barriers to improved access (supply- vs. demand-side); (e) the time and investments needed to achieve universal coverage; and (f) cost and subsidy issues. It concludes with a review of progress and remaining challenges in the basic services sector for poverty reduction. The chapter draws primarily on an extensive analysis of the ENCOVI 2000.[1]

The Benefits of Basic Services
Modern utility services offer important economic, productivity, and health benefits. Data from the ENCOVI reveal that households that have access to modern utility services reap important advantages:[2]

- First, the cost of modern utility services is often considerably lower than traditional alternatives. The clearest example is that of households without electricity who pay implicit prices of more than US$11 per kilowatt-hour (more than 80 times the price of electricity) to illuminate with candles and wick lamps and power appliances with dry cell batteries.
- Second, access to modern services can substantially enhance the productivity of households and household-based micro-enterprises. Rural households with access to piped water and liquid propane gas for cooking save around six man-hours per week compared with households who must go out to collect water and fuel wood.[3] Furthermore,

---

1. See Foster and Araujo (2002) for a detailed presentation of this analysis.
2. Foster and Araujo (2002).
3. Moreover, the ENCOVI demonstrates clear gender specialization in collection activities, with men and boys accounting for 65% of the labor devoted to the collection of fuel wood, and women and girls accounting for 74% of the labor devoted to the collection of water. See GUAPA Technical Paper 7 (Foster and Araujo, 2002).

micro-enterprises with access to water and electricity are twice as profitable than comparable enterprises without access to these services, and the effect of a cellular telephone on micro-enterprise profitability is even larger.

▇ **Third, some traditional substitutes for modern utility services are associated with adverse health impacts** and may contribute to infant mortality. Although it is difficult to isolate the underlying causality, children from households with access to piped water and adequate sanitation are significantly less likely to suffer from diarrhea and overall physical stunting (malnutrition). These effects would likely be even stronger with improvements in the quality of piped water (e.g., potability).

Sectoral Overview

Reflecting these benefits, the 1996 Peace Accords acknowledged the pivotal importance of modern utility services in the Guatemalan development process and made a commitment to expanding coverage to disadvantaged groups in order to make-up for historic neglect. This commitment was not an empty one and has indeed given rise to very significant and tangible changes in the utilities sectors in Guatemala.

On the one hand, Guatemala took major steps to allow private sector participation and promote the development of competition. Specifically:

▇ The national **telecommunications** operator TELGUA (previously GUATEL) was privatized in 1998, three new cellular licenses were issued, and the local and long distance markets were opened-up to immediate competition as part of one of the most radical liberalization processes in LAC.

▇ The three main **electricity** distribution companies EEGSA, DEORSA, and DEOCSA were also privatized, and the generation market opened up to competition, although the state-owned enterprise INDE continues to hold have of the generation capacity and to control the transmission network.

▇ **Water and sanitation** was the only sector where reform measures did not prove possible. As such, service continues to be provided by municipal utilities in urban areas and community-based organizations in rural areas. The metropolitan region is partly served by the state-owned enterprise EMPAGUA, but small-scale private sector operators also play and important role.

At the same time, the volume of resources channeled towards expanding rural service provision has increased substantially through a variety of new and existing institutional mechanisms. First, the investments made by the three main social funds (FIS, FONAPAZ, and FSDC) in rural electrification, water and sanitation, climbed from US$17 million in the period prior to the Peace Accords (1993–96) to US$152 million in the period since the accords (1997–2001). It is important to note, however, that this increase reflected an overall increase in social fund expenditures, rather than a shift towards infrastructure sectors. Moreover, there is evidence

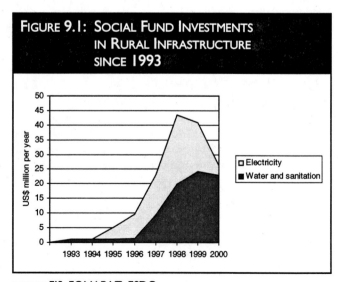

FIGURE 9.1: SOCIAL FUND INVESTMENTS IN RURAL INFRASTRUCTURE SINCE 1993

US$ million per year

□ Electricity
■ Water and sanitation

1993 1994 1995 1996 1997 1998 1999 2000

sources: FIS, FONAPAZ, FSDC

that water, sanitation and electricity investments by the social funds have begun to tail off (Figure 9.1). Second, in an example of a successful attempt to improve both equity and efficiency via market-based reforms, part of the sales proceeds from the privatization process were earmarked to finance rural service expansions. Thus, the US$110 million raised from the sale of the electricity distribution companies will be used to cover one third of the cost of a new Rural Electrification Program, which aims to connect 2,633 communities to the national grid during the period 2000/05. In addition, US$7.5 million raised from spectrum auctions for mobile telephony services were allocated to a special fund (FONDETEL) designed to support the expansion of public telephones in rural areas.

Access and Equity

Current Coverage and Equity
A significant share of Guatemalan households lack access to basic services. Overall, about 70% of Guatemalan households have water[4] and electricity. Almost 90% have some kind of basic sanitation,[5] though fewer than half have sewerage. About 20% subscribe to either a fixed line and/or a cellular telephone service. Around 16% of Guatemalan households do not have access to any kind of modern network utility service. Interestingly, households who only have one utility service (23% in all) are most likely to choose electricity, even when other services (such as piped water) are available in their communities. While overall coverage rates are average for Central America, they lag slightly the average for Latin America and other lower-middle income countries (Table 9.1).

TABLE 9-1: INTERNATIONAL COMPARISONS COVERAGE OF BASIC SERVICES (Percentage of households with access)				
	Electricity	**Piped water⁺**	**Basic sanitation⁺**	**Telephone**
Guatemala	73	69	87	20
El Salvador	80	52	81	20
Nicaragua	69	61	84	16
Panamá	79	86	93	41
LAC Average	n.a.	85	78	n.a.
Lower-middle income average	n.a.	80	54	n.a.

Notes: ⁺Piped water in dwelling or yard. ⁺Includes toilets and latrines. El Salvador and Honduras quintiles based on income aggregate.

Sources: El Salvador (Encuesta de Hogares de Propósitos Múltiples 1997); Guatemala (ENCOVI 2000, Instituto Nacional de Estadística—Guatemala); Honduras (Encuesta Nacional de Ingresos y Gastos de los Hogares, 1999); Nicaragua (LSMS 1998–99); Panama (LSMS 1997); averages for LAC and lower-middle income countries (World Bank 2001b).

Access to modern utility services is highly inequitable. While piped water and electricity are almost universal in urban areas, they reach little more than half of rural households (Table 9.2). Relative to the poorest quintile, the richest quintile of the population are twice as likely to have a water or electricity connection, and four times as likely to have sewerage (Figure 9.2). Just over half of all poor households are connected to water or electricity. Sanitation is more equitable, reaching close to 80% of poor or rural households. Almost no poor, rural, or indigenous households have telephone connections. Households living in the Norte and Peten regions are the most underserved for all services. About one third of rural households lack access to *any* kind of modern utility service. This figure rises to 40% for households in the lowest quintile. These inequities are typical in the Central American region.[6]

---

4. Defined as piped water to property (dwelling or yard). Not necessarily potable.
5. Broadly defined to include latrines, septic tanks, and sewerage.
6. Foster and Araujo (2002).

TABLE 9.2: COVERAGE OF BASIC SERVICES, BY AREA AND QUINTILE
(Percent of households in each group)

	National	By area		By quintile				
		Urban	Rural	1	2	3	4	5
Electricity	73	95	56	39	64	78	90	95
Water	69	88	54	50	62	63	76	92
Sanitation	87	97	79	73	80	88	95	98
Sewerage	38	76	09	06	18	32	54	81
Fixed telephone	15	31	03	0.3	01	03	14	58
Cellular telephone	10	18	03	0.1	01	03	11	34
Community public telephone	64	89	44	37	53	65	79	83
Lack access to any service	16	2	27	39	21	15	6	2

No service = lack of all network services and latrine. Network services = electricity, piped water in dwelling or field, telephone (fixed or cellular), and toilet connected to sewerage.

Source: World Bank calculations using the ENCOVI 2000, Instituto Nacional de Estadística—Guatemala. Quintiles are individual consumption quintiles.

Significant Progress Since the Peace Accords

Guatemala has witnessed significant progress since the Peace Accords, in terms of expanding coverage and reducing inequities. Coverage has accelerated considerably in recent years, reflecting increased levels of investment in the utilities sector (as discussed above). Coverage indices for electricity, water and sanitation increased by about 15 percentage points in the period after the Peace Accords (1997–2000) versus about 10 percentage points for the period preceding the accords (1993–96). Taking into account population growth, the expansion of *new* connections was in general about 50% higher in the years following the Peace Accords.[7] Furthermore, the acceleration of coverage was quite generalized affecting both urban and rural areas, as well as poor and non-poor populations. For telephones, the overall teledensity index rose almost fivefold from the period from 1997–01, largely due to the explosion of cellular telephony.

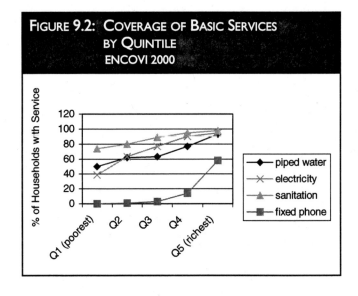

FIGURE 9.2: COVERAGE OF BASIC SERVICES BY QUINTILE ENCOVI 2000

Moreover, disparities in coverage were reduced, with new connections going disproportionately to traditionally disadvantaged groups. This is not surprising, since most other groups were already being served. To detect whether there has been an improvement in the targeting of services towards excluded groups, it is necessary to compare the probability that an unserved household in any particular category would become connected during the period immediately

7. See GUAPA Technical Paper 7 (Foster and Araujo, 2002). These differences were statistically significant.

TABLE 9.3: PROBABILITY THAT AN UNSERVED HOUSEHOLD WAS CONNECTED
(Proportion of unserved households receiving a connection)

	Electricity	Piped water*	Sanitary services*
National			
1993–1996	.19***	.19***	.31***
1997–2000	.36	.34	.55
% change	89%	79%	77%
Urban			
1993–1996	.38***	.31***	.50***
1997–2000	.70	.53	.82
% change	84%	71%	64%
Rural			
1993–1996	.13***	.14***	.22***
1997–2000	.29	.28	.48
% change	123%	100%	118%
Extreme poor			
1993–1996	.06***	.13***	.21***
1997–2000	.17	.26	.37
% change	183%	100%	76%
All Poor			
1993–1996	.13***	.15***	.25***
1997–2000	.28	.29	.44
% change	115%	93%	76%
Non-poor			
1993–1996	.29***	.24***	.38***
1997–2000	.55	.41	.72
% change	90%	71%	89%
Indigenous			
1993–1996	.16***	.18***	.30***
1997–2000	.30	.32	.52
% change	88%	78%	73%
Non-indigenous			
1993–1996	.21***	.19***	.31***
1997–2000	.42	.35	.57
% change	100%	84%	84%

Notes: The null hypothesis of equality of the probability of coverage before and after Peace Accord is rejected at: ***99% level. **95% level, *90% level. *Piped water in dwelling or yard. *Includes toilets and latrines.

Source: World Bank calculations using the ENCOVI 2000, Instituto Nacional de Estadística—Guatemala.

preceding and following the Peace Accords (Table 9.3).[8] At the national level, the probability of an unserved household receiving a connection increased by approximately 80% for electricity, water and sanitation. All types of households experienced a significant increase in the probability of being connected. Importantly, however, disadvantaged groups gained *disproportionately*, increasing their probability of being connected by well over 100% in most cases (Table 9.3). For example, the probability of being connected to electricity increased by 183% for the extreme poor, 115% for the poor, and 90% for the non-poor. This disproportionate gain has not been enough, however, to

---

8. This has the effect of normalizing the number of new connections received against the size of the corresponding unserved population in each group.

compensate for their historic disadvantage. Thus, notwithstanding the large gains, in absolute terms, the probability of being connected to electricity for a poor household (0.28) is still lower than for a non-poor household (0.55).

For telephones, although the richest quintile accounts for about half of new cellular subscriptions (as second telephones), there is evidence that cellular telephones are having a wider social impact. In rural areas, cellular telephones are as common as fixed lines and two-thirds represent first telephones for households that lack a fixed-line service. Moreover, there is considerable anecdotal evidence that cell phones are being used to provide an informal public "pay phone" service for rural communities. Rural access to telecommunications has improved substantially, with the number of rural public telephones increasing by 80% since the Peace Accords. Thus, 50% of rural households now have a public telephone in their community, and 80% live within 6 kilometers (about half an hour) of a public telephone.[9]

Remaining Coverage Gaps

Notwithstanding this momentous progress, a significant coverage gap remains. Well over half a million households are still without electricity and piped water (Table 9.4). Some 200,000 are without any form of sanitation, while about 1.3 million rely on latrines as opposed to conventional sewerage. The households that remain unserved are predominantly rural and predominantly poor.

TABLE 9.4: COVERAGE GAP FOR MODERN UTILITIES
(Number of unserved households)

	Electricity	Piped water*	Basic sanitation*	Improved sanitation	Total no. of households
National	585,933	686,893	288,807	1,353,895	2,191,451
By area					
Urban	45,189	113,235	24,156	224,291	951,654
Rural	540,744	573,658	264,651	1,129,604	1,239,797
By quintile					
1	266,931	220,182	116,340	411,318	438,437
2	155,116	163,797	84,249	349,173	427,908
3	98,428	164,199	52,064	304,708	446,068
4	44,513	104,894	25,003	203,850	442,583
5	20,945	33,821	10,161	84,846	436,455
% unserved—Nat'l	27	31	13	62	n.a.

Notes: *piped water in dwelling or yard; *includes toilets and latrines.

Source: World Bank calculations using the ENCOVI 2000, Instituto Nacional de Estadística–Guatemala. Quintiles are individual consumption quintiles.

Barriers to Improved Access: Supply vs. Demand-Side

The availability of basic infrastructure is not the only constraint to improved access–demand-side factors play an important role too. Disentangling these constraints is crucial for policy decisions. For some households, the service is simply not available in the communities in which they live. This is essentially a supply-side problem that requires increased investment in infrastructure expansion. Other households, however, simply fail to take-up the service even when it is available in the community. This is essentially a demand-side problem that will not be solved by building more infrastructure. The relative importance of demand- and supply-side constraints is revealed by decomposing the coverage deficit into the share of unserved households that:

---

9. For households in the ENCOVI community questionnaire sample.

(a) live in communities where the service is available but don't connect (pure demand-side constraints); (b) would connect if the service were made available (pure supply-side constraints); and (c) that live in communities where the service is not available but would still not connect even if it were (mixed supply- and demand-side constraints). According to this decomposition,[10] between 20–40% of the coverage gap is caused purely by demand-side factors and could be resolved without major investments in infrastructure (Figure 9.3). Between 32–59%

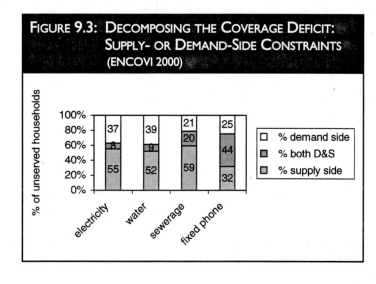

FIGURE 9.3: DECOMPOSING THE COVERAGE DEFICIT: SUPPLY- OR DEMAND-SIDE CONSTRAINTS (ENCOVI 2000)

is caused primarily by supply-side factors. Finally, between 8–44% of the coverage gap, depending on the service, would require both physical expansion and demand-side measures.

Economic factors are important demand-side barriers for lower-income households. Controlling for other factors, household consumption is significantly correlated with the take-up of all modern utilities, except electricity.[11] This finding suggests that connection charges for all services may represent a barrier for lower-income households. Indeed, connection charges for all services except electricity in urban areas represent a significant proportion of the poverty line. Furthermore, the cost of connecting to utility services often goes beyond the direct connection charge. There is often a substantial complementary investment that must be made in adapting the dwelling to the new service. For example, internal wiring for electricity can cost around US$100, while internal plumbing for water and sewerage can cost several hundred dollars. In addition, once connected, households face recurring costs of using the service, as discussed further below. Other significant demand side factors include gender (male headed households less likely to connect), years of education, ethnicity (indigenous less likely to connect to sewerage and telephone), the presence of a household business (more likely to be connected to electricity and telephone), and area (urban more likely to connect to all services).

Achieving Universal Coverage: Time and Costs

It will take more than eight years to reach universal coverage for all services except basic sanitation, given current levels of population growth and actual average annual rates of service expansion (Table 9.5.[12] Only a doubling of current rates of expansion, or a stabilization of population, would permit universal coverage to be reached in the medium term; that is between 3 to 12 years depending on the service.

---

10. Foster and Araujo (2002).

11. This paragraph presents the results of multi-variate probit regressions in which take-up is the dependent variable (for all households that live in communities in which the service is available). See Foster and Araujo (2002) for details.

12. Present average rates of service expansion were around 115,000 new connections for electricity, water, and sanitation. Population growth rates are around 2.6% p.a. See Foster and Araujo (2002). These projections differ from those presented in Chapter 5 as they are based on projections of rates of service expansion that were observed since the Peace Accords, where as those in Chapter 5 are based on average international rates of service expansion (worldwide panel of growth-service elasticities).

TABLE 9.5: HOW FAR AWAY IS UNIVERSAL COVERAGE?
(Anticipated date of universal coverage)

	Present effort levels sustained	Present effort levels doubled
Electricity	2006	2003
Water	2007	2004
Basic sanitation	2003	2002
Improved sanitation	2014	2007

World Bank calculations using the ENCOVI 2000, Instituto Nacional de Estadística—Guatemala.

Based on typical unit costs for service expansion, the total cost of meeting universal coverage across the electricity, water and sanitation services is estimated at US$1.5 billion.[13] The electricity service, owing to its relatively high unit cost, accounts for over 40% of this total expenditure, compared with 24% for piped water. Sanitation would absorb about 32% of these costs, with public telephones accounting for the remainder (about 4%).[14] For water and sewerage services, the costs of universalizing access could be reduced by as much as 40% with a "condominial" approach whereby a single branch from the main network is provided to a whole block ("condominium") of houses, who then make their connections along this common branch instead of providing a separate branch to each household.[15] It is important to note, however, that these estimates assume that supply-side factors account for the full coverage gap. The decomposition of the coverage gap above suggests that this is not the case, and that a significant share of the deficit could be bridged by removing demand-side barriers that prevent households from connecting to existing networks. Overall, it is estimated that this factor could reduce the cost of meeting universal access by as much as 30%, from US$1.5 billion to US$1.0 billion, provided appropriate interventions were instituted.

Costs and Subsidies for Basic Services

Households spend about 10% of their budgets on basic services. Over half of this expenditure goes to energy for cooking and heating, and another quarter covers the costs of lighting and powering appliances. Less than 1% of total consumption is spent on water services. The overall budget share is higher for households in poorer quintiles, though the composition shifts away from cooking fuels towards telecommunications for richer households (Figure 9.4).

In Guatemala, there has been a conscious policy decision to use subsidies to keep water and electricity tariffs artificially low. To some extent, this is understandable, given that providing access to utility services is only ultimately meaningful if these services are available to poor households to use. However, the evidence suggests that the policies have been mistargeted, failing to reach desired outcomes, and that their disadvantages are substantial.

In the *electricity sector*, subsidies via the "social tariff" are not well targeted to the poor. Introduced following the privatization of distribution companies, the objective of the *"tarifa social"* is to keep domestic tariffs for those consuming up to 300 kilowatt-hours per month capped

---

13. Foster and Araujo (2002).

14. In the case of sanitation, two levels of universal service are defined. The first level is universal *basic* sanitation, which basically entails providing latrines to the 288,807 households that currently have no form of sanitation, and would cost less than US$15 million to achieve. The second level is universal *improved* sanitation. This entails providing sewerage to all households in conurbations with greater than 50,000 population (notably the Metropolitan area, Quetzaltenango, and Escuintla), and upgrading all other households to a flush toilet with a septic tank. This is a very much more expensive proposition, accounting for almost a third of the overall expansion costs. See GUAPA Technical Paper 7 (Foster and Araujo, 2002).

15. Foster (2001).

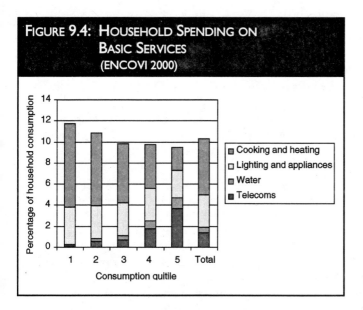

FIGURE 9.4: HOUSEHOLD SPENDING ON BASIC SERVICES (ENCOVI 2000)

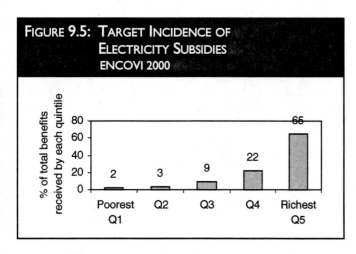

FIGURE 9.5: TARGET INCIDENCE OF ELECTRICITY SUBSIDIES ENCOVI 2000

at a fixed price of US$0.08 per kilowatt-hour.[16] An analysis of the ENCOVI, however, reveals that this costly subsidy has been misguided for several reasons. **First,** the thresholds that have been set for the social tariff are very high in relation to typical residential consumption. The average household consumes 102 kWh per month, with poor households consuming 48 kWh per month on average and non-poor households consuming 128 kWh per month. As a result, virtually all residential customers—rich and poor alike—qualified for the subsidy.[17] **Second,** coverage of the poor is relatively low owing to relatively low connection rates among poorer households. While three quarters of households in the top quintile benefit from the subsidy, only 38% of those in the bottom two quintiles benefit. About 65% of the beneficiaries are non-poor households. **Third,** the subsidy is regressive in terms of its distributional incidence. The richest quintile receives two thirds of total subsidies transferred, as compared with the poorest quintile, which only receives 2% (Figure 9.5).[18] By poverty group, 90% of the benefits accrue to the non-poor. Simulations using ENCOVI data suggest that lowering the threshold from 300 to 100 kWh per month would improve matters somewhat by lowering the number of non-poor beneficiaries. Nonetheless, even with this lower threshold, an estimated 75% of benefits would still accrue to the non-poor.

A more pro-poor policy would be to instead channel these resources towards expanding coverage of electricity to unserved households. As discussed above, households without electricity

---

16. This threshold of eligibility was reduced from 500 kWh to 300 kWh per month in January 2001, leading to an estimated cost savings of US$7.1 million annually. The new law also obliged distributors to finance the subsidy via cross-subsidization across consumer categories (transferring the subsidy from industrial users to households). Prior to these changes, the cost of the subsidy, estimated at US$57 million per year, was met by INDE on the basis of state transfers.

17. An estimated 99% of residential customers qualified for the social tariff under the original threshold of 500 kWh, and 94% still qualify with the recently lowered threshold of 300 kWh. Source: World Bank calculations using the ENCOVI 2000, *Instituto Nacional de Estadística–Guatemala*.

18. These incidence estimates differ slightly from those presented in Chapter 12 because they assessed at the household (rather than per capita) level.

pay some 80 times more per kilowatt hour for traditional fuel sources. From this perspective, it would appear to make much more sense to channel the US$50 million annual cost of the 'tarifa social' towards increasing connections to unserved households. It is estimated that an additional 50,000 new connections each year could be financed in this way. Moreover, given that over 70% of households without electricity belong to the poorest segments of the population, such a policy would be quite well targeted.

In the *water and sanitation* sector, tariffs are well below true economic costs and international parameters of willingness to pay. Households pay bills of less than US$2 per month in Guatemala City, and less than US$1 per month in other urban areas. The underlying tariffs are barely US$0.10 per cubic meter compared with typical costs of around US$0.40 per cubic meter for the Latin American region. In spite of these low tariffs, as many as 30% of households with piped water reported that they did not pay for the service in the last month, compared with only 8% for electricity. As a result, households spend barely 0.5% of their budgets on water and sanitation services, which is a fraction of the 3%-5% World Health Organization guideline for what households are typically willing to pay. Moreover, many households spend three times as much on bottled water as on piped water.

While low water tariffs may seem attractive, they are also associated with poor service quality. There is substantial evidence that the precarious financial position of water utilities is contributing to a very poor quality of service. In fact, piped water in Guatemala is generally not potable. Three quarters of households with piped water feel it necessary to either buy bottled water or perform some kind of self-treatment. It is particularly striking that the practice regular boiling drinking water is equally prevalent among households with and without piped water (some 40% of both groups). Moreover, water service is irregular. Households report that on average they receive only 17 hours of water per day and face 3.6 days per month without water. Such findings were confirmed in the QPES, where informants in most communities complain about non-potable water and irregular service provision.

Summary of Key Issues and Priorities

There has been significant progress in expanding the equitable provision of basic utility services since the signing of the Peace Accords in 1996. Notably,

- Sectoral reforms have improved competition and efficiency;
- The volume of resources channeled towards the expansion of rural service provision has increased substantially through a variety of new and existing institutional mechanisms;
- Overall coverage of basic services has accelerated considerably since 1996; and
- This expansion has been well-targeted, with new connections going disproportionately to traditionally disadvantaged groups.

Nonetheless, important challenges remain. In particular,

- Despite improvements, significant coverage gaps remain;
- Access to modern utility services remains highly inequitable;
- A significant share of those without access to basic services live in communities where the services are present but do not connect due to demand-side barriers, such as the direct costs of connecting to and using services; as such, interventions other than simply supplying the basic infrastructure will be needed;
- Given existing rates of expansion, it will take more than eight years to reach universal coverage for all services except sanitation, and the total cost of meeting universality is estimated at between US$1–1.5 billion;
- Energy subsidies (under the "*tarifa social*") are poorly targeted, benefiting primarily the non-poor; and
- The quality of piped water services is poor (non-potable and irregular).

A number of policy recommendations seem appropriate in light of these challenges. Specifically:

- To maintain and, if possible, increase the current level of resources channeled towards the expansion of modern utility services so as to reach universal coverage within a 10-year horizon.
- To better target service expansion efforts to traditionally disadvantaged groups, in particular, poor, rural and indigenous households (for example, using the poverty map).
- To develop a strategy for removing the barriers that prevent a significant proportion of excluded households from making connections to services even when these are available in their communities.
- To find new financial resources for the FONDETEL rural telephony program and to consider using these to subsidize the extension of cellular networks into commercially marginal areas.
- To reform the 'tarifa social' policy by at least reducing the eligibility threshold to 100 kilowatt-hours per month, and preferably replacing it with a program to fund new connections.
- To allow water tariffs to rise to a level that allows water utilities to become financially sustainable and thereby improve the quality of service that they offer to the public.
- To encourage social funds and other providers to consider measures to improve the quality of water when expanding coverage
- To complement expansion of water and sanitation programs with measures to improve household hygiene practices so as to reap the full health benefits of the service.
- To complement expansion of electricity and telecommunications coverage in rural areas with measures to promote the productive use of these services by micro-enterprises.

CHAPTER 10

TRANSPORT, POVERTY, AND ISOLATION

"During the rainy season, the community is affected because the road is blocked by the mud and the landslides . . . The result is that we can't buy or transport products to the market."

Mam Villager, M2 (QPES)

As an "intermediate good," transport[1] is widely viewed as critical to reducing poverty and promoting growth by providing access to opportunities, markets, and basic services. Transport also empowers people, providing them with physical, social, and political access. Finally, easy access also reduces vulnerability to natural and man-made disasters. This chapter seeks to provide a "poverty-transport" profile that can simultaneously inform strategies to reduce poverty and expand rural access.[2] Specifically, this chapter will examine (a) the correlations between poverty and road access; (b) the issues of road dependability and quality; (c) the correlations between poverty and access to public transport services; and (d) the effects of physical isolation in terms of increased travel times associated with a lack of access to motorable roads. The chapter concludes with a review of key challenges and recommendations for the transport-poverty nexus.[3]

Access to Roads

Relative physical isolation is not uncommon in Guatemala due to a limited road network. As discussed in Chapter 4, the country is not physically united and many villages are fairly isolated, with long-inter-village distances, due to an inadequate road network. The classified road network is approximately 14,000[4] kilometers in length (4,000 km of main and secondary roads that are mostly paved and 10,000 km of unpaved tertiary and rural roads), or 1.2 km per 1,000 people. This compares with Costa Rica—a country that is half the size of Guatemala—which boasts a road network of about 35,600 kilometers, or 11.1 kilometers per 1,000 people.

---

1. Transport in this means "accessibility-providing infrastructure and services," including roads and transport services.

2. A subsequent phase of the work will attempt to quantify the impact of transport infrastructure on service access and poverty.

3. This chapter is largely based on an analysis of the ENCOVI 2000 that was jointly sponsored by the GUAPA Program and the World Bank's transport team. See Puri (2002) for details.

4. The classified road network covers surfaced, gravel, and unsurfaced roads. It does not include dirt roads, tracks or paths—which are the only form of access for numerous villages in Guatemala. This unclassified road network is estimated at 12,000 km. Source: Dirección General de Caminos.

Indeed, access to roads is limited, with a non-poor and urban bias. Some 13% of households in the ENCOVI PSU sample[5] lack access to a **motorable road** (surfaced or unsurfaced) (Table 10.1). This share is higher in rural areas than urban. It also rises with poverty with a higher share of those in the lower quintiles lacking access (Figure 10.1). Regionally, a lack of access to motorable roads is highest in the Region Nor-Occidente and Norte, which are also the regions with the highest rates of poverty (Figure 10.2). This geographic correlation between poverty and road access can also be seen in more detail in Figure 10.3, which overlays the poverty map with the roads map. The patterns for access to **surfaced roads** are similar, but with a larger share lacking access (60% overall, with over 70% of ENCOVI PSU households in the lowest two quintiles lacking access). The apparent correlation between poverty and the road network could be by design. In other words, since roads are not randomly distributed, it is likely that they were placed according to some sort of strategy that likely favored the development of the coffee sector and the *finca* zone, as well as urban areas. Nonetheless, regardless of the direction of causality, the fact remains that the poor are relatively more access-constrained, which limits their opportunities and access to basic services, as discussed below.

Road Quality and Dependability

Road reliability is also a problem. Road closures are common in Guatemala. Indeed, while significant

> ### BOX 10.1: CLASSIFICATION OF ROADS IN THE ENCOVI
>
> ***Type A** roads are surfaced (asphalted or metaled) and accessible to motorized transport (*carretera pavimentada o balustrada*).
>
> ***Type B** roads are gravel or unsurfaced and accessible to motorized transport (*carretera de tierra o terraceria*), though their surface quality varies greatly.
>
> ***Type C** roads are dirt roads or tracks (*caminos de herradura sin balastre*) and are mainly used for beasts of burden or walking.
>
> ***Type D** consists of paths (*veredas*) that are mainly for pedestrians.
>
> ***Motorable roads** consist of Types A and B.

FIGURE 10.1: LACK OF ACCESS TO PAVED AND MOTORABLE (PAVED+UNPAVED) ROADS, BY QUINTILE, ENCOVI 2000

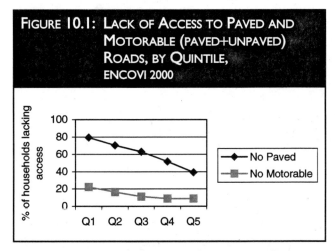

FIGURE 10.2: POVERTY AND ROAD ACCESS, BY REGION ENCOVI 2000

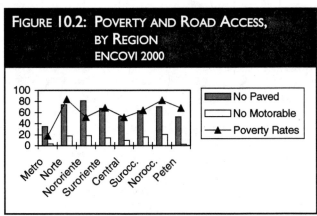

---

5. Road information is only available for households in the ENCOVI sample for which community-level data were collected. Community level data was collected for 481 Primary Sampling Units (PSUs). Due to difficulties in administering the community questionnaire in certain areas (particularly urban areas, where "community" boundaries are less clear), this represents about two-thirds of all households in the ENCOVI household survey (with relatively higher coverage of rural areas). All ENCOVI information presented in this chapter refers to this sub-sample, which, while large, is not statistically representative of the population. See GUAPA Technical Paper 8 (Puri, 2002) for details.

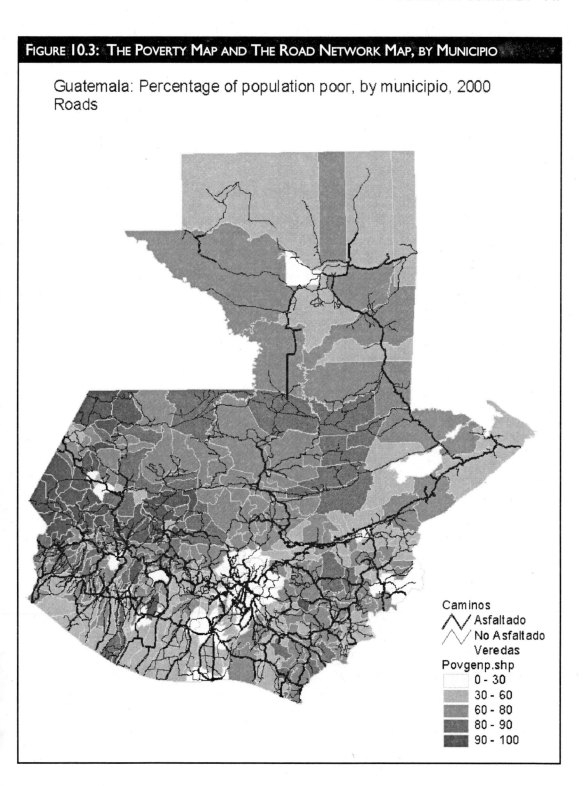

FIGURE 10.3: THE POVERTY MAP AND THE ROAD NETWORK MAP, BY MUNICIPIO

Guatemala: Percentage of population poor, by municipio, 2000
Roads

Caminos
Asfaltado
No Asfaltado
Veredas
Povgenp.shp
0 - 30
30 - 60
60 - 80
80 - 90
90 - 100

TABLE 10.1: ACCESS TO ROADS BY TYPE OF ROAD
(Households for which PSU level information is Available)

	HHs with Access to Road Type/Total HHs (%)					Among those with access to Road Type: Share by Characteristic (%)				
	Type A	Type B	Type C	Type D	No Motorable Roads*	Type A	Type B	Type C	Type D	No Motorable Roads*
All	**39.8**	**69.9**	**37.9**	**62.5**	**13.3**	**100**	**100**	**100**	**100**	**100**
Urban	65.3	58.7	22.3	34.9	10.1	51.1	26.1	18.3	17.4	23.9
Rural	28.3	75	44.9	75	14.7	48.9	73.9	81.7	82.6	76
Poverty Levels										
Non-Poor	52	67.4	32	58.8	8.9	60.4	44.7	39.1	81.1	31
All Poor	29.4	72.1	43	86.1	17	39.6	55.3	60.9	18.9	69
Extremely Poor	20.5	69.4	42.4	86.1	23.4	7.1	13.6	15.3	18.9	24.3
Regions										
Metropolitan	65.2	57.3	22.3	34.3	3.2	33	16.5	11.8	11	4.7
North	25.8	66.3	15	75.1	17.8	6.5	9.5	4	12.1	13
North-East	18.7	77.2	51.2	34.9	18.3	4.3	10.2	12.5	5.2	13.7
South-East	32.6	73.4	69.9	77.8	14.4	7.9	10.2	17.8	12	10.1
Central	47.4	83.6	30	61.5	9.5	12.4	12.5	8.3	10.3	7.4
South-West	37	76.2	38.7	69.3	16.1	22.7	26.7	25	27.1	31
North-West	29.3	61.7	48.2	91.7	20.5	9.6	11.5	16.6	19.1	19.5
Peten	47.7	70	51.1	67	2.3	3.6	3	4.1	3.2	0.5

Quintiles										
First	20.7	70.5	43.5	86.3	22.3	9.2	17.8	20.3	24.4	29.7
Second	29.6	71.7	44.1	77.9	16.4	15.1	20.9	23.7	25.4	25.1
Third	37.1	74.4	40.4	61.3	11.3	18.7	21.4	21.4	19.7	17.3
Fourth	48.3	70.8	33.7	52.5	8.9	26.4	22.1	19.4	18.3	14.4
Fifth	60.7	62.2	28.7	38	8.9	30.6	17.8	15.2	12.2	13.5
Ethnic Groups										
Non-Indigenous	44.5	69.5	41.8	49.7	11.2	62.5	55.7	61.8	44.6	47.2
Indigenous	33.9	70.4	32.9	78.9	15.9	37.5	44.3	38.2	55.4	52.8
Kiche	43.6	71.7	27.7	86.9	4.4	9.8	9.1	6.5	12.4	2.9
Qeqchi	21.3	59.3	13.2	67.6	23	4.5	7.1	2.9	9	13.9
Kaqchikel	43.1	86.6	30.2	69.2	14	9.5	10.8	7	9.7	9.9
Mam	28.9	72.6	41.4	89.7	17.9	6.3	9	9.5	12.5	11.7
Other Indigenous	32.1	61.9	50.2	80	20.5	7.5	8.2	12.3	11.9	14.4

Type A road is surfaced (*Carretera pavimentada o balastrada*); Type B = gravel/unsurfaced (*Carretera de tierra o terraceria*); Type C = dirt roads/tracks (*Carretera de herradura sin balastre*); Type D = paths (*Veredas*). HHs can have access to more than one type of road. A motorable road is a Type A or Type B road. Source: World Bank calculations using ENCOVI 2000, Instituto Nacional de Estadistica, Guatemala

progress has been made over the period from 1994–2000 in the rehabilitation and maintenance of the surfaced road network (such that 75% is in good or fair condition), only 45% of the unsurfaced classified road network is in maintainable condition.[6] Some 28% of households in the ENCOVI sample report road closures. Close to three quarters of these (or 20% of all ENCOVI households) report closures lasting longer than five days. While the differences between urban and rural areas are not significant, road closures are more common in the Norte (34%), Sur-Oriente (48%) and Central (32%) regions. The main causes of road closures according to households in the ENCOVI PSU sample are: flooding and winter (36%) and landslides (28%). There appears to be a slight correlation between road type and dependability, with a larger share of households (32%) without access to motorable roads reporting road closures. These findings are consistent with those in the QPES: several villages (e.g., M2 and KA1) note that heavy rains make their single dirt access roads impassable, completely isolating the villages during the rainy season.

Road closures further constrain access to opportunities and services. The main activities affected by road closures include: school attendance (36% of those reporting closure), work (28%), and market access (11%). The interruptions of access to work and school are reportedly higher in rural areas. Households in the poorest quintile (45%) are more likely to report interruptions in their lack of access to work than those in the richest quintile (12%).

Road quality appears to have improved since the Peace Accords, but with improvements favoring the urban and non-poor populations. Overall, 44% of households in the ENCOVI PSU sample perceive improvements in road quality since 1995, with 16% perceiving worsening conditions. Perceptions are generally more favorable in urban areas (53% perceive improvements in quality) than rural (only 40% perceive improvements). They are much more favorable among non-poor than poor (55% among top quintile vs. 34% among poorest quintile perceive improvements). Finally, there are significant differences by region, with more favorable perceptions in the Metropolitan (53% perceiving improvements) and Sur-Occidente (57%) regions and much less favorable in the Norte (only 28%) and Nor-Occidente (22%) regions. Again, this seems to mimic an apparent historical bias towards urban areas and the *finca* zone, since many of the municipalities in the Sur-Occidente are dominated by plantations.

Public Transport

Access to public transport is limited in Guatemala, with biases towards urban areas and the non-poor. Less than half of the households in the ENCOVI PSU sample report access to public transport. Access is reportedly higher in urban areas than rural and among the non-indigenous than the indigenous (Figure 10.4). There also appears to be a strong correlation between economic status and access to transport services: 66% of those in the top quintile have access compared with only 29% in the poorest quintile. This is important because the poor also generally lack alternative modes of transport (few own vehicles for example). There are significant differences in access by region, with three quarters of those in the Metropolitan region reporting access versus one third in the Norte, Nor-Oriente, Sur-Occidente, and Nor-Occidente regions.

When available, demand for public transport services is high. Among those who report having access to pub-

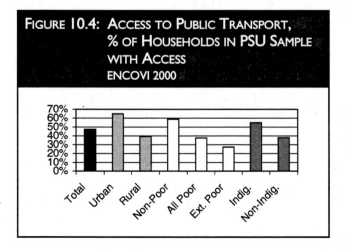

FIGURE 10.4: ACCESS TO PUBLIC TRANSPORT, % OF HOUSEHOLDS IN PSU SAMPLE WITH ACCESS
ENCOVI 2000

---

6. Project Concept Document for the proposed new Rural Roads Project.

lic transport services, 92% report using it every day. While 41% of households in the ENCOVI PSU sample perceive improvements in public transport since 1995, many also report problems with public transport. The main problems cited are insufficient busses (51%), particularly in rural areas (56%). The second main problem cited is the bad condition of busses, particularly in urban areas.

The road network seems to be a constraining factor for expanding public transport services. There is a significant correlation between the motorable road network and availability of public transport. While half of all households in the ENCOVI PSU sample with motorable road access report access to public transport services, only a quarter of those without access to motorable roads have access to public transport services. This effect is particularly strong in rural areas.

The Effects of Isolation: Limited Access to Services and Opportunities

Access to motorable roads confers significant benefits in terms of reduced travel times to key services and opportunities. Travel times were compared for those households with and without access to motorable roads using data from the ENCOVI PSU sample. The results suggest rather striking benefits of road access:

- **Health Services.** Travel times to health services are significantly longer for those without motorable roads access (Figure 10.5). Physical isolation is particularly serious in rural areas and among the poor: for these populations, a lack of motorable roads puts health services just out of reach according to the WHO definition of access (travel times of less than an hour). These findings are consistent with the QPES: two villages (KA1 and M2) note that inadequate access roads constrain their access health services, particularly when the rains make their single dirt access roads impassable. In fact, when discussing vulnerability, the villagers of KA1 specifically identify "giving birth" as a risk because laboring mothers cannot access health services due to inadequate road access, par-

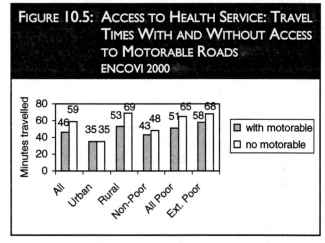

FIGURE 10.5: ACCESS TO HEALTH SERVICE: TRAVEL TIMES WITH AND WITHOUT ACCESS TO MOTORABLE ROADS
ENCOVI 2000

ticularly in the rainy season. Interestingly, road access has no effect on urban travel times, likely reflecting the much stronger coverage of urban populations by health services (Figure 10.5).

- **Access to Opportunities (Markets, Commercial Inputs).** In rural areas, road access also appears to be a significant determinant of access to opportunities, such as markets and other commercial inputs (Figure 10.6). Travel times to markets and post offices, for example, are

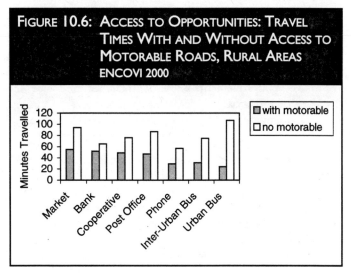

FIGURE 10.6: ACCESS TO OPPORTUNITIES: TRAVEL TIMES WITH AND WITHOUT ACCESS TO MOTORABLE ROADS, RURAL AREAS
ENCOVI 2000

almost doubled for rural households in the ENCOVI PSU sample without access to motorable roads. Access to inter-urban and urban bus stops is significantly constrained by a lack of motorable roads. Travel times are also longer for urban households without access to motorable roads (compared to those with access), but still shorter than those in rural areas (even with motorable roads), reflecting a much more extensive network of markets and commercial services in Guatemala's cities. Moreover, as discussed in Chapter 6, households located in smaller municipalities (with less infrastructure including roads) have higher chances of being poor and fewer employment opportunities than those living in larger municipalities (with more extensive infrastructure networks).

■ **Access to Institutions.** Likewise, road access seems to play an important role in determining access to institutions in rural areas. Access to police and municipal services, for example, is significantly constrained by limited road access (Figure 10.7). Church access is the least dependent on the road network, reflecting the extensive presence of churches in rural areas. This finding is consistent with the QPES, in which all but one of the ten communities report at least one church, with most having more than one (and one village, KI1, boasting 17 churches).

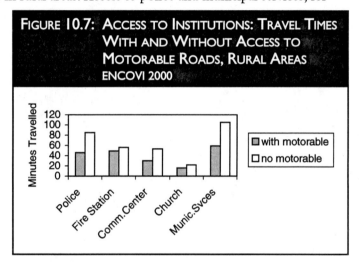

FIGURE 10.7: ACCESS TO INSTITUTIONS: TRAVEL TIMES WITH AND WITHOUT ACCESS TO MOTORABLE ROADS, RURAL AREAS ENCOVI 2000

Summary of Key Issues and Priorities

Although households do report improvements in the road network and public transport, important challenges remain to extend this infrastructure to the poor, particularly in rural areas. In particular:

■ Rural residents and the poor are relatively more isolated. There is a significant inverse correlation between access to the motorable road network and poverty;

■ Year-round access is also crucial, with road closures from rains and landslides further cutting off access to opportunities and services;

■ The poor also lack access to public transportation, which appears to be correlated with a lack of adequate road networks, particularly in rural areas;

■ Road improvements implemented since the Peace Accords appear to have favored the non-poor and urban residents; and

■ Inadequate road access significantly constrains the access of the poor and rural residents to health services, opportunities, and institutions, further exacerbating their isolation.

In light of these challenges, policymakers should seek to improve the targeting of future transport investments. First, a shift in focus towards rural roads is needed. Second, while decisions on future transport investments (improvements, rehabilitation, and new roads) clearly must take into account economic calculations (population density, economic returns), equity concerns should be given more weight than has been done in the past. The poverty map, combined with the roads map and other information on economic activity and service access, should be used by policy makers to determine funding allocations and project location decisions so as to better favor the poor.

PART 3

KEY CHALLENGE:
REDUCING VULNERABILITY

"As for the earthquake (of 1976), it affected the families because the majority of houses were destroyed. Most had to build shelters between the fields and in the road. . . . Many still haven't repaired their houses."

Kaqchiqel villagers in KA1 (QPES)

The limited assets of the poor (and the near-poor)—discussed in previous chapters—also makes them particularly vulnerable to the impact of adverse shocks as they lack the means to be able to cope with them. With a wave of recent shocks in Guatemala (Hurricane Mitch in 1998, the recent coffee crisis, droughts and recent deaths from extreme acute malnutrition), the issue of vulnerability has taken center stage in policy discussions.

This section of the report brings the "vulnerability lens" to the traditionally static, asset-based poverty analysis. It thus shifts the emphasis from a passive or reactive approach (given poverty, what can be done to reduce it?), to a dynamic or proactive approach (given vulnerability, poverty and risks, what can be done to get help the current poor escape from poverty and reduce the likelihood that others will fall into poverty?). It also helps further characterize the nature of poverty in Guatemala: (a) is it more chronic, with a mass of people statically living in poverty and transmitting it across generations? or (b) is it more transient, with many moving in and out of poverty? or (c) is it a specific set of sub-groups that are chronically poor and vulnerable due to specific features or circumstances? The implications of each of these scenarios for policy and targeting are clearly quite different.

Chapter 11 provides an operational assessment of vulnerability, while Chapter 12 reviews existing social protection and social risk management mechanisms to assess their adequacy and offer insights into ways in which to strengthen them.

VULNERABILITY AND VULNERABLE GROUPS

T his chapter presents the findings of an operational assessment of vulnerability. Vulnerability comes from the notion that certain groups in society are more vulnerable to shocks that threaten their livelihood and/or survival. Other groups are so vulnerable that they live in a chronic state of impoverishment where their livelihood remains a constant state of risk due to certain structural features (structurally or chronically vulnerable groups). The concept of vulnerability as used here has two elements: (a) a person or household's resilience to a given shock, which is largely based on the portfolio of assets at their disposition (the higher the resilience, the lower the vulnerability); and (b) the severity of the impact of the shock (the more severe the impact, the higher the vulnerability). The sources of risk may be natural (for example, hurricanes) or the result of human activity (for example, job loss or conflicts). By identifying the sources of vulnerability, and—in a broad sense—the nature of poverty and vulnerability in Guatemala, this chapter seeks to deepen our understanding of the dynamic nature of poverty, with a view towards informing policy and highlighting priorities for poverty reduction *and* prevention.

Vulnerability is analyzed using a combination of quantitative and qualitative data, as well as administrative information on shocks in Guatemala (for example, mappings of natural disasters). The primary quantitative data source is the ENCOVI 2000, which included a risks and shocks module in both its household and community questionnaires. The household module covers shocks that occurred during the past 12 months, examining (a) whether the shocks triggered a loss in consumption, income or wealth; (b) the main coping strategies used to compensate for these losses; (c) whether the households were able to compensate or resolve the welfare loss; and (d) the estimated time until successful resolution of the situation. Similar information was collected via focus group discussions at the survey cluster level (primary sampling units, PSUs) in the ENCOVI community questionnaire but using a five-year time horizon (rather than 12 months). Although panel data would better facilitate the analysis of the dynamic concept of vulnerability, such data are not available. Instead, these retrospective modules provide a unique opportunity to analyze vulnerability using available cross-section data. Qualitative information primarily comes from the risks and shocks module of the 10 village QPES study. Detailed results and methodological considerations are discussed in GUAPA Technical Paper 9 (Tesliuc, 2002).

This chapter is divided into two sections. The first analyzes shocks as a source of vulnerability in Guatemala, painting a portrait of shocks in the year 2000, their occurrence, severity, duration, distribution by poverty group, and estimated impact. The main coping strategies used by Guatemalan households and communities are also examined. Finally, the first section postulates likely future sources of vulnerability and their potential impact, building on the impacts revealed for the year 2000. The second section examines vulnerable groups in Guatemala in two ways. First, it analyzes the chronic or transient nature of poverty and vulnerability in Guatemala. Second, it broadens the concept of vulnerability beyond the income and consumption sphere to look at groups that are structurally vulnerable due to other dimensions (e.g., malnutrition or education) over the life cycle. Finally, the chapter concludes with a review of key issues and priorities.

Shocks as a Source of Vulnerability in Guatemala

This section seeks to describe the sources of vulnerability in Guatemala by (a) analyzing the characteristics of shocks that affected the country in recent years (particularly in 2000, the year the ENCOVI data were collected); (b) reviewing the mitigation and coping strategies used by households when faced with these shocks; and (c) estimating the potential impact of these shocks on welfare, poverty and inequality.

Shock Characteristics: Frequency and Correlation Structure

Guatemala was largely spared any major "macro" shocks in the year 2000. Macroeconomic indicators were stable, with modest growth (3.3%), low inflation (6% p.a.), and negligible unemployment (1.8%). Indeed, a recent regional World Bank study classifies Guatemala as a low macroeconomic risk country.[1] No massive natural disasters hit the country that year, the latest major disasters were Hurricane Mitch in 1998 and earthquakes in previous years (particularly the 1976 earthquake).

Nonetheless, Guatemalan households reported a high incidence of shocks in 2000. Respondents in the QPES recalled all types of shocks: natural, health, economic, social, life-cycle related, political and environmental. Over half (53%) of households reported one or more shocks in the ENCOVI 2000.[2] A quarter (23%) reported natural shocks, 17% cited man-made (e.g., economic) shocks, and 13% reported having experienced both types.[3] The most common types of shocks are agricultural-related: pest infestations and harvest losses, (Figure 11.1). Other shocks, such as a "fall in income," accident of the breadwinner, job loss, drought, worsened terms-of-trade, tempest, criminal offense, or floods are reported by 2–10% of the population. Not all reported shocks resulted in material losses, which can be interpreted as the result of the households' ability to entirely mitigate the impact of the shock or as "false" complaints. Some shocks without serious material losses could have impacted other dimensions of household well-being, such as social or psychological effects, that were not captured in the ENCOVI (but nonetheless reported in the QPES, Table 11.1). Such could be the case, for example, for the death of household members other than the main breadwinner, land or family disputes, or public protests.

Most households experienced multiple shocks. The majority of households reporting shocks in 2000 were hit by more than one shock. A quarter reported having experienced two shocks that year, and another quarter reported three or more shocks. The incidence of multiple shocks is similar for the (ex-post) poor and non-poor. The large share of households reporting multiple shocks signals accumulated vulnerabilities as a possible cause of poverty.

---

1. de Ferranti, Perry, Gill, and Servén (2000).

2. Gaviria (2001) reports that in the first semester of 2000, 36% of urban Guatemalans reported income losses and 26% reported falling consumption.

3. These estimates omit inflation, which was mentioned by 68% of households as a shock. Nonetheless, inflation was quite low in 2000 (6% p.a., falling from 11% in 1996) and none of the respondents in the QPES reported inflation as a shock. It is believed that ENCOVI respondents were simply indicating a general complaint about the level of prices (the cost of living), as they did in their perceptions of poverty and welfare responses.

Consistent with the absence of any major macro shock, the analysis reveals that all reported shocks were localized (idiosyncratic). A variance decomposition test found that location alone explains less than 25% of shocks that were classified a-priori as covariate. The shocks with higher degree of covariance at the local level were harvest losses and income losses.

Shocks tend to hit in bunches. There is strong empirical evidence about the effect of shock-bunching on household welfare. The impact of a shock is harder if the affected household was hit by other shocks as well. A factor analysis revealed the following major types of bunched shocks: (a) agricultural (drought, pests, harvest or terms-of-trade losses); (b) idiosyncratic economic shocks (job loss, bankruptcy, accident or death of the breadwinner, lost remittances); (c) social / violence (family or land disputes, criminal offense); (d) covariate economic shocks (enterprise closure; mass lay-offs); and (e) natural (earthquake, floods, tempests, hurricanes, landslides, or forest fires).

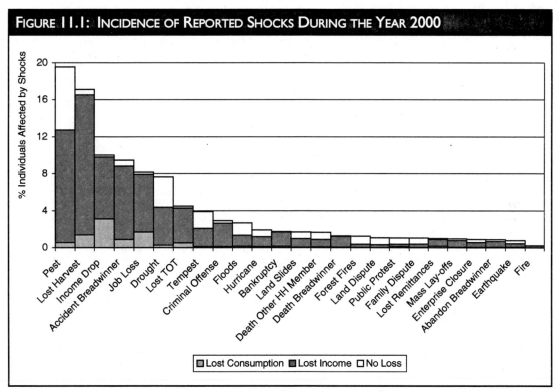

FIGURE 11.1: INCIDENCE OF REPORTED SHOCKS DURING THE YEAR 2000

World Bank calculations using the ENCOVI 2000, *Instituto Nacional de Estadísticas—Guatemala*

Shocks are difficult to predict. A comparison of the information on the incidence of reported shocks from the ENCOVI, the QPES, and administrative and secondary sources reveals that there are important changes in the shock profile over time. The evidence suggests sizeable differences in the incidence of shocks when different reporting periods are used. For example, while no one was affected by a hurricane in 2000, 45% report hurricanes over the past five years. To some extent, this reflects the rare nature of certain shocks (such as hurricanes, earthquakes)—although these shocks can have catastrophic impacts. An implication of this finding is that the cross-sectional incidence of shocks in 2000 is a poor predictor of the future distribution of shocks. It does not allow us to predict how many shocks of specific types will hit the country next year. Nonetheless, while the profile of shocks does not allow us to predict which types of shocks will hit in the future, it does shed light on the likely impact of various types of shocks, as discussed below.

Natural shocks are an exception. Exposure to some natural shocks does seem to be largely determined by location and geographic factors. Administrative maps of vulnerability to drought, seismic activities, hurricanes, storms or tempests, frosts, and landslides are highly consistent with the results reported in the ENCOVI 2000. For example, both the flood maps prepared by the Ministry of Agriculture and the FAO, and the data from the ENCOVI, classify the Nororiente Region as a high risk area and the Nor-Occidente Region as a low risk area. As such, vulnerability maps are useful instruments for risk management planning. They can be even more powerful in targeting assistance to those less able to cope with such shocks when combined with poverty maps. Guatemala has experience in collecting information on areas with high vulnerability to natural disasters and some institutional mechanisms to implement disaster-relief programs (Box 11.1). However, these mechanisms face implementation problems (for example. inadequate financing and human resources to respond in a timely manner) and actual interventions have mainly focused on ex-post coping rather than risk mitigation or prevention.

> **BOX 11-1: DISASTER MANAGEMENT PROGRAMS**
>
> The *Coordinadora Nacional para la Reducción de Desastres* (CONRED) is a disaster management program (early-warning and early-response) employing about 1,300 people and providing training to communities exposed to natural risks and special housing arrangements to reduce vulnerability to earthquakes. The initiative relies primarily on foreign funding (90%). The budget for CONRED is quite small (about Q130 mn, or 0.09% of GDP). The Ministry of Health (MSPAS) also has a Unidad Nacional de Prevención de Desastres.

The Effects of Shocks: Multi-Dimensionality, Severity, Duration

The effects of shocks are multi-dimensional. Respondents in the QPES identified a wide range of impacts of shocks (Table 11.1). In addition to economic effects, such as wealth and income, reported impacts include: (a) psychological, such as the demoralizing impacts of job loss, the traumatic impacts of violence (fear, post-traumatic stress syndrome or *susto*); (b) social (destroying trust and social capital within villages); (c) damage or destruction of community assets (loss of road access, school destroyed, water tank damaged); and (e) impacts on health (death, illness) and education (children can't attend school). In the ENCOVI, covariant shocks tend to be reported more often even if they do not trigger income or wealth losses (perhaps because they resulted in other non-economic impacts). Idiosyncratic shocks are almost always associated with income or wealth losses. Social shocks (for example, violence, unrest) are less likely to cause income or wealth losses (but clearly have other psychological and social impacts, as found in the ENCOVI). Some shocks, like earthquakes, fire, or hurricanes, mainly affect household wealth and community assets. Other natural shocks primarily affect income.

The duration of impact varies by type of shock. In the QPES, which did not restrict respondents to a particular reference period, several villages note long-lasting effects of shocks. For example, many villages report that families still live in homes that were badly damaged by the Earthquake of 1976 (some 25 years later). The shock simply shifted these households from an already poor level of living conditions to an even worse state, with no resolution. Hurricane Mitch also seemed to have catastrophic consequences on some villages, completely wiping out the main productive base of the villages (see Box 11.2). The social and psychological impacts of the conflict of the 1980s also clearly have had lasting effects, according to respondents in the QPES. The ENCOVI 2000 suggests a broad diversity by type of shock in terms of the share of households that were able to resolve the shocks by the time of the interview. Most households were, in fact, able to resolve the shocks and restore their (economic) welfare within 12 months. For example, close to 70% of households reporting fire were able to resolve their situation within a year. The duration of impact seems longer among more frequent shocks, however: less than 20% of households were able to restore their welfare within a year when faced with a worsening terms-of-trade, income (earnings) losses, enterprise closure, public protest, criminal offense, or bankruptcy. Only a third of those

TABLE 11.1: SHOCKS REPORTED IN THE QPES: TYPES OF SHOCKS AND IMPACTS

Types of Shocks	# of Villages Reporting Shock (out of 10)	Types of Impacts Cited					
		ECON WEALTH	ECON INCOME	PSYCH. SOCIAL	COMM. ASSETS	HEALTH	EDUC.
Natural							
Earthquakes (1976, 86)	7	X		X	X	X	
Tremors	1			X			
Hurricane (1998, 2000)	5	X	X		X	X	
Flooding	2	X	X		X		
Landslides	1				X		
Tornado	1				X		
Freezing/frost	2		X				
Forest Fire	1				X		
Drought	2		X				
Crop Loss	3		X				
Man-Made							
Violence of 1980s	3	X	X	X		X	X
Debt/Collective Debt	2	X					
Land conflict^a	1	X		X	X		
Conflict in Community^a	1			X	X		
Job loss	4		X	X			
Domestic Violence	3			X			
Crime and Violence	2			X			
Terms-of-Trade losses	1		X	X			
Abandonment from migration	1		X	X			
Health							
Cholera, dengue epidemic	2					X	
Birth (maternal mortality)	3					X	
Sickness	7		X			X	
Automobile accidents	1	X				X	
Death	5					X	

Source: QPES. PSYCH = psychological (fear, *susto*); COMM = community assets, such as damaged water tank, road blocked, etc. ECON = economic. EDUC = educational (kids couldn't attend school due to violence). a. Many other communities identified these conflicts as occurring in their villages (land, religious), but only a few identified them as shocks.

reporting pest infestation, harvest losses, lost remittances, or job loss were able to overcome the shock within a year.

Moreover, not all income or wealth losses result in a reduction in consumption. Most households were able to smooth their consumption even when faced with shocks. In fact, just over a quarter of all shocks that resulted in income or asset losses forced households to cut their consumption as a way of coping with the shock. In the majority of cases, households were able to mitigate the effects of shocks or use coping strategies other than reducing consumption, as discussed in more detail below. The shocks with harsher impacts on household consumption include economic

---

BOX 11.2: CATASTROPHIC CONSEQUENCES OF HURRICANE MITCH: THE CASE OF L1 (QPES)

The Ladino village of L1, located in the Nororiente Region of the country has faced a drastic worsening of living conditions since Hurricane Mitch struck in 1998. Prior to the hurricane, the main source of income was agriculture, with a somewhat diverse range of production: lemons, papaya, tobacco, melons, eggplant, palms for raw material from artisan work, corn for subsistence, and livestock. Hurricane Mitch severely damaged the land, however, rendering it largely infertile and covered with rocks (the flooding basically washed away the productive topsoil and dumped rocks all over the fields). It also destroyed livestock animals and farm implements. Now most have to search for day labor jobs elsewhere, with some 400 (half the village population) migrating to the capital or the US and leaving their families behind.

Moreover, despite having certain community assets, such as electricity and water, the hurricane clearly exposed vulnerabilities in the asset base of the village, which lacks proper drainage and contamination, as well as health services. The villagers blame an ensuing dengue epidemic on Mitch, as a result of stagnant waters, which generated an infestation of mosquitos. The effects of this epidemic were exacerbated by the lack of health services in the village.

---

shocks that most often force households to reduce their income streams: falling earnings (32%), job loss (21%), lost remittances (19%), and worsening terms-of-trade (12%). Somewhat surprisingly, public protests are also associated with reduced consumption (27%).

In terms of severity, economic shocks had the highest negative impact on household income, consumption and wealth. Using data from the ENCOVI, shocks were classified by the severity of their impact on income or wealth by creating an index equal to the mean rank of three variables:[4] (a) the percentage of households that lost income or wealth given the shock; (b) the share of households that reported reduced consumption as a main coping strategy; and (c) the proportion of households that did not resolve the shock by the time of the interview (Table 11.2). According to this index, economic shocks—including job loss, lost remittances, bankruptcy, worsened terms-of-trade, a fall in income, or inflation—seem to have the highest impact. Using this index, it also appears that there is a positive correlation between shock frequency and severity, with frequent shocks, such as harvest or income losses, having a severe negative impact on household income or wealth. This ranking of the severity of shocks, however, is likely to hold only for the current distribution of shocks, as the ENCOVI was conducted during a year in which no large catastrophic disasters (such as hurricanes or earthquakes) occurred.

Shocks for the Rich and Shocks for the Poor?

The poor are more exposed to natural shocks. Consistent with international experience, the poor are more likely to be hit by natural shocks (Table 11.3), probably reflecting their dependence on agriculture as a source of living and their geographic location (more likely to live in marginal areas). The non-poor are more often the victims of economic shocks. This relationship holds in multi-variate regressions controlling for the impact of shocks on welfare. The probability of experiencing a welfare loss following harvest losses, droughts, pest infestation or worsening terms-of-trade drops significantly with higher household wealth, after controlling for other potential determinants. The reverse is true for economic shocks, such as job loss, bankruptcy, and accidents of the main breadwinner.

The poor have lower resilience than the rich. The probability of restoring incomes to levels prevailing before the occurrence of shocks rises with income. Some 88% of the extreme poor and 86% of the poor suffered losses in response to shocks, compared with 83% of the non-poor. This is particularly notable for natural shocks: while half of those in the top quintile that experienced natural shocks suffered resulting welfare losses, two thirds of those in the bottom quintile did (Table 11.3).

---

4. The ENCOVI did not collect information on the magnitude of income or consumption losses due to shocks. As such, this analysis combines the information on the shares of households that lost income, wealth or consumption and the share that did not resolve the shock within a year, as a way to rank the severity of shock impact.

TABLE 11.2: RANKING THE SEVERITY OF SHOCKS	Lost Income	Reduced Cons.	Shock Not Overcome	Mean Rank	Median Rank
Low Impact					
Forest_Fires	33	3	60	4	3
Land_Dispute	31	0	75	7	1.5
Land_Slides	63	4	57	7	6
Drought	57	6	59	8	8
Family_Dispute	39	7	66	9	10
Death_Other_HH_Member	57	9	50	9	7
Moderate-Low Impact					
Pest	65	4	68	9	11
Earthquake	61	9	46	9	9
Fire	100	0	31	10	1.5
Tempest	55	6	72	10	8
Floods	52	10	54	10	5
Hurricane	66	11	53	12	13
Moderate-High Impact					
Criminal_Offense	90	5	80	14	16
Public_Protest	38	27	80	15	18
Death_Breadwinner	97	5	72	15	16
Accident_Breadwinner	94	10	65	15	18
Lost_Harvest	97	8	69	16	14
Abandon_Breadwinner	77	7	86	16	14
Enterprise_Closure	65	7	86	16	13
Mass_Lay_offs	82	7	85	16	15
High Impact					
Lost_Remittances	92	19	70	18	17
Job_Loss	97	21	69	20	23
Bankruptcy	98	9	82	20	20
Lost_TOT	96	12	86	22	21
Income_Drop	98	32	83	24	25
Inflation	96	46	88	24	26

Source: World Bank calculations using the ENCOVI 2000, *Instituto Nacional de Estadísticas—Guatemala*

Main Coping Strategies

Faced with shocks, Guatemalan households rely on their own assets as their main coping strategy; few receive public assistance. For the majority of shocks, the ENCOVI reveals that the main coping strategies include reducing consumption or self-help (supplying more labor, selling or mortgaging assets, drawing down savings), as shown in Table 11.4. Few households report receiving Government or NGO/donor assistance (Table 11.4). Informal coping mechanisms ("social capital"), such as borrowing or receiving help from friends, relatives or neighbors, were the primary coping strategy in instances of family disputes, accidents of the bread-winner, or death of other members of the household. Formal insurance (market-based mechanisms such as credit and private insurance) were most common for insurable risks, mitigating the risks of fire, earthquakes, hurricanes, or land slides. Consumption losses were the main "coping strategy" used in the face of falling household incomes (earnings) and public protests. These findings are very consistent with the findings of the QPES, where self-help and collective (community) action were the prime coping strategies, with little evidence of government or formal assistance (Table 11.5).

TABLE 11.3: SHOCKS FOR THE RICH AND POOR?

% of households	Total	Wealth Quintiles[5]				
		Q1 poorest	Q2	Q3	Q4	Q5 richest
Reported Shocks						
Natural	28.7	35.4	28.2	32.0	26.7	21.2
Economic	32.8	32.8	31.5	34.7	33.0	31.8
Social	5.7	2.2	3.1	6.4	7.1	9.8
Life-Cycle	12.4	10.8	12.4	11.8	14.2	12.7
Shocks that Reduced Welfare[a]						
Natural	18.6	23.0	21.2	22.2	15.9	10.6
Economic	31.7	32.1	30.8	33.6	31.7	30.2
Social	3.7	1.0	1.8	5.5	4.6	5.8
Life-Cycle	11.0	9.8	11.4	11.0	12.0	11.0

Source: World Bank calculations using the ENCOVI 2000, *Instituto Nacional de Estadística—Guatemala.* Natural shocks include: earthquake, drought, floods, tempests, hurricanes, pests, land slides, fire, forest fire; Economic shocks include: enterprise closure, mass lay-offs, job loss, income losses, bankruptcy, lost remittances, worsened terms-of-trade, lost harvest; Social shocks include: public protests, criminal offense, land disputes, family disputes; Life-cycle shocks include: accident of the breadwinner, death of breadwinner or other, abandonment of breadwinner.
a. Income or wealth.

TABLE 11.4: MAIN COPING STRATEGIES, BY WEALTH QUINTILES

% of households reporting shocks	Total	Wealth Quintiles				
		Q1 poorest	Q2	Q3	Q4	Q5 richest
Self-Help	35.3	39.4	39.2	31.8	33.6	33.1
Informal/Social Capital	7.4	11.0	8.1	7.4	5.8	5.1
Private Insurance/Credit	12.6	7.7	14.4	13.9	14.7	11.9
Government Assistance	0.2	0.4	0.0	0.2	0.0	0.3
NGO/Int'l Assistance	0.5	0.6	0.5	0.7	0.0	0.5
Reduced Consumption	44.0	40.9	37.7	46.1	46.0	49.0
Total	100.0	100.0	100.0	100.0	100.0	100.0

Source: World Bank calculations using the ENCOVI 2000, *Instituto Nacional de Estadística—Guatemala.*

The poor are less equipped than the rich to fight shocks. The poorest quintiles were far more likely to rely on themselves (self-help) or use informal, social capital networks to resolve shocks than the better off (Table 11.4). In contrast, the wealthier quintiles were more likely to rely on private insurance or credit to resolve their situations. Indeed, a multinomial model contrasting three coping strategies (market-based and informal coping versus self-help) reveals that for all shocks, the probability of choosing market-based strategies over self-help increases with household wealth and education of the household head. Interestingly, informal coping mechanisms ("social capital" networks) are more often used by female-headed households and the probability of using market-based coping mechanisms is lower for indigenous people (*ceteris paribus*).

---

5. Wealth quintiles are used to circumvent the circularity of being poorer and being affected by a shock, households were ranked from poorest to richest using a wealth index instead of observed consumption. As suggested by Filmer and Pritchett (1998), this factor is a latent variable that captures the long-term socio-economic status of the household. This measure of wealth correlates strongly with (log) household consumption (Pearson coefficient = 0.77), as well as other indicators of well-being such as education and health status.

TABLE 11.5: MAIN COPING STRATEGIES AND FORMAL ASSISTANCE IN 10 RURAL VILLAGES
(for main collective shocks, QPES)

| Community | Shock Description | Main Coping Strategy/Response | | Any Formal Assistance? |
		Type	Description	
KA1	Earthquake 1976	SELF COLLECTIVE	Tried to rebuild homes, mill Using mill at neighboring finca	Received a few housing materials from unknown bilateral donors ("los gringos de francia o italia")
	Massive labor dismissals by finca (labor dispute)	SELF	Tried to get union help (pending action) Sought temporary employment on nearby fincas	None
KA2	Earthquake 1976	COLLECTIVE	Organized development committee	Received housing materials, food, helicopter help for injured
	Violence of 1980s	SELF, COLLECTIVE	Villagers fled to nearby town, now have organized development committee to protect town	None during the violence Did receive a school, housing project after the conflict
K11	Earthquake 1976	SELF (market-based)	Went into debt and then had to migrate to find work to pay back debt	UNEPAR provided some housing materials
	Cholera epidemic 1990	SELF	Went to hospital, received medicine, now treat water	Health education campaign at health center (promoting water treatment)
	Hurricane Mitch 1998	SELF	Went into debt, had to migrate to find work to pay back debt	None
L1	Hurricane Mitch	SELF	Migration in search of work	None
	Dengue epidemic	SELF	Illness, sought treatment	None
L2	Earthquake 1976	SELF	Each family rebuilt home	None
	Tornado 1998	SELF	Each family rebuilt home	None
M1	Violence 1980s	SELF, COLLECTIVE	Villagers fled, helped each other repair homes, provide shelter and food	Some unknown external agency provided housing materials
	Forest Fire 1990s	COLLECTIVE	Village tried to fight fire	None
M2	Earthquake 1976	SELF	Family rebuilt home	Municipality provided some housing materials and food
	Rains, road washed out	COLLECTIVE	Village worked together to transport products and repair roads	None

(continued)

Community	Shock Description	Main Coping Strategy/Response		Any Formal Assistance?
		Type	Description	
QE1	Drought 1998	None	None	None
	Hurricane Mitch 1998	COLLECTIVE	Water committee, collective action	None
	Collective debt	COLLECTIVE	Collective action but little progress	Some advice from NGO/MAGA
	Land conflict with neighboring community	COLLECTIVE	Contacted government officials	Yes, soldiers withdrawn (see Box 13-1 in Chapter 13).
QE2	Drought 1998	SELF	Temporary migration in search of work	None
	Conflict within community	None	None ("voluntad de Dios")	None

TABLE 11.5: MAIN COPING STRATEGIES AND FORMAL ASSISTANCE IN 10 RURAL VILLAGES (for main collective shocks, QPES) (CONTINUED)

For some shocks, such as income or job losses, poorer households are more likely to resort to a reduction in consumption rather than other strategies. In contrast, for pests, worsening terms-of-trade, or harvest losses, the reverse is true, with richer households more likely to cut consumption when faced with such shocks. Other studies shed light on this phenomenon: while shocks can trigger a reduction in consumption among the rich and poor alike, the poor will be forced to cut their consumption of an undiversified basket of basic staples, whereas the rich will reduce their consumption of luxury goods. The interpretation of these findings is that poor households cannot smooth their consumption when faced with income or job shocks. The poor do seem more able to smooth consumptions by using their assets (mainly labor) when faced with agricultural shocks (drought, pests, or harvest losses). Self-help is more often used by the poor. However, while the poor respond to such shocks by seeking job elsewhere (either by augmenting the labor of those already working or of other members of the family, including children), the better off use their physical and financial assets (savings, formal insurance) to cope with the effects of shocks.

The Impact of Shocks

The cost of shocks is significant. Two different methodologies were used to estimate the impact of shocks: a multivariate regression model[6] and propensity-score matching techniques.[7] The overall impact of shocks on average income and consumption in 2000 was estimated at 4% and 1% respectively using the multivariate model, and 8% and 6% respectively using propensity-matching techniques. The shocks increased income inequality by 2% under the multivariate model and 16% under the propensity-matching model. Poverty was also worsened by the shocks, by 2% using the multivariate model and 20% using propensity-score matching. While the absolute impact of the shocks was larger for the non-poor, the relative impact was greater among the poor (as a share of their counterfactual consumption or income) using both models.

The most severe impact is associated with economic shocks,[8] with an average loss of income of 28% for job loss, 19% for accidents of the breadwinner, and 17% each for lower earnings

---

6   Counterfactual income and consumption was first estimated using an augmented specification of the typical consumption regression including "dummy" variables for the main shocks and interactions between shocks and wealth. The consumption or income in the absence of the shock was then estimated by setting al shock variables to zero, and welfare "with and without" the shocks was then compared. See GUAPA Technical Paper 9 (Tesliuc, 2002) for details.

7. Tesliuc (2002).

8. Patterns in this paragraph come from regression results from the multivariate model.

and bankruptcy. Natural, agricultural shocks had an important, but less severe, impact on household income: 11% for harvest loss, 10% for pest infestation, and 9% each for drought and worsened terms-of trade. These estimates confirm the severity ranking discussed above that signaled larger impacts from economic shocks.

Current and Future Sources of Vulnerability

Key future sources of vulnerability include worsening terms-of-trade, reduced remittances, and natural disasters—all shocks that could hurt the poor. While the composition of shocks in the year 2000 should not be used to predict which shocks might occur in subsequent years, it can help shed light on the potential impact of various types of shocks, especially when combined with structural information on the likelihood of various shocks. Given the small share of the public sector and its under-developed financial institutions, Guatemala is likely to be relatively cushioned from international financial contagion, debt or currency crises.[9] Rather, the main "macro" and covariant shocks that are more likely to affect Guatemalans in the future (2001 and beyond) include: (a) worsening terms-of-trade; (b) a reduction of international remittances; and (c) natural disasters. The profile of shocks discussed above suggests that these shocks could all have significant poverty impacts:

- **Coffee shocks: severe and lasting impact likely.** The recent fall in the prices of coffee (and to a lesser extent, sugar) has been a substantial blow to a sector that a large number of poor workers depend on for seasonal and permanent livelihoods (see Chapter 6). As discussed above, the profile of shocks shows that this type of shock (job loss and worsening terms-of-trade could indeed have significant adverse impacts in terms of: (a) severity and magnitude of impact: both job loss (for coffee workers) and worsened terms-of-trade (for coffee producers) resulted in large average income and consumption losses (9–28%, see above); and (b) duration of impact: only a small share of households (20–30%) were able to overcome the impact of this type of shocks within a year (see above).
- **Natural disasters: high and lasting impact, particularly for the poor.** Compared with many other countries, Guatemala is very prone to natural disasters, especially earthquakes and hurricanes. The country is located at the confluence of three tetonic plates, with 30 volcanos that pepper its southwestern highlands. Although the latest massive earthquake dates back to 1976, a series of medium-scale earthquakes have hit Guatemala in recent years. Hurricane Mitch in 1998 affected the coastal regions of the country, with lasting effects on soil erosion and destruction of livelihoods (see Box 11.2). Droughts have also been a problem in 2001. The profile of shocks analyzed above suggests that natural disasters affect a disproportionate share of poor households, either because they are pushed to live in marginal areas and/or because of their limited ability to manage these risks. Moreover, the QPES suggests that such shocks have multiple effects, including economic (reducing wealth and income), communal (damaging community assets), and psychological (causing fear and post-traumatic stress syndrome or *susto*). Finally, the QPES suggests that the effects of catastrophic natural disasters are lasting, shifting the poor to an even lower standard of living for the long-run.

Vulnerable Groups in Guatemala

As discussed above, the notion of vulnerability encompasses two elements: (a) the severity of the impact of shocks; and (b) people's resilience to shocks. While the above discussion examines shocks (the event) as a source of vulnerability in Guatemala, this section examines the characteristics of particular households and groups (the people) in an attempt to discern a which groups (or characteristics) might be more vulnerable to the impact of shocks (due to structural features or lower resilience). The first sub-section examines household characteristics to form a type of "vulnerability

---

9. Although recent problems in Guatemala's own financial sector have damaged overall confidence, as discussed in Chapter 5.

profile" that predicts the probability that households will be poor in the future. The second sub-section examines structural features of different groups across the life-cycle to identify which might be inherently more vulnerable due to special circumstances.

Classifying the Vulnerable: The Probability of Being Poor in the Future

The profile of vulnerability is similar to that of poverty, but there are differences particularly for urban areas. Vulnerability to consumption-poverty was estimated using a stochastic model of consumption and its variance, taking into account household characteristics (including assets and other risk management instruments) as well as the likelihood of experiencing shocks.[10] The results reveal significant overlaps, as well as some differences, between the profiles of poverty and vulnerability in Guatemala (Table 11-6). Overall, while 56% of the population was poor in 2000, 64% had a probability larger than 50% of falling into poverty in future years (the group called "vulnerable" to consumption poverty). The general patterns of poverty and vulnerability are similar—higher poverty *and* vulnerability for rural than urban residents, for indigenous than non-indigenous, for those with little education, for those dependent on agricultural incomes, and so forth (Table 11.6). Nonetheless, while the overall number of vulnerable is 14% higher than the number of poor, this difference is higher for certain groups. Most notably, higher vulnerability-poverty ratios were observed in the Metropolitan region (2.2 times higher), and urban areas in general (33% higher). In other words, while observed poverty is low in urban areas and the capital, there is a significant share of the population that is vulnerable to poverty.

Education is a strong predictor of both poverty and vulnerability. Households headed by individuals with less education are more likely to be poor and vulnerable to poverty than those with more education. The exception to this is secondary education, which records the lowest level of vulnerability (10%). Those with higher education are vulnerable (30%), this vulnerability is all due to high volatility of consumption (HV vulnerability, as discussed below) rather than low expected mean consumption (LM vulnerability, see below).

Certain shocks are more likely to hit the vulnerable. The ENCOVI suggests that agriculture-related natural shocks like drought, pest infestation, and harvest losses are mostly reported by households vulnerable to poverty. Other shocks, such as tempests, worsened terms-of-trade, and accidents of the breadwinner, are equally likely to hit vulnerable and non-vulnerable households. Shocks associated with the formal labor market or entrepreneurship—such as job loss or falling earnings—are reported primarily by non-vulnerable households. Strengthening the ability of the poor and vulnerable to reduce, mitigate or cope with agricultural-related shocks is important for reducing vulnerability.

Most poverty and vulnerability arises due to chronic rather than transient conditions in Guatemala. The proximate cause of poverty is low consumption, which can either be a relatively chronic condition (e.g., due to a low level of assets and endowments) or a transient situation (for example, due to a temporary setback from a recent shock). For vulnerability, there are two proxi-mate causes: low expected consumption and high variance of consumption.[11] For policy formula-

---

10. Specifically, in addition to the typical household characteristics, the model included the likelihood of experiencing a loss following any of the seven most frequent shocks: drought, pests, job loss, income (earnings) losses, accident of the breadwinner, worsened terms-of-trade, and harvest losses. Separate models were estimated for the Metropolitan Region and for the remaining rural and urban areas. See GUAPA Technical Paper 9 (Tesliuc, 2002) for details.

11. Chaudhuri and Datt (2001) elaborate on the parallel that exists between the classification in Figure 18 and the more familiar distinction between transient and chronic poverty: "Loosely speaking, households who are HV-vulnerable are in a sense more likely to be only transitorily poor, whereas households who are LM-vulnerable are more likely to be chronically poor . . . The two taxonomies differ fundamentally because of the different questions they pose. The distinction between the transient poor and the chronic poor is based on the question: *how often* is the household poor? . . . . [Whereas] the distinction between HV-vulnerable and LM-vulnerable households is based on the question: *why* is the household poor?"

TABLE 11.6: PROFILE OF POVERTY AND VULNERABILITY

	Population share	Share of poor	Share of vulnerable	Poverty Headcount	Mean vulnerability	Vulnerability Headcount	Vulnerability to poverty ratio
Total	100.0	100.0	100.0	56.2	0.58	64.1	1.14
Area of Residence							
Rural	61.4	81.4	78.3	74.5	0.75	81.8	1.10
Urban	38.6	18.6	21.7	27.1	0.27	36.1	1.33
Region							
Metropolitan	21.7	6.9	13.6	18.0	0.10	40.21	2.24
Norte	8.1	12.1	10.7	84.0	0.79	84.58	1.01
Nororiente	8.2	7.6	7.6	51.8	0.56	59.41	1.15
Suroriente	8.8	10.7	9.2	68.6	0.64	67.25	0.98
Central	10.7	9.8	9.5	51.7	0.55	57.03	1.10
Sur-Occidente	26.5	30.1	28.6	64.0	0.65	69.16	1.08
Nor-Occidente	12.9	18.8	17.3	82.1	0.80	85.88	1.05
Peten	3.3	4.0	3.7	68.0	0.67	71.59	1.05
Ethnicity of the HH Head							
Ladino	57.5	42.4	46.1	41.4	0.44	51.5	1.24
Indigenous	42.6	57.6	53.9	76.1	0.75	81.2	1.07
Gender of the HH Head							
Male	85.3	87.5	88.8	57.6	0.60	66.7	1.16
Female	14.7	12.5	11.2	47.8	0.46	48.8	1.02
Age of the HH Head							
<25 years old	4.7	3.8	4.2	45.9	0.52	57.4	1.25
25–59 years old	81.3	82.8	82.9	57.2	0.59	65.3	1.14
60 years old and over	14.0	13.4	13.0	53.7	0.54	59.2	1.10
HH Head ST Migrant							
Non Migrant	92.7	90.3	90.8	54.8	0.57	62.8	1.15
Short Term Migrant	7.3	9.7	9.2	74.6	0.75	80.5	1.08
Education Status of the HH Head							
No_School	38.3	52.9	49.9	77.7	0.76	83.5	1.07
Primary	45.0	43.3	45.8	54.1	0.59	65.2	1.20
Secondary	11.4	3.3	1.9	16.4	0.12	10.4	0.64
Higher	5.3	0.4	2.5	4.2	0.03	30.5	7.32
HH Head Industry of Employment							
Agriculture	47.0	66.0	61.6	80.8	0.80	86.6	1.07
Mining	0.4	0.1	0.4	18.3	0.32	67.9	3.71
Manufacturing	10.1	6.2	6.8	35.5	0.38	44.3	1.25
Gas, Electricity, Water	0.5	0.3	0.5	31.7	0.45	65.7	2.07
Construction	8.3	7.2	8.0	50.2	0.54	64.1	1.28
Commerce	15.2	9.7	9.6	36.8	0.35	41.9	1.14
Transport	3.9	2.5	3.5	36.8	0.47	59.3	1.61
Financial	2.6	0.7	1.5	14.9	0.21	38.9	2.61
Community	12.0	7.3	8.0	35.1	0.33	44.4	1.26

Mean vulnerability is the mean probability of being poor for a particular group (the mean vulnerability index for persons in that group). World Bank calculations using data from the ENCOVI 2000, *Instituto Nacional de Estadística—Guatemala*.

tion, it is useful to decompose the pool of vulnerable into two mutually exclusive groups: (a) those who are vulnerable due to high volatility of consumption (labeled the "HV vulnerable"); and (b) those who are vulnerable due to low expected mean consumption (labeled the "LM vulnerable"), as shown in Figure 11.2.[12] An analysis of the ENCOVI suggests that low expected consumption rather than volatility is the primary cause of both poverty and vulnerability in Guatemala:

- **Chronic poverty dominates:** While 56% of Guatemala's population was poor in 2000, the majority of these (79%) were chronically poor (44% of the total population), whereas only a fifth were transient poor (12% of the total population), as shown in Figure 11.2.
- **Chronic vulnerability dominates:** Similarly, while 64% of Guatemala's population was estimated to be vulnerable to poverty in the future, the main reason for their vulnerability is low expected mean consumption (LM vulnerability), which accounted for 79% of total vulnerability (or 51% of the total population), whereas only a fifth are vulnerable due to high volatility of consumption (13% of the total population), as shown in Figure 11.2.

The chronic nature of poverty and vulnerability has important policy implications. Namely, interventions should emphasize building the assets of the poor, as discussed in previous chapters (Chapters 5–10) and emphasized in the Peace Accords (see Chapter 4) and in the Government's poverty reduction strategy (see Chapter 14).

Other Types of Vulnerability: Chronically Vulnerable Groups and a Life-Cycle Approach
Certain groups are highly vulnerable due to special circumstances. There are other sources of vulnerability in Guatemala besides consumption poverty. Figure 11.3 uses a classification of risks

FIGURE 11.2: CLASSIFICATION OF POVERTY AND VULNERABILITY: TRANSIENT VS. CHRONIC?
Numbers = % of total population

		Observed Poverty Status Based on Consumption			
		Poor 56.2%	**Non-Poor** 43.8%		
Vulnerability	**Vulnerable** >50% chance of being poor in future **64.2%** (LM = 51.4%) (HV = 12.8%)	Chronic Poor (LM vulnerable) **44.4%**	Vulnerable to Chronic Poverty (LM vulnerable) **6.9%**	Expected consumption < poverty line **51.3%**	**Expected Consumption**
		Frequently Poor (HV vulnerable) **4.1%**	Vulnerable to frequent poverty (HV vulnerable) **8.7%**	Expected consumption > poverty line = 12.8 (frequently poor) + 35.9 (non-vulnerable) = **48.7%**	
	Non-Vulnerable < 50% chance **35.8%**	Infrequently Poor **7.7%**	Non-vulnerable non-poor **28.2%**		

Poor = Chronic poor + transient poor; **transient poor** = frequently poor + infrequently poor. **Vulnerable group** = LM vulnerable + HV vulnerable. **LM vulnerability group** = chronic poor + vulnerable to chronic poverty; **HV vulnerability group** = frequently poor + vulnerable to frequent poverty. Classification scheme adapted from Bidani and Richter (2001). Estimates from World Bank calculations using data from the ENCOVI 2000, *Instituto Nacional de Estadística—Guatemala*. Numbers may not add exactly to 100% due to rounding.

---

12. Specifically, the HV vulnerable have estimated vulnerability in excess of 0.5, but estimated mean consumption above the poverty line. In absence of shocks (or more generally, consumption volatility), these households will not experience poverty. The LM vulnerable have mean consumption below the poverty line and may or may not have high consumption volatility. Even in the absence of shocks, this group will remain in poverty (and their vulnerability may even increase).

FIGURE 11.3: RISKS BY MAIN AGE GROUP, LEADING INDICATORS OF RISKS, UNCOVERED POOR/VULNERABLE, AND SUGGESTED INTERVENTIONS

Years / Age Groups	Main Risks	Leading Indicators of Selected Risks	Indicator Value – Extreme Poor (1)	Total Poor (2)	Vulnerable (3)	Total (4)	Number of Affected Persons – Extreme Poor (5)	Total Poor (6)	Vulnerable (7)	Total (7a)	Priority (8)	Risk Prevention/Mitigation (9)	Risk Coping (10)
0-5	Malnutrition	Stunting	63%	52%	49%	44%	293,988	756,379	794,321	945,974	***	ECD, growth monitoring	Care of malnourished
		Wasting	4%	3%	3%	3%	16,742	39,570	51,355	60,611	***	ECD Programs	Care of malnourished
		Pre-school Not Covered	98%	97%	96%	94%	456,270	1,416,582	1,545,838	2,052,302			
6-13	Low HumanDev	Not enrolled in school	32%	22%	20%	16%	155,673	357,962	368,047	420,585	***	Incr. coverage primary, demand-side interventions	Income support tied to school attendance
		Late entry	41%	33%	31%	27%	200,492	545,399	585,965	700,076	***	Raise quality	Remedial education
	Child Labor	Child labor	20%	18%	17%	15%	97,846	294,398	312,749	387,542	**	Improve and enforce child labor legislation	Income support tied to school attendance
14-17	Low HumanDev	Not enrolled in school	75%	67%	63%	54%	124,284	410,297	446,765	577,502	**	Incr. coverage secondary (supply and demand-side)	Income support Targeted schollarships
		Late entry	29%	21%	19%	16%	47,182	128,470	135,445	172,339	**	Raise quality	Remedial education
	Child Labor	Child labor	53%	56%	53%	51%	87,222	344,399	380,651	541,197	*	Improve and enforce child labor legislation	Income support tied to school attendance
18-24	Low HumanDev	Not enrolled in school	93%	91%	87%	81%	153,344	610,756	676,519	1,104,339		Incr. coverage high-school	Income support Targeted schollarships
	Employment	Youth Unemployment	2%	1%	2%	2%	2,971	8,871	12,344	27,488			Income support Job search support
		Underemployment	17%	18%	18%	17%	27,324	124,149	139,972	237,094		Labor intensive growth	Remedial education; Income support Job search support
		Low wages	29%	24%	23%	18%	48,028	160,453	174,993	249,785	**	Labor intensive growth	Remedial education
25-60	Low income	Unemployment	0%	1%	1%	1%	2,046	10,075	17,000	41,031			Workfare
		Underemployment	24%	22%	21%	22%	103,380	379,571	419,473	758,109		Labor intensive growth	Income support Job search support; Remedial education
		Low wages	31%	25%	22%	18%	134,991	423,077	436,873	627,033	**	Labor intensive growth	Income support Job search support
		No IGSS coverage	62%	64%	63%	63%	272,712	1,082,284	1,244,863	2,207,606	**	Enforce regulations	Remedial education
	Nutrition	Obesity	0%	0%	1%	2%	345	7,798	22,384	78,121			Expand TAM
over 60	Chronic diseases	No Health insurance	97%	95%	92%	86%	63,641	288,072	288,683	584,217	*	Provide Health Insurance for Poor Elderly	
	Low income	No pension coverage	96%	96%	94%	88%	63,327	290,292	294,995	597,826	*	Institute Social Pension	
	Nutrition	Obesity	0%	0%	0%	1%	-	242	758	4,033			
Other Population groups													
Housing	Poor housing	Poor housing conditions	10%	8%	7%	5%	183,827	509,251	516,144	582,134	**	Promote savings and mortgages	Target Housing subsidies titling / Land
Basic Services	Poor basic services	No Water	50%	41%	39%	31%	884,601	2,638,151	2,858,295	3,524,266	***	Improve coverage (supply and demand-side interventions)	Subsidize connections for poorest
		No Sewage	96%	86%	81%	66%	1,715,914	5,500,787	5,904,965	7,548,734	***	Improve coverage (supply and demand-side interventions)	Subsidize connections for poorest; Eliminate user subsidy; subsidize connections for poor
		No Electricity	66%	44%	40%	29%	1,182,669	2,833,552	2,884,040	3,282,762	**	Improve coverage (supply and demand-side interventions)	
Natural Disasters		Damages due to ND	26%	31%	31%	29%	468,110	1,957,760	2,270,000	3,267,620	**	Disaster management, incentives for relocation; Improved housing	Temporary shelter provision; Supply of food/medicine

(1) Share of extreme poor individuals in the age-category affected by the risk (e.g., first row: share of children aged 0-5 years old in extreme poverty affected by stunting)
(2) Share of poor individuals in the age-category affected by the risk (e.g. share of children aged 0-5 years old in poverty affected by stunting)
(3) Share of vulnerable individuals in the age-category affected by the risk (e.g. share of children aged 0-5 years old classified as vulnerable affected by stunting)
(4) Share of individuals affected by the risk in that age category (e.g. share of children aged 0-5 years old affected by stunting)
(5) Number of extreme poor persons in the age-category affected by the risk (e.g. number of extremely poor children aged 0-5 years old affected by stunting)
(6) Number of poor persons in the age-category affected by the risk (e.g. number of poor children aged 0-5 years old affected by stunting)
(7) Number of vulnerable persons in the age-category affected by the risk (e.g. number of vulnerable children aged 0-5 years old affected by stunting)
(8) *** = top priority; ** = medium priority; * = priority.
(9) Lists suggested public, private or informal interventions that can be used in Guatemala to reduce the occurrence of the risk or mitigate (credit, insurance, hedging, portfolio diversification) the impact of the risk
(10) Lists suggested public, private or informal interventions that can be used in Guatemala to help households cope with the impact of the risk
Underemployment is defined as working less than 40 hours a week, and low pay as recording earning in the lowest decile of the earning distribution (less than 150 Qz per month)

by life-cycles, to expand the vulnerability concept in other areas, such as nutrition, education, health, access to basic services and exposure to natural disasters. For each type of risk, the share of people at risk is presented for four categories: the extreme poor, total poor, vulnerable to poverty, and total population in that group. There is a monotonic increase in the incidence of risks and household welfare, with the highest exposure to these other vulnerabilities among the extreme poor. For each type of risk, the risk matrix lists possible interventions that may contribute to risk reduction, mitigation or coping. The matrix also offers a subjective prioritization of risk groups, based on two criteria: the relative size of the group (particularly the number of poor that also fall into that group), and whether the risks or circumstances are likely to have lasting, even inter-generational effects on the transmission of poverty (education and malnutrition-related risks). Among the risks that are of particular concern include: malnutrition; low school enrollment, late school entry and grade repetition; child labor; low earnings; low health coverage of the elderly; lack of access to basic services among the poor; and higher exposure to natural disasters (Figure 11.3). Seasonal migrants and their families also appear to have higher poverty and vulnerability rates than those who migrate permanently or the general (non-migrating) population.

Summary of Key Issues and Priorities

This chapter highlights a number of key findings with respect to vulnerability and the dynamics of poverty. Specifically:

- Households in Guatemala experienced a high incidence of shocks in 2000, and most experienced multiple shocks with varying duration of impact.
- The effects of shocks are multi-dimensional, affecting not only income, wealth and consumption, but also community assets, the psychological and social well-being of individuals, families and communities, health and education.
- The poor are more exposed to natural disasters and agriculture-related shocks. They also have lower resilience to shocks than the non-poor.
- The cost of shocks is significant. Economic shocks have larger and more severe impacts than other types of shocks.
- Faced with shocks, Guatemalan households tend to rely primarily on their own assets. The main coping strategies include reduced consumption or self-help. Few households report receiving any formal governmental or non-governmental assistance in the face of shocks. The poor are less equipped than the non-poor to fight shocks, and are more likely to reduce consumption (regrettable, of basic staples) or use existing assets (particularly labor). The non-poor are more likely than the poor to use market-based insurance mechanisms.
- Key sources of vulnerability in the future include: (a) worsening terms-of-trade and job loss, such as those associated with the crisis in the coffee sector; (b) lost remittances from the global economic slowdown; and (c) natural disasters. All are likely to have lasting and severe impacts on the poor.
- Poverty and vulnerability are primarily a chronic (rather than transient) phenomena in Guatemala, reflecting low average consumption (current and expected) due to low levels of overall assets (for example, education).
- Certain sub-groups of the population are inherently or structurally vulnerable due to special circumstances. Specifically, key vulnerable groups include young children, who are vulnerable to malnutrition and lack of development; school-aged children, who are vulnerable due to lack of educational opportunities and child labor; the working poor, particularly those in agriculture, due to low earnings and susceptibility to natural shocks; poor households lacking basic services; seasonal migrants and their families; and poor, rural households living in areas prone to natural disasters.

In light of these findings, a number of policy recommendations seem appropriate as options for a strategy to reduce vulnerability. Notably, strategies to reduce vulnerability should emphasize:

- **Children.** A strategic emphasis on children—particularly child-focused interventions to reduce malnutrition (see Chapter 8) and promote early childhood development) crucial to avoid an inter-generational transmission of poverty and vulnerability;

- **Building the assets of the poor.** Given the chronic nature of poverty and vulnerability implies that interventions should emphasize building the assets of the poor, as discussed in previous chapters and emphasized in the Peace Accords and the Government's poverty reduction strategy. As discussed in Chapter 12, social protection programs can play an important role in building the assets of the poor. Specifically, when designed properly, conditional-transfer programs can be quite effective in helping ease demand-side constraints, which have been shown to constitute important limitations for improved coverage of key assets, such as education (Chapter 7), health (Chapter 8) and basic utility services (Chapter 9).

- **Disaster management and relief,** which should be expanded and improved, given the disproportionate exposure of the poor and vulnerable to natural disasters and agriculture-related shocks. The introduction of catastrophic insurance may also merit consideration. Such interventions should be well-targeted to the poor and delivered in a timely manner. Since exposure to some natural disasters does seem to be largely determined by location and geographic factors, administrative maps of vulnerability to drought, seismic activities, hurricanes, storms, frosts, and landslides could be quite useful instruments for risk management planning. Many such maps have been prepared by the Ministry of Agriculture and FAO, and are available to policy makers. Their ability to target limited funds for disaster relief would be greatly enhanced if used in conjunction with poverty maps (since those who are already poor are less equipped to cope with shocks). Since the impact of natural disasters often includes damage to, or destruction of, community infrastructure (in addition to income and wealth losses at the household level), the social funds may serve as the institutional channel by which such relief and infrastructure rehabilitation is implemented.

CHAPTER 12

SOCIAL PROTECTION, PRIVATE TRANSFERS, AND POVERTY

This chapter reviews the effectiveness and efficiency of Guatemala's numerous and scattered social protection programs with a view to informing policy and highlighting priorities for reducing poverty and vulnerability. An adequate social protection system is an important element of a comprehensive strategy to reduce poverty and vulnerability. *Social protection* (SP) has been traditionally defined as "a set of public measures aimed at providing income security for individuals."[1] The final goal of public social protection policies is to increase the welfare of the population, and to that end, these schemes have generally included social assistance (SA) and social insurance (SI) programs. *Social assistance* programs are generally designed to help individuals or households cope with chronic poverty or transient declines in income that would cause them to live in a situation of poverty or worsening poverty. As such, they help alleviate poverty and reduce vulnerability to poverty. SA programs as a whole make up what is commonly referred to as "the social safety net," and include programs such as transfers (in cash or kind),[2] subsidies,[3] and workfare.[4] *Social insurance* schemes include publicly-provided or mandated insurance for unemployment, old age (pensions), disability, survivorship, sickness, and so forth, which are designed to help mitigate income risks. Private transfers can complement public social protection interventions. In Guatemala, private transfers (particularly remittances), are a particularly important source of income. As such, this chapter also considers private transfers.

---

1. (Holzmann and Jørgensen 2000).
2. Transfer schemes include non-contributory payments in cash (e.g., family or child allowances), near cash (e.g., food stamps, vouchers), and in-kind (e.g., food supplementation, school feeding).
3. Subsidies, such as those on food, energy and housing, artificially lower the price of certain goods or services either for the entire population (generalized subsidies) or for certain sub-groups (e.g., self-targeted food subsidies). Subsidies are explicit if their cost is paid for by the government and implicit if it is borne by the producers of the goods or services.
4. Workfare programs are transfer schemes that require the beneficiaries to work for their benefits. Workfare benefits are paid either in cash or kind (e.g., food-for-work schemes) or some combination.

The chapter begins with an overview of SP programs. It then assesses the coverage, targeting incidence, adequacy, and overall effectiveness of these schemes. It examines the potential impacts of social protection programs on poverty and inequality, and assesses their cost effectiveness. Finally, the chapter concludes with a review of key issues and priorities. It builds on an inventory of social protection programs conducted by the *Universidad Rafael Landívar* (2001), an analysis of this inventory by Santiso (2001), and an in-depth analysis of the effectiveness and efficiency of SP programs using the ENCOVI 2000.[5]

Overview of SP Programs: Types, Magnitudes and Spending

Overall Magnitude and Trends in Public SP Spending

Public spending on social protection is low by international standards, reflecting the low level of overall public resources in Guatemala. Numerous social protection programs are managed by many different agencies in Guatemala, as discussed below. As such, accounting for SP spending is complicated and estimates of the total magnitude of such spending vary. Two approaches are generally used: (a) disaggregating official government spending accounts by type of spending (usually by major category or ministry); and (b) building up spending estimates from an inventory of programs. Using the **first** approach, IMF estimates indicate that total public spending on social protection ("social security and welfare") absorbed 1.0% of GDP and 8.3% of total government spending in 2000 (Table 12.1). This compares with reported spending on education and health of 2.5% and 1.1% of GDP respectively (representing 18.3% and 7.9% of total government spending).[6] It also compares with spending on social investment funds, which accounted for 0.6% in 2000.[7] With these estimates, the level of public SP spending has increased from 0.7% of GDP in 1996 to 1.0% in 2000. Using the **second** approach, an analysis of an inventory of programs conducted by the University of Rafael Landívar (URL, 2001) yields a slightly higher estimate, with total public spending on social protection absorbing 1.8% of GDP and 12.4% of total government spending in 2000 (Table 12.1).[8] Using these estimates, the level of public SP spending has increased from 0.8% of GDP in 1996 to 1.8% in 2000. Although SP spending appears to be rather low by international standards (Table 12.1), it is not so low relative to other social sectors in Guatemala and current levels mainly reflect low overall public finance base in Guatemala (total public revenues represented about 10.5% of GDP in 2000).

SP spending is also quite low in relation to the poverty gap. The estimated annual cost of eliminating to total poverty gap is Qz11.1 billion, or 8.4% of GDP. Total SP spending pales in comparison to this gap (Table 12.1). As such, poverty reduction via redistribution is unlikely; growth is necessary. The low level of spending on social protection (and the social sectors in general) is one of the reasons Guatemala ranks so poorly on poverty and social indicators (such as life expectancy, infant mortality, nutrition, literacy, and school coverage), as discussed in Chapter 2.

Overview of Public SP Programs

The public social protection system in Guatemala is fragmented, reflecting the lack of an overall strategy and a scattering of programs across many agencies. In 2000, there were some 36 different public social protection programs (39 if sub-programs are included, Table 12.2), including two main social insurance programs (accounting for 40% of total SP spending) and 34 social assistance programs (absorbing 60% of total SP spending).

Guatemala's social insurance system provides minimal coverage of the population, risks financial crisis, faces allegations of corruption, and is regressive. Social insurance is run by

---

5. Tesliuc and Lindert (2002a).

6. SIAF/Ministry of Finance (communication of 2-12-02).

7. IMF estimates. IMF (2001). Other estimates put social funds spending at 1.64% of GDP in 2000. Santiso (2001).

8. Inventory conducted by URL (2001); analysis conducted by Santiso (2001).

TABLE 12.1: PUBLIC SPENDING ON SOCIAL PROTECTION, 2000

	Million Qz.	% of GDP	% of TS	% of SS	% of SPS
IMF estimates					
Social Security/Welfare	1,524	1.0	8.3	17.5	n.a.
MEMO: Total Government Spending	18,317	12.4	100.0	n.a.	n.a
MEMO: Total Social Spending	8,722	5.9	47.6	100.0	n.a.
URL/Santiso estimates					
Social Protection—total	2,698	1.8	12.4	29.3	100.0
Social Insurance	1,090	0.7	5.0	11.6	40.4
Social Assistance	1,608	1.1	7.4	17.7	59.6
MEMO: Social Investment Funds	2,418	1.7	11.1	26.3	n.a.
Some International Comparisons					
Argentina—SP	n.a.	5.0	n.a.	32.0	100.0
SI	n.a.	4.1	n.a.	26.0	82.0
SA	n.a.	0.9	n.a.	6.0	18.0
Brazil—SP	n.a.	10.8	45.0	n.a.	100.0
SI	n.a.	10.3	42.9	n.a.	95.4
SA	n.a.	0.5	2.1	n.a.	4.6
Mexico—SP	n.a.	4.3	27.0 (fed)	44.0 (fed)	100.0
SI	n.a.	3.2	20.1	32.7	74.4
SA	n.a.	1.1	6.9	11.3	25.6
Nicaragua—SP	n.a.	1.10	3.00	7.30	100.0
SI	n.a.	0.01	0.03	0.09	0.9
SA	n.a.	1.10	2.90	7.21	99.1

Sources: IMF (April 2001); URL (2001); Santiso (2001); international comparisons: Lindert/World Bank (on-going database)

the Instituto Guatemalteco de Seguridad Social (IGSS) and covers workers in the formal private and public sectors across the country.[9] Established in 1946, social security includes several main sub-programs: accident coverage; maternity and sickness; disability; old age (pensions) and survival. More recently, a pilot program (TAM) was launched in 1998 to provide social insurance to agricultural migrant workers and their families in the departments of Escuintla and Suchitepequez. While the social security system is said to cover the entire country, not all services are available in all departments. For example, employee contributions in the Department of Guatemala are 4.83%, as compared with only 2.83% in Alta Verapaz. This is due to the fact that all programs are covered in the capital, but only accident and disability, old age and survival programs are available in Alta Verapaz. The social security system is in disarray and at risk of a financial crisis. As of the end of 1997, the Guatemalan State owed an estimated Q148 million to the IGSS due to its failure to pay contributions as an employer. More fundamentally, the inability to match expenditures with social security contributions raises questions about the sustainability of the system as currently designed. In mid 2001, for example, the IGSS accident-maternity-sickness (IVS) program had a deficit of Q166 million, contrasting with its own surplus of Q178 million in 1998. Moreover, the IGSS has been embroiled in recent corruption allegations, with the General Accounting Office reporting irregularities and unreliability of the accounting system of IGSS in 2000. Finally, as shown below, coverage of IGSS programs is minimal and the incidence of IGSS benefits regressive.

---

9. Much of this paragraph is based on Santiso (2001), which draws largely on the inventory conducted by URL (2001).

TABLE 12.2: OVERVIEW OF PUBLIC SOCIAL PROTECTION PROGRAMS

Types & No. of Programs (incl. sub-programs)	Cost 2000	Description of Program	Number of beneficiaries (official fig)	Agency Responsible	Covered in the ENCOVI (Category)
Social Insurance					
Social Security (IVS)	Q1,090 mn 0.74% GDP 5.0% TS 11.9% SS 21.3% SPS	Covers formal private and public sector workers, including accident coverage, maternity and sickness, disability, old age, and survival	n.a.	IGSS	Yes—Partial Old Age Survivorship Alimony[a]
TAM	n.a.	New program for agricultural migrant workers and their families; pilot in Suchitepéquez and Escuintla	50,021	IGSS?	No
Social Assistance					
Scholarships (7 programs)	Q13 mn 0.01% GDP 0.06% TS 0.14% SS 0.25% SPS	7 programs covering students in primary, secondary (basic and intermediaγ) schools; focus is on rural areas; some focused on girls (programa atencion de la nina); some have sub-nat'l focus	broad range: 80–31,195 total approx: 35,000	Being restructured Various agencies (MINEDUC has largest, FONAPAZ)	Yes Beca escolar Bolsa utiles escolar
In-kind transfers, mainly food-for-work (4 programs)	Q35 mn 0.02% GDP 0.16% TS 0.38% SS 0.69% SPS	4 food-for-work programs with varying geographic coverage and size	broad range: 175–65,000 total approx: 11,575	FONAPAZ/WFP WFP FIS Municipalities	No
Various Social Assistance Programs (9 programs)	Q129 mn 0.09% GDP 0.59% TS 1.41% SS 2.53%SPS	Various programs covering variety of groups: babies, children, orphans, youths, young delinquents, breast-feeding mothers, poor rural women, single mothers, poor elderly, victims/perpetuators of domestic violence, poor marginalized, etc.	broad range. total approx: 31,106 o/w: SBS: 7,921 SOSEP: 23,185 SAS: n.a.	SBS SOSEP SAS MINEDUC and MSPAS	Partially "Other SA benefits, gov't aid"

Program	Spending	Description	Amounts	Institutions	Targeted
School Feeding (3 programs)	Q143 mn 0.10% GDP 0.66% TS 1.56% SS 2.8% SPS	School snack (refacción) School breakfast School lunches	992,692 903,177 7,000 total: 1,089,869	Being restructured and in flux. Mainly MINEDUC (also PRONADE NGOs)	Yes galleta escolar desayuno, leche en polvo, vaso de leche, vaso de atol
PRONADE (1 program, multiple benefits)	Q357 mn 0.24% GDP 1.64% TS 3.88% SS 6.98% SPS	Decentralized, community-managed education program. Provides primary schooling, school meals,[b] cash transfers, training, TA for construction of classrooms	294,041	PRONADE	Yes for SA parts, as captured under school feeding, scholarship, bolsa utiles transfers
Micro-credit (2 programs)	n.a.	Nat'l micro and small enterprise program under MINECON FONAPAZ PDP Program	n.a.	MINECON FONAPAZ	No
Disaster Management (2 programs)	Q130 mn 0.09% GDP 0.60% TS 1.41% SS 2.54% SPS	Programs to help communities vulnerable to natural and environmental risks and shocks (national coverage)	n.a.	CONRED MSPAS- unidad nacional de prevención de desastres	No
Subsidies 6 (9) programs	Q801 mn 0.55% GDP 3.67% TS 8.71% SS 15.65% SPS	Land Fund (Q106 mn (4 progs)) Housing Subsidy (Q295 mn) School Transport Subsidy (Q27 mn) Electricity Subsidy (Q372 mn)	land: 12,915 housing: 7,623 Sch.transp: 76,374 Electricity: 10,212,000	FONTIERRAS FOGUAVI FONAPAZ Comision de Vivienda MINEDUC INDE	Yes, partial Sch. transport Electricity

TS = total spending; SS = social spending; SPS = social protection spending

a. Alimony pensions are included in the social insurance system as they are a mechanism regulated by social norms and enforced by the state authority, although implemented outside IGSS

b. PRONADE school meals program costs covered under PRONADE category rather than school feeding

Guatemala lacks a comprehensive social safety net, with numerous programs scattered across many agencies, shifting institutional responsibility, duplications, gaps, and often regressive benefits. Social assistance is provided by numerous agencies and includes at least 34 different programs (Table 12.2). The main categories of programs include: (a) scholarships; (b) food-for-work programs; (c) various social assistance/service programs; (d) school feeding; (e) PRONADE, a decentralized program that provides cash transfers and school meals along with education services; (f) micro-credit; (g) disaster management; and (h) a variety of subsidies (land, housing, school transport and electricity). Institutional responsibility for these programs is dispersed among many agencies and duplications in types of programs abound. The seven different scholarship programs, for example, are currently being restructured in an attempt to improve their coherence. Possible options for restructuring including transferring responsibility for coordination to the Vice Presidency, with MINEDUC as the main implementing agency. Likewise, responsibility for the three main school feeding programs has been transferred several times in the past year, from MINEDUC to the Vice Presidency and then to the Estado Mayor Presidencial (military). Delays in food delivery and quality problems with school feeding programs have also been highlighted recently in the press, with questions regarding nutritional value and taste. Criteria for targeting the various SA programs differs widely across programs, with some using geographic criteria (though rarely based on the poverty map) and others using broad categorical eligibility (girls in poor rural areas, victims of human rights violations, orphans, poor elderly, landless peasants, breast-feeding mothers, refugees, etc.). As a result, many social assistance programs are regressive, as shown below.

Overall Magnitude of Private Transfers
Private transfers (including remittances and private charity) are an important source of income in Guatemala. As analyzed in more detail below, private transfers account for 46% of all transfers received by households in Guatemala (10% for charity and 36% for remittances from family members, as compared with 29% for public SA programs and 26% for public SI benefits).[10] Charity is provided by a range of agencies, including international donors, NGOs, churches, private-sector agencies and so forth. In addition, several private-sector industries have established private foundations to provide social assistance, social services, and basic infrastructure to workers and their families in these sectors as part of a recent wave of "social business responsibility" (the largest are FUNDAZUCAR and FUNRURAL, representing the sugar and coffee sectors respectively).[11]

Average Magnitude of Household-Level Benefits
There is considerable variation in the average benefit level per household of various SP programs and private transfers in Guatemala (Figures 12.1 and 12.2). For public programs, the ENCOVI 2000 shows that the smallest transfer is the electricity subsidy, which provides beneficiaries with an equivalent cash benefit of Q.132 per year. At the other extreme, beneficiaries of old-age pensions receive an average of Q.14,500 per household per year. These compare with private transfers, which average Qz 5,800 in total, Q.5,700 for remittances and Qz 3000 for charity. The variation between benefit levels within programs is even higher. For instance, the ratio between the pension of the top 95% recipient household (p95) and the bottom 5% (p5)—shown on Figure 12.1 through the vertical bands—is over 100 times for all types of pensions. Most social assistance programs exhibit lower dispersion in benefit level across households, with p95/p5 ratios ranging from 10 to 30 times. The largest dispersion in benefit levels for each type of transfer is to be found, as expected, for private transfers, with p95/05 ratios between 100 and 300 times.

Coverage of SP Programs and Private Transfers
This section analyzes the coverage of SP programs using data from the ENCOVI (the distribution or "incidence" of benefits is discussed in the next section). The ENCOVI collected data at both

---

10. World Bank calculations using the ENCOVI 2000, *Instituto Nacional de Estadísticas—Guatemala*.
11. Fuentes & Asociados (2001).

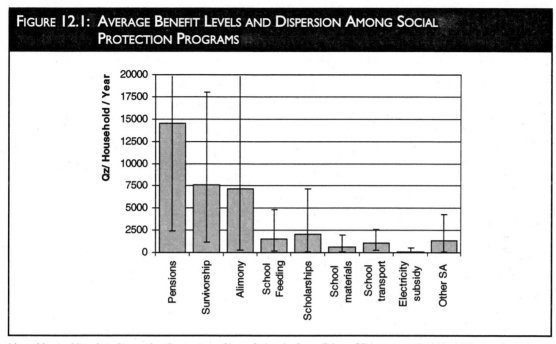

FIGURE 12.1: AVERAGE BENEFIT LEVELS AND DISPERSION AMONG SOCIAL PROTECTION PROGRAMS

Note: Vertical bands indicate the dispersion of benefit levels, from 5th to 95th percentile. World Bank calculations using the ENCOVI 2000, *Instituto Nacional de Estadísticas—Guatemala*

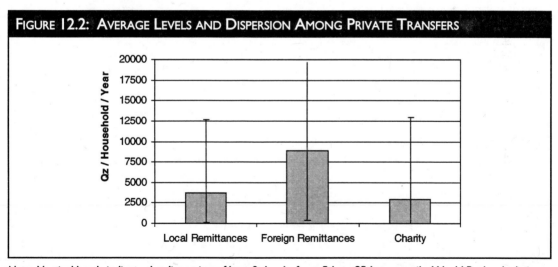

FIGURE 12.2: AVERAGE LEVELS AND DISPERSION AMONG PRIVATE TRANSFERS

Note: Vertical bands indicate the dispersion of benefit levels, from 5th to 95th percentile. World Bank calculations using the ENCOVI 2000, *Instituto Nacional de Estadísticas—Guatemala*

the household and the individual level for a variety of SP programs. Unfortunately, these do not cover the full range of SP programs provided in Guatemala (see comparison in Table 12.2 above).[12] As such, unless otherwise noted, the remainder of the paper adopts categories of programs collected in the ENCOVI. We estimate that these programs cover between two thirds and three quarters of total social protection spending in Guatemala.

---

12. Programs with low beneficiary coverage, such as land or housing subsidies, were only scarcely captured in the ENCOVI and will be omitted for lack of estimability.

Coverage of Public SP Programs

Coverage of social insurance programs is extremely limited, with non-poor and urban biases. Overall, 7% of the population lives in households[13] that receive social insurance, with only 3% receiving old-age pensions (Table 12.3). Coverage of social insurance is eight times higher for the top quintile as the bottom quintile, and higher for urban residents and the non-indigenous.

Coverage of social assistance programs is much more extensive and more evenly distributed. Close to four-fifths of the population receives some form of social assistance, and this share is fairly uniform across quintiles, ethnicities and areas (Table 12.3). Nonetheless, coverage differs substantially by specific program, both in terms of overall coverage and by poverty group (Figure 12.3). The electricity subsidy, for example, covers almost all households with electricity, and thus covers a higher share of the non-poor than the poor. The majority of the population also lives in households benefiting from school feeding programs, and these have a slight coverage bias in favor of the poor. Scholarship and transport subsidies have minimal coverage that favors the non-poor.

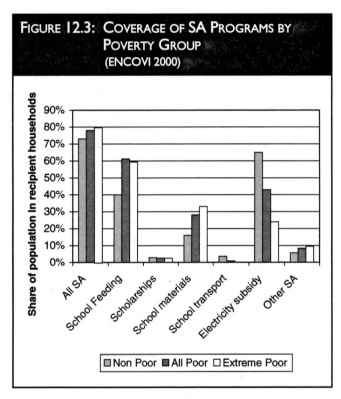

FIGURE 12.3: COVERAGE OF SA PROGRAMS BY POVERTY GROUP (ENCOVI 2000)

Coverage of Private Transfers

Private transfers accrue more to non-poor, urban and non-indigenous residents (Table 12.3). Overall, about 28% of the population lives in households that receive private transfers, including remittances (local and foreign) and private donations (charity). The non-poor are twice as likely to receive private transfers as the extreme poor. Urban and non-indigenous residents are also more likely to receive such transfers. Remittances are even more biased towards advantaged groups, particularly those from relatives living abroad. Other market-based risk mitigation mechanisms are also biased towards the non-poor (Box 12.1).

---

13. This analysis uses the household, not the individual as a reference unit. Nonetheless, to ensure comparability with poverty statistics, coverage figures are reported as on a per capita basis (weighted by household size). There are several reasons for this presentational format. First, although most SP benefits provide individual benefits, some target households (e.g., energy subsidies and some form of government aid). Moreover, private transfers are recorded only at the household level. Thus the household is the smallest common denominator where all transfers can be presented and compared. Second, benefits provided for one individual will have spillover effects for the other members in the households, which will adequately be captured at this level of aggregation. Coverage is thus presented as the share of people residing in recipient households in a particular population group.

TABLE 12.3: COVERAGE OF SOCIAL PROTECTION PROGRAMS AND PRIVATE TRANSFERS
Beneficiaries as % of population in each group

	Total	By Quintile					By Poverty Group			By Ethnicity		By Area	
											Non-		
		Q1	Q2	Q3	Q4	Q5	XP	AP	NP	Ind.	Ind	Rural	Urban
All Public SP Programs	80	75	80	83	83	79	74	79	81	79	81	78	84
All Social Insurance (SI)	7	2	3	5	8	15	2	4	11	3	9	4	11
Pensions	3	1	1	2	3	9	1	1	6	1	5	1	6
Survivorship	1	1	0	0	2	3	1	1	2	1	2	1	2
Alimony	3	1	2	3	3	5	0	2	4	1	4	1	5
All Social Assistance (SA)	79	74	79	83	83	76	73	78	80	79	79	77	82
School Feeding	52	60	63	60	51	25	59	61	40	57	48	58	42
Snack	38	39	43	46	42	21	38	42	33	42	36	38	39
Breakfast	28	36	40	34	21	7	34	37	16	32	24	41	6
Powdered Milk	2	2	2	2	2	1	1	2	1	2	1	2	1
Glass of Milk	5	5	7	5	4	2	5	6	3	6	4	6	3
Glass of Atol	35	41	40	42	34	18	41	41	28	39	33	38	31
Scholarships	3	3	2	4	3	3	3	3	3	3	3	2	4
School Materials	23	22	26	24	21	10	33	28	16	26	20	26	18
School Transport Subsidy	2	0	1	2	5	3	0	1	4	1	3	0	5
Electricity Subsidy	53	28	45	58	65	67	24	43	65	49	56	44	66
Other SA	7	9	8	7	7	5	9	8	6	10	5	7	7
All Private Transfers	28	17	24	28	34	36	16	23	35	23	31	24	34
Remittances	21	12	18	19	24	31	11	16	27	17	23	19	24
Local	13	8	12	12	13	19	7	10	16	10	15	11	16
Foreign	9	4	7	8	11	13	3	6	12	7	10	8	9
Charity	13	8	12	14	16	14	7	10	16	10	15	10	17
Public + Private	84	78	83	87	88	87	77	82	87	82	86	82	89
Memo for Comparison													
Share of total population	100	20	20	20	20	20	16	56	44	43	58	61	39
Share of poor population	100	36	36	29	0	0	n.a.	n.a.	n.a.	58	42	81	19

Source: World Bank calculations using the ENCOVI 2000, *Instituto Nacional de Estadística—Guatemala*. Categories are not additive as people can receive more than one type of transfer. Quintiles are individual consumption quintiles.

BOX 12-1: ACCESS TO MARKET-BASED RISK MITIGATION MECHANISMS

Only 2% of the population is covered by at least one form of private insurance. The entire group of insured is non-poor.

Financial deposits are also used exclusively by the non-poor. Overall 18% of Guatemalan households have financial deposits, most with private banks (85%). By poverty status, access to financial deposits varies from 30% for the non-poor to 3% for the poor. The main cause of not having financial deposits is a lack of savings (92% of cases).

The use of **credit services** is more evenly spread across the population. Overall, 13% of households applied for and received loans in 2000. Although this share is fairly constant across the poverty groups, loan sizes differ significantly, with the non-poor receiving an average of Q11,091 as compared with Q2,129 for the poor.

Source: World Bank calculations using the ENCOVI 2000

Duplications and Gaps in Coverage
Duplications and gaps in coverage of social protection and private transfers abound (Figure 12.4). Specifically:

■ **Duplications in Public and Private Transfers.** The degree of overlap between public social protection and private transfers is large (upper left-hand panel of Figure 12.4). Specifically, 23% of all households receive support from both the Government and private sources. Private transfers reach only 6% of households not covered by public social protection schemes.

■ **Overlaps between Social Insurance and Social Assistance.** Major duplications exist between SI and SA at the household level (upper right-hand panel of Figure 12.4). Three quarters of households that receive pensions also receive other social assistance benefits (such as the energy subsidy). Besides the energy subsidy, one quarter of households that receive pensions also receive other social assistance benefits (mainly programs for children). These duplications are difficult to detect by the administration as most programs target individuals not households.

■ **Duplications between Social Assistance Programs.** Given the extensive coverage of school feeding programs, overlaps between SA programs also abound (lower right-hand panel of Figure 12.4). Most children who receive scholarships, school materials, or other social assistance programs also receive school feeding or have siblings that do. Besides school feeding, there is little overlap between the rest of the programs.

■ **Duplications of Private Transfers.** The degree of overlapping of private transfers is smaller (lower left-hand panel of Figure 12.4). Households that receive local remittances are generally not the same as those that receive foreign remittances. About half of those receiving private donations do not receive remittances.

■ **Gaps in Coverage.** Some 23% of the extreme poor and 18% of all poor were not covered by any type of public or private transfers, as compared with only 13% of the non-poor. The public social protection system fails to reach a quarter of the extreme poor and a fifth of the poor. Virtually all of the poor are excluded from the social insurance system.

Distributional Incidence (Targeting Outcomes) of SP Programs

While the last section examined the coverage of programs (in terms of "people" or beneficiaries), this section examines the distribution of benefits (the target "incidence") of social protection programs using data from the ENCOVI 2000. Two concepts are used: (a) absolute target incidence, which measures average benefits received by any particular group as a share of total benefits (or the targeting outcomes of a program); and (b) relative incidence, which measures the average benefits received by any particular group as a share of average total consumption for that group (i.e., the relative "importance" of a program).

Incidence of Public SP Programs
Overall, public social transfers in Guatemala are regressive in absolute terms, but progressive in relative terms. Specifically, the top quintile receives close to half (46%) of all public social protection spending, as compared with the bottom quintile, which receives only 8% (absolute incidence, Table 12.4). In other words, the richest receive significantly larger absolute public transfers than the poorest. Nonetheless, these transfers are relatively more important to the poor than the non-poor (relative incidence, Table 12.5). Specifically, public transfers represent 9% of total consumption for the poorest quintile, as compared with 5% for the top quintile. Looked at another way, public transfers were less regressive than the existing distribution of total consumption and income.

In contrast, social insurance is highly regressive in both absolute and relative terms. Three quarters of all social insurance benefits go to those in the richest quintile of the population; the

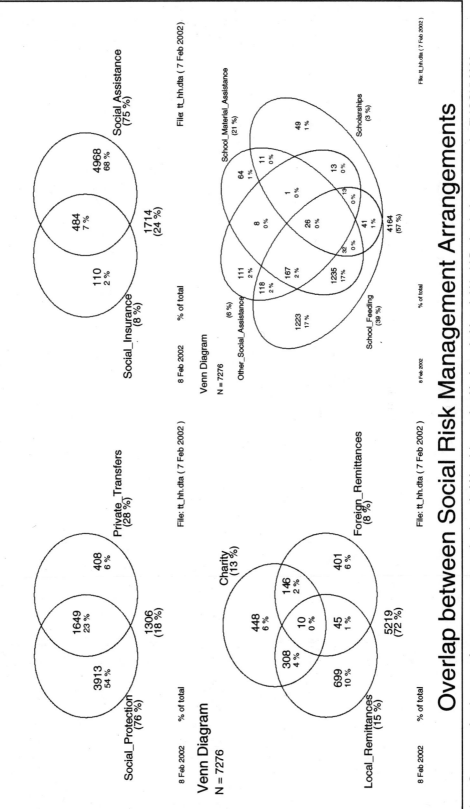

FIGURE 12.4: DUPLICATIONS AND GAPS IN SOCIAL RISK MANAGEMENT ARRANGEMENTS

Overlap between Social Risk Management Arrangements

Note: Coverage of each group of programs is estimated at household level (unweighted by household size). World Bank calculations using the ENCOVI 2000, Instituto Nacional de Estadísticas—Guatemala.

TABLE 12.4: ABSOLUTE TARGET INCIDENCE OF SOCIAL PROTECTION PROGRAMS AND PRIVATE TRANSFERS

Average transfers received by each group as % of total transfers received by entire population

	Total	By Quintile					By Poverty Group			By Ethnicity		By Area	
		Q1	Q2	Q3	Q4	Q5	XP	AP	NP	Ind.	Non-Ind	Rural	Urban
All Public SP Programs	100	8	13	15	18	46	6	33	67	25	75	45	55
All Social Insurance (SI)	100	1	3	5	15	76	1	9	91	9	91	20	80
Pensions	100	1	2	4	12	81	1	6	94	9	91	17	83
Survivorship	100	4	4	4	13	75	2	11	89	9	91	16	84
Alimony	100	1	6	10	24	60	0	16	84	10	90	30	70
All Social Assistance (SA)	100	14	21	24	21	20	10	54	46	39	61	66	34
School Feeding	100	16	25	27	20	11	12	63	37	43	57	79	21
Snack	100	13	21	26	26	14	10	55	45	39	61	59	41
Breakfast	100	17	28	29	17	9	12	68	32	43	57	92	8
Powdered Milk	100	30	26	14	16	14	7	65	35	62	38	56	44
Glass of Milk	100	16	29	25	19	12	11	65	35	49	51	75	25
Glass of Atol	100	17	22	25	23	14	13	57	43	42	58	64	36
Scholarships	100	9	4	23	16	48	3	30	70	47	53	28	72
School Materials	100	18	24	24	20	13	14	60	40	35	65	69	31
School Transport Subsidy	100	0	2	15	56	27	0	16	84	8	92	3	97
Electricity Subsidy	100	2	3	9	22	65	1	12	88	16	84	18	82
Other SA	100	13	20	16	17	34	11	48	52	46	54	53	47
All Private Transfers	100	4	8	14	21	54	2	22	78	24	76	41	59
Remittances	100	4	8	14	20	55	2	23	77	24	76	43	57
Local	100	4	8	11	16	63	3	20	80	18	82	31	69
Foreign	100	4	7	16	23	49	2	25	75	29	71	52	48
Charity	100	2	9	13	24	51	2	20	80	22	78	32	68
Public + Private	100	6	10	14	19	50	4	28	72	24	76	42	58
Memo for Comparison													
Share of total population	100	20	20	20	20	20	16	56	44	43	58	61	39
Share of poor population	100	36	36	29	0	0	n.a.	n.a.	n.a.	58	42	81	19
Share of total consumption	100	5	9	13	20	54	4	24	76	24	76	37	63
Share of total income	100	2	7	11	18	62	4	24	76	23	77	35	65

Source: World Bank calculations using the ENCOVI 2000, Instituto Nacional de Estadística—Guatemala. Categories are not additive as people can receive more than one type of transfer. Quintiles are individual consumption quintiles.

poorest quintile receives only 1% (Table 12.4). Moreover, social insurance benefits represent 4% of total consumption for the richest quintile, as compared with less than 1% for the poorest (Table 12.5).

Social assistance programs are generally better targeted, though target outcomes vary significantly by program. Overall, the top quintile receives a larger share of social assistance transfers than the poorest quintile (Table 12.4). Nonetheless, SA programs are relatively more important to the poor (contributing 8.4% of total consumption of the poorest quintile) than the rich (accounting for just 1.1% of total consumption of the top quintile, Table 12.5). Target outcomes vary significantly by program. Scholarships, for example, are very poorly targeted, with the top quintile capturing close to half of all scholarship benefits (Table 12.4). Similarly, the top two quintiles receive 83% of all subsidies to school transport. Likewise, 65% of all electricity subsidies accrue

TABLE 12.5: RELATIVE INCIDENCE OF SOCIAL PROTECTION PROGRAMS AND PRIVATE TRANSFERS (THE "IMPORTANCE" OF THE TRANSFERS)
Average transfers received by each group as % of average total consumption for each group

	Total	Q1	Q2	Q3	Q4	Q5	XP	AP	NP	Ind.	Non-Ind	Rural	Urban
			By Quintile				By Poverty Group			By Ethnicity		By Area	
All Public SP	5.8	9.1	8.5	6.8	5.3	5.0	8.9	8.0	2.5	5.9	5.8	7.0	5.1
All SI	2.8	0.8	1.0	1.1	2.1	3.9	0.7	1.0	0.3	1.1	3.3	1.5	3.5
Pensions	1.8	0.4	0.4	0.5	1.1	2.7	0.5	0.4	0.1	3.3	2.2	0.9	2.3
Survivorship	0.4	0.2	0.2	0.1	0.2	0.5	0.2	0.2	0.1	0.7	0.4	0.2	0.5
Alimony	0.6	0.1	0.4	0.5	0.7	0.7	0.0	0.4	0.1	0.1	0.7	0.5	0.7
All SA	3.0	8.4	7.5	5.7	3.2	1.1	8.2	7.0	2.1	4.8	2.5	5.5	1.6
School Feeding	1.9	6.2	5.7	4.2	2.0	0.4	6.0	5.2	1.6	3.4	1.5	4.2	0.6
Snack	0.4	1.0	0.9	0.8	0.5	0.1	1.0	0.9	0.3	0.6	0.3	0.6	0.2
Breakfast	1.1	3.6	3.5	2.4	0.9	0.2	3.5	3.1	1.0	1.9	0.8	2.7	0.1
Powdered Milk	0.0	0.1	0.1	0.0	0.0	0.0	0.0	0.1	0.0	0.0	0.0	0.0	0.0
Glass of Milk	0.1	0.2	0.2	0.1	0.1	0.0	0.2	0.2	0.0	0.1	0.0	0.1	0.0
Glass of Atol	0.4	1.3	1.0	0.8	0.5	0.1	1.4	1.0	0.3	0.7	0.3	0.7	0.2
Scholarships	0.1	0.2	0.1	0.3	0.1	0.1	0.1	0.2	0.1	0.3	0.1	0.1	0.2
School Materials	0.4	1.3	1.1	0.7	0.4	0.1	1.4	0.9	0.3	0.5	0.3	0.7	0.2
Sch. Transport Subsidy	0.1	0.0	0.0	0.1	0.2	0.0	0.0	0.1	0.0	0.0	0.1	0.0	0.1
Subsidy													
Electricity Subsidy	0.3	0.1	0.1	0.2	0.3	0.4	0.1	0.1	0.0	0.2	0.3	0.1	0.4
Other SA	0.2	0.6	0.5	0.3	0.2	0.1	0.6	0.4	0.1	0.4	0.2	0.3	0.2
All Private Transfers	5.0	3.5	4.7	5.3	5.2	5.0	3.0	4.7	5.3	4.8	5.0	5.5	4.6
Remittances	3.9	3.1	3.5	4.2	3.9	3.9	2.5	3.8	4.0	3.9	3.9	4.6	3.5
Local	1.6	1.3	1.3	1.4	1.3	1.9	1.3	1.4	1.8	1.2	1.8	1.4	1.8
Foreign	2.3	1.8	2.3	2.8	2.6	2.0	1.2	2.4	2.6	2.6	2.1	3.2	1.7
Charity	1.1	0.4	1.2	1.1	1.3	1.0	0.5	0.9	1.2	1.0	1.1	0.9	1.1
Public + Private	10.8	12.6	13.2	12.1	10.5	10.0	11.9	12.7	3.9	10.7	10.8	12.5	9.8
Memo:													
Avg Total Cons.	6161	1580	2639	3884	6076	16632	1460	2580	10754	3531	8108	3668	10122

Source: World Bank calculations using the ENCOVI 2000, *Instituto Nacional de Estadística—Guatemala.* Categories are not additive as people can receive more than one type of transfer. Quintiles are individual consumption quintiles.

to the top quintile. These programs are quite small however, in terms of their contribution to average consumption in any quintile (Table 12.5). In contrast, school feeding and the school materials assistance program (*bolsa de utiles escolares*) benefit primarily the middle quintiles (Table 12.4), but are still relatively more important to the poorest (Table 12.5).

Incidence of Private Transfers
Private transfers are regressive in both absolute and relative terms. The top quintile receives over half of all private transfers (remittances and donations) in Guatemala (Table 12.4). Private transfers are also relatively more important for the rich, contributing 5% of total consumption for the top quintile as compared with 3.5% for the bottom quintile (Table 12.5). Interestingly, local remittances are more regressive than foreign remittances or charity in absolute terms.

Overall Effectiveness of SP Programs

The indicators of coverage, absolute target incidence, and relative target incidence (importance/adequacy) all reveal important information about the effectiveness of SP programs. This section seeks to combine those multiple indicators for a more comprehensive review of these programs, in particular with respect to their effectiveness in reducing poverty.

Figures 12.5 and 12.6 plot in a single graphs the three related concepts of coverage, absolute target incidence, and adequacy for various social protection programs and private transfers based on a simulated model that classifies the poor based on a counterfactual of consumption *without* the transfers. The x-axis presents the coverage of the "ex ante" poor (the poor without the transfers, which represent 61% of the population). The share of total benefits received by the "ex ante" poor is plotted on the y-axis (absolute target incidence). Adequacy (relative incidence) is captured by the size of the "bubbles" in the graphs. A "perfectly-targeted program" would be located on the upper right-hand side of these graphs, with a large bubble (equal to the size of the poverty gap before the transfer).

While none of the programs are close to "perfect" in terms of targeting or coverage, some are better than others (Figure 12.5). In particular, only social assistance provides relatively

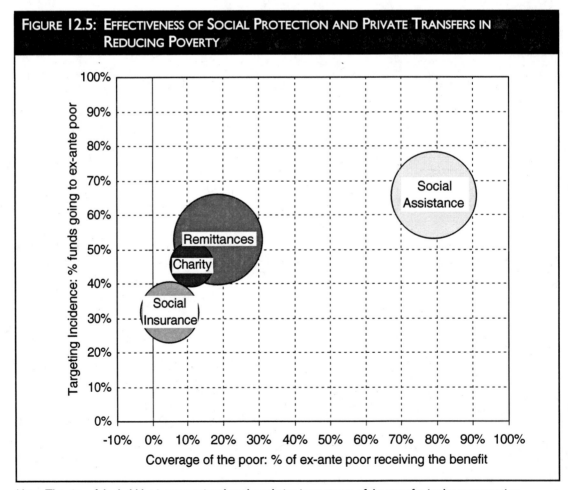

FIGURE 12.5: EFFECTIVENESS OF SOCIAL PROTECTION AND PRIVATE TRANSFERS IN REDUCING POVERTY

Note: The size of the bubbles is proportional to the relative importance of the transfer in the consumption of the recipient.

World Bank calculations using the ENCOVI 2000, *Instituto Nacional de Estadísticas—Guatemala*

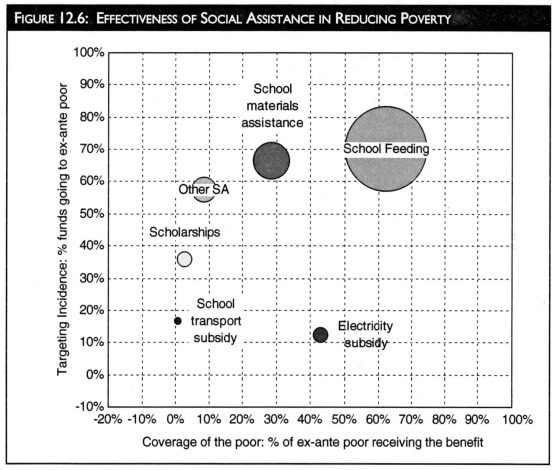

FIGURE 12.6: EFFECTIVENESS OF SOCIAL ASSISTANCE IN REDUCING POVERTY

Note: The size of the bubbles is proportional to the relative importance of the transfer in the consumption of the recipient.

World Bank calculations using the ENCOVI 2000, *Instituto Nacional de Estadísticas—Guatemala*

high coverage with relatively large transfers. Social insurance and private transfers all cover a smaller fraction of the poor. In terms of adequacy (relative importance), remittances and social insurance are the most important for their poor recipients (as a share of ex ante consumption). None of the programs are very well targeted in terms of the absolute share of funds going to the ex ante poor. Since the ex ante poor represent 61% of the population, even social assistance is at best a neutral benefit in terms of absolute target incidence (with 66% of all benefits going to the ex ante poor).

Within social assistance, the effectiveness of programs varies significantly (Figure 12.6). Three types of programs are observed. First, the school feeding programs (combined) and the school materials program have the best target incidence and relatively high coverage. Second, the two subsidy programs, for electricity and school transport, have extremely low targeting incidence and adequacy. From a poverty-alleviation perspective, these programs should be redesigned or eliminated. Third, scholarships have extremely low coverage of the poor, target incidence, and adequacy. Again, these programs should be redesigned to better target the poor.

Impact on Poverty and Inequality
Simulations suggest little impact of social protection programs on poverty or inequality.
Data from the ENCOVI 2000 were used to simulate poverty and inequality in an absence of social

protection programs or transfers.[14] Total transfers (public and private) succeed in reducing poverty from 61% without the transfers to 56%, and the poverty gap index from 0.29 to 0.23 and the poverty severity index from 0.19 to 0.12. Nonetheless, these reductions were only significant for the poverty gap (depth) and severity indices, but not the headcount index. In other words, total transfers will not lift many people out of poverty, but will reduce the depth and severity of their destitution. While social insurance has *no* significant impact on poverty, social assistance does have a significant impact on the depth and severity of extreme poverty. Similarly, while an elimination of all transfers (public and private) would increase inequality from a Gini of 48 to a Gini of 51, some transfers (for example, social insurance and the electricity subsidy) actually contribute to an increase in inequality.

Cost-Benefit Analysis

Comparing the costs[15] and benefits of social protection programs reveals that social assistance programs are the most efficient in reducing poverty. Social assistance programs cost between Q1.4 to Q2 to reduce the poverty gap by Q1. School feeding programs, for example, costs Q1.5 on average for each Q1 reduction in the poverty gap. Some social assistance programs, however, are quite cost inefficient: school transport subsidies and scholarships cost Q6 and Q3 to reduce the poverty gap by Q1. The energy subsidy is even less efficient, costing Q8 for every Q1 reduction in the poverty gap. In contrast, social insurance programs are extremely inefficient for poverty reduction, costing between Q5 to Q9 for a reduction of Q1 in the poverty gap.

Summary of Key Issues and Priorities

The above analysis reveals a number of key messages and recommendations:

- **Strategic priorities** for social protection in Guatemala should (a) seek to maintain the current focus on children, given their inherent vulnerabilities and prospects for long-term transmission of poverty; and (b) seek to build the assets of the poor, given the dominance of chronic, rather than transient, poverty as discussed in Chapter 11. Public social protection programs can play an important role in building the assets of the poor. Specifically, when designed properly, conditional-transfer programs can be quite effective in helping ease demand-side constraints, which have been shown to constitute important limitations for improved coverage of education (Chapter 7), health (Chapter 8) and basic utility services (Chapter 9). Some transfers (social assistance) could also be desirable to alleviate the poverty and suffering of the *extreme* poor.
- Although low by international standards, **public spending** on social protection has increased since the Peace Accords. Much could be done within the existing budget envelope to improve the effectiveness and efficiency of public social protection spending as an instrument to reduce poverty and vulnerability, including: (a) eliminating programs that are poorly targeted, inefficient and ineffective; and (b) consolidating, rationalizing, improving the targeting and expanding coverage of remaining programs.
- **Better targeting** could be achieved using various tools, including geographic targeting via the poverty map (for example, selecting eligible municipalities with high concentrations of poor or extreme poor people, as has recently been done for scholarships), categorical targeting (for example, no connection to electricity, which is a very good proxy for the extreme poor), piggy-backed targeting via self-targeted services (for example, channeling

---

14. See Tesliuc and Lindert (2002a) for details on methodology and results.

15. Due to data limitations, the costs used for this analysis include only the value of the benefits provided by the programs as reported by the beneficiaries in the ENCOVI. They do not include administrative costs or potential incentive effects. See Tesliuc and Lindert (2002a) for details.

benefits through health posts or community health centers which are well targeted to the poor), or some form of means testing (or a combination of targeting tools).

- Certain **social assistance** programs should be eliminated due to extremely poor targeting, ineffectiveness, and cost inefficiencies. The **electricity subsidy** is a candidate ripe for elimination—the funds would be better used to further expand electricity coverage for the rural poor (as discussed in Chapter 9). If a sudden single elimination seems politically unfeasible, the eligibility threshold could be substantially reduced (for example, to 100 KwH or less) as an intermediate step on the way to a phased elimination. The **school transport subsidy** is another candidate for elimination or redeployment to rural areas (where a lack of public transport to school *is* an issue) since, as currently designed, it offers virtually no benefits to the poor and is virtually entirely urban focused.

- The seven miniscule and poorly-targeted **scholarship programs** should be consolidated, streamlined, and explicitly targeted to the poor. A well-designed scholarship program has the potential to be an effective conditional-transfer that could ease demand-side constraints to enrollment and attendance for the poor (as discussed in Chapter 7). To do so, the programs should be effectively targeted to the poor (individuals or entire schools in very poor communities) and benefits should be tied to well-monitored daily attendance (preferably paid on a more frequent basis according to attendance registries). At present the dispersed set of programs do not satisfy either condition.

- **School feeding programs** can also provide strong incentives for regular school attendance in poor communities. Indeed, children in the QPES study cited the "refacción" (school snack) as one of the main reasons the like going to school. School feeding programs should not, however, be considered as nutrition interventions, since (a) malnutrition occurs at a much younger age; and (b) Guatemala's nutrition problems do not arise primarily from a lack of food (see Chapter 8). Guatemala's school feeding programs could be strengthened by: (a) improving the targeting of school eligibility based on the poverty map combined with educational attendance and enrollment information; (b) consolidating and rationalizing the implementation of the various programs to improve efficiency and institutional responsibility (and avoiding the recent state of flux that has commonly disrupted program execution); and (c) decentralizing food procurement and preparation to the communities by providing eligible and certified communities (or hub communities serving several eligible satellite communities) block grants to purchase and prepare food locally, which would have the benefits of improving community participation, stimulating local economies, and reducing the costs of shipping and storage of food (and possibly improving quality by allowing for discretion and local tastes). The programs should also investigate the use of powdered milk, which could actually be dangerous for children if combined with unpotable water.

- The **school materials program** (bolsa de utiles) could be improved with explicit targeting (see above).

- Regarding the creation of new **social assistance programs,** Guatemala may want to consider **conditional transfer programs** channeled through self-targeted health services (health posts and community health centers) that require certain health interventions for children to be eligible (for example, growth monitoring, vaccinations). These have the dual advantage of alleviating short-term poverty (by providing relief via a transfer payment) and reducing long-term poverty (by providing incentives to build incentives). Well-targeted conditional transfers have proven to be quite effective in other countries (for example, Progresa in Mexico). An expansion of well-targeted **workfare** programs may also be considered to help provide seasonal employment alternatives, particularly for those dependent on migration to the coffee fincas, in light of recent terms-of-trade shocks.

- **Disaster management and relief** should be expanded and improved, since Chapter 11 shows that the poor in Guatemala are disproportionately more exposed to natural disasters and agriculture-related shocks. Such interventions should be well-targeted to the poor and delivered in a timely manner. Since exposure to some natural disasters does seem to be largely determined by location and geographic factors, administrative maps of vulnerability to drought, seismic activities, hurricanes, storms, frosts, and landslides could be quite useful instruments for risk management planning. Many such maps have been prepared by the Ministry of Agriculture and FAO, and are available to policy makers. Their ability to target limited funds for disaster relief would be greatly enhanced if used in conjunction with poverty maps (since those who are already poor are less equipped to cope with shocks, as shown in Chapter 11). Since the impact of natural disasters often includes damage to, or destruction of, community infrastructure (in addition to income and wealth losses at the household level, see Chapter 11), the social funds may serve as the institutional channel by which such relief and infrastructure rehabilitation is implemented.

- When budgets and administrative capabilities permit, the Government should seek ways to improve the public **social insurance** coverage of the poor. Recent attempts to cover specific vulnerable groups, such as agricultural migrant workers, seem promising and should be considered for expansion.

- **Private transfers** do constitute an important source of income, accounting for almost half of all transfers between households in Guatemala. Nonetheless, they should not be viewed as a substitute for government assistance of the poor, since they are highly regressive. Nonetheless, attention should be paid to the effects of global economic recessions on such transfers, since they do contribute to the incomes of the poor.

PART 4

KEY CHALLENGE: EMPOWERMENT

"The services at the municipality are deficient. Sometimes there are lots of people and you have to wait two days [to obtain documentation] . . . When there's a political campaign, they treat you well, after that, no . . . They always tell us 'wait over there' and when a Ladino enters, they always say 'come on in' (pasen adelante)."

Q'eqchi villagers, QE1 (QPES)

CHAPTER 13

BUILDING INSTITUTIONS AND EMPOWERING COMMUNITIES

As discussed in Chapter 4, one of the key remaining challenges for the Peace Agenda is the modernization of the state and a strengthening of community and social participation.[1] This chapter contends that these institutional forces are also crucial for the "Poverty Agenda," influencing the menu of options available to the Government in future efforts to reduce poverty and the way in which these options are carried out. Indeed, poverty is not only the result of economic processes, but also of interacting economic, social and political forces. In particular, it is driven by the accountability and responsiveness of state institutions. Social institutions (kinship systems, community organizations, and informal networks) also greatly affect poverty outcomes, helping communities manage public goods, cope with risks and shocks, and leverage external assistance. In light of the importance of these factors for both poverty and the Peace Agenda, this chapter reviews key institutional challenges in the areas of (a) public sector management; (b) governance; and (c) community participation and social capital. The chapter also considers the role of other important actors in development, namely the private sector, NGOs, and religious organizations.

Public Sector Management

Guatemala's democratic transition faces a number of challenges regarding effective public sector management. An effective government is a vital necessity for development and poverty reduction. At a minimum, governments should effectively seek to create an environment that is conducive to economic growth, provide basic public goods (such as defense, law and order, protection of property rights, public health and stable macroeconomic management) and protect the poor via anti-poverty programs and disaster relief. Other important functions include the management of externalities (basic education, pollution), the regulation of monopoly power, and the provision of social insurance, financial regulation and consumer protection to overcome imperfect information and improve equity.[2] Although Guatemala has made serious efforts since the Peace

---

1. MINUGUA (2001a).
2. World Bank (1997).

Accords to improve living conditions and promote a more inclusive, democratic society (as discussed in Chapter 4), these efforts have been hampered by a weak public sector. Such weaknesses curb the Government's ability to deliver services, create an environment conducive to growth, and reduce poverty. Key challenges in this area include: (i) a fragile and inadequate fiscal base; (ii) weak public expenditure management; (iii) a weak civil service; and (iv) an overly centralized government. These issues are treated in turn below.

Inadequate Tax Base

Despite some progress, Guatemala's inadequate tax base remains a fundamental challenge to improving the government's ability to deliver effectively and to fulfilling a key target established by the Peace Accords. Successive post-war governments have made some progress in increasing total government revenues, which rose from 9.2% of GDP in 1996 to an estimated 11.1% in 2001.[3] Such increases were aided by the adoption of a variety of tax measures, including increasing the VAT rate from 7% to 10% in 1996, and again from 10% to 12% in August 2001 amid strong popular opposition, as well as efforts to improve the efficiency of the tax collection agency and clamp down on tax evasion. Nonetheless, the current level of revenues fails to meet the targets set by the Peace Accords (see Chapter 4) and remains relatively low. In comparison, current revenue averaged 14.2% for lower-middle income countries and 20.1% for all of LAC for 1998.[4] Moreover, the outlook for public finances in coming years is blurred by the weak state of the domestic economy, the likely impact of the US and global recession, and the cost of consolidating and modernizing the country's financial system. Without adequate resources, the Government's hands are tied in its ability to deliver the services and investments needed to reduce poverty. The inadequate revenue base thus constitutes one of the key challenges for both the Peace Agenda and the "Poverty Agenda."

Public Spending and Public Expenditure Management

The Government has made considerable progress in increasing public spending and improving public expenditure management. Public spending has increased since the signing of the Peace Accords, with notable gains in sectors that are crucial for poverty reduction (Table 13.1). Moreover, progress has been made in improving the management of public expenditures with the introduction and implementation of the Integrated Financial Management System (SIAF) since 1998. Accomplishments include *inter alia:* extending SIAF coverage to some 82% of public spending for budget formulation, execution, cash management and internal audit; eliminating arrears to suppliers; improving transparency with full, real-time open access to account information; implementing reforms in public procurement processes; and improving public investment planning and better coordination with SEGEPLAN. Furthermore, the gap between planned and executed spending has improved since the introduction of SIAF (Table 13.1).

Nonetheless, public spending remains low and public expenditure management still suffers from a number of weaknesses. Despite increases, the overall level of public spending remains relatively low as a share of GDP (Table 13.1), hampered largely by the inadequate revenue base (see above). In comparison to Guatemala, the averages for lower-middle income countries and the LAC region overall were 18.8% and 21.0% of GDP respectively in 1998.[5] In addition, despite widespread coverage of the SIAF, the system needs to be extended to cover the remaining 18% of government spending, most notably to bring in the municipalities and social funds. Spending allocations are also fairly inflexible, with a substantial share of the budget earmarked for specific uses by legal mandates (24% of the total budget).[6] Moreover, the current budget planning process is weak,

---

3. World Bank macroeconomic database for Guatemala.
4. World Bank (2001b).
5. World Bank (2001b).
6. CIEN (2000).

TABLE 13.1: PUBLIC SPENDING, 1996–2001	1996	1997	1998	1999	2000	2001
Total Spending, mn Q.[a]	9,914.8	12,618.2	16,637.0	19,239.2	19,801.2	22,182.2
% of Total Spending:	100%	100%	100%	100%	100%	100%
Health	6.3	6.9	7.1	8.3	7.9	7.9
Water, sanitation, environment	1.8	1.9	1.2	1.8	2.2	2.2
Education	15.2	15.1	15.7	17.1	18.3	20.0
Housing	0.0	0.5	4.0	2.1	0.1	0.6
Justice	3.0	3.6	3.3	3.5	3.9	4.2
Urban and Rural Development	7.0	7.6	7.3	6.8	6.3	8.2
Spending/GDP (%):[a]						
Total	10.4	11.7	13.4	14.2	13.4	13.8
Health	0.7	0.8	0.9	1.2	1.1	1.1
Water, sanitation, environment	0.2	0.2	0.2	0.2	0.3	0.3
Education	1.6	1.8	2.1	2.4	2.5	2.8
Housing	0.0	0.1	0.5	0.3	0.0	0.1
Justice	0.3	0.4	0.4	0.5	0.5	0.6
Urban and Rural Development	0.7	0.9	1.0	1.0	0.8	1.1
Executed/Planned						
Total	78	83	100	91	93	100
Health	62	92	92	90	94	134
Water, sanitation, environment	51	69	97	74	87	134
Education	112	93	95	92	98	96
Housing	7	96	95	98	83	53
Justice	98	100	100	93	91	95
Urban and Rural Development	92	91	83	97	78	90

Sources: SIAF/Ministry of Finance (Feb. 12, 2002). a. Spending amounts refer to executed amounts (*devengado*). Note that the executed/planned ratio may be underestimated for 2001 since some executed amounts may not have been recorded at the time the figures were provided.

involving an overly detailed focus on incremental changes in budget line items or agency spending ceilings rather than a more comprehensive understanding and review of national priorities and government spending tradeoffs by all stakeholders (as would occur under a medium-term expenditure framework). Annual budgeting also hinders proper planning for multi-year projects and makes them more susceptible to political maneuvering and electoral cycles.

In addition, public spending is poorly targeted, with a limited share of public resources actually reaching the poor. As shown in Table 13.2, the poor receive a slightly smaller share of public spending on education and heath than their relative share in the population, and disproportionately less public spending on social protection. Investments by the social funds are slightly better targeted, though they still only transfer a slightly disproportionate share to the poor (62%) as compared with their share in the population (56%), as shown in Figure 13.1.[7] Nonetheless, social spending is relatively more progressive than the current distribution of income and consumption (Table 13.2), and would thus be inequality reducing.

---

7. The target incidence of public spending by social funds should be treated as a rough estimate. It was calculated using regional spending figures by the social funds (source: UNDP 2001b), combined with poverty rates (source: ENCOVI 2000) for each region (hence assuming that within each region, spending is allocated neutrally according to population shares).

TABLE 13.2: DISTRIBUTIONAL INCIDENCE OF PUBLIC SPENDING, BY SECTOR AND SOCIO-ECONOMIC GROUP
% of total benefits received by each group

	Total	By Quintile					By Poverty Group			By Ethnicity		By Area	
		Q1	Q2	Q3	Q4	Q5	XP	AP	NP	Ind.	Non-Ind	Rural	Urban
Education—Total	100	17	21	21	21	21	13	55	45	37	63	59	41
Health—Total	100	17	18	23	25	17	12	53	47	40	60	64	36
Social Protection—Total	100	8	13	15	18	46	6	33	67	25	75	45	55
Social Insurance—Total	100	1	3	5	15	76	1	9	91	9	91	20	80
Social Assistance—Total	100	15	23	25	21	16	11	58	42	41	59	70	30
Memo for Comparison													
Share of total population	100	20	20	20	20	20	16	56	44	43	58	61	39
Share of poor population	100	36	36	29	0	0	n.a.	n.a.	n.a.	58	42	81	19
Share of total consumption	100	5	9	13	20	54	4	24	76	24	76	37	63
Share of total income	100	2	7	11	18	62	4	24	76	23	77	35	65

Source: World Bank calculations using the ENCOVI 2000, *Instituto Nacional de Estadística—Guatemala.*
See Chapters 7, 8, 9, and 12 for details on the breakdown of the target incidence by sector. Quintiles are individual consumption quintiles.

A Weak Civil Service

The ability of the Government to deliver key public services and programs is hampered by low administrative capabilities and a weak civil service. Weak hiring practices, a lack of continuity, and uncertainty regarding policies and budgets hinder the effectiveness of Guatemala's civil service:

- **Relatively small civil service.** Reflecting the relatively low share of public sector spending in GDP, Guatemala's civil service is quite small by international standards.[8] The ENCOVI suggests that just over 200,000 people were employed by the public sector, representing just 5% of total employment and 3% of the labor force. The largest public employers were education (62%), the Ministry of Interior and National Security (*Gobernación,* 16%), and health (14%).[9] The number of civil service has been growing at a rate of 1.5% per year since 1996, or by about 10,000 workers

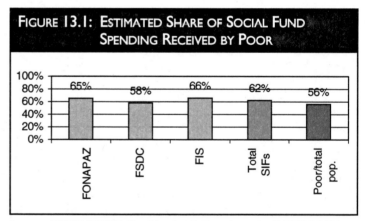

FIGURE 13.1: ESTIMATED SHARE OF SOCIAL FUND SPENDING RECEIVED BY POOR

Sources: UNDP (2001b) Combined with Data from the ENCOVI 2000.

---

8. Estimates of the size of the civil service vary, ranging from 150,000–205,000CIEN (August 2001) and Perlman (1995). These estimates translate into a ratio of approximately 132–180 civil service workers per 10,000 population. Comparable figures were 867 for Uruguay, 648 for Venezuela, 641 for Argentina, 340 for Peru, 330 for Ecuador, and 252 for Chile (all in 1990–91). World Bank (1996).

9. CIEN (2001c).

in total for the five years since the Peace Accords were signed. The main areas of growth have been in education, which grew by 3.8% p.a., and Ministry of Interior and National Security (*Gobernación*), which almost doubled in the five years since the Peace Accords (growing at an annual rate of 16.7%).

▧ **Weak incentives, lack of continuity.** Because the official civil service salary structure is lower than for comparable professions in the private sector,[10] the Government has resorted to hiring temporary workers and "consultants" as a widespread practice in order to offer better incentives for hiring qualified people. As a result, the ENCOVI reveals that only 15% of public-sector workers have permanent contracts, while 62% have temporary contracts and 23% report having no contract at all.[11] Such temporary status has obvious adverse impacts for efficient public sector management, including an undermining of institutional memory, continuity, technical capacity, and staff motivation.

▧ **Arbitrary hiring and evaluation practices.** Moreover, hiring practices appear to be fairly arbitrary. According to a survey of current and former civil servants, carried out by CIEN (August 2001), although 64% of survey respondents indicate having been hired based on merit criteria, some 77% also respond that other factors, such as political connections, factored in hiring decisions. Two-thirds indicate that changes in government yield substantial changes in the policies they are implementing. Some 88% complain of uncertainty in their budgets, with divergences between planned and actual spending allocations yielding significant changes in their work programs. In addition, almost half (47%) indicate that their work is not evaluated according to clear performance standards. Finally, there is little representation of the indigenous in the government structure or the ethnic make-up of the civil service.

Decentralization

Finally, the government is overly centralized, particularly in light of Guatemala's heterogeneity. The Central Government accounts for 68% of total public spending.[12] The budget and financial management are also highly centralized under the Ministry of Finance, though a recent pilot with the Ministries and Health and Education gave them increased control over their own budgets. Government offices and services are disproportionately concentrated in the capital. Given the heterogeneity of Guatemala's population, economy, and topography, decentralization of many public functions could bring the government closer to the client and improve the delivery of public services. Guatemala has made some initial progress on the long path towards enabling decentralization, for example with the introduction of general revenue transfers to municipalities in the 1980s,[13] some deconcentration of sectoral management to department levels, the channeling of resources via newly created and elected Regional and Departmental Councils, and the creation of the Presidential Commission for the Modernization and Decentralization of the State. Since the early 1990s, several mechanisms have emerged with decentralized management of specific programs and activities, such as the Sistema Integral de Atención de Salud (SIAS) and the Programa Nacional de Autogestión para el Desarollo Educativo (PRONADE). Social funds, which work directly with communities to expedite the delivery of infrastructure and services, have also increased their share of government spending (though they remain centralized agencies). As for decentralization to municipalities *per se*, Congress recently passed three laws to broadly define areas of responsibility (the *Ley de los Consejos de Desarrollo Urbano y Rural*, the *Código Municipal*, and

---

10. CIEN (2001c). Indeed, the ENCOVI shows that hourly earnings for those with permanent contracts are lower than those with temporary contracts (Q15.3 per hour as compared with Q19.1 per hour on average).

11. It is important to note, however, that although the ENCOVI is representative for households in Guatemala, it is not representative for public civil servants.

12. Some of this "central government" spending, however, is transferred to decentralized programs such as PRONADE or SIAS. World Bank draft Project Appraisal Document for a proposed Third Integrated Financial Management Reform Loan.

13. Rojas (1999).

TABLE 13.3: COMPOSITE GOVERNANCE INDICATORS, INTERNATIONAL COMPARISONS, 2001
World Rankings (lower is better), Numbers in parentheses refer to Guatemala's ranking out of LAC countries

	Voice and Accountability	Political Instability	Government Effectiveness	Regulatory Burden	Rule of Law	Corruption
Guatemala	105 (21/26)	130 (23/26)	112 (21/26)	83 (15/27)	147 (25/27)	116 (21/26)
El Salvador	68	49	87	23	119	86
Honduras	84	70	108	104	153	111
Nicaragua	86	65	116	106	134	122
Panamá	49	50	81	25	80	94
Costa Rica	16	24	37	26	50	32
CA Median	76	58	98	55	127	99
Number of Countries (N=)	173	161	159	169	170	161

Source: Kaufmann, Kraay, and Zoido-Lobatón (January 2002). Database and definitions can be accessed at the following website: http://www.worldbank.org/wbi/governance/govdata2001.htm

the *Ley General de Descentralización*), although leaving the final definition of responsibilities to laws pertaining to specific sectors and central government decisions (reflecting the differing sectoral needs and characteristics). Such laws now need to be put into effect.

Governance
Related to its weaknesses in public sector management, Guatemala scores fairly poorly on most governance indicators. There is strong empirical evidence of a causal relationship between good governance and better development outcomes, including higher per capita incomes, lower infant mortality, and higher literacy.[14] World Bank researchers recently compiled a massive cross-country database of some 300 governance indicators, yielding six key clusters of composite measures: voice and accountability, political instability, government efficiency, regulatory burden, rule of law, and corruption.[15]

Guatemala scores poorly for most of these (Table 13.3). Nonetheless, a summary indicator of country policy and institutional quality (CPIA) suggests that Guatemala has made some progress over time, particularly since the Peace Accords (Figure 13.2). Key challenges for the development and poverty reduction agenda include fighting corruption, improving the rule of law and the justice system, and reducing political instability, as discussed in more detail below.

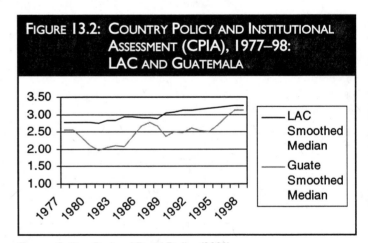

FIGURE 13.2: COUNTRY POLICY AND INSTITUTIONAL ASSESSMENT (CPIA), 1977–98: LAC AND GUATEMALA

Source: Collier, Paul and David Dollar (2002).

14. Kaufmann, Kraay, and Zoido-Lobatón (2002).
15. Database compiled by Kaufmann, Kraay, and Zoido-Lobatón (1999). Database and documentation can be found at the following website: http://www.worldbank.org/wbi/governance/wp-governance.htm

Corruption

Guatemala's corruption problem is serious. Indeed, Guatemala ranks among the worst 28% of countries in the world on an international composite measure of corruption (Table 13.3). The current Government has been plagued by a stream of corruption scandals, including allegations of misuse of public funds, mis-procurement, embezzlement, and cover-ups.[16] A recent public opinion survey found that 92% of Guatemalans perceive that corruption is high.[17] A recent report by Transparency International alleges that 24% of the annual national budget in 2001 would be lost to corruption and financial mismanagement[18]—a particularly serious problem given Guatemala's already low public finance base. Guatemala was also recently placed on the OECD-backed Financial Action Task Force (FATF) "money-laundering blacklist," though the recent passage of the "anti-money laundering" law in November 2001 should contribute to improving the country's standing in this respect.[19] Although a special public prosecutor's office was set up in 2000 to deal with corruption cases, to date only 13 cases have been taken to court, with just two convictions.[20] Corruption occurs not only at government levels, but even at the village level; in the QPES, numerous villages reported problems with misuse of funds by community development committees (or specialized committees such as the water committee). On-going extension and implementation of the SIAF system should help improve transparency and reduce discretional spending and misuse of public funds. In addition, the Government has recently launched an important initiative to combat corruption. This initiative—formalized in a Letter of Intent from the Government—involves the creation of a national program to promote global transparency in Guatemala. With support from the World Bank and the international community and the participation of civil society, it will seek to further diagnose and analyze the issue of corruption in Guatemala and develop a national plan to combat corruption. This initiative represents an important step in improving governance and promoting transparency in Guatemala.

Corruption affects the poor in several ways. Corruption affects the poor indirectly via it's adverse impact on economic growth, which is critical for poverty reduction.[21] The poor are also affected directly, since corruption (e.g., bribes) levies a type of "regressive tax," (though such "taxes" are worse than income taxes because their amounts are uncertain and the revenues are not plowed back into the provision of public services). In fact, households in the ENCOVI ranked corruption/bad government as the second main cause of poverty in Guatemala (tied with "high prices" and following a lack of adequate employment opportunities, which was ranked as the top cause). There are also clear links between Guatemala's political instability, protests and corruption—both recently and historically with corruption at the roots of the original uprisings in the civil war (see above). The Government's credibility for raising taxes has also been intimately tied with corruption and misuse of funds in popular opinion and media commentary. Simply put, unless the Government can clean up the use of public funds, continued resistance to increased funding of the public sector is likely, further jeopardizing the Government's ability to deliver services and reduce poverty.

The Rule of Law, Justice, Crime and Violence

Guatemala is also plagued by a widespread lack of the "rule of law." Empirical evidence clearly links an efficient justice system and an upholding of the rule of law with better economic

---

16. EIU (November 2001); numerous articles in La Prensa, Siglo-XXI, and other daily newspapers.

17. Survey carried out by Vox Latina—Acción Ciudadana (April 2001), as cited by CIEN (2001a).

18. Transparency International (2001) and EIU (2001).

19. Problems included poor secrecy rules, failure to classify money-laundering (other than that related to drug trafficking) as a criminal offense, laws preventing the authorities from sharing information with other countries in investigations, and the lack of a specific body to investigate such transactions. EIU (2001).

20. EIU (2001).

21. There is ample cross-country evidence that higher levels of corruption are associated with lower growth. World Bank (2002).

performance.[22] The justice system is crucial for enforcing property rights, convicting criminals, and protecting citizens' rights. Such guarantees are particularly crucial for the poor, who cannot afford to protect themselves or seek legal representation. Guatemala ranks among the worst 14% of countries in the world for a composite indicator of "rule of law," which measures the extent to which people have confidence in and abide by the rules of society, including the incidence of crime, the effectiveness and predictability of the judiciary, and the enforceability of contracts (Table 13.3).[23] Within LAC, only Haiti and Honduras rank worse than Guatemala for effective rule of law. Some progress is evident, however, with improvements since the 1980s and in the period since signing of the Peace Accords in 1996.[24]

Indeed, Guatemala has a very weak administration of justice, indicated by lengthy case delays, limited and unequal access to justice, a lack of transparency and predictability in court decisions, extremely formal application of written law, and a lack of training of judges. In a 1998 user perception and public opinion survey of justice administration,[25] 89% of those interviewed indicated that there is a lack of adequate justice, characterizing the system as "corrupt," "inefficient" and "overly-centralized." The main obstacles for effective justice were identified as corruption, impunity, and violence. Over three quarters of those interviewed perceive the justice system as expensive, not only because of high legal fees, but also because of difficult access to justice services (including insufficient number of courts, geographic isolation, and language barriers). Frustrations towards the justice system are also evident because the general public does not have a unified understanding of the authorities responsible for justice administration. The ENCOVI 2000 reveals that most Guatemalans perceive justice to be in the hands of a variety of centralized authorities, including the Supreme Court (77%), Justice Ministry (72%), judges (86%), the President (55%), as well as the National Civil Police (PNC, 56%), and the Army (45%). The latter attribution is particularly surprising since the responsibility of the Army is to defend citizens, and not administer justice. This likely reflects the experiences of the civil war when the Army arbitrarily assumed the role of the justice system. In addition, a third of the population perceives communities as responsible for providing justice, with a higher share of the poor (41%) perceiving community-responsibility for justice than the non-poor (26%), perhaps reflecting relatively less access of the poor to the formal justice system than the non-poor. Indigenous groups were also more likely to perceive community-responsibility for justice, probably reflecting the historical exclusion and isolation of these groups. Such findings are echoed in the QPES, in which villagers report resolving conflicts either by going directly to top Government officials or locally within the community with little of decentralized courts (see Box 13.1).

Closely related to the weak justice system are the extra-judicial killings, which occur in Guatemala with alarming frequency. Indeed, lynchings have become a well-known practice in Guatemala, as citizens decide to enforce the law themselves due to perceived failures in the formal justice system. Between 1996 and 2000, some 337 lynchings were reported by MINUGUA, resulting in some 635 victims.[26] One third of these occurred in 1999 alone. Over half were executed in the western regions of the country (Nor-Occidente and Sur-Occidente), which also claim relatively high poverty rates and were heavily involved in the civil war (as discussed in Chapter 4). The 1998 justice survey revealed that 69% of those interviewed approved of lynchings as a form of justice (76% among the indigenous).[27]

Likewise, crime and violence—particularly in urban areas—have increased in the wake of the armed conflict. Indeed, the ENCOVI suggests that "violence, alcoholism, and family prob-

---

22. World Bank (2002).

23. Kaufmann, Kraay, and Zoido-Lobatón (2002).

24. For example, Guatemala's ranking on the International Country Risk Guide's Rule of Law index roe from 1.1 in the 1980s to 2.3 in the period from 1990–96 to 2.8 in the period from 1996–98 (on a scale of 1–7 where 1 is the most risky).

25. Aragon and Associates (1998).

26. MINUGUA (2000).

27. Aragon and Associates (1998).

lems" was ranked by households as the third most common "community problem" in Guatemala (8%). This figure is particularly high in the Metropolitana Region (26%), where such problems were ranked second only to public services. Those in the richest quintile perceive such problems to be relatively more important than those in lower quintiles. Some 15% of all households report the occurrence of a violent event in the past 12 months, with theft (9%) being the most common type of crime reported, followed by assault (5%). Such events are reportedly more likely in urban areas (with 24% of urban households reporting them), in the Metropolitan Region (29%), and among the non-poor (21%), even when other factors are taken into account.[28] A qualitative study of urban violence also suggests that crime and violence is on the rise in the post-conflict period, inflicting significant intra-family, social, economic, and human capital costs.[29] Alcohol consumption was perceived as the most critical cause of violence in all communities studied. Rebuilding trust in the judicial and law enforcement system was seen as crucial for reducing the occurrence of crime and violence. Nonetheless, for communities in which the reformed PNC were present, a higher degree of trust was reported. In rural communities, the QPES suggests that domestic violence and conflicts with and between villages (over land, religious difference in particular) are fairly widespread problems, but with little or no involvement of the formal justice system in their resolution (Box 13.1).

BOX 13.1: INTERNAL AND EXTERNAL CONFLICTS: THE CASE OF QE1 (QPES)

Despite being small and ethnically homogeneous (Q'eqchi), the village of QE1 has been plagued by internal and external conflicts, relating primarily to differences over land and religion. Located in the Renion Norte, the village was founded about 30 years ago when the founding families migrated from other regions in search of land. Distribution of the land was managed by the founding families (particularly a prominent village leader), who led the initiative to gain access to the land and distribute the plots (primarily to males) in accordance with the procedures of INTA (the National Institute for Agrarian Transformation). Unequal land distribution has generated conflicts within the community. Although some residents are grateful to the leader for his initiative in managing the land, others complain that his family secured access to bigger and better pieces of land. Not all families have plots.

The village of QE1 has also experienced a serious land conflict with a neighboring community. Apparently the other community hired soldiers to force the villagers of QE1 to abandon their land by burning their houses, damaging their plantations, and whipping their community leader. In response, the community sent a letter to the President of the Republic and visited the Ministry of the Interior (Gobernación). As a result, the soldiers were withdrawn and numerous residents from the other community were arrested. It is interesting to note, however, that the village did not turn to any local judicial authorities for help in resolving the conflict—the only way they were able to get action was through centralized authorities in Guatemala City.

Religious affiliation also generates conflicts inside the community that started due to confrontation between Evangelical (majority) and Catholic religious leaders. The tone of these confrontations has heightened and villagers now indicate that they attend services in other villages to avoid problems.

Political Instability

Political instability continues to reign in Guatemala. Although the country is currently experiencing its longest effort at sustaining a democratic system, which was bolstered by the Peace Accords, political instability remains a pervasive feature. Indeed, Guatemala still ranks among the top 20% of most politically unstable countries in the world (Table 13.3). Within LAC, only Colombia and Haiti rank worse than Guatemala for this indicator. Recent confrontations between the Government and private sector, divisions within the ruling party, a series of corruption scandals, various allegations of unconstitutional modifications of laws, weak management of public finances, protests and strikes in response to increases in the VAT, and perceived inadequate

---

28. Logit regression results provide the significance of these factors, controlling for other characteristics; figures in parentheses are cross-tabulations. Source: World Bank calculations using data from the ENCOVI—Instituto Nacional de Estadística—Guatemala.

29. Moser and McIlwaine (2001).

response to economic shocks and natural disasters have all contributed to a current climate of heightened instability.[30] Indeed, Guatemala maintains a score of "D" on the Economist Intelligence Unit's political risk ratings (with "E" being the highest risk), though the EIU does not forecast the risk of a military coup as likely.[31] Such instability further worsens Guatemala's prospects for growth and poverty reduction at a time when economic crisis calls for strong leadership and effective government.

Community Participation and Social Capital[32]

Communities have an important role to play in promoting their own development and ultimately in reducing poverty. Government is not the only actor in development and poverty reduction. In fact, in the absence of effective Government provision of public goods and services, communities are often forced to rally together to make decisions, manage public goods and collective resources, cope with shocks, and leverage external assistance. Moreover, the empowerment of communities and the promotion of participation are central themes in the Peace Accords (as discussed in Chapter 4).

Social capital is an important asset that can reduce vulnerability, increase opportunities, and empower local communities. Social capital is typically defined as norms, trust, and reciprocity networks that facilitate mutually beneficial cooperation in a community. Social capital generally develops in social interaction within, between and beyond communities, and can therefore be defined in three dimensions:

- First, **bonding social capital** develops *within* communities and constitutes the strong ties connecting family members neighbors, close friends and business associates. These ties connect people who share similar demographic characteristics. Some examples of bonding social capital are religious groups and neighborhood committees.
- Second, **bridging social capital,** created *between* communities, is defined as horizontal connections to people with broadly comparable economic status and political power. School committees, professional associations, groups that manage community-level public goods, and social groups are examples of bridging social capital.
- Finally, **linking social capital** describes interaction *beyond* communities and consists of the vertical ties between individuals and people or formal institutions in positions of influence. Connections to politicians and representatives of formal development organizations are examples of linking social capital.

International evidence suggests that better off individuals and communities tend to have "more" social capital, particularly more extensive networks (e.g., bridging, linking).[33]

Impact of Civil War on Social Capital

Despite decades of civil war, the overall level of participation in organizations and collective action is comparable to that of other countries. In terms of participation in organizations, the ENCOVI 2000 shows proportions of individuals participating in any type of formal group sum to 23%. This compares with Argentina, where participation in any group is close to 20%.[34] On aver-

---

30. EIU (January 2002a).

31. EIU (January 2002b) and EIU (2001). These risk ratings range from "A" (lowest risk) to "E" (highest risk). In Central America, Honduras and Nicaragua also scored a "D" on political risk, while Panama and El Salvador ranked as "C," and Costa Rica ranked as "B."

32. All numbers presented in this section come from World Bank calculations using the ENCOVI 2000, *Instituto Nacional de Estadística—Guatemala* unless otherwise specified. Village examples come from the QPES. For additional details, see GUAPA Technical Paper 12 (Ibáñez, Lindert and Woolcock, 2002).

33. World Bank (2001e).

34. Lederman (2002).

age, Guatemalans participate in 1.09 organizations and households participate in 1.11.[35] In the United States and Tanzania,[36] the mean value of membership in organizations per person is 1.8 and 1.5 respectively. In Indonesia and Bolivia,[37] the average number of associations each household is member is 5.5 and 1.4 respectively. Participation rates for collective action activities are significantly higher than membership rates in organizations, with 58% of the population participating in bridging activities and 23% participating in linking activities.[38] Unlike membership in organizations, community activities do necessarily not entail long-term commitments and time and monetary investments, which have been identified as barriers to participation (see below).

Social capital appears to have been both undermined and strengthened by the prolonged civil war. In some cases, the war encouraged solidarity and community cohesion: confronting the war further enhanced villagers' resolve to work as a unit and protect themselves from other threats. In the Kaqchiqel village of KA2 (QPES), for example, the war had devastating consequences, including a severe massacre in which the village's leadership was exterminated and the burning of crops and homes, which forced villagers to flee for two years. Nonetheless, the community has since organized several committees (for example, development committee, women's groups, a support group for widow victims of the war, a school committee). The development committee now acts as the "maximum authority," not only to solve problems, leverage assistance, and organize community activities, but also as a protective, security body (for example, protecting the village against a recent onslaught of gangs). The village of M1 provides another example of strong social capital despite the war (Box 13.2). On the other hand, the violence of the 1980s tested community

---

BOX 13.2: STRONG VILLAGE BONDS: THE CASE OF M1 (QPES)

Horizontal connections (**bonding social capital**) within the Mam village of M1 are quite strong, despite the fact that the village was invaded by both the army and the guerrillas during the civil war. Numerous formal organizations are active in the community, including a development committee that boasts representation of all families; sub-committees for education, water, and irrigation; an agricultural organization; and two women's groups. The community also operates a fairly successful revolving credit fund, which started with seed money from a Canadian organization but is now run entirely by the community, and a micro-enterprise committee for women. The village also appoints two rangers (*guardabosques*) to manage the common woods and their use (charging fees for people to gather wood). Villagers cite examples of mutual assistance: helping an orphan family, helping those facing a death in the family (with men providing firewood and women providing food), and financial transfers being provided by the church to poor families. The villagers also reportedly helped each other when they were ransacked during the conflict of the 1980s (and their homes were burned). Nonetheless, despite their participation in specific groups, the women of M1 acknowledge that they have little influence on community decisions.

The community also seems to have significant ties to external organizations (**linking social capital**), receiving aid and projects from FODIGUA, DECOPAZ, PRONADE, UNICEF, the E.U. and NGOs.

In contrast, other than remittances from migrant members in the US and Mexico, the community does not seem to have much in the way of "**bridging**" networks. This relative lack of influence over others perhaps explains their almost paradoxical complaints that they "lack organization, leaders" unlike "the ladinos who do help each other and collaborate with each other." They also indicate that they feel excluded from broader Guatemalan society due to the fact that most do not speak Spanish and to their physical isolation and distance from other communities. They likewise perceive discrimination in being treated or receiving medicines from the nearest hospital.

---

35. The average number of organizations at the household and individual level has a downward bias because the survey asked respondents to identify only the three main groups in which the individual is member. This bias however might not be significant since from 29,414 who answered this portion of the questionnaire, 8,316 participate in one group, 732 participate in a two groups and 105 participate in three groups.

36. Glaeser, E., D. Laibson, J. Scheinkman, and C. Soutter (2000).

37. Grootaert, C. (1999) and Grotaert and Narayan (2001).

38. Collective action activities include the following. For bridging: collecting funds, community workshops, labor agreements, donations in cash or kind, community childcare, construction of community infrastructure. For linking: contacting government officials, information campaigns, electoral campaigns, contacting local politicians, notifying judicial authorities.

ties and trust in the village of KI1 (see Box 4.3 in Chapter 4). Moreover, the ENCOVI also shows that participation rates in any type of organization are far lower for residents of the Region Norte, which is one of the epicenters of the later phase of the war. Such results suggest that the war may have prompted fear of involvement in organizations (or actively repressed them), and hence undermining social capital.

Stronger Within Village Bonds, Weaker Bridges

Social capital in Guatemala is mainly concentrated in strong horizontal, within-village connections. This pattern is reflected in both the QPES, where most connections are within villages and sometimes with external development agencies (see for example the case of M1 in Box 13.2) and in the ENCOVI 2000. Overall, participation rates in bonding organizations (18%) are over three times higher than those for bridging organizations (5%), with many communities having become somewhat closed in upon themselves as a result of war and physical isolation. Membership rates in bonding organizations is mainly driven by participation in religious groups (18% of the population), which constitutes the most common form of social capital in Guatemala. Recreation (3%) and groups that supervise public goods (2%) are the next most common forms of participation in organizations. Participation in income-generation groups, school committees, community service associations, and social and special interest groups is below one percent (each). Likewise, participation in collective activities reflects a rather limited scope of networks. The most common collective action activities are community construction, participation in labor exchange agreements, the provision of voluntary labor, and the collection of monetary or in-kind donations (all bridging activities); linking activities such as contacting local politicians, contacting government officials, participating in information or electoral campaigns, or notifying judicial authorities, are the least common.

Concentration of Social Capital Among Privileged Groups

Importantly, social capital seems to be concentrated among the privileged groups in Guatemalan society. As such, programs considering community-based targeting or community-driven development (CDD); such schemes should seek to ensure participation of excluded groups (e.g., women, the poor, the illiterate) so as to avoid a continuation of these patterns. These patterns are confirmed in both the QPES and the ENCOVI, and robust to specifications in multivariate logit regressions[39]:

- **Regional variations** are strong and significant. The Metropolitan Region reports significantly higher membership rates for formal organizations, whereas participation rates in the Norte Region, which had been one of the epicenters of the civil war, are significantly lower. By type of organization, participation in recreation groups was far stronger in the Metropolitan Region, whereas participation in religious groups was far lower in the Norte Region (than all other regions). Interestingly, the opposite is true for collective action, which is significantly weaker in the Metropolitana Region—perhaps because metropolitan residents can rely more on government-provided services to solve their problems for them. Indeed, Metropolitan residents were far less likely to participate in collective activities such as community construction, labor agreements, or community workshops, than those in other regions.
- Similar patterns are noted by **urban and rural areas.** Urban residents participate more than their rural counterparts in bridging organizations, particularly recreation groups. In contrast, rural residents participate more in organizations that supervise public goods and in collective action activities (particularly labor agreements and community construction)—perhaps reflecting a relative lack of the state's rural outreach in these activities.

---

39. Ibáñez, Lindert and Woolcock (2002).

- **Guatemalan men** tend to participate more than women (Figure 13.3). This is true for both membership in organizations and participation in collective action. The only exception is for participation in bonding organizations, which are dominated by religious organizations and in which women tend to participate more than men. Villagers in the QPES communities confirmed this finding: in virtually all villages, men and women agreed that women do not participate in community decision-making. Some women indicate that when the do try to participate, they are "mocked" by the men (due to *machista* attitudes; see for example the case of KI2 in Annex 5).

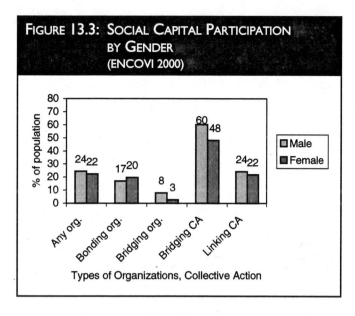

FIGURE 13.3: SOCIAL CAPITAL PARTICIPATION BY GENDER (ENCOVI 2000)

- **The non-poor** participate more than the poor in formal organizations (Figure 13.3). Such differences even stronger for bridging organizations. The dominance of formal organizations by elite or better off families is confirmed in the QPES villages. In the Ladino village of L1, for example, the distribution of water is managed by the local authority ("el comité"), which has been presided over by the same person for the past 20 years. Participation in this comité is not democratic and excludes those who cannot afford the operations expenses of being members. Study participants also repeatedly complained that the comité manages resources arbitrarily and has no accountability. Those who feel discontent, however, seem to have little power to make any changes and this produces divisions within the community. In the K'iché village of KI2, the poor are self-excluded from community activities. They explain that they have "too much work" and don't have time to participate. Informants in other QPES villages also note that time and financial costs of participation present barriers for participation by the poor in organizations. The ENCOVI suggests that the poor participate slightly more in collective action activities, but the differences are not significant.

- **Education** is also highly correlated with all types of participation (collective action and organizations), as is Spanish-speaking ability among the indigenous, and age. Education not only provides skills at the individual level, but also contributes to the community by preparing individuals to assume leadership roles, leverage external assistance, and represent the community in local and national institutions. Informants in several QPES villages do indicate that illiterate members are excluded from community decision making (see Box 4.3 in Chapter 4).

- Although there are some differences by **ethnicity,** for example with much lower participation rates among the Q'eqchi, these are not systematically significant when other factors, such as region, education, or language ability, are taken into account.

Benefits of Social Capital

Nonetheless, the benefits of social capital to community welfare are significant and diverse. First, the QPES offers a rich array of examples of how communities organize to manage public goods and collective resources, and make community decisions. In the QPES village of KI1, for example, the community organized to solve problems with drinking water and to acquire improved stoves to protect women's health while cooking (though there are allegations of misuse of funds by the water committee, see Box 4.3 in Chapter 4). In M1, the community has established rangers (*guardabosques*) to protect communal woods (see Box 13.2). **Second,** social capital is often called upon in the face of shocks. This is evident in both the ENCOVI, in which community-based actions are second only to self-help for dealing with shocks, and in the QPES, in which communities report various forms of mutual assistance when hit with shocks (see for example Box 13.2). **Third,** higher social capital seems to be strongly associated with the ability of communities to leverage external assistance. Communities in the

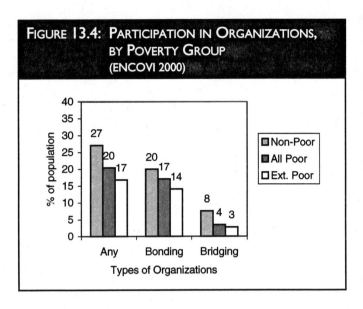

FIGURE 13.4: PARTICIPATION IN ORGANIZATIONS, BY POVERTY GROUP (ENCOVI 2000)

ENCOVI sample with higher than average participation in organizations also report more help from formal institutions and more success in leveraging funds (see Table 13.4 below).

TABLE 13.4: SOCIAL CAPITAL AND EXTERNAL ASSISTANCE
(Percentage of Total Communities in ENCOVI sample)

	Number of Organizations in the Community	
	Below Median	**Above Median**
Help from any Institution[a]	61.8	94.2
Help from Government	23.5	42.6
Help from Social Funds[b]	29.5	60.4
Help from Institutions[c]	9.7	35.2
Help from NGO	21.2	32.8
Success Leveraging Funds	84.1	90.1
Success in Project Application	59.0	65.6
Success Obtaining Support from Institutions	64.6	77.4

Source: World Bank calculations using ENCOVI 2000, Instituto Nacional de Estadística—Guatemala. a. The Institutions include: Government, Politicians, Church, School, NGOs and Social Funds. b. Social Funds include: FIS, FONAPAZ, FSDC and other Social Funds. c. Institutions include: Politicians, Church and School.

Recent Legal Reforms to Empower Communities

The recent passage of three laws[40] pertaining to citizen participation and decentralization constitutes an important step in empowering local communities in Guatemala. Specifically, the passage of these laws represents a significant step towards creating the framework and legal structures for bringing the Government closer to the community, developing certain responsibilities to the local level, and empowering communities and their councils (consejos comunitiarios) to participate in decision-making. Building on the findings of the ENCOVI and QPES (above), efforts should be made to ensure the participation of women, the poor and other traditionally excluded groups in the implementation of this new framework.

---

40. Specifically, the *Ley de Consejos de Desarrollo Urbano y Rural (Decreto 11-2002), the Código Municipal (Decreto 12-2002), and the Ley General de Descentralización (Decreto 14-2002).*

Role of Other Actors

In addition to communities and governments, other actors (such as the private sector, NGOs, and religious organizations) have an important role to play in reducing poverty and promoting development. While it is beyond the scope of this study to do a full stakeholder or institutional analysis, it is important to acknowledge the role of these other actors, particularly in Guatemala where the limited size and effectiveness of the state makes their participation all the more crucial.

- Historically, the **private sector,** has had somewhat of a mixed relationship with the poor. On the one hand, certain segments of the private sector (particularly large-scale, formal enterprises) had vested interests that supported the exclusionary policies that afforded them land and cheap labor inputs over the past centuries. On the other hand, today's private sector has a vested interest in progress on development, which relies on the success of the peace process, which in turn relies on a reversal of the exclusionary forces that sparked the later phases of the war in the first place. Perhaps reflecting acknowledgement of this basic reality, the private sector has explicitly developed organizations, or "fundaciones" to promote social business responsibility in many industries. As of 1995, nine such foundations from various industries had united under the *Consejo de Fundaciones Privadas de Guatemala,* the largest of which are the Sugar Foundation and the Foundation for Rural Development (FUNRURAL, representing ANACAFE and the coffee sector).[41] Projects supported by the foundations commonly support activities in education, training, housing, municipal development, health, environment, and social protection. Such projects are commonly co-financed with joint participation of the public sector or donors. There has also been a recognition among several private-sector business groups that bold reforms are needed to enhance productivity and promote development and security in the country. Moreover, the private sector is not homogeneous, and a significant share of private sector activity is conducted by micro-enterprises in Guatemala, with self-employment accounting for one third of all employment in 2000.[42] Indeed the strong entrepreneurial spirit that characterizes much of Guatemala seems to be one of the country's main sources of growth and employment.

- Hundreds of **NGOs** are also active in Guatemala, providing services in education, health, agriculture, environment, culture, human rights, and so forth.[43] Geographically, there are distinct patterns in the distribution of NGOs between development-oriented organizations and those focusing on human rights. There has recently been a conversion of several NGOs that are shifting from providing humanitarian assistance towards playing the role of effective development brokers, often partnering for the delivery of public services (under the PRONADE and SIAS programs). Development-focused NGOs are concentrated largely in the Metropolitana Region (Department of Guatemala) and the center and alti-plano of the country. Human rights organizations are concentrated largely in the Departments of Quiché, Huehuetenango, Alta Verapaz, Solola, San Marcos and Chimaltenango (many of which were largely affected by the war) as well as Guatemala. There is a significant under-coverage of NGOs in departments in the Eastern regions of the country.

- As discussed above, membership in **religious organizations** is the most common form of social capital in Guatemala (based on results of the ENCOVI 2000). Besides providing moral and spiritual support, QPES communities suggest many examples of churches providing faith-based assistance to the needy (to orphan families in M1 or helping villages mitigate the effects of shocks like the earthquake of 1976, Hurricane Mitch, and the war). The villagers also clearly associate spiritual relations with welfare (see Chapter 2). To promote the links between poverty reduction, development and religion, an Inter-Faith Development Dialogue was recently established in Guatemala, with representation from the Mayan, Catholic, Protestant, and Jewish faiths. Nonetheless, conflicts between religions can be

---

41. Fuentes & Asociados (2001).
42. Source: World Bank calculations using the ENCOVI 2000, *Instituto Nacional de Estadística—Guatemala.*
43. Browning et al. (1998)

quite divisive in Guatemala's villages. Indeed, conflicts between religious leaders or groups were also a common theme raised by informants in the QPES study villages.

Summary of Key Issues and Priorities
The above analysis reveals a number of key messages and policy implications:

▓ The effectiveness of Guatemala's Government affects the menu of options for reducing poverty and the ways in which these options are carried out. Despite some progress, Guatemala's efforts to improve living conditions and promote a more inclusive and democratic society have been hampered by a weak public sector. Key challenges in this area include:
  ● Improving the tax base to generate more revenues for increased public spending, particularly in the social sectors, basic utility services and rural development;
  ● Improving public expenditure management, with stronger links to policy, planning and priorities;
  ● Improving the targeting of public spending to the poor;
  ● Making the public sector more accountable and responsive;
  ● Strengthening administrative capabilities and the civil service; and
  ● Bringing the government closer to the client and improving service delivery, particularly given the heterogeneity of Guatemala's population and communities.
▓ Good governance is also important for growth and poverty reduction. Guatemala scores poorly on most governance indicators, despite some progress. Key challenges for the development and poverty reduction agenda include: (a) fighting corruption; (b) improving the rule of law and the justice system; and (c) reducing political instability, which further hurts the climate for growth and investment. While it is beyond the scope of this study to propose a governance strategy, some actions that could be effective include: report cards for key ministries and services to track perceptions of service quality and corruption, client satisfaction surveys, and formal adoption and implementation of an anti-corruption charter. Recent initiatives to fight corruption should be expanded and implemented.
▓ Improving governance and public sector management are prerequisites to expanding tax revenues and public spending. Without sincere improvements in public sector effectiveness, accountability and transparency, continued opposition to increased funding of the state is likely. The recent passage of three laws[44] pertaining to citizen participation and decentralization constitutes an important step in promoting greater social accountability in Guatemala.
▓ Communities have an important role to play in promoting their own development, particularly in light of Guatemala's weak public sector. Social capital can offer significant benefits to community welfare, including managing public goods, coping with shocks, and leveraging external assistance. Nonetheless, social capital in Guatemala is mainly concentrated in strong horizontal, within-village connections, reflecting the physical isolation of many communities and decades of exclusion and war. Moreover, social capital appears to be concentrated among the more privileged groups in Guatemalan society, to the exclusion of women, the poor, and those with less education. An important policy implication of these findings is the importance of explicitly promoting the participation of these traditionally excluded groups in programs that rely on community-driven development (CDD) or community-based targeting. The recent passage of three laws[45] pertaining to citizen participation and decentralization constitutes an important step in empowering local communities in Guatemala.
▓ Other actors—particularly the private sector, NGOs, and religious groups—are active players in the fight against poverty. Given the limited size and scope of the Government, partnerships should be sought with these actors to help advance the poverty-reduction agenda.

---

44. Specifically, the *Ley de Consejos de Desarrollo Urbano y Rural (Decreto 11-2002)*, the *Código Municipal (Decreto 12-2002)*, and the *Ley General de Descentralización (Decreto 14-2002)*.

45. Specifically, the *Ley de Consejos de Desarrollo Urbano y Rural (Decreto 11-2002)*, the *Código Municipal (Decreto 12-2002)*, and the *Ley General de Descentralización (Decreto 14-2002)*.

PART 5

CONCLUSIONS AND RECOMMENDATIONS

CHAPTER 14

PRIORITY ACTIONS TO REDUCE POVERTY

This chapter builds on the empirical findings in the rest of the report to build an agenda for poverty reduction in Guatemala. Broadly speaking, a concerted strategy should be adopted to reduce poverty by building opportunities and assets, reducing vulnerability, improving institutions and empowering communities. This broad agenda for poverty reduction largely coincides with the central tenets of both the Peace Accords and social policy in Guatemala. Progress on advancing this agenda has occurred, and is possible. Nonetheless, significant challenges remain, particularly those involving improvements in key outcomes and deeper institutional reforms. In light of these main issues, this chapter proposes a set of priority actions within the broad agenda for poverty reduction. While these actions are needed in general, they can be made more effective if targeted to specific priority groups. As such, this chapter identifies a set of priority target groups and offers suggestions on ways explicit targeting criteria can be built into poverty reduction efforts so as to improve their effectiveness. Finally, the chapter offers some suggestions on monitoring and evaluation.

Three caveats are important to emphasize at the outset:

▨ **First, while there is no single "blueprint" for poverty reduction, there are some key levers that take central stage for national efforts to reduce poverty,** and these are the emphasis of this chapter. Nonetheless, efforts should be made to tailor this broad agenda to local conditions, particularly in a country as heterogeneous as Guatemala. To this end, efforts are underway in Guatemala to develop not only a national poverty reduction strategy, but also localized strategies at the department and municipal levels.[1]

▨ **Second, the policy discussion is aimed primarily at the perspective of policy makers and the role of the public sector;** hence it emphasizes interventions that both (a) would have a substantial impact on poverty; and (b) merit the use of public resources in a market-oriented economy. Nonetheless, other actors, such as the private sector and other facets of

---

1. These efforts are being led by SEGEPLAN under the ERP initiative.

civil society (for example, communities, NGOs, religious organizations), also have an important role to play in reducing poverty. The private sector, in particular, will provide the central arena for economic growth and productive activities, which are crucial for poverty reduction. Other facets of civil society (for example, communities, NGOs, religious organizations) are clear partners in this poverty reduction agenda, and will play crucial roles in prioritization and implementation of public sector actions, as well as the provision of other services and interventions that are beyond the scope of the public sector.

- **Third, poverty reduction is a multi-dimensional and long-term process.** There is no single magic bullet to reduce poverty. Rather, efforts should be made to attack the poverty problem from a multitude of angles, including those to foster opportunity, build assets, reduce vulnerability, and improve institutions and empower communities. Moreover, poverty reduction does not occur over night. Implementation of key actions to reduce poverty takes time, and often the impact of such actions occurs over an even longer time frame (for example, into subsequent political cycles—or even subsequent generations). That said, the sooner actions are undertaken, the more quickly the inter-generational cycle of poverty can be broken.

A Broad Agenda for Poverty Reduction in Guatemala

Broadly speaking, a concerted strategy should be adopted to reduce poverty in Guatemala by building opportunities and assets, reducing vulnerability, and improving institutions and empowering communities. A broad agenda of actions in these areas is outlined in Table 14.2 (at the end of the chapter).

- **Building opportunities.** Economic growth is necessary for poverty reduction, particularly given the relatively small size and capabilities of Guatemala's public sector. Moreover, a recurring theme that arises in the analysis is the fact that the poor, particularly the rural poor, women and the indigenous, are not able to fully participate in, or benefit from, the overall economic system. Therefore, improving employment and earnings opportunities is essential, and this depends largely on the actions of the private sector. The pattern of growth needs to be made more "pro-poor," with an emphasis on building opportunities for the rural poor, women and the indigenous. This will depend on two other key areas: building the assets of the poor, as well as improving institutions and the investment climate. Specific actions are outlined in Table 14.2 below and detailed in Chapters 5 and 6.[2]
- **Building the assets of the poor.** This is arguably the most important area for poverty reduction in Guatemala, given the chronic nature of poverty in Guatemala, existing disparities, and linkages to the other key areas—including promoting growth, reducing vulnerability, and empowering the excluded. Key assets include: education, health, basic utility services (particularly water and sanitation), land and physical capital, and rural roads. Specific actions for each of these assets are outlined in Table 14.2, and detailed in Chapters 7–10.
- **Reducing vulnerability.** Again, the central path for reducing vulnerability is to build the assets of the poor, since most vulnerability in Guatemala is associated with low expected earnings (due to weak assets) rather than high volatility of consumption. Nonetheless, disaster management is important, given the poor's exposure to natural and agriculture-related shocks. Moreover, much could be done to improve the efficiency and effectiveness of existing public social protection programs. Many of these (such as scholarships, school feeding) could also play a role in building the assets of the poor by easing demand-side constraints to improved coverage. Some transfers (social assistance) could also be used to alleviate the poverty and suffering of the *extreme* poor, particularly when tied to participation in health

---

2. The "priority" column in Table 14.2 reflects not only a rating of relative priorities for poverty reduction (based on the relative importance of these factors for poverty and growth), but also judgments about the feasibility (administrative and political) of certain interventions.

and education activities. Specific actions in this area are outlined in Table 14.2 and further detailed in Chapters 11–12.

▨ **Improving institutions and empowering communities.** Weaknesses in the public sector and poor governance strongly shape the menu of feasible options and effectiveness of poverty reduction efforts. They also influence the overall climate for investment and economic growth. As such, improvements in this area are deemed to be of high priority, consistent with the strategic emphasis on "modernization of the state" in the Peace Accords, as discussed in Chapters 4 and 13. The role of communities in promoting their own development is also important, as acknowledged in the Peace Accords, and poverty reduction efforts should seek to partner with communities in determining priorities. Nonetheless, explicit efforts should be made to reach out to groups typically excluded from community decision-making (namely, the poor, women, and the uneducated), as discussed in Chapter 13. Partnerships should likewise be sought with private-sector and NGOs to extend and improve service delivery.

This broad agenda for poverty reduction largely coincides with the central tenets of the Peace Accords. Indeed, reducing poverty and improving living conditions is central to lasting peace in Guatemala. As discussed in Chapter 4, the Peace Accords went well beyond formalizing the end to Guatemala's civil war, outlining a broad policy agenda that signaled a significant shift towards a more inclusive development path. Key areas of emphasis related to economic development and poverty reduction include: a focus on human development, goals for productive and sustainable development, a program for the modernization of the democratic state, and strengthening and promoting participation. The rights of the indigenous and women were also highlighted as cross-cutting themes throughout the accords, in an attempt to reverse the historical exclusion of these groups.

Moreover, this broad agenda for poverty reduction is consistent with the current thrust of social policy in Guatemala. Given the importance of improving living conditions to lasting peace, poverty reduction has taken center stage on the current social policy agenda. In particular, the Government recently outlined its poverty reduction strategy in an important policy document "Estrategia de Reducción de la Pobreza" (ERP),[3] presented at the Consultative Group meetings in February 2002. General principles emphasized in the ERP include: a rural focus, using the poverty map for targeting (see Box 14.1 below); efficient and transparent public spending; decentralization; and participation. Key action areas ("ejes vitales") include: (a) promoting growth with equity; (b) investing in human capital (emphasizing health, education and food security); and (c) investing in physical capital (particularly water and sanitation, rural roads, electricity, and rural development). Cross-cutting issues ("temas transversales") in the ERP include multiculturalism and interculturalism, gender equity, and vulnerability.

Some Progress . . . and Key Issues

Progress has occurred—and *is* possible. In the six years since the signing of the Peace Accords, Guatemala has taken important steps on this new, more inclusive development path. In particular, progress has occurred in the areas of building assets and improving institutions:

▨ **Public sector management,** particularly public financial management with the introduction and implementation of the Integrated Financial Management System (SIAF) since 1998, as discussed in Chapters 4 and 13;

▨ **Public revenues and spending,** with increases in revenues and public spending, particularly for the education and basic utility services sectors, as discussed in Chapters 4, 7, 9, and 13;

▨ **Education coverage,** with notable increases in improving coverage and narrowing disparities between genders, ethnicities and poverty groups, particularly since the signing of the Peace Accords in 1996, as discussed in Chapter 7; and

---

3. SEGEPLAN (November 2001).

▨ **Basic utility services,** with an expansion of coverage of water, sanitation and electricity services and a reduction in disparities in access to these services, particularly since the signing of the Peace Accords in 1996, as discussed in Chapter 9.

Progress has also occurred in other areas. For example, for land, numerous entities have been created and initiatives launched, though their reach has been limited to only a few thousand households (see Chapter 6).

Importantly, these steps signal that progress *is* possible, despite the magnitude of the challenge of changing the course of the country's history.

Nonetheless, significant challenges remain to build opportunities and assets, reduce vulnerability, improve institutions and promote empowerment. Within this broad agenda, several key issues should be considered as top priority:

▨ **Growth has slowed, particularly in rural areas.** As discussed in Chapter 5, economic growth has slowed in recent years, with a sharp decline in coffee prices and the global economic slowdown, as well as concerns relating to the overall investment climate and weaknesses in the banking sector. Taking into account population growth rates of 2.7% p.a., GDP per capita actually fell and poverty is projected to have risen in 2001 and 2002. Rural growth rates in particular have declined over time. Given the high concentration of the poor in rural areas, economic growth rates—particularly those in rural areas—need to improve if Guatemala is to make significant progress in reducing poverty and meeting the goals set by the Peace Accords, the MDGs, and the ERP. Related to the meager performance of the overall economy, households do not perceive significant improvements in living conditions. While communities in the ENCOVI do indicate they perceive progress—and attribute it to improvements in basic services—households are decidedly more pessimistic about changes in their welfare since the Peace Accords, as discussed in Chapter 2. They attribute these perceptions to economic factors, such as a lack of increases in incomes and opportunities (factors that directly affect "their wallets").

▨ **Coverage of education, health and basic services remains insufficient and biased against the poor.** Despite progress, significant gaps and disparities remain, particularly for the poor, girls (for education and health), and rural and indigenous residents. Demand-side barriers, not just a lack of physical infrastructure, largely account for inadequate access to these services. Quality of education, health and basic services also appears to be deficient, as discussed in Chapters 7, 8 and 9.

▨ **Health outcomes (particularly malnutrition and infant/maternal mortality) have not improved** in line with targets set by the Peace Accords or the MDGs, as discussed in Chapter 8.

▨ **Weaknesses in public sector management and governance continue to hamper Guatemala's quest for a more inclusive and prosperous society,** as discussed in Chapter 13. Additional reforms are needed to make the public sector more accountable and responsive, strengthen administrative capabilities and the civil service, strengthen public financial management, and bring the government closer to the client. Key governance challenges for promoting economic development and reducing poverty include: (a) fighting corruption; (b) improving the rule of law and the justice system; and (c) reducing political instability, which further hurts the climate for growth and investment.

▨ **Public revenues and spending are still inadequate, and could be better targeted.** First, existing levels of revenues remain insufficient for Guatemala to make a significant dent in poverty reduction by expanding assets and service delivery, as discussed in Chapters 4 and 13. However, improving governance and public sector management is a prerequisite to expanding tax revenues and public spending. Without sincere improvements in public sector effectiveness, accountability and transparency, continued opposition to increased funding of the state is likely. Second, public spending is poorly targeted, with a significant share going to the non-poor, as discussed in Chapter 13.

Priority Actions for Poverty Reduction in Guatemala

In light of these issues, certain actions stand out as *top priority*. As discussed above, a broad, multi-dimensional strategy should be adopted to reduce poverty in Guatemala by building opportunities and assets, reducing vulnerability, and improving institutions and empowering communities. A broad agenda of actions in these areas is outlined in Table 14.2 below. Within this broad agenda, actions should be further prioritized using the following criteria: (a) likely poverty impact; (b) political, institutional, and administrative feasibility; (c) economic feasibility and costs; and (d) their need and justification for public sector resources. Such prioritization will likely require further dialogue and analysis (e.g., institutional assessments, costing of actions, public expenditure analysis). As a first cut, certain actions should be considered as top priority, based on a cursory review of such criteria:

(1) **Promoting economic growth and productive opportunities, particularly in rural areas.** Guatemala must raise its rate of economic growth if it is to make significant progress in achieving key development and peace targets (as discussed in Chapter 5). This is true internationally, but particularly relevant for Guatemala, given the limited scope for public sector action and redistribution. In this context, the main engine of growth is likely to come from the private sector, with the public sector playing a supporting role affecting growth mainly insofar as it stimulates private-sector investment and productive activities. Yet the actions of the public sector in this supporting role are crucial. In particular, *priority actions* include:

▓ Maintaining macroeconomic stability;

▓ Enforcing a tight fiscal position, with a careful plan for strengthening tax collection and redirecting public spending towards the social sectors so as to build assets that are crucial to both growth and poverty reduction;

▓ Fostering a climate that is conducive to private investment and growth, including improvements in governance and public sector management (see Chapter 13);

▓ Promoting growth with special emphasis on sectors that are likely to generate substantial employment for the poor. Additional analytical work is needed to define a more comprehensive pro-growth strategy (see below). Nonetheless, while a thorough sectoral analysis of growth is beyond the scope of this study, available data do suggest certain levers that would have stronger impacts on poverty reduction than others for urban and rural areas:

   ● In urban areas, this requires policies to support labor-intensive sectors, particularly micro-, small- and medium-enterprises (MSMEs), as well as education and technical training.

   ● In rural areas, this means developing non-agricultural activities that are better remunerated and have better long-term prospects than traditional agriculture. As discussed in Chapter 6, key interventions to support growth in non-farm activities include: (a) increasing and improving the targeting of investments in education and technical training; (b) increasing investments in transport and basic infrastructure, which are crucial for the diversification, growth and inclusion of the poor in the rural economy and with facilitating the adjustment to the coffee crisis; and (c) policies that promote micro-, small- and medium-enterprises (MSMEs), a segment of the private sector that tends to generate a lot of employment. While agriculture is unlikely to generate enough additional employment opportunities to reduce poverty on a large scale in the medium term, it will continue to be an important source of incomes for the poor (at least in the short run). In this context, diversification efforts should focus on non-traditional products with better demand and price prospects than traditional export crops (as discussed in Chapter 6). Policies should also continue to facilitate productivity improvements (such as technical assistance), so as to boost the earnings of those who remain in agriculture. Investments in infrastructure (e.g., rural roads to improve marketing opportunities and education to improve farm-management practices) will likewise be important.

(2) **Investing in education, with priority actions to improve quality and access to pre-primary and primary education.** Both theory and empirical analysis of the ENCOVI demonstrate the crucial role of education in promoting economic growth;[4] reducing poverty and malnutrition; reducing vulnerability by making the labor force more agile and able to adjust to shocks; and reducing inequality, social disparities and exclusion. Since Guatemala is still a "primary" country on average (with average attainment of 4.3 years) and since the poor in particular fail to complete primary school, investments should still focus on expanding and improving primary education, as discussed in Chapter 7. Investments in early childhood education (pre-primary) are also crucial as they (a) increase the likelihood of success at the primary level and (b) reach children at a critical phase of their physical, cognitive, and social development. As such, *priority actions* should focus on:

  ▨ Increasing access to primary education, largely through demand-side interventions, since supply-side constraints are no longer binding for most of the population. This expansion should be implemented via the PRONADE program given the benefits of this program in terms of community and parental participation (see Chapter 7). However, as supply-side gaps are filled, the Government should consider easing eligibility criteria so as to allow poor communities that already have schools to be eligible for the PRONADE-type community-based school-management model. To target this expansion, the poverty map could be used to identify eligible schools and preserve PRONADE's exemplary targeting record;

  ▨ Improving the quality of education, curriculum and performance standards so as to improve internal efficiency and the returns to education, particularly at the primary level; and

  ▨ Investing in early childhood development to promote: (a) improved child nutrition at an early age, since nutritional status is a significant factor in determining enrollment and attainment and since nutritional deficiencies emerge at a young age (see Chapter 8); and (b) early educational opportunities, including links between traditional schooling and pre-primary schooling (see Chapter 7).

(3) **Investing in health, with an emphasis on expanding access and usage using both supply- and demand-side interventions.** Again, both theory and empirical analysis using the ENCOVI point to important linkages between health and productivity (economic growth), vulnerability (health shocks), and poverty. Guatemala's health outcomes have lagged significantly behind those in other countries as well as the targets set by the Peace Accords and the MDGs, as discussed in Chapters 4 and 5. A significant share of the population still lacks access to health facilities—or fails to use them when available—due to a mix of supply- and demand-side constraints, as discussed in Chapter 8. As such, *priority actions* should seek to improve health outcomes by:

  ▨ Expanding access to affordable health care using both supply- and demand-side interventions (see Chapter 8). Such interventions should be targeted to the poor and priority groups (for example, using the poverty map, as discussed below);

---

4. Indeed, Loening (2002) demonstrates the empirical impact of education on economic growth in Guatemala.

▓ Emphasizing preventative care, infectious and parasitic diseases, reproductive health, and key outcomes (mortality, malnutrition); and

▓ Expanding access to potable (not just piped) water and improved sanitation to complement the basic health care package.

(4) **Integrating actions to reduce malnutrition into the basic health-care package.** The high and stagnant rates of malnutrition in Guatemala are unacceptable, as discussed in Chapter 8. Their lasting effects also result in inter-generational transmission of poverty. Reducing malnutrition should be designated as a top priority. Malnutrition interventions should be integrated into the MSPAS basic health care package and provided at the community level through outreach workers, so as to improve their effectiveness and reach and foster the integration of malnutrition as a key concern into the health system. The target population for these schemes should be pre-school children (particularly those under 24 months of age) and mothers (including pregnant and lactating women). *Priority actions* include:

▓ Promotion of proper health, hygiene, and feeding practices;

▓ Growth monitoring of pregnant women and children under aged two;

▓ Micronutrient supplementation (particularly for iron); and

▓ Deworming treatments and oral rehydration therapy.

(5) **Reducing isolation and improving communications by investing in rural transport and roads.** Many communities in Guatemala are still relatively isolated due to a lack of road access, as discussed in Chapter 10. Empirical analysis using the ENCOVI has demonstrated the effects of isolation on opportunities, productivity, vulnerability (shocks), and access to services (as discussed in Chapters 6, 10 and 11). Expanded rural transport helps build the assets of the poor, promote economic growth and opportunity, reduce vulnerability, and empower communities. *Priority actions* in this area include focusing on improving and expanding the network of motorable roads in rural areas, particularly those with untapped economic potential *and* a high concentration of poor people.

(6) **Improving governance and the effectiveness of the public sector.** Actions are needed to reduce corruption, improve transparency, improve public expenditure management, and better target existing resources to the poor, as discussed in Chapter 13. Such actions will have multiple benefits, including: (a) making the most of existing scarce resources and improving service delivery, which is crucial under any scenario, but even more important in the event that growth were to slow; (b) fostering a climate that is more conducive to economic growth; (c) assuring that public resources reach the poor (needed for impact); and (d) improving the credibility of government and its ability to increase revenues in the future (without such improvements, the Government will face continued resistance to tax increases). *Priority actions* include:

▓ Improving the tax base and increasing public spending, which will depend on improvements in governance and the effectiveness and credibility of the public sector;

▓ Improving the targeting of public spending, particularly for investments in education, health, basic utility services, and transfers (for example, using the poverty map as an explicit criteria for allocations, as discussed in more detail below);

▓ Improving public expenditure management, with stronger links to policy, planning and priorities;

▓ Expanding and building on recent initiatives to fight corruption (for example, adopting an anti-corruption charter);

▓ Improving incentives for better service delivery (for example, decentralization, local "*control social*," and service "report cards" and client satisfaction surveys); and

▓ Improving the rule of law and the justice system.

While a range of short-, medium- and long-term actions are outlined in Table 14.2, some can be undertaken immediately, including:

- Promoting economic growth by maintaining macroeconomic stability and fiscal balances, while redirecting public spending towards the social sectors and rural areas (for 2002 and 2003 budgets), as discussed above and in Chapter 5.
- Undertaking extensive study of economic growth with a view towards formulating a pro-poor development strategy (see below);
- Using the poverty map prepared by SEGEPLAN-INE-URL as a tool for improving the targeting of public spending and poverty reduction interventions in key sectors (education, health, basic services, as discussed below). This should be applied immediately for the execution of the 2002 budget. It should also be systematized as a criteria for allocating spending during the planning of the 2003 budget.
- Reviewing quality, curriculum and performance standards in education, particularly for grades 1, 7, and 10 (transition years associated with high levels of repetition and drop-out), as discussed in Chapter 7.
- Consolidating and improving scholarship, school feeding, and other demand-side programs in education for the next school year, as discussed in Chapter 7.
- Acknowledging the high priority of reducing malnutrition and conducting a critical review of existing malnutrition interventions (across agencies, both public and private) with a view towards (a) identifying programs that have worked (both in Guatemala and internationally); (b) streamlining and restructuring existing programs to better focus on young children, growth monitoring, information and behavioral change via community-based interventions as part of the basic health-care package, as discussed in Chapter 8.
- Encouraging the social funds and other providers to adopt measures to improve the quality of water and complement water and sanitation programs with measures to improve household hygiene and water treatment practices, as discussed in Chapter 9.
- Promoting community-based development for better local accountability (and "social control"), while taking steps to ensure the participation of groups traditionally excluded from community decision-making (e.g., women, indigenous, uneducated), as discussed in Chapter 13.
- Drafting and adopting an anti-corruption charter, as discussed in Chapter 13.

Areas for further work and analysis include:

- Conducting an in-depth analysis of the (potential and existing) sources of growth in Guatemala with a view to formulating a pro-poor development strategy. The study should not only adopt a "macro" perspective, but should also look at more "micro" issues and a sectoral perspective (for example, specific economic activities in agricultural and non-agricultural spheres, and productive activities relying on credit, technical assistance, and microenterprises). While this type of analysis is beyond the scope of the present report, it is a top priority for further research (see Chapters 5 and 6). The planned up-coming Country Economic Memorandum (CEM) should make some headway on such analysis;
- Conducting additional analysis of public expenditures in the social sectors with the objective of finding ways in which their efficiency and effectiveness could be improved (see Chapters 7, 8, and 13);
- Reviewing quality, curriculum and performance standards in education (see Chapter 7);
- Conducting critical review of malnutrition interventions (see Chapter 8); and
- Reviewing supply-side issues in the health sector, including an evaluation of the institutional capacity of MSPAS and of the effectiveness and impact of the SIAS system, in particular with respect to its ability to improve health outcomes (see Chapter 8 for specific issues).

Priority Target Groups for Poverty Reduction in Guatemala

The broad agenda for poverty reduction can become even more effective by focusing efforts on key priority groups. For example, while economic growth is needed in general, growth that provides opportunities for the rural poor will be even more effective in reducing poverty. While building assets of the poor in general is essential, priority is needed to tackle the issues of malnutrition and the relative disparities against poor women and indigenous residents.

As such, the Government should prioritize among poverty groups, according to the prevalence of poverty, specific risks, and demographic circumstances. Specifically, the analysis reveals several priority groups that should be emphasized in poverty reduction efforts: (a) poor and malnourished children; (b) poor women and girls; (c) poor indigenous households; (d) the rural poor; and (e) specific geographic areas (Table 14.1). Clearly, these groups can have considerable overlaps. For example, a poor or malnourished indigenous girl living in rural areas in the North or North-Western parts of the country would probably qualify for just about any anti-poverty intervention.

- **Poor and malnourished children.** The developmental status of children renders them extremely vulnerable to the risks of living in an impoverished environment. Youth (particularly early childhood) is the point in the life cycle when physical, cognitive, and psycho-social development occurs at its most accelerated pace and is most susceptible to abnormal development from poverty conditions. As such, childhood poverty also increases the likelihood of inter-generational transmission of poverty. About two-thirds of all Guatemalan children live in poverty. Close to half (44%) are stunted, putting Guatemala among the worst performers in the world for malnutrition, as discussed in Chapter 8. Four-fifths of malnourished children are poor. Pre-school children are particularly vulnerable to malnutrition (especially those between 6–24 months). Infant mortality is also alarmingly high. A significant share of poor pre-school and primary-aged children also fail to enroll in school, as discussed in Chapter 7. Finally, child labor is common, particularly among poor children, further compromising their chances of attending school, as discussed in Chapters 6 and 7. In this context, poverty reduction efforts should confer top priority to poor and malnourished children as a key target group.
- **Poor girls and women.** Girls and women face cumulative disadvantages in Guatemala, reflecting historically exclusionary policies (for example, in land and education, see Chapter 4) and a general culture of *machismo*. They face limited access to education (with fewer girls attending school even when schools are available, see Chapter 7), constrained employment opportunities, explicit wage discrimination (even after taking into account differences in endowments, see Chapter 6), and traditional exclusion from land ownership. Women are also at risk for health shocks, with Guatemala recording extremely high levels of maternal mortality, as discussed in Chapter 8. Furthermore, women participate significantly less in community decision-making (limited social capital networks), as discussed in Chapter 13. Yet women's roles are crucial in promoting long-term development, with a strong influence, for example, on the nutritional status of children.
- **Poor indigenous households.** The indigenous likewise suffer cumulative disadvantages, reflecting the historical pattern of exclusion and decades of conflict. Poverty is higher among the indigenous. Indigenous children also suffer higher rates of malnutrition and less access to education, which affect their earnings ability in the future, as discussed in Chapters 7 and 8. The indigenous also have less access to health and basic utility services (see Chapters 8 and 9). They are further constrained in employment opportunities (particularly those who don't speak Spanish), and face considerable wage discrimination (even after taking into account disparities in endowments), as analyzed in Chapter 6. Finally, they also report perceptions of discrimination by public officials and service providers (see Chapters 4 and 13).

TABLE 14.1: PRIORITY TARGET GROUPS

Priority Target Groups	Key Constraints/Challenges	Possible Targeting Tools
Poor and malnourished children, especially pre-school (age 0–6) and primary-aged children (7–13)	▪ Poverty ▪ Malnutrition (stunting) ▪ Not enrolled in school ▪ Child labor ▪ Vulnerable phase of life cycle ▪ Inter-generational transmission of poverty	▪ Poverty map combined with information on malnutrition and educational enrollment ▪ Self-targeting via health posts and community health centers (e.g., a growth monitoring program channeled through these facilities) ▪ Community-based targeting ▪ Proxy means testing
Poor women and girls	▪ Historical pattern of exclusion ▪ Less access to education ▪ Constrained in employment and earnings opportunities ▪ Face wage discrimination ▪ Face discriminatory attitudes (culture of *machismo*) ▪ Excluded from participating in community decision making (social capital)	▪ Poverty map ▪ Gender-based targeting (e.g., programs that restrict eligibility to girls, such as scholarships) ▪ Community-based targeting ▪ Proxy means testing
Poor indigenous	▪ Historical pattern of exclusion ▪ Higher poverty and malnutrition ▪ Less access to education, health services ▪ Less coverage by basic utility services ▪ Constrained in employment and earnings opportunities ▪ Face wage discrimination ▪ Face discrimination in treatment by public officials and other service providers	▪ Poverty map combined with language map ▪ Proxy means testing
The rural poor, particularly small land-holders, agricultural day laborers, seasonal migrant agricultural workers	▪ Higher poverty and malnutrition ▪ Less access to education, health services ▪ Less coverage by basic utility services ▪ Geographic constraints (isolation, roads, small municipalities) ▪ Constrained employment and earnings opportunities ▪ Low returns, limited coverage of labor and IGSS benefits ▪ Susceptible to shocks	▪ Poverty map ▪ Vulnerability maps (e.g., natural disasters) ▪ Proxy means testing, with certain proxies emphasized (e.g., land holdings, electricity connections, etc.) ▪ Migration maps (that could be developed from census data) showing municipalities with significant concentrations of seasonal migrants
Specific geographic areas, especially in the "poverty belt" (Norte, Nor-Occidente, San Marcos)	▪ Higher poverty rates, malnutrition ▪ Lower access to basic services ▪ Geographic isolation, limited road network	▪ Poverty map, combined with other asset-specific maps/info. (e.g., gaps in coverage of roads, education, health services, utilities, etc.)

▨ **Rural poor.** Poverty is higher in rural areas, and even higher among specific rural sub-groups, including small land-holders, agricultural day laborers, and seasonal migrant agricultural workers (see Chapter 6). The rural poor (particularly these sub-groups) have relatively limited access to services and infrastructure (education, health, utilities, transport, markets), as discussed in Chapter 9. They also have limited employment and earnings opportunities, particularly those living in more geographically isolated areas and smaller municipalities, as analyzed in Chapter 6. They also face lower returns to their labor and are rarely covered by formal labor and IGSS benefits. Finally, they are quite susceptible to shocks, particularly natural disasters, agricultural-related shocks, and recent economic shocks (such as the coffee crisis which has worsened the terms-of-trade for producers and caused job loss for day laborers), as discussed in Chapter 11. The emphasis of the ERP on rural areas is thus correct and should be maintained.

▨ **Specific geographic areas.** While poverty is clearly a national problem in Guatemala, poverty is significantly higher in the "poverty belt" in the Northern and North-Western regions as well as the departments of San Marcos. The poverty map helps further pinpoint specific municipalities with higher incidence of poverty (see Chapter 2 and Annex 4). The ERP's inclusion of the poverty map as a key tool is thus appropriate.

Explicit efforts to target resources and interventions could greatly improve their impact. As discussed in Chapter 13 (and throughout the report), public spending on the social sectors is not well targeted to the poor. Specifically, the poorest quintiles receive disproportionately less public spending on health, education and social protection, than their share in the population. Yet targeting is crucial for many of the actions outlined above if they are to have a real impact on reducing poverty and improving social indicators. The rationale for targeting is that, given budget constraints, stronger impacts are achieved when resources are concentrated on those who need them the most. In Guatemala, this means that explicit efforts are needed to reverse historically contrary tendencies whereby most resources have traditionally been captured by elites as a matter of policy (as discussed in Chapter 4). These efforts should involve explicit criteria for, and monitoring of, budget allocations, eligibility, and project site selection. These mechanisms should be built into existing institutional processes, such as the public expenditure management system.

Given budget constraints, certain activities should be actively targeted to the poor. As a "rule of thumb," incremental increases in public spending on areas such as education, health, basic utility services, core communication links, social assistance transfers, or employment schemes should be explicitly targeted to the poor in order to better integrate them into the economy and improve social indicators. In contrast, decisions regarding the allocation of investments in other services, such as more intensive infrastructure, institutional support, or banking services, should generally follow indicators of economic potential (for example, opportunities for intensification of agricultural or non-agricultural activities), which could also be combined with targeting criteria (for example, the poverty map). Ideally, a strategy to promote pro-poor growth and reduce poverty would focus on areas that have both a large concentration of poor people, but also a strong potential for future economic activity.

The Government can use a variety of tools to better target programs to priority groups. Improved use of limited public resources is crucial for poverty reduction efforts. Ensuring such resources are channeled to key poverty groups (Table 14.1) is a first step in improving the effectiveness of public spending and poverty reduction efforts. The Government has at its disposition several potentially potent tools for targeting its poverty reduction efforts to these priority groups. First, the *poverty map,* recently constructed by SEGEPLAN-INE-URL (Box 14.1), can be extremely useful (alone or with other targeting tools) in ensuring that resources get channeled to municipalities with high concentrations of the poor. Second, considerable efforts have been made to develop other geographic-based maps and databases, such as an extensive road network inventory/map, vulnerability maps (showing areas prone to specific natural disasters), conflict maps, municipal-level databases

---

BOX 14.1: POVERTY MAP

Poverty maps can be extremely useful tools for Government policy, in terms of improving the targeting of programs and public spending (either alone or in conjunction with other information and maps), promoting transparency in resource allocation and helping agencies resist political pressures (because allocations are based on objective poverty criteria), monitoring public spending, and tracking poverty trends.

New methodologies have greatly improved the construction of poverty maps. Traditionally, poverty maps are constructed using census data and a composite index of basic needs. The disadvantage of this approach is that weights must be assigned in order to weight the relative importance of the various components (or "needs"). These weights are subjective (or arbitrary). The World Bank[5] has recently developed a new methodology for constructing poverty maps which gets around this problem by estimating the empirical relationship between these "basic-need" type variables with monetary measures of poverty (usually consumption). The weights used are thus empirical rather than subjective. The methodology combines census data (which provides the needed disaggregated sample) and household survey data (which provide monetary measures of welfare and poverty) in order to construct a map based that predicts poverty down to the municipal level (or lower).

The multi-agency technical team of SEGEPLAN-INE-URL recently developed a poverty map using this new methodology with technical assistance from the World Bank under the GUAPA Program. The map was first developed using data from the Census and the ENIGFAM 1998–99, and will be updated using data from the upcoming census and the ENCOVI 2000. The poverty map was widely disseminated, both in a technical publication and in a "popular" publication prepared by SEGEPLAN and FLACSO.

The map is already serving important uses. Specifically, the map was included as an official part of the Government's poverty strategy (ERP). It was also used to design criteria for allocation decisions for the 2002 public investment budget—the first time such decisions were based on objective poverty criteria. It is currently being used in conjunction with roads maps to develop the rural roads strategy and to determine eligibility for a proposed new rural roads project. Finally, it has been used to verify geographic allocations for a re-targeting and expansion of the scholarships program.

---

on education and health services, etc. The upcoming census will help update many of these maps. A unified geographic information system could combine the poverty map with these other maps and databases to better target specific interventions to the poor. Third, certain services, such as health posts and community health centers, are self-targeted to the poor. Other programs could be channeled through these facilities to take advantage of this inherent self-targeting (and perhaps even promote use of these facilities, which would have positive spill-over effects). Fourth, community-based targeting could be used (perhaps after broader program allocations are made using the poverty map) to select specific individuals eligible for programs (such as poor or malnourished children, girls or women). Given the traditional exclusion of certain groups from community decision-making (see Chapter 13), however, care should be taken to ensure that these patterns are not repeated with such mechanisms. Fifth, a unified proxy-means database (such as those in Costa Rica or Colombia) could be developed for programs targeted to individuals, though this could require significant administrative capabilities.

Monitoring Poverty Reduction Efforts

Monitoring of both poverty and poverty reduction interventions is necessary, and adequate resources should be made available for this task. First, the MECOVI program seeks to develop an integrated system of household surveys to track living conditions and provide data for the evaluation of the impact of interventions. The system will build on the ENCOVI 2000, and should execute similar surveys every 3–5 years. In addition, INE is currently developing an employment and incomes survey that would be executed on a more regular basis, to fill crucial gaps in Guatemala's information base. Finally, the upcoming Population Census will provide additional information for the monitoring of poverty, including an opportunity to update the poverty map (combined with data from the ENCOVI), as well as infrastructure maps.

---

5. For technical details, see Hentschel, Jesko, Lanjouw, et al. (2000).

TABLE A: MENU OF OPTIONS AND KEY ACTIONS FOR POVERTY REDUCTION		
Main Constraints	**Main Recommendations**	
Key Issues	**Priority**	**Key Actions & Time Period for Actions and Impact**
BUILDING OPPORTUNITIES AND LIVELIHOODS: Priority overall, especially in rural areas		
● **Growth has slowed and isn't very "pro-poor."** Economic growth is crucial for reducing poverty and building opportunities, particularly given the relatively small size and limited capabilities of Guatemala's public sector. ● **Households do not perceive improvements,** largely due to constrained opportunities and limited earnings ● **Limited opportunities and earnings** for the poor, particularly the rural poor, women, and the indigenous: ✓ Discrimination for women, indigenous ✓ Low profitability in agriculture ✓ Constrained entry for non-farm opportunities	▣▣▣ ▣▣▣ ▣ ▣▣▣▣ ▣▣ ▣ ▣ ▣	● Maintaining macroeconomic stability, with a careful plan for allocating public expenditures and strengthening tax collection; ACT: on-going, IMP: ST, MT ● Improving the climate for growth, including governance and public sector management; ACT: ST, MT; IMP: MT, LT ● Improving regulation and supervision of financial sector; ST ● Promoting growth with emphasis in sectors that are likely to generate employment, such as non-agricultural sectors, via education and training, transport, basic infrastructure, and support to SMEs.; ACT: ST, MT; IMP: LT ● Reducing transactions costs in accessing markets (e.g., with road access, basic services); ACT: ST, MT; IMP: MT, LT ● Creating mechanisms to discourage labor-market discrimination for women and the indigenous; ACT: MT; IMP: LT ● Expanding land titling and land markets programs; establishing financial institutions in rural areas; ACT: MT; IMP: MT ● Expanding seasonal employment creation programs (such as existing food-for-work programs) to provide opportunities for the rural poor; ACT: MT; IMP: MT
BUILDING THE ASSETS OF THE POOR—EDUCATION: Priority for poor overall, especially for girls, indigenous, rural		
● **Disparities, gaps in access:** ✓ Pre-primary: all poor, esp. rural ✓ Primary: poor, esp. girls, indigenous ✓ Secondary: all poor ● **Demand-side constraints** (both primary and secondary) ● **Supply-side constraints** (mainly at secondary) ● **Internal efficiency, quality** ● **Weak targeting of pubic spending, education programs** ● **Health outcomes**—malnutrition, infant and maternal mortality, and morbidity—are inadequate and not improving fast enough	▣▣ ▣▣▣ ▣▣ ▣▣▣▣ ▣▣ ▣▣▣ ▣▣▣	● Continuing increases in public spending on education, particularly at primary and pre-primary levels; ACT: ST, MT; IMP: MT, LT ● Expanding coverage, especially for girls and indigenous. Expansion should be implemented via decentralized PRONADE program using poverty map to replace supply-side restrictions as targeting mechanism; ACT: ST, MT; IMP: MT, LT ● Lowering official age of entry for primary school from 7 to 6; ACT: ST; IMP: MT ● Reviewing and improving quality, curriculum and performance standards, particularly at grades 1, 7, and 10 (transition years); ACT: ST, MT; IMP: MT, LT ● Promoting, expanding, consolidating and improving demand-side programs, with emphasis on girls and indigenous children (e.g., scholarships, school feeding, bolsa de utiles); ACT: ST, MT; IMP: MT, LT ● Increasing investments in early childhood development; ACT: ST, MT; IMP: MT, LT ● Using poverty map and other mechanisms, to better target public spending and demand-side programs (e.g., scholarships, school feeding, bolsa de utiles); ACT: ST; IMP: MT

(continued)

TABLE A: MENU OF OPTIONS AND KEY ACTIONS FOR POVERTY REDUCTION (*CONTINUED*)		
Main Constraints	**Main Recommendations**	
Key Issues	Priority	Key Actions & Time Period for Actions and Impact

BUILDING THE ASSETS OF THE POOR—HEALTH:
Priority for poor overall, especially for girls, indigenous, rural

Key Issues	Priority	Key Actions & Time Period for Actions and Impact
● **Public spending inadequate and not well targeted** ● **Significant share of population lacks access to affordable health care,** particularly the rural poor and indigenous ● **Supply-side constraints,** including fragmented services, minimal insurance coverage, waste in public spending, lack of medicines, doctors, staff ● **Demand-side constraints,** including cost and cultural barriers	▪▪▪	● Increasing public spending and expanding access to health care combined with better targeting (via poverty maps and health posts/community centers); ACT: ST, MT; IMP: MT
	▪▪▪	● Emphasizing preventative care, infectious and parasitic diseases, reproductive health, ey outcomes (mortality, malnutrition); ACT: ST, MT; IMP: MT
	▪▪	● Conducting a critical review of existing malnutrition interventions; ACT: ST; IMP: ST
	▪▪▪	● Implementing specific interventions for malnutrition as a top priority: community-based information and behavioral change programs; growth monitoring for pregnant women and children under age two; micro-nutrient supplements. ACT: ST, MT; IMP: MT, LT
	▪	● Focusing on demand-side interventions (e.g., conditional transfers) that could be channeled through self-targeted health posts/community centers; ACT: ST, MT; IMP: MT
	▪▪	● Promoting culturally-sensitive health care practices; ACT: ST, MT; IMP: MT
	▪	● Conducting full review of supply-side issues; ACT: ST; IMP: MT
	▪	● Developing monitoring system for health outcomes, including better and more regular measurement of infant and maternal mortality; ACT: ST; IMP: MT
	▪▪	● Adopting measures to improve efficiency and quality of services delivered (see Chapter 8); ACT: MT, LT; IMP: LT
	▪▪	● Facilitating increased awareness of family planning options so as to reduce Guatemala's high population growth rates, which constrain per capita income growth; ACT: ST, MT; IMP: LT

BUILDING THE ASSETS OF THE POOR—BASIC SERVICES:
Priority for poor overall, especially for rural, indigenous

Key Issues	Priority	Key Actions & Time Period for Actions and Impact
● **Significant coverage gaps and disparities,** especially among rural poor and indigenous ● **Demand-side factors** (connections costs) ● **Supply-side constraints** (not available) ● **Energy subsidies** poorly targeted ● **Quality of water is poor** (not potable, irregular) ● **Geographic isolation** for rural poor, due to limited road network and public transport services	▪▪	● Maintaining and, if possible, increasing resources for expansion of services; ACT: ST, MT; IMP: MT
	▪▪	● Targeting service expansion to poor (particularly rural) using poverty map combined with geographic information on coverage gaps; ACT: ST; IMP: MT
	▪▪	● Developing strategy for demand-side constraints; ACT: ST; IMP: MT
	▪	● Eliminating "tarifa social" energy subsidy and using resources to fund new connections instead; ACT: ST, but gradually; IMP: MT
	▪	● Allowing water tariffs to rise to a level that allows water utilities to become financially sustainable and improve the quality of service offered; ACT: ST but gradually; IMP: ST-MT
	▪▪	● Encouraging social funds and other providers to consider measures to improve quality of water; ACT: ST; IMP: ST
	▪▪	● Complementing water and sanitation programs with measures to improve household hygiene and water treatment practices; ACT: ST; IMP: ST

Main Constraints	Main Recommendations	
Key Issues	**Priority**	**Key Actions & Time Period for Actions and Impact**

BUILDING THE ASSETS OF THE POOR—TRANSPORT: Priority for rural poor

Key Issues	Priority	Key Actions & Time Period for Actions and Impact
● **Road quality and closures** limit year-round access ● **Road improvements have favored non-poor, urban areas** ● **Inadequate road access significantly constrains access of rural poor to health services, opportunities, institutions**	▪▪ ▪▪▪ ▪	● Focusing public spending on transport on rural areas; ACT: ST; IMP: ST, MT ● Expanding and improving *motorable* road network in rural areas, particularly by improving existing roads (including dirt roads); ACT: ST, MT; IMP: ST, MT ● Targeting expansion and rehabilitation using combination of poverty map with road maps; ACT: ST, MT; IMP: ST, MT

REDUCING VULNERABILITY:
Priority for all poor/vulnerable, particularly rural and specific vulnerable groups

Key Issues	Priority	Key Actions & Time Period for Actions and Impact
● **Lack of assets makes poor vulnerable to shocks,** particularly natural disasters and agriculture-related shocks ● **Key sources of future vulnerability:** (a) coffee crisis; (b) lost remittances from global slowdown; (c) natural disasters ● **Certain sub-groups** are particularly vulnerable due to special circumstances ● **Faced with shocks, households rely on own assets with little formal assistance** ● **Existing social protection programs are poorly targeted and inefficient**	▪▪▪ ▪▪ ▪ ▪▪ ▪ ▪▪ ▪▪	● Building assets of poor and key vulnerable groups (see Table B); ACT: ST, MT; IMP: MT, LT ● Expanding and improving disaster management relief; ACT: ST, MT; IMP: MT ● Introducing catastrophic insurance schemes; ACT: MT; IMP: MT ● Improving targeting of social protection programs; ACT: ST, MT; IMP: MT ● Eliminating energy subsidy and school transport subsidy; ACT: ST; IMP: ST ● Consolidating and improving scholarships and school feeding programs; ACT: ST, MT; IMP: ST, MT ● Improving targeting of *bolsa de utiles* program; ACT: ST, MT; IMP: ST, MT

IMPROVING INSTITUTIONS AND EMPOWERING COMMUNITIES: Priority for all poor

Key Issues	Priority	Key Actions & Time Period for Actions and Impact

● **Weak public sector hampers poverty reduction efforts**
  ✓ Weak tax base, limited public spending
  ✓ Public exp. management needs strengthening
  ✓ Public spending poorly targeted
  ✓ Weak civil service
  ✓ Overly centralized
● **Governance weak, constrains growth and poverty reduction efforts:** corruption, lack of rule of law, inadequate justice system, political instability.
● **Social capital limited, concentrated among privileged**
  ✓ Limited networks outside villages
  ✓ Community participation limited for women, poor, uneducated
	▪▪
	
	▪▪▪
	
	▪▪▪
	
	▪▪
	▪▪
	
	▪▪▪
	
	▪▪▪
	
	▪▪
	
	▪▪
		● Improving tax base and tax collection; ACT: ST, MT; IMP: ST, MT
		● Increasing and improving targeting of public spending; ACT: ST, MT; IMP: ST, MT
		● Improving public expenditure management, with stronger links to policy, planning, and priorities; ACT: ST, MT; IMP: ST, MT
		● Strengthening the civil service; ACT: MT; IMP: MT
		● Improving incentives for better service delivery (e.g., implementing recently-passed laws on decentralization, local *"control social,"* and service "report cards" and client satisfaction surveys); ACT: MT, LT; IMP: MT, LT
		● Expanding and building on recent initiatives to fight corruption (e.g., an anti-corruption charter) and making it a top priority. ACT: ST, MT; IMP: ST, MT
		● Improving rule of law, justice system; ACT: ST, MT; IMP: ST, MT
		● Promoting community-based development but with explicit outreach programs to ensure participation of excluded groups (women, poor, uneducated) in community-decision making; ACT: ST, MT; IMP: ST, MT
		● Partnering with private sector, NGOs to extend services; ACT: ST, MT; IMP: ST, MT

▪▪▪ = top priority; ▪▪ = medium priority; ▪ = priority; ST = one year period; MT = 1–3 years; LT = more than 3 years; ACT = period for implementation of actions; IMP = period needed for impact on poverty

Second, SEGEPLAN is also developing **tools to monitor actions to reduce poverty** under the ERP, including: further elaborating the ERP (fleshing out details for specific sectors and developing poverty reduction strategies at the department- and municipal-levels), and developing a system of monitoring indicators for the targets set by the ERP. Ideally, a goal-based poverty reduction strategy would involve a system that relates actions and external conditions to progress in reaching the goals, incorporating evaluation mechanisms and feedback loops. The development of this type of system should clearly be coordinated with: (a) efforts to gather data (e.g., with the MECOVI program); (b) efforts to monitor the targets set by the Peace Accords and the MDGs, (c) the SIAF, which is developing performance monitoring indicators for public expenditure management; and (d) the various executing agencies (e.g., sectoral ministries). Adequate financial and technical resources should be made available to the concerned agencies for the purposes of strengthening these two facets of the monitoring system.

ANNEXES

MEASURING CONSUMPTION USING THE ENCOVI 2000

Measuring Welfare: total Consumption

Assessing poverty relies on some measure of welfare. Since well-being, or utility, cannot be measured directly, consumption is used as an indirect measure of welfare. Consumption is used instead of income for several reasons. **First,** consumption is considered a better indicator of standards of living since it fluctuates less than income during a month or year. When incomes change (e.g., in different seasons), individuals tend to use their savings (in cash and kind) to smooth consumption throughout the year. **Second,** consumption data tend to be more accurate than information on individuals' incomes. International experience has shown that respondents tend to provide more accurate information on consumption than income. The latter is often underestimated or difficult to measure due to informal or in-kind income. **Finally,** using consumption as a measure of welfare has the advantage that poverty lines can be derived from the same data and not from other information sources.

Consumption also has several advantages over other welfare measures, such as indicators of basic needs (as access to water, electricity, and schooling; malnutrition; etc.). While consumption is an *objective* measure of welfare, indicators of basic needs are based on various *subjective* definitions, including the level at which such needs would be "satisfied" and the respective weights assigned to their components. Moreover, indicators of basic needs are not responsive to short-term changes, since they mainly reflect public investments. As such, they are less useful for monitoring changes in economic conditions. Although the Poverty Assessment uses consumption as the basis to measure welfare and poverty, the vast array of data available from the ENCOVI 2000 allow for the use of basic social indicators (as malnutrition access and use of basic services) to complement this quantitative measure of poverty.

Components of Total Consumption

Overview

The ENCOVI 2000 includes the data necessary to construct a measure of total consumption. This measure includes the annual consumption of food (both purchased and non-purchased, including

229

own-production), housing (using an imputed value for owned housing), durable goods, spending on consumer goods and services, basic services (water, gas, electricity), and outlays on health and education. These components are described in detail below. The prices used to value the consumption of these components come mainly from the household and community surveys. A price index was established to adjust for geographical cost differentials (see below). Finally, information on household members was used to con-

---

BOX A1.1: COMPONENTS OF TOTAL CONSUMPTION

Consumption of purchased food
Consumption of non-purchased food (own-production, gifts, donations)
Transport and communication
Spending on consumer goods
Household services and legal costs
Basic services (water, electricity, gas)
Annual use value of housing
Annual use value of durable goods
Education
Health

---

vert household consumption (collected in the survey) into a measure of the individual (per capita) welfare, taking into account household size.

Food Consumption

Purchased Food. The main data source for purchased foods is Section 12.A of the ENCOVI 2000 household questionnaire ("Spending and Consumption of Food, Drinks, and Tobacco"). Question 3 (variable P12A03) indicates if household members purchased each item during the last 12 months. Using this section, the number of months (question 4, variable P12A04) in which each food item was consumed was multiplied by the average monthly value (question 5, variable P12A05) to obtain the annual value of consumption.

To calculate annual spending on foods purchased in supermarkets,[1] Section 12.B of the ENCOVI 2000 ("Place and Frequency Purchases" of food) was used, multiplying the total value of purchases (question 12, variable P12B12) by the annual frequency of purchases (question 11, variable P12B11[2]). In addition, the annual value of food consumed *outside* the household was calculated by multiplying weekly expenditures in food and drinks consumed outside the home (variable GHOGAR for variable ITEM = 105) in Section 12.C (spending the last 7 days) by 52 (weeks per year).

Adding the annual expenses of all purchased foods, food purchased in supermarkets, and food consumed outside the home yields the total annual spending on purchased foods.

Non-Purchased Food. Even though the consumption of these items does not involve a monetary outlay, household welfare increases in the same way as with purchased food. The main data source for the consumption of non-purchased foods is Section 12.A in the ENCOVI 2000 household questionnaire ("Spending and Consumption of Food, Drinks, and Tobacco"). Question 7 (variable P12A07) indicates whether the item was obtained by own production or through other means (donations, partial reimbursement, or from a business) during the last 12 months. To obtain the annual *quantity,* the number of months in which each food was consumed (question 8, variable P12A08) was multiplied by the average monthly amount (question 9, variable P12A09A[3]) and by the corresponding price.

To obtain the annual *value* of non-purchased food consumption, the annual amount was multiplied by a *price*. In the case of non-purchased food, however, prices and values were not reported (since such quantities were never purchased or sold). Therefore, prices were imputed as follows. **First,** if the household also purchased the item (in addition to being consumed from non-purchase

---

1. If no individual information for food purchases was provided
2. For daily purchases, the frequency was 365, for weekly purchases it was 52, for monthly purchases it was 12 and for annual purchases the frequency was one.
3. After taking into consideration the product unit from question GA109B.

acquisitions), the price paid for the purchased quantities was used. To impute this paid price, the total value of purchases during the last 15 days (question 6d, variable P12A06D) was divided by the amount purchased during the last 15 days (question 6a, variable P12A06A).[4] **Second,** if this price was unknown (because the good was never purchased), its value was estimated using the prices paid by nearby households (geographically), since they would presumably have access to similar markets. Information from the price questionnaire was used when no price information was available for an specific item in the nearby households.

The consumption of food from social programs was also included (from Section 4.c, "Participation and Benefits from Social Programs"). To obtain the annual value of free food consumed outside the home,[5] the social programs "School Cookie," "School Breakfast," "Powder Milk," "Glass of Milk," and "Glass of atoll" were selected (question 1, variable P04C01 with values of 1, 2, 3, 4 or 5) and the reported value from questions 4, 8 and 12 (variables P04C04, P04C08 and P04C12) was multiply by 12 for the "powder milk" program, and by 10 for the other programs (month of services related to the school calendar).

The total annual value of non-purchased food consumption is obtained by adding the imputed annual expenses of all non-purchased foods consumed at home (internal consumption, gifts, donations) and food from social programs.

Spending on Consumer Goods and Services

The main data source for outlays on goods and services that are generally consumed in one year or less (such as matches, soap, detergent, newspaper, deodorants, books, school or non-work related transportation expenses, shoes, clothing, etc.) are include in section 12.c of the ENCOVI 2000. All expenses were reported in question 4 (variable GHOGAR). For expenses during the last 7 days, the value reported was multiplied by 52 weeks to obtain the annual value, for expenses during the last month, the value was multiplied by 12 months for the annual value, and annual expenses were included directly. Question 3 from the same section (variable ITEM) include all expenditures from the last seven days (codes 101–111), from last month (codes 201–231), and from last year (codes 301–326). **Transport and communication** included the annual value from questions 101, 102, 103, 104, 107, and 314. **Spending on consumer goods** included the annual value from questions 106, 108 through 217, 221, 222, 223, 225, 301, 302, 303, 305, 308 through 313, 315 and 325. It also includes information provided in Section 4.c, questions 4, 8 and 12 (variables P04C04, P04C08 and P04C12) for the non food social programs benefits (variable P04C01 with values between 6 and 11[6]). **Household services and legal** included the annual value from questions 218, 220, 224, 231, 319, 322 and 326.

Household Services: Energy, Water, Telephone

Data on household water, sanitation and communication services expenses come from Section 1.a of the ENCOVI 2000 ("Housing conditions"). To obtain the annual value of household water consumption, monthly values from "piped water" (question 17, variable P01A17), and "non piped water" (question 24, variable P01A24) were multiplied by 12 months. For garbage recollection, the monthly expenditure from question 33 (variable P0A22) was multiplied by 12. To obtain annual spending on regular telephone, cellular telephone, beeper, internet and cable connections, the monthly consumption (question 29, variables P01A29A, B, C D and E) were multiplied by 12 months. Data on monthly spending on household energy sources consumption (candles, kerosene, gas, coal, batteries, electricity, firewood and others) come from Section 1.b ("Sources of

---

4. Unit weight information was collected from several local markets. This information was used to transform the units reported into pounds or units

5. Not all the food was 100% free.

6. School transport subsidy, scholarships, school materials, health program, female children program and others.

Energy"). Yearly values were derived by multiplying monthly consumption (question 7, variable P01B07) by 12 months. Total annual spending on household services equals the sum of annual spending for each of the household services.

Annual Use Value of Housing

The annual use value of the housing must be included in total consumption for each household. Data on housing come from Section 1.c of the ENCOVI 2000 household questionnaire ("Housing ownership").

Rented housing. Rent is considered to be a good estimate of the use value of housing for those households that pay for the use of their house, apartment, or other type of home. As such, for rented housing, the annual rent value was calculated by multiplying monthly rent (question 8, variable P01C08) by 12 months and included in the consumption aggregate.

Owned Housing (not rented). The annual use value of owned housing was imputed as follows: (i) in most cases, the value estimated by the owners was used; or (ii) for households that did not provide an estimated value, the use value of housing was estimated by a regression (as discussed below).

(i)   *Value estimated by owners.* The use value estimated by owners was used for most cases of owned housing. Fortunately, the ENCOVI 2000 asked households that did not rent: "If you had to pay rent for this housing, how much would you pay on a monthly basis?" (question 7, variable P01C07). The answer to this question was used as an estimate of the rental value of the housing and therefore as an estimate of its use value (the estimated value was multiplied by 12 months to obtain the annual value).

(ii) *Value not estimated by owners.* In 0.36% of the 7,276 households, the respondents did not provide an estimate of the rental value for owned housing; consequently, their value was estimated from the average value of nearby households.

Value of the Annual Use of Durable Goods

Many goods are only partially consumed during the study period, such as cars, refrigerators, stoves, etc. Even if a television set has been purchased during the time period of the survey, it is expected to be used (and hence consumed) during many years to come. To reflect the current welfare that these goods provide to the household, the "value of one year of use" (annual use value) must be estimated and incorporated (rather than the actual purchase cost of these goods), whether the item was purchased in the current year or in previous years.

Data on the consumption value of household durables come from Section 14 of the ENCOVI 2000 ("Household durable goods"). Since these goods are generally not entirely consumed during one year, the value of their use during the past year had to be estimated. For example, if someone bought a television set this year for Q/.3,000.00, the annual consumption value of this television set is not Q/.3,000.00, since the individual can also use the television during the following year, i.e., the Q/.3,000.00 will be consumed during a time period of more than one year. Food and other consumer goods do not have this characteristic, because if someone buys one liter of milk, this milk will be consumed in less than one year.

Three data points are needed to estimate the consumption value of the household durables (i) the age of the durable good (question 3, variable P14A03); (ii) the remaining use life of the durable good; and (iii) the current value of the durable good (question 5, variable P14A05).

To obtain the remaining use life of durable goods, we need to know the average lifetime of each good[7] or, as commonly referred to, its use life or expected lifetime. If the use life of the durable good is known, we will only need to subtract its age to obtain the remaining lifetime. Fortunately, ENCOVI 2000 data allow for an estimate of the expected lifetime of each durable good.

---

7. Each item is identify in question 1, variable ITEM.

Assuming that in one year a similar percentage of the population buys a durable good (say a television), it is likely that some individuals will have a new television, some will have televisions that are one-year old, others two-years old, etc. As such, calculating the average age of all televisions sets (average of P14A03) yields the mean life or average age of all televisions. By multiplying the mean life by two, the result would be the expected lifetime of a television set in years. If the reported age (variable P14A03) is subtracted from the expected lifetime of a television set, the remaining use life of each television set is obtained. Finally, dividing the current value of a television set (variable P14A05) by the remaining use life yields the annual use value of the television set.

Applying this procedure for all durable good and adding the values of each item yields the annual value of the consumption of household durable goods.

Education

Data on household expenses on education (such as registration and enrollment fees, uniforms, books or material, travel) come from Section VII of the ENCOVI 2000. The ENCOVI 2000 asked households for *annual* pre-primary school expenses for children under 6 years (questions 3,4 and 5, variables P07A03, P07A04 and P07A05 in Section 7.a) and for students aged 6 and over (questions 12, 13 and 17; variables P07B12, P07B13 and P07B17 in Section 7.b). Households were also asked for the *monthly* expenses for children under 6 (questions 6–9, variables P07A06–P07A09 in Section 7.a) and students aged 6 and over (questions 19 through 22; variables P07B19 through P07B22 in Section 7.b). To obtain the annual value of the monthly expenses, they were multiplied by 10 months.

Total annual education consumption is obtained by adding the educational expenses and scholarships for all household members.

Health

The data source for health expenses for the past month is Section 6. Health spending for children 5 years and younger for diarrhea and respiratory problems are in Section 6.c, question 9 (variables P06C09A–P06C09F and P06C09T). Section 6.d has the information for all the household members expenditures during last month[8] on doctor fees (question 11, variable P06D11), medicines (question 12, variable P06D12), X-rays and tests (question 13, variable P06D13), transport to medical facilities (question 14, variable P06D14), orthopedic equipment (question 15, variable P06D15), glasses, hearing aid, dentures, etc (question 16, variable P06D16), hospitalization (question 18, variable P06D18), and health insurance premiums (question 19, variable P06D19). Expenditures related to pregnancy were reported in an yearly basis in Section 11 (questions 14 and 23, variables P11A14 and P11A23).

Section 12.c has the information for health expenditures for the last 12 months (excluding the previous month and all pregnancy expenses) in question 20 variable GHOGAR (for ITEM = 320). Monthly expenses on accident and death insurance reported in questions 28, 29, and 30 of Section 12.c (variable GHOGAR for ITEM = 228, 229 and 230) were also included.

Monthly expenses on accident and death insurance reported in questions 28, 29, and 30 of Section 12.c (variable GHOGAR for ITEM = 228, 229 and 230) were also included (multiplied by 12 months to obtain the annual value).

Total annual health spending is obtained by adding all expenditures reported in these questions.

Other

Total consumption did not include donations (Section 13.b) because it was difficult to avoid double counting. Out of 7,276 households 517 (7.1%) household reported receiving food consumed outside the house or goods (question 2, variables P13B02B or P13B02C = 1). Since the type of donation received accepted multiple answers, it is not always possible to differentiate from valid

---

8. Excluding expenditures reported in section 6.c and pregnancy related health expenditures.

from invalid types.[9] Only 328 households reported valid types of donation and at the same time did not report invalid types. Finally, it was not possible to differentiate from this donations and information provided (and already included) from the social programs. Due to this problems, no information was included from this section.

Total Consumption

Finally, by adding all consumption values for each component (by household), we obtain the **total consumption** variable. Thirty three households were excluded from the original figure of 7,309 households (yielding a total of 7,276) because a large share of the consumption aggregate had to be estimated or imputed due to missing values.[10]

Weighting Total Consumption by the Regional Price Index

The cost of living is not uniform throughout the country; as such, the value of total consumption was adjusted to account for regional variation in prices. Price indices were constructed for each Department (22), Area (Urban/Rural) combination (44 indices) using the information collected in the price questionnaire and the household questionnaire (Section 12.a) in the following manner.

Using consumption data from Section 12.a, **"national average consumption in pounds"** was calculated for each food article. This was achieved by dividing the national average value of annual *purchased and non purchased food*[11] (without the Social Programs component) by the national average price derived from question 6 (estimated dividing variables P12A06D by P12A06A).[12] The result is a file with one variable (pounds) for each of the 99 food articles (99 entries).

Next, prices for each article were estimated for each Department/Area combination. The average prices were estimated using the Household questionnaire (estimated dividing variables P12A06D by P12A06A). If such information was not available in the ENCOVI 2000 household questionnaire, prices reported in the price questionnaire were used.[13] With these prices, the purchase cost of the **"national average consumption in pounds"** in each Department/Area was estimated. The cost of the national average consumption in pound in each Department/Area was divided by the cost in Guatemala City to produce the **Geographical Food Index.**

To obtain a similar Index for the non-food items, the Price questionnaire, Section B was used. A weighted average for each Department/Area was computed. Items also present in the Guatemalan Consumer Price Index (CPI) were selected (questions 1–12 and 14–22, Variable PRECIO for ITEM = 41–52 and 54–62). The same weight values used in the CPI were applied.

Similar to the Geographical Food Index, all the non-food Department/Area values were divided by the Guatemala City value to produce the **Geographical Non-Food Index.**

Finally, to obtain the overall **Geographical Index** for each Department/Area, the weighted average of the Geographical Food and Non Food Indexes was computed. The weight used is the same proportions between food and non-food observed in the consumption aggregate: 40.5% for the food component, and 59.5% for the non food component. The resulting variable allows for standardization of any expense at the Guatemala City level (to be used as a divisor).

Using the Guatemala City average as a basis (Guatemala City = 1), the FACT.GEO variable was found to vary between 0.99 and 1.07.

---

9. Valid types: food consumed outside the house or goods. Invalid types: food consumed in the house (already included in non-purchased food), or cash (people do not consume cash)

10. Also, only households with complete interviews were selected.

11. Described previously under "Food Consumption."

12. This national average price per item was used only for the estimation of the average national consumption quantities. Later, another "national average price" is estimated using a methodology based in the price questionnaire information.

13. A minimum of 15 prices per article for each department/area combination were required. If neither the ENCOVI 2000 household questionnaire, nor the Price questionnaire had enough data points, the average for the Region(8)/Area combination was used (with a minimum of 25 data points), or the Departmental average (with a minimum of 35 data points) or the Regional average (with a minimum of 45 data point).

Value of Total Consumption Per Capita

For the final step to rank the population by welfare level (consumption) from the lowest to the highest, a share of the total consumption must be allocated to each household member. Per capita consumption is used in the Poverty Assessment, i.e., the total value of consumption of the household divided by the number of household members. There are several other ways of allocating household consumption to the different members, taking into account different requirements, economies of scale, and the presence of public services in the household. Per capita consumption was used due to its transparency, but other methods were used for sensitivity tests of the consumption aggregate.

Levels of Total Consumption Per Capita: Guatemala 2000

The population was ranked from the lowest to the highest level according to total per capita annual consumption (welfare). Per capita consumption varies considerably in Panama (see Fig. A1.1). On average, annual per-capita consumption is Q/.6,180. The richest ten percent of the population has an average consumption level of Q/.23,543 while the poorest ten percent has an annual average per-capita consumption of Q/.1,287.

FIGURE A1.1: LEVELS OF CONSUMPTION: REPUBLIC OF GUATEMALA, 2000

% of population	Level of average annual per-capita consumption (Q/.)
100	
	23,543
90	
	9,862
80	
	6,940
70	
	5,243
60	
	4,240
50	
	3,537
40	
	2,916
30	
	2,369
20	
	1,876
10	
	1,287
0	

Lowest level of consumption

Source: ENCOVI 2000 2000

MEASURING INCOME USING THE ENCOVI 2000

Introduction

This note summarizes the components and the methodology used to construct the income aggregate using the ENCOVI 2000, Guatemala.

The income aggregate measures the income obtained by a household in a year. The total household income can be divided between (i) income earned from labor activities; and (ii) income not related to labor activities. In addition, labor income can be further divided between wage and self-employed income, agricultural and non-agricultural, formal and informal. Non-labor income consists of income such as interest earned from savings, pensions and remittances.

The above income components are calculated for each household member and transformed in annual income. The total household income is the sum of each of these components for each household member. All variables are previously "cleaned" and reviewed to remove "outliers," missing data and other data problems. All values are also adjusted to account for regional price differences.

This notes continues as follows: the next section summarizes the components of the income aggregate. Then the labor income components are discussed in specific detail, followed by a discussion of the non-labor income components (directly using the information in the ENCOVI 2000 data). A list of all the variables used is then provided at the end.

Income Aggregate Components

Household income can be divided between labor and non-labor activities. The components for each category are summarized as:

Labor income

- Wages from formal non-agricultural activities
- Wages from informal non-agricultural activities
- Wages from formal agricultural activities
- Wages from informal agricultural activities
- Self-employed income from formal non-agricultural activities

- Self-employed income from informal non-agricultural activities
- Self-employed income from agricultural activities

Non-labor income

- Rental of equipment and property
- Interest and dividends
- Remittances
- Public assistance and donations
- Private assistance and donations
- Pensions and compensations
- Other income (inheritance, scholarships, lottery winnings)

Labor Income

Labor Income Classifications

Labor income is constructed using chapters X (economic activities) and XVI (agricultural activities) of the ENCOVI 2000. The first issue to address is the classification of labor activities. Labor activities are divided between wages and self-employed income. Income is defined as wages if a person is an employee in the government or a private company (P10B14B < 5 or >6).[1] Otherwise, labor income is classified as self-employed. Income is derived from agricultural activities if the person works in any of the agricultural occupational classifications (P10B02 = 1 or 2 or 5) and as non-agricultural otherwise. Finally, income is classified as formal if a person works for the government, or in the private sector in a company with more than 5 workers, or in a farm that employs more than 5 people (P10B14 = 1, P10B12 > 2 and P10B14 = 2 or 3 or P10B14 > 4). Otherwise, it is classified as informal.

Wages. For each person, the ENCOVI 2000 reports up to three jobs. The following components of annual wages are constructed for each of the three jobs:

- Wages and salaries times months worked during the year;
  (P10B04 * P10B22, P10C05 * P10C16, P10D05 * P10D10);
- Bono 14 (P10B20B, P10C14B, P10D08B);
- Payment in aguinaldo (P10B27B);

less

- Payment to social security—IGSS (P10B13 * P10B04);
- Income tax.[2]

The level of annual wage income is constructed by first summing the above components for each of the three jobs and then aggregating them at the household level. The income is divided between agricultural and non-agricultural as well as formal and informal based on the definitions above to give the following four wage income categories:

- Wages and salaries from formal non-agricultural activities;
- Wages and salaries from informal non-agricultural activities;

---

1. In parenthesis, the corresponding variable names and appropriate formulae to construct each variable is provided.

2. Income taxes in Guatemala are based on disposable income (DI). This is calculated as: Net income— Q 36,000 (exempt income)—less social security contributions. Given that, the tax rates are: (i) DI less than Q 65,000: 15%; (ii) DI between Q 65,000 – Q 180,000 : Q 9,750 + 20% of amount in excess of Q 65,000; and (iii) DI between Q 180,000 – Q 295,000 : Q 61,500 + 31% of amount in excess of Q 295,000.

▓ Wages and salaries from formal agricultural activities;
▓ Wages and salaries from informal agricultural activities;

Self-employed non-agricultural income. This refers to independent entrepreneurs that work in non-agricultural activities. For them, their income is the reported net income multiplied by the number of months that they received it for each of the three possible jobs (P10B15A * P10B15C, P10B15A * P10B15C, P10B15A * P10B15C). The total income from this activity is constructed by summing income from same type jobs for every person in the household. Self-employed income from non-agricultural activities is divided between formal and informal:

▓ Self-employed income from formal non-agricultural activities
▓ Self-employed income from informal non-agricultural activities

Self-Employed Income from Agricultural Activities

Income from independent agricultural activities is the sum of all income minus the costs related to that. In this context, this income represents the net income from agricultural activities.

In particular, household self-employed agricultural income is derived from the following:

▓ Revenue from the rent of owned land to others (P16A11)
▓ Revenue from the sale of crops (P16B06)
▓ Revenue from the sale of processed crop products (P16H03CA through p16H03CG)
▓ Revenue from the sale of forest products (P16I04A through P16I04E)
▓ Revenue from animal sales (P16J08B and P16J11B)
▓ Revenue from the sale of animal products (P16L03CA through P16L03CJ)
▓ Consumption of own produced output (constructed in the consumption aggregate)

less

▓ Cost for renting land from others (P16A22 if P16A21> 1 and P16A23A * Period (using P16A23B) if P16A21 = 1)
▓ Cost for agricultural inputs. These are further divided in:
  ✔ Crop and forest production related inputs (P16C02A through P16C02E, P16D02A through P16D02I)
  ✔ Labor inputs (P16E02A * P16E02B, P16E03A * P16E03B, P16E05, P16E06C)
  ✔ Cost for technical assistance (P16F05)
  ✔ Cost for inputs related to livestock activities (P16M02A through P16M02E)
  ✔ Depreciation of agricultural capital equipment.[3]

Non-Labor Income

Income from non-labor income is divided in the following categories:

▓ Rental of equipment and property. This includes the income received from rental of properties, construction, equipment and goods[4] (P13A02A) and the estimated rental value of owned housing (P010C7 and constructed in the consumption aggregate).

---

3. This represents the value of the annual use of durable goods used in agricultural activities. To estimate this value, the average age of each equipment is calculated (average of P16G04 by equipment type if P16G01 = 1). This is multiplied by 2 to obtain the expected lifetime of the equipment. Then, the reported age is subtracted from the expected lifetime to get the remaining lifetime of the equipment for each household.[3] Finally, the current value of the equipment (P16G07) is divided by the remaining lifetime to obtain the annual use of the equipment.

4. Not related to agricultural activities.

- Interest and dividends from savings accounts and stock holdings (P13A02B)
- Remittances. This is support in cash by friends and family (P10E09, P13B03E if in cash)
- Donations. These include donations and help in cash or in kind gifts received by the government, church, private organizations and friends and family (P10E06, P13B03A through P13B03E) and public program assistance (P04C04, P04C08, P04C12, P13A02H-I). The support in cash by friends and family is reported as remittances. This income is divided between private and public.
- Pensions and compensations. This includes child care allowances, orphan and widow pensions, retirement benefits, compensations for work or contract termination, life insurance. (P10E01B*12, P10E02B*12, P10E03B*12, P13A02C, P13A02D, P13A02E, P13A02G).
- Other income. This income includes inheritance, scholarships and lottery winnings. (P13A02F, P13A02H through P13A02L).

MEASURING POVERTY USING THE ENCOVI 2000

This annex uses the following method to classify individuals as extreme poor, poor, or non-poor: (i) individuals are ranked according to their level of welfare, as measured by total consumption (Annex 1); (ii) the value of the full poverty line and extreme poverty line is calculated; and (iii) individuals whose consumption levels fall below these lines are classified accordingly.

(I) Ranking Individuals

Defining Welfare. Since welfare, or well-being, cannot be measured directly consumption was used as an indirect measure of welfare. Consumption is used because it is not subject to the under-estimation and biases of an income measure, and because it avoids the subjectivity associated with measures of basic needs and indicators of human development. Annex 1 provides details on the construction of total consumption as a measure of welfare.

Individuals were ranked from the lowest to the highest level of annual per-capita consumption (welfare). Figure A3.1 shows major differences in the current per-capita consumption in Guatemala. On average, annual per-capital consumption is Q.6,180. Consumption ranges from an average of Q/.23,543 for the richest ten percent of the population to an average of Q/.1,287 for the poorest ten percent.

(II) Constructing Poverty Lines

Two poverty lines were constructed for this study: an extreme poverty line and a full poverty line.

The Extreme Poverty Line. The extreme poverty line represents the yearly cost of the minimum daily caloric requirement recommended for Guatemala (2,172 on average, see Table A3.1), using the observed consumption basket of the entire- population. When the consumption level of any individual is below such value, he/she is unable to consume the minimum recommended calorie level. That is, even if the individual spends all his/her resources on food, he/she would still not be able to acquire the minimum level of recommended calories.

FIGURE A3.1: LEVELS OF CONSUMPTION: REPUBLIC OF GUATEMALA, 2000

% of population	Level of average annual per-capita consumption (Q/.)
100	
	23,543
90	
	9,862
80	
	6,940
70	
	5,243
60	
	4,240
50	
	3,537
40	
	2,916
30	
	2,369
20	
	1,876
10	
	1,287
0	

Lowest level of consumption

Source: ENCOVI 2000 2000

The extreme poverty line was calculated as follows:

a) Using the ranking based on total annual per-capita consumption, households with the lowest and highest consumption level were dropped (those in the lowest 2% and highest 2% of the population were not included).

b) On the basis of the food consumption *patterns* of the households in the 3%—98% range, the amount of calories supplied by each type of food[1] and the percentage of these calories in the total was calculated. For example, for this group of households, corn provides more calories than any other type of food (36.5 percent of the calories consumed). Next in importance are bread (sweet) and sugar, which supply 10.2 and 9.4 percent respectively of the total calories consumed (see Table A3.2 for consumption patterns of all products).

c) The minimum average calorie requirements of a Guatemalan were calculated using data from INCAP: 2,172 kcal/day (see Table A2-1).

d) The amount of food required to satisfy the minimum calorie requirements were calculated, using the shares (consumption patterns) for each type of food for households within the 3–98% of consumption. The absolute amounts consumed by this group are adjusted to meet the amounts required to achieve the recommended calorie level (2,172) using their consumption shares.

e) On the basis of these amounts, the cost of food required to satisfy the minimum calorie requirements was determined.

f) An adjustment to account for "wasted food" was apply. According to nutritional experts in Guatemala only 90% of acquired food reach the mouth of the consumer.[2] The cost of food to get 2,172 Kcal./day was divided by 0.9 This is the cost of the minimum calorie requirements, in other words, the value of the extreme poverty line. For Guatemala in 2000, the extreme poverty line was calculated as Q/.1,869 per-capita per year.

Figure A3.2 below shows the method used for calculating the extreme poverty line.

---

1. Using food calorie composition data from "Valor Nutritivo de los alimentos de Centroamérica." Instituto de Nutrición de Centro América y Panamá (INCAP) y la Organización Panamericana de la Salud (OPS). Ciudad de Guatemala, Guatemala, 1998.

2. The rest is left in the plate, thrown away, dropped, etc. Ma. Teresa Menchú, Central America Nutritional Institute (INCAP).

TABLE A3.1: GUATEMALA: MINIMUM CALORIE REQUIREMENTS: AVERAGE BY AGE AND GENDER

Age in Years	Population Persons	%	Daily Kcal requirement	Daily Kcal contribution
< 1 year				
< 1 breast feeding	316,928	3	0	0
< 1 not breast feeding	69,570	1	738	4.5
1–2	743,855	7	1,200	78.4
3–4	714,964	6	1,400	87.9
5–6	687,707	6	1,675	101.2
Male				
7–9	496,022	4	2,000	87.1
10–11	309,554	3	2,200	59.8
12–13	293,825	3	2,350	60.6
14–15	281,364	2	2,650	65.5
16–17	268,573	2	3,000	70.8
18–64	2,604,682	23	3,100	709.2
65 & +	193,786	2	2,200	37.4
Female				
7–9	475,556	4	1,700	71.0
10–11	296,833	3	1,900	49.5
12–13	281,798	2	2,000	49.5
14–15	228,955	2	2,100	42.2
16–17	135,127	1	2,150	25.5
18–49	1,665,876	15	2,100	307.3
50–64	368,327	3	2,100	67.9
65 & +	209,958	2	1,850	34.1
Pregnant				
14–15	8,137	0	2,385	4.9
16–17	42,176	1	2,435	15.0
18–49	374,835	3	2,385	69.5
Breast feeding		0		
14–15	6,047	0	2,600	4.0
16–17	31,350	0	2,650	12.2
18–49	279,531	2	2,600	56.5
TOTAL	**11,385,336**	**100**		**2172**
Minimum Calorie Requirements: Weighted Average				2172

Source: *Instituto de Nutrición de Centro América y Panamá* (INCAP)
CEPAL/CELADE—División de Población, Boletín Demográfico No. 66, Julio 2000

The Full Poverty Line. Total consumption, even among the poorest, almost always includes the consumption of non-food goods and services. As such, the general poverty line includes an additional amount for the percentage of the **non-food** consumption. The share of non-food consumption is based on the observed consumption patterns of individuals whose food consumption is close to the extreme poverty line.

The full poverty line equals the extreme poverty line plus an allowance for non-food consumption, as follows:

a) Individuals with *food consumption* (C_A) levels close to (+/−5%) the extreme poverty line ($C_A = Z_{pe} = 1,869$) were selected. These individuals barely meet their minimum calorie requirements.

TABLE A3.2: CALCULATION OF FOOD CONSUMPTION PATTERNS FOR EXTREME POVERTY LINE

ITEM	Quetzals per			Lb./year/ HH	Consumed daily Kcal			Kcal to get 2,172/day/ person	Yearly cost of 2,172	
	Kcal/ Lb.	Lb.	1,000 Kcal		Household (5 persons)	Person	%		without waste	with 10% waste
Corn (grain)	1,639	0.94	0.57	1,125.2	5,052.4	1,010.5	36.5%	791.8	166.06	184.51
Bread (sweet)	1,707	1.78	1.04	303.3	1,418.4	283.7	10.2%	222.3	84.39	93.77
Sugar	1,743	1.81	1.04	272.9	1,303.2	260.6	9.4%	204.2	77.22	85.80
Tortillas	1,018	1.34	1.32	353.7	987.0	197.4	7.1%	154.7	74.31	82.56
Beans (frijoles)	1,530	2.59	1.69	156.6	656.5	131.3	4.7%	102.9	63.61	70.67
Bread (French)	1,353	2.12	1.57	165.2	612.3	122.5	4.4%	96.0	55.01	61.12
Oil	4,013	4.43	1.10	51.3	563.9	112.8	4.1%	88.4	35.57	39.53
Rice	1,634	2.35	1.44	92.4	413.9	82.8	3.0%	64.9	34.00	37.78
Pasta	1,684	3.44	2.04	52.1	240.6	48.1	1.7%	37.7	28.13	31.25
Eggs	591	3.75	6.34	102.8	166.5	33.3	1.2%	26.1	60.42	67.14
Chicken or Hens	573	7.15	12.48	87.0	136.6	27.3	1.0%	21.4	97.49	108.33
Corn tamales	499	2.49	4.98	98.1	134.2	26.8	1.0%	21.0	38.25	42.50
Beef Meat	970	13.78	14.21	49.4	131.3	26.3	0.9%	20.6	106.72	118.57
Potato	307	1.15	3.73	135.1	113.6	22.7	0.8%	17.8	24.26	26.96
Oatmeal	1,716	4.31	2.51	22.6	106.4	21.3	0.8%	16.7	15.29	16.99
Bread (slice)	1,212	1.34	1.11	29.9	99.4	19.9	0.7%	15.6	6.29	6.99
Powder Milk	2,252	13.56	6.02	14.4	89.0	17.8	0.6%	13.9	30.66	34.07
Flour (Incaparina)	1,689	3.87	2.29	19.2	88.9	17.8	0.6%	13.9	11.65	12.95
Milk Cream	1,235	6.48	5.25	24.1	81.4	16.3	0.6%	12.8	24.46	27.17
Margarine	3,264	5.61	1.72	8.8	78.9	15.8	0.6%	12.4	7.76	8.62
Cheese	1,230	9.74	7.91	22.7	76.6	15.3	0.6%	12.0	34.68	38.54
Milk Cream	238	1.78	7.47	112.7	73.3	14.7	0.5%	11.5	31.36	34.84
Candy 1	2,336	11.46	4.91	11.1	70.9	14.2	0.5%	11.1	19.91	22.13
Beef Meat with bone	515	7.34	14.26	49.2	69.4	13.9	0.5%	10.9	56.58	62.87
Flour (Corn)	1,657	2.48	1.50	15.3	69.3	13.9	0.5%	10.9	5.93	6.59
Plantains	382	0.97	2.53	50.9	53.3	10.7	0.4%	8.3	7.72	8.58
Flour (Wheat)	1,653	2.35	1.42	11.1	50.2	10.0	0.4%	7.9	4.09	4.54
Panela o rapadura	1,616	2.36	1.46	10.5	46.6	9.3	0.3%	7.3	3.89	4.32
Bananas	269	0.80	2.99	58.9	43.3	8.7	0.3%	6.8	7.40	8.22

Cakes	1,766	10.53	5.96	7.9	38.1	7.6	0.3%	6.0	13.00	14.44
Dry Seeds	2,626	5.56	2.12	5.1	36.8	7.4	0.3%	5.8	4.47	4.96
Corn Flakes	1,766	19.58	11.08	7.5	36.1	7.2	0.3%	5.7	22.86	25.40
Chocolate	2,075	5.50	2.65	5.4	30.7	6.1	0.22%	4.8	4.66	5.17
Cookies	2,111	15.54	7.36	5.3	30.7	6.1	0.2%	4.8	12.93	14.36
Sausages (Pork)	2,996	19.87	6.63	3.7	30.7	6.1	0.2%	4.8	11.65	12.94
Sausages	1,004	12.01	11.96	10.9	29.9	6.0	0.2%	4.7	20.49	22.76
Fat (Pork)	3,991	5.28	1.32	2.7	29.2	5.8	0.2%	4.6	2.21	2.46
Tomatoes	93	1.87	20.04	113.9	29.2	5.8	0.2%	4.6	33.42	37.14
Soups	1,292	14.97	11.58	8.2	29.1	5.8	0.2%	4.6	19.31	21.45
Powder Milk (children)	2,302	17.75	7.71	4.2	26.6	5.3	0.2%	4.2	11.74	13.05
Pork Meat	978	11.73	12.00	9.6	25.8	5.2	0.2%	4.0	17.70	19.67
Güisquil	108	1.17	10.78	86.6	25.7	5.1	0.2%	4.0	15.87	17.63
Carrots	168	1.34	7.98	54.4	25.1	5.0	0.2%	3.9	11.47	12.75
Tostadas	1,874	9.32	4.97	4.6	23.7	4.7	0.2%	3.7	6.75	7.50
Cabbage	100	0.54	5.36	81.0	22.3	4.5	0.2%	3.5	6.83	7.59
Candy 2	1,630	9.83	6.03	4.6	20.4	4.1	0.1%	3.2	7.04	7.82
Chicken or Hens inners	763	4.44	5.83	9.6	20.1	4.0	0.1%	3.2	6.71	7.46
Avocado	378	2.26	5.99	19.0	19.6	3.9	0.1%	3.1	6.73	7.48
Oranges and Tangerines	110	0.80	7.34	59.6	17.9	3.6	0.1%	2.8	7.51	8.34
Onions	143	2.38	16.65	43.5	17.0	3.4	0.1%	2.7	16.22	18.02
Ice cream	549	4.91	8.95	10.9	16.3	3.3	0.1%	2.6	8.37	9.30
Other Atoll	275	2.49	9.06	20.7	15.6	3.1	0.1%	2.4	8.09	8.99
Pork Mean with bone	808	8.53	10.56	6.9	15.4	3.1	0.1%	2.4	9.29	10.33
Soda pop	202	3.27	16.21	27.1	15.0	3.0	0.1%	2.4	13.91	15.46
Ayote, chilacayote	70	0.40	5.68	71.9	13.8	2.8	0.1%	2.2	4.48	4.98
Paches	499	3.19	6.39	9.6	13.1	2.6	0.1%	2.1	4.80	5.34
Corn Dough (fresh)	779	2.56	3.28	5.9	12.6	2.5	0.1%	2.0	2.37	2.64
Spices	146	2.98	20.49	29.7	11.9	2.4	0.1%	1.9	13.91	15.45
Fish (fresh)	296	8.30	28.02	14.1	11.5	2.3	0.1%	1.8	18.37	20.41
Cattle inners	554	8.36	15.10	6.8	10.3	2.1	0.1%	1.6	8.88	9.87
Corn Atoll	173	2.33	13.51	20.7	9.8	2.0	0.1%	1.5	7.58	8.42
Honey and molasses	1,280	8.53	6.66	2.5	8.9	1.8	0.1%	1.4	3.41	3.78

(continued)

TABLE A3.2: CALCULATION OF FOOD CONSUMPTION PATTERNS FOR EXTREME POVERTY LINE (CONTINUED)

| ITEM | Kcal/ Lb. | Quetzals per | | Lb./year/ HH | Consumed daily Kcal | | | Kcal to get 2,172/day/ person | Yearly cost of 2,172 | |
		Lb.	1,000 Kcal		Household (5 persons)	Person	%		without waste	with 10% waste
Ketchup & tomato paste	427	8.38	19.64	6.5	7.6	1.5	0.1%	1.2	8.59	9.54
Fat (Vegetable)	3,954	4.87	1.23	0.7	7.3	1.5	0.1%	1.1	0.51	0.57
Cassava	374	2.18	5.84	6.9	7.1	1.4	0.1%	1.1	2.37	2.63
Beer	186	7.21	38.74	13.9	7.1	1.4	0.1%	1.1	15.66	17.40
Garlic	572	6.24	10.91	4.4	7.0	1.4	0.1%	1.1	4.34	4.83
Limes	67	1.39	20.67	36.4	6.7	1.3	0.0%	1.0	7.92	8.80
Alcohol	1,049	17.56	16.74	2.3	6.5	1.3	0.0%	1.0	6.20	6.88
Beets	126	1.42	11.27	18.5	6.4	1.3	0.0%	1.0	4.11	4.57
Cucumber	52	1.30	24.79	37.9	5.4	1.1	0.0%	0.9	7.72	8.58
Tuna and Sardines	909	15.01	16.51	2.1	5.1	1.0	0.0%	0.8	4.83	5.37
Butter	2,742	11.73	4.28	0.6	4.8	1.0	0.0%	0.8	1.17	1.30
Mangos	121	2.86	23.63	14.1	4.7	0.9	0.0%	0.7	6.33	7.03
Pine Apple	139	1.09	7.84	11.8	4.5	0.9	0.0%	0.7	2.01	2.23
Papaya	109	1.15	10.52	14.9	4.4	0.9	0.0%	0.7	2.67	2.97
Bell peppers	162	6.28	38.77	10.0	4.4	0.9	0.0%	0.7	9.84	10.93
Dry Fruit	1,103	6.92	6.27	1.1	3.2	0.6	0.0%	0.5	1.15	1.28
Juice (pre packed)	215	3.09	14.37	5.3	3.1	0.6	0.0%	0.5	2.54	2.82
Marmalade	1,117	14.78	13.24	1.0	2.9	0.6	0.0%	0.5	2.22	2.46
Lettuce	68	2.10	30.86	15.6	2.9	0.6	0.0%	0.5	5.14	5.71
Watermelon	49	0.90	18.49	15.2	2.0	0.4	0.0%	0.3	2.15	2.39
Yogurt	327	6.67	20.41	2.2	2.0	0.4	0.0%	0.3	2.28	2.54
Arveja	368	4.11	11.17	1.6	1.6	0.3	0.0%	0.3	1.04	1.16
Melons	81	1.04	12.83	7.1	1.6	0.3	0.0%	0.2	1.16	1.28
Condensed & Evaporated Milk	1,033	8.61	8.34	0.5	1.3	0.3	0.0%	0.2	0.64	0.71
Celery	73	4.87	67.04	1.4	0.3	0.1	0.0%	0.0	1.05	1.17
Mushrooms	54	9.98	183.27	0.5	0.1	0.0	0.0%	0.0	0.73	0.82
Salt	—	0.65	n/a	15.4	—	—	0.0%	—	1.56	1.73
Sum				4,528		2,771		2,172	1,682	1,869

Source: ENCOVI 2000, Guatemala

FIGURE A3.2: CALCULATING THE EXTREME POVERTY LINE

A. Ranking Individuals

Highest level of total annual per-capita consumption lowest 3-98%.

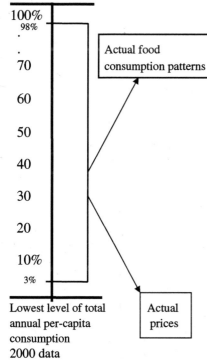

Lowest level of total annual per-capita consumption 2000 data

B. Calculating the Value of Minimum Caloric Requirements

Actual level of average calories for households in the

Total level in this group = 2,025/person. *For example*:
36.5% of calories comes from corn
10.2% of calories comes from bread (sweet)
9.4% of calories comes from sugar
7.1% of calories comes from tortillas

See patterns for all products in Table A2.2

The number of calories corresponds to a physical amount of food (in pounds)

Average recommended calorie level = 2,172

The quantity of each food item is adjusted to obtain a basket that provides the 2,172 calories maintaining the *consumption patterns* of households in the 3-98% per-capita consumption range.

C. Value of the Extreme Poverty Line
The value is calculated by adding the quantity of items estimated in the last step using the prices actually faced by households in the 3-98% group. Using THE ENCOVI and allowing for a 10% "waste", the annual value of the extreme poverty line is Q/.1,682 per capita. $Z_{pe} = Q\backslash\ 1,682$

b) *Consumption coefficients* were calculated for this group: that is, the share of total consumption allocated to food (in this case, 44.2%) and non-food products (55.8%).

c) To obtain the full poverty line, the value of the extreme poverty line was divided by this share of food consumption (44.2%).

Figure A3.3 below shows the method used to calculate the general poverty line.

(III) Poverty Measures

The poverty indices used in this study are three special cases of additively separable measures developed by Foster, Greer and Thorbecke (FGT, 1984). The general poverty measure is:

$$P_\alpha = \frac{1}{n} \sum_{n=1}^{q} \left(\frac{Z - y_i}{Z} \right)^\alpha \qquad \text{[Eq. 1]}$$

FIGURE A3.3:   CALCULATING THE FULL POVERTY LINE

Ranking Individuals
Highest level of total
per-capita consumption (Quetzales)

23,543
.
.   .   .   .   .
4,240

3,537

2,916

2,369

1,876

1,287

Lowest level of
total consumption

Shares of food
and non-food
consumption

$C_A = Z_{pe} = 1,869$

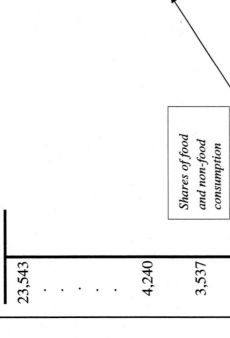

The full poverty line includes the cost of the extreme poverty line, Z_{pe}, plus an additional amount for non-food consumption.

$C_T = C_A + C_{NA}$
C_T = Total consumption
C_A = Food consumption
C_{NA} = Non-food consumption

What share of total consumption is allocated to non-food?
To calculate the poverty line, actual *consumption coefficients* of the group of individuals with a *food consumption near (+/-5%)* the extreme poverty line (Z_{pe}) were used.
In this case, this group allocates 55.8% to non-food consumption and 44.2% to food consumption.

These consumption shares were used to calculate the full poverty line:
$C_A = (1-.5584)Z_{pg}$
$Z_{pg} = 519/.4416$

Zpe = Extreme Poverty Line = 1,869
Zpg = General Poverty Line = 4,233

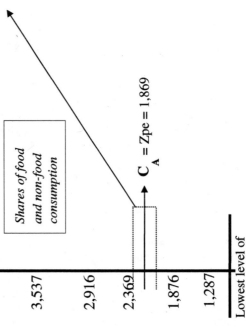

where:

y_i = estimated consumption of the ith person in a population of size n

Z = the poverty line

q = number of persons whose y_i is below poverty line Z and;

α = is a non-negative parameter that reflects the measure's aversion to poverty

Head Count Index. The first case is that where a = 0. This is the Head Count measure (H) and, as can be seen from Eq. 1, it is simply q/n or the proportion of the population below the poverty line. In short, the Head Count Index provides information on the incidence of poverty. It says nothing about the depth or severity of poverty and treats as equal any two populations where the proportion of the population living in poverty is the same.

Poverty Gap. To determine the depth of poverty, a second version of the FGT poverty measure, called the Poverty Gap index (PG), is used. This index is the case where a = 1 (in Eq. 1). The index is the aggregate poverty deficit of the poor relative to the poverty line.

FGT P2 (Severity). The third case of the poverty measure is that where $\alpha = 2$. This measure, often called the Foster-Greer-Thorbecke P_2 measure (FGT P_2), identifies the severity of poverty and demonstrates the relative inequalities among the poor. It is distributionally sensitive and, essentially, weights the average poverty gaps by the population at each level.

Ravaillion (1992[3]) presents a good example to illustrate the differences between the FGT P_2 index and the previous two. For example, it is possible for two populations to have the same head count and poverty gap indices but have very different distributions of levels of poverty. Ravaillion (1992) presents the example of two populations A and B where A is made up of four individuals with consumption levels 1, 2, 3, 4 and B is made up of four individuals with consumption levels 2, 2, 2, 4. If the poverty line equals three, the head count for both populations is 75 percent, the poverty gap measure is 25 percent. But the FGT P_2 measure is 14 in population A and 8 in population B, thus demonstrating that the poorest person in Population A has half the expenditures of the poorest person in Population B.

(IV) Sensitivity Analysis

In order to assess the robustness and sensitivity of the poverty lines calculated above, poverty rates are recalculated by varying the poverty line so as to evaluate how sensitive the results are to the specific choice of poverty line. Tables A3.4 and A3.5 present the results of the exercise for general and extreme poverty lines, respectively.

For example, for general poverty, a 5 percent increase raises the poverty line from Q\4,319 (the baseline) to Q\4,534 (Table A3.4). Based on the latter, the new national poverty rate would be 58.9% (compared with the baseline 56.1%). This represents a 2.8 percentage point difference with the baseline poverty rate, or a 5 percent difference. In addition, there is an implied elasticity of poverty line changes to changes in the poverty rate of 1. In fact the last column listing these implied elasticities for different levels of poverty line increases or decreases, shows that there are no extreme changes in poverty rates due to changes in poverty lines. The above also holds for the extreme poverty calculations.

Finally, Tables A3.6–A3.8 evaluate the impact of the different ways to compute the consumption aggregate. Specifically, they compare how individuals' classification would change by using per capita consumption as opposed to per adult equivalent consumption. The adult equivalent base used in this exercise was the average for Guatemala (2,172 Kcal/day). Since the extreme poverty line is the cost to buy 2,172 Kcal/day, the same line was used for the annual consumption per adult equivalent and the per capita one.

In summary, using consumption per capita or per adult equivalent as the unit to classify welfare does not seem to significantly change the results. For example, in classifying individuals in poverty groups (extreme poor, non-extreme poor, non-poor), 91% of the population is the same irrespective of the unit of analysis (as shown by the diagonal cells). Similarly, for quintile classification 83% of the population is the same using either unit of analysis.

---

3. Ravallion, Martin, "Poverty Comparisons: A Guide to Concepts and Methods," World Bank LSMS Working Paper No. 88, 1992.

TABLE A3.4: POVERTY LINE SENSITIVITY: GENERAL POVERTY

Line Change	Ql.	New Poverty %					Change in % points					Change as % of original poverty rate					Nation elasticity
		Urban	Rural	Indig.	Non In	Nation	Urban	Rural	Indig.	Non In	Nation	Urban	Rural	Indig.	Non In	Nation	
Original	4,319	27.1%	74.5%	76.0%	41.4%	56.1%	27.1%	74.5%	76.0%	41.4%	56.1%	27.1%	74.5%	76.0%	41.4%	56.1%	
-10%	3,887	20.9%	68.5%	70.9%	34.6%	50.0%	-6.2%	-6.0%	-5.1%	-6.8%	-6.1%	-22.9%	-8.1%	-6.7%	-16.4%	-10.9%	1.09
-9%	3,930	22.6%	68.9%	71.2%	36.0%	50.9%	-4.5%	-5.6%	-4.8%	-5.4%	-5.2%	-16.6%	-7.5%	-6.3%	-13.0%	-9.3%	1.03
-8%	3,973	22.9%	69.7%	71.7%	36.8%	51.6%	-4.2%	-4.8%	-4.3%	-4.6%	-4.5%	-15.5%	-6.4%	-5.7%	-11.1%	-8.0%	1.00
-7%	4,016	23.6%	70.3%	72.3%	37.4%	52.2%	-3.5%	-4.2%	-3.7%	-4.0%	-3.9%	-12.9%	-5.6%	-4.9%	-9.7%	-7.0%	0.99
-6%	4,059	24.0%	70.9%	72.9%	37.8%	52.7%	-3.1%	-3.6%	-3.1%	-3.6%	-3.4%	-11.4%	-4.8%	-4.1%	-8.7%	-6.1%	1.01
-5%	4,103	24.3%	71.3%	73.3%	38.1%	53.1%	-2.8%	-3.2%	-2.7%	-3.3%	-3.0%	-10.3%	-4.3%	-3.6%	-8.0%	-5.3%	1.07
-4%	4,146	25.0%	72.0%	74.2%	38.7%	53.8%	-2.1%	-2.5%	-1.8%	-2.7%	-2.3%	-7.7%	-3.4%	-2.4%	-6.5%	-4.1%	1.02
-3%	4,189	25.7%	72.6%	74.7%	39.4%	54.4%	-1.4%	-1.9%	-1.3%	-2.0%	-1.7%	-5.2%	-2.6%	-1.7%	-4.8%	-3.0%	1.01
-2%	4,232	26.0%	73.1%	75.0%	39.9%	54.8%	-1.1%	-1.4%	-1.0%	-1.5%	-1.3%	-4.1%	-1.9%	-1.3%	-3.6%	-2.3%	1.16
-1%	4,275	26.6%	74.0%	75.4%	41.0%	55.6%	-0.5%	-0.5%	-0.6%	-0.4%	-0.5%	-1.8%	-0.7%	-0.8%	-1.0%	-0.9%	0.89
0%	4,319	27.1%	74.5%	76.0%	41.4%	56.1%	0.0%	0.0%	0.0%	0.0%	0.0%	0.0%	0.0%	0.0%	0.0%	0.0%	
1%	4,362	27.3%	75.3%	76.4%	42.1%	56.6%	0.2%	0.8%	0.4%	0.7%	0.5%	0.7%	1.1%	0.5%	1.7%	0.9%	0.89
2%	4,405	28.1%	75.9%	76.9%	42.9%	57.3%	1.0%	1.4%	0.9%	1.5%	1.2%	3.7%	1.9%	1.2%	3.6%	2.1%	1.07
3%	4,448	28.3%	76.5%	77.3%	43.5%	57.8%	1.2%	2.0%	1.3%	2.1%	1.7%	4.4%	2.7%	1.7%	5.1%	3.0%	1.01
4%	4,491	29.1%	76.8%	77.9%	43.8%	58.3%	2.0%	2.3%	1.9%	2.4%	2.2%	7.4%	3.1%	2.5%	5.8%	3.9%	0.98
5%	4,534	29.3%	77.6%	78.6%	44.3%	58.9%	2.2%	3.1%	2.6%	2.9%	2.8%	8.1%	4.2%	3.4%	7.0%	5.0%	1.00
6%	4,578	29.6%	77.9%	78.9%	44.6%	59.2%	2.5%	3.4%	2.9%	3.2%	3.1%	9.2%	4.6%	3.8%	7.7%	5.5%	0.92
7%	4,621	29.8%	78.3%	79.5%	44.8%	59.5%	2.7%	3.8%	3.5%	3.4%	3.4%	10.0%	5.1%	4.6%	8.2%	6.1%	0.87
8%	4,664	30.1%	79.0%	79.9%	45.4%	60.1%	3.0%	4.5%	3.9%	4.0%	4.0%	11.1%	6.0%	5.1%	9.7%	7.1%	0.89
9%	4,707	30.6%	79.4%	80.1%	45.9%	60.5%	3.5%	4.9%	4.1%	4.5%	4.4%	12.9%	6.6%	5.4%	10.9%	7.8%	0.87
10%	4,750	31.1%	79.9%	80.9%	46.2%	61.0%	4.0%	5.4%	4.9%	4.8%	4.9%	14.8%	7.2%	6.4%	11.6%	8.7%	0.87

TABLE A3.5: POVERTY LINE SENSITIVITY: EXTREME POVERTY

Line Change	Ql.	New Poverty %					Change in % points					Change as % of original poverty rate					
		Urban	Rural	Indig.	Non In	Nation	Urban	Rural	Indig.	Non In	Nation	Urban	Rural	Indig.	Non In	Nation	elasticity
Original	1,912	2.8%	23.8%	26.4%	7.7%	15.7%	2.8%	23.8%	26.4%	7.7%	15.7%	2.8%	23.8%	26.4%	7.7%	15.7%	
-10%	1,721	1.8%	18.2%	20.6%	5.4%	11.8%	-1.0%	-5.6%	-5.8%	-2.3%	-3.9%	-35.7%	-23.5%	-22.0%	-29.9%	-24.8%	2.48
-9%	1,740	1.9%	18.9%	21.4%	5.7%	12.3%	-0.9%	-4.9%	-5.0%	-2.0%	-3.4%	-32.1%	-20.6%	-18.9%	-26.0%	-21.7%	2.41
-8%	1,759	2.1%	19.6%	21.9%	6.1%	12.8%	-0.7%	-4.2%	-4.5%	-1.6%	-2.9%	-25.0%	-17.6%	-17.0%	-20.8%	-18.5%	2.31
-7%	1,778	2.1%	19.9%	22.1%	6.3%	13.0%	-0.7%	-3.9%	-4.3%	-1.4%	-2.7%	-25.0%	-16.4%	-16.3%	-18.2%	-17.2%	2.46
-6%	1,797	2.2%	20.4%	22.7%	6.5%	13.4%	-0.6%	-3.4%	-3.7%	-1.2%	-2.3%	-21.4%	-14.3%	-14.0%	-15.6%	-14.6%	2.44
-5%	1,816	2.3%	20.9%	23.3%	6.6%	13.7%	-0.5%	-2.9%	-3.1%	-1.1%	-2.0%	-17.9%	-12.2%	-11.7%	-14.3%	-12.7%	2.55
-4%	1,835	2.4%	21.7%	24.3%	6.8%	14.2%	-0.4%	-2.1%	-2.1%	-0.9%	-1.5%	-14.3%	-8.8%	-8.0%	-11.7%	-9.6%	2.39
-3%	1,854	2.6%	22.4%	25.3%	7.0%	14.7%	-0.2%	-1.4%	-1.1%	-0.7%	-1.0%	-7.1%	-5.9%	-4.2%	-9.1%	-6.4%	2.12
-2%	1,873	2.7%	22.9%	25.5%	7.3%	15.0%	-0.1%	-0.9%	-0.9%	-0.4%	-0.7%	-3.6%	-3.8%	-3.4%	-5.2%	-4.5%	2.23
-1%	1,893	2.8%	23.3%	26.1%	7.4%	15.3%	0.0%	-0.5%	-0.3%	-0.3%	-0.4%	0.0%	-2.1%	-1.1%	-3.9%	-2.5%	2.55
0%	1,912	2.8%	23.8%	26.4%	7.7%	15.7%	0.0%	0.0%	0.0%	0.0%	0.0%	0.0%	0.0%	0.0%	0.0%	0.0%	
1%	1,931	2.9%	24.4%	27.1%	7.9%	16.1%	0.1%	0.6%	0.7%	0.2%	0.4%	3.6%	2.5%	2.7%	2.6%	2.5%	2.55
2%	1,950	3.0%	25.0%	27.7%	8.2%	16.5%	0.2%	1.2%	1.3%	0.5%	0.8%	7.1%	5.0%	4.9%	6.5%	5.1%	2.55
3%	1,969	3.2%	25.6%	28.6%	8.3%	16.9%	0.4%	1.8%	2.2%	0.6%	1.2%	14.3%	7.6%	8.3%	7.8%	7.6%	2.55
4%	1,988	3.3%	26.0%	29.1%	8.4%	17.2%	0.5%	2.2%	2.7%	0.7%	1.5%	17.9%	9.2%	10.2%	9.1%	9.6%	2.39
5%	2,007	3.5%	26.5%	29.7%	8.6%	17.6%	0.7%	2.7%	3.3%	0.9%	1.9%	25.0%	11.3%	12.5%	11.7%	12.1%	2.42
6%	2,026	3.6%	27.3%	30.4%	9.0%	18.1%	0.8%	3.5%	4.0%	1.3%	2.4%	28.6%	14.7%	15.2%	16.9%	15.3%	2.55
7%	2,046	3.6%	27.6%	30.8%	9.1%	18.3%	0.8%	3.8%	4.4%	1.4%	2.6%	28.6%	16.0%	16.7%	18.2%	16.6%	2.37
8%	2,065	3.7%	28.4%	31.6%	9.4%	18.8%	0.9%	4.6%	5.2%	1.7%	3.1%	32.1%	19.3%	19.7%	22.1%	19.7%	2.47
9%	2,084	4.0%	29.0%	32.4%	9.6%	19.3%	1.2%	5.2%	6.0%	1.9%	3.6%	42.9%	21.8%	22.7%	24.7%	22.9%	2.55
10%	2,103	4.1%	29.3%	32.8%	9.7%	19.5%	1.3%	5.5%	6.4%	2.0%	3.8%	46.4%	23.1%	24.2%	26.0%	24.2%	2.42

TABLE A3.6: POVERTY SENSITIVITY TO PER CAPITA/PER ADULT EQUIVALENT, BY POVERTY
Poverty (per capita)

Poverty (adult equivalent)	Extreme	Non extreme	Non Poor
Extreme	13.0%	0.9%	0.0%
Non Extreme	2.7%	36.9%	2.4%
Non Poor	0.0%	2.7%	41.4%
No change	91.3%		
change in one	8.7%		
change in two	0.0%		

TABLE A3.7: POVERTY SENSITIVITY TO PER CAPITA/PER ADULT EQUIVALENT, BY QUINTILES
Quintile (per capita)

Quintile (adult equivalent)	1	2	3	4	5
1	18.1%	1.9%	0.0%	0.0%	0.0%
2	1.9%	15.5%	2.6%	0.0%	0.0%
3	0.0%	2.6%	15.1%	2.3%	0.0%
4	0.0%	0.0%	2.3%	16.1%	1.6%
5	0.0%	0.0%	0.0%	1.5%	18.5%
No change	83.3%				
change in one	16.7%				
change in two or more	0.0%				

TABLE A3.8: POVERTY SENSITIVITY TO PER CAPITA/PER ADULT EQUIVALENT, BY DECILES
Deciles (per capita)

Deciles (adult equivalent)	1	2	3	4	5	6	7	8	9	10
1	8.90%	1.10%	0.00%	0%	0%	0%	0%	0%	0%	0%
2	1.10%	7.00%	1.80%	0.10%	0%	0%	0%	0%	0%	0%
3	0%	1.80%	6.10%	2.00%	0.10%	0%	0%	0%	0%	0%
4	0%	0.00%	2.10%	5.40%	2.30%	0.20%	0%	0%	0%	0%
5	0%	0%	0.00%	2.40%	5.20%	2.10%	0.10%	0%	0%	0%
6	0%	0%	0.00%	0.10%	2.20%	5.50%	2.10%	0.00%	0%	0%
7	0%	0%	0%	0.00%	0.10%	2.20%	6.00%	1.70%	0.00%	0%
8	0%	0%	0%	0%	0%	0.00%	1.80%	6.70%	1.50%	0%
9	0%	0%	0%	0%	0%	0%	0%	1.50%	7.70%	0.70%
10	0%	0%	0%	0%	0%	0%	0%	0.00%	0.70%	9.30%
No change	67.8%									
change in one	31.1%									
change in two	0.7%									
change in three or more	0.0%									

STATISTICAL APPENDIX

List of Tables

TABLE A4.1: GUATEMALA: SELECT POVERTY AND SOCIAL INDICATORS AT A GLANCE

Demographics	1989	1994	1998	2000	Source/Comments
Population (million)	8.5	9.7	10.8	11.4	WDI
Population growth rate (%)	2.5%	2.7	2.7	2.7	WDI
Infant Mortality (per 1000 live births)	72.7	51.1	45.1	38.8	DHS (other estimates suggest 40 for 1998); except 2000 = WDI
Under 5 Mortality (per 1000 live births)	na	68	59	49.4	DHS; except 2000 = WDI
Urban Population (% of the total)	38	38.5	39.2	38.6	WDI; except 2000 = ENCOVI 2000
Life expectancy at birth (years)	59.7	63.6	64.2	65.2	
Male	57.3	60.8	61.4	62.4	WDI (1987 instead of 1989; 1995 instead of 1994; 1997 instead of 1998)
Female	62.2	66.5	67.2	68.2	
Total fertility rate (births per woman)	5.4	5.1	5	4.6	WDI (1995 instead of 1994; 1997 instead of 1998)
Education	**1989**	**1994**	**1998**	**2000**	
Adult illiteracy rate (%)	39.7	35.8	32.8	31.1	WDI; except 2000 = ENCOVI 2000
Primary school enrollment, gross (%)	NA	85.8	101.9	99	WDI; except 2000 = ENCOVI 2000
Male	NA	91.5	107.5	103	WDI; except 2000 = ENCOVI 2000
Female	NA	79.9	96	95	WDI; except 2000 = ENCOVI 2000
Primary school enrollment, net (%)	NA	NA	82.7	79	WDI; except 2000 = ENCOVI 2000
Male	NA	NA	85.1	81	WDI; except 2000 = ENCOVI 2000
Female	NA	NA	80.2	76	WDI; except 2000 = ENCOVI 2000
Illiteracy rate, young adult total (% of people 15–24)	27.3	24	21.8	20.7	WDI
Ratio of illiterate females to males (% ages 15–24)	NA	NA	NA	1.76	WDI; except 2000 = ENCOVI 2000
Public spending on education (% of GDP)	1.8	1.5	2.1	2.5	WDI; except 1998, 2000 = Ministry of Finance/SIAF
Health & Nutrition	**1987**	**1995**	**1998/99**	**2000**	
Child Malnutrition					
Height for age (stunting/chronic malnutrition)	57.8	49.7	46.4	44.2	DHS except ENCOVI 2000
Weight for age (underweight)	33.2	26.6	24.2	22.3	DHS except ENCOVI 2000
Weight for height (wasting/acute malnutrition)	1.3	3.3	2.5	2.8	DHS except ENCOVI 2000
Immunization, DPT (% of children under 12 months)	16	77	78	NA	WDI
Immunization, measles (% of children under 12 months)	24	83	81	NA	WDI
Public health expenditure (% of GDP)	NA	0.7	0.9	1.1	SIAF/Ministry of Finance

(continued)

TABLE A4.1: GUATEMALA: SELECT POVERTY AND SOCIAL INDICATORS AT A GLANCE (CONTINUED)

Poverty & Income Distribution	1989	1995	1998/99	2000	Source/Comments
Living on less than $1 per day (PPP) (% of people)	20	NA	NA	16	1989 = Encuesta Socio Economica; 2000 = ENCOVI; UNDP
Urban (living on less than $1 day (PPP))	9	NA	NA	5	1989 = Encuesta Socio Economica; 2000 = ENCOVI; UNDP
Rural (living on less than $1 day (PPP))	26	NA	NA	22	1989 = Encuesta Socio Economica; 2000 = ENCOVI; UNDP
Extreme Poverty (% of population below national extreme poverty line)	NA	NA	NA	15.7	2000 = ENCOVI; WB analysis (using consumption as indicate)
Urban (% below urban extreme poverty line)	NA	NA	NA	2.8	2000 = ENCOVI; WB analysis (using consumption as indicate)
Rural (% below rural extreme poverty line)	NA	NA	NA	23.8	2000 = ENCOVI; WB analysis (using consumption as indicate)
Poverty (% of population below national poverty line)	62	NA	NA	56.2	
Urban (% below urban poverty line)	NA	NA	NA	27.1	1989 = Encuesta Socio Economica (adjusted); 2000 = ENCOVI; WB analysis (using consumption as indicator)
Rural (% below rural poverty line)	NA	NA	NA	74.5	
GINI Index					
Using Consumption	NA	NA	NA	48	ENCOVI 2000
Using Income	NA	NA	NA	57	ENCOVI 2000
Percentage share of income: highest 20%	NA	NA	NA	62	ENCOVI 2000
Percentage share of income: lowest 20%	NA	NA	NA	3	ENCOVI 2000
Percentage share of consumption: highest 20%	NA	NA	NA	5	ENCOVI 2000
Percentage share of consumption: lowest 20%	NA	NA	NA	53	ENCOVI 2000
Public expenditure on social security and welfare (% of GDP)	NA	NA	NA	1.8%	WB estimates; IMF estimates at 1%

Environment & Infrastructure	1989	1994	1998	2000	
Surface area (sq. km)	108890	108890	108890	108890	WDI
Population density (people per sq. km of land area)	78.8	89.6	99.6	105	WDI
GDP per unit of energy use (PPP $ per kg of oil equivalent)	5.8	6.5	6.5	NA	WDI
CO_2 emissions (kt)	4234.5	6863.4	9669.3	NA	WDI
Access to an improved water source (% of population)	NA	NA	NA	69	ENCOVI 2000 (GUAPA)
Urban (% of urban population)	NA	NA	NA	88	ENCOVI 2000 (GUAPA)
Rural (% of rural population)	NA	NA	NA	54	ENCOVI 2000 (GUAPA)
Access to improved sanitation facilities (% of population)	NA	NA	NA	87	ENCOVI 2000 (GUAPA)
Urban (% of urban population)	NA	NA	NA	97	ENCOVI 2000 (GUAPA)
Rural (% of rural population)	NA	NA	NA	79	ENCOVI 2000 (GUAPA)
Access to electricity, urban (% of urban population)	NA	NA	NA	95	ENCOVI 2000 (GUAPA)
Access to electricity, rural (% of rural population)	NA	NA	NA	56	ENCOVI 2000 (GUAPA)
Telephone mainlines (per 1,000 people)	18.1	25.1	47.8	57	ENCOVI 2000 (GUAPA)
Mobile phones (per 1,000 people)	0	1.1	10.3	61.2	WDI
Personal computers (per 1,000 people)	NA	2	8.3	11.4	WDI

TABLE A4.2: POPULATION, CONTRIBUTION TO POVERTY (CONTR%), PERCENTAGE OF POOR (P0), POVERTY DEPTH INDEX (P1) & POVERTY SEVERITY INDEX (P2), AND COST TO ELIMINATE POVERTY (VALOR DE LA BRECHA): NATIONAL

| | # de personas y su contribución | | | | | | | | P 0, P 1, & P 2 | | | | | | Valor ($) de la brecha de pobreza | | | |
| | Todos | | Pobre extremo | | Todos pobres | | No Pobre | | Pob. General | | | Pob. Extrema | | | P. General | | P. Extrema | |
	Personas	%	Personas	Contr%	Personas	Contr%	Personas	Contr%	P 0	P 1	P 2	P 0	P 1	P 2	Ql. 000,000	%	Ql. 000,000	%
NACIONAL																		
TOTAL	11,385,441	100.0	1,786,682.0	100.0	6,397,903	100.0	4,987,538	100.0	56.2	22.6	11.7	15.7	3.7	1.3	11,122.0	100.0%	807.5	100.0%
POBREZA																		
Extrema	1,786,682	15.7	1,786,682.0	100.0	1,786,682	27.9	—	—	100.0	66.2	44.3	100.0	23.6	8.1	5,107.1	45.9%	806.8	99.9%
Pobre (todos)	6,397,903	56.2	1,786,682.0	100.0	6,397,903	100.0	—	—	100.0	40.3	20.8	27.9	6.6	2.3	11,121.0	100.0%	807.2	100.0%
No pobre	4,987,538	43.8	—	—	—	—	4,987,538	100.0	—	—	—	—	—	—	—	—	—	—
QUINTIL																		
1	2,277,561	20.0	1,786,682.0	100.0	2,277,561	35.6	—	—	100.0	63.4	40.9	78.5	18.5	6.4	6,237.9	56.1%	806.8	99.9%
2	2,277,056	20.0	—	—	2,277,056	35.6	—	—	100.0	38.9	15.7	—	—	—	3,825.3	34.4%	—	0.0%
3	2,276,907	20.0	—	—	1,843,286	28.8	433,621	8.7	81.0	10.8	1.9	—	—	—	1,057.0	9.5%	—	0.0%
4	2,276,239	20.0	—	—	—	—	2,276,239	45.6	—	—	—	—	—	—	—	0.0%	—	0.0%
5	2,277,678	20.0	—	—	—	—	2,277,678	45.7	—	—	—	—	—	—	—	0.0%	—	0.0%
AREA																		
Urbana	4,397,854	38.6	123,583.0	6.9	1,192,551	18.6	3,205,303	64.3	27.1	7.8	3.3	2.8	0.6	0.2	1,471.9	13.2%	50.4	6.2%
Rural	6,987,587	61.4	1,663,099.0	93.1	5,205,352	81.4	1,782,235	35.7	74.5	32.0	17.0	23.8	5.7	2.0	9,647.4	86.7%	756.1	93.6%

REGION

Metropolitana	2,465,957	21.7	15,524.0	0.9	443,704	6.9	2,022,253	40.6	18.0	3.4	1.1	0.6	0.2	0.1	366.3	3.3	9.0	1.1%
Norte	919,834	8.1	359,308.0	20.1	772,610	12.1	147,224	3.0	84.0	42.3	24.6	39.1	10.1	3.8	1,678.3	15.1%	177.6	22.0%
Nororiente	932,583	8.2	83,313.0	4.7	483,087	7.6	449,496	9.0	51.8	18.1	8.2	8.9	1.3	0.3	730.2	6.6%	22.3	2.8%
Suroriente	998,505	8.8	200,942.0	11.3	684,509	10.7	313,996	6.3	68.6	27.6	14.2	20.1	4.6	1.4	1,191.4	10.7%	87.4	10.8%
Central	1,216,330	10.7	106,338.0	6.0	629,328	9.8	587,002	11.8	51.7	17.9	8.2	8.7	1.5	0.4	940.3	8.5%	34.9	4.3%
Suroccidente	3,013,789	26.5	511,249.0	28.6	1,927,904	30.1	1,085,885	21.8	64.0	25.7	13.2	17.0	4.1	1.4	3,341.0	30.0%	236.2	29.3%
Noroccidente	1,466,733	12.9	462,130.0	25.9	1,204,094	18.8	262,639	5.3	82.1	38.5	21.3	31.5	7.7	2.6	2,436.1	21.9%	215.1	26.6%
Peten	371,710	3.3	47,878.0	2.7	252,667	4.0	119,043	2.4	68.0	27.2	13.3	12.9	3.4	1.3	436.5	3.9%	23.9	3.0%

ETNIA (2gr.)

Indígena	4,844,032	42.6	1,281,674.0	71.7	3,687,600	57.6	1,156,432	23.2	76.1	34.2	18.6	26.5	6.6	2.4	7,154.4	64.3%	614.0	76.0%
No indígena	6,541,409	57.5	505,008.0	28.3	2,710,303	42.4	3,831,106	76.8	41.4	14.0	6.5	7.7	1.5	0.5	3,966.2	35.7%	192.6	23.8%

ETNIA (6 gr.)

K'iche	1,073,324	9.4	204,493.0	11.5	691,009	10.8	382,315	7.7	64.4	26.2	13.6	19.1	4.3	1.5	1,214.9	10.9%	88.0	10.9%
Q'eqchi	736,163	6.5	279,377.0	15.6	614,315	9.6	121,848	2.4	83.5	42.0	24.5	38.0	10.3	4.1	1,334.9	12.0%	144.8	17.9%
Kaqchiquel	1,011,802	8.9	137,603.0	7.7	633,523	9.9	378,279	7.6	62.6	24.2	11.9	13.6	2.9	0.9	1,057.0	9.5%	55.5	6.9%
Mam	940,865	8.3	321,545.0	18.0	844,308	13.2	96,557	1.9	89.7	43.0	24.2	34.2	9.7	3.6	1,745.5	15.7%	174.1	21.6%
Otros indig	1,081,878	9.5	338,656.0	19.0	904,445	14.1	177,433	3.6	83.6	38.6	21.1	31.3	7.3	2.4	1,802.1	16.2%	151.6	18.8%
No indígena	6,541,409	57.5	505,008.0	28.3	2,710,303	42.4	3,831,106	76.8	41.4	14.0	6.5	7.7	1.5	0.5	3,966.2	35.7%	192.6	23.8%

SEXO JEFE

Masculino	9,716,582	85.3	1,622,618.0	90.8	5,599,652	87.5	4,116,930	82.5	57.6	23.5	12.3	16.7	3.9	1.4	9,873.6	88.8%	730.0	90.4%
Femenino	1,668,859	14.7	164,064.0	9.2	798,251	12.5	870,608	17.5	47.8	17.3	8.4	9.8	2.4	0.8	1,246.1	11.2%	76.2	9.4%

TABLE A4.3: Population, Contribution to Poverty (Contr%), Percentage of Poor (P0), Poverty Depth Index (P1) & Poverty Severity Index (P2), and Cost to Eliminate Poverty (Valor de la Brecha): Urban

	# de personas y su contribución								P 0, P 1, & P 2						Valor ($) de la brecha de pobreza			
	Todos		Pobre extremo		Todos pobres		No Pobre		Pob. General			Pob. Extrema			P. General		P. Extrema	
	Personas	%	Personas	Contr%	Personas	Contr%	Personas	Contr%	P 0	P 1	P 2	P 0	P 1	P 2	Ql. 000,000	%	Ql. 000,000	%
Urbana																		
TOTAL	4,397,854	100.0	123,583.0	100.0	1,192,551	100.0	3,205,303	100.0	27.1	7.8	3.3	2.8	0.6	0.2	1,471.9	100.0%	50.4	100.0%
POBREZA																		
Extrema	123,583	2.8	123,583.0	100.0	123,583	10.4	—	—	100.0	65.2	43.0	100.0	21.4	7.1	347.9	23.6%	50.4	100.0%
Pobre (todos)	1,192,551	27.1	123,583.0	100.0	1,192,551	100.0	—	—	100.0	28.6	12.0	10.4	2.2	0.7	1,472.4	100.0%	50.4	99.9%
No pobre	3,205,303	72.9	—	—	—	—	3,205,303	100.0	—	—	—	—	—	—	—	—	—	—
QUINTIL																		
1	188,259	4.3	123,583.0	100.0	188,259	15.8	—	—	100.0	61.1	38.0	65.7	14.0	4.6	496.6	33.7%	50.4	100.0%
2	386,320	8.8	—	—	386,320	32.4	—	—	100.0	38.2	15.1	—	—	—	637.8	43.3%	—	0.0%
3	745,276	17.0	—	—	617,972	51.8	127,304	4.0	82.9	10.5	1.8	—	—	—	338.3	23.0%	—	0.0%
4	1,237,370	28.1	—	—	—	—	1,237,370	38.6	—	—	—	—	—	—	—	0.0%	—	0.0%
5	1,840,629	41.9	—	—	—	—	1,840,629	57.4	—	—	—	—	—	—	—	0.0%	—	0.0%
AREA																		
Urbana	4,397,854	100.0	123,583.0	100.0	1,192,551	100.0	3,205,303	100.0	27.1	7.8	3.3	2.8	0.6	0.2	1,471.9	100.0%	50.4	100.0%
Rural	—	—	—	—	—	—	—	—	—	—	—	—	—	—	—	0.0%	—	0.0%

REGION																		
Metropolitana	2,078,474	47.3	7,154.0	5.8	289,418	24.3	1,789,056	55.8	13.9	2.3	0.6	0.3	0.1	0.0	203.8	13.8%	3.2	6.3%
Norte	146,174	3.3	11,406.0	9.2	69,747	5.9	76,427	2.4	47.7	17.0	8.1	7.8	2.1	0.8	107.6	7.3%	5.7	11.4%
Nororiente	240,983	5.5	10,296.0	8.3	60,760	5.1	180,223	5.6	25.2	8.1	3.6	4.3	0.9	0.3	84.1	5.7%	4.1	8.1%
Suroriente	230,079	5.2	5,394.0	4.4	97,518	8.2	132,561	4.1	42.4	11.8	4.5	2.3	0.5	0.1	117.5	8.0%	2.3	4.6%
Central	536,293	12.2	26,214.0	21.2	204,577	17.2	331,716	10.4	38.2	11.4	4.8	4.9	0.7	0.2	264.7	18.0%	6.9	13.6%
Suroccidente	817,755	18.6	29,812.0	24.1	319,395	26.8	498,360	15.6	39.1	12.7	5.5	3.7	0.6	0.2	448.2	30.4%	8.9	17.7%
Noroccidente	245,867	5.6	29,546.0	23.9	114,362	9.6	131,505	4.1	46.5	18.5	9.6	12.0	3.6	1.3	195.9	13.3%	16.8	33.3%
Peten	102,229	2.3	3,761.0	3.0	36,774	3.1	65,455	2.0	36.0	11.4	5.0	3.7	1.2	0.4	50.5	3.4%	2.3	4.6%
ETNIA (2gr.)																		
Indigena	1,231,941	28.0	99,619.0	80.6	621,997	52.2	609,944	19.0	50.5	17.3	8.0	8.1	1.8	0.6	917.7	62.4%	42.2	83.6%
No indigena	3,165,913	72.0	23,964.0	19.4	570,554	47.8	2,595,359	81.0	18.0	4.1	1.4	0.8	0.1	0.0	555.1	37.7%	8.5	16.8%
ETNIA (6 gr.)																		
K'iche	338,438	7.7	22,342.0	18.1	134,345	11.3	204,093	6.4	39.7	12.6	5.8	6.6	1.3	0.5	184.2	12.5%	8.7	17.2%
Q'eqchi	126,729	2.9	16,073.0	13.0	57,384	4.8	69,345	2.2	45.3	18.6	9.6	12.7	2.8	0.9	102.0	6.9%	6.7	13.2%
Kaqchiquel	394,595	9.0	17,084.0	13.8	171,649	14.4	222,946	7.0	43.5	13.4	5.8	4.3	1.0	0.3	227.8	15.5%	7.5	15.0%
Mam	124,695	2.8	12,853.0	10.4	102,876	8.6	21,819	0.7	82.5	29.9	12.8	10.3	0.7	0.1	161.0	10.9%	1.7	3.4%
Otros indíg	247,484	5.6	31,267.0	25.3	155,743	13.1	91,741	2.9	62.9	22.7	11.4	12.6	3.7	1.4	242.8	16.5%	17.6	35.0%
No indigena	3,165,913	72.0	23,964.0	19.4	570,554	47.8	2,595,359	81.0	18.0	4.1	1.4	0.8	0.1	0.0	555.1	37.7%	8.5	16.8%
SEXO JEFE																		
Masculino	3,562,698	81.0	99,681.0	80.7	971,630	81.5	2,591,068	80.8	27.3	7.8	3.3	2.8	0.6	0.2	1,195.5	81.2%	42.2	83.7%
Femenino	835,156	19.0	23,902.0	19.3	220,921	18.5	614,235	19.2	26.5	7.7	3.1	2.9	0.5	0.1	276.6	18.8%	8.1	16.1%

TABLE A4.4: Population, Contribution to Poverty (contr%), Percentage of Poor (P0), Percentage of Poor (P0), Poverty Depth Index (P1) & Poverty Severity Index (P2), and Cost to Eliminate Poverty (Valor de la Brecha): Rural

	# de personas y su contribución								P 0, P 1, & P 2						Valor ($) de la brecha de pobreza			
	Todos		Pobre extremo		Todos pobres		No Pobre		Pob. General			Pob. Extrema			P. General		P. Extrema	
	Personas	%	Personas	Contr%	Personas	Contr%	Personas	Contr%	P 0	P 1	P 2	P 0	P 1	P 2	Ql. 000,000	%	Ql. 000,000	%
Rural																		
TOTAL	6,987,587	100.0	1,663,099.0	100.0	5,205,352	100.0	1,782,235	100.0	74.5	32.0	17.0	23.8	5.7	2.0	9,647.4	100.0%	756.1	100.0%
POBREZA																		
Extrema	1,663,099	23.8	1,663,099.0	100.0	1,663,099	32.0	—	—	100.0	66.3	44.4	100.0	23.8	8.2	4,758.9	49.3%	756.4	100.0%
Pobre (todos)	5,205,352	74.5	1,663,099.0	100.0	5,205,352	100.0	—	—	100.0	42.9	22.8	32.0	7.6	2.6	9,648.3	100.0%	756.3	100.0%
No pobre	1,782,235	25.5	—	—	—	—	1,782,235	100.0	—	—	—	—	—	—	—	—	—	—
QUINTIL																		
1	2,089,302	29.9	1,663,099.0	100.0	2,089,302	40.1	—	—	100.0	63.6	41.2	79.6	18.9	6.5	5,741.2	59.5%	756.1	100.0%
2	1,890,736	27.1	—	—	1,890,736	36.3	—	—	100.0	39.0	15.8	—	—	—	3,187.7	33.0%	—	0.0%
3	1,531,631	21.9	—	—	1,225,314	23.5	306,317	17.2	80.0	10.9	1.9	—	—	—	719.0	7.5%	—	0.0%
4	1,038,869	14.9	—	—	—	—	1,038,869	58.3	—	—	—	—	—	—	—	0.0%	—	0.0%
5	437,049	6.3	—	—	—	—	437,049	24.5	—	—	—	—	—	—	—	0.0%	—	0.0%
AREA																		
Urbana	—	—	—	—	—	—	—	—	—	—	—	—	—	—	—	0.0%	—	0.0%
Rural	6,987,587	100.0	1,663,099.0	100.0	5,205,352	100.0	1,782,235	100.0	74.5	32.0	17.0	23.8	5.7	2.0	9,647.4	100.0%	756.1	100.0%

REGION																		
Metropolitana	387,483	5.6	8,370.0	0.5	154,286	3.0	233,197	13.1	39.8	9.7	3.7	2.2	0.8	0.3	162.1	1.7%	5.6	0.7%
Norte	773,660	11.1	347,902.0	20.9	702,863	13.5	70,797	4.0	90.9	47.0	27.7	45.0	11.6	4.4	1,570.6	16.3%	171.9	22.7%
Nororiente	691,600	9.9	73,017.0	4.4	422,327	8.1	269,273	15.1	61.1	21.6	9.8	10.6	1.4	0.3	646.0	6.7%	18.2	2.4%
Suroriente	768,426	11.0	195,548.0	11.8	586,991	11.3	181,435	10.2	76.4	32.4	17.1	25.5	5.8	1.8	1,073.9	11.1%	85.2	11.3%
Central	680,037	9.7	80,124.0	4.8	424,751	8.2	255,286	14.3	62.5	23.0	10.9	11.8	2.2	0.6	675.5	7.0%	28.0	3.7%
Suroccidente	2,196,034	31.4	481,437.0	29.0	1,608,509	30.9	587,525	33.0	73.3	30.5	16.1	21.9	5.4	1.9	2,893.5	30.0%	227.5	30.1%
Noroccidente	1,220,866	17.5	432,584.0	26.0	1,089,732	20.9	131,134	7.4	89.3	42.5	23.6	35.4	8.5	2.9	2,240.2	23.2%	198.4	26.2%
Peten	269,481	3.9	44,117.0	2.7	215,893	4.2	53,588	3.0	80.1	33.2	16.5	16.4	4.2	1.6	385.9	4.0%	21.6	2.9%
ETNIA (2gr.)																		
Indigena	3,612,091	51.7	1,182,055.0	71.1	3,065,603	58.9	546,488	30.7	84.9	40.0	22.3	32.7	8.3	3.0	6,238.1	64.7%	571.8	75.6%
No indigena	3,375,496	48.3	481,044.0	28.9	2,139,749	41.1	1,235,747	69.3	63.4	23.4	11.4	14.3	2.9	0.9	3,409.6	35.3%	184.6	24.4%
ETNIA (6 gr.)																		
K'iche	734,886	10.5	182,151.0	11.0	556,664	10.7	178,222	10.0	75.8	32.5	17.2	24.8	5.7	2.0	1,031.1	10.7%	79.4	10.5%
Q'eqchi	609,434	8.7	263,304.0	15.8	556,931	10.7	52,503	3.0	91.4	46.9	27.6	43.2	11.9	4.8	1,233.0	12.8%	138.2	18.3%
Kaqchiquel	617,207	8.8	120,519.0	7.3	461,874	8.9	155,333	8.7	74.8	31.1	15.9	19.5	4.1	1.2	829.5	8.6%	47.9	6.3%
Mam	816,170	11.7	308,692.0	18.6	741,432	14.2	74,738	4.2	90.8	45.0	25.9	37.8	11.1	4.2	1,584.7	16.4%	172.4	22.8%
Otros indig	834,394	11.9	307,389.0	18.5	748,702	14.4	85,692	4.8	89.7	43.3	24.0	36.8	8.4	2.7	1,559.2	16.2%	134.0	17.7%
No indigena	3,375,496	48.3	481,044.0	28.9	2,139,749	41.1	1,235,747	69.3	63.4	23.4	11.4	14.3	2.9	0.9	3,409.6	35.3%	184.6	24.4%
SEXO JEFE																		
Masculino	6,153,884	88.1	1,522,937.0	91.6	4,628,022	88.9	1,525,862	85.6	75.2	32.7	17.5	24.8	5.9	2.0	8,677.0	89.9%	688.2	91.0%
Femenino	833,703	11.9	140,162.0	8.4	577,330	11.1	256,373	14.4	69.3	26.9	13.6	16.8	4.3	1.5	969.6	10.1%	68.1	9.0%

TABLE A4.5: POPULATION, CONTRIBUTION TO POVERTY (CONTR%), PERCENTAGE OF POOR (P0), POVERTY DEPTH INDEX (P1) & POVERTY SEVERITY INDEX (P2), AND COST TO ELIMINATE POVERTY (VALOR DE LA BRECHA): INDIGENOUS

	# de personas y su contribución								P 0, P 1, & P 2						Valor ($) de la brecha de pobreza			
	Todos		Pobre extremo		Todos pobres		No Pobre		Pob. General			Pob. Extrema			P. General		P. Extrema	
	Personas	%	Personas	Contr%	Personas	Contr%	Personas	Contr%	P 0	P 1	P 2	P 0	P 1	P 2	Ql. 000,000	%	Ql. 000,000	%
Indigena																		
TOTAL	4,844,032	100.0	1,281,674.0	100.0	3,687,600	100.0	1,156,432	100.0	76.1	34.2	18.6	26.5	6.6	2.4	7,154.4	100.0%	614.0	100.0%
POBREZA																		
Extrema	1,281,674	26.5	1,281,674.0	100.0	1,281,674	34.8	—	—	100.0	66.8	45.2	100.0	25.1	9.0	3,699.0	51.7%	614.0	100.0%
Pobre (todos)	3,687,600	76.1	1,281,674.0	100.0	3,687,600	100.0	—	—	100.0	44.9	24.5	34.8	8.7	3.1	7,155.2	100.0%	614.0	100.0%
No pobre	1,156,432	23.9	—	—	—	—	1,156,432	100.0	—	—	—	—	—	—	—	—	—	—
QUINTIL																		
1	1,621,160	33.5	1,281,674.0	100.0	1,621,160	44.0	—	—	100.0	64.0	41.7	79.1	19.8	7.1	4,481.4	62.6%	613.9	100.0%
2	1,311,576	27.1	—	—	1,311,576	35.6	—	—	100.0	39.1	15.8	—	—	—	2,215.8	31.0%	—	0.0%
3	933,321	19.3	—	—	754,864	20.5	178,457	15.4	80.9	11.4	2.1	—	—	—	457.5	6.4%	—	0.0%
4	672,133	13.9	—	—	—	—	672,133	58.1	—	—	—	—	—	—	—	0.0%	—	0.0%
5	305,842	6.3	—	—	—	—	305,842	26.5	—	—	—	—	—	—	—	0.0%	—	0.0%
AREA																		
Urbana	1,231,941	25.4	99,619.0	7.8	621,997	16.9	609,944	52.7	50.5	17.3	8.0	8.1	1.8	0.6	917.7	12.8%	42.2	6.9%
Rural	3,612,091	74.6	1,182,055.0	92.2	3,065,603	83.1	546,488	47.3	84.9	40.0	22.3	32.7	8.3	3.0	6,238.1	87.2%	571.8	93.1%

REGION

Metropolitana	394,537	8.1	13,292.0	1.0	148,318	4.0	246,219	21.3	37.6	9.7	4.1	3.4	1.1	0.4	165.6	2.3%	8.6	1.4%
Norte	749,127	15.5	340,054.0	26.5	665,569	18.1	83,558	7.2	88.9	46.5	27.6	45.4	11.8	4.5	1,504.0	21.0%	169.0	27.5%
Nororiente	168,804	3.5	50,374.0	3.9	134,770	3.7	34,034	2.9	79.8	35.8	18.7	29.8	4.6	1.1	261.2	3.7%	14.8	2.4%
Suroriente	53,385	1.1	5,252.0	0.4	43,438	1.2	9,947	0.9	81.4	29.8	13.2	9.8	3.3	1.3	68.7	1.0%	3.4	0.5%
Central	558,674	11.5	77,822.0	6.1	356,928	9.7	201,746	17.5	63.9	24.9	12.1	13.9	2.4	0.7	599.8	8.4%	25.1	4.1%
Suroccidente	1,674,345	34.6	374,507.0	29.2	1,247,389	33.8	426,956	36.9	74.5	32.2	17.1	22.4	5.9	2.1	2,324.7	32.5%	187.2	30.5%
Noroccidente	1,147,353	23.7	408,908.0	31.9	1,019,638	27.7	127,715	11.0	88.9	42.7	23.9	35.6	9.1	3.2	2,113.3	29.5%	198.7	32.4%
Peten	97,807	2.0	11,465.0	0.9	71,550	1.9	26,257	2.3	73.2	27.9	13.3	11.7	3.7	1.6	117.8	1.6%	6.8	1.1%

ETNIA (2gr.)

Indigena	4,844,032	100.0	1,281,674.0	100.0	3,687,600	100.0	1,156,432	100.0	76.1	34.2	18.6	26.5	6.6	2.4	7,154.4	100.0%	614.0	100.0%
No indigena	—	—	—	—	—	—	—	—	—	—	—	—	—	—	—	0.0%	—	0.0%

ETNIA (6 gr.)

K'iche	1,073,324	22.2	204,493.0	16.0	691,009	18.7	382,315	33.1	64.4	26.2	13.6	19.1	4.3	1.5	1,214.9	17.0%	88.0	14.3%
Q'eqchi	736,163	15.2	279,377.0	21.8	614,315	16.7	121,848	10.5	83.5	42.0	24.5	38.0	10.3	4.1	1,334.9	18.7%	144.8	23.6%
Kaqchiquel	1,011,802	20.9	137,603.0	10.7	633,523	17.2	378,279	32.7	62.6	24.2	11.9	13.6	2.9	0.9	1,057.0	14.8%	55.5	9.0%
Mam	940,865	19.4	321,545.0	25.1	844,308	22.9	96,557	8.4	89.7	43.0	24.2	34.2	9.7	3.6	1,745.5	24.4%	174.1	28.4%
Otros indig	1,081,878	22.3	338,656.0	26.4	904,445	24.5	177,433	15.3	83.6	38.6	21.1	31.3	7.3	2.4	1,802.1	25.2%	151.6	24.7%
No indigena	—	—	—	—	—	—	—	—	—	—	—	—	—	—	—	0.0%	—	0.0%

SEXO JEFE

Masculino	4,227,160	87.3	1,171,387.0	91.4	3,261,747	88.5	965,413	83.5	77.2	35.1	19.2	27.7	6.9	2.5	6,400.3	89.5%	560.0	91.2%
Femenino	616,872	12.7	110,287.0	8.6	425,853	11.6	191,019	16.5	69.0	28.4	14.5	17.9	4.6	1.7	755.5	10.6%	53.9	8.8%

TABLE A4.6: POPULATION, CONTRIBUTION TO POVERTY (CONTR%), PERCENTAGE OF POOR (P0), POVERTY DEPTH INDEX (P1) & POVERTY SEVERITY INDEX (P2), AND COST TO ELIMINATE POVERTY (VALOR DE LA BRECHA): NON-INDIGENOUS

	# de personas y su contribución								P 0, P 1, & P 2						Valor ($) de la brecha de pobreza			
	Todos		Pobre extremo		Todos pobres		No Pobre		Pob. General			Pob. Extrema			P. General		P. Extrema	
	Personas	%	Personas	Contr%	Personas	Contr%	Personas	Contr%	P 0	P 1	P 2	P 0	P 1	P 2	Ql. 000,000	%	Ql. 000,000	%
No indigena																		
TOTAL	6,541,409	100.0	505,008.0	100.0	2,710,303	100.0	3,831,106	100.0	41.4	14.0	6.5	7.7	1.5	0.5	3,966.2	100.0%	192.6	100.0%
POBREZA																		
Extrema	505,008	7.7	505,008.0	100.0	505,008	18.6	—	—	100.0	64.6	42.1	100.0	20.0	5.9	1,408.2	35.5%	192.7	100.1%
Pobre (todos)	2,710,303	41.4	505,008.0	100.0	2,710,303	100.0	—	—	100.0	33.9	15.8	18.6	3.7	1.1	3,965.5	100.0%	192.7	100.1%
No pobre	3,831,106	58.6	—	—	—	—	3,831,106	100.0	—	—	—	—	—	—	—	—	—	—
QUINTIL																		
1	656,401	10.0	505,008.0	100.0	656,401	24.2	—	—	100.0	62.0	38.9	76.9	15.4	4.5	1,756.1	44.3%	192.7	100.1%
2	965,480	14.8	—	—	965,480	35.6	—	—	100.0	38.6	15.4	—	—	—	1,609.4	40.6%	—	0.0%
3	1,343,586	20.5	—	—	1,088,422	40.2	255,164	6.7	81.0	10.3	1.7	—	—	—	599.4	15.1%	—	0.0%
4	1,604,106	24.5	—	—	—	—	1,604,106	41.9	—	—	—	—	—	—	—	0.0%	—	0.0%
5	1,971,836	30.1	—	—	—	—	1,971,836	51.5	—	—	—	—	—	—	—	0.0%	—	0.0%
AREA																		
Urbana	3,165,913	48.4	23,964.0	4.8	570,554	21.1	2,595,359	67.7	18.0	4.1	1.4	0.8	0.1	0.0	555.1	14.0%	8.5	4.4%
Rural	3,375,496	51.6	481,044.0	95.3	2,139,749	79.0	1,235,747	32.3	63.4	23.4	11.4	14.3	2.9	0.9	3,409.6	86.0%	184.6	95.8%

REGION																	
Metropolitana	2,071,420	31.7	2,232.0	0.4	295,386	10.9	1,776,034	46.4	14.3	2.2	0.5	0.1	0.0	—	200.4	5.1%	0.4	0.2%
Norte	170,707	2.6	19,254.0	3.8	107,041	4.0	63,666	1.7	62.7	23.6	11.3	11.3	2.6	0.8	174.1	4.4%	8.5	4.4%
Nororiente	763,779	11.7	32,939.0	6.5	348,317	12.9	415,462	10.8	45.6	14.2	5.9	4.3	0.5	0.1	469.0	11.8%	7.4	3.9%
Suroriente	945,120	14.5	195,690.0	38.8	641,071	23.7	304,049	7.9	67.8	27.5	14.3	20.7	4.7	1.4	1,122.8	28.3%	84.2	43.7%
Central	657,656	10.1	28,516.0	5.7	272,400	10.1	385,256	10.1	41.4	12.0	4.9	4.3	0.8	0.2	340.2	8.6%	9.7	5.0%
Suroccidente	1,339,444	20.5	136,742.0	27.1	680,515	25.1	658,929	17.2	50.8	17.6	8.3	10.2	1.9	0.6	1,016.9	25.6%	49.2	25.5%
Noroccidente	319,380	4.9	53,222.0	10.5	184,456	6.8	134,924	3.5	57.8	23.4	11.8	16.7	2.7	0.6	322.9	8.1%	16.3	8.5%
Peten	273,903	4.2	36,413.0	7.2	181,117	6.7	92,786	2.4	66.1	26.9	13.4	13.3	3.3	1.2	318.7	8.0%	17.2	8.9%
ETNIA (2gr.)																		
Indigena	—	—	—	—	—	—	—	—	—	—	—	—	—	—	—	0.0%	—	0.0%
No indigena	6,541,409	100.0	505,008.0	100.0	2,710,303	100.0	3,831,106	100.0	41.4	14.0	6.5	7.7	1.5	0.5	3,966.2	100.0%	192.6	100.0%
ETNIA (6 gr.)																		
K'iche	—	—	—	—	—	—	—	—	—	—	—	—	—	—	—	0.0%	—	0.0%
Q'eqchi	—	—	—	—	—	—	—	—	—	—	—	—	—	—	—	0.0%	—	0.0%
Kaqchiquel	—	—	—	—	—	—	—	—	—	—	—	—	—	—	—	0.0%	—	0.0%
Mam	—	—	—	—	—	—	—	—	—	—	—	—	—	—	—	0.0%	—	0.0%
Otros indig	—	—	—	—	—	—	—	—	—	—	—	—	—	—	—	0.0%	—	0.0%
No indigena	6,541,409	100.0	505,008.0	100.0	2,710,303	100.0	3,831,106	100.0	41.4	14.0	6.5	7.7	1.5	0.5	3,966.2	100.0%	192.6	100.0%
SEXO JEFE																		
Masculino	5,489,422	83.9	451,231.0	89.4	2,337,905	86.3	3,151,517	82.3	42.6	14.7	6.9	8.2	1.6	0.5	3,475.4	87.6%	170.0	88.3%
Femenino	1,051,987	16.1	53,777.0	10.7	372,398	13.7	679,589	17.7	35.4	10.8	4.8	5.1	1.1	0.3	490.7	12.4%	22.3	11.6%

TABLE A4.7: POVERTY INDICATORS BY WELFARE MEASURE, CENTRAL AMERICA COMPARISONS

	All Poor (below FPL)			Extreme Poor (below XPL)			GNI Per Capita, PPP
	% Poor[a]	Depth[b]	Severity[c]	% Poor[a]	Depth[b]	Severity[c]	
Using Consumption as Welfare Measure							
Guatemala (2000)	56.2%	22.6	11.7	15.7%	3.7	1.3	$3,630
Nicaragua (1998)	47.9%	18.3	9.3	17.3%	4.8	2.0	$2,060
Panamá (1997)	37.3%	16.4	9.7	18.8%	7.7	4.2	$5,450
Using Income as Welfare Measure							
Guatemala (2000)	65.6%	35.1	25.9	31.9%	15.1	22.2	$3,630
Nicaragua (1998)	55.1%	26.2	16.0	29.9%	12.2	6.6	$2,060
Panamá (1997)	42.1%	22.8	17.1	26.2%	14.2	13.3	$5,450
Honduras (1996)	62.9%	33.4	22.3	35.0%	16.3	10.6	$2,270
LAC Average (1996)	36.7%	16.9	10.7	16.1%	7.4%	5.1	$6,620

Sources: GNI (gross national income) per capita estimates for 1999 in PPP US$, from World Bank, World Development Indicators 2001. Guatemala poverty estimates calculated by INE-SEGEPLAN-URL with technical assistance from World Bank using the ENCOVI 2000, *Instituto Nacional de Estadística—Guatemala.* Nicaragua poverty estimates from World Bank (2001a). Panama poverty estimates from World Bank (2000a). Honduras estimates from World Bank (2001c). Other countries: from Wodon (2001). a. Incidence of poverty or headcount index (% of population whose total consumption or income falls below poverty line, FPL or XPL). All poor includes extreme poor (throughout study). b. The Poverty Depth Index (P1) represents the amount needed to bring all poor individuals up to the poverty line (FPL or XPL), expressed as a percent of the poverty line taking into account the share of the poor population in the national population. c. The Poverty Severity Index (P2) is a derivation of P1 that takes into account the distribution of total consumption among the poor. In other words, it is a measure of the degree of inequality among the population below the poverty line. CAVEATS: International comparisons of poverty are always difficult due to various methodological differences (welfare measures, poverty lines, survey samples).

TABLE A4.8: INCOME INEQUALITY AND DISTRIBUTION

	Population Share (%)	Income Share (%)	Gini (%)
All Guatemala	100	100	57
Area			
Urban	39	66	54
Rural	61	34	47
Region			
Metropolitana	22	45	54
Norte	8	4	50
Nororiente	8	7	47
Suroriente	9	6	50
Central	11	9	47
Suroccidente	26	19	51
Noroccidente	13	7	51
Peten	3	2	53
Ethnic group[a]			
Indigenous	43	23	46
Non-indigenous	57	77	56
Language ability[b]			
Monolingual Spanish	62	80	56
Monolingual indigenous	9	3	39
Bilingual	29	17	48
Income quintiles			
1 (Low)	20	3	22
2	20	6	9
3	20	11	7
4	20	18	11
5 (High)	20	62	38

a. Based on household definition of ethnicity.
b. Based on household head's language ability.

Source: World Bank calculations using ENCOVI 2000, Instituto Nacional de Estadística—Guatemala.

TABLE A4.9: CONSUMPTION INEQUALITY AND DISTRIBUTION			
	Population Share (%)	Income Share (%)	Gini (%)
All Guatemala	100	100	48
Area			
Urban	39	63	44
Rural	61	37	35
Region			
Metropolitana	22	43	44
Norte	8	4	38
Nororiente	8	8	39
Suroriente	9	6	37
Central	11	10	38
Suroccidente	26	20	40
Noroccidente	13	7	36
Peten	3	2	39
Ethnic group[a]			
Indigenous	43	24	36
Non-indigenous	57	75	47
Language ability[b]			
Monolingual Spanish	62	79	46
Monolingual indigenous	9	3	29
Bilingual	29	18	36
Consumption quintiles			
1 (Low)	20	5	13
2	20	9	7
3	20	13	6
4	20	20	9
5 (High)	20	53	30

a. Based on household definition of ethnicity.
b. Based on household head's language ability.

Source: World Bank calculations using ENCOVI 2000, Instituto Nacional de Estadística—Guatemala.

TABLE A4.10: CONSUMPTION QUINTILES: LEVELS AND DISTRIBUTION

	National	Urban	Rural	K'iche	Q'ueqchi	Kaqchiquel	Man	Other Mayan	Non-indigenous	All Mayan	All Indigenous
Value in Quetzales											
Q.1	1,579.92	2,742.81	1,383.42	1,506.13	1,139.60	1,673.58	1,152.45	1,296.81	2,054.91	1,313.15	1,313.44
Q.2	2,638.52	4,633.97	2,123.30	2,418.41	1,706.94	2,503.60	1,764.82	1,868.20	3,548.78	2,016.68	2,018.45
Q.3	3,883.52	6,930.03	2,903.94	3,409.92	2,250.62	3,566.45	2,305.85	2,479.54	5,181.96	2,740.08	2,741.54
Q.4	6,074.55	10,593.92	4,014.67	4,713.51	3,157.54	4,760.47	3,054.48	3,285.28	8,225.38	3,851.17	3,851.36
Q.5	16,626.48	25,704.65	7,916.11	8,851.28	6,371.75	9,526.52	5,149.32	6,994.22	21,322.54	7,703.71	7,735.95
National average	6,161.00	10,121.85	3,668.12	4,179.06	2,919.70	4,407.09	2,684.36	3,183.34	8,065.97	3,524.85	3,531.18
% of 5th quintile											
Q.1	9.5%	10.7%	17.5%	17.0%	17.9%	17.6%	22.4%	18.5%	9.6%	17.1%	17.0%
Q.2	15.9%	18.0%	26.8%	27.3%	26.8%	26.3%	34.3%	26.7%	16.6%	26.2%	26.1%
Q.3	23.4%	27.0%	36.7%	38.5%	35.3%	37.4%	44.8%	35.5%	24.3%	35.6%	35.4%
Q.4	36.5%	41.2%	50.7%	53.3%	49.6%	50.0%	59.3%	47.0%	38.6%	50.0%	49.8%
Q.5	100.0%	100.0%	100.0%	100.0%	100.0%	100.0%	100.0%	100.0%	100.0%	100.0%	100.0%
National average	37.1%	39.4%	46.3%	47.2%	45.8%	46.3%	52.1%	45.5%	37.8%	45.8%	45.7%
% National average											
Q.1	5.1%	5.4%	7.5%	7.2%	7.8%	7.6%	8.6%	8.2%	5.1%	7.5%	7.4%
Q.2	8.6%	9.2%	11.6%	11.6%	11.7%	11.4%	13.2%	11.7%	8.8%	11.4%	11.4%
Q.3	12.6%	13.7%	15.8%	16.3%	15.4%	16.2%	17.2%	15.6%	12.9%	15.6%	15.5%
Q.4	19.7%	20.9%	21.9%	22.6%	21.6%	21.6%	22.8%	20.6%	20.4%	21.9%	21.8%
Q.5	54.0%	50.8%	43.2%	42.4%	43.7%	43.2%	38.4%	43.9%	52.9%	43.7%	43.8%
National average	100.0%	100.0%	100.0%	100.0%	100.0%	100.0%	100.0%	100.0%	100.0%	100.0%	100.0%
Ratios											
Q.2/Q.1	1.67	1.69	1.53	1.61	1.50	1.50	1.53	1.44	1.73	1.54	1.54
Q.3/Q.2	1.47	1.50	1.37	1.41	1.32	1.42	1.31	1.33	1.46	1.36	1.36
Q.4/Q.3	1.56	1.53	1.38	1.38	1.40	1.33	1.32	1.33	1.59	1.41	1.40
Q.5/Q.4	2.74	2.43	1.97	1.88	2.02	2.00	1.69	2.13	2.59	2.00	2.01
Q.5/Q.1	10.52	9.37	5.72	5.88	5.59	5.69	4.47	5.39	10.38	5.87	5.89

TABLE A4.11: INCOME QUINTILES: LEVELS AND DISTRIBUTION

	National	Urban	Rural	K'iche	Q'ueqchi	Kaqchiquel	Man	Other Mayan	Non-indigenous	All Mayan	All Indigenous
Value in Quetzales											
Q.1	655.00	1,348.60	558.92	865.01	401.24	759.62	445.39	599.61	855.74	581.83	585.24
Q.2	1,813.14	3,280.76	1,377.46	1,696.34	1,091.62	1,881.33	947.51	1,260.70	2,479.06	1,316.17	1,322.12
Q.3	2,986.43	5,361.18	2,157.37	2,546.41	1,670.32	2,968.19	1,503.04	1,835.05	4,022.18	2,072.34	2,076.09
Q.4	5,110.92	9,215.44	3,343.75	3,763.83	2,515.92	4,228.64	2,337.07	2,855.85	6,913.64	3,197.96	3,205.39
Q.5	17,326.64	28,083.08	8,243.51	8,960.39	6,056.60	9,664.25	5,255.46	7,257.54	22,922.18	7,766.79	7,822.60
National average	5,578.57	9,458.37	3,136.71	3,569.50	2,344.48	3,896.83	2,097.58	2,763.00	7,444.01	2,987.16	3,001.10
% of 5th quintile											
Q.1	3.8%	4.8%	6.8%	9.7%	6.6%	7.9%	8.5%	8.3%	3.7%	7.5%	7.5%
Q.2	10.5%	11.7%	16.7%	18.9%	18.0%	19.5%	18.0%	17.4%	10.8%	17.0%	16.9%
Q.3	17.2%	19.1%	26.2%	28.4%	27.6%	30.7%	28.6%	25.3%	17.6%	26.7%	26.5%
Q.4	29.5%	32.8%	40.6%	42.0%	41.5%	43.8%	44.5%	39.4%	30.2%	41.2%	41.0%
Q.5	100.0%	100.0%	100.0%	100.0%	100.0%	100.0%	100.0%	100.0%	100.0%	100.0%	100.0%
National average	32.2%	33.7%	38.1%	39.8%	38.7%	40.3%	39.9%	38.1%	32.5%	38.5%	38.4%
% National average											
Q.1	2.4%	2.9%	3.6%	4.9%	3.4%	3.9%	4.3%	4.3%	2.3%	3.9%	3.9%
Q.2	6.5%	6.9%	8.8%	9.5%	9.3%	9.7%	9.0%	9.1%	6.7%	8.8%	8.8%
Q.3	10.7%	11.3%	13.8%	14.3%	14.3%	15.2%	14.3%	13.3%	10.8%	13.9%	13.8%
Q.4	18.3%	19.5%	21.3%	21.1%	21.5%	21.7%	22.3%	20.7%	18.6%	21.4%	21.4%
Q.5	62.1%	59.4%	52.6%	50.2%	51.7%	49.6%	50.1%	52.5%	61.6%	52.0%	52.1%
National average	100.0%	100.0%	100.0%	100.0%	100.0%	100.0%	100.0%	100.0%	100.0%	100.0%	100.0%
Ratios											
Q.2/Q.1	2.77	2.43	2.46	1.96	2.72	2.48	2.13	2.10	2.90	2.26	2.26
Q.3/Q.2	1.65	1.63	1.57	1.50	1.53	1.58	1.59	1.46	1.62	1.57	1.57
Q.4/Q.3	1.71	1.72	1.55	1.48	1.51	1.42	1.55	1.56	1.72	1.54	1.54
Q.5/Q.4	3.39	3.05	2.47	2.38	2.41	2.29	2.25	2.54	3.32	2.43	2.44
Q.5/Q.1	26.45	20.82	14.75	10.36	15.09	12.72	11.80	12.10	26.79	13.35	13.37

TABLE A4.12: INCOME SOURCES, BY INCOME QUINTILES						
	Income quintiles					
	1	**2**	**3**	**4**	**5**	**Total**
Income per capita (Q)	653	1,810	2,983	5,110	17,319	5,578
Labor Income (%)	43	72	74	78	73	73
Agricultural	*20*	*44*	*30*	*17*	*5*	*13*
Salaries	28	21	15	8	2	6
Formal sector	9	10	8	5	1	3
Informal sector	19	11	7	3	1	3
Net inc. from production	–8	23	15	9	3	7
Non-Agricultural	*23*	*28*	*44*	*61*	*68*	*60*
Salaries	12	18	33	43	47	42
Formal sector	6	10	19	30	42	35
Informal sector	6	8	14	13	5	7
Own business	11	10	11	18	21	18
Formal sector	0	1	1	2	6	4
Informal sector	11	9	10	16	15	14
Non-labor income (%)	55	27	26	22	27	27
Return to capital[a]	*31*	*14*	*12*	*10*	*14*	*14*
Donations, gifts	*22*	*12*	*12*	*10*	*6*	*8*
Remittances	5	3	4	6	4	4
Private	1	1	1	1	1	1
Public	16	8	7	3	1	3
Pensions, indemnizaciones	**2**	**1**	**2**	**2**	**4**	**3**
Other[b]	**0**	**0**	**0**	**0**	**3**	**2**

Percentages may not add up to 100 due to rounding.
a. As interest received was negligible, the return to capital includes: income from rental of equipment, rental of property and the interest received.
b. For example, inheritance or lottery winnings.

Source: World Bank calculations using ENCOVI 2000, Instituto Nacional de Estadística—Guatemala.

TABLE A4.13: INCOME SOURCES, BY CONSUMPTION QUINTILES

	Consumption quintiles					
	1	2	3	4	5	Total
Income per capita (Q)	**1,429**	**2,408**	**3,487**	**5,064**	**15,503**	**5,578**
Labor Income (%)	**77**	**78**	**77**	**76**	**70**	**73**
Agricultural	*49*	*38*	*24*	*14*	*3*	*13*
Salaries	30	18	11	6	1	6
Formal sector	13	9	6	4	1	3
Informal sector	17	9	5	2	0	3
Net inc. from production	19	20	13	8	2	7
Non-Agricultural	*28*	*40*	*53*	*62*	*67*	*60*
Salaries	17	25	39	47	46	42
Formal sector	8	13	26	36	42	35
Informal sector	9	12	13	11	4	7
Own business	11	15	14	15	21	18
Formal sector	1	1	1	1	7	4
Informal sector	10	14	13	14	14	14
Non-labor income (%)	**22**	**22**	**24**	**26**	**30**	**27**
Return to capital[a]	*10*	*8*	*10*	*11*	*16*	*14*
Donations, gifts	*11*	*12*	*12*	*10*	*6*	*8*
Remittances	3	4	5	5	4	4
Private	1	2	1	2	1	1
Public	7	6	6	3	1	3
Pensions, indemnizaciones	*1*	*1*	*1*	*3*	*5*	*3*
Other[b]	*0*	*1*	*1*	*2*	*3*	*2*

Percentages may not add up to 100 due to rounding.

a. As interest received was negligible, the return to capital includes: income from rental of equipment, rental of property and the interest received.

b. For example, inheritance or lottery winnings.

Source: World Bank calculations using ENCOVI 2000, Instituto Nacional de Estadística—Guatemala.

TABLE A4.14: INCOME SOURCES, BY POVERTY CLASSIFICATION

	Extreme Poor	All Poor	Non-Poor
Income per capita (Q)	1,345	2,349	9,721
Labor Income (%)	78	77	71
Agricultural	49	34	6
Salaries	31	17	3
Formal sector	13	8	2
Informal sector	18	9	1
Net inc. from production	18	17	3
Non-Agricultural	29	43	65
Salaries	17	29	46
Formal sector	9	17	40
Informal sector	8	12	6
Own business	12	14	19
Formal sector	1	1	5
Informal sector	11	13	14
Non-labor income (%)	20	22	27
Return to capital[a]	9	9	15
Donations, gifts	10	11	6
Remittances	3	4	4
Private	1	1	1
Public	6	6	1
Pensions, indemnizaciones	1	1	4
Other[b]	0	1	2

Percentages may not add up to 100 due to rounding.

a. As interest received was negligible, the return to capital includes: income from rental of equipment, rental of property and the interest received.

b. For example, inheritance or lottery winnings.

Source: World Bank calculations using ENCOVI 2000, Instituto Nacional de Estadística—Guatemala.

TABLE A4.15: Consumption Patterns: National

	Food	Housing	Personal goods	Education	Health	Durable goods	Transport	Other	Services	Total
NACIONAL										
TOTAL	2,489	860	577	320	225	244	383	953	111	6,161
POBREZA										
Extrema	840	149	186	21	20	9	28	205	3	1,460
Pobre (todos)	1,413	267	280	69	45	33	80	386	8	2,580
No pobre	3,869	1,620	957	642	456	516	771	1,681	243	10,754
QUINTIL										
1	911	163	194	25	22	10	31	221	4	1,580
2	1,477	273	289	64	44	31	76	376	9	2,639
3	2,029	411	380	128	80	66	156	617	16	3,884
4	2,840	755	572	251	155	167	329	957	49	6,075
5	5,187	2,696	1,447	1,130	825	949	1,320	2,594	479	16,626
AREA										
Urbana	3,442	1,617	929	657	456	480	706	1,581	252	10,122
Rural	1,889	383	355	107	80	96	179	557	23	3,668
REGION										
Metropolitana	3,890	2,087	1,112	812	624	588	937	1,897	337	12,284
Norte	1,566	293	329	105	68	89	108	492	26	3,076
Nororiente	2,697	699	516	186	166	214	334	870	59	5,741
Suroriente	2,085	521	417	128	99	111	218	654	35	4,268
Central	2,528	733	525	255	159	179	310	865	79	5,632
Suroccidente	2,123	539	445	236	121	187	247	726	56	4,679
Noroccidente	1,641	346	340	100	80	75	149	507	26	3,265
Peten	2,219	467	391	195	92	127	206	730	53	4,480
ETNIA (2gr.)										
Indígena	1,721	398	371	136	77	81	175	543	29	3,531
No indígena	3,057	1,201	728	456	335	366	536	1,256	172	8,108
ETNIA (6 gr.)										
K'iche	1,938	489	419	191	103	132	201	668	38	4,179
Q'eqchi	1,596	249	323	70	56	42	101	467	16	2,920
Kaqchiquel	1,910	569	467	188	111	110	304	695	53	4,407
Mam	1,383	306	295	90	38	53	112	392	16	2,684
Otros indíg	1,708	329	335	115	70	54	132	460	19	3,222
No indígena	3,057	1,201	728	456	335	366	536	1,256	172	8,108
SEXO										
Masculino	2,486	821	564	304	223	245	385	944	109	6,081
Femenino	2,492	897	589	335	228	244	380	961	113	6,237
EDAD										
0–6	2,062	561	424	164	160	136	246	753	64	4,571
7–12	2,212	618	456	310	159	183	301	811	74	5,124
13–18	2,375	726	525	436	165	224	370	887	86	5,794
19–24	2,711	975	649	403	264	305	474	1,147	152	7,080
25–59	2,830	1,057	688	379	300	330	500	1,141	153	7,378
>=60	3,000	1,753	911	200	352	323	394	967	171	8,070

Annual consumption levels (per capital, in Quetzales)

			Percent of total annual consumption per capita						
Food (%)	Housing (%)	Personal goods (%)	Education (%)	Health (%)	Durable goods (%)	Transport (%)	Other (%)	Services (%)	Total (%)
40.4%	14.0%	9.4%	5.2%	3.7%	4.0%	6.2%	15.5%	1.8%	100.0%
57.5%	10.2%	12.8%	1.4%	1.4%	0.6%	1.9%	14.1%	0.2%	100.0%
54.8%	10.3%	10.8%	2.7%	1.8%	1.3%	3.1%	14.9%	0.3%	100.0%
36.0%	15.1%	8.9%	6.0%	4.2%	4.8%	7.2%	15.6%	2.3%	100.0%
57.6%	10.3%	12.3%	1.6%	1.4%	0.6%	2.0%	14.0%	0.2%	100.0%
56.0%	10.3%	11.0%	2.4%	1.7%	1.2%	2.9%	14.2%	0.3%	100.0%
52.2%	10.6%	9.8%	3.3%	2.0%	1.7%	4.0%	15.9%	0.4%	100.0%
46.8%	12.4%	9.4%	4.1%	2.6%	2.7%	5.4%	15.8%	0.8%	100.0%
31.2%	16.2%	8.7%	6.8%	5.0%	5.7%	7.9%	15.6%	2.9%	100.0%
34.0%	16.0%	9.2%	6.5%	4.5%	4.7%	7.0%	15.6%	2.5%	100.0%
51.5%	10.4%	9.7%	2.9%	2.2%	2.6%	4.9%	15.2%	0.6%	100.0%
31.7%	17.0%	9.1%	6.6%	5.1%	4.8%	7.6%	15.4%	2.7%	100.0%
50.9%	9.5%	10.7%	3.4%	2.2%	2.9%	3.5%	16.0%	0.8%	100.0%
47.0%	12.2%	9.0%	3.2%	2.9%	3.7%	5.8%	15.2%	1.0%	100.0%
48.8%	12.2%	9.8%	3.0%	2.3%	2.6%	5.1%	15.3%	0.8%	100.0%
44.9%	13.0%	9.3%	4.5%	2.8%	3.2%	5.5%	15.4%	1.4%	100.0%
45.4%	11.5%	9.5%	5.0%	2.6%	4.0%	5.3%	15.5%	1.2%	100.0%
50.3%	10.6%	10.4%	3.1%	2.5%	2.3%	4.6%	15.5%	0.8%	100.0%
49.5%	10.4%	8.7%	4.3%	2.1%	2.8%	4.6%	16.3%	1.2%	100.0%
48.7%	11.3%	10.5%	3.8%	2.2%	2.3%	4.9%	15.4%	0.8%	100.0%
37.7%	14.8%	9.0%	5.6%	4.1%	4.5%	6.6%	15.5%	2.1%	100.0%
46.4%	11.7%	10.0%	4.6%	2.5%	3.1%	4.8%	16.0%	0.9%	100.0%
54.6%	8.5%	11.1%	2.4%	1.9%	1.4%	3.5%	16.0%	0.5%	100.0%
43.3%	12.9%	10.6%	4.3%	2.5%	2.5%	6.9%	15.8%	1.2%	100.0%
51.5%	11.4%	11.0%	3.3%	1.4%	2.0%	4.2%	14.6%	0.6%	100.0%
53.0%	10.2%	10.4%	3.6%	2.2%	1.7%	4.1%	14.3%	0.6%	100.0%
37.7%	14.8%	9.0%	5.6%	4.1%	4.5%	6.6%	15.5%	2.1%	100.0%
40.9%	13.5%	9.3%	5.0%	3.7%	4.0%	6.3%	15.5%	1.8%	100.0%
39.9%	14.4%	9.4%	5.4%	3.7%	3.9%	6.1%	15.4%	1.8%	100.0%
45.1%	12.3%	9.3%	3.6%	3.5%	3.0%	5.4%	16.5%	1.4%	100.0%
43.2%	12.1%	8.9%	6.1%	3.1%	3.6%	5.9%	15.8%	1.4%	100.0%
41.0%	12.5%	9.1%	7.5%	2.8%	3.9%	6.4%	15.3%	1.5%	100.0%
38.3%	13.8%	9.2%	5.7%	3.7%	4.3%	6.7%	16.2%	2.1%	100.0%
38.4%	14.3%	9.3%	5.1%	4.1%	4.5%	6.8%	15.5%	2.1%	100.0%
37.2%	21.7%	11.3%	2.5%	4.4%	4.0%	4.9%	12.0%	2.1%	100.0%

TABLE A4.16: CONSUMPTION PATTERNS: URBAN

	Food	Housing	Personal goods	Education	Health	Durable goods	Transport	Other	Services	Total
				Annual consumption levels (per capital, in Quetzales)						
Urbana										
TOTAL	3,442	1,617	929	657	456	480	706	1,581	252	10,122
POBREZA										
Extrema	789	179	204	49	27	10	22	220	4	1,504
Pobre (todos)	1,486	393	358	148	63	43	98	483	12	3,084
No pobre	4,170	2,073	1,142	847	603	642	933	1,990	341	12,740
QUINTIL										
1	888	215	208	52	33	11	31	236	5	1,681
2	1,284	366	329	120	49	34	84	393	9	2,668
3	1,852	491	435	191	83	59	144	619	17	3,890
4	2,717	860	604	317	177	158	330	974	58	6,196
5	5,288	2,988	1,548	1,250	924	1,008	1,387	2,766	553	17,712
AREA										
Urbana	3,442	1,617	929	657	456	480	706	1,581	252	10,122
Rural	—	—	—	—	—	—	—	—	—	—
REGION										
Metropolitana	4,127	2,323	1,209	917	703	653	1,010	2,061	385	13,390
Norte	2,547	849	625	388	185	302	310	1,060	115	6,381
Nororiente	3,509	1,071	726	404	343	422	484	1,354	155	8,468
Suroriente	2,708	944	659	314	197	281	441	1,082	78	6,704
Central	2,939	1,016	673	393	198	260	415	1,104	128	7,127
Suroccidente	2,776	1,014	711	497	251	375	471	1,188	148	7,430
Noroccidente	2,346	860	582	358	230	264	370	992	122	6,124
Peten	2,885	968	680	534	218	298	442	1,302	160	7,486
ETNIA (2gr.)										
Indígena	2,309	742	561	307	158	154	322	859	76	5,489
No indígena	3,883	1,958	1,073	794	573	607	856	1,862	320	11,925
ETNIA (6 gr.)										
K'iche	2,430	772	598	306	177	189	308	939	78	5,797
Q'eqchi	2,394	650	559	203	150	141	270	824	70	5,262
Kaqchiquel	2,443	843	605	326	153	162	391	944	88	5,956
Mam	1,448	548	466	272	70	77	203	582	67	3,735
Otros indíg	2,319	684	487	350	189	138	320	773	62	5,321
No indígena	3,883	1,958	1,073	794	573	607	856	1,862	320	11,925
SEXO										
Masculino	3,434	1,541	911	631	457	482	723	1,579	251	10,008
Femenino	3,449	1,687	946	681	456	477	692	1,584	253	10,226
EDAD										
0–6	2,902	1,096	688	377	359	302	487	1,333	164	7,708
7–12	3,030	1,174	745	682	337	375	560	1,377	180	8,459
13–18	3,188	1,337	827	906	327	407	672	1,412	193	9,269
19–24	3,723	1,734	1,007	793	499	564	854	1,866	320	11,361
25–59	3,824	1,845	1,053	709	560	594	853	1,796	313	11,547
>=60	3,919	3,240	1,440	368	647	618	701	1,490	351	12,775

			Percent of total annual consumption per capita						
Food (%)	Housing (%)	Personal goods (%)	Education (%)	Health (%)	Durable goods (%)	Transport (%)	Other (%)	Services (%)	Total (%)
34.0%	16.0%	9.2%	6.5%	4.5%	4.7%	7.0%	15.6%	2.5%	100.0%
52.5%	11.9%	13.6%	3.3%	1.8%	0.7%	1.5%	14.6%	0.3%	100.0%
48.2%	12.8%	11.6%	4.8%	2.1%	1.4%	3.2%	15.6%	0.4%	100.0%
32.7%	16.3%	9.0%	6.6%	4.7%	5.0%	7.3%	15.6%	2.7%	100.0%
52.8%	12.8%	12.4%	3.1%	2.0%	0.7%	1.9%	14.1%	0.3%	100.0%
48.1%	13.7%	12.3%	4.5%	1.8%	1.3%	3.1%	14.7%	0.3%	100.0%
47.6%	12.6%	11.2%	4.9%	2.1%	1.5%	3.7%	15.9%	0.4%	100.0%
43.9%	13.9%	9.7%	5.1%	2.9%	2.6%	5.3%	15.7%	0.9%	100.0%
29.9%	16.9%	8.7%	7.1%	5.2%	5.7%	7.8%	15.6%	3.1%	100.0%
34.0%	16.0%	9.2%	6.5%	4.5%	4.7%	7.0%	15.6%	2.5%	100.0%
n/a	n/a	n/a	n/a	n/a	n/a	n/a	n/a	n/a	n/a
30.8%	17.4%	9.0%	6.8%	5.3%	4.9%	7.5%	15.4%	2.9%	100.0%
39.9%	13.3%	9.8%	6.1%	2.9%	4.7%	4.9%	16.6%	1.8%	100.0%
41.4%	12.6%	8.6%	4.8%	4.0%	5.0%	5.7%	16.0%	1.8%	100.0%
40.4%	14.1%	9.8%	4.7%	2.9%	4.2%	6.6%	16.1%	1.2%	100.0%
41.2%	14.3%	9.4%	5.5%	2.8%	3.6%	5.8%	15.5%	1.8%	100.0%
37.4%	13.6%	9.6%	6.7%	3.4%	5.0%	6.3%	16.0%	2.0%	100.0%
38.3%	14.0%	9.5%	5.8%	3.8%	4.3%	6.0%	16.2%	2.0%	100.0%
38.5%	12.9%	9.1%	7.1%	2.9%	4.0%	5.9%	17.4%	2.1%	100.0%
42.1%	13.5%	10.2%	5.6%	2.9%	2.8%	5.9%	15.7%	1.4%	100.0%
32.6%	16.4%	9.0%	6.7%	4.8%	5.1%	7.2%	15.6%	2.7%	100.0%
41.9%	13.3%	10.3%	5.3%	3.0%	3.3%	5.3%	16.2%	1.4%	100.0%
45.5%	12.4%	10.6%	3.9%	2.8%	2.7%	5.1%	15.7%	1.3%	100.0%
41.0%	14.2%	10.2%	5.5%	2.6%	2.7%	6.6%	15.9%	1.5%	100.0%
38.8%	14.7%	12.5%	7.3%	1.9%	2.1%	5.4%	15.6%	1.8%	100.0%
43.6%	12.9%	9.2%	6.6%	3.5%	2.6%	6.0%	14.5%	1.2%	100.0%
32.6%	16.4%	9.0%	6.7%	4.8%	5.1%	7.2%	15.6%	2.7%	100.0%
34.3%	15.4%	9.1%	6.3%	4.6%	4.8%	7.2%	15.8%	2.5%	100.0%
33.7%	16.5%	9.3%	6.7%	4.5%	4.7%	6.8%	15.5%	2.5%	100.0%
37.7%	14.2%	8.9%	4.9%	4.7%	3.9%	6.3%	17.3%	2.1%	100.0%
35.8%	13.9%	8.8%	8.1%	4.0%	4.4%	6.6%	16.3%	2.1%	100.0%
34.4%	14.4%	8.9%	9.8%	3.5%	4.4%	7.2%	15.2%	2.1%	100.0%
32.8%	15.3%	8.9%	7.0%	4.4%	5.0%	7.5%	16.4%	2.8%	100.0%
33.1%	16.0%	9.1%	6.1%	4.9%	5.1%	7.4%	15.6%	2.7%	100.0%
30.7%	25.4%	11.3%	2.9%	5.1%	4.8%	5.5%	11.7%	2.7%	100.0%

TABLE A4.17: CONSUMPTION PATTERNS: RURAL

	Food	Housing	Personal goods	Education	Health	Durable goods	Transport	Other	Services	Total
Rural										
TOTAL	1,889	383	355	107	80	96	179	557	23	3,668
POBREZA										
Extrema	843	146	185	19	19	9	28	204	3	1,457
Pobre (todos)	1,396	238	262	51	41	31	75	363	8	2,465
No pobre	3,328	806	625	272	192	287	480	1,124	67	7,182
QUINTIL										
1	913	158	192	23	21	9	31	219	3	1,571
2	1,517	254	281	52	43	30	75	372	8	2,633
3	2,116	373	354	98	78	70	163	615	15	3,880
4	2,987	630	534	172	129	177	327	937	38	5,930
5	4,761	1,463	1,023	624	408	701	1,039	1,869	167	12,054
AREA										
Urbana	—	—	—	—	—	—	—	—	—	—
Rural	1,889	383	355	107	80	96	179	557	23	3,668
REGION										
Metropolitana	2,619	821	588	252	199	240	541	1,017	78	6,356
Norte	1,381	188	273	52	46	49	70	385	9	2,452
Nororiente	2,413	570	442	110	104	141	282	702	26	4,791
Suroriente	1,898	395	344	73	70	60	151	526	22	3,539
Central	2,203	510	408	146	128	116	228	676	40	4,454
Suroccidente	1,880	362	345	138	73	117	164	554	21	3,655
Noroccidente	1,500	243	291	48	50	37	105	409	7	2,690
Peten	1,967	277	282	66	45	62	116	513	13	3,340
ETNIA (2gr.)										
Indígena	1,521	281	307	77	50	56	124	435	13	2,864
No indígena	2,283	492	406	139	112	140	237	688	33	4,529
ETNIA (6 gr.)										
K'iche	1,712	359	336	138	69	105	152	543	20	3,434
Q'eqchi	1,429	166	274	43	36	21	66	393	5	2,433
Kaqchiquel	1,569	394	378	100	84	77	249	536	30	3,417
Mam	1,373	269	268	62	33	49	98	363	8	2,524
Otros indíg	1,527	223	290	46	35	29	76	367	6	2,599
No indígena	2,283	492	406	139	112	140	237	688	33	4,529
SEXO										
Masculino	1,912	385	354	106	81	101	181	561	24	3,705
Femenino	1,866	380	355	108	78	92	176	554	22	3,632
EDAD										
0–6	1,663	307	298	63	65	58	132	476	16	3,077
7–12	1,790	331	306	118	67	85	167	518	19	3,401
13–18	1,884	357	342	153	67	114	187	570	22	3,697
19–24	1,955	408	382	112	89	111	190	611	26	3,885
25–59	2,049	439	402	120	95	123	222	627	28	4,105
>=60	2,299	622	508	72	128	98	160	568	34	4,489

Annual consumption levels (per capital, in Quetzales)

			Percent of total annual consumption per capita						
Food (%)	Housing (%)	Personal goods (%)	Education (%)	Health (%)	Durable goods (%)	Transport (%)	Other (%)	Services (%)	Total (%)
51.5%	10.4%	9.7%	2.9%	2.2%	2.6%	4.9%	15.2%	0.6%	100.0%
57.9%	10.0%	12.7%	1.3%	1.3%	0.6%	1.9%	14.0%	0.2%	100.0%
56.6%	9.7%	10.6%	2.1%	1.7%	1.3%	3.1%	14.7%	0.3%	100.0%
46.3%	11.2%	8.7%	3.8%	2.7%	4.0%	6.7%	15.7%	0.9%	100.0%
58.1%	10.1%	12.3%	1.5%	1.4%	0.6%	2.0%	14.0%	0.2%	100.0%
57.6%	9.6%	10.7%	2.0%	1.6%	1.2%	2.8%	14.1%	0.3%	100.0%
54.5%	9.6%	9.1%	2.5%	2.0%	1.8%	4.2%	15.9%	0.4%	100.0%
50.4%	10.6%	9.0%	2.9%	2.2%	3.0%	5.5%	15.8%	0.6%	100.0%
39.5%	12.1%	8.5%	5.2%	3.4%	5.8%	8.6%	15.5%	1.4%	100.0%
n/a	n/a	n/a	n/a	n/a	n/a	n/a	n/a	n/a	n/a
51.5%	10.4%	9.7%	2.9%	2.2%	2.6%	4.9%	15.2%	0.6%	100.0%
41.2%	12.9%	9.3%	4.0%	3.1%	3.8%	8.5%	16.0%	1.2%	100.0%
56.3%	7.7%	11.1%	2.1%	1.9%	2.0%	2.9%	15.7%	0.4%	100.0%
50.4%	11.9%	9.2%	2.3%	2.2%	3.0%	5.9%	14.6%	0.5%	100.0%
53.6%	11.2%	9.7%	2.1%	2.0%	1.7%	4.3%	14.9%	0.6%	100.0%
49.5%	11.4%	9.2%	3.3%	2.9%	2.6%	5.1%	15.2%	0.9%	100.0%
51.4%	9.9%	9.5%	3.8%	2.0%	3.2%	4.5%	15.1%	0.6%	100.0%
55.8%	9.0%	10.8%	1.8%	1.9%	1.4%	3.9%	15.2%	0.2%	100.0%
58.9%	8.3%	8.4%	2.0%	1.3%	1.8%	3.5%	15.4%	0.4%	100.0%
53.1%	9.8%	10.7%	2.7%	1.7%	2.0%	4.3%	15.2%	0.5%	100.0%
50.4%	10.9%	9.0%	3.1%	2.5%	3.1%	5.2%	15.2%	0.7%	100.0%
49.8%	10.5%	9.8%	4.0%	2.0%	3.1%	4.4%	15.8%	0.6%	100.0%
58.8%	6.8%	11.3%	1.8%	1.5%	0.9%	2.7%	16.1%	0.2%	100.0%
45.9%	11.5%	11.1%	2.9%	2.5%	2.2%	7.3%	15.7%	0.9%	100.0%
54.4%	10.7%	10.6%	2.5%	1.3%	1.9%	3.9%	14.4%	0.3%	100.0%
58.8%	8.6%	11.2%	1.8%	1.3%	1.1%	2.9%	14.1%	0.2%	100.0%
50.4%	10.9%	9.0%	3.1%	2.5%	3.1%	5.2%	15.2%	0.7%	100.0%
51.6%	10.4%	9.6%	2.9%	2.2%	2.7%	4.9%	15.1%	0.6%	100.0%
51.4%	10.5%	9.8%	3.0%	2.2%	2.5%	4.9%	15.3%	0.6%	100.0%
54.0%	10.0%	9.7%	2.1%	2.1%	1.9%	4.3%	15.5%	0.5%	100.0%
52.6%	9.7%	9.0%	3.5%	2.0%	2.5%	4.9%	15.2%	0.6%	100.0%
51.0%	9.7%	9.3%	4.1%	1.8%	3.1%	5.1%	15.4%	0.6%	100.0%
50.3%	10.5%	9.8%	2.9%	2.3%	2.9%	4.9%	15.7%	0.7%	100.0%
49.9%	10.7%	9.8%	2.9%	2.3%	3.0%	5.4%	15.3%	0.7%	100.0%
51.2%	13.8%	11.3%	1.6%	2.9%	2.2%	3.6%	12.7%	0.8%	100.0%

TABLE A4.18: CONSUMPTION PATTERNS: INDIGENOUS

	Food	Housing	Personal goods	Education	Health	Durable goods	Transport	Other	Services	Total
Indígena										
TOTAL	1,721	398	371	136	77	81	175	543	29	3,531
POBREZA										
Extrema	818	144	188	20	18	8	30	205	3	1,433
Pobre (todos)	1,285	244	274	63	38	30	77	359	8	2,378
No pobre	3,111	891	680	367	202	242	486	1,130	98	7,208
QUINTIL										
1	888	157	194	26	20	9	33	223	3	1,554
2	1,450	266	296	67	41	34	81	386	8	2,629
3	1,913	415	420	134	78	71	180	632	18	3,861
4	2,759	640	583	218	141	168	342	915	64	5,830
5	4,435	1,659	1,020	833	394	499	944	1,824	213	11,821
AREA										
Urbana	2,309	742	561	307	158	154	322	859	76	5,489
Rural	1,521	281	307	77	50	56	124	435	13	2,864
REGION										
Metropolitana	2,665	916	663	298	208	129	545	886	53	6,363
Norte	1,398	224	291	73	47	42	72	417	16	2,578
Nororiente	1,805	296	352	46	69	36	127	449	10	3,191
Suroriente	1,935	354	351	95	73	46	199	548	32	3,633
Central	1,935	580	432	203	108	133	271	710	70	4,441
Suroccidente	1,685	408	372	162	79	102	158	558	30	3,555
Noroccidente	1,495	258	299	69	38	44	101	411	12	2,727
Peten	2,164	277	346	94	61	41	135	631	14	3,763
ETNIA (2gr.)										
Indígena	1,721	398	371	136	77	81	175	543	29	3,531
No indígena	—	—	—	—	—	—	—	—	—	—
ETNIA (6 gr.)										
K'iche	1,938	489	419	191	103	132	201	668	38	4,179
Q'eqchi	1,596	249	323	70	56	42	101	467	16	2,920
Kaqchiquel	1,910	569	467	188	111	110	304	695	53	4,407
Mam	1,383	306	295	90	38	53	112	392	16	2,684
Otros indíg	1,708	329	335	115	70	54	132	460	19	3,222
No indígena	—	—	—	—	—	—	—	—	—	—
SEXO										
Masculino	1,730	394	369	136	82	85	180	544	30	3,550
Femenino	1,712	402	374	135	73	77	170	542	28	3,512
EDAD										
0–6	1,523	327	320	88	71	58	132	474	24	3,018
7–12	1,565	317	311	127	51	69	133	474	20	3,067
13–18	1,708	374	353	196	65	93	194	563	34	3,581
19–24	1,842	432	411	159	88	92	221	620	36	3,900
25–59	1,889	476	421	152	93	100	216	608	35	3,991
>=60	2,073	580	522	87	124	68	161	561	27	4,201

Annual consumption levels (per capital, in Quetzales)

			Percent of total annual consumption per capita						
Food (%)	Housing (%)	Personal goods (%)	Education (%)	Health (%)	Durable goods (%)	Transport (%)	Other (%)	Services (%)	Total (%)
48.7%	11.3%	10.5%	3.8%	2.2%	2.3%	4.9%	15.4%	0.8%	100.0%
57.1%	10.0%	13.1%	1.4%	1.3%	0.6%	2.1%	14.3%	0.2%	100.0%
54.0%	10.2%	11.5%	2.6%	1.6%	1.3%	3.2%	15.1%	0.3%	100.0%
43.2%	12.4%	9.4%	5.1%	2.8%	3.4%	6.7%	15.7%	1.4%	100.0%
57.1%	10.1%	12.5%	1.7%	1.3%	0.6%	2.1%	14.3%	0.2%	100.0%
55.1%	10.1%	11.3%	2.5%	1.6%	1.3%	3.1%	14.7%	0.3%	100.0%
49.5%	10.8%	10.9%	3.5%	2.0%	1.9%	4.7%	16.4%	0.5%	100.0%
47.3%	11.0%	10.0%	3.7%	2.4%	2.9%	5.9%	15.7%	1.1%	100.0%
37.5%	14.0%	8.6%	7.0%	3.3%	4.2%	8.0%	15.4%	1.8%	100.0%
42.1%	13.5%	10.2%	5.6%	2.9%	2.8%	5.9%	15.7%	1.4%	100.0%
53.1%	9.8%	10.7%	2.7%	1.7%	2.0%	4.3%	15.2%	0.5%	100.0%
41.9%	14.4%	10.4%	4.7%	3.3%	2.0%	8.6%	13.9%	0.8%	100.0%
54.2%	8.7%	11.3%	2.8%	1.8%	1.6%	2.8%	16.2%	0.6%	100.0%
56.6%	9.3%	11.0%	1.4%	2.2%	1.1%	4.0%	14.1%	0.3%	100.0%
53.3%	9.7%	9.7%	2.6%	2.0%	1.3%	5.5%	15.1%	0.9%	100.0%
43.6%	13.1%	9.7%	4.6%	2.4%	3.0%	6.1%	16.0%	1.6%	100.0%
47.4%	11.5%	10.5%	4.6%	2.2%	2.9%	4.5%	15.7%	0.9%	100.0%
54.8%	9.5%	11.0%	2.5%	1.4%	1.6%	3.7%	15.1%	0.4%	100.0%
57.5%	7.4%	9.2%	2.5%	1.6%	1.1%	3.6%	16.8%	0.4%	100.0%
48.7%	11.3%	10.5%	3.8%	2.2%	2.3%	4.9%	15.4%	0.8%	100.0%
n/a	n/a	n/a	n/a	n/a	n/a	n/a	n/a	n/a	n/a
46.4%	11.7%	10.0%	4.6%	2.5%	3.1%	4.8%	16.0%	0.9%	100.0%
54.6%	8.5%	11.1%	2.4%	1.9%	1.4%	3.5%	16.0%	0.5%	100.0%
43.3%	12.9%	10.6%	4.3%	2.5%	2.5%	6.9%	15.8%	1.2%	100.0%
51.5%	11.4%	11.0%	3.3%	1.4%	2.0%	4.2%	14.6%	0.6%	100.0%
53.0%	10.2%	10.4%	3.6%	2.2%	1.7%	4.1%	14.3%	0.6%	100.0%
n/a	n/a	n/a	n/a	n/a	n/a	n/a	n/a	n/a	n/a
48.7%	11.1%	10.4%	3.8%	2.3%	2.4%	5.1%	15.3%	0.8%	100.0%
48.7%	11.4%	10.6%	3.8%	2.1%	2.2%	4.8%	15.4%	0.8%	100.0%
50.4%	10.8%	10.6%	2.9%	2.4%	1.9%	4.4%	15.7%	0.8%	100.0%
51.0%	10.3%	10.1%	4.1%	1.7%	2.3%	4.3%	15.4%	0.7%	100.0%
47.7%	10.5%	9.9%	5.5%	1.8%	2.6%	5.4%	15.7%	0.9%	100.0%
47.2%	11.1%	10.5%	4.1%	2.3%	2.4%	5.7%	15.9%	0.9%	100.0%
47.3%	11.9%	10.5%	3.8%	2.3%	2.5%	5.4%	15.2%	0.9%	100.0%
49.4%	13.8%	12.4%	2.1%	2.9%	1.6%	3.8%	13.3%	0.6%	100.0%

TABLE A4.19: CONSUMPTION PATTERNS: NON-INDIGENOUS

			Annual consumption levels (per capital, in Quetzales)							
	Food	**Housing**	**Personal goods**	**Education**	**Health**	**Durable goods**	**Transport**	**Other**	**Services**	**Total**
No indígena										
TOTAL	3,057	1,201	728	456	335	366	536	1,256	172	8,108
POBREZA										
Extrema	895	162	184	24	23	9	24	207	3	1,530
Pobre (todos)	1,586	298	287	77	55	37	83	422	10	2,856
No pobre	4,098	1,840	1,041	724	533	598	857	1,847	287	11,825
QUINTIL										
1	967	177	193	23	27	10	26	216	4	1,643
2	1,514	281	280	60	48	28	70	361	9	2,652
3	2,110	408	353	124	81	62	140	606	15	3,899
4	2,874	804	567	264	161	166	323	975	43	6,177
5	5,303	2,857	1,513	1,176	892	1,019	1,378	2,713	521	17,372
AREA										
Urbana	3,883	1,958	1,073	794	573	607	856	1,862	320	11,925
Rural	2,283	492	406	139	112	140	237	688	33	4,529
REGION										
Metropolitana	4,124	2,310	1,197	910	703	676	1,011	2,090	391	13,412
Norte	2,304	596	499	247	161	299	267	822	68	5,262
Nororiente	2,894	788	552	217	187	253	380	963	70	6,304
Suroriente	2,093	531	420	130	101	114	219	661	35	4,304
Central	3,031	863	603	299	202	219	343	996	87	6,644
Suroccidente	2,671	703	535	328	173	293	358	936	88	6,085
Noroccidente	2,165	664	487	211	234	186	324	851	76	5,198
Peten	2,239	535	408	231	103	157	231	766	68	4,737
ETNIA (2gr.)										
No indígena	—	—	—	—	—	—	—	—	—	—
No indígena	3,057	1,201	728	456	335	366	536	1,256	172	8,108
ETNIA (6 gr.)										
K'iche	—	—	—	—	—	—	—	—	—	—
Q'eqchi	—	—	—	—	—	—	—	—	—	—
Kaqchiquel	—	—	—	—	—	—	—	—	—	—
Mam	—	—	—	—	—	—	—	—	—	—
Otros indíg	—	—	—	—	—	—	—	—	—	—
No indígena	3,057	1,201	728	456	335	366	536	1,256	172	8,108
SEXO										
Masculino	3,052	1,141	710	430	329	365	539	1,245	169	7,979
Femenino	3,062	1,258	746	481	341	366	534	1,268	175	8,231
EDAD										
0–6	2,545	771	517	232	238	206	349	1,001	99	5,958
7–12	2,738	863	573	459	247	276	438	1,084	117	6,796
13–18	2,880	992	655	618	240	324	503	1,132	126	7,471
19–24	3,270	1,324	803	560	377	441	637	1,487	227	9,125
25–59	3,442	1,436	862	527	435	480	684	1,489	230	9,585
>=60	3,591	2,503	1,159	273	499	485	543	1,226	263	10,542

			Percent of total annual consumption per capita						
Food (%)	Housing (%)	Personal goods (%)	Education (%)	Health (%)	Durable goods (%)	Transport (%)	Other (%)	Services (%)	Total (%)
37.7%	14.8%	9.0%	5.6%	4.1%	4.5%	6.6%	15.5%	2.1%	100.0%
58.5%	10.6%	12.0%	1.6%	1.5%	0.6%	1.5%	13.5%	0.2%	100.0%
55.6%	10.5%	10.1%	2.7%	1.9%	1.3%	2.9%	14.8%	0.3%	100.0%
34.7%	15.6%	8.8%	6.1%	4.5%	5.1%	7.2%	15.6%	2.4%	100.0%
58.9%	10.8%	11.7%	1.4%	1.7%	0.6%	1.6%	13.1%	0.2%	100.0%
57.1%	10.6%	10.6%	2.3%	1.8%	1.0%	2.6%	13.6%	0.3%	100.0%
54.1%	10.5%	9.1%	3.2%	2.1%	1.6%	3.6%	15.5%	0.4%	100.0%
46.5%	13.0%	9.2%	4.3%	2.6%	2.7%	5.2%	15.8%	0.7%	100.0%
30.5%	16.4%	8.7%	6.8%	5.1%	5.9%	7.9%	15.6%	3.0%	100.0%
32.6%	16.4%	9.0%	6.7%	4.8%	5.1%	7.2%	15.6%	2.7%	100.0%
50.4%	10.9%	9.0%	3.1%	2.5%	3.1%	5.2%	15.2%	0.7%	100.0%
30.7%	17.2%	8.9%	6.8%	5.2%	5.0%	7.5%	15.6%	2.9%	100.0%
43.8%	11.3%	9.5%	4.7%	3.1%	5.7%	5.1%	15.6%	1.3%	100.0%
45.9%	12.5%	8.8%	3.4%	3.0%	4.0%	6.0%	15.3%	1.1%	100.0%
48.6%	12.3%	9.8%	3.0%	2.3%	2.7%	5.1%	15.3%	0.8%	100.0%
45.6%	13.0%	9.1%	4.5%	3.0%	3.3%	5.2%	15.0%	1.3%	100.0%
43.9%	11.5%	8.8%	5.4%	2.8%	4.8%	5.9%	15.4%	1.4%	100.0%
41.7%	12.8%	9.4%	4.1%	4.5%	3.6%	6.2%	16.4%	1.5%	100.0%
47.3%	11.3%	8.6%	4.9%	2.2%	3.3%	4.9%	16.2%	1.4%	100.0%
n/a	n/a	n/a	n/a	n/a	n/a	n/a	n/a	n/a	n/a
37.7%	14.8%	9.0%	5.6%	4.1%	4.5%	6.6%	15.5%	2.1%	100.0%
n/a	n/a	n/a	n/a	n/a	n/a	n/a	n/a	n/a	n/a
n/a	n/a	n/a	n/a	n/a	n/a	n/a	n/a	n/a	n/a
n/a	n/a	n/a	n/a	n/a	n/a	n/a	n/a	n/a	n/a
n/a	n/a	n/a	n/a	n/a	n/a	n/a	n/a	n/a	n/a
n/a	n/a	n/a	n/a	n/a	n/a	n/a	n/a	n/a	n/a
37.7%	14.8%	9.0%	5.6%	4.1%	4.5%	6.6%	15.5%	2.1%	100.0%
38.3%	14.3%	8.9%	5.4%	4.1%	4.6%	6.8%	15.6%	2.1%	100.0%
37.2%	15.3%	9.1%	5.8%	4.1%	4.5%	6.5%	15.4%	2.1%	100.0%
42.7%	12.9%	8.7%	3.9%	4.0%	3.5%	5.9%	16.8%	1.7%	100.0%
40.3%	12.7%	8.4%	6.7%	3.6%	4.1%	6.4%	16.0%	1.7%	100.0%
38.5%	13.3%	8.8%	8.3%	3.2%	4.3%	6.7%	15.2%	1.7%	100.0%
35.8%	14.5%	8.8%	6.1%	4.1%	4.8%	7.0%	16.3%	2.5%	100.0%
35.9%	15.0%	9.0%	5.5%	4.5%	5.0%	7.1%	15.5%	2.4%	100.0%
34.1%	23.7%	11.0%	2.6%	4.7%	4.6%	5.1%	11.6%	2.5%	100.0%

TABLE A4.20:   PERCEPTIONS OF WELFARE CHANGES DURING LAST 5 YEARS HOUSEHOLD QUESTIONNAIRE
(Percentage of Total Households and Standard Deviation)

	Worse	Same	Better
Total Population	21.3 (0.9)	47.6 (1.1)	31.0 (0.9)
Regions			
Metropolitan	28.8 (2.6)	34.9 (2.9)	36.3 (2.3)
North	16.5 (2.8)	58.2 (2.8)	25.3 (2.7)
North East	23.9 (3.0)	47.0 (2.1)	29.1 (3.0)
South East	23.0 (2.1)	51.6 (2.2)	25.4 (2.1)
Central	22.8 (1.6)	48.1 (2.0)	29.1 (1.8)
North West	11.7 (1.3)	55.7 (2.1)	32.5 (1.8)
South West	17.2 (1.4)	52.2 (2.3)	30.6 (2.2)
Petén	23.1 (3.3)	48.8 (2.1)	28.2 (3.1)
Rural/Urban Area			
Rural	17.3 (0.9)	55.6 (1.3)	27.1 (1.2)
Urban	26.6 (1.6)	37.1 (1.6)	36.2 (1.4)
Household Head			
Male	20.1 (1.0)	48.5 (1.2)	31.4 (1.0)
Female	26.8 (1.7)	43.6 (2.0)	29.7 (1.8)
Poverty level			
Non-Poor	23.6 (1.3)	39.5 (1.4)	36.8 (1.3)
Poor	18.6 (1.1)	57.2 (1.4)	24.2 (1.2)
Extremely Poor	16.2 (2.0)	65.9 (2.4)	17.8 (1.8)
Consumption Quintile			
First	16.9 (1.8)	64.6 (2.1)	18.5 (1.6)
Second	16.4 (1.5)	58.4 (1.9)	25.1 (1.7)
Third	23.3 (1.8)	48.0 (2.2)	28.6 (1.8)
Fourth	21.6 (1.6)	44.6 (2.2)	33.7 (1.9)
Fifth	25.0 (1.7)	34.5 (1.5)	40.5 (1.7)
Ethnic Group			
Indigenous	15.3 (1.6)	55.4 (1.6)	29.2 (1.3)
K'iqche	18.3 (2.0)	48.3 (3.2)	33.3 (2.7)
Q'eqchi	12.6 (2.7)	56.8 (3.9)	30.7 (4.3)
Kaqchiquel	21.0 (3.6)	54.3 (3.7)	24.6 (2.3)
Mam	10.2 (2.2)	62.8 (3.6)	27.0 (3.2)
Non-Indigenous	25.1 (1.1)	42.6 (1.3)	32.3 (1.3)

Note: Numbers may not sum to total because of rounding.

Source: World Bank calculations using ENCOVI 2000, Instituto Nacional de Estadística—Guatemala.

TABLE A4.21: PERCEPTIONS OF WELFARE CHANGES DURING LAST 5 YEARS
COMMUNITY QUESTIONNAIRE
(Percentage of Total Communitiesa)

	Household Welfare			Community Welfare		
	Worse	Same	Better	Worse	Same	Better
Total Communities	19.8	45.3	34.9	9.6	39.2	51.1
Regions						
Metropolitan	20.0	28.9	51.1	6.8	25.0	68.2
North	14.3	58.7	27.0	9.5	39.7	50.8
North East	20.3	37.5	42.5	12.5	45.0	42.5
South East	17.6	47.1	35.3	9.8	39.2	51.0
Central	26.2	43.7	30.0	13.7	45.0	41.2
South West	22.4	43.4	34.2	16.2	32.4	51.3
North West	16.7	48.9	34.4	2.2	42.9	54.9
Petén	20.6	47.1	32.3	5.9	41.2	52.9
Rural/Urban Area						
Rural	22.6	46.4	30.1	9.3	39.7	50.9
Urban	14.1	43.0	42.9	10.3	38.1	51.6
Main Language						
K'iqche	16.0	40.0	44.0	0.0	28.0	72.0
Q'eqchi	9.8	68.3	21.9	4.9	31.7	63.4
Kaqchiquel	15.1	42.4	42.4	6.1	39.4	54.5
Mam	18.5	70.4	11.1	7.7	46.1	46.1
Spanish	22.2	40.1	37.7	12.3	40.3	47.3

Note: Numbers may not sum to total because of rounding.

a. The sample for the ENCOVI(2000) was based on dwellings, not communities. Results reported at the community level are not representative of communities in Guatemala.

Source: World Bank calculations using ENCOVI 2000, Instituto Nacional de Estadística—Guatemala.

TABLE A4.22: PERCEPTIONS CAUSES OF WELFARE CHANGE, CAUSES OF POVERTY AND COMMUNITY PROBLEMS HOUSEHOLD QUESTIONNAIRE
(Percentage of Total Households and Standard Deviation)

	Causes Welfare Change	Causes Poverty	Community Problems
Unemployment	21.0 (0.9)	39.2 (0.9)	2.6 (0.2)
Public services[a]	2.9 (0.2)	1.4 (0.1)	49.7 (1.3)
Lower income/salary/profits	23.8 (0.8)	6.2 (0.4)	0.3 (0.1)
Health[b]	2.1 (0.4)	0.3 (0.0)	11.2 (0.8)
Education[c]	0.2 (0.0)	6.6 (0.5)	4.6 (0.5)
Violence/alcoholism/family problems	1.6 (0.3)	2.4 (0.2)	8.2 (0.9)
Corruption/bad government	0.5 (0.1)	10.3 (0.6)	0.3 (0.1)
High Prices	20.1 (0.8)	10.0 (0.6)	0.5 (0.2)
Lack of land/land titling/loss yields	5.9 (0.5)	5.0 (0.4)	1.6 (0.3)
Lack credits/high interest rates	0.3 (0.0)	0.3 (0.1)	0.5 (0.1)
Lack technical assistance/training	0.2 (0.0)	0.8 (0.1)	0.6 (0.1)
Other	21.1 (1.0)	17.1 (0.8)	19.6 (0.9)

Note: Numbers may not sum to total because of rounding.
a. Public services include: water, electricity, transportation, communication services, garbage collection and housing
b. Health includes: poor health and insufficient quantity of clinics and hospitals.
c. Education includes: Insufficient quantity of schools and teachers.
Source: World Bank calculations using ENCOVI 2000, Instituto Nacional de Estadística—Guatemala.

TABLE A4.23: PERCEPTIONS OF CAUSES OF WELFARE CHANGE COMMUNITY QUESTIONNAIRE
(Percentage of Total Communities[a])

	Household Welfare			Community Welfare		
	Better	Same	Worst	Better	Same	Worst
Labor market	23.5	33.5	27.6	6.8	12.9	12.2
Public services[a]	11.8	5.3	3.4	53.4	25.3	24.4
Sources of income	32.0	22.8	20.7	2.3	9.0	14.6
Health[b]	1.3	0.0	1.1	1.4	4.5	7.3
Education[c]	3.9	3.4	2.3	13.1	6.2	2.4
Violence/alcoholism/family problems	0.6	0.0	0.0	2.7	1.1	9.8
Government performance	1.3	4.8	0.0	0.4	0.0	2.4
Prices	0.0	11.2	23.0	0.0	0.0	0.0
Land/land titling/loss yields	0.0	4.4	1.1	2.7	6.7	2.4
Credits/Interest rates	0.6	0.0	0.0	0.4	0.0	0.0
Technical assistance/training	0.0	0.5	0.0	0.0	0.0	0.0
Community Cohesion	7.2	0.0	0.0	0.0	14.6	0.0
Other	17.6	14.1	13.8	16.7	19.7	24.4

Note: Numbers may not sum to total because of rounding.
a. The sample for the ENCOVI(2000) was based on dwellings, not communities. Results reported at the community level are not representative of communities in Guatemala.
Source: World Bank calculations using ENCOVI 2000, Instituto Nacional de Estadística—Guatemala.

TABLE A4.24: PERCEPTIONS OF CAUSES OF WELFARE CHANGE–HOUSEHOLD QUESTIONNAIRE DIVIDED BY REGIONS
(Percentage of Total Households and Standard Deviation)

	Causes Welfare Change							
	Metropolitan	North	Northeast	Southeast	Central	Southwest	Northwest	Petén
Unemployment	13.0 (2.0)	22.4 (2.3)	25.7 (3.7)	18.5 (2.0)	18.9 (1.7)	25.1 (2.0)	30.6 (2.3)	17.8 (2.8)
Public services[a]	1.4 (0.5)	3.1 (0.8)	3.8 (1.1)	3.3 (0.8)	1.4 (0.4)	3.0 (0.7)	6.6 (1.2)	3.3 (0.9)
Lower income/salary/profits	26.0 (2.2)	27.4 (3.3)	19.9 (3.2)	21.5 (2.2)	25.6 (1.7)	22.6 (1.8)	22.8 (1.8)	21.9 (2.4)
Health[b]	0.6 (0.4)	1.4 (0.6)	1.0 (0.4)	3.2 (1.0)	1.8 (0.5)	4.2 (1.7)	2.2 (0.1)	2.0 (0.8)
Education[c]	0.0 (0.0)	0.6 (0.4)	0.1 (0.1)	0.7 (0.4)	0.2 (0.1)	0.3 (0.2)	0.2 (0.1)	0.3 (0.2)
Violence/alcoholism/family problems	1.7 (1.1)	1.4 (0.5)	2.3 (1.1)	1.1 (0.4)	1.7 (0.5)	1.5 (0.4)	1.3 (0.4)	1.5 (0.6)
Corruption/bad government	0.5 (0.2)	0.0 (0.0)	0.7 (0.6)	1.3 (0.6)	0.5 (0.3)	0.3 (0.2)	0.4 (0.2)	0.7 (0.4)
High Prices	20.9 (2.0)	22.1 (2.6)	21.0 (3.1)	19.2 (2.5)	26.5 (1.9)	20.3 (1.8)	9.8 (1.5)	19.0 (2.4)
Lack of land/land titling/loss yields	0.0 (0.0)	10.5 (2.3)	7.8 (2.3)	12.1 (2.4)	4.1 (0.9)	5.9 (1.4)	8.5 (1.5)	16.0 (2.9)
Lack credits/high interest rates	0.0 (0.0)	0.0 (0.0)	0.0 (0.0)	0.8 (0.4)	0.8 (0.3)	0.4 (0.3)	0.3 (0.3)	0.0 (0.0)
Lack technical assistance/training	0.0 (0.0)	0.0 (0.0)	0.0 (0.0)	0.2 (0.2)	0.0 (0.0)	0.6 (0.3)	0.3 (0.2)	0.1 (0.1)
Other	35.7 (2.7)	10.5 (1.7)	17.6 (2.8)	17.7 (2.5)	18.4 (1.7)	15.9 (1.9)	16.8 (1.8)	17.2 (2.6)

Note: Numbers may not sum to total because of rounding.
a. Public services include: water, electricity, transportation, communication services, garbage collection and housing
b. Health includes: poor health and insufficient quantity of clinics and hospitals.
c. Education includes: Insufficient quantity of schools and teachers.

Source: World Bank calculations using ENCOVI 2000, Instituto Nacional de Estadística—Guatemala.

TABLE A4.25: PERCEPTIONS OF CAUSES OF POVERTY CHANGE–HOUSEHOLD QUESTIONNAIRE DIVIDED BY REGIONS
(Percentage of Total Households and Standard Deviation)

	Causes Welfare Change							
	Metropolitan	North	Northeast	Southeast	Central	Southwest	Northwest	Petén
Unemployment	38.8 (2.4)	31.2 (3.0)	48.0 (4.2)	43.7 (2.6)	34.7 (1.9)	40.3 (2.0)	38.2 (2.2)	34.7 (3.1)
Public services[a]	0.2 (0.2)	1.8 (0.6)	0.8 (0.4)	1.7 (0.7)	1.7 (0.4)	2.0 (0.5)	2.9 (0.6)	0.7 (0.4)
Lower income/salary/profits	4.6 (1.0)	8.2 (1.3)	3.7 (1.0)	3.9 (1.2)	8.7 (0.9)	7.8 (0.9)	6.9 (1.0)	5.3 (1.2)
Health[b]	0.2 (0.1)	0.2 (0.2)	1.0 (0.6)	0.5 (0.2)	0.1 (0.0)	0.2 (0.1)	0.3 (0.2)	0.9 (0.6)
Education[c]	6.4 (1.1)	9.6 (2.4)	6.7 (2.8)	5.4 (1.3)	6.1 (0.9)	6.4 (1.0)	6.8 (1.4)	9.2 (1.9)
Violence/alcoholism/family problems	1.8 (0.5)	3.1 (0.8)	2.7 (1.0)	3.5 (0.7)	2.1 (0.5)	2.4 (0.5)	2.6 (0.6)	1.7 (0.5)
Corruption/bad government	11.8 (1.9)	8.0 (1.5)	11.1 (2.0)	10.8 (1.7)	13.1 (1.1)	8.1 (1.0)	9.4 (1.1)	12.3 (2.1)
High Prices	10.0 (1.6)	16.8 (2.6)	9.0 (1.7)	10.1 (1.4)	10.8 (1.0)	9.6 (1.6)	6.0 (1.1)	12.1 (1.5)
Lack of land/land titling/loss yields	0.6 (0.3)	9.8 (2.1)	1.8 (0.6)	7.2 (1.6)	4.2 (0.7)	6.8 (1.2)	9.0 (1.3)	6.1 (1.6)
Lack credits/high interest rates	0.0 (0.0)	0.4 (0.3)	1.0 (0.6)	0.3 (0.2)	0.3 (0.2)	0.5 (0.4)	0.4 (0.2)	0.0 (0.0)
Lack technical assistance/training	0.0 (0.0)	0.9 (0.4)	1.0 (0.9)	1.7 (0.8)	1.6 (0.6)	1.1 (0.3)	1.0 (0.3)	0.4 (0.3)
Other	25.7 (2.3)	9.8 (1.4)	13.0 (2.4)	11.3 (1.2)	16.6 (1.4)	14.7 (1.6)	16.4 (1.7)	16.3 (1.6)

Note: Numbers may not sum to total because of rounding.
a. Public services include: water, electricity, transportation, communication services, garbage collection and housing
b. Health includes: poor health and insufficient quantity of clinics and hospitals.
c. Education includes: Insufficient quantity of schools and teachers.

Source: World Bank calculations using ENCOVI 2000, Instituto Nacional de Estadística—Guatemala.

TABLE A4.26: PERCEPTIONS OF COMMUNITY PROBLEMS—HOUSEHOLD QUESTIONNAIRE DIVIDED BY REGIONS
(Percentage of Total Households and Standard Deviation)

	Causes Welfare Change							
	Metropolitan	North	Northeast	Southeast	Central	Southwest	Northwest	Petén
Unemployment	1.9 (0.7)	2.6 (0.7)	6.2 (1.7)	2.4 (0.7)	1.9 (0.5)	2.6 (0.6)	2.1 (0.6)	2.8 (0.9)
Public services[a]	35.8 (3.1)	57.6 (3.8)	45.5 (5.4)	49.4 (3.6)	50.2 (2.3)	57.2 (2.6)	60.0 (2.4)	59.5 (3.7)
Lower income/salary/profits	0.0 (0.0)	0.0 (0.0)	0.0 (0.0)	0.7 (0.3)	1.1 (0.3)	0.6 (0.2)	0.2 (0.1)	0.5 (0.3)
Health[b]	2.4 (0.6)	11.2 (2.8)	18.5 (5.7)	15.7 (2.2)	10.7 (1.5)	13.4 (1.9)	17.1 (2.0)	12.0 (2.1)
Education[c]	3.3 (1.0)	4.1 (1.2)	3.4 (1.0)	4.2 (1.4)	5.2 (0.8)	7.5 (2.4)	2.4 (0.5)	3.3 (1.2)
Violence/alcoholism/family problems	26.3 (3.1)	0.9 (0.4)	1.2 (0.5)	2.0 (0.6)	6.6 (1.3)	1.4 (0.4)	1.1 (0.3)	1.8 (0.6)
Corruption/bad government	0.7 (0.3)	0.0 (0.0)	0.0 (0.0)	0.3 (0.2)	0.1 (0.1)	0.4 (0.2)	0.4 (0.2)	0.0 (0.0)
High Prices	0.5 (0.3)	0.3 (0.2)	0.0 (0.0)	1.4 (0.7)	1.1 (0.3)	0.2 (0.1)	0.5 (0.4)	0.2 (0.1)
Lack of land/land titling/loss yields	1.5 (1.0)	3.8 (1.0)	1.1 (0.5)	2.1 (0.7)	1.6 (0.4)	1.2 (0.4)	1.2 (0.4)	1.4 (0.7)
Lack credits/high interest rates	0.0 (0.0)	0.3 (0.2)	1.5 (0.7)	1.9 (0.7)	0.5 (0.2)	0.3 (0.2)	0.3 (0.2)	1.0 (0.7)
Lack technical assistance/training	0.0 (0.0)	0.9 (0.4)	0.2 (0.2)	1.4 (0.8)	0.5 (0.2)	1.0 (0.4)	0.6 (0.2)	0.2 (0.2)
Other	27.3 (2.8)	18.0 (2.6)	22.2 (4.7)	18.4 (2.4)	20.3 (1.6)	14.1 (1.7)	14.2 (1.4)	17.2 (2.7)

Note: Numbers may not sum to total because of rounding.
a. Public services include: water, electricity, transportation, communication services, garbage collection and housing
b. Health includes: poor health and insufficient quantity of clinics and hospitals.
c. Education includes: Insufficient quantity of schools and teachers.

Source: World Bank calculations using ENCOVI 2000, Instituto Nacional de Estadística—Guatemala.

TABLE A4.27: PERCEPTIONS OF CAUSES OF WELFARE CHANGE, CAUSES OF POVERTY AND COMMUNITY PROBLEMS—HOUSEHOLD QUESTIONNAIRE DIVIDED BY RURAL AND URBAN AREAS
(Percentage of Total Households and Standard Deviation)

	Causes of welfare change		Causes of poverty		Community problems	
	Rural	Urban	Rural	Urban	Rural	Urban
Unemployment	23.1 (1.2)	18.0 (1.4)	37.2 (1.3)	41.9 (1.4)	2.2 (0.4)	3.0 (0.4)
Public services[a]	3.5 (0.4)	2.2 (0.4)	1.9 (0.3)	0.8 (0.2)	55.4 (1.7)	42.2 (1.8)
Lower income/salary/profits	22.6 (1.1)	25.5 (1.4)	7.3 (0.6)	5.0 (0.6)	0.5 (0.1)	0.2 (0.0)
Health[b]	2.7 (0.8)	1.4 (0.3)	0.4 (0.1)	0.2 (0.0)	16.1 (1.4)	4.8 (0.6)
Education[c]	0.3 (0.1)	0.0 (0.0)	6.4 (0.8)	7.0 (0.7)	5.1 (0.8)	4.0 (0.6)
Violence/alcoholism/family problems	1.4 (0.3)	1.8 (0.7)	2.3 (0.3)	2.2 (0.3)	0.7 (0.2)	18.0 (1.8)
Corruption/bad government	0.4 (0.1)	0.6 (0.2)	9.3 (0.7)	11.7 (1.1)	0.2 (0.0)	0.6 (0.2)
High Prices	18.7 (1.1)	22.0 (1.2)	11.6 (0.9)	8.0 (0.8)	0.3 (0.1)	0.8 (0.2)
Lack of land/land titling/loss yields	9.1 (0.9)	1.4 (0.4)	7.4 (0.7)	1.8 (0.3)	1.8 (0.3)	1.4 (0.6)
Lack credits/high interest rates	0.4 (0.1)	0.1 (0.0)	0.5 (0.2)	0.0 (0.0)	0.8 (0.2)	0.0 (0.0)
Lack technical assistance/training	0.4 (0.1)	0.0 (0.0)	1.1 (0.2)	0.6 (0.2)	0.8 (0.2)	0.3 (0.1)
Other	17.1 (1.1)	26.8 (1.8)	14.2 (0.9)	20.9 (1.4)	15.9 (1.2)	24.4 (1.6)

Note: Numbers may not sum to total because of rounding.
a. Public services include: water, electricity, transportation, communication services, garbage collection and housing
b. Health includes: poor health and insufficient quantity of clinics and hospitals.
c. Education includes: Insufficient quantity of schools and teachers.

Source: World Bank calculations using ENCOVI 2000, Instituto Nacional de Estadística—Guatemala.

TABLE A4.28: PERCEPTIONS OF CAUSES OF WELFARE CHANGE, CAUSES OF POVERTY AND COMMUNITY PROBLEMS— COMMUNITY QUESTIONNAIRE DIVIDED BY GENDER OF HOUSEHOLD HEAD
(Percentage of Total Households and Standard Deviation)

	Causes of welfare change		Causes of poverty		Community problems	
	Male	Female	Male	Female	Male	Female
Unemployment	21.8 (1.0)	17.7 (1.7)	38.3 (1.0)	43.4 (1.9)	2.2 (0.3)	4.2 (0.9)
Public services[a]	3.1 (0.3)	2.4 (0.6)	1.4 (0.2)	1.4 (0.4)	50.8 (1.3)	44.7 (2.4)
Lower income/salary/profits	24.5 (1.0)	20.9 (1.8)	6.1 (0.4)	6.8 (1.2)	0.4 (0.0)	0.2 (0.1)
Health[b]	2.2 (0.6)	2.0 (0.6)	0.3 (0.0)	0.6 (0.3)	11.6 (0.9)	9.5 (1.1)
Education[c]	0.2 (0.0)	0.4 (0.2)	6.6 (0.6)	6.7 (1.0)	5.0 (0.6)	3.0 (0.8)
Violence/alcoholism/family problems	0.7 (0.1)	5.4 (1.5)	2.3 (0.2)	2.8 (0.6)	7.7 (1.0)	10.8 (2.3)
Corruption/bad government	0.5 (0.1)	0.5 (0.2)	11.1 (0.7)	6.8 (0.8)	0.2 (0.0)	1.0 (0.4)
High Prices	19.5 (0.1)	22.6 (1.9)	10.1 (0.7)	9.4 (1.2)	0.6 (0.1)	0.3 (0.1)
Lack of land/land titling/loss yields	6.6 (0.6)	2.8 (0.6)	5.4 (0.5)	3.0 (0.7)	1.6 (0.3)	1.6 (0.7)
Lack credits/high interest rates	0.3 (0.1)	0.2 (0.1)	0.4 (0.1)	0.0 (0.0)	0.6 (0.1)	0.2 (0.1)
Lack technical assistance/training	0.2 (0.0)	0.1 (0.1)	0.9 (0.2)	0.7 (0.3)	0.7 (0.1)	0.2 (0.2)
Other	20.2 (1.0)	25.1 (2.0)	16.8 (0.8)	18.4 (1.7)	18.5 (0.9)	24.3 (2.2)

Note: Numbers may not sum to total because of rounding.
a. Public services include: water, electricity, transportation, communication services, garbage collection and housing
b. Health includes: poor health and insufficient quantity of clinics and hospitals.
c. Education includes: Insufficient quantity of schools and teachers.

Source: World Bank calculations using ENCOVI 2000, Instituto Nacional de Estadística—Guatemala.

TABLE A4.29: PERCEPTIONS OF CAUSES OF WELFARE CHANGE, CAUSES OF POVERTY AND PROBLEMS IN COMMUNITY—HOUSEHOLD QUESTIONNAIRE DIVIDED BY POVERTY LEVEL
(Percentage of Total Households and Standard Deviation)

	Causes of welfare change			Causes of poverty			Community problems		
	Non-Poor	Poor	Ext. Poor	Non-Poor	Poor	Ext. Poor	Non-Poor	Poor	Ext. Poor
Unemployment	18.5 (1.3)	23.6 (1.2)	24.1 (2.1)	42.0 (1.3)	36.0 (1.4)	32.5 (2.5)	3.1 (0.4)	1.9 (0.3)	2.3 (0.9)
Public services[a]	2.1 (0.3)	3.8 (0.5)	5.1 (0.9)	0.8 (0.2)	2.1 (0.3)	1.2 (0.4)	45.7 (1.6)	54.5 (1.7)	58.0 (2.8)
Lower income/salary/profits	24.6 (1.2)	23.0 (1.2)	22.8 (2.1)	5.1 (0.5)	7.7 (0.7)	7.0 (1.0)	0.3 (0.0)	0.6 (0.1)	0.6 (0.3)
Health[b]	1.9 (0.7)	2.4 (0.4)	2.6 (1.0)	0.4 (0.1)	0.3 (0.0)	0.7 (0.3)	7.7 (0.7)	15.3 (1.3)	16.7 (2.1)
Education[c]	0.0 (0.0)	0.5 (0.1)	0.7 (0.4)	7.0 (0.7)	6.2 (0.7)	7.0 (1.2)	3.8 (0.5)	5.6 (1.0)	5.6 (1.3)
Violence/alcoholism/family problems	1.8 (0.6)	1.4 (0.3)	1.7 (0.6)	2.2 (0.3)	2.6 (0.3)	1.4 (0.4)	13.9 (1.5)	1.6 (0.5)	0.5 (0.3)
Corruption/bad government	0.6 (0.2)	0.4 (0.1)	0.1 (0.1)	11.1 (0.9)	9.4 (0.7)	8.6 (1.2)	0.4 (0.2)	0.3 (0.1)	0.4 (0.1)
High Prices	22.5 (1.2)	17.6 (1.1)	14.0 (1.7)	9.2 (0.8)	10.9 (0.9)	10.6 (1.7)	0.7 (0.2)	0.3 (0.0)	0.6 (0.1)
Lack of land/land titling/loss yields	2.6 (0.4)	9.3 (0.9)	14.5 (2.1)	2.3 (0.3)	8.1 (0.8)	13.5 (1.9)	0.9 (0.3)	2.4 (0.4)	3.1 (0.7)
Lack credits/high interest rates	0.2 (0.1)	0.4 (0.1)	0.4 (0.3)	0.2 (0.0)	0.5 (0.2)	1.2 (0.6)	0.3 (0.1)	0.8 (0.2)	0.4 (0.2)
Lack technical assistance/training	0.0 (0.0)	0.4 (0.2)	0.0 (0.0)	0.6 (0.1)	1.2 (0.3)	1.9 (0.6)	0.3 (0.1)	0.9 (0.2)	0.6 (0.3)
Other	25.0 (1.4)	17.1 (1.3)	13.7 (1.8)	19.0 (1.2)	14.9 (1.0)	14.1 (1.9)	22.7 (1.4)	15.9 (1.1)	12.2 (1.6)

Note: Numbers may not sum to total because of rounding.
a. Public services include: water, electricity, transportation, communication services, garbage collection and housing
b. Health includes: poor health and insufficient quantity of clinics and hospitals.
c. Education includes: Insufficient quantity of schools and teachers.

Source: World Bank calculations using ENCOVI 2000, Instituto Nacional de Estadística—Guatemala.

TABLE A4.30: PERCEPTIONS OF CAUSES OF WELFARE CHANGE—HOUSEHOLD QUESTIONNAIRE DIVIDED BY CONSUMPTION QUINTILE
(Percentage of Total Households and Standard Deviation)

	First	Second	Third	Fourth	Fifth
Unemployment	23.3 (1.8)	24.5 (1.8)	22.1 (1.7)	21.2 (1.7)	16.1 (0.9)
Public services[a]	4.9 (0.7)	3.7 (0.6)	2.7 (0.5)	2.0 (0.5)	2.1 (0.3)
Lower income/salary/profits	23.3 (1.9)	24.0 (1.9)	21.7 (2.1)	27.2 (1.7)	22.7 (1.8)
Health[b]	2.5 (0.8)	2.3 (0.5)	2.5 (0.8)	2.6 (1.1)	1.2 (0.3)
Education[c]	0.8 (0.3)	0.3 (0.2)	0.2 (0.1)	0.0 (0.0)	0.0 (0.0)
Violence/alcoholism/family problems	1.9 (0.6)	0.9 (0.4)	1.5 (0.5)	2.0 (1.3)	1.6 (0.4)
Corruption/bad government	0.2 (0.1)	0.5 (0.3)	0.7 (0.3)	0.3 (0.2)	0.7 (0.3)
High Prices	15.4 (1.6)	18.8 (1.7)	19.2 (1.9)	21.7 (1.9)	23.3 (1.7)
Lack of land/land titling/loss yields	14.1 (1.9)	8.2 (1.2)	5.6 (1.0)	3.4 (0.7)	1.5 (0.4)
Lack credits/high interest rates	0.4 (0.2)	0.6 (0.4)	0.0 (0.0)	0.3 (0.2)	0.1 (0.1)
Lack technical assistance/training	0.1 (0.1)	0.7 (0.4)	0.4 (0.2)	0.0 (0.0)	0.0 (0.0)
Other	12.7 (1.6)	15.3 (1.5)	23.3 (2.3)	19.2 (1.8)	30.5 (1.8)

Note: Numbers may not sum to total because of rounding.
a. Public services include: water, electricity, transportation, communication services, garbage collection and housing
b. Health includes: poor health and insufficient quantity of clinics and hospitals.
c. Education includes: Insufficient quantity of schools and teachers.

Source: World Bank calculations using ENCOVI 2000, Instituto Nacional de Estadística—Guatemala.

TABLE A4.31: PERCEPTIONS OF CAUSES OF POVERTY—HOUSEHOLD QUESTIONNAIRE DIVIDED BY CONSUMPTION QUINTILE
(Percentage of Total Households and Standard Deviation)

	First	Second	Third	Fourth	Fifth
Unemployment	33.7 (2.3)	36.5 (2.0)	37.2 (2.1)	43.2 (2.3)	41.8 (1.6)
Public services[a]	1.5 (0.4)	2.5 (0.5)	2.0 (0.5)	0.9 (0.2)	0.6 (0.2)
Lower income/salary/profits	6.6 (0.9)	7.8 (1.0)	8.6 (1.3)	5.4 (0.8)	4.3 (0.6)
Health[b]	0.6 (0.3)	0.1 (0.0)	0.1 (0.0)	0.4 (0.2)	0.4 (0.1)
Education[c]	6.9 (1.1)	6.1 (0.9)	5.2 (0.8)	4.6 (0.7)	9.5 (1.0)
Violence/alcoholism/family problems	1.5 (0.4)	2.5 (0.5)	3.5 (0.7)	2.5 (0.5)	2.0 (0.4)
Corruption/bad government	8.7 (1.1)	9.6 (1.0)	11.7 (1.4)	9.7 (1.2)	11.2 (1.1)
High Prices	10.4 (1.4)	11.1 (1.3)	11.1 (1.4)	13.0 (1.4)	6.0 (0.7)
Lack of land/land titling/loss yields	13.1 (1.6)	6.6 (0.9)	5.0 (0.7)	2.6 (0.5)	1.7 (0.4)
Lack credits/high interest rates	1.0 (0.5)	0.6 (0.3)	0.2 (0.1)	0.2 (0.1)	0.2 (0.0)
Lack technical assistance/training	2.0 (0.5)	1.3 (0.4)	0.3 (0.1)	0.4 (0.2)	0.7 (0.2)
Other	13.9 (1.7)	15.2 (1.3)	15.0 (1.5)	16.7 (1.6)	21.6 (1.6)

Note: Numbers may not sum to total because of rounding.
a. Public services include: water, electricity, transportation, communication services, garbage collection and housing
b. Health includes: poor health and insufficient quantity of clinics and hospitals.
c. Education includes: Insufficient quantity of schools and teachers.

Source: World Bank calculations using ENCOVI 2000, Instituto Nacional de Estadística—Guatemala.

TABLE A4.32: PERCEPTIONS OF COMMUNITY PROBLEMS—HOUSEHOLD QUESTIONNAIRE DIVIDED BY CONSUMPTION QUINTILE
(Percentage of Total Households and Standard Deviation)

	First	Second	Third	Fourth	Fifth
Unemployment	2.0 (0.7)	2.0 (0.4)	2.4 (0.5)	3.0 (0.6)	3.0 (0.6)
Public services[a]	59.6 (2.5)	54.5 (2.2)	50.5 (2.2)	49.5 (2.2)	41.4 (2.0)
Lower income/salary/profits	1.1 (0.4)	0.2 (0.1)	0.4 (0.2)	0.1 (0.0)	0.3 (0.1)
Health[b]	15.6 (1.8)	15.3 (1.7)	15.3 (1.6)	9.9 (1.2)	4.8 (0.7)
Education[c]	4.8 (1.1)	6.2 (1.3)	5.0 (1.3)	4.5 (7.7)	3.3 (0.5)
Violence/alcoholism/family problems	0.6 (0.3)	0.7 (0.2)	3.1 (1.1)	10.2 (2.1)	18.5 (2.1)
Corruption/bad government	0.0 (0.0)	0.2 (0.1)	0.5 (0.3)	0.3 (0.2)	0.5 (0.3)
High Prices	0.0 (0.0)	0.4 (0.1)	0.4 (0.2)	0.8 (0.3)	0.7 (0.2)
Lack of land/land titling/loss yields	2.8 (0.6)	1.5 (0.4)	3.2 (1.4)	0.6 (0.2)	0.7 (0.4)
Lack credits/high interest rates	0.4 (0.2)	1.0 (0.4)	0.7 (0.3)	0.5 (0.3)	0.1 (0.0)
Lack technical assistance/training	0.8 (0.3)	1.2 (0.4)	0.5 (0.2)	0.2 (0.1)	0.4 (0.2)
Other	12.1 (1.4)	16.7 (1.9)	17.8 (1.5)	20.2 (1.9)	25.8 (1.7)

Note: Numbers may not sum to total because of rounding.
a. Public services include: water, electricity, transportation, communication services, garbage collection and housing
b. Health includes: poor health and insufficient quantity of clinics and hospitals.
c. Education includes: Insufficient quantity of schools and teachers.

Source: World Bank calculations using ENCOVI 2000, Instituto Nacional de Estadística—Guatemala.

TABLE A4.33:   PERCEPTIONS OF CAUSES OF WELFARE CHANGE—HOUSEHOLD QUESTIONNAIRE DIVIDED BY ETHNICITY
(Percentage of Total Households and Standard Deviation)

	Indigenous	K'iche	Q'eqchi	Kaqchiquel	Mam	Non-Indigenous
Unemployment	25.5 (1.4)	32.6 (3.6)	18.3 (2.2)	20.3 (2.8)	24.7 (3.3)	18.2 (1.1)
Public services[a]	3.5 (0.5)	3.2 (1.0)	3.9 (1.2)	0.9 (0.4)	5.5 (1.3)	2.6 (0.3)
Lower income/salary/profits	24.8 (1.7)	24.4 (3.0)	29.1 (4.0)	29.8 (3.2)	18.7 (3.3)	23.1 (1.2)
Health[b]	1.7 (0.4)	2.3 (1.1)	0.9 (0.5)	1.1 (0.5)	2.2 (1.1)	2.5 (0.7)
Education[c]	0.3 (0.1)	0.0 (0.0)	0.8 (0.5)	0.3 (0.2)	0.4 (0.4)	0.2 (0.0)
Violence/alcoholism/family problems	1.5 (0.4)	1.6 (0.6)	2.4 (1.6)	1.0 (0.5)	1.7 (1.0)	1.6 (0.5)
Corruption/bad government	0.3 (0.1)	0.5 (0.4)	0.0 (0.0)	0.1 (0.1)	0.1 (0.1)	0.7 (0.2)
High Prices	17.3 (1.3)	15.6 (2.6)	20.7 (3.0)	22.9 (3.8)	12.9 (2.3)	21.9 (0.1)
Lack of land/land titling/loss yields	8.3 (1.0)	3.4 (1.1)	14.4 (3.3)	3.5 (1.0)	16.0 (3.4)	4.4 (0.6)
Lack credits/high interest rates	0.3 (0.1)	0.0 (0.0)	0.0 (0.0)	0.6 (0.3)	0.0 (0.0)	0.3 (0.1)
Lack technical assistance/training	0.3 (0.2)	0.0 (0.0)	0.0 (0.0)	0.1 (0.1)	1.2 (0.8)	0.1 (0.0)
Other	16.0 (1.1)	16.4 (2.4)	8.8 (1.9)	19.3 (2.4)	16.6 (3.0)	24.3 (1.4)

Note: Numbers may not sum to total because of rounding.

a. Public services include: water, electricity, transportation, communication services, garbage collection and housing

b. Health includes: poor health and insufficient quantity of clinics and hospitals.

c. Education includes: Insufficient quantity of schools and teachers.

Source: World Bank calculations using ENCOVI 2000, Instituto Nacional de Estadística—Guatemala.

TABLE A4.34: PERCEPTIONS OF CAUSES OF POVERTY—HOUSEHOLD QUESTIONNAIRE DIVIDED BY ETHNICITY
(Percentage of Total Households and Standard Deviation)

	Indigenous	K'iche	Q'eqchi	Kaqchiquel	Mam	Non-Indigenous
Unemployment	33.1 (1.4)	39.9 (2.8)	25.8 (3.2)	27.6 (2.3)	32.9 (3.9)	43.1 (1.3)
Public services[a]	1.7 (0.3)	2.4 (0.7)	1.8 (0.7)	1.0 (0.3)	1.8 (0.7)	1.2 (0.2)
Lower income/salary/profits	7.2 (0.6)	6.3 (1.2)	6.1 (1.4)	8.3 (1.3)	7.3 (1.6)	5.7 (0.6)
Health[b]	0.3 (0.1)	0.2 (0.1)	0.2 (0.2)	0.0 (0.0)	0.8 (0.4)	0.3 (0.1)
Education[c]	7.6 (0.8)	6.4 (1.8)	12.1 (2.9)	6.0 (1.3)	6.3 (1.4)	6.1 (0.7)
Violence/alcoholism/family problems	2.5 (0.3)	3.8 (0.8)	1.5 (0.6)	2.5 (0.8)	1.7 (0.7)	2.3 (0.3)
Corruption/bad government	9.6 (1.0)	8.3 (1.6)	7.7 (1.8)	14.7 (3.2)	6.0 (1.5)	10.8 (0.8)
High Prices	10.6 (0.9)	9.1 (1.2)	15.2 (2.6)	13.1 (2.4)	7.0 (1.7)	9.6 (0.9)
Lack of land/land titling/loss yields	8.5 (0.9)	4.3 (1.4)	11.9 (2.5)	5.7 (1.1)	15.2 (2.7)	2.8 (0.4)
Lack credits/high interest rates	0.6 (0.2)	0.3 (0.2)	0.3 (0.3)	0.3 (0.2)	1.5 (0.8)	0.2 (0.0)
Lack technical assistance/training	1.1 (0.2)	0.6 (0.3)	1.0 (0.5)	1.5 (0.7)	1.4 (0.7)	0.7 (0.2)
Other	17.0 (1.2)	18.5 (2.5)	16.1 (3.5)	19.2 (2.3)	17.6 (3.2)	17.1 (1.1)

Note: Numbers may not sum to total because of rounding.
a. Public services include: water, electricity, transportation, communication services, garbage collection and housing
b. Health includes: poor health and insufficient quantity of clinics and hospitals.
c. Education includes: Insufficient quantity of schools and teachers.

Source: World Bank calculations using ENCOVI 2000, Instituto Nacional de Estadística—Guatemala.

TABLE A4.35: PERCEPTIONS OF COMMUNITY PROBLEMS—HOUSEHOLD QUESTIONNAIRE DIVIDED BY ETHNICITY
(Percentage of Total Households and Standard Deviation)

	Indigenous	K'iche	Q'eqchi	Kaqchiquel	Mam	Non-Indigenous
Unemployment	2.2 (0.4)	3.2 (1.0)	2.1 (0.8)	2.7 (1.1)	0.6 (0.4)	2.8 (0.4)
Public services[a]	54.8 (1.8)	52.3 (3.1)	53.7 (5.9)	53.6 (3.7)	55.6 (4.7)	46.5 (1.8)
Lower income/salary/profits	0.5 (0.2)	0.4 (0.3)	0.1 (0.1)	0.6 (0.3)	0.9 (0.6)	0.3 (0.0)
Health[b]	14.2 (1.4)	14.9 (2.0)	18.6 (6.1)	12.3 (2.4)	14.5 (3.4)	9.3 (1.0)
Education[c]	6.1 (1.1)	80 (1.8)	4.5 (1.4)	3.7 (0.8)	11.0 (5.0)	3.7 (0.5)
Violence/alcoholism/family problems	2.3 (0.4)	2.4 (0.7)	1.9 (0.9)	3.8 (1.2)	0.5 (0.4)	12.0 (1.4)
Corruption/bad government	0.3 (0.1)	0.7 (0.3)	0.0 (0.0)	0.0 (0.0)	0.6 (0.5)	0.4 (0.1)
High Prices	0.4 (0.1)	0.3 (0.2)	0.0 (0.0)	1.0 (0.4)	0.2 (0.2)	0.6 (0.2)
Lack of land/land titling/loss yields	2.1 (0.4)	1.7 (0.6)	6.3 (2.3)	1.2 (0.6)	0.3 (0.2)	1.3 (0.4)
Lack credits/high interest rates	0.4 (0.1)	0.0 (0.0)	0.4 (0.3)	0.6 (0.3)	0.8 (0.5)	0.6 (0.2)
Lack technical assistance/training	0.7 (0.2)	0.0 (0.0)	0.8 (0.4)	1.2 (0.4)	0.5 (0.3)	0.5 (0.2)
Other	15.9 (1.2)	15.8 (2.3)	11.5 (2.3)	19.1 (2.3)	14.4 (3.3)	21.8 (1.4)

Note: Numbers may not sum to total because of rounding.

a. Public services include: water, electricity, transportation, communication services, garbage collection and housing

b. Health includes: poor health and insufficient quantity of clinics and hospitals.

c. Education includes: Insufficient quantity of schools and teachers.

Source: World Bank calculations using ENCOVI 2000, Instituto Nacional de Estadistica—Guatemala.

TABLE A4.36: PERCEPTIONS OF CAUSES OF CONFRONTATION IN THE COMMUNITY—HOUSEHOLD QUESTIONNAIRE HOUSEHOLDS PERCEIVING CONFRONTATION IS CAUSED BY [. .]
(Percentage of Total Households and Standard Deviation)

	Education	Wealth	Poverty	Native	Political Affiliation	Religion	Ethnic Group	Age
Total Population	26.1 (1.2)	17.4 (1.1)	13.0 (0.8)	12.3 (1.0)	13.0 (0.9)	11.9 (0.7)	4.8 (0.4)	10.7 (0.7)
Regions								
Metropolitan	39.1 (3.0)	23.2 (2.9)	14.9 (1.9)	21.1 (3.2)	10.6 (2.2)	8.1 (1.3)	3.7 (0.9)	12.1 (1.9)
North	17.8 (3.3)	15.6 (3.3)	8.3 (1.7)	8.9 (2.3)	5.4 (1.5)	9.4 (2.0)	2.8 (1.1)	6.6 (2.1)
North East	19.1 (3.5)	14.5 (3.8)	7.6 (1.5)	8.7 (2.4)	10.6 (2.5)	9.8 (2.0)	1.5 (0.9)	7.9 (2.8)
South East	20.1 (2.5)	11.7 (1.5)	9.1 (1.5)	7.6 (1.4)	12.2 (2.0)	6.0 (1.0)	1.6 (0.4)	7.4 (1.6)
Central	28.6 (2.3)	22.4 (2.2)	17.7 (2.1)	15.7 (1.9)	16.9 (1.7)	16.5 (1.5)	7.8 (1.1)	12.3 (1.5)
South West	25.2 (2.4)	16.6 (2.1)	16.4 (2.2)	9.3 (1.5)	18.2 (2.1)	18.4 (2.0)	8.7 (1.6)	13.5 (1.7)
North West	13.3 (2.0)	9.8 (2.0)	6.5 (1.2)	5.4 (1.1)	11.5 (2.1)	10.7 (1.7)	2.8 (0.6)	8.5 (1.9)
Petén	20.1 (3.1)	14.8 (2.6)	12.8 (2.6)	9.6 (1.8)	7.5 (1.6)	6.3 (1.1)	2.4 (0.6)	5.6 (1.5)
Rural/Urban Area								
Rural	20.4 (1.5)	14.6 (1.3)	10.7 (1.1)	8.7 (1.0)	11.1 (1.1)	11.6 (1.0)	3.5 (0.6)	9.3 (1.0)
Urban	33.6 (1.9)	21.0 (1.8)	16.0 (1.3)	17.0 (1.9)	15.3 (1.4)	12.3 (1.1)	6.6 (0.8)	12.5 (1.2)
Household Head								
Male	25.7 (1.3)	16.9 (1.2)	12.4 (0.9)	11.8 (1.1)	12.9 (0.9)	11.6 (0.7)	4.6 (0.5)	10.7 (0.8)
Female	27.9 (2.0)	19.8 (2.0)	15.3 (1.8)	14.7 (1.9)	13.2 (1.4)	13.1 (1.4)	5.8 (1.0)	10.6 (1.2)

(continued)

TABLE A4.36: PERCEPTIONS OF CAUSES OF CONFRONTATION IN THE COMMUNITY—HOUSEHOLD QUESTIONNAIRE HOUSEHOLDS PERCEIVING CONFRONTATION IS CAUSED BY [. . .] (CONTINUED)
(Percentage of Total Households and Standard Deviation)

	Education	Wealth	Poverty	Native	Political Affiliation	Religion	Ethnic Group	Age
Poverty level								
Non-Poor	32.8 (1.5)	21.5 (1.4)	15.4 (1.0)	16.4 (1.5)	14.4 (1.1)	12.4 (0.9)	6.1 (0.6)	12.5 (1.0)
Poor	18.2 (1.3)	12.6 (1.2)	10.1 (1.1)	7.5 (0.8)	11.3 (1.1)	11.4 (1.0)	3.3 (0.6)	8.6 (0.9)
Extremely Poor	10.5 (1.5)	9.6 (1.5)	6.4 (1.1)	4.7 (1.2)	8.3 (1.7)	9.1 (1.6)	1.6 (0.6)	6.6 (1.5)
Consumption Quintile								
First	11.4 (1.5)	10.0 (1.4)	6.4 (1.0)	4.8 (1.0)	8.4 (1.4)	9.3 (1.4)	1.7 (0.5)	6.4 (1.3)
Second	16.0 (1.5)	11.0 (1.4)	9.3 (1.3)	6.0 (0.9)	12.0 (1.5)	10.8 (1.3)	4.1 (1.0)	8.1 (1.1)
Third	26.1 (2.1)	16.8 (1.9)	14.1 (1.7)	11.2 (1.5)	12.7 (1.7)	12.6 (1.4)	4.2 (0.8)	10.7 (1.3)
Fourth	32.2 (2.6)	23.5 (2.6)	17.9 (1.6)	16.2 (2.1)	14.3 (1.5)	13.1 (1.4)	6.5 (1.1)	11.5 (1.3)
Fifth	34.9 (1.8)	20.5 (1.5)	13.9 (0.8)	17.6 (1.7)	14.9 (1.6)	12.5 (1.2)	6.0 (0.8)	13.8 (1.3)
Ethnic group								
Indigenous	20.7 (1.6)	15.0 (1.4)	15.9 (1.4)	10.2 (1.3)	15.0 (1.3)	14.0 (1.2)	7.6 (1.1)	10.6 (1.1)
K'iche	22.9 (3.2)	13.8 (2.2)	17.3 (3.6)	9.9 (1.7)	18.9 (2.7)	19.1 (3.4)	13.5 (3.5)	12.2 (2.1)
Q'eqchi	16.6 (4.4)	17.7 (4.8)	11.1 (4.1)	12.6 (4.4)	8.0 (3.4)	6.5 (1.7)	1.0 (0.3)	6.7 (2.4)
Kaqchiquel	27.6 (3.8)	19.2 (3.0)	15.4 (2.4)	17.2 (3.0)	21.2 (2.5)	19.1 (2.2)	13.6 (2.3)	14.8 (2.4)
Mam	13.5 (2.5)	8.1 (2.3)	9.4 (3.0)	3.3 (1.4)	7.7 (1.7)	10.2 (2.0)	2.9 (1.0)	7.5 (1.8)
Non-Indigenous	29.5 (1.6)	18.9 (1.4)	13.0 (0.9)	13.7 (1.2)	11.7 (1.1)	10.6 (0.8)	3.1 (0.3)	10.7 (1.0)

Note: Numbers may not sum to total because of rounding.

Source: World Bank calculations using ENCOVI 2000, Instituto Nacional de Estadística—Guatemala.

TABLE A4.37: PERCEPTIONS OF CAUSES OF CONFRONTATION IN THE COMMUNITY—COMMUNITY QUESTIONNAIRE COMMUNITIES PERCEIVING CONFRONTATION IS CAUSED BY [. . .]
(Percentage of Total Communitiesb)

	Education	Wealth	Political Affiliation	Religion	Ethnic Group	Age
Total Population	17.8	13.4	12.8	10.0	3.3	16.1
Regions						
Metropolitan	35.6	24.4	17.8	11.1	4.4	17.8
North	4.8	4.8	4.8	4.8	1.6	9.7
North East	15.0	12.5	12.5	5.0	2.5	15.0
South East	29.4	17.6	19.6	9.8	2.0	19.6
Central	24.0	19.0	19.0	11.4	5.1	19.0
South West	13.2	15.8	9.2	10.5	1.3	13.2
North West	14.3	8.8	11.0	16.5	4.4	22.0
Petén	8.8	2.9	8.8	2.9	5.9	5.9
Rural/Urban Area						
Rural	16.1	11.5	8.4	10.2	3.1	15.2
Urban	21.1	17.3	21.8	9.6	3.8	17.9
Main Language						
K'iche	32.0	20.0	16.0	28.0	8.0	40.0
Q'eqchi	5.0	2.5	2.5	0.0	2.5	10.0
Kaqchiquel	21.2	18.2	18.2	12.1	9.1	18.2
Mam	0.0	0.0	0.0	3.7	0.0	3.7
Non-Indigenous	21.9	16.9	15.3	11.6	3.3	17.3
Confrontation causes discrimination[a]	16.5	35.9	6.6	2.1	37.5	2.6

Note: Numbers may not sum to total because of rounding.
a. Percentage of communities that perceive [. . .] causes confrontation.
b. The sample for the ENCOVI(2000) was based on dwellings, not communities. Results reported at the community level are not representative of communities in Guatemala.

Source: World Bank calculations using ENCOVI 2000, Instituto Nacional de Estadística—Guatemala.

TABLE A4.38: PERCEPTIONS OF EXCLUSION HOUSEHOLDS PERCEIVING COMMUNITY MEMBERS ARE EXCLUDED FROM ASSETS
(Percentage of Total Households and Standard Deviation)

	Human Capital	Physical Assets	Social Security	Justice
Total Population	4.2 (0.4)	6.1 (0.5)	7.4 (0.6)	5.4 (0.6)
Regions				
Metropolitan	4.0 (1.1)	4.0 (1.1)	5.1 (1.2)	4.3 (1.3)
North	4.4 (1.0)	7.1 (1.6)	14.4 (3.6)	15.6 (4.4)
North East	4.3 (1.3)	6.8 (2.0)	6.0 (1.4)	7.4 (2.5)
South East	3.7 (1.0)	3.4 (0.9)	5.7 (1.3)	5.2 (1.6)
Central	5.7 (0.8)	8.2 (1.2)	9.1 (1.1)	3.1 (0.6)
South West	3.4 (0.8)	7.7 (1.4)	7.6 (1.5)	5.1 (1.2)
North West	5.1 (1.2)	6.5 (1.2)	7.3 (1.2)	3.3 (0.8)
Petén	5.8 (1.8)	5.7 (1.5)	10.1 (1.9)	1.9 (0.6)
Rural/Urban Area				
Rural	4.4 (0.6)	5.8 (0.7)	7.7 (1.0)	5.8 (1.0)
Urban	4.0 (0.5)	6.6 (0.7)	6.9 (0.6)	4.8 (0.7)
Household Head				
Male	4.4 (0.4)	6.0 (0.6)	7.7 (0.7)	5.7 (0.7)
Female	3.3 (0.7)	6.9 (1.0)	5.7 (0.9)	4.0 (0.9)
Poverty level				
Non-Poor	4.6 (0.5)	5.6 (0.6)	7.5 (0.8)	5.3 (0.6)
Poor	3.9 (0.6)	6.7 (0.7)	7.2 (0.8)	5.5 (0.9)
Extremely Poor	3.1 (0.7)	6.3 (1.2)	6.8 (1.3)	5.5 (1.3)
Consumption Quintile				
First	3.1 (0.6)	7.1 (1.1)	7.2 (1.3)	5.3 (1.3)
Second	4.2 (0.9)	7.2 (6.0)	7.1 (1.0)	4.6 (0.9)
Third	4.2 (0.9)	6.0 (1.0)	7.3 (0.9)	6.0 (1.2)
Fourth	5.3 (0.8)	6.6 (1.1)	8.7 (1.2)	6.4 (1.0)
Fifth	3.9 (0.6)	4.8 (0.7)	6.6 (0.9)	4.5 (0.7)
Ethnic group				
Indigenous	4.2 (0.6)	7.2 (0.9)	9.4 (1.1)	7.2 (1.2)
K'iche	3.6 (1.0)	6.8 (1.6)	8.1 (1.5)	4.6 (1.1)
Q'eqchi	4.1 (1.2)	4.8 (1.3)	17.5 (4.3)	13.3 (4.4)
Kaqchiquel	4.2 (0.8)	7.1 (1.5)	9.3 (1.7)	8.7 (3.1)
Mam	4.3 (2.2)	8.6 (3.0)	6.6 (2.3)	2.6 (1.3)
Non-Indigenous	4.3 (0.6)	5.5 (0.6)	6.1 (0.7)	4.2 (0.6)

Note: Numbers may not sum to total because of rounding.

Source: World Bank calculations using ENCOVI 2000, Instituto Nacional de Estadística—Guatemala.

TABLE A4.39: PERCEPTIONS OF JUSTICE PERFORMANCE
(Percentage of Total Population and Standard Deviation)

	Good quality	Average	Poor
Total Population	16.5 (0.7)	65.3 (0.8)	18.2 (0.8)
Regions			
Metropolitan	9.7 (1.3)	60.3 (2.0)	30.0 (2.2)
North	27.7 (3.3)	55.5 (3.2)	16.9 (1.6)
North East	21.4 (2.9)	65.1 (3.4)	13.5 (2.1)
South East	21.8 (2.0)	65.7 (3.4)	13.5 (2.1)
Central	11.2 (1.0)	70.7 (1.5)	18.1 (1.2)
South West	15.8 (1.3)	70.3 (1.7)	13.9 (1.5)
North West	23.0 (1.9)	66.2 (1.9)	10.8 (1.2)
Petén	16.2 (1.9)	65.2 (2.0)	18.5 (2.2)
Rural/Urban Area			
Rural	20.7 (1.0)	65.8 (1.1)	13.5 (0.9)
Urban	11.0 (0.7)	64.6 (1.3)	24.4 (1.3)
Gender			
Female	16.5 (0.7)	66.6 (0.9)	16.9 (0.8)
Male	16.5 (0.8)	63.8 (1.0)	19.7 (0.9)
Poverty level			
Non-Poor	11.9 (0.6)	64.6 (1.0)	23.5 (1.0)
Poor	21.4 (1.0)	66.0 (1.2)	12.5 (1.0)
Extremely Poor	24.0 (1.9)	64.2 (2.1)	11.7 (1.1)
Consumption Quintile			
First	24.1 (1.7)	64.1 (1.8)	11.8 (1.1)
Second	21.4 (1.4)	66.9 (1.5)	11.7 (1.0)
Third	18.0 (1.5)	66.9 (2.3)	15.1 (2.4)
Fourth	14.7 (1.0)	67.9 (1.2)	17.3 (1.3)
Fifth	9.1 (0.7)	61.6 (1.4)	29.3 (1.4)
Ethnic Group			
Indigenous			
K'iqche	17.8 (2.2)	71.6 (2.4)	10.6 (1.3)
Q'eqchi	32.4 (4.1)	50.8 (4.1)	16.8 (1.9)
Kaqchiquel	9.7 (1.4)	68.7 (2.9)	21.5 (3.5)
Mam	18.2 (2.8)	74.2 (3.0)	7.6 (1.8)
Non-indigenous			

Note: Numbers may not sum to total because of rounding.

Source: World Bank calculations using ENCOVI 2000, Instituto Nacional de Estadística—Guatemala.

QUALITATIVE POVERTY AND EXCLUSION STUDY (QPES): OVERVIEW OF 10 RURAL VILLAGES (SUMMARY)

Overview of the QPES

Qualitative instruments are useful for gathering information on the influence of motives, attitudes and preferences on economic behavior, on perceptions, and on the barriers and opportunities that determine poverty and mobility. They are not intended to be statistically representative or reflect measures of central tendency. Rather, they yield information that is primarily descriptive but can broaden the field of inquiry to include questions, issues and factors which are otherwise likely to be missed with quantitative instruments.

The QPES: General Objectives. As part of the GUAPA Program, a Qualitative Study of Poverty and Exclusion (QPES) was conducted in 10 rural villages during the year 2000 by a multi-ethnic team of local researchers led by COWI Consultants.[1] The objectives of the QPES were to gather information on perceptions and the nature of constraints to and opportunities for economic mobility so as to better understand the dynamic processes that perpetuate or reduce poverty and exclusion. Specifically, the QPES has four objectives:

(a) To identify factors linked to the perpetuation of indigenous and non-indigenous rural poverty which might be known to the poor themselves, but may not be fully reflected in conventional quantitative surveys;

(b) To provide, through example and case history, an understanding of the specific mechanisms through which poverty and exclusion arise and are perpetuated in the study villages;

(c) To build theories and hypotheses that will help in analyzing the ENCOVI; and

(d) To better understand vulnerability and coping mechanisms, which will help in improving social service delivery and in improving and designing social safety net mechanisms for Guatemala.

---

1. See QPES Terms of Reference, April 6, 2000 and QPES Final Report 2002 for more details on the broader study.

The QPES Sample. The QPES involved data collection and substantial field work in 10 rural communities. The sample was drawn from the ENCOVI community/census segment sample so as to allow for integrated analysis of the qualitative and quantitative and to introduce a random element into sample selection for the QPES. Based on that, the sample was selected using a few intentional criteria, including ethnicity (2 villages per ethnicity), presence of certain programs (e.g., PRONADE, a decentralized school management program) in at least a few of the villages, and history with a large covariant shock (e.g., natural disaster) in at least a couple of the villages. The team was instructed explicitly not to seek out villages that had suffered substantial massacres or destruction during the violence of the 1980s, but not to avoid them either; nonetheless, several seem to have randomly been captured the sample (see KA2, KI1, M1). The configuration of these villages seeks to examine perceptions of poverty and exclusion for a number of ethnicities; as such, the sample includes two villages from each of the following ethnic groups: Mam, K'iché, Q'ekchi, Katchiquel, and Ladino (non-indigenous). To protect the anonymity of the villagers and informants, the villages are given "code names" in the QPES: KI1 and KI2 are predominantly K'iché villages, QE1 and QE2 are predominantly Keqchi villages, KA1 and KA2 are predominantly Kaqchiquel villages, M1 and M2 are predominantly Mam villages, and L1 and L2 are predominantly ladino villages.

Modules and Instruments. The field work covered a number of key themes, including: perceptions of poverty and welfare; perceptions of risk, shocks and vulnerability; social capital; user perceptions of public programs; community perceptions of education; and gender roles and issues. In addition, the teams conducted a village overview and social mapping to better understand the context of each village. The research teams spent a little over a week in each village and the main research instruments included: community focus groups (often split by gender), direct interviews, the social mapping exercise, and direct observation.

The objectives of this note are to present an overview of the context and main features of each of the 10 villages included in the study. A summary matrix is included at the end of this note. Detailed information about the study and the field work can be found in the QPES main report and 10 village reports (Participatory Poverty Assessments, PPAs). An analysis of perceptions of poverty and welfare is presented in Chapter 2 of the GUAPA main report, while an analysis of social capital is presented in GUAPA Technical Paper 12 (Ibáñez, Lindert and Woolcock, 2002), an analysis of Vulnerability, Risks and Shocks is included in GUAPA Technical Paper 9 (Tesliuc and Lindert, 2002) the other modules (public programs, education, gender) have been incorporated throughout the GUAPA.

Summary of QPES Villages: Key Characteristics and Context

Kaqchiqel 1 (KA1): Extremely Poor and Vulnerable Finca Village, with Few Hopes or Assets
This small village consists of workers[2] and their families (about 200 people) who live on a privately-owned coffee plantation (*finca*)[3] in the Central Region.[4] The majority of residents were born on the finca, their ancestors (mainly grandparents) having migrated here in previous generations. Although the finca previously did not permit the presence of evangelical religions, the village now has two evangelical churches as well as a catholic church.

Physical Assets and Basic Services. The villagers of KA1 own almost zero physical capital; the finca owns the houses and small plots of land that they are allowed to use for subsistence production (mainly of corn). When their spouses pass away, widows are not allowed to maintain use of

2. In addition to the permanent residents of the finca, a number of temporary workers (*cuadrillas*) migrate to the finca during the harvest season and live in *galeras* (collective dormatories).
3. The finca has had numerous different owners, none of whom live nearby (most based in Guatemala city). The current owner is a commercial bank. The finca is administered by an administrator (*mayordomo*) and his auxiliary (*caporal*).
4. The Central Region includes the Departments of Chimaltenango, Escuintla, and Sacatepequez.

these plots or houses, unless they move in with relatives who are actively employed by the finca. The houses are in terrible condition, with incomplete walls of wood and metal roofs. The villagers lack most basic services, such as water, sanitation, or energy. The only access to the finca comes from an unpaved road (*camino de terracería*), which gets flooded during heavy rains and becomes impassable. Financial capital is virtually non-existent, as the villagers have little opportunity to acquire surplus or borrow.

Education. Almost all adults are illiterate and none of the children attend school past grade 3. The elementary school is owned by the finca,[5] and has one teacher (of Kaqchiqel ethnicity), offering grades 1–3 with a current enrollment of 31 students. The school lacks basic infrastructure, with insufficient chairs and tables, walls in bad condition, and a lack of a latrine. The teacher notes that child labor is a serious obstacle to educational attainment, causing drop out and seasonal absences, primarily for boys but also for girls. In fact, current enrollment of girls is twice as high as that of boys (21 girls and 10 boys). The villagers do not send their children for additional schooling to schools in other fincas or villages because they are very far and they fear the children would be assaulted[6] en route to school.

Health Services. The finca does not have any pharmacy or health clinic. Some villagers report that they do have a midwife (who possibly travels between fincas), and one women notes that her husband has a gift for healing (a curandero).

Labor Benefits. Workers on the finca receive benefits according to their labor classification (see Box 1). Permanent workers ("rancheros") and the deputy plantation administrator/supervisors, who all live and work on the finca, do receive benefits. However, many "permanent residents" of the finca (particularly members of the labor union) have been classified as "volunteers" and have much more tenuous job security, facing periodic suspensions in an apparent strategy by the finca owners to avoid paying labor benefits and discourage labor union affiliation.[7] Their classification as volunteers derives from the fact that they seek work on other fincas during the period of suspension (as a survival strategy). Women on the fincas do not receive any of these benefits, despite contributing to the production process, both directly (especially during the harvest) and indirectly by maintaining the workers via household chores and cooking (women not only have to prepare the meals of their family members, but also for the temporary migrant workers).

Social Capital. Social capital and capacity to engage in collective action is virtually non-existent. The villagers do not feel they belong to the community. Vertical authoritarian relations between the finca administrators and the village workers rule daily life and discourage the formation of horizontal connections or organization within the village. Whereas the previous plantation owner gave Christmas gifts to the children, paid for their school lunches, provided school necessities, and made the feel welcome, the current owner is apparently more authoritarian and discourages any attempt to organize community activities. The highest authority on the finca is the "mayordomo" (administrator).

---

5. By law, plantations are required to provide schooling to child residents.
6. They apparently report presence of gangs along the rural roads, citing examples of others (including a midwife) being assaulted while walking between fincas.
7. As one focus group participant put it: "Es que el patrón no le conviene que los trabajadores estén organizados y exijen sus derechos . . . por eso nos 'joden.' " (PPA KA1).

BOX A5.1: LABOR CLASSIFICATION, JOB SECURITY, AND JOB BENEFITS ON THE FINCA OF KA1[8]

Labor Classification	Job Status	Job Security	Labor Benefits
Los "03"	Called "rancheros," these workers live and work on the finca (except those mentioned in 06).	Permanent[9]	Receive benefits: bono 14, IGSS, aguinaldo, martes o miercoles Santo (vacation)
Los "04"	These are considered "voluntarios," but with a higher standing since they serve as "auxiliares" (deputy administrator/supervisor of the finca).	Permanent	
Los "06"	The least secure category. It includes two types of workers: ■ "Volontarios." Workers who live on the finca more or less "permanently" but have been classified as "voluntarios" because they also work on other fincas. Many of these were classified into this category by the finca as a result of their union association. When the unionized workers were dismissed by the finca, they sought work at other fincas during that longer-term dismissal period. That resulted in them being classified as "voluntarios" and hence as "06." The sons of the "rancheros" are also classified as "06." ■ "Cuadrillas" or temporary migrant workers who come seasonally for the harvest	Voluntarios are laid off (suspended) 2–3 times per year (for 15 days to 2 months per suspension). During this period, they have to find work at other fincas (or be unemployed, which they can hardly afford).	Do not receive formal labor benefits. Voluntarios are permitted to remain on the finca and harvest their corn ("milpa") during the period of suspension.

Some workers did organize a union to protect their rights.[10] The finca owners, however, laid off union workers and reclassified them as "volunteers" (see Box 1) with worse contract terms. Since many workers do not join for fear of retaliation by the finca, a minority of villagers is unionized. Solidarity among union members, however, is strong, and the union helps provide lawyers and benefits when they are dismissed. There are no other collective action organizations in the community. Contacts with external agencies or bodies is negligent.

Loss of Cultural Identity. In addition to a lack of these basic assets, the villagers of KA1 seem to have lost their cultural identity, identifying themselves and their language not as the mayans that they are,[11] but simply as "natives" of the finca. While they have little roots to establish themselves

---

8. This classification is based on a compilation of information from numerous discussions in the focus groups and in individual interviews during the fieldwork. It was verified several times with many participants.

9. It's interesting that the non-unionized ranchero workers are not dismissed periodically, although if they were, they would organize in protest. The investigador asked a Grupo Focal: "¿A los que no están afiliados [al sindicato] les quitan el trabajo?" To which the respondants answered: "No porque somos del 04 y además si suspenden a alguien todos vamos a hablar con el administrador, por eso no lo hacen."

10. Associated with UNSITRAGUA, the Union de Sindicatos de Trabajadores de Guatemala.

11. While predominantly Kaqchiqel, residents also include K'ichés and a few Ladinos.

at the finca or create a sense of belonging, they have little or no ties beyond the finca and "no where else to go." While adults speak mayan languages (Kaqchiqel and K'iché), they don't identify them as such, calling what they speak "una lengua." Children only speak Spanish, though they do understand the mayan languages. Few residents wear traditional indigenous clothing (traje).

Shocks and Vulnerability. On top of this situation of extreme poverty, the villagers of KA1 have been subject to several significant shocks and the effects of these shocks have been lasting, forcing them into an even deeper state of extreme poverty. Given their lack of assets of any kind, they have been little equipped to respond to these shocks, which basically pushed them down from one already-low level of welfare to an even more impoverished state.

Collective shocks identified by the villagers include: (a) the earthquake of 1976; (b) large-scale labor shocks; and (c) other recurring natural disasters including flooding and landslides. With respect to the earthquake of 1976, focus group participants were fairly unanimous in identifying the shock as having substantially impacted virtually all in the community with lasting effects. Most houses were destroyed—and only partially rebuilt in the quarter century since the quake. The earthquake also destroyed the village's mill. Women seem to have been particularly affected by the earthquake, perhaps because it directly affected their productive assets more (houses, garden plots, mill). The community was clearly hard-pressed to handle a shock as big as the earthquake. Their main responses consisted of a patchwork of basic self-help survival strategies, including going to a neighboring finca to mill their corn, making purchases on credit, going into debt, and partially (but not fully) repairing their homes. They did not receive any help from the finca owners or the Government, though they apparently did receive some housing materials from "unos gringos de Francia" and some food and milk from some Italians.

The most serious risk identified by the community is unemployment. This importance comes as no surprise, given that labor is the main (only) asset of the majority of the community members. During the discussions, the informants identified two types of massive labor shocks: (a) vengeful dismissals of union workers; and (b) periodic dismissals of workers classified as "volunteers" (see Box 1 above) as part of an apparent scheme by the finca owners to avoid paying labor benefits. In terms of the vengeful dismissals, apparently, several years ago[12] a substantial share of community members were fired from the finca due to their association with the union (UNSITRAGUA). The dismissal lasted over two years. Similar dismissals were repeated in subsequent years. Although union lawyers helped the worker recuperate lost wages in some of the instances, the most recent case has not yet been resolved. According to the villagers, the impacts of this shock were multiple, including: (a) the obvious immediate economic loss of earnings, job security, and benefits; (b) the lasting economic losses associated with the workers' reclassification as "volunteers" (06, see Box 1 above) and resulting periodic dismissals; (c) the discouragement of collective action within the village; (d) the withholding of other assistance by the finca owners for those involved (e.g., the finca won't repair the homes of those affiliated with the union); and (e) social and psychological effects, including a constant feeling of insecurity, demoralization,[13] helplessness, and exclusion, as well as estranged labor relations between the workers and the finca managers. Responses and coping strategies for these labor shocks reported by the villagers included: (a) seeking temporary employment in other fincas; (b) selling some of their (subsistence) food production, with families compensating and cutting back on their own dietary intake and diversity; and (c) increased child labor to generate additional income.

The villagers also identify a number of **idiosyncratic risks and shocks,** including sickness (dengue, malnutrition, stomach ailments, fever, diarrhea, anemia, etc.) sometimes resulting in

---

12. Specific dates withheld to protect the anonymity of the village.

13. As one focus group participant describes it: "Aqui cada año hay despidos. Lo hacen para *desmoralizarnos. Lo que pasa es que ya no quieren pagar las prestaciones . . . El interés es destituir a toda la gente poco a poco.*" (KA1 PPA).

death; giving birth, maternal and infant mortality (clearly associated with the lack of nearby health services); domestic violence associated with alcoholism; and crime and violence in the area (including when walking on rural roads due to the reported presence of gangs).

Perceptions of Changes Over Time; Aspirations for the Future. The villagers of KA1 expressed that they haven't experienced any improvements in their living standards: "Everything stays the same on the finca, without potable water, without lighting, without drainage or latrines," voiced one participant. Moreover, they perceive access to health services as having worsened: "whereas before there was a nurse and a clinic in the municipality head, now there isn't. This changed with the new owner of the finca who doesn't want to invest money to offer these health services." They seem to have few aspirations for a better life—or one away from the finca. When asked if they had any intention of leaving in search of better conditions, the villagers responses made it clear that they "don't think of doing something different" and that they "don't leave because they have no where else to go." The children of KA1 have little hope for a different future either; when asked what they would like to be when they grow up, the boys responded "working in the coffee harvest, cleaning the hillside," and the girls answered "cleaning the house."

Kaqchiqel 2 (KA2): Rebuilding after the Violence of the 1980s

This ethnically homogenous, largely bilingual[14] village of 1000 people, located in the Central Region,[15] was seriously marked by the violence of the armed conflict in the early 1980s, in which numerous members of the village were massacred (including the village leaders and religious leaders), kidnapped or disappeared, crops and houses were burned, and remaining villagers fled to a nearby town for two years. As a result, the remaining population is quite young ("hay pocos ancianos"), with 40 widows and two orphan families. Even though the Catholic and Evangelic Churches are present, ethnic bonds are reportedly stronger than religious affiliation. Divisions between religions are not perceived to be problems because "we are all Kaqchiqels." Indeed, the villagers appear quite proud of their ethnic heritage, with most women and children wearing traditional dress. Despite it's violent history, the village seems better off than many of the other QPES communities.

Economic Activities, Land. The village depends largely on agriculture, with a diverse range of crops: corn (for subsistence), potatoes, tomatoes, radishes, apples, and peaches. Women are primarily engaged in domestic responsibilities, as well as the weaving of *guilpiles* for personal use and sale; widows work as day-laborers (*jornaleras*). Land is privately owned, though those who don't have enough for cultivation rent additional land within the municipality. Some have irrigation, allowing them to cultivate two harvests per year. Some young people have migrated to the capital.

Infrastructure and Services. The village has most basic services, including a paved access road, dirt interior roads, piped water, electricity, and latrines. Many families either burn their trash, or use it as organic fertilizer to conserve natural resources. The village also has 10 stores, 4 mills, and two churches (one catholic and one evangelical). They also use an old schoolhouse that was abandoned during the violence as a community meeting place. With regards to water, most have connections to piped water (though not the poorer households), though villagers complain of irregular service in the summer. The community has developed norms for rationing water during this time, putting priority to cooking, while laundry washing must be done using well water.

Health and Education. The community has a SAIS health post and a midwife. The villagers report that these services are generally good. The village has a primary school, offering grades 1–6 with 5 teachers for 159 students, though teachers note problems with school drop out, particularly for girls who leave early to help their mothers, and a lack of teachers, classrooms, materials and texts.

---

14. Most are bilingual Kaqchiqel-Spanish.
15. The Central Region includes the Departments of Chimaltenango, Escuintla, and Sacatepequez.

Social Capital. Social capital is "medium-high," and relations in the community still appear strained by the violence of the 1980s due to on-going fears of associating and assuming leadership roles, and a lack of trust.[16] Since the village was abandoned for two years and the leadership exterminated, community cohesion was weakened and social organizations were lost. Nonetheless, the community has organized several committees (development committee, women's groups including a group to support the widows of the violence, a school committee). The Development Committee acts as the "maximum authority" in the village, not only to solve the village problems, organize community activities and leverage external assistance, but also as a protective/security enforcing body, as was the case with the gangs (maras), which recently threatened the village. Against this threat, the community organized itself via the development committee, caught the gang members, wet them down (los mojaron), and threatened them with lynching. Although women have organized specific support groups and participated in specific activities (school lunches, church charity groups), women reportedly do not participate actively in the decisions of the community. They also do not vote in the elections of the auxiliary mayor.

Municipal Services; External Contacts. The villagers of KA2 note that they've seen an improvement in services at the municipality over the past decade, largely because civil servants there are now Kaqchiqel. The villagers have few connections outside the village, though they have received assistance from FONAPAZ, which paved the road in a tripartite arrangement with the municipality and the community (which provided the labor).

Shocks. The village of KA2 has faced two major collective shocks: the earthquake of 1976, which destroyed some houses and resulted in a few deaths, and the horrific violence of the early 1980s (discussed above). In terms of response and coping strategies, the community did receive some external assistance after the earthquake (received some housing materials and a helicopter helped evacuate the injured). The main response mechanism for the violence was self-help (fleeing for two years), and the follow up actions have been to organize the Development Committee to protect the community. Though villagers perceive the effects of the earthquake to have been largely overcome, the impact of the violence appears to be lasting, particularly by creating an on-going obstacle to greater community unity and fear. The violence of the 1980s was also the primary idiosyncratic shock identified by villagers in the community, with consequences persisting even in daily life (broken families, widows, lost earnings, on-going fear, etc.).

Perceptions of Changes Over Time; Aspirations for the Future. Villagers perceive that living conditions have improved somewhat, attributing these gains to the construction of the paved access road, potable water, and electricity connections obtained five years ago. The children do seem to have aspirations for a stronger future, noting that they want to "continue studying . . . study through secondary school . . . become a teacher."

K'iché 1 (KI1): Fairly Well Endowed; Rebuilding Community After Violence of 1980s

Socio-Economic Situation. KI1 is an ethnically homogeneous K'iché village of 2,840 people (568 households) in the North-West Region[17] that was founded over a hundred years ago. The village was rocked by violence during the armed conflict of the 1980s, during which time the population significantly dropped (reportedly due to people fleeing and some being murdered). Since the 1990s, the village has been a recipient of in-migration, and its population has expanded rapidly. The community appears to be largely bilingual (Spanish and K'iché).

---

16. "El proceso de recomposición de las formas de la organización social y del capital social ha sido lento porque en ellos persiste el temor . . . 'miedo, temor de asociarse, hay secuelas sicológicas, ya que varios vieron o fueron testigos de masacres y secuestros. . . . No se quieren organizar en grupos porque tienen miedo que pueda perjudicarles, así como pasó en la violencia." Source: QPES, PPA-KA2.

17. The North-West Region includes the Departments of Quiché and Huehuetenango.

Land. Land inequality[18] is high. About 2% of the population owns plots as large as 50 cuerdas, 5% owns plots as large as 10 cuerdas, and the remainder owns plots of 1–2 cuerdas, often no larger than what is needed for their homes. Unclear definitions of borders between properties cause land conflicts, and the auxiliary mayor and president of the Development Committee are charged with resolving these. By tradition, women cannot hold legal title to land.

Diversified Economic Activities. Major sources of livelihoods are fairly well diversified and include (a) agriculture (corn and fruits such as apples); and (ii) non-farm activities, such as artisan crafts (tejidos típicos), making clothes, and commercialization. Many men (especially landless) work as day laborers (jornaleros) in apple and corn cultivation, while others work off farm, while women focus primarily on domestic activities, as well as the production of artisan crafts for sale. There is little migration, although a few men (mainly the landless) do migrate to work on the coffee fincas in Guatemala.

Assets: Well Endowed. The community is well endowed in terms of physical and social assets, with extensive road access, water (which covers 95% of homes, but is scarce in summer), latrines, and electricity (which covers 95% of homes). The community also boasts substantial communal infrastructure, including a market, 17 churches, sports fields, mills, and a cooperative. They've also received assistance to develop improved stoves (estufas mejoradas) and credit.

Education and Health. Health services seem to be a gap in coverage in the village of KI1, and they only have midwives. In contrast, the village boasts relatively extensive school coverage, with a preschool, primary school, secondary school, and a bilingual teacher training center. The primary school has nine teachers offering grades 1–6 with 10 classrooms for 385 students. Problems of dropout, seasonal absences, or discrimination against girls do not seem to be a problem, according to the teachers.

Social Capital and Village Relations. The violence of the 1980s tested community ties and trust. "Envious" villagers "wrongfully" accused other residents of being guerrilla members. People were afraid to talk even inside their homes for fear of being listened to and reported by their neighbors. Nonetheless, the community seems to have rebuilt its organization to a fairly high level of social capital. It boasts numerous committees, including the Development Committee, committees for water, electricity, stoves, the parent-teacher school committee, a cooperative and a farmers association. The water committee was created to solve the drinking water problem. The committee contacted FONAPAZ to leverage external assistance. People in the community contributed by buying construction materials, providing unpaid labor, and covering the expenses of the committee. The project benefited 100 households (18% of the village). Despite the success of the project, the committee faced corruption charges due to misuse of funds. Following the success of the water committee, the village established the stove committee to submit a proposal to FIS to improve women's health while cooking. In contrast to these connections, religious conflicts (between catholics, evangelicals, and mayan faiths) do seem to be causing some divisions within the community. Clashes within the Evangelical church have also created divisions in subgroups. In addition to bonds within the community, the villagers of KI1 seem to have built fairly strong links to external bodies, and are receiving assistance from the municipality, various bilateral agencies, social funds (FIS and FONAPAZ), the "Programa K'iché," and the Ministry of Health. Women are not active in community decision making, with the exception of initiatives spearheaded by the churches. The illiterate also seem to be excluded ("nobody takes them into account"). Links between poor and wealthy families are scarce, with little mutual support.

Shocks. The violence of the early 1980s is the main **collective shock** that has hit the village of KI1.[19] The shock was apparently severe, with numerous families losing relatives (killed or missing), girls

---

18. Land titles are apparently only inherited by males according to the traditions of their ancestors; only over the past few years have a few women gained title to their homes. About 90% of the households possess public titles (escritura pública), 5% have registered titles, and 5% have no titles, which has spurred conflicts on occasion.

being raped, and houses being looted. A huge share of the population fled to the capital in fear, returning only in the 1990s. In addition to the obvious psychological trauma suffered by the victims and their families, agricultural production halted, children didn't attend school, and communication between neighbors and families was severed out of fear and lack of trust. The village did receive some donations in the aftermath of the violence, including a school and housing project. Focus group participants consider that this shock has mainly been overcome; as one participant put it: "Now there is more freedom to travel, to go to the market, for children to go to school, to celebrate *fiestas patronales,* to visit between families." Village members also report being hit by the 1976 earthquake, in which some people died and homes were destroyed. Solidarity in response to this quake was fairly strong, with the community participating in rescue operations and burying victims and the churches helping reconstruct houses and providing food.

Idiosyncratic shocks reported by the villagers include: (a) individual job loss and insecurity; (b) sickness and other health shocks); (c) automobile/pedestrian accidents on the well-traveled roads; (d) loss of tourist markets for their artisan crafts associated with a reduction in "foreigners" coming through the town due to local crime ("delincuencia") and assaults; and (e) terms-of-trade problems with low producer prices for apples and high inputs costs (e.g., for fertilizer).

Perceptions of Changes and Strong Aspirations for the Future. The villagers perceive that poverty has increased in the community, mainly due to population pressures on the land and natural resources and increases in the cost of living. In contrast, the children seem quite empowered in their aspirations for the future, and education seems to play an important role in getting them there. Indeed they aspire to a range of diverse professions with many attached to social causes, including: "President because I want to help the poor . . . a lawyer for land titling . . . a solder to protect our nation . . . a teacher to teach other children . . . the mayor to help people . . . a doctor to help the sick and children . . . a legislator to be president." Others aspire to be artists, merchants, sports players.

K'iché 2 (KI2): Fairly Poor, Seasonal Migrants; With Internal Ethnic Conflicts and Series of Shocks

Although the majority of KI2's population of 1,254 (144 households) is K'iché, there is an influential minority of Ladinos who arrived in this town in the North-Western Region[20] 15 years ago and bought land for cultivation. Relations between these two groups are conflictive, with the K'ichés complaining that the Ladinos have more land and allow their cattle to roam freely, intruding on the plots of the K'iché families. The majority of residents are Catholic, with a number of people practicing Evangelism.

Land and Natural Resources. Land ownership is private, with plots averaging 10–20 cuerdas, though not all possess titles; ownership of forests and grasslands is communal. Overexploitation of common natural resources is leading to forest depletion, water scarcity, and infertile land.

Economic Activities: Agriculture and Seasonal Migration. Agricultural production (corn, beans, greens/verduras, vegetables) is the primary source of income in the community, and the community only has one merchant. Reflecting their poverty, seasonal labor migration is necessary to supplement incomes, and the majority of families migrate to the coffee and sugar plantations on the *Costa Sur.*[21] School drop out, temporary absences, and child labor are an immediate effect of this migration—with long-run impacts for the inter-generational transmission of poverty.[22]

---

19. Some also note being hit by the earthquake of 1976, but the village does not appear to have been hit hard and the lasting effects are minimal.

20. The North-West Region includes the Departments of Quiché and Huehuetenango.

21. Typically for two months (November and December). Villagers of KI2 indicate that working conditions on the fincas are not adequate, with low pay, high rates of illness, and inadequate food rations. Source: QPES PPA for KI2.

22. Villagers note this impact with regret: "Si van, todos pierden el estudio . . . La mayoría de los niños está triste porque ha dejado de estudiar . . . El papá y la mamá tienen la culpa porque no tienen dinero, los tienen que llevar porque no hay quien le de comer." Source: QPES PPA-KI2/Raw notes.

Basic Services and Infrastructure. The village of KI2 only has minimal basic and social infrastructure: while most have piped water (with the exception of 10 households),[23] less than half have latrines and none have energy connections. There are problems with irregular water supply and pressure, particularly in the summer. The village is accessible only by one unpaved road and 12 unpaved small roads.

Education and Health. The village has a bilingual primary school,[24] offering grades 1–6 with 3 teachers for 112 students, though teachers note serious problems with school drop out and temporary absences due to child labor (associated with labor migration) and early marriage of girls,[25] and a lack of materials and texts. The only health services available come from two midwives in the village.

Social Capital. Social capital in the village is "medium." Within the K'iché majority, the village is a close and tightly bonded community that mistrusts strangers. The Development Committee leverages assistance and solves community problems. For example, it submitted an application to FONAPAZ to build the school. During the project, the community provided unpaid labor, FONAPAZ donated the funds and the municipality supplied the materials. The committee is also searching for additional water sources and considering a water sewage project to reduce pollution. The school and PTA committees are also active in the village, with parents providing school lunches and allocating school expenses, and teachers helping leverage external assistance to construct basketball and soccer fields. The village also operates a credit cooperative for agricultural producers.

Although village leaders suggest that no one is excluded from community activities, certain groups present substantial evidence to the contrary. Women feel excluded from community decision making, and mocked when they try to participate. They are not allowed to vote in elections for community authorities. The poor are also auto-excluded from community activities. They explain that they "have too much work and do not want to get in contact with anyone from the community." Moreover, the conflictive relations between the K'ichés and the Ladinos does not contribute to community cohesiveness.

Municipal Services and External Assistance. With respect to municipal services, the villagers perceive a history of exclusion and poor treatment, with recent improvements because more civil servants are now indigenous. Contact with formal external institutions is scarce, though the community has benefited from a UNEPAR water project, assistance from FONAPAZ (basketball and soccer fields), and NGO assistance (land terracing, roads, latrines, training for youth on drugs, health, child care, etc.).

Shocks. The village of KI2 has been hit by a series of collective shocks, including the earthquake of 1976, the earthquake of 1986, a cholera epidemic in which one person died in 1990, and hurricane Mitch, which destroyed and damaged crops and houses in 1998. The villagers perceive that the effects of the first earthquake and Hurricane Mitch have not been overcome even despite the passage of time: in the case of the latter, houses remain cracked and damaged and as a result of the former, villagers remain indebted and still have to migrate to the coast to supplement their incomes. There was little collective action in response to these shocks; most coping strategies relied on self-help (going into debt, migrating in search of work). The villagers did receive some external assistance after the 1976 earthquake, with UNEPAR providing housing materials. Health officials also ran a health education campaign after the cholera epidemic, teaching the villagers about the importance and practice of treating water. Individual households also report having been hit with additional shocks, such as death of a family member (including spouse), sickness, and crop loss.

---

23. Villagers perceive that piped water has improved their living conditions substantially, reducing the domestic burden on women in particular. QPES PPA-KI2.

24. Escuela Oficial Rural Mixta run by DIGEBI (Dirección General de Educación Bilingüe Intercultural).

25. At around age 13, the last year of primary school.

Perceptions of Changes; Aspirations for the Future. Villagers perceive an increase in poverty, associated with a lack of material assets (such as cars), problems with their livestock, the need to migrate to the fincas in search of work (lack of opportunity), and land fertility problems. Despite their poverty, the children express high hopes and aspirations for their future. When they grow up, the boys claim they want to be: "lawyers to become president of the republic and to help the poor . . . doctors . . . teachers . . . police," while girls express their aspirations as: "secretary . . . doctor . . . lawyer . . . nurse . . . teacher . . . mayor . . . police to resolve problems between people that the men don't resolve . . . and president to govern our country."

Ladino 1 (L1): Shock-Induced Poverty

This ethnically-homogeneous Ladino village of about 420 people, located in the North East Region[26] has faced a drastic worsening of living conditions since Hurricane Mitch struck in 1998.

Economic Activities. Prior to Hurricane Mitch, the main source of income was agriculture, with a somewhat diverse range of production: lemons, papaya, tobacco, melons, eggplant, palms for raw material for artisan work, corn for subsistence, and livestock. Women also earn money from artisan basket-based crafts, such as sombreros, brooms, straw mats, etc. Hurricane Mitch severely damaged the land, however, rendering it largely infertile and covered with rocks. Now most have to search for day labor jobs elsewhere, with some 400 migrating to the capital and the US and leaving their families behind.

Physical Assets, Services. Despite having certain physical assets, such as electricity, water,[27] and soccer fields,[28] the hurricane clearly exposed vulnerabilities in the asset base of the village. The productive and employment base, which was highly dependent on land, was largely wiped out by the hurricane. The village also lacks proper drainage and sanitation, causing contamination—and hence malnutrition and diseases—in the wake of Hurricane Mitch. The village is accessible only via an unpaved road. Villagers complain of a lack of access to credit.

Health and Education. Other than a midwife, health services within the village are non-existent, and informants report that travel costs to services in other localities are often prohibitive. Although the village does have a primary school, offering grades 1–6 with a three teachers serving 72 students, most adults have less than a complete primary education and many women are illiterate. As such, the more "mobile" human capital base is weak, such that when the villagers have to migrate in search of work, their opportunities are limited. Moreover, the teachers note that school drop out and temporary absences are common due to child labor and domestic duties.

Social Capital. Social capital is "low-medium." On the one hand, the development, school, and electricity committees all play important roles in the community, and the villagers emphasize the importance of soccer games and fiestas (celebrations) in bringing the community together. Community cohesion also seems to increase when the village is confronted with a shock, with examples of villagers providing transportation when residents are seriously ill, sharing food, and providing interest-free short-term loans to those in need during emergencies. On the other hand, participation in collective action in the village is low due to apathy, mistrust in organizations, and lack of information. Some residents believe they should be compensated in kind or cash for attending community meetings. Teachers note that parents participate in school meetings only when they derive a direct benefit. Women are excluded from community activities and decision making.

---

26. The North East Region includes the departments of El Progreso, Izabal, Chiquimula, and Zacapa.

27. Although villagers perceive water quality to be good (due to chlorination), there are problems with water pressure, and hence rationing across three sectors of the village each day.

28. Moreover, water service is irregular and has to be rotated among the three sectors of the village during the day.

Municipal Services and External Assistance. The villagers of L1 perceive good treatment by municipal and departmental authorities when they seek services for registry, land registry/titling, etc. They don't believe that the government invests enough in their community however, and some indicate a mistrust of politicians and their "forgotten promises." The village receives a fair amount of external assistance: with cooperative chicken project for women supported by Holland, Japan and Australia; a housing project and child sponsorship project supported by Plan International;[29] an electricity project installed by INDE; and a DICOR extension project. They don't have contact with Social Funds, however.

Shocks. The village of L1 has been hit with several collective shocks, including the earthquake of 1976 (the effects of which have largely been overcome), hurricane Mitch in 1998, and an epidemic of dengue in 1999. In addition to wiping out the productive base and rendering their land infertile, Hurricane Mitch also destroyed livestock animals, and agricultural tools (including tractors). The villagers also blame the dengue epidemic on Mitch, as a result of stagnant waters, which generated an infestation of mosquitoes in the village causing an outbreak of dengue. This effects of this epidemic were exacerbated by the lack of health services in the village. On top of this, villagers note risks from various idiosyncratic shocks, including sickness (primarily, diarrhea, flu, and respiratory infections); risks of maternal mortality due to the absence of health services and ambulances for transportation; death in the family (including of spouses); unemployment (largely as a result of Mitch); and domestic violence and alcoholism.

Perceptions of Changes over Time; Aspirations for the Future. The villagers clearly perceive a worsening of poverty and living conditions, largely associated with the wake of Hurricane Mitch and the depletion of soil fertility. This hasn't seemed to dampen the children's aspirations for the future, however. When they grow up, boys indicate they'd like to be: "a doctor to cure people . . . to work in the maquila (textile industry) . . . teacher . . . a soldier to carry a big shotgun (escopeta) . . . an engineer . . . police." The girls aspire to be: "a lawyer . . . teachers . . . secretaries." The children also express an interest in learning English so as to be able to travel and migrate to the U.S.

Ladino 2 (L2): Divisions between Rich and Poor, Vulnerability among the Landless

This small agricultural community of 160 people (24 houses) is located in the North East Region[30] of Guatemala. Despite being so small and ethnically homogeneous, the village has conflicts and divisions related to inequalities in the ownership and management of resources, as discussed below.

Land: A Source of Conflict. Ownership of agricultural land is the most important element in terms of differentiation between rich and poor. A few households own most of the land, and what they own is the higher quality land with large pastures and water nearby. The remaining households own little more land than the property on which they've built their houses. The only mechanism for the poor to access land is through sharecropping agreements. The larger, better off land owners have significant advantages, including access to credit, participation in the local government, and a more advantageous position in the sharecropping relationship because in case of a loss, the tenant has to pay back the landlord for any expenditures on inputs.

Economic Activities. Men in the village are largely farmers. They grown corn, beans, tomatoes, rice and chili. The more powerful families in the village also have cattle and some are in the business of transporting products to local markets; these are the same families who participate in the comité. Farmers complain that while their products have become cheaper, inputs are always more expensive.

---

29. Plan International sponsors a number of children in the village, giving them food, clothing, school supplies. While clearly appreciated by beneficiaries, this seems to have caused some divisions and jealousies within the village, particularly from those families whose children are not sponsored.

30. The North East Region includes the departments of El Progreso, Izabal, Chiquimula, and Zacapa.

They also consider that commercializing their products has high transactions costs (transportation charges and payments to intermediaries). The community receives inflows of migrant agricultural workers during the harvest season. Few members migrate out of the community. Women are primarily in charge of housework, which seasonally may imply getting involved in farm work. They are also the ones to participate in school activities (preparation of children's lunches, meetings) as well as in religious practices.

Physical Assets and Basic Services: Inequality and Conflict. Although piped water has been an improvement over their previous source of water (the river), access to piped water has also been a matter of conflict and inequality. While most households have piped (not potable) water,[31] the distribution of water is managed by the local authority ("el comité"), which has been presided over by the same person for the last 20 years. Participation in the local government does not appear democratic and excludes those who cannot afford the operations expenses related to being part of the comité. Participants in the study regularly complained that the comité manages resources arbitrarily and has no accountability. Those who feel discontent, however, seem to have little power to make any changes and this produces divisions within the community. A few households have access to electricity via a solar project sponsored by an NGO, but only those who an afford the connections costs. The village is accessible via a single surfaced road (*camino balustrada*). Environmental problems appear to plague the community. Land quality has decreased significantly and more fertilizers and fungicides are needed. The river, which used to be their source of drinking water, is now very polluted. There is no adequate waste disposal service and most dwelling do not have latrines or toilets. There are no churches within the community, but members attend churches in other nearby communities. Community members complain of lack of access to credit.

Education and Health. About 75% of people in the community are literate. There is one elementary school with three teachers and two classrooms, serving 70–80 students through grade six. Teachers note that there are problems with school drop out, low achievement, and seasonal absenteeism, all associated with child labor. Though villagers claim equality between girls and boys for school enrollment, only 40% of those currently enrolled are girls. In terms of health services, a doctor visits the community twice a month under the SAIS program.

Social Capital. Social capital in L2 is fairly weak. Some villagers question the performance and usefulness of the Development Committee due to unfair and preferential decision making and management of resources (for example, with water, per above), misuse of funds, elite capture, and authoritarian stance. The school committee, which oversees use of government funds, however, is well regarded. Parents participate by providing labor and preparing school lunches. The poor are excluded from community activities.[32] Women's participation is also low. Although they can elect committee members, few attend the meetings since they are busy with household chores and men do not invite them. During national elections, many women do not vote because they lack documentation and don't see the benefits of participating.

Municipal Services and External Assistance. The villagers appear satisfied with the treatment they receive by the municipality (for citizenship documents, etc.), though many women don't get their documents. The villagers complain that land titling and cadastre services are prohibitively costly (they are only available in Guatemala City and require costly lawyers). In addition to SIAS, the village has received external assistance from PRODER, which has promoted three projects: water, extension, and the construction of the road. Other than that, external contacts are scarce.

---

31. The piped water is not treated; households do treat it with chlorine, but only for drinking water.

32. As one informant expressed: "a poor person cannot be a member of the committee because he does not have enough means for moving around and time to lead initiatives. They would have to provide some time for the committee and they have to work and eat." L2 PPA.

Shocks. The community identified several collective shocks that have hit them in recent memory: the earthquake of 1976, Hurricane Mitch in 1998, a tornado in 1998, and a tremor (temblor) in 1998. The earthquake and tremor had strong psychological effects, causing fear and nausea among women and children, as well as *susto* (post-traumatic stress syndrome). The hurricane and tornado had stronger economic impacts, ruining the tomato crop and damaging other crops, as well as a few houses. Informants report that these effects have largely been overcome, though in none of the instances did they receive any formal assistance. Villagers also report a number of idiosyncratic shocks, including sickness (primarily flu and diarrhea), crop loss (which is particularly difficult for sharecroppers who still have to pay the landlords for their inputs and who lack credit), and unemployment for the landless (particularly for women, who can't seem to find work outside their domestic duties). Some women also report domestic violence, alcoholism among spouses, and family disintegration as shocks they've faced.

Perceptions of Changes over Time; Aspirations for the Future. The villagers perceive that in some respects, living conditions have improved in their community, attributing these improvements to: improved road access, piped water, the elementary school. However, they note concerns about land fertility and environmental contamination. The children have high hopes for the future, with boys aspiring to be: "teachers . . . a veterinarian . . . an accountant/auditor . . . a divorce lawyer," while girls hope to become: "a lawyer . . . a seamstress . . . a secretary . . . a accountant/auditor to count money and not steal from us . . . a teacher to teach children to read and write." The children also express an interest in learning English so as to be able to travel and migrate to the U.S.

Mam 1 (M1): Better Off Despite Land Pressures, With Migration Playing a Key Role

This mountainous village of less than 1000 people (104 households) is located in the North West Region[33] of Guatemala. The ethnically-homogeneous Mam population is quite young, with the majority under age 35. Most adults are illiterate.

Land: Population Pressures and Minifundización. Land is privately owned via inheritance (with sons inheriting). Land pressures are a problem, as plots get divided up between more and more sons through the process of *minifundización* (average plot size is now 1–5 cuerdas).

Economic Activity: Diversification and Migration. The economic base is fairly diversified, with a range of agricultural crops (potatoes, onions, cabbage, carrots, broccoli, beans, corn, and herbs), construction, freight transport, and tailoring (sewing) providing a substantial share of incomes. Land pressures have caused many to migrate in search of jobs. Indeed, most families depend on some form of migration for additional income. Migration patterns have evolved and vary substantially: (a) a decreasing share of families still migrate to the fincas of Guatemala or Chiapas as seasonal day-laborers to harvest coffee (in August/September and November/December); (b) some families have land holdings in other municipalities (coffee plots of 10–20 cuerdas) and they go there for harvests; (c) others (mainly young men) migrate to Cancún, Mexico to work in construction for a year or more; and (d) others (mainly young) go to the USA. Those with family members in the USA enjoy many benefits associated with significant remittances, such as television, larger houses, funds to send their children in school, and the ability to purchase more land. These remittances seem to be creating inequalities within a village that was historically fairly equal. Largely as a result of remittances from migration and access to credit (via the revolving community fund, see below)—and in spite of population pressures on the land—the villagers of M1 perceive that living standards have improved and poverty has declines.

---

33. The North West Region includes the departments of Huehuetenango and Quiché.

Physical and Communal Infrastructure. The village of M1 seems to be fairly well endowed in terms of other physical and social assets and services. They have piped water, latrines, drainage installed by the European Union that covers 40% of the community, and electricity covering 90% of households. The main access road is an unsurfaced (gravel) road (*carretera de terracería*), and the villagers communicate with other nearby villagers via footpaths (*veredas*). The main forms of transport are: pickup trucks, small trucks, and other vehicles. Communal infrastructure is also extensive, with three mills, stores, one cellular telephone (that is private, but operated as a public "pay" phone service), and a church. The villagers also maintain communal woods, with two representatives serving as rangers (*guardabosques*) to manage the common woods and their use (charging fees for people to gather wood).

Education and Health. The village also has an elementary school that is managed by the community under the PRONADE program, with three teachers serving 105 students through grade six. Teachers note that while drop out is not a serious problem, low achievement is, primarily due to lack of support from parents, many of whom (particularly the fathers) have migrated. Seasonal absenteeism, associated with child labor, is also a problem during the corn and coffee harvests (about a month or two), according to the teachers. The teachers don't note any serious problems of discrimination against girls' enrollment in the village. Health services are also abundant, with several midwives, SAIS representatives, a health clinic (but that lacks a doctor and medicine), health promoters (*promotores*), and a hospital in another town (though villagers note "discrimination" in being served or receiving medicines, due to their indigenous ethnicity and their lack of Spanish speaking ability).

Social Capital. Social capital within the village (bonding social capital) is quite strong, with a development committee that boasts representation from all families, sub-committees for education, water, irrigation, an agricultural organization, two women's groups, etc. The community also operates a fairly successful revolving credit fund (started by a grant from a Canadian organization, but run entirely by the community) and a micro-enterprise committee for women. They also have two appointed rangers (*guardabosques*) designated to maintain and guard the communal forests. Villagers cited examples of mutual assistance: helping an orphan family, helping those with death in the family, and financial transfers being provided by the church to poor families. The community also seems to have significant ties to external organizations (linking social capital), receiving aid and projects from FODIGUA, PRONADE, DECOPAZ, UNICEF, the E.U. and NGOs. Despite their participation in specific groups, women acknowledge that they have little influence on community decisions.

Shocks. The villagers of M1 identified four main collective shocks: (a) violence during the armed conflict of the 1980s; (b) a forest fire during the 1990s; (c) freezing and frost (*heladas*) in 1994 and 2000; and (d) a hurricane in 2000. The violence in the 1980s was perceived as very severe, with lasting effects. Apparently both the army and the *guerrillas* came through the village, and the army reportedly burned eight houses. Few of the villagers were hurt because they had fled into the mountains. The villagers helped each other, providing the newly homeless shelter and food. Some external agency sent them materials (metal plates—laminas) to help rebuild their houses, but they don't know who sent them. Lasting effects are largely psychological, with reports of fear and *susto* (post-traumatic stress syndrome). The forest fire swept through the municipal and communal woods during the 1990s. The cause was unknown. Once again, the villagers organized to try to stop it, reflecting their strong social capital, but they were not equipped to extinguish it. The villagers note that the frosts in 1994 and 2000 were quite severe, generating substantial economic and crop losses (particularly for potatoes). The villagers provided little information about the effects of the hurricane. Idiosyncratic shocks identified by the villagers include: sickness (including *susto*), death in the family (particularly of spouse or parents), uncertainties or abandonment for those left behind when a family member migrates. Widows and an orphan family were identified by the village as being particularly vulnerable.

Perceptions of Changes over Time; Aspirations for the Future. The members of M1 definitely perceive that living standards have improved. "We used to migrate to the fincas [in Guatemala] because we weren't organized and we didn't know how to produce better from our lands. Now there are fewer who migrate [to the fincas of Guatemala], because now we have credit in the community, we harvest vegetables or potatoes . . . at least we don't go to the fincas anymore." The children have aspirations for a very different life than that of their parents. When they grow up, the boys of M1 indicate they do not want to work the fields, rather, they want to "work in factories . . . in an office . . . be radio disk jockeys . . . be a teacher to give classes in both languages . . . to be an engineer . . . to study computers." Girls aspire to work as teachers or secretaries, with the hopes of returning to their community to teach what they have learned.

Mam 2 (M2): Poor, with Inequalities in Land, Services, Remittances and Social Capital

Population. M2 is a larger, ethnically homogeneous mountainous village of some 3000 people (277 houses) located in the South Western Region[34] of Guatemala. The community has existed for close to 200 years. Villagers are monolingual Mam speakers, and children learn Spanish only when they attend school.

Denial of Emerging Inequalities. Productivity within the community seems to have reach its limit. In this context, the only way to increase one's wealth is to take it from someone else or seek opportunities (land, work) elsewhere.[35] The villagers seem uncomfortable with this reality—and the growing inequality associated with it. During the field work, they repeatedly denied inequality within the village, insisting that "everyone in the community is equally poor, nobody has more than the rest"— perhaps as an effort to "protect" themselves from the conflicts that may derive from envy and greed.[36] Despite these denials, emerging inequalities are indeed apparent, in access to land and productive opportunities, services access (water, education, electricity), control of the local government (comité), income from remittances, etc.

Land. Land in the community is privately owned via inheritance through the sons.[37] Population pressures have resulted in smaller and smaller plot sizes, and many plots are of poor quality. Due to altitude and wind, land in the region has low productivity and people either rent land in other parts of the municipality or migrate to look for temporary off-farm jobs.

Economic Activities: Agriculture and Migration. Men in M2 are farmers. They grow corn, beans, potatoes, peaches, and apples. Some of the better-off families also raise lambs, although no one has more than 20 animals. Those with livestock are the ones within the community who participate in school meetings as well as in the local government (comité). The main problems identified by the farmers are related to the low productivity of the soil, the lack of irrigation and technical assistance, and high transactions costs associated with the commercialization of their products. Women are in charge of the housework; they also collect firewood and help with farm work. Women have been involved in two communal projects related to water and energy with an NGO. Some 90% of the villagers (including children) migrate once a year to other regions of Guatemala or Chiapas (Mexico) to harvest coffee. The money that is earned when the family migrates is what

34. The South West Region includes the departments of Sololá, Totonicapán, Suchitepequez, Quetzeltenango, Retalhuleu, and San Marcos.

35. Barring any major innovations, of course.

36. There is a large literature in anthropology (Foster (XXXX): Tzintzuntzan) that analyzes how this is a very coherent behavior in a context where productivity has reached its limits. In this context, it's hard to expand productive opportunities and therefore people see individual advancement as a "zero sum game:" that an increase in wealth is only possible if you take away from someone else. In order to "protect" itself from the conflicts that may derive from envy and greed, the society needs to see itself as an "equal" society, even in the face of emerging inequalities.

37. Only men inherit the land because "they contribute more to the family."

sustains the agricultural inputs of the family farm, as well as their own consumption of food. Some have permanently migrated to Mexico, Belize or the U.S., and those households with a permanent migrant member sending back remittances are better off than the rest.

Basic Services and Infrastructure. Less than a quarter of the dwellings have access to electricity, and about 13% have piped (not potable) water. Connections and operations costs seem to be the prohibitive barrier for most households to acquire access to these services. Very few dwellings have latrines. A dirt road connects the community with other villages and the municipality head. Rains from July through September damage the access road and isolate the village completely.

Education and Health. There is one elementary school offering through grade six, with four teachers serving 215 students. The teachers not that school dropout and achievement are problems due to (a) early drop out associated with marriage (around age 12–13); (b) migration; (c) child labor; (d) malnutrition; and (e) lack of understanding of Spanish among the students. A fewer share of students are girls; teachers attribute this to domestic responsibilities and a lack of Spanish ability among the girls. Most adults are illiterate. In terms of health services, the village has some midwives and a health care worker (promotor). They rarely go to the doctor in municipal head because it's expensive and because access is difficult due to the poor quality of their access road.

Social Capital. Social capital within the village is "low-medium," and unequally distributed and plagued by some internal conflicts. Within the community, the Development Committee (comité) and the auxiliary mayor are prominent members leading development projects and contacting government and non-government institutions. They convene meetings with the community to inquire whether residents are willing to participate in development projects, When households want to participate, they must contribute to fund transportation costs, food, and other expenses. This system restricts access to the poorer families. Women are also excluded from most community activities and decision making, though they did participate in two development projects (water and energy). The school committee (PTA) is also active in the community, particularly in the preparation of school lunches and teacher recruiting. Only men are members of the PTA. Divisions between the Evangelical and Catholic churches, as well as the Mayan religion, have spurred conflicts within the community. The community has very few links outside the village and strangers are not trusted.

Government Services and External Aid. Regarding access to municipal and other government services, the villagers note that they perceive discrimination in these services and that they are treated like "second class people because they are not given attention and when they say hello, no one answers them. They are viewed as 'dirty people.' " They have received assistance from FIS and FONAPAZ (for the electricity project, their access road, and an irrigation project), as well as training from DICOR representatives for both men (agriculture, fertilizer use) and women (cooking, weaving, vegetable cultivation). CONALFA has given a few adults (10–15) literacy teaching, and the village has received some support from two NGOs (on child nutrition and pregnancy, food preparation, and school feeding).

Shocks. The community of M2 identified the following collective shocks: (a) the earthquake of 1976; (b) heavy rains in July and September; and (c) freezing/frost in December through February. The effects of the earthquake were relatively minor (one family lost its house) and have largely been overcome. The other two shocks are interesting because they are predictable and repeated. First, in the case of the heavy rains, the village becomes extremely vulnerable, since their only access road (dirt) become impenetrable. This impedes their ability to transport their products or make purchases in the market. It also creates a barrier for travel to the health clinic in the municipality. To mitigate the impact of this situation, the community has developed two "survival" strategies: (a) the whole village participates in transporting products between the closest point trucks can come and the community by foot and with beasts of burden; and (b) the men work to repair and maintain the roads (without any external assistance). They classify this risk and shock as severe, and don't believe it to have been overcome. Second, the villagers repeatedly lose their potato harvest due to frost in December and January. They don't seem to have a strategy to prevent these losses.

In terms of idiosyncratic shocks, the villagers of M2 focus on a variety of health shocks, such as sickness, death in the family, maternal mortality (which they cite as the most common cause of death among women). The lack of a dependable access road complicates their ability to seek treatment outside the village, and many seem to die of common illnesses (such as dysentery, fever). About 15–20 widows also lost their husbands, who contracted common illnesses in the fincas or died of alcoholism.

Perceptions of Changes Over Time, Aspirations for the Future. The villagers of M2 perceive that poverty has increased over time and attribute this to a number of factors: (a) low productivity of the land that requires them to migrate to the fincas; (b) fertility and household size; (c) increases in cost of living and agricultural inputs; and (d) alcoholism and problems between couples. They note that the ones who have experienced improvements in living conditions "are those who have relatives in the United States who help them with remittances, or those who run their own businesses, such as clothing or stores (tiendas)." In terms of aspirations for the future, the girls of M2 want to "work in the kitchen . . . work . . . go to the capital to work as domestic employees," while boys aspire to "be merchants . . . work the land . . . be farmers . . . be a bricklayer."

Q'eqchi 1 (QE1): Poor, with Internal and External Conflicts and Exclusion

This small ethnically homogeneous village, located in the Northern Region,[38] was founded about 30 years ago when the founding families migrated from other regions in search of land. The village is composed of 72 households and 350 families. The Q'eqchi population is mostly monolingual and illiterate, with only a few residents speaking any Spanish. The villagers believe that learning Spanish is crucial because those who do "have access to the Ladino world, the world of better opportunities . . . they can communicate with Ladinos and spearhead community initiatives in Government offices."

Communal Land: Source of Internal and External Conflicts. Land is communal property and with each family being assigned a plot (averaging 90 *cuerdas* plus 25 square meters for houses). Distribution of the land was managed by the founding families (particularly a prominent leader), who led the initiative to gain access to the land and distribute the plots (primarily to males) in accordance with the INTA (National Institute for Agrarian Transformation). Unequal land distribution has generated conflicts within the community. Although some residents are grateful to the community leader for his initiative in managing the land, others complain that his family secured access to bigger and better pieces of land. Not all families have plots (particularly those who arrived later). The village of QE1 has also experienced a serious land conflict with a neighboring community. The neighboring community hired soldiers to force them to abandon their land by burning their houses, damaging their plantations, and whipping their community leader. "Many fled, but those who remained united to face the problem." The community sent a letter to the President of Guatemala and visited the Ministry of the Interior (*Gobernación*). As a result, soldiers were withdrawn and 25 residents from the other community were arrested.

Economic Activities. Agriculture provides the main source of earnings for the community. Cardamom is the main crop, followed by coffee, and corn for subsistence consumption. While migration is scant, a few young men do migrate to work in nearby coffee and cardamom plantations. Men primarily work in agriculture and are responsible for collecting and transporting firewood. Women are primarily responsible for domestic duties, but also help during the cardamom harvest. Children also work during the harvest season, causing absenteeism at school.

---

38. The Northern region includes the departments of Alta Verapaz and Baja Verapaz.

Basic Services and Infrastructure. Most (86%) of households have access to piped water,[39] although the village has an insufficient water supply and water pressure is low. Contamination is also a problem, and villagers allege that this may come from the two houses that live closest to the water tank. A water committee was created to handle these issues and collect funds for maintenance. Some residents allege misuse of funds collected by the committee. There is no electricity in the village. Access to the village is provided by the surfaced road (*carretera de balastrada*), which was recently constructed by FONAPAZ, as well as dirt roads (*caminos comunales de herradura*) that connect them to nearby villages. The village has one public phone.

Health Services. The village has a health post that belongs to the SIAS system and is attended by a rural health worker (nurse). The nurse is Q'eqchi and people from other communities come to the village of QE1 for treatment. The villagers note that there is a lack of medicines at the health post. The village also has a midwife.

Education. The village has an elementary school with three teachers offering up to grade five and serving 99 students. The school belongs to the PRONADE program and is managed by the community via the COEDUCA (comité de educación). The classes are bilingual (Q'eqchi and Spanish). A new school building was apparently built by the FIS, but at the time of the study had not been officially presented to the community (entregada) and was not being used. Teachers did not perceive school drop out to be a problem, though attendance does dip during the harvest season (July-August and October-November) when the children have to work. There do not seem to be large biases against girls' attendance or enrollment.

Social Capital: Dominance and Exclusion. Social capital in the community is "low," with exclusion and conflict pervading even existing organizations. The community has a few formal committees: the development committee (*comité promejoramiento*), the COEDUCA school committee, and the water committee. The prominent member of the founding family postulated himself as the development committee, which is responsible for distributing land. Respondents perceive the president as authoritarian, although they praise the committee for leveraging external assistance. As discussed above, informants allege misuse of funds by the water committee. The poor and women are excluded from participation in community decision making and committees. Men acknowledge that women do not participate, but do not appear eager to change this pattern.

Religious Conflicts. The majority of QE1 is Evangelic, but a small number of villagers practice Catholicism. Religious affiliation generates conflicts inside the community that started due to confrontations between religious leaders. The tone of these confrontations has heightened; participants in focus groups indicated that they attend services in other villages to avoid problems.

Government Services and External Contacts: Discrimination and Mistrust. Residents of QE1 perceive that they face discrimination when seeking municipal services such as citizenship registry, birth and marriage certificates, etc. They claim that when they go to the municipality (alcalde) they are always told to "wait over there (*espere allá*)" (for up to two days) but when a Ladino comes in, they serve him immediately, telling him "come right up (*pase adelante*)." They have received assistance from the FIS (school construction), SIAS, a government housing program, PRONADE, FONAPAZ, and two NGOs. Nonetheless, contacts with formal institutions and other communities are scarce because the community mistrusts strangers and is disenchanted by unfulfilled government promises. Although the village was not directly affected by the war, PACs[40] recruited residents of QE1 prompting mistrust of strangers.

---

39. For which they pay about Qz.30 per year.

40. PACs, or Self Defense Patrols, were created as counterinsurgency instruments during the armed conflict of the 1980s.

Shocks. The village identified four collective shocks: (a) drought in the summer of 1998, which affected the corn and bean harvests; (b) Hurricane Mitch in 1998, which affected cultivation along the river and damaged the water tank and piping (though these have since been fixed); (c) collective debt to a commercial bank;[41] and (d) the land conflicts with a neighboring community (discussed above). The collective debt problem seems to be the main lingering problem; they have received some assistance from an NGO and had contacts with the Ministry of Agriculture to try to obtain fertilizers, but have been frustrated by inaction on the part of the ministry to help them solve their problems. Idiosyncratic shocks identified by the villagers include: sickness (primarily diarrhea, fever, stomach ailments); and death of a spouse (viudez) due to alcoholism.

Perceptions of Changes over Time; Aspirations for the Future. The villagers of QE1 perceive that poverty has worsened in their village, largely due to the unequal distribution of land, population pressures on the land (particularly for those with small plots that have to be divided up among more and more inheritors), and because the price of their main product, cardamom, is low. The villagers note that as a result of population pressures on the land, they have to cut down the woods, and now firewood is becoming scarce. In the discussions of solutions to poverty, the villagers identify re-parcelization (more equal distribution) with a formalization of property rights, taking into account the communal woods, as the solution. The children link their aspirations for the future to education, and identify their goals as "Having a good job so that they don't have to suffer working the earth, receiving a salary."

Q'eqchi 2 (QE2): Extremely Poor and Deeply Divided
Located in the Northern Region, the village of QE2 belongs administratively to a Cooperative. The village is quite small, consisting of 40 households and 200 residents, and was founded about 70 years ago. It is extremely poor, lacking the most basic services and assets. Most are illiterate and few speak Spanish. Lack of Spanish-speaking ability is perceived by the villagers to be a strong disadvantage and source of their exclusion.

Deep Divisions, Despite Homogeneity. The community is homogeneous in the sense that residents all belong to the same ethnic group (Q'eqchi), all have the same occupation, belong to the same cooperative and grow cardamom. However, despite this homogeneity, divisions and conflicts permeate the community. The conflict originated as an outcome of discord between two families, which resulted in dividing the community in two groups. Tensions deepened during the construction of the school and road because one of the groups did not participate. Today, each group is affiliated with a separate church and each has its own entrance to the village to avoid conflict. Residents expressed that "this problem is terrible and dangerous. A war is about to start."

Cooperative Land Arrangements. The Cooperative owns the land and assigns plots to the families under the agreement that the households work the cooperative's lands. Some residents note that plot distribution is unequal, with those having arrived in the village first receiving the largest plots. Today, land is scarce due to migration and population increments.

Economic Activities. The main sources of earnings in the community are the harvesting of cardamom and coffee. Although residents don't normally migrate, in situations of crisis (such as the drought of 1998 that ruined their harvests, see below), they were forced to migrate in search of work.

---

41. Apparently one of the borrowers misused his funds, while others invested in harvests. The collective borrowers apparently couldn't repay in the time required by the Bank, and now they've had to mortgage their land at the Bank. If they don't repay, they risk losing their land.

Basic Services and Infrastructure. None of the households have access to piped or potable water. Water is obtained from streams (riacheulos) and channeled to dwellings in open ducts (poliducto). Houses have metal roofs and only two have cement walls. There is no electricity or telephone. The village is accessed by two caminos balustrados and one footpath (vereda) that connects to the municipal head. In terms of communal infrastructure, the village has two stores, three churches, and one mill.

Health Services. The village does not have a health center or post, but does receive support from SIAS promoters (promotores) and a midwife. Lack of medicines is a problem. Health problems—and the lack of health services—rank high as key problems in the minds of the villagers, as expressed in virtually all interviews.

Education. The village has an elementary school that belongs to the PRONADE system, offering through grade four with one teacher and 45 students. Classes are bilingual, in both Spanish and Q'eqchi (the teacher is Q'eqchi). Although the teacher does not report early drop out to be a problem, he does indicate problems with seasonal absenteeism associated with harvests. None of the children attend school past grade four, since the school does not offer beyond that. There do not appear to be strong biases against girls' enrollment or attendance.

Social Capital: Weak and Divided. The authoritarian relations dictated by the cooperative and the Evangelical Church, combined with the deep divisions in the community, have hindered the development of social capital in QE2. Solidarity among community members is scant, and the village lacks associations, committees and special groups (except the COEDUCA). Villagers are extremely dependent on the cooperative for internal management and external contacts. Women are excluded from community decision-making and participation. During focus group exercises, women acknowledged misinformation about government programs stems from their husbands' reluctance to update them. Women do participate in school activities, preparing school lunches. Links with formal institutions is negligible and only one NGO has had any presence in the community via a coffee project (no other institutions identified).

Government Services and External Contacts. Villagers report acceptable treatment by municipal authorities, who speak Q'eqchi, for services such as the processing of formal documents. Other than SIAS and PRONADE, the village does not receive any direct Government support (including no social funds).

Shocks. Two main collective shocks were identified by the community: (a) the drought of 1998, which also involved insect and rodent infestations and destroyed their coffee and cardamom crops; and (b) the conflicts and divisions in the community. While the conflict and its impacts are on-going, the villagers were able to overcome the impacts of the drought by migrating in search of work to protect their consumption and earnings. Numerous idiosyncratic shocks were also identified, including: (a) health shocks in almost all case interviews, including sickness and death, exacerbated by the lack of health services in the community; (b) loss of a spouse or family member (particularly for widows); (c) the malicious burning of one family's cardamom crop by another member of the community as part of the on-going conflict in the village; and (d) failure of a household enterprise (affecting one family).

Perceptions of Changes Over Time; Aspirations for the Future. The villagers of QE2 perceive that poverty has increased and they attribute this to population pressures on the land (and resulting smaller plot sizes via *minifundización*) and degradation in soil quality and productivity. Aspirations of children essentially repeat the life they know: boys aspire to work in agriculture like their fathers and girls in domestic work like their mothers.

QPES: SUMMARY OVERVIEW OF 10 RURAL VILLAGES IN GUATEMALA

Community	Characteristics	Poverty Inequality	Changes over time	Land	Economic activities
KA1 K A Q C H I Q E L	–Village consists of a workers and families living on a privately owned finca –Most born on the finca –Ethnic mix; lost cultural identity; they do not identify themselves as indigenous, just "natives" of the finca. –200 people, 40 households –Bilingual, but with children speaking Spanish, adults speaking indigenous languages –Central Region	–Extremely poor –Relatively homogeneous	–Same or worse –Little hope or aspirations for a better future	–Villagers use small plots owned by the finca (2–3 cuerdas) –Villagers do not own their own land	–Workers on coffee plantation –Subsistence production of corn, small garden plots
KA2 K A Q C H I Q E L	–Village seriously affected by violence of 1980s –1000 people, 220 HH –Bilingual –Ethnically homogeneous –Central Region	–Relatively better off –Some within village inequality	–Improved living conditions –Stronger aspirations for better future	–Private –Some also rent land –Some have irrigation	Agriculture: –Corn (subs.) –Potatoes –Tomatoes –Radishes –Apples –Peaches Non-Ag. –Weaving *guilpiles* (women)
KI1 Q U I C H E	–Village seriously affected by violence of 1980s –2840 people, 568 HH –Bilingual –Ethnically homogeneous –Some land conflicts –Some religious conflicts –North West Region	–Relatively better off –High within village inequality	–Poverty increased –Strong aspirations for better future	–Private –High inequality –2% own plots of 50 cuerdas –5% own plots of 10 cuerdas –Rest own plots of 1–2 cuerdas	Agriculture Corn Fruits Apples (day laborers and self-emp) Non-Ag. –Artisan crafts –Making clothes –Commerce
KI2 Q U I C H E	–Ethnic conflicts between K'iché majority and Ladino minority –Villagers dependent on seasonal migration –1254 people, 144 HH –Some bilingualism –North West Region	–Very poor –Small degree of within village inequality	–Poverty increased –Strong aspirations for the future	–Private –Plots avg. 10–20 cuerdas –Fertility problems –Communal forests and grasslands	Agriculture –Corn –Beans –Vegetables Non-Ag. –limited; only one merchant Finca Migration –Most

Migration patterns	Basic & social services	Social capital & relations	Gender	Shocks
−Ancestors migrated to the fincas −Current residents rarely leave −Finca receives temporary inflow of migrant workers during harvests	MINIMAL −NO water, latrines, sanitation, electricity −Primary school with 1 teacher, 1:31 ratio, grades 1–3 −NO health clinic or pharmacy; one midwife −Village accessible by one dirt road, impassable after heavy rains	−WEAK −finca authorities dominate −little collective action −almost no external links	Household: No Community: No Land: No Girls Enroll: Same	Collective: Earthquake Labor Other nat. Idiosync. Sickness Mat. mort. Dom. vio. Crime
−Little migration (a few young people have migrated to the capital) −Villagers fled during violence	ADEQUATE −Piped water but irregular service −Electricity −Latrines −Paved access road and dirt interior roads −Lots of communal infrastructure −Primary school with 1:32 ratio, grades 1–6 −SIAS health post, midwife	−MED-HIGH −Having to rebuild after violence	Household: Yes Community: No Land: CHECK Girls Enroll: Girls less	Collective Earthquake Violence of 1980s Idiosync. Violence of 1980s
Little migration, though a few men (landless) do migrate to the coffee fincas of Guatemala	ADEQUATE −Piped water, summer scarcity −Electricity −Latrines −Extensive road access −Lots of communal infrastructure −Primary school with 1:39 ratio, grades 1–6 −Pre-school, secondary school, teacher training center −NO clinic, just midwives	−Fairly HIGH −Rebuilding after violence −Some internal conflicts (land, religious) −Somewhat exclusive	Household: No Community: No Land: No Girls Enroll: Same	Collective Violence of 1980s Earthquake Idiosync. Job loss Sickness Accidents Loss of markets Terms of trade problems
−Most families migrate temporarily to work on the coffee and sugar plantations of the Costa Sur	MINIMAL −Most have piped water, but pressure problems −Few have latrines −NO energy −Village accessible by one unpaved road −No health post; has two midwives −Primary school with 1:37 ratio, grades 1–6	MEDIUM −Some external contacts −Internal ethnic conflicts −Somewhat exclusive	Household: Yes Community: No Land: Not clear Girls Enroll: Same	Collective: Earthquakes Cholera Hurricane Mitch Idiosyncrasy. Sickness Death Crop loss

(continued)

QPES: SUMMARY OVERVIEW OF 10 RURAL VILLAGES IN GUATEMALA (CONTINUED)

Community	Characteristics	Poverty Inequality	Changes over time	Land	Economic activities
L1 **L A D I N O**	−Shock-induced poverty −Hurricane Mitch destroyed productive base −420 people, 74 HH −Ethnically homogeneous −Monolingual Spanish −North East Region	−Poor, especially since Hurricane Mitch −Some within village inequality	−Poverty increased due to Mitch −Strong aspirations for the future	−Private −Those who don't own land, rent −Largest plots are 4 manzanas	Pre-Mitch −Lemons −Papaya −Tobacco −Melons −Eggplant −Palms −Corn (subsist.) −Livestock Post-Mitch Mainly have to search for jobs else-where; land infertile
L2 **L A D I N O**	−Inequality, divisions between rich and poor −Vulnerability among landless −Conflicts over management of resources −160 people, 24 HH −Ethnically homogeneous −Monolingual (Spanish) −North East Region	−Poor −Within village inequality	−Improved living conditions −Strong aspirations for future	−Private −Highly unequal −A few households own most of the land (esp. better quality) −Other HH work the land via share-cropping arrangements	Agriculture −Corn −Beans −Tomatoes −Rice −Chili −Cattle (wealthier HH) Non-Agric. (wealthier HH) −Transport of agric. to local markets
M1 **M A M**	−Better off despite land pressures −Migration and remittances play a key role −About 1000 people (104 HH) −Ethnically homogeneous −Largely monolingual −North-West Region −Affected by Violence of 1980s	−Relatively better off −Within village inequality	−Definitely perceive living conditions have improved −Strong aspirations for future	−Private −Average plot size small 1–5 cuerdas −Population pressure problem (minifun-dización) −Some own plots in other municipios −Communal woods	Agriculture −Potatoes −Onions −Cabbage −Carrots −Broccoli −Beans −Corn −Herbs Non-Agric. −Construction −Freight transp. −Tailoring −Remittances from migration
M2 **M A M**	−Poor and unequal, but villagers deny inequalities −3000 people (277 HH) −Ethnically homogeneous −Largely monolingual	−Very poor −Inequalities in land, services, remittances, social capital −Denial of inequalities by villagers	−Poverty increased −Modest aspirations for future	−Private −Small plot sizes −Unequal, ranging from 2–50 cuerdas	Agriculture −Corn −Beans −Potatoes −Peaches −Apples

Migration patterns	Basic & social services	Social capital & relations	Gender	Shocks
−Heavy out-migration, spurred largely by Hurricane Mitch's destruction of productive base −400 village members now living in capital or US	SOME GAPS −Most have piped water, but service irregular −Electricity −Communal infrastructure such as soccer fields −Inadquate drainage and sanitation −Village accessible only by unpaved road −NO health clinic or post; does have a midwife −Primary school with 1:24 ratio, grades 1–6	LOW-MEDIUM −Community does have number of organizations −Fairly significant presence of external aid agencies −Collective action low due to apathy, women excluded	Household: Yes Community: Some Land: Not clear Girls Enroll: Same	Collective Earthquake Hurricane Mitch Dengue Idiosync. Sickness Mat. Mort. Death Unemploy. Dom.vio.
−Village receives inflow of temporary migrant workers for harvest season −Few migrate out	MINIMAL −Piped water, not potable (most HH) −A few HH have electricity via solar project −Few latrines −No adequate sanitation, waste disposal −Village accessible via surfaced road −Doctor visits community twice per month under SIAS −Primary school, with 1:25 ratio, grades 1–6	LOW −Conflicts within community over resource management −Committees dominated by elite −Poor excluded −Women's participation low −Few external contacts	Household: Yes Community: No Land: Not clear Girls Enroll: Girls less	Collective Earthquake H. Mitch Tornado Tremors Idiosync. Sickness Crop loss Unempl. Dom. vio.
−Major feature −Remittances represent large % of incomes −Fewer migrate to fincas in Guatemala −Some go to land holdings in other municipalities −Cancun, Mexico (construction) −USA	WELL-ENDOWED −Piped water −Latrines −Drainage (40%) −Electricity (90%) −Access road: unpaved road −A lot of communal infrastructure −PRONADE elem. school, with 1:35 ratio, grades 1–6 −Several midwives, SIAS representatives, health clinic	HIGH −Strong internal bonds −Successful revolving credit fund (example) −Norms −Significant links to external organizations −Women little participation	Household: Yes Community: Some Land: No Girls Enroll: Girls less	Collective Violence of 1980s Forest fire Frost Hurricane Idiosync. Sickness Death Abandonment of families by migrants
−Major feature −90% of villagers (including children) migrate temporarily to coffee fincas of Guatemala or Chiapas	MINIMAL −Only 13% have piped water −<25% have electricity −Few latrines −Dirt access road, rains make road impassable, isolating village from July-Sept.	LOW-MED −Some internal committees −Elite capture and dominance −Conflictive −Poor, women excluded	Household: No Community: No Land: No Girls Enroll: Girls less	Collective Earthquake Heavy rains Frost Idiosync. Sickness Death Mat. Mort.

(continued)

QPES: SUMMARY OVERVIEW OF 10 RURAL VILLAGES IN GUATEMALA (CONTINUED)

Community	Characteristics	Poverty Inequality	Changes over time	Land	Economic activities
	–South West Region			–Those with remittances from US have more land	–Lambs (wealthier HH) Other –Income from day-labor work on fincas –Remittances
QE1 Q ` E Q C H I	–Poor, with serious internal and external conflicts, exclusion –350 people (72 HH) –Ethnically homogeneous –Monolingual, illiterate –Northern Region	–Very poor –Inequalities with unequal distribution of land	–Poverty increased –Modest aspirations for future	–Communal –Each family assigned a plot –Average plot size 90 cuerdas –Unequal distribution –Land conflicts (internal and external) –Some landless	Agriculture –Cardamom –Coffee –Corn
QE2 Q ` E Q C H I					

Source: QPES Main Report and village PPAs

(1) <u>Poverty:</u> A subjective description of the village based on qualitative information on villager perceptions of living conditions; basic and social services/assets; migratory patterns and employment (including work on fincas in Guatemala, which is an indication of relatively low earnings opportunities); diversification of economic activities. <u>Inequality:</u> subjective description of relative economic homo- or heterogeneity within the village based on welfare and assets (e.g., inequality of access to land, other assets).

(2) <u>Changes in living conditions over time, aspirations for future:</u> Perceptions of villagers as reported in QPES (focus groups for perceptions of changes; children for aspirations)

(3) <u>Basic Services:</u> As reported in QPES; XX:XX ratio refers to the teacher-student ratio. Most schools have multi-grade classes.

Migration patterns	Basic & social services	Social capital & relations	Gender	Shocks
–Some have relatives who permanently migrated to US, Mexico, Belize	–Primary school, with 1:52 ratio, grades 1–6 –Midwives, health worker	–Religious conflicts –Few external links, but have received some formal assistance		
Little migration	MINIMAL –Most have piped water, but pressure and contamination problems –No electricity –Road access: surfaced road + dirt roads –PRONADE elem. school, with 1:33 ratio, grades 1–5 –SIAS health post, with nurse, lack of medicines –Midwife	LOW –Internal conflicts –Exclusionary organizations –Elite capture –Misuse of committee funds –Poor and women excluded –Religious conflicts	Household: Yes Community: No Land: Not clear Girls Enroll: Same	Collective Drought H. Mitch Collective debt Land conflicts with neighboring community Idiosync. Sickness Death due to alcoholism
			Household: Yes Community: Some Land: No Girls Enroll: Girls less	Collective Idiosync.

(4) Social Capital: Overall ranking is a subjective description based on apparent degree of both formal (organizations) and informal (solidarity, collective action, trust) social capital, as well as bonding SC (within community), bridging SC (external), and linking SC (links to formal organizations); exclusion/inclusion of certain groups (women, poor); and relations within village (harmonious, conflictive, divided). See text above and Social Capital Paper for additional details.

(5) Gender: As reported in QPES (a) household: women participate in household decision making; (b) community: women participate in household decision making; (c) land: women inherit land or hold title; (d) girls enrollment: significant differences or discrimination in enrollment between girls and boys; all as reported by the villagers in the QPES.

(6) Shocks: Mat. Mort = maternal mortality (risks of birth); Dom. Vio. = domestic violence (usually associated with alcoholism)

QUALITATIVE STUDY RESULTS: CLUSTERING OF ASSETS AT VILLAGE LEVEL?

Villages (KI = k'iche, M = mam, L = ladino, KA = kaqhiqel, QE = q'eqchi

	KI1	M1	KA2	L1	KI2	L2	M2	QE1	QE2	KA1
POPULATION	2840	1000	1000	420	1254	160	3000	350	200	200
INCOME DIVERSIFICATION										
Agriculture	Diverse	Diverse	Diverse	Diverse	Medium	Diverse	Diverse	Little	Finca	Finca
Non-agriculture	Diverse	Diverse	Weaving	Weaving		Some				
Migration	Little	Int'l	Coping	Int'l, coping	Fincas	Inflow	Fincas		Coping	
ASSETS										
School with grades 1-3	YES	YES*	YES	YES	YES	YES	YES	YES*	YES*	YES
Midwife/health promoter	YES	YES	YES	YES	YES	YES	YES	YES	YES	YES
School with grades 3-6	YES	YES	YES	YES	YES	YES	YES	to 5	to 4	
Piped water	YES	YES	YES	YES	Most	YES	few HH	YES		
Social Capital	HIGH	HIGH	MED.	LOW	MED.	LOW	med-low	LOW	LOW	LOW
Electricity	YES	YES	YES	YES		few HH	few HH			
Communal infrastructure	LOTS	LOTS	LOTS	LOTS			few HH			
Road access	good	med	good	med	med	bad	verybad	bad	bad	verybad
Latrines	YES	YES	YES	most	few HH	few HH	few HH			
Health clinic/post		YES	YES					YES		
Preschool	YES									
Secondary School	YES									
SHOCKS/COHESION										
Major shocks	80s-Violence	80s-Violence	80s-Violence	serious				some		some
Social Cohesion	conflict				conflict	conflict	conflict	serious conflict	serious conflict	conflict**
POVERTY & INEQUALITY										
Pov-Subjective Judgement	Modpoor	Modpoor	Modpoor	Modpoor	Modpoor	Modpoor	Poor	Extpoor	Extpoor	Extpoor
Poverty Map-municipality	86%	70%	57%	75%	77%	18%	90%	84%	86%	43%
Inequality-subjective	High	High	Med.	Med.	Low	Med.	High	High	Low	Low
SUMMARY JUDGEMENT										
Endowment summary	"ALL", but still poor			"Mixed" and poor				"NOTHING" very poor		
Key Problem		Livelihoods		Assets, Livelihoods				Everything		

Notes: * = PRONADE school

Income diversification: little means not very diversified, few or single crop dependence

Migration: coping = migrated only in response to shock; inflow = receives seasonal migrants for harvest

Finca: either the village IS a finca (or coop) or many villagers migrate seasonally to fincas

Poverty, inequality: subjective judgement based on assets, income diversification, perceptions of villagers themselves, photos

**Conflict with finca owners/managers; other conflicts mainly over land/religious disputes

QPES: Inventory of Collective Shocks, Impacts and Responses in Ten Rural Guatemalan Villages

Community	Shock		Impacts			
	Description	Type	Description	Type	Severity	Duration
KA1	Earthquake 1976	NAT	Houses destroyed, damaged (and still are)	ECO-W	severe	lasting
	Massive dismissals, unemp. early 1990s	ECO	Union members vengefully dismissed by finca, incomes, benefits lost	ECO-Y	severe	lasting
			Social and psychological impacts (demoralizing, destroying trust)	PSYCH-SOC		
	Flooding from river (recurrent)	NAT	Blocks access road to finca; can't leave or enter	COMM-ASSET	moderate	lasting
	Landslides from heavy rains (recurrent)	NAT	n.a.	n.a.	moderate	n.a.
KA2	Earthquake 1976	NAT	Lost family members (death)	HEALTH	severe	overcome
			Houses destroyed	ECO-W		
	Violence/conflict 1980s	PO	Mass murder/disappearances (leaving 40 widows and 2 orphan families)	HEALTH	severe	lasting
			Fear/susto	PSYCH		
			Crops burned	ECO-Y		
			Houses destroyed	ECO-W		
			Community disintigrated, fear of collective association	SOC		
KI1	Earthquake 1976	NAT	Some people died	HEALTH	severe	overcome
			Houses destroyed	ECO-W		
	Violence 1980s	PO	People murdered/disappeared; girls raped	PSYCH/SOC/HEALTH	very severe	overcome but memories remain
			Fear/susto	PSYCH		
			Couldn't work, lost crops, houses looted	ECO-W,Y		
			Children couldn't go to school	EDUCATION		
			Social capital damaged, mistrust	SOC		
KI2	Earthquake 1976	NAT	Fear	PSYCH.	severe	lasting
			Homes destroyed and damaged (many still not fixed)	ECO-W	severe	lasting
	Earthquake 1986	NAT	Fear/susto	PSYCH.	sev-mod.	overcome
			Destroyed homes; lack of water	ECO-W, HEALTH		
	Cholera epidemic 1990	HEALTH	Six people caught it; one died	ECO-Y, W	moderate	overcome
	Hurricane Mitch 1998	NAT	Crops destroyed and damaged, homes damaged	ECO-Y, W HEALTH	severe	lasting
			Children got sick	HEALTH		
LI	Earthquake 1976	NAT	Destroyed some homes and the school	ECO-W, COMM.ASSETS	severe	overcome
			Fear	PSYCH.		

(continued)

QPES: INVENTORY OF COLLECTIVE SHOCKS, IMPACTS AND RESPONSES IN TEN RURAL GUATEMALAN VILLAGES (CONTINUED)

Community	Shock Description	Shock Type	Impacts Description	Impacts Type	Severity	Duration
	Hurricane Mitch 1998	NAT	Completely wiped out main productive asset: land	ECO-W, Y	very severe	lasting
			Destroyed livestock, agricultural tools (tractors)			
			Widespread unemployment as a result			
	Dengue Epidemic 1999	HEALTH	Caused outbreak of dengue (see below)	HEALTH		
			Illness; lingering risk of dengue due to stagnant water	HEALTH	moderate	risk lasting
L2	Earthquake 1976	NAT	Psychological/fear/susto	PSYCH/HEALTH	moderate	overcome
	Hurricane Mitch 1998	NAT	Ruined tomato crops, damaged other crops and houses	ECO-Y, W	severe	overcome
	Tornado 1998	NAT	Damage to some houses	ECO-W	severe	overcome
	Tremor 1999	NAT	Psychological/fear/susto	PSYCH/HEALTH	moderate	overcome
MI	Violence 1980s	PO	Houses burned	ECO-W	very severe	overcome
			Violence	SOC	very severe	overcome
			Fear, susto (post-traumatic stress syndrom)	PSYCH/HEALTH	very severe	lasting
	Forest Fire 1990s	NAT	Communal woods burned, lost wood for homes, animals destroyed	COMM. ASSETS	severe	lasting
	Freezing/frost 1994/2000	NAT	Potato crop losses	ECO-Y	n.a.	n.a.
	Hurricane 2000	NAT	Crop losses, homes swept away	ECO-Y, W	n.a.	n.a.
M2	Earthquake 1976	NAT	Fear in village; one family lost house	SOC/ECO-W	moderate	overcome
	Rains/flooding (recurrent)	NAT	Road becomes impassable, can't transport products or reach health services	ECO-W,Y	severe	lasting
	Freezing frost (recurrent)	NAT	Damage/destroy potato crops	ECO-Y	severe	repeated
QEI	Drought 1998	NAT	Affected corn and bean harvests	ECO-income	moderate	overcome
	Hurricane Mitch 1998	NAT	Damaged water tank and piping	COMM. ASSETS	moderate	overcome
	Collective Debt	ECO	Villagers had to mortgage land, putting them at risk	ECO-Wealth	mod-severe	lasting
	Land conflict with neighboring community	SOCIAL	Violence, whipping of committee member	SOC/COMM	severe	lasting
			Burning houses, cutting crops	ECO-W, Y		
QE2	Drought 1998	NAT	Destroyed coffee/cardamom crops	ECO-income	severe	overcome
	Conflict within community	SOCIAL	Broken social capital	SOC/COMM	severe	lasting
			Inefficient management of communal resources/infrastructure	COMM. ASSETS		

QPES: INVENTORY OF COLLECTIVE SHOCKS, IMPACTS AND RESPONSES IN TEN RURAL GUATEMALAN VILLAGES

Community	Strategy/Response — Description	Type	Formal Assistance
KA1	Tried to rebuild homes, mill; debt; using mill at neighboring finca	SELF, FORMAL	Received some housing materials from bilateral donors
	Tried to get union help (lawyers)—pending action	COLLECTIVE	Union lawyers
	Seeking temporary employment on nearby fincas	SELF	
	n.a.	n.a.	n.a.
	n.a.	n.a.	n.a.
KA2	Organized devel. committee; received ext'l assistance	COMM/FORMAL	Received housing materials, food
			Helicopter help for injured
	Villagers fled to nearby town	SELF	None
	Now have organized with devel. committee that also has role to protect community	COLLECTIVE	
KI1	Churches helped rebuild houses, hand out food	COLLECTIVE	None
	People helped each other	SELF	None-during
	Villagers fled to capital	FORMAL	After-school and housing project
KI2	People had to go into debt and then migrate to pay debt	SELF, FORMAL	UNEPAR provided housing materials
	n.a.	n.a.	n.a.
	Went to hospital, received medicine; woman who died refused to go. Now treat water	SELF, FORMAL	Health education campaign at health center
	Villagers went into debt and then had to migrate to pay debt	SELF	None
L1	n.a. (community rebuilt school, homes?)	n.a.	None
	Migration in search of work	SELF	None
	n.a.	n.a.	None
L2	None	NONE	None
	Each family rebuilt, community helped one family	SELF	None
	Each family rebuilt	SELF	None
	None	NONE	None

(continued)

QPES: INVENTORY OF COLLECTIVE SHOCKS, IMPACTS AND RESPONSES IN TEN RURAL GUATEMALAN VILLAGES (CONTINUED)

Community	Strategy/Response Description	Type	Formal Assistance
M1	Villagers fled, helped each other repair homes, provide shelter and food; some external unknown external agency provided housing materials	COLLECTIVE FORMAL	Housing materials
	Collective action to try to fight fire	COLLECTIVE	None
	None	NONE	None
	n.a.	n.a.	None
M2	Family rebuilt house with help from municipality	SELF/FORMAL	Municipality provided housing materials, food
	Village works together to transport products and repair roads	COLLECTIVE	None
	None	NONE	None
QE1	None	NONE	None
	Water committee/collective action	COLLECTIVE	None
	Collective action, but little progress	COLLECTIVE	Some advice from NGO/MAGA
	Contacted Government officials	COLLECTIVE	Yes—military withdrawn
QE2	Temporary migration in search of work	SELF	None
	None; voluntad de Dios	NONE	None

SUPPLY VERSUS DEMAND-SIDE CONSTRAINTS TO COVERAGE OF EDUCATION, HEALTH, AND BASIC UTILITY SERVICES: CLUSTER METHODOLOGY

Objectives

This annex presents a methodology for analyzing the coverage gaps for education, health and basic utility services (water, sanitation, electricity). Specifically, it seeks to decompose these gaps into (a) pure supply-side barriers (lack of facilities in the community); (b) pure demand-side barriers (facilities exist but people do not use them due to demand-side constraints); and (c) mixed supply- and demand-side factors. The results are presented in Chapters 7, 8, and 9.

Coverage is the traditional indicator of access to services. For a particular service (e.g. access to electricity), coverage shows how many people or households use it. However, the drawback of this indicator is that it does not distinguish between supply- or demand-side constraints. Such a distinction is critical, as it leads to very different policy implications (e.g., build more schools or provide scholarships). This annex presents a methodology that can be used to decompose coverage gaps into supply-side, demand-side and mixed constraints. While the methodology itself has its limitations (see below) it can nevertheless provide crucial insights related to access and usage of services that can inform policy makers.

Basic Concepts and Methodology

Definitions. The following concepts are first defined:

1. Coverage rate (C): the number of households that use a particular service divided by the total number of households;[1]
2. Unserved population (U): 100—Coverage rate

---

1. This analysis can be applied to both individuals as well as households, depending on the type of service considered. For example, access to electricity would use households as the level of analysis where access to schools would use individuals.

3. Availability rate (A): the number of households living in communities where the service is available divided by the total number of households;

4. Take-up rate (T): the number of households using the service divided by the total number of households living in communities where the service is available; and

5. Primary sampling unit (PSU): the PSU defines a community based on geographical proximity. Households within the same PSU (or cluster) are said to belong in the same community. In the ENCOVI, a sub-set of households in each PSU were sampled.[2]

Decomposing Constraints for Non-Usage. This methodology first takes advantage of the PSUs to infer the existence of particular services or facilities within a specific PSU and extending it to the whole community. Specifically, if a household within a PSU uses a particular service, it can then be inferred that the service is available to everyone within that same PSU. Then, the gap (lack) of usage for those households that do not use the service can be classified in one of three categories: (i) demand-side; (ii) supply-side; and (iii) mixed.

Demand-side gap. This applies to households residing in PSUs where the service was available but did not use it, indicating that usage constraints are related to demand-side factors such as affordability (incomes to low to afford the service) or cultural factors. This is calculated as:

$$\text{Demand-side gap} = A - C$$

Supply-side gap. This refers to households residing in PSUs where the service is not available but would use it if it existed. It is given by:

$$\text{Supply-side gap} = (U - (A - C)) * T$$

Mixed supply and demand gap. In some cases, households face both supply- and demand-side constraints to usage of services. In other words, the service is not presently available, but even if it were made available, the households would not use it due to demand-side constraints. As such, while supply is the first binding constraint, demand-side factors would also be binding were the service made available. This is calculated as:

$$\text{Mixed supply and demand gap} = (U - (A - C)) * (100 - T)$$

The final step of this methodology is to normalize these indicators to show the actual proportion of any service deficit that is attributable to supply side factors, demand-side factors or both. This is achieved by dividing each of the above indicators by the unserved population (U):
Proportion of deficit attributable to demand side factors only:

$$\frac{A - C}{U}$$

Proportion of deficit attributable to supply side factors only:

$$\frac{(U - (A - C)) * T}{U}$$

---

2. However, this concept of community is a loose one does not necessarily have the usual meaning of a community. For example, within an urban area, a PSU could define a geographically based neighborhood (i.e. community) of 10 households that nevertheless belong to two different administrative units.

Proportion of deficit attributable to both demand and supply side factors only

$$\frac{(U - (A - C)) * (100 - T)}{U}$$

Example

To help illustrate the methodology, the following example decomposes the gaps in electricity usage:

Coverage rate = 40%
Availability rate = 80%
Take-up rate = 50%
Unserved population = 100% − 40% = 60%

Given the above, the unserved population is decomposed as follows:

Pure demand-side gap = 80% − 40% = 40%
Pure supply-side gap = (60% − (80% − 40%)) * 50% = 10%
Mixed demand and supply-side gap= (60% − (80% − 40%)) * (100% − 50%) = 10%

Finally normalizing the above indicators can be done by dividing each of them by the unserved population:

Proportion of deficit attributable to demand side factors only = 40%/60% = 66%
Proportion of deficit attributable to supply side factors only = 10%/60% = 17%
Proportion of deficit attributable to both demand and supply side factors only = 10%/60% = 17%

Limitations

While this methodology can provide useful information about the underlying constraints for using particular services, a number of caveats need to be taken into account. **First,** as mentioned above, the definition of a community relies on the survey specific definition of the PSUs. As such, there can be cases in which a service were available within a PSU, but none of the households surveyed used it. Using the above methodology this would overestimate the role of supply-side constraints for the particular service.

Second, applying this methodology to identify availability for some services may lead to overestimating the importance of supply-side constraints. For example, for health services, the under-coverage gap is examined by looking at those who reported illness, but didn't seek treatment (in the past month). To determine if a facility exists in a community, the reference population is those who reported illness and sought treatment. As such, the results could overestimate supply-side constraints by concluding a facility does not exist because no one in the community sough treatment, when in fact they may not have sought treatment because they did not perceive the need for medical attention.

Finally, the methodology could also lead to an incorrect assessment if a substitute to the particular service exists. In the example of health facilities, households that need medical attention may decide to treat the illness at home because they viewed the condition as not urgent. Still, if others in the PSU have used a medical facility, the inference using the methodology would imply a demand-side constraint. In the extreme case where everyone in the PSU that needed medical attention treated it at home, a supply-side constraint would be inferred when there was none.

Therefore, this type of analysis need to viewed as indicative and can be easily complemented by additional analysis in order to correctly assess the limiting factor in using different services.

REFERENCES

Anderson, Maria Elena. 2001. "Guatemala: the Education Sector." Draft prepared for the World Bank.

Arcia, Gustavo. 2002. "Educación y Reducción de Pobreza—Estrategia para el período 2002–2005." Draft.

Arragon and Associates. 1998. "User Perceptions of Justice Administration in Guatemala." Draft.

Asociación de Investigación y Estudios Sociales (ASIES). 2000. "Características y Funcionamiento del Mercado Laboral en Guatemala."

Asociación Gremial de Exportadores de Productos No Tradicionales (AGEXPRONT). 2000. "Exportaciones La Experiencia de Una Década."

Bachrach Ehlers, Tracy. *Silent Looms: Women and Production in a Guatemalan Town.* University of Texas Press.

Barrios, Lina Eugenia. 2001. *El Papel de la Alcaldía Indígena en el Desarrollo.*

Britnell, G. E. 1951. " Problems of Economic and Social Change in Guatemala." *The Canadian Journal of Economics and Political Science.*

Browning, Felix Alvarado, Maribel Carrera Guerra and Abel Girón. 1998. *Perfil de las Organizaciones No Gubernamentales en Guatemala.*

CEPAL. 1991. *Magnitud de la Pobreza en America Latina en los Años Ochenta.*

Centro de Investigaciones Económicas Nacionales (CIEN). 2000a. "Proyecto del Presupuesto General de Ingresos y Egresos del Estado del Ejercicio Fiscal 2001." Informe al Congreso No. 45.

Centro de Investigaciones Económicas Nacionales (CIEN). 2000c. " Carta Económica: El Problema de la Corrupción." Carta No. 227. By Maria del Carmen Aceña de Fuentes and Vilma de Liú.

Centro de Investigaciones Económicas Nacionales (CIEN). 2001a. "Del Autoritarismo a la Democracia: Democracia, Transparencia e Instituciones."

Centro de Investigaciones Económicas Nacionales (CIEN). 2001b. " Informe al Congreso: Ejecución del Presupuesto de Ingresos y Egresos del Ejercicio Fiscal 2000." No. 46.

Centro de Investigaciones Económicas Nacionales (CIEN). 2001c. " Carta Económica: En Busca de una Bureaucracia Eficiente." Carta No. 224. By Vilma de Liú.

Clert, Carine and Ana-María Ibáñez. 2002. "Exclusion and Poverty in Guatemala's Rural Villages: The Challenge of Tackling Cumulative Barriers." Guatemala Poverty Assessment Report Technical Background Paper. The World Bank.

Collier, Paul and David Dollar. 2002. "Aid Allocation and Poverty Reduction." European Economic Review.

Comisión para el Esclarecimiento Histórico (CEH, Truth Commission). 1999. *Guatemala: Memoria del Silencio.*

Comisión de Acompañamiento del Cumplimiento de los Acuerdos de Paz. 2000. *Cronograma de Implementación, Cumplimiento, y Verificación de los Acuerdos de Paz: 2000–2004.*

Cosminsky, S. and M. Scrimshaw. " Medical Pluralism on a Guatemalan Plantation." *Social Science and Medicine.* Vol. 148: 267–278.

Davis, Shelton H. 1988. "Sowing the Seeds of Violence." In *Harvest of Violence: The Maya Indians and the Guatemalan Crisis.* Robert M. Carmack (Ed). University of Oklahoma Press: Norman and London.

Davis, Shelton H. 2001. *El Potencial de los Recursos Culturales Para el Desarrollo.*

de Ferranti, David, Guillermo Perry, Indermit Gill and Luis Servén. 2000. *Securing our Future in a Global Economy.* The World Bank.

Edwards, John. 2002. "Education and Poverty in Guatemala." Guatemala Poverty Assessment Report Technical Background Paper. The World Bank.

EIU-Economist Intelligence Unit. 2001. "Guatemala Country Report," November.

EIU-Economist Intelligence Unit. 2002a. "Guatemala Country Report," January.

EIU-Economist Intelligence Unit. 2002b. "Guatemala Country Risk Service Report," January.

Eveleth, P. B. and J. M. Tañer. 1976. *Worldwide Variation in Human Growth.* Cambridge: Cambridge University Press.

Eveleth, P. B. and J. M. Tañer. 1990. *Worldwide Variation in Human Growth.* Second Edition. Cambridge: Cambridge University Press.

Ferreira, F. H. G. and Litchfield, J. A. 1997. "Poverty and Income Distribution in a High-Growth Economy: Chile: 1987–1995." Capitulo 2 "Income Distribution and Poverty: A Statistical Overview."

FLACSO. 2001. *Pueblos Indígenas y Pobreza.*

Foro de Coordinaciones de ONG de Guatemala. *Perfil de las Organizaciones No Gubernamentales en Guatemala.*

Gacitua Mario, E. and C. Sojo, with S. Davis. 2000. *Social Exclusion and Poverty Reduction in Latin America.* World Bank and FLACSO, Washington, DC.

Foster, Vivien and Araujo, Caridad. 2002. "Poverty and Modern Utility Services." Guatemala Poverty Assessment Report Technical Background Paper. The World Bank.

Fuentes & Asociados. 2001. "Intervenciones de Protección Social Financiadas con Fondos Empresariales Privados."

Glaeser, E., D. Laibson, J. Scheinkman, and C. Soutter 2000, "Measuring Trust" Quarterly Journal of Economics.

Gragnolati, Michele and Marini, Alessandra. 2002. "Health and Poverty in Guatemala." Guatemala Poverty Assessment Report Technical Background Paper. The World Bank.

Grandin, Greg. 2000. *The Blood of Guatemala: A History of Race and Nation.* Duke University Press.

Grootaert, C. 1999. "Social Capital, Household Welfare and Poverty in Indonesia." Local Level Institutions Working Paper No. 6. World Bank.

Habicht, J.-P., R. Martorell, C. Yarbrough, R. M. Malina, and R. E. Klein. 1974. "Height and Weight Standards for Preschool Children. How Relevant Are Ethnic Differences in Growth Potential." *Lancet* 6:61–614.

Hansen, John R. 1978. *Guatemala: Economic and Social Position and Prospects.* A World Bank Country Study.

Hentschel, Jesko, Jean Olson Lanjouw, Peter Lanjouw, and Javier Poggi. "Combining Census and Survey Data to Trace the Spatial Dimensions of Poverty: A Case Study of Ecuador." *World Bank Economic Review,* Vol 14, No. 1, 2000.

Heuveline, P. and N. Goldman. 1998. "A Description of Child Illness and Treatment Behavior in Guatemala." Mimeo (Office of Population Research, Princeton NJ).

Ibanez, Ana-Maria, Kathy Lindert, and Michael Woolcock. 2002. "Social Capital in Guatemala: A Mixed Methods Analysis." Guatemala Poverty Assessment Report Technical Background Paper. The World Bank.

Instituto Nacional de Estadística—Guatemala. 1999. "Encuesta Nacional de Ingresos y Gastos Familiares 1998–1999."

Instituto Nacional de Estadística—Guatemala. 2001. "Encuesta Nacional sobre Condiciones de Vida ENCOVI 2000: La Pobreza en Guatemala, Principales Resultados."

Instituto Nacional de Estadística—Guatemala and FNUAP. 1989. "Perfil de la Pobreza: Encuesta Nacional Sociodemografica 1989."

Instituto Nacional de Estadística—Guatemala (INE), Secretaría General de Planificación y Programación de la Presidencia (SEGEPLAN), Universidad Rafael Landívar (URL), y Programa de Naciones Unidas para el Desarrollo (PNUD). 2002. "Encuesta Nacional de Condiciones de Vida 2002: Perfil de la Pobreza en Guatemala."

International Bank for Reconstruction and Development. 1951. "The Economic Development of Guatemala." Report of a World Bank Mission.

International Monetary Fund. 2001a. Guatemala: Recent Economic Developments.

International Monetary Fund. 2001b. Guatemala: Staff Report for the 2001 Article 2001 IV Consultation.

Jonas, Susanne. 2000. Of Centaurs and Doves: Guatemala's Peace Process. Westview Press.

Kaufman, Daniel, Aart Kraay, and Pablo Zoido-Lobatón. 1998. "Governance Matters." World Bank Policy Research Working Paper No. 2196.

Kaufmann, Kraay, and Zoido 2002. "Governance Matters II: Updated Indicators for 2000/01." Policy Research Working Paper No. 2772. The World Bank.

Lederman, Daniel. 2002, "Income, Wealth, and Socialization in Argentina: Provocative Responses from Individuals." Policy Research Working Paper No. 2821. The World Bank.

Loening, Ludger J. 2002. "The Impact of Education on Economic Growth in Guatemala." Discussion Paper No. 87, Ibero-America Institute for Economic Research, Georg-August-Universität Gottingen.

Logan, M. H. 1973. Human Medicine in Guatemala and Peasant Acceptance of Modern Medicine. *Human Organization.* Vol 32(4): 385–395.

Lopez, Humberto. 2000. "The Cost of Armed Conflict in Centro-America." draft paper.

Lopez Rivera, Oscar Augusto. *Guatemala: Intimidades de la Pobreza.* Universidad Rafael Landívar, Instituto de Investigaciones Económicas y Sociales.

Marini, Alessandra and Michele Gragnolati. 2002. "Malnutrition and Poverty in Guatemala." Guatemala Poverty Assessment Report. The World Bank.

McCreery. 1976. "Coffee and Class: The Structure of Development in Liberal Guatemala." *Hispanic American Historical Review,* vol. 56.

McCreery. 1983. "Debt Servitude in Rural Guatemala, 1876–1930." *Hispanic American Historical Review,* vol. 64.

McCreery. 1994. Rural Guatemala: 1760–1940. Stanford University Press.

MINUGUA. 2000. "Informe de Verificación: Los Linchamientos: un Flagelo Contra la Dignidad Humana."

MINUGUA. 2001a. "Sexto Informe del Secretario General de las Naciones Unidas Sobre la Verificación de los Acuerdos de Paz de Guatemala."

MINUGUA. 2001b. "Duodécimo Informe Sobre Derechos Humanos de la Misión de Verificación de las Naciones Unidas en Guatemala."

Moser, Caroline and Cathy McIlwaine. 2001. *Violence in a Post-Conflict Context: Urban Poor Perceptions from Guatemala*. The World Bank.

MSPAS, OPS/OMS. 2001. Propuesta: Establecimiento de las Redes Sociales Locales, su Epidemiología Cultural, Recursos Etno-terapéuticos, su Interacción con el Medio Social y las Redes del Sistema Oficial de Salud. Guatemala.

Narayan, D. and L. Pritchett. 1999 "Cents and Sociability: Household Income and Social Capital in Rural Tanzania," *Economic Development and Cultural Change* 47(4): 871–97.

Nugent, Jeffrey B. and James A. Robinson. 2000. "Are Endowments Fate?" Unpublished draft paper.

Nuñez, César Antonio (2001). "Exclusión social y VIH-SIDA en Guatemala." United Nations.

ODHAG. 1998. *Guatemala Nunca Más*. Volume IV: Victims of Conflict. Guatemala.

Pebley, A. R., E. Hurtado, and N. Goldman. 1997. "Beliefs about Children's Illness Among Rural Guatemalan Women." In *Journal of Biosocial Sciences*.

Plant, Roger. 1995. *Rebuilding Civil Society: Rural Workers' Organizations in Guatemala*. International Labor Office: Issues in Development Discussion Paper No. 5.

Psacharopoulos, George and Ying Chu Ng. 1992. "Earnings and Education in Latin America: Assessing Priorities for Schooling Investments." World Bank Policy Research Working Papers Series no. 1067.

Psacharopoulos, George. 1993. "Returns to Investment in Education: A Global Update." World Bank Policy Research Working Papers Series No. 1067.

Psacharopoulos, George and Harry Anthony Patrinos, Eds. 1994. *Indigenous People and Poverty in Latin America: An Empirical Analysis*. World Bank Regional and Sectoral Studies.

Puri, Jyotsna. 2002. "Transport and Poverty in Guatemala: a Profile Using Data from the ENCOVI 2000." Guatemala Poverty Assessment Report Technical Background Paper. The World Bank.

Rodriguez Santana, Martha. 2001. "Percepciones Sobre la Educación: Un Estudio Cualitativo y Multi-Etnico En Guatemala." Guatemala Poverty Assessment Report Technical Background Paper. The World Bank.

Rojas, Fernando. 1999. "A Strategic View of Decentralization in Guatemala." Draft paper.

Sabino, Carlos A. Guatemala: "Dos Paradojas y Una Incógnita." Atlas Economic Research Foundation.

Santiso, Carlos. 2001. *Guatemala: Analysis of Social Protection Interventions in the Public Sector in Guatemala in 2000*. The World Bank.

Secretaria de Planificación y Programación, SEGEPLAN. 2001a. "El Drama de la Pobreza en Guatemala: Sus Rasgos y Efectos Sobre la Sociedad."

Secretaria de Planificación y Programación, SEGEPLAN. 2001b. Mapas de Pobreza: Informe Final.

Secretaria de Planificación y Programación, SEGEPLAN. 2001c. Estrategia de Reducción de la Pobreza: El Camino de la Paz. Gobierno de Guatemala.

Secretaria de Planificación y Programación, SEGEPLAN. 2001d. Mapas de Pobreza de Guatemala: Un Auxiliar para Entender el Flagelo de la Pobreza en el País.

Solares, J, 1992. *Guatemala: Etnicidad y Democracia en Tierra Arrasada, en Problemas de la democracia*, Cuidad de Guatemala. FLACSO.

Solares, Jorge. 1997. *Etnicidad, Salud y Riesgo en Guatemala*. OPS/OMS-BID.

Tax, Sol. 1953. "Penny Capitalism: A Guatemalan Indian Economy." Smithsonian Institution, Institute of Social Anthropology, No. 16.

Tesliuc, Emil and Kathy Lindert. 2002a. "Social Protection, Private Transfers and Poverty: a Quantitative and Qualitative Assessment." Guatemala Poverty Assessment Report Technical Background Paper. The World Bank.

Tesliuc, Emil and Kathy Lindert. 2002b. "Vulnerability: a Quantitative and Qualitative Assessment." Guatemala Poverty Assessment Report Technical Background Paper. The World Bank.

Tierney, Nancy Leigh. 1997. *Robbed of Humanity: Lives of Guatemalan Street Children.*

Tovar Gómez, Marcela. 1998. *Perfil de los Pueblos Indígenas de Guatemala.* The World Bank.

Transparency International. 2001. Global Corruption Report. September.

Universidad Rafael Landívar, Instituto de Investigaciones Económicas y Sociales. 2001. *Inventario de Intervenciones de Protección Social con Fondos Públicos.*

United Nations. 2001. *World Population Prospects: The 2000 Revision Highlights.*

United Nations Development Programme. 1999. *Guatemala: el rostro rural del desarrollo humano.*

United Nations Development Programme. 2000. *Guatemala: la fuerza incluyente del desarrollo humano.*

United Nations Development Programme. 2001a. *Human Development Report.*

United Nations Development Programme. 2001b. *Informe de Desarrollo Humano 2001: Guatemala: El Finaciamiento del Desarrollo Humano.*

Vakis, Renos. 2002. "Guatemala: Livelihoods, Labor Markets and Rural Poverty." Guatemala Poverty Assessment Report Technical Background Paper. The World Bank.

Villamar Contreras, Marco Antonio. 1993. *Significado de la Década 1944–1954 Conocido Como la Revolución Guatemalteca de Octubre.*

von Hoegen, Miguel. 2000. *Tres Retos para la Inclusión en Guatemala: La Inversión Pública, la Educación Formal, y el Empleo en el Sector Formal.* Universidad Rafael Landívar/Instituto de Investigaciones Económicas y Sociales.

von Hoegen, M. 2001. *Las Macro Tendencias del Empleo Formal en la Década de 1990.* Universidad Rafael Landívar, Guatemala.

von Hoegen, M. and Palma. 1999. *Los Pobres Explican la Pobreza.* Universidad Rafael Landívar, Guatemala.

World Bank. 1995. "Guatemala: An Assessment of Poverty." Report No. 12313-GU.

World Bank. 1996. "Guatemala: Building Peace with Rapid and Equitable Growth;" Country Economic Memorandum, Report No. 15352-GU.

World Bank. 1997. *World Development Report 1997: The State in a Changing World.*

World Bank. 2000a. *Panama Poverty Assessment: Priorities and Strategies for Poverty Reduction.* A World Bank Country Study.

World Bank. 2000. "Guatemala: Expenditure Reform in a Post-Conflict Country." Report No. 19617-GU.

World Bank. 2001a. " Nicaragua Poverty Assessment: Challenges and Opportunities for Poverty Reduction." Report No. 20488 NI.

World Bank. 2001b. *World Development Indicators 2001.*

World Bank. 2001c. *Honduras Poverty Assessment.*

World Bank. 2001d. *The Little Green Data Book 2001.*

World Bank. 2001e. *World Development Report 2000/2001: Attacking Poverty.*

World Bank. 2001f. "Rural Poverty reduction in Brazil: Towards an Integrated Strategy." Report No. 21790-BR.

World Bank. 2002. *World Development Report 2002: Building Institutions for Markets.*

World Bank and the Carter Center. 1997. *From Civil War to Civil Society: The Transition from War to Peace in Guatemala and Liberia.*

World Faiths Development Dialogue. 1999. *Poverty & Development: An Inter-faith Perspective.*

Wodon, Quentin. 2000. "Guatemala: Preliminary Poverty Diagnostic." The World Bank.

Wodon, Quentin. 2001. "Poverty and Policy in Latin America and the Caribbean." World Bank Regional Study Number 467.

Woolcock, Michael and Deepa Narayan. 2000. "Social Capital: Implications for Development Theory, Research, and Policy." *World Bank Research Observer* 15(2): 225–49